INSIDE

Macromedia®

Director® 6
with Lingo™

Lee Allis
Jay Armstrong
Matt Davis
Rob Dillon
Tab Julius
Kirk Keller
Matthew Kerner
David Miller
Raúl Silva

New
Riders

New Riders Publishing, Indianapolis, Indiana

Inside Macromedia Director 6 with Lingo

By Lee Allis, Jay Armstrong, Matt Davis, Rob Dillon, Tab Julius, Kirk Keller, Matthew Kerner, David Miller, and Raúl Silva

Published by:
New Riders Publishing
201 West 103rd Street
Indianapolis, IN 46290 USA

Printed in the United States of America 1 2 3 4 5 6 7 8 9 0

Library of Congress Cataloging-in-Publication Data

Inside Macromedia Director 6 with Lingo/Lee Allis…[et al.].

    p. cm.

  Includes index.

  ISBN 1-56205-728-6

  1. Director (Computer file) 2. Lingo (Computer program language) 3. Multimedia systems. I. Allis, Lee, 1969–
QA76.575.I5682 1997
006.6--dc21
97-8061 CIP

Warning and Disclaimer

Publisher	*Don Fowley*
Associate Publisher	*David Dwyer*
Marketing Manager	*Mary Foote*
Managing Editor	*Carla Hall*
Director of Development	*Kezia Endsley*

Product Director
Alicia Buckley

Senior Editors
Sarah Kearns
Suzanne Snyder

Development Editors
Laura Frey
Laurie McGuire

Project Editor
Karen Walsh

Copy Editors
Gina Brown
Keith Cline
Wendy Garrison
Cricket Harrison
Matt Litten
Michelle Warren

Technical Editors
Scott Hamlin
Bentley Wolfe

Software Specialist
Steve Flatt

Assistant Marketing Manager
Gretchen Schlesinger

Acquisitions Coordinator
Stacey Beheler

Administrative Coordinator
Karen Opal

Manufacturing Coordinator
Brook Farling

Cover Designer
Karen Ruggles

Cover Production
Aren Howell

Book Designer
Sandra Schroeder

Director of Production
Larry Klein

Production Team Supervisors
Laurie Casey
Joe Millay

Graphics Image Specialists
Steve Adams, Kevin Cliburn
Wil Cruz, Brad Dixon, Tammy
Graham, Oliver Jackson

Production Analysts
Dan Harris
Erich J. Richter

Production Team
Dan Caparo, Lori Cliburn, Kim Cofer,
Rowena Rappaport, Scott Tullis

Indexer
Nicholas Schroeder

About the Authors

Lee Allis has worked at Macromedia since 1993, always working with Director in some way. Currently, she is the Technical Support Supervisor for Director and Authorware. Many developers know her from when she was the Director sysop on the Macromedia CompuServe forum. As Director lead for technical support, she worked on the Director 5 Quality Assurance Team. Prior to joining technical support, Lee produced the *Director 4.0 Lingo Dictionary* and *Using Lingo* manuals, and at one time was the assistant product manager for Director and Authorware. Prior to Macromedia, Lee worked for other small multimedia and data-compression software companies.

Lee made her debut with New Riders Publishing last year as the primary author for *Inside Macromedia Director 5 with Lingo*. Lee graduated from the University of Michigan and lives in Oakland, California.

Jay Armstrong manages the developers center on the support section of Macromedia's web site. He first started playing around with computers in the days of the Atari 800.

Jay graduated with a BS in psychology from UC Santa Cruz in 1991. He served as Director of West Coast's largest canoe and kayak school from 1991–1995 (including all IS functions) and was a CBT consultant from 1995–1996.

Matt Davis is Director of Graphics and IT at Project Multimedia Ltd., a leading multimedia and event production company in the UK. Matt has worked with Macromedia Director for seven years, following a previous life producing TV graphics for the BBC.

Aside from corporate work with clients such as IBM, Toshiba, and Sun, Matt produced Power Presentations® (presentation software), ClickTracks™ (a software based "toy"), and Router™ (a navigation package).

Matt continues to live with a Chapman Stick, a Peer Gynt recumbent bicycle, and a passion for fencing.

Rob Dillon has been a media producer for more than twenty years. This career began with some work in communications with the US Army. Rob continued his communication career at the Instructional Production Service at the University of Pittsburgh where he produced shows in video, film, and multi-image. Rob moved on to work as the cinematographer and eventually the supervisor of the Media Production Services for the Allegheny Intermediate Unit, a regional educational support agency. While there, Rob produced motion pictures, video, and wide screen multi–image shows. He also supervised the print design and production services. Rob's next stop was at Mindbank, Incorporated, a Pittsburgh-based interactive videodisc production company. At Mindbank, Rob was an Interactive Producer responsible for the production of a videodisc-based instructional program to be used in business. Rob went on to The SLIDEing Board, Inc. as the General Manager. The SLIDEing Board was a multi-image and slide production service business. In a little more than three years Rob moved the business from a mechanical composition and design production focus to one using computer graphics and digitally mastered media.

Rob founded the Digital Design Group as a reaction to an almost complete lack of multimedia production services available in the Pittsburgh, PA area. In business since 1993, Digital Design has produced CD-based and web-based digital media for business.

Rob has written two "Survival Guides" for Apple Computer's Apple Media Program. He also writes an occasional column (more occasional than the editor likes) on technology and the Internet for a Pittsburgh news weekly newspaper. Rob has a BA in Mass Communication from the University of Pittsburgh.

The Digital Design Group Limited can be found on the web at `http://www.ddg-designs.com` and Rob can be reached at `rob@ddg-designs.com`.

Tab Julius is extremely active in the Macromedia Director community, both as President/CEO of Penworks Corporation, a leading developer of software written with, and Xtras written for, Macromedia Director, and as publisher of the *Lingo User's Journal*, the only publication dedicated to Lingo programming. He is author of *Lingo! An Advanced Guide to Director's Scripting Language* (New Riders, 1996) and contributor to many other books, including *Director Power Solutions* (New Riders, 1996), *More Tricks of the Game Programming Gurus* (Sams Publishing, 1995), and *PC Techniques C/C++ Power Tools* (Bantam Books, 1992). He can be reached at `tab@penworks.com` or via `www.penworks.com`.

Kirk Keller has been developing multimedia for almost a decade and authoring in Macromedia Director for more than four years. He has created two web applications that have been selected as Macromedia's Shocked Site of the Day—one of them being the first Shockwave application ever selected for this honor.

Kirk has acted as co-author or technical editor on several books on multimedia development and Director authoring, one of them being *Director Power Solutions* (New Riders, 1996).

Kirk currently develops multimedia applications for CD-ROM, kiosk and the web for the Missouri Department of Conservation. When he's not writing or editing books on multimedia development, he teaches courses on Director authoring at the University of Missouri and does independent multimedia development.

You can find out more about Kirk and the projects he has developed at his web site, `http://www.grommett.com`, or you can contact him at `kirk@grommett.com`.

Matthew Kerner is a third year Communication student at the University of Missouri, Columbia. His research interests include human-computer interaction and computer-mediated communication channels. He currently serves as the student director of the Bingham Multimedia Site where he helps coordinate collaborative multimedia projects between students and faculty on the MU campus. He previously worked as a multimedia researcher at MU's Digital Media Center.

In a nonacademic setting, Matthew is a principal of Cedar Lake Consulting, a design and development group for multimedia, database, and network solutions. He also serves as a new media consultant to several organizations.

Matthew began learning Director as a high school student in Independence, MO. His programming efforts diverged to more traditional routes as he began developing applications in C and C++. Matthew returned to Director development when he began his studies at MU, and he continues to actively program Lingo.

David Miller is a Multimedia Application Developer and Instructional Technology Specialist for the School of Education and New Media Center at Stanford University. He is a web site administrator, designer, and programmer in the San Francisco Bay area and teaches classes in instructional technology, designing learning environments with technology, and web multimedia. Dave is completing his Ph.D. at Stanford. His home page is `http://www-leland.stanford.edu/~dmiller/`.

Raúl Silva was born and raised in Puerto Rico. He came to Chicago to attend the Art Institute of Chicago where he concentrated in Art and Technology. At the Art Institute, Raúl served as Multimedia Coordinator, working on interactive multimedia titles and coordinating production efforts with various museum departments. Raúl is a multimedia programming veteran and has more than 17 years of computer experience. Raúl is also an accomplished graphics and interface designer. Most recently, he co-founded AfterShock, a company that develops interactive content for the World Wide Web and creates complete web solutions. He has also developed custom authoring tools and is a contributing writer for industry-related books and magazines.

Raúl has won several excellence awards and is recognized as a leading multimedia authority in the city of Chicago and around the world. AfterShock's page can be reached at http://www.ashock.com. Raúl's page can be reached at http://www.tezcat.com/~Raúl.

Acknowledgment

from Lee Allis

This book is dedicated to James Hayes, for all of his love and support. Thank you for putting up with me doing this again!

Special thanks to my parents, Susan and Harry Allis, for their loving help through this time of doing the book and planning the wedding.

A special thanks to my family for their support: Tom, Bob, Carol, Melissa, Shelly, Emily, Ashley, Katie, and Scott Allis. You should now understand where I was when you called.

To Carolyn Hyland, Aimee VanDragt, Shauna Andrews, Heidi Spaly, Jane Spray, Shelley Wagner, Allison Schuster, Cariad Hayes, Peter Baty, Bill Bird, and Sesi Kodali for sticking with me through my crazy schedule.

To Gretchen Macdowall, without whom much of this edition could not have happened.

Thanks to the following Macromedians:

John Dowdell for his infinite knowledge; Kevin Mullet, Diana Wynne, Joe Schmitz, Ben Melnick, John "JT" Thompson, Anders Walgren, and the Director engineering team; Bud Colligan, Sherry Flanders-Page, and Ed Krimen for giving me the opportunity; Brian Ellertson, Lennart Isaccson, Sue McHugh, Jay Armstrong, Bentley Wolfe, Brian Schmidt, Craig Goodman, Peter DeCrescenzo, Fred "asparagus" Green, Henry Warwick, Tyson Norris, Jeff Schick, Dan Read, Jeff Kafer, S Page, Charles Corley, Leslie Alperin, Bill Mowery, Calvin Kwan, Alan Felgate, Luiz Lanna, Ed Baldwin, Brian Payne, Phil Royer, Hank Hansen, Victoria Avdienko, Traci Dos Santos, Suzanne Porta, and Karen Tucker.

At New Riders Publishing:

To Alicia Buckley, thanks for believing in me again and thanks for all of your encouragement. Vertigo was great!

To Karen Walsh and Laurie McGuire, the dynamic editing team. Thank you for catching everything and making it all work out. To Steve Weiss, for building a great previous version.

To David Dwyer and Don Fowley: I know you're still watching this book come alive. Thanks for trusting in our project.

Trademark Acknowledgments

All terms mentioned in this book that are known to be trademarks or service marks have been appropriately capitalized. New Riders Publishing cannot attest to the accuracy of this information. Use of a term in this book should not be regarded as affecting the validity of any trademark or service mark.

Contents at a Glance

Part VI: Extending Director with Xtras   817

Part VII: Appendices   847

Index   923

Table of Contents

3 The Strategy: Product Analysis and Design   51

4 Delivering the Goods   69

Part II: Working with Director   99

5 Working with Director 6: Understanding the Metaphor   101

10   Text: The Story   351

12 Digital Video: The Movie Within the Movie 433

Part IV: Multimedia on the Web with Director and Shockwave   507

15   Mastering Shockwave   595

Part VI: Extending Director with Xtras   817

21   The Xtra Step   819

Part VII: Appendices   847

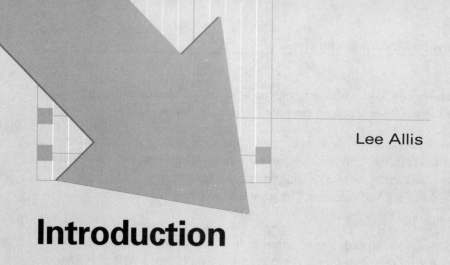

Lee Allis

Introduction

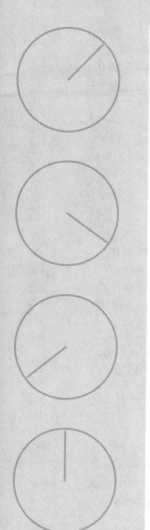

All the world's a stage.

—William Shakespeare

Inside Macromedia Director 6 with Lingo is not just another Director book. In fact, it's more like a Director production. It is a compilation of work by a group of Director developers, each specializing in different aspects of the development process.

Approach *Inside Macromedia Director 6 with Lingo* as a seminar given by nine experts in the field. The cast of authors have been using Director for years, some since 1985, when Director was still VideoWorks. They've posted thousands of online messages, they've worked through thousands of issues with other developers, and they're here to share their knowledge and love for the product with you.

Why "With Lingo"?

When we started the first edition of this book, *Inside Macromedia Director 5 with Lingo*, "with Lingo" was not a part of the title. We wanted to make an intermediate to advanced, beyond-the-documentation Director book. Like many people, we saw over twenty basic Director books out there and knew that people wanted more. The trouble with writing a book on Director is that there's so much information to cover. You can write 800 pages on the basic information and never touch Lingo. Or you can write an entire book on Lingo. That's what you find today: basic Director books or Lingo-specific books, but never the two together. Even the Director documentation divides its books between the basics and Lingo. But the truth is that after you reach the intermediate level with Director, you'll be using Director with Lingo each step of the way. Thus, *Inside Macromedia Director 5 with Lingo* was born.

Director basics take a while to understand. But after you get used to placing cast members in the score, making them animate and play sounds, you need to learn the facts about memory management and how to play your 650 MB CD-ROM in a 4 MB partition. The most effective way is to scale back the production and to use more Lingo.

With Lingo, you can craft a production to fit any environment whether it's a 14.4 modem, a floppy disk, or a Windows 95 machine with 8 MB of RAM. You can do it, but many things must be learned. Scanning 24-bit images; recording CD-quality, 16-bit, 44 kHz sounds; and capturing 80 MB QuickTime files is fun. The real test, though, is learning how to use the best tools to edit those media elements to a size with an acceptable quality. At that point, you'll need to know how to bring them all together in Director, use the score or Lingo to control them, and deliver your movie onto a low-end machine. There's a lot to learn, and that's why the authors of *Inside Macromedia Director 6 with Lingo* are here. The book covers how to take each step in the Director development process, and with each step, how Lingo can help you achieve the best results.

What's New in This Edition?

Inside Macromedia Director 6 with Lingo has a number of new features in this edition of which you should be aware. We have added a complete section on Shockwave and Director on the Internet. You'll find that there are many more tutorials in this edition, that some chapters have moved around, and that extra steps have been taken to blend the writings of nine authors more clearly.

Of course, the book has been updated to include all of the new information on Director 6. You'll also notice that some of the authors are new to the group.

Who Should Read This Book?

Inside Macromedia Director 6 with Lingo is intended for people who are serious about Director. It is for people who need to know all the little-known facts about Director and don't have time to learn them on their own. It takes into consideration that you're familiar with the Macintosh or Windows environment and Director. You may have already taken a class in Director or worked through the tutorials and still have many unanswered questions.

If you are new to Director, this book gives a jump start in Director development. It offers background information about each step of the Director development process; it is intended to be a companion to the basic Director 6 documentation set.

If you do not yet own Director 6 or the products in the Director 6 Studio, you can request working demos from Macromedia free-of-charge. All the demos are on the Showcase CD which can be ordered by calling 1-800-326-2128.

How to Read This Book in a Non-Linear Fashion

This book is not necessarily meant to be read from start to finish. You can read it that way, but you can also easily turn to a chapter on a subject for which you're looking and start there. Take a look at the section that follows on how the book is organized. You should understand the road map before you jump around, but you should be able to find your way. If you do jump around the book, remember that there may be information in other sections that will help you with what you are doing.

How This Book Is Organized

Inside Macromedia Director 6 with Lingo covers every part of a Director development process from pre-planning projects and prototyping to working with each media type to delivering the goods. The main text is divided into six parts: "Director Inside and Out," "Working with Director," "Director's Multimedia Components," "Multimedia on the Web with Director and Shockwave," "Lingo," and "Extending Director with Xtras." Part VII is comprised of four Appendices.

Part I: Director Inside and Out

The first part of this book introduces Macromedia Director and the role it plays in the multimedia world. It also covers planning your Director production, as well as steps you will need to take to deliver your project to your audience.

Chapter 1, "Introducing Director 6," discusses Macromedia Director's role and the advantages of Director, and it gives background and perspectives on cross-platform development. Chapter 1 also introduces Director 6 with all its new features, providing a short description of each and describing where the new features may be found within the rest of the text.

Chapter 2, "Before You Get Started: Planning Your Director Project," and Chapter 3, "The Strategy: Product Analysis and Design," help you plan your Director project with advice and steps to take through the entire development process. Chapter 4, "Delivering the Goods," covers all the issues you'll need to know when putting together a Director piece for distribution. It covers testing your Director production and setting up the Director projector, and tells the files you need to include with your Director projector.

Part II: Working with Director

Part II, "Working with Director," covers the basics of Director, creating animations, and working with multiple casts.

Chapter 5, "Working with Director 6: Understanding the Metaphor," is an introduction to Director, setting the scene for the application and how its parts work together. This chapter is intended to provide background information for new to intermediate users as well as provide useful tips for working with each part of Director.

Chapter 6, "Director as an Animator," explores creating animations within Director and some of the new ways to use Director 6 for animation. Chapter 7, "Multiple Casts," teaches you the powerful authoring techniques available when you use multiple casts.

Part III: Director's Multimedia Components

Part III should be used as a reference section for every multimedia element in the Director application. If you have a question about sound, for example, you will turn to Chapter 11, "Sound: The Soundtrack." If you'd like to add three-dimensional animations to your Director piece, you will turn to Chapter 9, "Adding the Third Dimension."

Chapter 8, "Graphics: The Visuals," describes tips and techniques for creating and using graphics for Director. You will learn how to work with all the new graphics file formats supported in Director 6.

Chapter 9, "Adding the Third Dimension," brings these graphics elements into the third dimension and teaches you how to create a 3D illusion in your movie.

Chapter 10, "Text: The Story," covers things you'll need to know about using text in Director, including fields and rich text.

Chapter 11, "Sound: The Soundtrack," incorporates sound to the picture, describing tips and techniques for using realistic soundtracks and sound effects in Director.

Chapter 12, "Digital Video: The Movie Within the Movie," teaches you the black art of creating perfect digital video for use in your Director production.

Part IV: Multimedia on the Web with Director and Shockwave

Part IV is a new section in *Inside Macromedia Director 6 with Lingo* that was not in the previous edition. It covers Shockwave and techniques for delivery on both the Internet and network–aware CD-ROMs.

Chapter 13, "Designing Multimedia for the Web," provides a comprehensive guide to the many issues involved in web-based multimedia and provides tips and tricks for creating and delivering effective multimedia on the web.

Chapter 14, "Creating Shockwave Movies," discusses Director 6's new relationship to the Internet. You'll learn how to author Director movies *live* on the Internet, including new features such as linked Internet content and streaming playback.

Chapter 15, "Mastering Shockwave," further discusses Shockwave movies, Shockwave audio, and ways to implement advanced features such as browser scripting and dynamic web pages.

Part V: Lingo

The five chapters in the Lingo section move their way from the basics to the most advanced concepts, including: Chapter 16, "Lingo: The Basics," Chapter 17, "Managing Your Data," Chapter 18, "Movie in a Window," Chapter 19, "Advanced Concepts," and Chapter 20, "Object-Oriented Programming in Director."

Nothing is as satisfying as seeing a concept that minutes before existed only in your head take shape on-screen. Chapter 16, "Lingo: The Basics," helps you do just that. No tool quite matches Lingo's capability to help you realize ideas quickly.

Chapter 17, "Managing Your Data," shows you methods to control and manipulate data in your production. You'll learn how to use variables and lists and how to store and retrieve data from outside Director.

Chapter 18, "Movie in a Window," presents the many creative possibilites of Movies in a Window (MIAWs). MIAWs can help you add novelty to your interface, overcome the 120 sprite barrier, or make tools for yourself and others. Learn all this and more in Chapter 18.

Chapter 19, "Advanced Concepts," challenges you a bit with some of the more advanced features of Director. Topics discussed include score animation versus Lingo animation, making games, behaviors, and coming to Lingo from C, among others.

Chapter 20, "Object-Oriented Programming in Director," covers the many topics related to building objects in Director. Learn about object creation, object properties, ancestors, escaping the score, and using parent and child scripts. If you want to learn all about object-oriented programming, this is the place to look.

Part VI: Extending Director with Xtras

Chapter 21, "The Xtra Step," features Tab Julius, an Xtras developer and author of *Lingo: An Advanced Guide*, by New Riders. This chapter takes you beyond Director 6 to explore all the capabilities that Xtras can add to Director.

Part VII: Appendices

You'll find four useful appendices at the back of *Inside Macromedia Director 6 with Lingo*. They include: Appendix A, "Lingo Library," Appendix B, "New Lingo Terms in Director 6," Appendix C, "Contacting Macromedia," and Appendix D, "Xtras Reference."

The Director 6 Challenge

Writing about a software package when it's under development is difficult. It's never clear how the new features will turn out or how you will use them. It would have been much easier for all of us to write about Director 5 now, one year after it's been out, but then you wouldn't have bought this book.

Changes to Director 6 will come after this book is published. And there will be errors, as with any publication. Please do not call Macromedia technical support about this book. Contact New Riders and the authors with suggestions for the next version.

Congratulations on buying *Inside Macromedia Director 6 with Lingo*.

New Riders Publishing

The staff of New Riders Publishing is committed to bringing you the very best in computer reference material. Each New Riders book is the result of months of work by authors and staff who research and refine the information contained within its covers.

As part of this commitment to you, New Riders invites your input. Please let us know if you enjoy this book, if you have trouble with the information and examples presented, or if you have a suggestion for the next edition.

Please note, however: New Riders staff cannot serve as a technical resource for Director 6 or for questions about software- or hardware-related problems. Please refer to the documentation that accompanies your software or to the application's Help system.

If you have a question or comment about any New Riders book, you can contact us in several ways. We will respond to as many readers as we can. Your name, address, or phone number will never become part of a mailing list or be used for any purpose other than to help us continue to bring you the best books possible.

You can write us at the following address:

New Riders Publishing
Attn: Alicia Buckley
201 W. 103rd Street
Indianapolis, IN 46290

If you prefer, you can fax New Riders Publishing at:

317-817-7448

You can also send electronic mail to New Riders at the following Internet address:

abuckley@newriders.mcp.com

New Riders Publishing is an imprint of Macmillan Computer Publishing. To obtain a catalog or information, or to purchase any Macmillan Computer Publishing book, call 800-428-5331 or visit our web site at http://www.mcp.com.

Thank you for selecting *Inside Macromedia Director 6 with Lingo*!

PART

I

Director Inside and Out

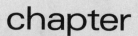

Lee Allis

Introducing Director 6

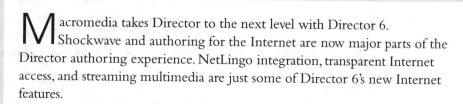

Macromedia takes Director to the next level with Director 6. Shockwave and authoring for the Internet are now major parts of the Director authoring experience. NetLingo integration, transparent Internet access, and streaming multimedia are just some of Director 6's new Internet features.

Director 6 is also easier to use than Director 5. The score, sprite objects, and interactivity are all more accessible in this version. Director is easier to learn and use from the very beginning. You'll find a tour of Director 6's enhancements in the section, "What's New in Director 6" (see fig. 1.1).

This chapter's coverage includes the following:

▶ Macromedia Director's role in the multimedia industry

▶ Director's strengths

▶ What's new in Director 6

▶ The Director community

Figure 1.1

Director 6 is the most powerful authoring tool for multimedia and the Internet.

Macromedia Director's Role

When you think of multimedia, what do you see? You should see vivid graphics, encompassing sounds, animated worlds, and digital videos coming together all at the same time. You should see fun web pages and beautiful CD-ROM titles, all presenting digital means to ideas and messages at the click of a button.

You have heard of the multimedia revolution. Perhaps you've heard that it will bring new life to your business presentations. Or perhaps your client wants to take their newsletter onto the Internet and add streaming audio, rich text, and animation. Maybe you are an artist ready to learn the new, emerging art forms of the future. Director is your vehicle to all this and more.

Director is the industry-standard authoring tool for multimedia production and the Internet. Director not only combines multimedia elements into a portable movie, but backs them up with Lingo, Director's own interactive scripting language. Lingo enables a Director developer and the movie's audience to control any situation in the production. They may interact with any of the media elements presented, navigate through volumes of information, play an interactive game, and so on. The only boundaries on Director with Lingo are the limits of your imagination.

Shockwave for Director

The World Wide Web is the hottest mode of communication today. The Internet offers a low-cost solution for distributing ideas to millions of people. And multimedia is taking over as the presentation method of choice on the Internet. Shockwave for Director is the number one Internet plug-in today (see fig. 1.2). Shockwave enables web pages to display Director movies full of streaming audio, rotating logos, transitions, sound effects, interactivity, and more.

Figure 1.2

Shockwave provides for the creation of dynamic multimedia Internet solutions.

Blinking text is no longer the hit of HTML. Check out Macromedia's web page at `http://www.macromedia.com`. Macromedia hosts the Shockwave Epicenter Gallery (see fig. 1.3), featuring the largest guide to Shockwave sites in the world. Every day there is a new Shocked site of the day, featuring the coolest sites on the web.

Figure 1.3

The Shockwave Epicenter Gallery is the guide to Shockwave sites. It features a site of the day every day.

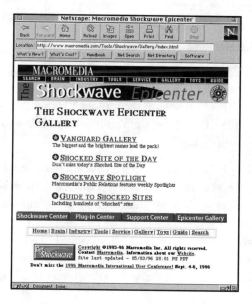

Corporations using Shockwave include Kodak, Chevron, Intel, CNN, Disney, Apple, @Home, General Motors, Netscape, MTV, Maytag, Nissan—the list grows every day (see fig. 1.4). Shockwave for Director is truly changing the face of the World Wide Web.

Figure 1.4

Macromedia features the top corporate Shockwave sites at http://www. macromedia.com.

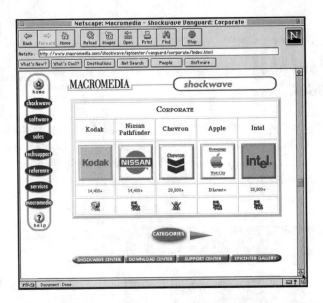

What is the secret to this Shockwave technology? It's actually quite easy—the main trick is to be able to use Director. You'll need to learn some details of the Internet delivery platform, but Director is the key.

The Shockwave Plug-In is a playback engine for Macromedia Director movies. The Plug-In integrates seamlessly into a web browser, such as Netscape Navigator, on both the Macintosh and Windows. Director 6 movies can now be saved as Shockwave movies directly from the File menu. This compresses the movie by approximately 60 percent. The Shockwave Plug-In is free from Macromedia on their web page at `http://www.macromedia.com`. The web page and the more specific address that enables you to download the Plug-In are shown in figure 1.5.

After your movie is completed and you save it as a Shockwave movie, you will put it on a web server and refer to it in your HTML document like any GIF or JPEG file, and that's it. Many more techniques exist, of course, but that is the basic concept. Part IV of this book covers multimedia on the web with Director and Shockwave in detail.

Figure 1.5

The Shockwave Download Center enables you to obtain Shockwave for both the Macintosh and Windows.

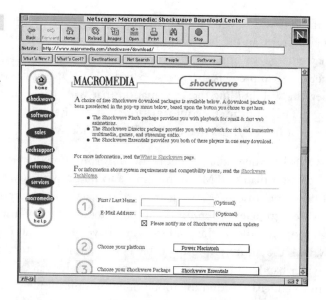

The key to Shockwave for Director development is understanding Director. The most successful Shockwave developers have probably been using Director for years. They understand how to work with the different media elements and how to use Lingo to create an animation in a very tight, Internet environment. Using Shockwave is easy, but it's even easier when you know Director. That's why you're reading this book.

Director and the CD-ROM Industry

CD-ROM drives are standard on personal computers today. CD-ROMs have replaced floppy disks in the computer industry just as they've replaced vinyl records in the music industry.

If you take a look at the statistics, CD-ROM drive sales have increased six-fold in the past three years. More and more software companies are shipping their products on CD-ROMs, and the prices of CD-ROM drives have continued to fall. Whether families purchase CD-ROM drives to play the latest educational titles with their children, or a programmer listens to an audio CD on one machine as he compiles his code on another, people today have access to CD-ROM drives. The market is there.

There is a debate these days over which delivery platform is more important. Is the future of multimedia success on the World Wide Web, and are CD-ROMs a thing of the past? Or, will CD-ROMs and the up-and-coming DVD-ROMs rule the future? Can the web and CD-ROMs work together? One scenario that may emerge is using the web for low-cost advertising of a CD-ROM title. Another scenario predicts that the web and CD-ROMs will eventually work together: the web holding the information that will change and the CD-ROM holding the bulk of the static information. Whatever the future holds, Director is there—for both CD-ROMs and the World Wide Web.

CD-ROMs have been the perfect medium for multimedia productions. What could be better than 650 MB of free space to fill up with *stuff*? The new DVD-ROM drives promise 4.7–8.5 gigabytes of storage space. Increasingly, 1.44 floppies are insufficient even for demo presentations—they just don't have enough room to hold all the cool stuff that developers want to promote. Finally, with the future promising cable connections for interactive television and a wider bandwidth for the Internet, we can only wait and see what happens to CD-ROMs and the mode of communication.

Director and the CD-ROM industry have developed together. Director was actually around first, and unquestionably, Director titles have helped define the interactive CD-ROM world. Director CD-ROM titles are being used for just about everything: museum and hospital kiosks, sales and marketing presentations, educational titles, games for adults and children, annual reports, family albums, and more. Again, take any idea, and you can make it come alive.

The Future of Multimedia

No one knows for certain where the future of multimedia will take us. All we know is that it's an exciting ride and will continue to change course. As a result, the mode of distribution for Director movies certainly will change over time. Whether the distribution is through CDs, DVDs, Shockwave over the Internet, or interactive television, one thing's for sure: It will become easier and faster to get the same idea across with each new technological breakthrough.

Director has proven itself again and again as the leader in multimedia. It lends itself to working with the finest media creation tools on the market and hitting every quality mark for delivery platforms. When new platforms grow to the size of the Macintosh and Windows, you can bet that Macromedia and Director will be there.

Director's Strengths

So what's Director's secret? Why is Director the industry-standard multimedia authoring tool? Why do 350,000 people use it? The words "really cool" come to mind, but for cold hard facts, you can break up its advantages into three categories: ease of use, power, and presence.

Ease of Use

It is possible to compare Director to C and Java, because all three demonstrate great versatility and power in creating software applications. Java and C are, of course, programming languages. Months of learning and years of programming experience generally are required to use those programming languages to their fullest capabilities. Director, on the other hand, offers an easy-to-use development environment similar to standard applications, in addition to the powerful scripting language, Lingo.

The Director score provides a visual interface in which movie elements can be examined at every moment in time. According to Marc Canter, the founder and later director of VideoWorks, "Time, as represented by the score in Director, is the single aspect that differentiates multimedia from flat media, such as paper. After all, time is what animation, sound, and video are all about. Combining the time-line score and WYSIWYG (what you see is what you get) layout capabilities, you create an intuitive system for multimedia composition."

The best thing about Lingo, in comparison to Java and C, is that Director's easy to use. Terms in Director are few, and their syntax is easy to understand. Actual English-like commands and events of on `mouseUp` or on `enterFrame` and simple `go to` commands make it easy for an artist to learn how to program. On the other hand, a programmer can take Lingo to the extent of a complete programming language, such as C.

Beyond Lingo and Director, if you would like to add a feature to Director that Lingo doesn't provide, you can obtain or create external C modules, called Xtras, that communicate with Director. Director 6 takes the Xtras technology introduced in Director 5 another step forward. The Macromedia Open Architecture, or MOA, provides easy use of external code in Director. With MOA, Xtras show up under the Xtras menu in the Director interface. Director 6 opens its internals further to Xtras developers. Xtras have evolved as an improvement over XObjects; XObjects require you to script most of the interaction with external code yourself. More information about Xtras can be found in Chapter 21, "The Xtra Step."

Director 6 ships with a number of third-party Xtras as well as an Xtras Development-ment Kit, or XDK, on both platforms. Macromedia also acts as host for a list of the current third-party Xtras found at `http://www.macromedia.com`. You can do almost anything with Director, Lingo, and Xtras. If you cannot do it in Director, you can certainly do it in C and easily integrate it into Director as an Xtra.

Other features that Director 6 has added to improve ease of use include drag-and-drop behaviors with scriptless authoring, a button editor, and a new score with object-oriented authoring capabilities. Sprites are now objects that span a range of frames. When you move sprites in the score, you move every instance of the sprite. When you move one of the keyframes, Director will re-inbetween the animation for you. Again, you will find a full description of the new features in Director 6 in the later section in this chapter entitled, "What's New in Director 6."

Power

The first thing you notice about a Director movie is the powerful media it presents. The audience might not know what's going on in the background, but if the movie is authored well they will see a production with moving animations, brilliant images, melodious sounds, and quick interactive control.

The time-based Director score allows for a true cell animation, updating the movements of 120 visual elements in each frame. Behind the stage is the Director engine capable of 120 frames per second. To top it all off, Director authors have the power to test for any user interaction, and given the interaction, change the production.

Director is where the media come together. It accepts and integrates media elements created in specialized tools for sound, digital video, and graphics. Director 5 introduced Photoshop-compatible filter support and onion skinning support in the Paint window for creating specialized content within Director. Director 6 introduces support for a multitude of new graphics file formats, including GIF, JPEG, PNG, Photoshop 3.0, LRG (xRes), and many more. Graphics artists authoring for the web have much more power now that they no longer have to edit everything to the PICT file format for Director for Macintosh.

Director 6 takes Director 5's relationship with external editors one step further. In Director 5, you could double-click on a sound cast member, launch SoundEdit 16, edit the sound, and return with the changes updated in Director. In Director 6, you now have an Editors Preference dialog box where you can specify any external editor for more than 16 file types.

One of Director 6's most powerful features is its integration with the Internet. With the new Internet dialog box, you can import and link to any object on the web. With Shockwave built into Director, you now can enjoy the compression within any Director movie that previously you could enjoy only in Shockwave. Shockwave movies can now stream because the files no longer have to download completely to begin playing.

Presence

Director 6 ships as an authoring tool on four platforms: the 68K Macintosh, Power Macintosh, Windows 95, and Windows NT. All four operating systems are available for both playback and authoring, and Windows 3.1 is part of the playback options in Windows. Director files are binary-compatible; the same file may be opened on the Macintosh and on Windows, without the need for any translation.

After the file or set of files is complete and ready to distribute, you will use the specific platform that you are targeting to create the Director executable, or *projector*. You need to have Director for Windows and a Windows machine to make a Director for Windows projector. The bonus is that the same file or set of files used to create a projector for the Macintosh may be made into a 16-bit or 32-bit Windows projector as well. This is why Macromedia is able to say "Author once, play anywhere." No other application on the market provides this binary-compatible authoring solution.

The Player Alternative

If you are new to Director, you might wonder why Director Macintosh movies cannot be converted through a playback-only converter for Windows. If you prefer the Windows platform, you might ask the opposite question for the Macintosh. Developers who used Director prior to version 4 have learned the hard way how painful a playback-only solution can be.

Macromedia (Macromind at that time) released its first version of a Windows Player, Director Player for Windows 1.0, in 1991. Prior to that, Macromedia had worked with Microsoft on the Multimedia Extensions for Windows 3.0. Microsoft's kit included a converter similar to the final Gaffer of Director Player for Windows. It worked with Director Macintosh 2.0 movies to convert them to Windows players that could be played back with MCI calls and the MCIMMP.DRV. Microsoft is no longer shipping the converter, nor is it compatible with Director for Macintosh 3.0 and later.

The first Macromind Windows Player 1.0 worked with Director 2.0 or 3.0 movies, on Windows 3.0. Through further incarnations of Director Macintosh and the Windows Player, the final version of Director Player for Windows 3.11 worked with Director for Macintosh 3.1.3. Even though these final versions made the road to Windows easier, many battles still had to be fought. The movies would look perfect on the Macintosh, but horrible on Windows. Palettes would have to be reversed manually, and font-mapping was a nightmare. It sometimes took an extra six months in development to iron out the problems.

Director for Windows

It was not until the release of Director for Windows 4.0 in July 1994 that the Windows world was truly opened to the Director community. Most of the cross-platform conversion issues were handled in the new, authoring version of Director for Windows. You could (and still can) troubleshoot and fix anything strange in the Windows movie within the Windows *or* Macintosh environment.

The marketplace for Director Macintosh productions opened up to the much wider Windows market. The future for the multimedia producer was solidified. Windows users found themselves with a mature, easy-to-use, multimedia authoring tool for both markets. Today with Shockwave for Director and Internet authoring, Director movies work seamlessly on both platforms through the use of Director's binary-compatible file format introduced in Director 4.

The best thing about the cross-platform development is that teams of Director producers are given a choice. Content for the Director movies can come from the Macintosh or Windows, regardless of the authoring platform. Graphics artists, animators, and sound designers may prefer the Macintosh, CAD designers may prefer Windows NT, and programmers may work on whatever platform they like. Director brings it all together in one unified file that can be opened on both platforms. The only platform-specific steps are testing and delivery.

The Secret to Cross-Platform Authoring

The secret to cross-platform authoring is this: You need to open and test your production in the target environment from the beginning of development. Don't develop for six months on the Macintosh without testing and at the last minute decide your movie should play on Windows. You might be lucky and have no problems, but why take that chance? Testing your Director production and the famous quotation of Macromedia's John Dowdell, "Test early, test often, test on all of your target machines" are covered in Chapter 4, "Delivering the Goods."

Director for Macintosh and Director for Windows are virtually the same applications. You'll find that the interface is the same, and that Lingo works the same. Director users are pretty spoiled after they have the dual platforms set up. After a file is transferred to the other platform, opening it up and making sure it runs well is amazingly easy. Director takes care of almost everything for you, but you'll still need to learn a few differences.

Taking on a cross-platform project may mean learning another operating system you don't know very well. You will not only need to have Director on whatever platform you want to eventually distribute to, but you will also need to have an IBM-compatible PC or a Macintosh system. Currently the Macintosh machines with Soft-Windows will not hold up to Director's minimum requirements on the PC.

An Interview with Two Director Developers

The release of Director for Windows created an interesting time in the Director community. With Director's roots in the Macintosh, many Director developers had to get used to the Windows operating system. Windows developers new to Director were forced to become familiar with Macintosh-centric books and training materials and accept the general consensus that the Macintosh was the platform of choice. Little did everyone know that Director for Windows would take off as well as it did.

Windows experts came on the scene to help many of the Macintosh users. David Goldsmith and Tab Julius, both volunteer sysops on Macromedia's CompuServe forum at that time, became the resident Windows gurus in the forum. David Goldsmith taught me a lot about the Windows video and sound cards and often informed me which installer programs and sound utilities the Windows world was really using. Tab Julius started his weekly *Lingo Users Journal* and told of the DLLs he wrote. David often mentioned his requisite Macintosh in the corner that he used for testing.

Some time ago, David and Tab participated in a question-and-answer session about Director for Windows and Director development.

Why did your company choose Director for their development platform, David?

I did an extensive evaluation of multimedia tools available at the time and found Director to be the most cost-effective solution for JourneyWare Media's multimedia development projects. Director was the only authoring tool that allowed us to develop on both of our target platforms: Windows and Macintosh. With our developers' expertise in Windows, and with 80% of our target audience running Windows, we were delighted that Macromedia had come up with a solution that let us develop on Windows and easily port to the Macintosh.

A key feature for us was the ability to use object oriented techniques in our development. With Director, we were able to get a good start on building a class library that we can reuse in future projects.

What can you tell me about working cross-platform? How hard was it to go from Windows to the Macintosh?

We had no problem at all. In my opinion, it's essential that you begin authoring on whatever platform the majority of your audience will have. We encountered none of the problems usually associated with Windows multimedia development using Director. And going to Director for Macintosh was easy.

Tab, how long have you used Director?

I honestly didn't start using Director until Director for Windows came out, but immediately decided to make it my development system of choice.

What did you do before you used Director?

I'd been doing commercial software for many years, but usually for other people who would hire their own Macintosh engineers to do the Macintosh version. However, as my business (Penworks Corporation) started growing, I'd get requests to provide both Windows and Macintosh versions. See, nowadays many products have both Macintosh and Windows versions on the same CD, and this perception has taken root that all you do is recompile for one or the other. Obviously it's not so, at least not in C, so when I heard about Director for Windows I became immediately interested.

Why do you like Director?

I like Director because it abstracts me from the gritty details specific to each platform and lets me write programs that run, basically unchanged, on Windows, the Macintosh, and now the web. It's hard enough being at the top of the learning curve for just one platform (Windows); there's no way I could be at the top of three platforms. Now, I just try to write good programs and I let Director do the porting for me.

As a C programmer, what do you think about Director?

I was willing to accept Director as my development environment of choice because it is still extensible if I need it. I can still write C code and plug it in if I need to, so effectively I get the best of both worlds.

Tab and his company, Penworks Corporation, have developed many Director Xtras. Tab is also the author of Chapter 21.

The initial investment of a cross-platform authoring environment may seem a bit high at first. The long-term rewards are much greater, though, with royalty-free distribution of commercial titles to the entire PC market and a chance to create a multimedia version of any idea you have.

What's New in Director 6

Let's take a look at Director 6. Some of the new features have already been mentioned, but this section briefly describes each of the new features and tells you where you can find out more about them in this book. The new features in Director 6 have been developed with the goal of making it easier to use, providing better Internet integration and giving you access to more powerful technology.

Easier to Use

Director has been known for years as the most powerful multimedia authoring tool, but some have felt Director is too difficult to learn. Macromedia listened to its developers, and consequently, a set of new and enhanced features is designed to be easier to use. Experienced developers may take a short time to get used to these features but in the long run, new and old developers alike will find them less time consuming and easier to use.

The New Score

Director's score is the most noticeable change in Director 6. Animators now have 120 channels with which to work—more than twice the number in Director 5. Sprites are now created as complete objects that span a period of time. Properties and behaviors can be attached to these objects as a whole, moving away from the cell-based properties and animations of earlier versions of Director (see fig. 1.6).

Figure 1.6

The new score in Director 6.

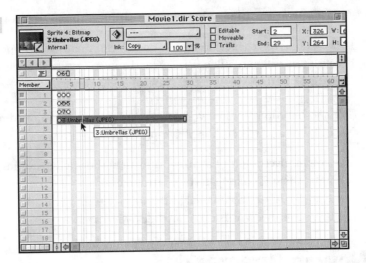

You can now open more than one score at a time, each with different views of the same movie information. The score can be expanded and zoomed, providing a flexible authoring environment. The new, red playback indicator displays in every channel in the active frame, and complete sprite information appears at the top of the score.

Sprite Overlay, Sprite Inspector, Sprite Paths

Sprite-level editing is much easier in Director 6 with the help of the new Sprite Overlay, Sprite Inspector, and Sprite Paths features (see fig. 1.7).

Sprite Overlay displays the most commonly edited sprite properties directly on the stage. Using Sprite Overlay with the new Sprite Inspector allows for quick, easy editing and more efficient authoring in Director 6.

Figure 1.7

The new Sprite Inspector and Sprite Overlay features help you edit sprites directly on the stage.

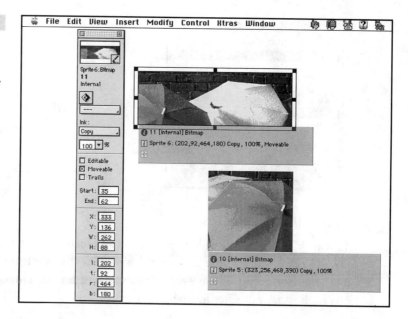

For increased animation control, Sprite Overlay has a feature that shows the path of a sprite. Sprite paths show up on the stage and can be edited directly there without ever using the score. Moving any keyframe in the animation on the stage or in the score automatically re-tweens the animation.

Using the new sprite information is covered in Chapter 5, "Working with Director 6: Understanding the Metaphor." Creating animations in Director 6 is covered in Chapter 6, "Director as an Animator."

Drag-and-Drop Behaviors

Scriptless authoring is now possible, via drag-and-drop behaviors, for people who do not want to use Lingo. Drag-and-drop behaviors offer an easier way to create interactivity in Director 6. Director 6 ships with a library of built-in behaviors that can easily be assigned to any object on the stage.

The Behavior Inspector, where you view, create, and edit these behaviors, has become one of the most integral windows in the Director authoring environment (see fig. 1.8). For the Lingo programmer, you can still create your own Lingo scripts. Behaviors actually create Lingo code. You can edit this code and create your own behaviors.

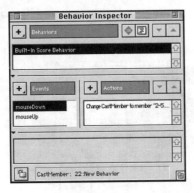

New Lingo Events

Many new Lingo events have been added to Director 6. Some of those that make Director easier to use include the `mouseEnter`, `mouseWithin`, `mouseLeave`, and `mouseUpOutside` events. These events make it easier for the Lingo programmer to detect rollovers and other mouse interaction.

For a list of the new Lingo terms in Director 6, take a look at Appendix B, "New Lingo Terms in Director 6." For information on using the new Lingo commands, turn to Part V, "Lingo."

Better Internet Integration

Shockwave for Director has defined the standard for multimedia on the Internet. Director 6 adds many new features to its authoring environment to support Shockwave, and the following features open themselves to the web right on your desktop.

Streaming Shockwave

Shockwave files no longer need to be downloaded completely onto the user's machine; they can stream over the Internet. Director developers can set up their files to begin playing immediately while the rest of the file downloads in the background. You can now create full multimedia titles to deliver over the Internet and have complete control over how they download onto the end user's machine.

Streaming Shockwave is covered in Chapter 14, "Creating Shockwave Movies."

Shockwave Integration

Director files can now take advantage of the Shockwave compression algorithm and files can be saved in the DCR file format. NetLingo is supported in the authoring environment and you can test your Shockwave movies directly, without launching a browser.

Transparent Internet Access

The Internet is available at all times in the Director 6 authoring environment. The new Network Preference dialog box enables you to set up a preferred browser, cache size, and other options from within Director, just like you would within a browser. This enables you to dynamically communicate with the web during both the authoring and playback environments.

Working with Director and the web is covered in Chapter 13, "Designing Multimedia for the Web."

Browser Scripting Support

Shockwave movies can now be controlled through standard browser scripting such as Live Connect, Active Script, Java Script, and ActiveX components. Shockwave movies and Java applets can communicate with one another.

More Powerful Technology

As with every new version of Director, Macromedia introduces some show-stopping new features that users have requested for years. Some of these features have been mentioned already, such as the support for 120 channels in the score. The following are other powerful new features that have been added to Director 6.

Media Synchronization

Director 6 now has the capability to synchronize animations with cue-points in sounds and digital video files. You can control Director's frame-based score to wait for specific times in these time-based media through the Tempo channel and Lingo control. Media synchronization was one of the most difficult techniques to accomplish in earlier versions of Director.

New File Format Support

Macintosh users will be happy to know that support for many new graphics file formats is available in Director 6. Besides the standard PICT, PICS, Scrapbook, and MacPaint options, you can also import GIF, JPEG, Photoshop, PNG, and xRes (LRG) files. Authoring for Shockwave with Internet file formats is much easier now.

Working with graphics in Director is covered in Chapter 8, "Graphics: The Visuals."

External Editors

Director 6 supports the launch and edit of its file formats, as mentioned earlier. The new Editors Preference enables you to designate which editor you would like to use for each file type. For example, you can launch Photoshop from Director's cast window when you double-click on a Photoshop file. The edits you make in Photoshop will automatically be updated in Director's cast.

Technology Adoption

In Windows 95, Director now supports Direct Draw API from Microsoft. This improves animation performance in 32-bit applications. Director 6 also supports the Microsoft Direct Sound technology in 32-bit applications, providing enhanced sound-mixing capabilities and performance.

On the Macintosh, Director 6 will be shipping with support for QuickDraw 3D and QuickTime VR.

The Director Community

One of the best things about Director is its supportive developer community. *Inside Macromedia Director 6 with Lingo* is actually a book by an entire group of developers who want to share what they have learned about Director. If you ever have a question about anything, someone will be there to help. Your first course of action should be to get online! The Director Internet Mailing list, called Direct-L, has developed into a respected community of high-level Director users. The Director engineers "lurk" around this forum to see what people are saying. Many Director-specific web pages created by third-party developers are also available.

Macromedia Users Groups are all over the world. A current list of these can be found at http://www.macromedia.com. To contact Macromedia technical support directly, you can access them on their CompuServe and America Online forums. The forums also publish library files with product updates, sample movies, techNotes from Macromedia technical support, and the KnowledgeBase, Macromedia's technical database of information.

Macromedia's web site will keep you up to date with all the Macromedia, Director, and multimedia and computer industry trends. As the product information, third-party information, and Shocked sites change, you will find the news first on the web site. More information on contacting Macromedia is included in Appendix C, "Contacting Macromedia."

If you are new to the Director community, welcome. You are not alone. If you've come from an artistic background, you'll feel right at home. If you are a programmer, you'll find Lingo easy to learn and the artistic aspects of Director intuitive. You're in store for a world of exciting technology and opportunities with a supportive development community. We look forward to seeing what you create.

In Practice

After this chapter's overview of Director, you probably know exactly which features and techniques you want to dive in to. If you are an experienced Director developer, you may want to charge ahead to specific chapters in this book. But if you are relatively new to Director or have not developed a project from start to finish, you will be in a much better position to tackle more detailed chapters if you first look at the big picture. Chapter 2 will get you started, with a look at how to plan and manage a Director project.

The central practical advice to take away from this chapter is the following:

- ▶ Mastering Director is a good investment in the multimedia future; Director is committed to standard distribution platforms and delivery methods that may emerge.

- ▶ Lingo, Xtras, and even C programming can extend Director's already considerable functions and capabilities.

- ▶ You can work in the platform of your choice and still produce cross-platform Director products.

- ▶ If you ever have a Director question, a wide and accessible community of users is eager to share their knowledge and expertise. You can reach the Director community via the Director Internet Mailing List, Macromedia users groups, and Macromedia's web page, among others.

Before You Get Started: Planning Your Director Project

This chapter discusses some issues to consider when setting up a production environment for your Director project. Large multimedia projects involve the coordination of programmers, interface designers, content experts, writers, graphic artists, audio specialists, videographers, and animators. At the outset, it's important to set standards for file naming, version control, documentation, and editing. Also, it's important to clearly define who has responsibility for the different parts of the production, such as graphics content, video content, audio content, script writing, programming, interface design, and so on.

Most of the recommendations in this chapter for setting up a production environment are relevant for simple projects and small teams as well as complex projects and large teams.

The model for multimedia production borrows from the publishing model, with authors and editors who both compose and revise information; the movie studio model, with a core staff of administrators, marketers, and creative directors who contract production to freelance talent; and the software development model, with full-time staff who support multiple systems, perform system integration, and create new versions and upgrades. Given the multiple media to be managed and their respective challenges and production models, the potential for complexity and frustration in developing a multimedia project is enormous. Careful and thorough planning and management of the process is critical.

The following subject areas are covered in this chapter:

▶ Production environment

▶ Production hardware

▶ Production software

▶ Content management

▶ Code documentation

Setting Up a Production Environment

This section covers some general recommendations for your production environment. Topics covered include setting up consistent production protocols and procedures. Although geared toward larger projects, most of the recommendations in this section are pertinent to smaller projects as well.

Document Everything You Do

Documentation of procedures is important. Documentation provides a database of tips and techniques that saves you time and money in future projects. Do not reinvent your workflow every time you want to burn a CD or retouch a scan. Carry a notebook with you and, as you perform tasks, jot down the steps you take, the problems that arise, and the solutions you derive. Set aside an hour or two a week to organize and write these notes and keep them in a three-ring binder for other team members to access. Provide a style sheet or form for documentation. If you are truly ambitious, you can create an online knowledge base that is accessible over a network.

For an online knowledge base or documentation form, include fields for date; name of person; functional category such as "Lingo programming," "Digital video editing," or "CD-ROM burning"; the purpose of the task, such as reducing 24-bit digital video to 8-bit; hardware and software used; a detailed list of steps taken; problems encountered; and results. For an online knowledge base, devise a consistent keyword scheme to facilitate searching and data normalization.

The documentation process is important on small projects you do yourself for use at another time. It is even more important, though, on projects with multiple people. If you hire contractors to help you build your project, require that they document what they have done.

Establish Naming Conventions

At the outset, determine a file-naming scheme for the Director movies, external casts, and final directories. If you are developing a hybrid HFS/ISO 9660 CD-ROM, the shared data must conform to the ISO 9660 naming conventions. Chapter 3, "The Strategy: Product Analysis and Design," discusses naming conventions in more detail. Be certain to create directories for Mac-specific data, PC-specific data, and shared data. Take a look at any hybrid CD-ROM, such as the CD that comes with this book, for an example. Create directories and subdirectories for external content and casts. The directory structure should mirror the organization of Director movies and score sequences. When you reference movies from Lingo, leave off the .DXR and .DIR extensions. If file names change, you can use Director's search-and-replace feature to change the names within Lingo scripts. Use a MacPerl, AppleScript, or Frontier script to change multiple file names at the System level on a Macintosh.

Devise a coding scheme for naming content in your project. Choose whatever works for you, but be consistent. Be certain that all team members use the same scheme. To make sorting easier, the first letter(s) of the file name should be a code for the most important aspect of that file, such as media type, color depth, or client name. Include a code for version tracking, which can be the initials of the person doing the current work, a version number, or an identifier such as "prototype1" or "final." If an intermediate step generates numerous auxiliary files or alternate versions, append an appropriate identifier, such as "edit1.1," and place them all in the same folder or directory.

If you are not constrained to the 8.3 DOS naming convention for Windows 3.11, for example, you could code QuickTime files as "QT"; the color depth as "8," "16," or "24"; movie dimensions as "160," "240," or "320"; presence of foreign language text tracks as "ENGL," "SPAN," "FREN," or "GERM"; and use an extension such as ".v1" for a version number. Then, if you want to arrange files on disc based on color depth, you could name your files something such as 24QT160SPAN.V1. If external media, such as digital video, will be delivered on Windows 3.11, you will have to conform to the DOS 8.3 naming convention. Chapter 4, "Delivering the Goods," contains more information on setting up a project for delivery.

Divide and Conquer

Consider dividing development responsibilities into manageable chunks based on function and content type. For example, one person can create interface elements, another can create digital video, and yet another can code the interface using external casts that contain placeholder or dummy cast members for the interface elements. Have the content developers create content as external casts. Then you can link the external casts to Director movies for testing during development.

Refer to your flowchart and storyboard (discussed in Chapter 3) and divide programming tasks based on the information flowchart and storyboard. Decide early the way in which the sections will interact. If the project consists of three main sections, for example, each of which contains 20 Director movies, then decide first the way in which the three primary sections interact at the top-most level and work your way down. Implement the most general data structures and most important features first, such as the basic navigation or help systems. Consider creating a "shell" or generic template into which you can add additional functionality as needed.

If you are working with the information flowchart, for example, you could decide to make each section of the flowchart a separate Director movie. First, code the navigation functions for the top-level Table of Contents screen. Then, create generic templates for the Symptoms screens and Treatment screens. These templates would provide basic navigational functionality and maybe a "shell" for a help system. The next step would be to add content, interface details, and context-specific help features to individual screens.

An alternative to this "top-down" approach is a "bottom-up" approach. In this approach, the lowest-level screens and Director movies are worked on first and the higher-level functions are laid on top of lower levels later in the development process. What works best for you depends on your project, the number of people working on it, and their particular preferences and programming styles.

Project management issues can have an impact on production infrastructure. If you have several workgroups working on different parts of a project and sharing files that are in different stages of development, you need to establish procedures for workflow, project tracking, and version control. A multimedia database on the back end helps manage content. You also must set production criteria and milestones to ensure that the project remains on time and on budget. Production plans can be shared verbally for small workgroups or shared in writing by recording task lists and process flowcharts for large workgroups.

Production Hardware

This section discusses the hardware requirements for authoring and digital media creation. Topics covered include authoring workstations, complementary hardware, production networks, and backup systems.

Authoring Workstations

The minimum authoring workstation requirements recommended by Macromedia are as follows:

Macintosh:

- ▶ 68040 processor or PowerPC
- ▶ System 7.1 or later
- ▶ 8 MB RAM
- ▶ 40 MB hard drive space

Windows:

- ▶ 486/66 or faster
- ▶ 8-bit video
- ▶ Windows 95, 3.1, 3.11, NT 3.5.1 or higher
- ▶ 8 MB RAM
- ▶ 40 MB hard drive space

Keep in mind that these requirements are the absolute bare minimum for authoring. You can never have enough RAM or a fast enough processor. An authoring workstation with a PowerPC or Pentium processor, 32+ MB of RAM, and 2 GB of internal hard drive space is probably more realistic.

Macromedia publishes a list of Windows Video and Sound drivers with which the Director authoring environment is compatible. See www.macromedia.com for details.

Complementary Hardware

You will probably want additional peripheral equipment for authoring and content creation. A 17-inch or larger monitor is beneficial for multimedia work, as are two-monitor systems. Graphics accelerator cards will speed up screen redraw. Most PowerPC Macintoshes come with built-in 16-bit, stereo audio. Generally, you will have to purchase a separate sound card for Windows PCs. Scanners and camcorders can be used to quickly create digital content. External storage and backups are important. Hardware for storage and backup is discussed later in this chapter in the section, "Backup Systems."

For CD-ROM development, a CD-ROM burner is essential. Even if you press your CDs at an external service bureau, CD-ROM burners are important for testing. You will probably want an external hard drive with at least 650 MB capacity to store an "image" of your CD content for burning. Probably even more important than the CD-burner is the software used to create CDs. Astarte's Toast Pro is a popular software package for creating CD-ROMs.

At some point, you may want to digitize audio and video for your project. Many Macintosh models, such as the PowerMac 8500/180, and some PCs come with built-in audio and video sub-systems that are suitable for digitizing tasks for web, intranet, and CD delivery. For more demanding digitizing requirements you will need a separate digitizing card. Capture audio and video to an "AV" rated drive (a drive optimized for the large file sizes and stable throughput required for digitizing). These drives are typically Fast or Fast/Wide SCSI drives. In addition, you will want off-line storage, for example, a 1 GB Jaz removable or magneto-optical drive. Chapter 11, "Sound: The Soundtrack" and Chapter 12, "Digital Video: The Movie Within the Movie" discuss audio and video digitizing issues in detail.

Ensure that drivers for multimedia peripherals, such as scanners, CD-ROM recorders, and digitizing boards, are compatible with your system hardware and software. This point is especially important for Windows systems, most notably Windows NT. Macromedia publishes a list of drivers supported by Director. Contact the vendors of a particular peripheral for information on compatibility.

Production Networks

Local area networks (LANs) can be an important productivity enhancer; however, if not optimized for multimedia production, LANs can result in a bottleneck. A large multimedia project involving multiple people on different workstations requires networking solutions to file sharing, asset storage, and backups. Even a small project involving a Mac and Windows authoring work-station, a couple of testing machines, and a tape drive back-up will benefit from a simple LAN for file sharing. Ethernet hubs that can link such a small LAN can be purchased for a couple hundred dollars.

The speed, bandwidth, and storage requirements of a multimedia production network can quickly overwhelm Ethernet-based LANs. If your multimedia production network is part of a larger enterprise network, you might need to isolate the production network from other network traffic. Fast Ethernet, Fiber Distributed Data Interface (FDDI), Asynchronous Transfer Mode (ATM), and Switched Multimegabit Data Service (SMDS) help reduce bottlenecks. Intelligent hubs enable individual workstations to optimize available bandwidth. Disk arrays and network-accessible optical jukeboxes can solve huge storage requirements.

The following is a possible model for a production network, illustrated schematically in figure 2.1, for a large multimedia project team involving several authors, programmers, and graphics people:

- ▶ Store master content on a magneto-optical or CD-ROM jukebox.

- ▶ Use a high-end Macintosh server or Silicon Graphics workstation as a file or application server.

- ▶ Attach a 9 GB disk array to your server with a 1 or 2 GB partition for each workgroup to store production files.

- ▶ Store edits and intermediate files in the workgroup partitions.

- ▶ Store personal archives on the local drives of client machines or on removable drives.

- ▶ Where necessary, mirror the directory structure of the final product on production drives.

- ▶ At the end of each day, move the material that meets the production criteria or milestone to a separate production archive that is a special drive with restricted write permissions. The material is now either eligible for further production processing by other workgroups or is frozen.

- ▶ Use file permissions to restrict who can access material from a drive or storage archive.

- ▶ Create disc images for test CDs from the production archive.

- ▶ Designate one person in each workgroup as the information "shepherd" to enforce version control and ensure that files are moved to correct locations.

Figure 2.1

Production network configuration.

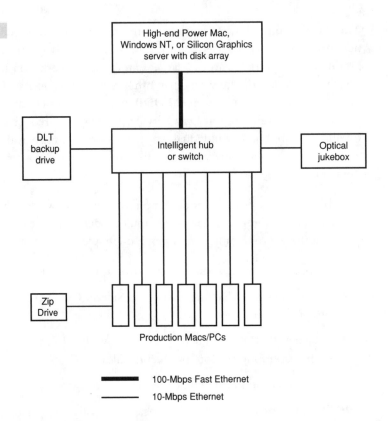

Backup Systems

A consistent and comprehensive backup strategy is critical. The backup system you choose depends on the amount of material you have to back up, the speed it takes to back up, the cost of drives and media, ease of use, and accessibility. Your backup system should be scaleable and expandable to accommodate the ever-increasing storage requirements of multimedia. The capability to perform unattended network backup is important for large networks. Having a centralized backup system is probably better than depending on each team member to back up his own workstation. You might consider using a dedicated server that backs up nightly to tape.

WARNING

Think of backups as an inexpensive insurance policy. Disasters happen. The first time you use one of your backups due to hardware failure, fire, earthquake, or another disaster, it pays for itself. Nobody thinks his system will be damaged or destroyed until it happens. Then it's too late.

Don't trust "fireproof" data safes. Store your backups in a location separate from your originals. If the building in which you store the backups burns down, you can still make new backups from your originals.

The software you use for backups should support scheduling, multiple volumes, remote network backups, and the capability to perform incremental and full backups. Retrospect backup software from Dantz Development Corporation is a popular choice. Keep a copy of your backups off-site.

Removable drives such as SyQuest drives, Zip drives, Jaz drives, and magneto-optical drives or external hard drives are generally cost-effective for backups in the 14 GB range or lower. The removable drives also provide fast backup rates and easy access to files. The removable drive market is changing rapidly. Read trade magazines for reviews of the latest technology and see whether it meets your current and projected requirements. Storage devices are frequently reviewed in *MacWeek, MacWorld, PC Magazine, InfoWorld, Byte,* and *New Media Magazine.*

Digital audio tape (DAT) drives provide up to 8 GB storage capacity per cartridge with transfer rates at approximately 20 MB per minute. DAT loaders provide higher storage capacities with multiple cartridges.

Digital linear tape (DLT) drives are more expensive than DAT drives but can back up files at rates up to 100 MB per minute. A single cartridge holds up to 30 GB of data using 2-to-1 hardware compression. DLT drives are designed for the backup of large files as opposed to several small files. DLT loaders provide higher storage capacities with multiple cartridges.

You can use recordable CD-ROMs for backups, but they have limited capacity and speed and are write-once. CDs are good for archiving purposes.

Production Software

You will probably use many different software programs during the production process. Asset management software is discussed in the following section, "Managing Content." This section includes coverage of categories of ancillary software such as media editors, project tracking, file exchange, and automation and batch processing.

Media Editors

Director comes with built-in media editors, such as the Paint window. This type of media editor is generally useful for touch-ups. However, you will most likely also create multimedia content in separate dedicated programs such as Premiere, After Effects, Photoshop, SoundEdit, xRes, and Extreme 3D, and then import content into Director. The additional software programs you choose to use depend on budget, expertise, the particular media on which you're working, and editing tasks you are doing.

Director 6 continues the trend of using Macromedia's content-editing applications, SoundEdit, xRes, and Extreme 3D for media editing. Double-clicking media in the Director cast typically will launch automatically one of these programs if it is available. You can also set a preferred editing application—such as Photoshop—for bitmaps in the Editors Preferences dialog box.

Project Tracking

Large productions may require dedicated project tracking software to manage workflow in complicated projects. Often, though, you can set up a spreadsheet, perhaps in Excel, to accomplish the same goals. In the spreadsheet, include fields for specific tasks, who is responsible for the task, time spent, milestones, deadlines, dependencies on other aspects of the production, and costs (see fig. 2.2).

Figure 2.2

A week in the life of a multimedia project.

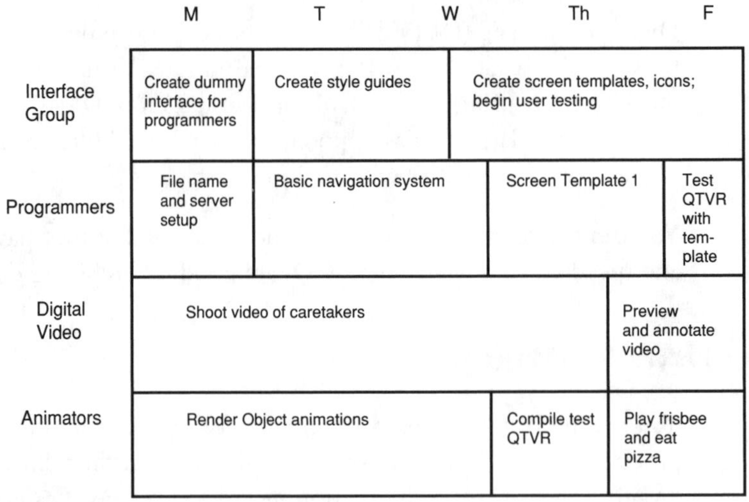

	M	T	W	Th	F
Interface Group	Create dummy interface for programmers	Create style guides	Create screen templates, icons; begin user testing		
Programmers	File name and server setup	Basic navigation system		Screen Template 1	Test QTVR with template
Digital Video	Shoot video of caretakers			Preview and annotate video	
Animators	Render Object animations			Compile test QTVR	Play frisbee and eat pizza

File Exchange

If you are developing cross-platform titles you will probably need to share files across platforms at some point. Macromedia has done an excellent job of making the file formats for their cross-platform products compatible on Macs and PCs. In addition, Macintosh can read and write to PC disks. Programs such as MacLAN enable sharing of files between PCs and Macs on a network. For additional network solutions, trade magazines such as *MacWorld* and *PC World* are good sources of information.

Automation and Batch Processing

Automating repetitive steps in Director can minimize production time. The following is a list of ideas to speed up the authoring process.

In Director 6, you can use Scriptable authoring and Lingo control of the score to streamline many tedious authoring tasks. Chapter 19, "Advanced Concepts," discusses scriptable authoring.

You can also use other automation solutions—such as CE Software's QuicKeys or WestCode's OneClick—to automate repetitive processes or ensure consistency in editing. An example of a task that would benefit from such a utility is when you want to repeatedly enter the same value in an editing dialog box.

With a Macintosh, scripting languages such as AppleScript, UserLand Frontier, or MacPerl provide even greater control over processes along with control over the system and other applications. All three languages support drag-and-drop and batch processing.

To batch process bit-depth reduction, resizing, file conversion, and many other image processing tasks, you can use Equilibrium Technology's DeBabelizer. To batch process audio processing, use Macromedia's SoundEdit 16 or Wave Technology's WaveConvert. Programs such as Adobe After Effects and Macromedia Extreme 3D enable you to set up batch renders that you can schedule to run at night or on weekends when computers are not being used for other tasks.

Managing Content

This section discusses content management. Managing content for a large project involves balancing the competing constraints of time, quality, and money. To produce a quality enhancement of 10 percent may take 50 percent of your budget and 80 percent of your time. Only you can decide whether it's worthwhile.

Multipurposing

Using existing content has the potential to save a lot of time and money, which you could then redistribute to other parts of your project. Snoop around for public domain material or collateral material to which you have the rights. Often, various departments in a large organization have collateral materials you can use. Many companies have media archives that contain videotapes, brochures, and training manuals. Maybe the facilities department has CAD-based maps of the company headquarters or perhaps there is a library where someone saved old photographs.

The downside of using existing content is that it often requires substantial investments in time and money to bring it up to acceptable quality. Corporate videos may be poorly lit or contain large areas of solid color that do not digitize well, making them unusable. Conversely, the video might be usable but you need additional footage. If you need to add material, such as additional video footage or voice-overs, it might be impossible to match the style or production values or to obtain the same talent used in the existing version.

When you have to create from scratch, you should design your original content with repurposing in mind. *Repurposing* means using the same content in different projects or on different media and delivery platforms. The content you create for your Director project might end up in print, broadcast video, CD-ROM, or the Internet. You can create the content once, then modify copies for a specific delivery platform. This usually is more efficient than creating new content for every project. Creating content once and repurposing it also helps to enforce a consistent look across multiple platforms and projects. Generally, creating original content at the highest resolution you can afford in time and disk space is a good idea. By using the highest resolution, the content survives the conversion to different formats and media. Consider such issues as what 24-bit graphics will look like dithered to 256 colors, what downsampling does to audio, and the trade-offs in different video compression formats.

Keep your high-resolution, original digital assets on a locked volume, such as a CD-ROM, to prevent accidental editing. Editing should only be done on *copies* of these originals. Keeping an edit log as you edit your content will prove useful. An edit log can be a text file in the same directory as the content and with the same name but with a .TXT extension. For example, GRPHC24.TXT would be the edit log for the file GRPHC24.PIC. Also, you can use an application-specific feature, such as Photoshop's File Info command from the File menu, to record information regarding the file.

You should always save intermediate versions of edited files in case you have to reconstruct a file after a bad edit. Save copies of your Premiere or After Effects projects because they provide a record of filters, effects, and compression settings. If you need to compress, reduce bit depth, resize, or in any way reduce the amount of actual information in your file, save this edit for last.

Master Content and Archives

Master content is the high-resolution, high-quality source that you use to create content for your Director project. High-quality master content facilitates repurposing, editing, and, if it is in analog form, digitizing. You should never edit or directly change master content; only edit copies.

One reason you want to spend time and money to create, digitize, or obtain high-quality master content is to save time and money when you need to generate derivative content for multiple products. If all you plan to do is create a one-shot, animated Shockwave banner, don't waste resources creating 24-bit graphics. If you intend to create corporate identity elements to use in different media and products, however, the benefits of high-quality master content are probably worth the cost. Look at the return on investment and evaluate whether it justifies the extra expense. Consider the "shelf life" of the content— the length of time before the material becomes dated. If you create and own original, high-quality content, consider licensing it to others as another way of earning back the investment.

Determine also the file formats you want to support based on compatibility with authoring and editing software and storage space. Save files in the format that preserves the most information. Devise a file-naming scheme that encodes information such as file type, file characteristics, client, and project name in the file name itself. Be certain to give master content files a special extension or identifier. For example, indicate master files with a capital "X," such as 24qt160span.X. On the Macintosh, you also could use the Label feature to give a common label to your master content files.

If your master content includes a multilayered Photoshop or Painter file, save the file in its native format to preserve the layering. The same is true for FreeHand artwork or other object-based drawing files. Make a copy of these files as PICT (or another format) for use in Director.

The resolution of a computer monitor is only 72 dots per inch (dpi), so you might think that you do not need to create files with more than 72 dpi. At some point in the future, however, you might use your digital assets in product packaging or the company's annual report. If repurposing for print is a possibility, you might want to create master content at a resolution greater than 72 dpi. Also, reducing the size and bit depth of graphic files usually works best if you start with high-resolution and high bit-depth originals. Another situation in which you might want to use a greater dpi is in scanning. Reduce the material to 72 dpi when you are ready to import it into Director. If you do not reduce the material to 72 dpi, a 144 dpi file, for example, will appear twice as large in Director.

Following are some typical file sizes for high-resolution digital media. When creating, storing, archiving, and editing master content keep these sizes in mind. At 72 dpi, a 640×480, 24-bit graphics file is approximately 900 KB in size. At 144 dpi, the same file is four times as large, or about 3.6 MB. For information about using graphics content in Director, see Chapter 8, "Graphics: The Visuals."

Digitize video at full-screen, 30 frames per second (fps) for master content purposes, and reduce the size and frame rate for your Director project. (Chapter 12, "Digital Video: The Movie Within the Movie," contains more information.) The file size of digital video depends on many factors, but 2–20 MB for every second of digital video is not unreasonable.

File sizes for one minute of uncompressed, digital audio range from 0.7 MB for telephone-quality (8-bit, 11 kHz, mono) to 10.6 MB for CD-quality (16-bit, 44 kHz, stereo). Chapter 11, "Sound: The Soundtrack," discusses digital audio in more detail.

Master content requires a lot of storage space. High-quality, high-resolution digital media—whether graphics, video, or audio—can consume vast amounts of storage space.

Maintaining libraries of videotapes, audio tapes, photographs, and printed source material can be costly and the materials can degrade over time. Digitized versions are more durable and easier to edit. After you spend the time and money digitizing material, you probably will want to archive it. One solution is to use one of the backup options discussed earlier in this chapter in the section, "Backup Systems." Storage on one-off CD-ROMs or a PhotoCD is another solution. CDs provide fast random access and write-protection, and they are accessible on any computer with a CD-ROM drive. CD-ROM jukeboxes provide access to multiple CDs from a network. (Remember to store a copy of the master content off site.) Other archive options are media servers and fast networks, provided you have a lot of money.

Asset Management Software

Organization, project tracking, version control, storage, and retrieval issues might be so sufficiently complex that you need to create a content database.

If so, you can use a general purpose database program, such as FileMaker Pro, a content browser, such as Extensis Fetch or Kudo Image Cataloguer, or an industrial-strength database designed specifically for multimedia content, such as the Cumulus Network Image Database from Canto Software. Your content database should include the following types of information:

- ▶ File name
- ▶ Keywords
- ▶ Licensing and copyright
- ▶ Size
- ▶ Dimensions
- ▶ Color depth
- ▶ Resolution
- ▶ Compression
- ▶ Edit history
- ▶ Project tracking information
- ▶ Source file
- ▶ Projects in which it is used
- ▶ Costs

Copyright and Intellectual Property

Copyright and intellectual property laws are murky, especially for digital media. The easiest way to handle copyright and intellectual property issues is to only use materials you own. If you do not own the material, purchase it and all rights to use it. If you cannot buy the material, you must obtain a license agreement, permission letter, or release form. If you use public domain material, make sure it is really free for you to use.

Even though you use material in one project, do not assume you can use it freely in subsequent products. As long as material is in the public domain, do not assume that all forms of it also are in the public domain. A piece of music may be in the public domain, but a recording of it by the San Francisco Symphony Orchestra probably is not. Also, you need to obtain a model release form when you use someone's likeness in a product. For more information about distributing Macromedia, Apple, and Microsoft products, refer to Chapter 4.

A comprehensive discussion of copyright and intellectual property issues is beyond the scope of this book, but several good references are available, including *The Multimedia Law and Business Handbook* by J. Diane Brinson and Mark F. Radcliffe, Ladera Press.

WARNING

The opinions set forth in this section do not constitute legal advice or counsel. Consult with a lawyer if you have any doubts about copyright or intellectual property issues for your project.

Code Documentation

Large Director projects generate a lot of Lingo code. The more code that must be maintained and debugged, the more important it is to document your code.

Code documentation consists of the following:

▶ Specifications and requirements for the project code. This includes such topics as the specific tasks the software will perform and the operating environment in which the software will be running.

▶ Descriptions of the algorithms and data structures.

▶ Descriptions of overall design and architecture.

Typically, keeping track of and maintaining an existing code base consumes the most time and effort in a large programming project. Consequently, making code readable and easy to maintain is important. Maintaining code involves fixing bugs that crop up, performing optimizations as bottlenecks in the shipping product become apparent, or adapting to new hardware and software requirements. For an extensive project, it is helpful to have a dictionary of the data structures used. The dictionary describes the data structures created for the specific project. The dictionary should list the names, data type, and purpose of the most important data structures. For example:

```
glUserHistory
```

The global variable `glUserHistory` is a list containing the names of the movies the user has visited. The list is modified by the user-defined `SetUserHistory` function in the `startMovie` handler of every movie. The user-defined `DisplayUserHistory` function takes the list and creates a pop-up menu when the user clicks on the Go button.

In addition to code documentation and a dictionary of data structures, it is helpful to have a written overview of the program design and architecture. The overview should indicate where important scripts reside in Director (score, frame, cast, movie), what these scripts do, and the way to implement an important feature such as navigation. The overview also should list any external files or Xtras you employ. If you use object-oriented techniques, prepare a class diagram that illustrates the relationships among classes.

Self-Documenting Code and Comments

Making your code self-documenting is a good idea. *Self-documenting* means that variables and functions have names that describe their purpose. Make your variable names reflect what the variable stands for, such as `ButtonSprite` or `NextMovie`. Nothing is more confusing than trying to read code in which all the variables are named x, y, z. Your functions should have names that reflect what they do, such as `HiliteButton` or `ProcessMouseDown`. Capitalize the first letter of multiword variable names. The goal is to make your code readable and understandable to someone else or to remind yourself, months later, what a variable stands for in case you forget. Lingo is generally case-insensitive. `HiliteButton` is the same as `hilitebutton` as far as Lingo is concerned; however, capitalizing the embedded words makes the code easier to read.

A common variable naming technique is to start every global variable with a lowercase g, such as `gMyGlobalVariable`. You also can start each variable name with a lowercase letter that stands for the data type of that variable. For example, use `sTodaysDate` for a variable that contains the date as a string; `iAge` for a variable that contains the user's age as an integer; or `lMovies` for a variable that contains a list of movies. Variables in Lingo can contain a string, integer, object, or any other data type. Coding the variable type into the variable name helps prevent the programmer from assigning the wrong data type to the variable. You can extend this technique to multiple characteristics. For example, `piAge` could be the property of an object that is an integer.

Comments are statements in your code that begin with a double dash (--). Director ignores these statements. Adding comments to your code is essential for readability, but you can overdo it. Don't clutter your code by commenting the obvious. The goal of comments is to make the code readable and maintainable. In general, it is a good idea to provide comments for the following:

- ▶ New variables
- ▶ Code structures such as if-then statements and repeat loops

▶ Functions

▶ Any nonobvious or obtuse code (of course, no one ever writes obtuse code!)

Include the following information in comments about a function:

▶ What information and data types are sent to the function

▶ What the function does

▶ What data the function returns

▶ Where the function is used in the overall program design

Because Lingo scripts can contain styled text, you can use colors and text styles to highlight different parts of your code. You can make all comments italicized, for example, or all references to a particular object a shade of red. To colorize your text, select the text you want to colorize and choose a new foreground color from the pop-up palette in the Tools palette.

Version Control

Document any changes you make to existing code. Create a comment section in a prominent place; for instance, the beginning of the `startMovie` handler, where programmers insert comments as they make changes. The comments should indicate the date, the programmer's initials, and the changes the programmer makes. Another good idea is to insert comments with the same information in the code itself, at the location where major changes are made.

In Practice

The rules of managing your production environment vary from project to project, but a few recommendations are useful:

▶ In many cases, the most efficient ways of working on your project reveal themselves as you confront problems and create and revise solutions. Document everything you do so that processes can be evaluated and optimized as you go, and so that optimal procedures are recorded for sharing with other team members and for future use.

▶ Define an intuitive, consistent file-naming convention at the beginning of the project.

▶ For projects with teams of people, define team roles and responsibilities clearly; make certain that all team members understand their own and others' roles.

▶ Spreadsheets or databases for project management, content management, or both can be useful or even necessary depending on the complexity of your project.

▶ Develop a plan for backing up your work—including a schedule—and use it!

▶ Make a careful analysis of whether the content you need already exists in some form or must be created from scratch. For all your content, consider whether it will need to be repurposed. The form and quality of content that needs to be repurposed may be different from content that will be used only once.

▶ Keep master content on a locked volume; use only *copies* of this content for editing and revision purposes.

▶ The rules of good programming apply to multimedia projects as much as to any other programming task. Document your code accurately and thoroughly.

There are no hard and fast rules in multimedia development. Borrow what you can from television, film, computer software, and publishing development models, but realize it's a new frontier. Rapid changes in hardware and software tools make multimedia development a continuously evolving process. The skills and tools you have today might not be used in two or three years—never stop educating yourself.

chapter 3

David Miller

The Strategy: Product Analysis and Design

This chapter looks at some of the issues you should consider if you think you are ready to begin authoring or if you are developing a proposal or budget for a multimedia project. What does the product do? Who is it for? What platform will it run on? Defining these issues at the outset saves you much grief and hair-pulling later on.

Director projects can take many forms, and no development strategy fits every project. Projects can be developed by single authors in garages or by production teams with seven-figure budgets. Each project has its unique design requirements and creative solutions. Still, all projects share the goal of trying to communicate information using rich, multimedia content. This chapter outlines a development strategy for going from concept to prototype and provides a framework that you can adapt to the goals of your specific project.

The road from concept to prototype consists of three primary steps:

1. Analysis: What are you doing?

2. Design: How are you going to do it?

3. Implementation and prototyping: Do it!

The steps are followed in chronological order. The goal of each step is to produce a set of design documents that provide a road map and reference point for the next step. The prototype step has the additional goal of producing a partial working model of the end product. The documents produced during analysis, design, and prototyping form the basis for manuals and user documentation.

While you are in the middle of each step, bounce ideas off colleagues; be creative; brainstorm. Do not be afraid to try new ideas. But at the end of each step, come to a consensus and freeze the design. If necessary, revise the budget and time line. Do this early in the development process before feature creep and design drift consume your resources.

Feature creep is the tendency to tack on features to your software that go beyond its core functionality. A lot of commercial software suffers from this syndrome whereby the pressure to create upgrades produces software with unnecessary complexity and a feature set that most people don't need or use.

Design drift occurs when you begin changing your design in ways that don't support your design goals (for example, adding a richly textured 3D interface just because it's the cool thing to do and not because it adds value or functionality to your product).

In general, the initial analysis, design, and prototyping should make up about a third of the total development time. Final authoring, production, and content creation should take another third, and quality assurance testing another third (if you're lucky!).

The project development strategy and design guidelines presented here are just that: guidelines. Know the rules but know when to break the rules if it suits the design goals of your project.

Analysis: What Are You Doing?

During the analysis phase, nail down the goals and project specifications. What exactly do you want the product to do? For whom? On what platform? Is the purpose of your project entertainment, education, reference, or some combination of these?

Define the Goals

The first step in defining your goals is to ask yourself, "What is this product trying to accomplish? Why does the product exist?" Are you trying to sell something, provide access to reference material, or reduce the client load for the customer support division? Write down these goals. In many ways, defining the goals is the most important part of the design process. At every decision point in your project, you should ask yourself, "Does this help me accomplish the product's goals?"

Another way to look at goal definition is to define the message that you want to convey. What story are you trying to tell? Why does the user want to use the product? What is the hook?

Write down a list of goals on a sheet of paper and ensure that everyone on the development team has a copy. Every element of the project—including graphics, layout, and information design—should reflect these goals.

Define the Audience

You can define your audience in many ways. Imagine that you are a typical user. Create a list of the demographics of your typical users. These might include education, age, and familiarity with computers and the subject matter, among others. Is the product for twelve-year-old gamers or computer-naive elders? What do these typical users want from your product? What assumptions and attitudes do they bring with them? Are they a captive audience? Will your product be a discretionary purchase for them? Your design will follow different tracks depending on the answers to these questions.

Talk to your users. A little informal market research cannot hurt, especially if you do not have access to market research data. Ask them what they like and dislike about products similar to the one you will be creating, and what they wish those products could do. If your product doesn't fill a perceived need, no one will want to use it.

After you define your audience, you may need to change—moderately or significantly—your product's goals. Do it now. It is easier to make changes early in the development process. The assumptions you make about your audience will affect every decision you make. If you reach the prototyping stage and your target audience finds the product unusable, annoying, or silly, you've just wasted a lot of time and money.

If your product will be distributed internationally, start keeping track of cultural and language-specific items as you become aware of them. Consult experts in localization and cross-cultural pitfalls. When designing screens, for example, you might need to leave extra space on the screen for the text of different languages. Be aware also of the cultural assumptions about visual symbols and colors. In some cultures, colors have special significance. In Islamic countries, for example, green is often a holy color, and in Japan, white is associated with death. With Director 6, you can create multiple casts each designed for a specific culture or language and then switch casts at run time based on the user's culture and background. Managing multiple casts is covered in Chapter 7, "Multiple Casts."

Is the product accessible to people with hearing loss, sight impairments, or limited motor skills? Designing maximum accessibility often improves the design for everyone. You could make your product more accessible by choosing fonts that make text more legible, creating buttons that are bigger and easier to click on, or adding speech recognition or voice synthesis.

Digital Dreams creates a speech recognition Xtra for Director. Find out more at

`http://www.surftalk.com/`

Define the Delivery Platform and Delivery Media

Decide on the minimum system requirements for running your project. Director 6 projects run on a broad range of operating systems and hardware. Macromedia provides a list of supported hardware, video cards, and sound cards. Although Macromedia has done well at making Director files transparently cross-platform, you still must be aware of cross-platform differences in such elements as file names, fonts, palettes, and the gamma values of monitors. You can find some of these differences in the "Using Director" manual that comes with the Director documentation. Chapter 4, "Delivering the Goods," goes into more detail on this critical topic.

Content Inventory

Now is a good time to take stock of content, such as text, graphics, digital audio and video, videotapes and audio tapes that you will need to digitize, and all other collateral material. If you can use existing content, you might be able to save time and money. Obtain the highest-quality originals of the content if you can.

Start a content inventory by making a list of existing content. Next to each content element, indicate the additional work that needs to be done to modify or repurpose the content for your project. You might need to break text into digestible chunks for the computer screen. Graphics, animation, and video might need to be edited or compressed so that they can be displayed on your minimum system. Do you have the copyright or license to use the material? If not, can you get a copyright, or is the material in the public domain?

Next, make a list or spreadsheet of the content that you need to create from scratch. Indicate media type, dimensions, resolution, time length, estimated cost, and anything else you think is important. Do not worry about accounting for all the content in your project now; just give a general picture of what needs to be done. Creating and editing content is often the most expensive part of a project, so making a list or spreadsheet is a good way to estimate costs and keep your budget in line. Keep this list nearby as you continue the development process and update it frequently. Your minimum system requirements place limits on the kind of content you can use. Beware of the technical limits of the media and playback systems you are using and how they restrict what is possible.

Look out for gratuitous media that can bloat a project. Creating original animation, video, and 3D graphics can quickly eat up time and budget. Whether you create original content or use stock content, it can consume memory and processor time, degrading the overall performance. Do you really need a CD-quality soundtrack to accompany the virtual reality tour of the company's corporate headquarters?

Consider devising a coding scheme to name content. If the dimensions of your graphics are an important element of the content, include the dimensions in the file name, such as HOUSE280.PIC. If color or black-and-white versions are available, call it HOUSE280C.PIC.

Organizing content into categories makes updating easier. It also makes using the multiple cast features of Director 6 easier. You could define a separate cast for each content category, making the content easier to find, organize, update, and change.

As discussed in Chapter 2, "Before You Get Started: Planning Your Director Project," organizing a great deal of content may require creating a content database.

Information Design and Flowchart

In this step, you design a structure for presenting your information. What is most important about the information? Try to organize the information into manageable chunks based on your stated project goals. Begin writing down topic headings and subheadings. Arrange them hierarchically and draw links between topics. What relationships in the information do you want to emphasize? The hierarchy should not be too deep; generally, anything more than three or four section levels deep is difficult for users to keep track of. Links between sections will become the paths that a user follows to access the information. Generally, links should flow logically between sections without unexpected jumps or leaps. The user should find it easy to get to the most important information. Does it take more than three jumps to get to any place in your information structure? If so, you should consider reorganizing, offering navigational shortcuts, or both.

What are the two or three most common tasks that the user will perform? Is it easy for her to do these tasks?

In addressing all these questions, focus on the information content and the logical connections among various forms of information. For now, do not worry about what media you will use, how the information will fit on a computer screen, or how Director will be used. At the end of this process, you should have a flowchart to be used as the information map for your project. Figure 3.1 illustrates two very simple flowcharts.

Figure 3.1

Examples of two flowcharts for the same information in a health-care education product.

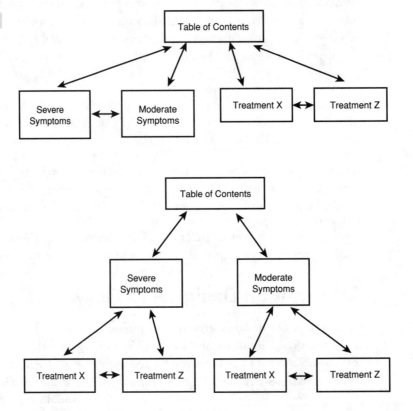

By breaking down the information into sections, drawing links, and creating a flowchart, you are setting the stage for the storyboard, in which you start adding media and designing interfaces.

You can break down the information into sections and subsections in several ways:

- ▶ By Category

- ▶ By Scaled Quantity

- ▶ Spatially

- ▶ By Time

- ▶ Alphabetically

Categories can be anything appropriate to the content. In Figure 3.1, the information for a health care product is categorized as symptoms and treatments. Be aware of the underlying assumptions in your categories. Are you inadvertently emphasizing one aspect of the information at the expense of another?

Information can be organized by scaled quantity, such as from cheap to expensive or from easy to difficult. Figure 3.1 incorporates this method, along with categories, by designating symptoms as moderate or severe. A catalog of real estate properties might be organized by price, or educational software might be organized by level of difficulty.

Spatial organization, such as a map, is perfect for geographical data, but other kinds of information can also be organized this way, with spatial proximity emphasizing relationships. You don't have to be constrained to two dimensions, either; three-dimensional spatial interfaces are becoming increasingly popular.

Arranging information temporally, such as in a time line, is a common organizational scheme. Temporal organization is good for historical information and narratives.

If text searching is important, you can arrange information alphabetically. An alphabetized hypertext index or glossary is a handy, familiar way for users to find topics and jump to specific sections.

If you are repurposing existing material, such as the script of a corporate video or a training manual, it will already have an informational structure. The Table of Contents, Glossary, and Index will already have an implied informational structure. You'll need to consider how well that structure meshes with the goals of your project.

After you have decided on an information flowchart for each section and subsection of your flowchart, ask these two questions:

- ▶ What task is the user going to perform in this section?

- ▶ What is the goal of this section?

Write down the tasks and goals for each section. These tasks and goals will form the basis for the navigational design and interface design. If you cannot articulate a task and a goal for a section, rethink your information structure.

End Result

At the end of the analysis phase you should have the following design documents:

▶ Statement of Goals

▶ Audience Definition

▶ Delivery Platform and Delivery Medium Specifications

▶ Content Inventory

▶ Flowchart

Make sure every member of the design team has a copy of the statement of goals, audience definition, and delivery platform specifications. These documents will guide every design decision you make.

Design: How Are You Going to Do It?

In the design phase, you merge the flowchart with content and sketch the user interface, screen layouts, and navigational controls. You determine the number of screens for each section of the flowchart and the content displayed on each screen. When designing screen layouts and interfaces, do not worry about the details. Just block out the positions of the main interface elements, such as buttons, text, graphics, and digital video. You can use paper and pen or a drawing program such as FreeHand or Director to sketch the interface—whatever works best for you.

Using a computer to design your storyboard has many benefits. Screen objects are easy to move and resize on a computer. Using a computer will help you figure out the quantity of text that will fit within a particular space and the way on-screen colors will look.

At the end of the design phase, you have a storyboard to use when you start creating your product in Director.

User Interface Principles

The way in which you design your interface depends on your product goals. Making your product easy to use is usually one of those goals. The easiest-to-use interfaces are transparent; they get out of the way and let the user get work done.

Users like to feel in control of the computer and be able to directly manipulate objects on the screen, so be careful about whether and how you limit user control. Be consistent in the ways that you indicate to the user which objects she can click, drag, or edit. When the user manipulates something, provide visual and aural feedback. If a user begins a process that will take more than a few seconds to complete, show a watch or other "busy cursor."

Also, design a consistent interface. A particular button should always have the same function and be in the same place. It should not disappear unexpectedly or suddenly do something different because it may confuse the user.

Let the user make mistakes and undo actions. Do not be rigid in your design. Consider enabling the user to customize the interface in some way. By enabling the user to customize the program, you increase their involvement and engagement with your product.

INSIDER TIP

Apple Computer has made their excellent user interface guidelines available free of charge on the Internet. You can find these guidelines—along with a lot of other useful material—at http://www.info.apple.com. "The Macintosh Human Interface Guidelines" can usually be found in the Developer Services-Technical Documentation-Human Interface directory.

Help

The interfaces you design are always completely transparent and intuitive, right? Even so, it is often a good idea to provide some kind of on-screen help. A help feature is especially important if your users are unfamiliar with computers. You can provide a help feature in several ways. You can create a separate help screen or a floating Movie in a Window (MIAWs are covered in Chapter 18, "Movie in a Window"), or create help balloons or pop-ups such as Director's ToolTips. You also can use Director's animation features to provide guided instruction and task emulation.

Navigation and Interactivity

In general, on each screen the user should be able to answer the following questions: Where am I? Where can I go? How do I get there? Navigation should be simple, consistent, and intuitive. In contrast, if you are designing a game, you might want the navigation to be difficult. An immersive, virtual reality environment will have different navigation than the navigation needed for a sales demo. Again, your design goals define your navigation.

As mentioned previously, try to design a navigational structure in which the most important information is easily accessible and users only need to jump three levels or so to get somewhere within the information structure. Providing a shortcut to a home screen, index, or table of contents on every screen can be a good way to minimize jumping through hoops to navigate an information structure.

It is a good idea to make all navigation reversible. If the user jumps somewhere, he should be able to jump back. You might want to include a list of the screens that the user has visited to help him keep track of where he has been. You can use Director's List data structure to keep track of user actions. If the user visits your product more than once, consider creating an external preference or bookmark file.

Generally, you should group together buttons and controls that have related functions. Keep these groups in a consistent screen location. If for some reason a button is inactive or unavailable, it is better to show this by dimming the button or by some other way than by having the button disappear.

Ensure that the function of each button and control is clear. Do not create similar-looking buttons that do different things. If the button that takes you to the next screen is a right-pointing arrow, do not use a similar right-pointing arrow for another function, such as playing digital video. If you use an icon for a button in one screen, do not reuse the icon as part of a nonclickable graphic somewhere else in the product. If you use drop-shadows or 3D, chiseled edges to indicate clickable regions, do not incorporate these elements in other graphics. The user will think they are buttons.

Consider using both icons and text to label your buttons. Clear, easy-to-understand icons can be difficult to design for certain functions. If you use text labels, it is generally best to capitalize the first letter of each main word in the label. Usability studies indicate that text is more readable on-screen this way.

Besides navigational elements, what other screen elements will the user be able to manipulate? What media controls will you provide? Is it necessary for the user to have frame-by-frame control of digital video? Of sound volume? In what way will the user interact with large pieces of related text that will not fit on one screen? Will she, for example, jump to a new screen, use scroll bars, or turn virtual pages?

Creating a Storyboard

The *storyboard* is the main outline for the project. It merges the flowchart, script, screen layout, and navigation design into a single document.

Script

Gather the narration and text (other than labels and buttons) and put them into one document in the order that they will appear in the product. This document is your text script.

Director's score gives you control of the flow of events over time. If your project is heavily time-based and requires synching audio, video, voice narration, and screen display, it might be a good idea to create a time line for each screen. Use your text script as a basis and insert audio, video, and animation cues when they should occur. Director 6 recognizes cue points in AIFF files created in SoundEdit to enable tighter synchronization. If your project contains extensive animation or digital video, consider writing separate screenplays to give to animators and videographers.

Screen Layout

Screen layout defines the position of interface objects and media on the computer screen. Designers in print media have traditionally used grids to provide consistency, balance, and structure in page design and layout. Screen layouts have many of the same design criteria as print pages, so consider using a grid as a framework for designing screens. Director comes with the capability to define grids on the stage during authoring, similar to many illustration and layout programs. An alternative to a grid is a 3D metaphor, such as a theatrical stage or desktop.

Create a grid using Director or another program or sketch it on a piece of paper. Add the navigation controls and screen objects that will be common to all screens. These might include such objects as headings and labels. Do you have any room for the content? You can use the layering features of Director or your illustration program to turn layers on and off.

After adding objects that will be common to all screens, begin adding other elements. At minimum, consider producing seven or eight layouts for each type of screen in your product. Then, you can narrow down your sketches to two or three basic designs. Do not worry about getting the screen layouts perfect. You will have time to do that during the prototyping phase.

Storyboard

Now it is time to create the storyboard. Get the project team together. (If you are the only person working on the project, invite yourself to a meeting.) To perform collaborative storyboard design, you can use a computer with a large screen display or a whiteboard, blackboard, or corkboard with slips of paper and thumbtacks. Determine the number of screens for each section of the flowchart and the content you want to display on each screen. Sketch each screen on a separate sheet of paper with references to content and script (see fig. 3.2), and thumbtack the papers to a corkboard. Try to visualize the big picture. Then, focus on the screen level and question the functionality of every element. In what way does each element help you meet your design goals?

Figure 3.2

Sample page from a storyboard.

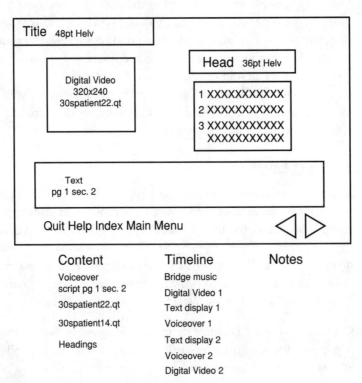

Show your storyboard and flowchart to potential users, colleagues, and friends. Potential users might reveal logical inconsistencies in your information structure and flowchart. If inconsistencies do exist, go back and revise your flowchart and navigational design. Correcting design flaws and inconsistencies early is generally cheaper and easier than doing so later.

End Result

At the end of the design phase you will have your project outline: the storyboard. This design document is the road map for production; it provides a visual overview of the entire project. By updating the storyboard to reflect completed, added, deleted, or revised elements as the project progresses, you can get a quick idea of how the development process is going. The storyboard also will provide a reference point for all team members. By sticking to the storyboard, you can help avoid potential design side trips that can throw your project off course.

Implementation: Do It!

During the implementation phase, use the storyboard and Director 6 to create a working model of your project. The working model is called a *prototype*. Director 5 introduced many features to help you create a prototype, including grids, multiple casts, and scriptable authoring and Lingo control of the score. Director 6 has added score enhancements and drag-and-drop behaviors to even further streamline the prototyping process.

Use the basic principles of user interface design and navigation design discussed earlier in this chapter to help you create your prototype. Prototyping may reveal serious design flaws and you might need to go back and revise your storyboard or flowchart. That is okay—better that you find out now, rather than a week before the ship date when changes could put you weeks or months behind deadline and thousands of dollars over budget.

Cross-Platform Considerations

If you are developing for cross-platform delivery, you need to develop a prototype for each platform. Windows and Mac programs typically follow certain interface conventions that users have come to expect from software. Quick and dirty ports from one platform to another are usually easy to spot for their non–Mac-like or non–Windows-like behavior. By developing a prototype for each platform, you can tailor the interface and functionality to the users of each platform and avoid the headache of incorporating interface and design changes late in development.

If you are delivering content for Windows 3.1, your file names—including linked, external files—must conform to the DOS 8.3 naming convention.

INSIDER TIP

If you are developing cross-platform, the following Lingo function will return the correct path delimiter for the current system.

```
on GetPathDelimiter

        if the machineType = 256 then

                return "\"

        else

                return ":"

        end if

end
```

You can build platform-independent path names, such as the following:

```
"MYDRIVE"&GetPathDelimiter()&"MOVIES"
```

Make sure your file and path names conform to the naming conventions of your minimum system.

For more information on using Lingo, see Part V, "Lingo."

If you use field cast members in Director (cast members that contain text), you must consider cross-platform differences in font display. Fonts on Windows systems tend to be larger than their Macintosh counterparts, taking up more screen real estate. You can use the FONTMAP.TXT file (described in the "Using Director" manual) to map different point sizes to each other on Mac and Windows systems. Still, differences in platform font display technology make achieving consistent cross-platform font display a matter of trial and error.

Pixel dissolves on Windows machines tend to look blockier and more ragged. Some Windows graphics drivers do not handle transitions and certain ink effects correctly. Test your product with as many different displays on Windows as you can. Windows systems also reserve certain colors in 8-bit palettes for interface elements. Check to see what your project looks like on 8-bit Windows systems if you use custom palettes. Graphics greater than 8-bit are not supported in Windows 3.1. Also, Windows monitors tend to display colors darker than Macintosh counterparts.

Many Windows systems cannot play two sounds simultaneously, such as a button click over background music. Macromedia has created a special DLL for Windows that enables you to mix AIFF and WAV sound files on Windows. See Chapter 11, "Sound: The Soundtrack," for more details on handling audio, including QuickTime audio in your project.

Prototypes

This section describes various prototyping strategies. Your prototype will probably be a mixture of these types. The goal of prototyping is to reproduce and evaluate the functionality of the final product as much as possible, without actually creating a complete, fully functioning final product. Prototyping enables you to test the most design-critical elements of your product before you begin serious authoring. Design-critical elements might include the most difficult or time-consuming components, the most central components, from which everything else derives, or the most expensive or labor-intensive.

Proof-of-Concept

You might want to try something in your product that has never been done before. For example, you might want to implement an artificial intelligence algorithm in Lingo or use a voice-recognition Xtra in a crowded computer lab. Can you do it? Who knows? It is time to create a *proof-of-concept demo*—which is a functioning prototype of your innovative element—to test its feasibility. You need to isolate the elements of the system that you need to test and begin a mini-design process.

Content

When you create your prototype, choose an extreme or most resource-intensive example (such as digital video or audio) from each of your content categories so that you can test playback and display. If the color-fidelity of 24-bit graphics is critical to your design goals, for example, make sure you include at least one 24-bit graphic in your prototype.

Broad Prototypes

In a broad prototype, you extensively develop a single layer within the information hierarchy. Screens in this layer are prototyped as fully as possible, and layers above and below are developed less completely.

Deep Prototypes

A deep prototype tunnels through your information structure. A screen from each layer is prototyped as fully as possible while adjacent screens on that layer remain sketchy.

Look-and-Feel Prototypes

A look-and-feel prototype emphasizes screen and interface design. Choose a representative screen or group of screens and bring them as close to the final version as possible. Adjacent or similar screens do not have to be as completely developed or as functional.

Using Director as a Prototyping Tool

Other chapters in this book contain many tips and techniques that you can use to help prototype your project.

You can use external casts to create cast libraries of different interface elements and rapidly switch between them at authoring time or run time. Find out how to use multiple external casts in Director 6 in Chapter 7.

You can use scriptable authoring to rapidly create reusable score templates. Chapter 19, "Advanced Concepts," discusses scripting the authoring process.

Use drag-and-drop behaviors to rapidly create user interfaces, buttons, sliders, and controls. Chapter 4, "Delivering the Goods," discusses using drag-and-drop behaviors.

User testing is a critical component of the prototyping phase. It can reveal design flaws that can be fixed before the product ships. User testing is covered in Chapter 4.

End Result

Now that you have reached the end of your analysis, design, and prototyping phases, you should have a well-defined prototype and a set of design documents to guide authoring and content creation. By following these design and implementation steps, you should save yourself trouble later on and be able to create a product of which you can be proud.

In Practice

Developing a strategy of analysis and design is as important and as creative as the actual implementation stage of your project. This chapter laid out a generic process of analysis, design, and implementation, in addition to some specific recommendations, that you can adjust to fit your project. Distribution is another strategic consideration you should consider sooner rather than later. The next chapter covers distribution and the role of testing, to close out our overview of product development.

▶ Analysis is the first phase of your project and includes defining goals, audience, delivery platform, delivery media, and content inventory. This information should be documented to provide formal, referential guidelines throughout the project.

▶ The analysis phase also should produce a flowchart that breaks the product into sections or components of information and illustrates their relationship to one another.

▶ In the design phase, you produce a storyboard that merges flowchart, script, content descriptions, screen layout, and navigation design into a single document. This process may reveal design flaws that require revising your information structure, navigational design, or both.

▶ In the implementation phase, you develop a prototype of the product. Prototyping should focus on the most critical or difficult (or both) components of the product.

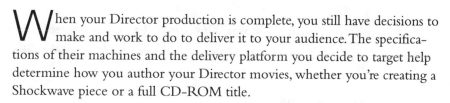

chapter 4

Lee Allis

Delivering the Goods

When your Director production is complete, you still have decisions to make and work to do to deliver it to your audience. The specifications of their machines and the delivery platform you decide to target help determine how you author your Director movies, whether you're creating a Shockwave piece or a full CD-ROM title.

Much of this chapter deals with the distribution issues you must deal with after your production is complete. Even though you won't be resolving these issues until late in your project, you need to anticipate them from the beginning because they have practical consequences for project planning and development. The reason for covering distribution issues so early in this book is so that you will know the tricks of delivery from the beginning and keep them in mind as you combine your graphics, videos, sounds, and animations into a final format. You'll want to turn back to this chapter for reference when you are truly ready to deliver the goods.

From a technical standpoint, delivering a Director project takes practice and attention to many details. This chapter discusses some of the best-known tips for testing and delivering a Director production, and it is organized by the following main topics:

- ▶ Testing your Director project
- ▶ Setting up the projector
- ▶ Deciding what to include with your projector
- ▶ Made with Macromedia
- ▶ Distributing the movie

Testing Your Director Project

Most everyone who has worked in the Director community recognizes the name John Dowdell. John is the senior technical support engineer at Macromedia and has taken many Director authors through troubleshooting issues related to delivering a project. John's famous quote is, "Test early; test often; test on all of your target machines." This testing section covers tips to complete each of these steps in detail.

Test Early

Test early. Don't wait until you're ready to ship your product to test what you've developed. Don't wait until the end to take your movie over to the Windows platform if your Director for Macintosh project is cross-platform. The following are some suggestions to follow as you test your Director production.

Test the Media

From the beginning of development, you need to test the media elements you introduce to your Director movie. Make sure each cast member—after you import it—works well within Director.

If you import a sound, play the sound from the Sound Cast Member Properties dialog box; if you import a digital video file, double-click on the file in the Cast window and preview it in the Video window; if you import a graphic, take a look at it in the Paint window. If these elements don't perform or appear to your satisfaction within Director, you might need to take them back to the digital video editing, sound editing, or graphics editing tools they came from for further editing.

INSIDER TIP

You can now specify external editors within the Director 6 Editors Preference to launch when you double-click a cast member in the Cast window. The external editor launches and immediately opens the cast member for editing. Changes made in the external editors are updated in the cast when you save the file in the editor.

When you import cast members, be aware of their location on the hard drive. If you link a sound or graphic, or if you import a QuickTime file, be aware that the path to that cast member is recorded in its member properties. If you end up moving the linked media element on the hard drive, you must relink or reimport it at a later time. Failing to do this causes the embarrassing "Where is..." dialog in your projector playback.

Create Small Movies

On a large Director project, create small movies and modules. It is easier to work with small files: They take less time to save; they make troubleshooting easier; and they also perform better on lower-end machines. If you divide your project into a series of smaller files, you can navigate among them with Lingo.

Director movies have no limit on size, and this can be problematic. If you are authoring for a 650 MB CD-ROM, you would never want your Director file to be 650 MB. Instead, you may want to create a series of five or six 10 MB Director movies that call to each other with Lingo. The file size limit in Director 3.1.3 was 16 MB. This limitation is nonexistent now, but you should keep it as a guideline. This guideline, of course, changes given your target machine.

If you have an idea, make it work in a small movie first. Say, for example, that you would like to create a custom slider for a QuickTime file in Director. Try to make this work in a small, test movie. Write the Lingo code, use sample artwork, and make it work on its own, away from the large project. After you know that your test movie works, you can either copy and paste it into your main score or keep it as a separate file among those that the project is branching.

If you encounter problems implementing your ideas, it is easier to test where the problems are in a small file than in a large one. When you work in a small file, you reduce the number of places problems can occur. If you can narrow the problem, you also can reduce the time it takes to solve the problem. Should it become necessary to call for technical support, for example, you only have to explain part of the movie to the person who is trying to help you, rather than having to explain the movie from start to finish.

The best reason for creating small Director movies is that you can save the files for later use. If you would like to use the same functionality in your next Director project, you can repurpose the code. Eventually, you might have an entire portfolio of Director movies, reducing development time on future projects.

Save Often

Saving your work and making backup copies is imperative when working in any application, but it's even more important in Director. A Director authoring session might consist of editing 10 different areas in the movie. You might work on the movie script; you might import 20 cast members; you might set the forecolor of 6 sprites with the tool palette and set 3 transitions. Saving often helps eliminate the pains of re-creating hours of work.

You can select from five Save commands with Director 6's File menu. They are:

▶ Save

▶ Save As

▶ Save and Compact

▶ Save All

▶ Save as Shockwave Movie

You need to understand the advantages of each. Regardless of which of the five Save commands you choose, remember that it is important to save your work often.

When Director saves a file using the regular Save command, changes are saved to the end of the file, leaving empty space where the now unused version of the modified object used to be. This command takes very little time to execute and is useful when you're doing a lot of production work, such as importing many graphics, working on your Lingo scripts, and so on. The disadvantage is that the Save command can actually increase the size of your file.

When you're ready to test your file, you should issue the Save As command or the Save and Compact command. Both of these commands write a completely new copy of the file. The Save As command rewrites the existing file with a different name or gives you the option to replace the existing file. The Save and Compact command rewrites the existing file with the same name and optimizes the file internally. Both the Save As and Save and Compact commands take longer to execute than a regular Save. Before you begin testing, you should use either the Save As or Save and Compact command. This ensures that the file you test is optimized and most like the final product that you will deliver.

Another useful technique is to issue a Save As command every half-hour or so and save incremental versions of the same project. This way, if you would like to revert to a previous version of the project, if the power goes out, or if one of your files becomes corrupted, you lose only thirty minutes of work.

You can use the Save All command to save the movie and its multiple casts: internal and external, both linked and unlinked. This was a new command in

Director 5. If your movie uses multiple casts, you can issue this command to save everything at once. If this is the first time you are saving the cast, Director prompts you to name it and choose a location at which to save it.

Director 6 has a new save command in its File menu: the Save as Shockwave Movie command. This command compresses your Director movie for use on the Internet, via the Shockwave technology. It also gives the file a .DCR extension, the Shockwave file name extension. This Save as Shockwave Movie command replaces the use of the AfterBurner technology in earlier versions of Shockwave.

Test Often

Testing often is assumed as an important step throughout this chapter and book, even when it's not implicitly stated. The most important idea is not to wait until the last minute to test your production. Whether you test every day or at the end of every week, make sure you consistently test your work.

Testing along the way is most important for cross-platform development. If you're developing for the Macintosh and Windows—or for the Internet, where you won't be able to tell whether the end user has a Macintosh or Windows machine—you need to test your project on both platforms each step of the way. You can do most of your development on one platform or the other, but you need to open and thoroughly test the movie on the other platform from time to time to see how things look and function on the other side.

The rest of this testing section is designed for those who are authoring a traditional Director CD-ROM production for mass distribution and who are unsure of the target machine that will be used. Shockwave tips are mixed within the rest of the chapter, but for a complete guide to Shockwave, take a look at Part IV, "Multimedia on the Web with Director and Shockwave."

Test from a Projector

The true test of a Director movie is when it plays as an executable file, or what Director calls a *projector*. Testing your movie or series of movies within Director is important, but even more important is testing your production in the environment that your audience has. To use the theatrical metaphor, there comes a time when you need to run through the scenes of your show and have a dress rehearsal before the audience arrives.

The Director projector's run-time engine is much smaller than the Director application. This way, you can distribute small Director projects on one or more floppy disks. It's important to understand that the versatility of the projector is different from the versatility of the application. Playing back your movie within the Director application can support the movie playback, open windows, and other system calls. When you test from a projector, you are testing the true capability of the small executable as your audience experiences it.

Many people create a single projector for both testing and final distribution. This is a projector with only one small movie in it that simply launches another Director movie outside the projector. In Director jargon, this file is called a *stub projector*. Using a stub projector eliminates the need to re-create a projector each time you want to test the file in the run-time environment.

Creating a Stub Projector

For use in the following tutorial, you will find a projector named Stub, and two movies with which to work, in the Chapter 4 folder on the *Inside Macromedia Director 6 with Lingo* CD-ROM.

Creating a Stub Projector

1. Create a new Director movie with the File, New command, and save it as STUB.DIR.

   The reason we've given this file a .DIR extension is so that it will run on all the Director playback platforms, including Windows 3.1. Windows 3.1 requires the 8.3 DOS naming convention. Windows 95 and Windows NT no longer require the .DIR extension for a Director for Windows movie.

2. In the Script channel of frame 1 in the score (see fig. 4.1), double-click and type:

```
on exitFrame

go to movie "intro.dir"

end
```

Figure 4.1

This Lingo script tells Director to go from the stub projector to the movie INTRO.DIR outside the projector.

3. Save the file again, and choose Create Projector from the File menu, adding the STUB.DIR file to the projector (see fig. 4.2).

Figure 4.2

Add the STUB.DIR file to the projector list.

4. Click the Create button and Director prompts you to name the file and asks where you would like to save it. Make sure that you save the projector in the same folder as the INTRO.DIR file.

As long as you have a movie file named INTRO.DIR (or whatever name you chose for your first movie) in the same folder as the stub projector, the stub projector is able to run that movie file.

Stub projectors enable you to quickly and easily test Director movies from a projector during authoring. If you keep a stub projector around for testing, you do not need to create a new projector more than once. The following sections discuss how to set up projectors.

Testing on All Your Target Machines

Testing your Director projects on all the target machines is very important. If you are authoring for a multimedia kiosk, you only need to test on that single machine. If you are authoring for a mass market, you need to define the minimum requirements for your project. The more systems with which you can test, the better, but at least you need to test on the system with the lowest common denominator specifications.

In addition to testing the minimum system requirements, try to test your project on as many different configurations as your audience will have. Test the low-end and the high-end. The closer your testing environment is to the audience's machine, the better you can judge what the audience's experience will be.

Defining the Minimum Requirements

Director's minimum system requirements are listed on the outside of its box. This saves customers' time and prevents misconceptions as to what they need to use the product. You should make such a list for your Director project if you plan to distribute it to a mass market, both as a preplanning tool and for your audience's convenience.

The intended platform, minimum available memory on the system, and processor speed are three of the most important issues to address when you write the minimum system requirements for your Director project.

Depending on the media included in your project, other important specifications include the following:

- ▶ Color depth setting
- ▶ System software or operating system
- ▶ Hard disk space
- ▶ Sound capabilities
- ▶ Monitor size
- ▶ Versions of QuickTime or Video for Windows

Macintosh Guidelines

When you define the Macintosh guidelines for your Director project, review the Director for Macintosh authoring and playback requirements defined by Macromedia.

The minimum authoring system requirements for Director 6 for Macintosh include the following:

- ▶ 68040 processor or faster, including PowerBook, AV, and PowerPC
- ▶ System Software version 7.1 or higher
- ▶ 8 MB or more application RAM
- ▶ 40 MB available hard disk space
- ▶ 640×480 (13-inch) monitor
- ▶ Double-speed or faster CD-ROM drive

The minimum playback system requirements for Director 6 for Macintosh are as follows:

- ▶ 68020 processor or faster
- ▶ System 7.0 or higher
- ▶ 4 MB RAM (8 MB or more recommended)
- ▶ 9-inch or larger monitor

Depending on what you have included in your project and who your audience is, you might want to expand on this list or edit it in some way. Following are some suggestions:

- ▶ **Minimum processor:** This should remain the same. It's your choice if you would like your project to play on a 68020 or a 68040. The minimum, however, cannot be below 68020.

- ▶ **System software version:** This should remain the same. If you require that your end user has the latest version of the system software, it will keep him up to date with the latest versions of the Sound Manager, Extension Manager, and other system inits.

- ▶ **Minimum RAM memory:** The amount of RAM your production requires depends on how you author your movie and the machine your audience has. A basic Macintosh today ships with 16 MB of RAM. The system software might take 4–5 MB, leaving you with 12 MB of RAM or less for your Director project. If this is the case, test run your projector, allocating 7–8 MB to it. Chapter 17, "Managing Your Data," discusses authoring your Director project for given memory requirements.

▶ **Minimum monitor capability:** Monitor requirements will depend on the stage size you've set for your movie.

▶ **Minimum free hard disk space:** This depends on the size of your project and supporting files. Find out the minimum storage space your project requires, and relay that to the end user.

Table 4.1 shows the suggested, minimum, and preferred memory allocations for the Director for Macintosh projectors, by default.

Table 4.1

Macintosh Memory Allocation

Macintosh Model	Suggested Size	Minimum Size	Preferred Size
Standard Macintosh	6144 K	2048 K	6144 K
Power Macintosh Native	7465 K	3369 K	7465 K
All Macintosh Models	7465 K	3369 K	7465 K

Follow these steps to control the memory allocation to the projector:

1. Select the projector on the hard drive.

2. Choose File, Get Info in the Finder, or press Command+I.

3. Adjust the Preferred size amount. Closing the Get Info window will save these changes.

By testing your Director movie or series of movies from a projector, you will be able to gauge how much memory your projector will require. If items play back to your satisfaction, the allocation should be correct. If items are playing back poorly or are dropping out altogether, you need to allocate more memory to the projector. Refer to Chapter 17 for more information.

Windows Guidelines

The basic system guidelines for defining the system requirements for your Director for Windows projector are the same as for the Macintosh. Take a look at the system requirements for authoring and playback for Director for Windows and customize it for your production.

The authoring system requirements for Director for Windows are as follows:

- ▶ 486/66 or faster with 8-bit or higher video
- ▶ Windows 95, NT 3.5.1, or higher
- ▶ 16 MB of RAM
- ▶ Hard drive with 40 MB free disk space
- ▶ Double-speed or faster CD-ROM drive

You cannot author in Director 6 for Windows in Windows 3.1. You can, however, play back on Windows 3.1.

The playback system requirements for Director for Windows are as follows:

- ▶ 386/33 or faster
- ▶ Windows 95, Windows 3.1, 3.11, NT 3.5.1, or higher
- ▶ 4 MB RAM on Windows 3.1, 8 MB or more required on Windows 95 and Windows NT.

Again, depending on what you have included in your project and who your audience is, you might want to expand on this list or edit it in some way. Here are some suggestions:

- ▶ **Minimum processor:** A Director for Windows projector requires a 386-enhanced processor or greater. Depending on your project, you might require your audience to have a 486 or higher processor. It's up to you. Animation speed and screen transition time are limited by processor speed. Be sure to test your project on the slowest recommended system to verify acceptable performance.

- ▶ **Minimum RAM memory:** For deciding on the RAM requirements for your Director for Windows projector, follow the same guidelines as described in the Macintosh scenario. You will want to test your projector in the lowest partition on the hard disk. Unlike the Macintosh, you can't directly allocate more or less memory to the projector in Windows. You can, however, adjust the size of the temporary memory accordingly to decide on your final recommendation.

- ▶ **Version of Windows:** When you create a projector with Director for Windows, it can be one of two types: Windows 3.x (16-bit) or Windows

95/NT (32-bit), but not both. If you want to distribute a projector to both categories of Windows platforms, you need to make two Windows projectors: one 16-bit and one 32-bit. An installation program to install the projector to the end user's computer will need to install either the 16- or 32-bit projector, but not both.

▶ **Minimum free hard disk space:** This depends on the size of your project and supporting files. Find out the minimum storage space your project requires and relay that to the end user.

Deciding on Additional Recommendations

You may also need to consider sound and CD-ROM capabilities in specifying requirements for the target machine.

▶ **Sound card:** Every Macintosh comes with built-in sound. If you want your end users to have a 16-bit sound card on the Macintosh, you might want to recommend it. In Windows, a sound card is not standard. You might recommend that your Windows end users install a sound card to hear the sound of your production.

If your Director movie plays sound and the machine does not have a sound card, there will not be an error message; the machine will simply not play the sound. A sound card might be a system recommendation rather than a requirement. That's up to you.

▶ **CD-ROM drive:** If you distribute your Director project on a CD-ROM, your end user needs a CD-ROM drive. You might want to specify a double- (2x) speed, quad- (4x) speed, six- (6x) speed, or even an eight- (8x) speed CD-ROM drive for your project. Again, testing your project in this environment is the only true way of deciding on these specifications.

Testing Tips

If you're authoring for Internet distribution, you should test download times on the slowest modem your audience might have. If you're authoring for CD-ROM distribution, you should test from the CD, especially if your movies contain digital video. If you're authoring for floppy-disk distribution, test the projector from both the floppy disk, if it is a single, uncompressed projector, and from the hard drive if files are going to be installed. The results of these tests help define the system requirements for your projector and structure your instructions for the end user.

Some Director developers take their CD-ROM titles to computer superstores to test their project on all the different systems and video cards. Some set up a beta program, which is a good idea if your resources are limited—you will not need to do all of the testing yourself. Go online and see whether people volunteer to help you test. Some companies have services to test your product for you. One such company is XXCAL Testing Laboratories. XXCAL Testing Laboratories can be reached at the following:

XXCAL Testing Laboratories
11500 W. Olympic Blvd., Suite 325
Los Angeles, CA 90064
(310)477-2902 ext. 1050

The results of your test can be put into a ReadMe file to accompany your project, or even a Help file to reduce the costs of technical support on your organization. Test, test, test. Doesn't sound like that much fun, does it? From those who have learned the hard way, however, testing is the most important thing to do from the very beginning.

Setting Up the Projector

Creating a Director projector is easy. You simply add the movie to the projector list and click the Create button. What takes more thought is how you should structure your Director project and how the projector works with the series of Director movies you've created. Like any software application, staging the delivery of the product onto the end users' machines takes planning and testing to ensure that the customer experiences what you intended.

The remainder of this section emphasizes setting up your production for hard disk delivery, touching only briefly on the Internet. For more Shockwave-specific information, take a look at Part IV.

Structuring Movies and Resources

When you create a Director projector, the Create Projector and Projector Options dialog boxes present you with many options. The choices you make in these dialog boxes depend on what your production includes and your target machine. After you save your movie, select Create Projector from the File menu (see fig. 4.3).

Figure 4.3

The Create Projector dialog box is where you add Director movies to a Director production for distribution.

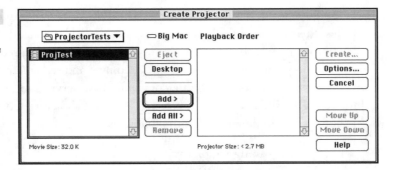

You can add one or many movies to your projector in the Create Projector dialog box. The Director projector plays the movies you add in the order that you select. Deciding which movies to add to a projector is a crucial part of finalizing your project.

Director projects can be divided into three categories: Shockwave applications for the Internet; simple, linear presentations; and interactive projects in which users randomly jump between files. The last two of these deal with the projector as their means of distribution. In the second case, when you know you will advance through the presentation in a slide-show manner, you can safely embed all the movies in your project within the projector. Director makes its way through each of them in the order that you put them into the projector. More commonly, in large-scale, interactive projects, you should add only one file to the projector and store the remaining movies external to the projector. The following example describes this situation.

Say, for example, that you're authoring a CD-ROM project and your target machine has 8 MB of RAM. Currently, the standard CD-ROMs hold 650 MB of data. Running a 650 MB projector through an 8 MB RAM partition is incredibly slow and much of the media is purged from memory.

Instead, most Director developers create a stub projector, described earlier in this chapter. The movie in the stub projector launches the first movie in the project with the go command. You then can call seamlessly between your first and subsequent Director movies with Lingo.

The Lingo used to navigate between movies is easy to use and is covered in detail in Chapter 16, "Lingo: The Basics." In short, to tell Director to go to another movie or to another frame in another movie, use the go command. To play specific movies or frames of specific movies and return at a later time, use the play command and the play done command.

When you set up your production for distribution, you might have a projector call to a subfolder or directory with 20–30 movies in it, which in turn call each other with Lingo. In a cross-platform project, one Macintosh and one Windows projector could call to the same folder of Director movies. Other folders can contain linked media elements, and the projector can launch the entire show.

Protecting Movies

Because most developers structure large projects according to the hierarchy previously described, it is common to protect the Director movies that remain outside the projector. Director 4 introduced the capability of protecting movies; in Director 6, you are given a choice of how you would like to protect the movies you leave outside the projector.

One choice—the one that has been available since Director 4—is to use the `Protect Movies` command, which strips out the scripts and cast thumbnails of your Director movie. The file extension of these movies is .DXR. After a file is protected, it can no longer be opened and edited in Director. This way you can freely distribute your movies without worrying that people may steal your original artwork or Lingo scripts.

Alternatively, Director 6 enables you to use the Shockwave compression technology to save your movie as a Shockwave movie (a process sometimes referred to as *shocking* a movie). The extension for this file is .DCR. Shockwave movies have the same "protected" features of protected movies, and they are also compressed. The `Save as Shockwave Movie` command is located in the Director 6 File menu.

If you are distributing on the Internet, you should obviously use the .DCR file format. If you are creating a CD-ROM and hard disk space is unlimited, use the `Protected Movies` command. Protected Movies load more quickly from the disk than Shockwave movies do because Protected Movies do not need to be decompressed upon playback.

After you protect or shock a movie, it can no longer be opened for editing within Director as a .DIR file can be. It can be played back only from a projector or on the Internet. Therefore, keep a backup copy of your .DIR files for editing. Both the `Save as Shockwave` and `Protect Movies` commands walk you through creating a new copy of the movie, instead of replacing the .DIR file on disk. If you do not protect your files, anyone with Director can open them. Be careful of your options when protecting movies.

Protecting movies is usually the last thing you do before you distribute your Director production. That is, of course, before you test it once again. To protect a movie or series of movies, select the Update Movies command from the Xtras menu (see fig. 4.4).

Figure 4.4

*Protecting movies
eliminates the cast
thumbnails and scripts
of your movie for
distribution.*

After you choose the Protect option in the Update Movies dialog box, you can select a folder in which to save the backup of the movies. You also can delete the original files, but that is not recommended. Always keep an unprotected archive of your master files; after you protect a movie, you can no longer open it from within Director. You can only call to it from a projector. Because you may want to later edit your Director movie, always keep a copy of the original.

As mentioned earlier, the extension of a Director movie changes to extension .DXR when you protect it and .DCR when you shock it. If you are authoring your movie for Windows 3.x, you might want to name your movie in the 8.3 naming convention: MYMOVIE.DIR. This file then becomes MYMOVIE. DXR when you protect it and MYMOVIE.DCR when you shock it.

Understanding the change in file-name extension is important when calling to new movies using Lingo. If a command looks for the MOVIE2.DIR, but you protect the movie, Director will not find it. Have your command look for MOVIE2—with no extension after the file name. This way the projector can find the movie whether it has a .DIR, .DXR, or .DCR extension. The extension in the file name is not necessary for Director to find the movie.

Director 5 enhanced the Protect Movies and Update Movies commands, enabling you to protect an entire project with one command. You can protect multiple movies simultaneously and maintain their linked resources and directory structure. Director 6 adds the Convert to Shockwave Movies command to the Update Movies dialog box, so you'll be able to batch-edit a series of Director files into the Shockwave file format.

Projector Options

The Projector Options dialog box offers many choices for the way in which the projector plays when launched. It's easy to overlook this button when you create a projector, but this dialog box determines many important settings. The following sections cover each of the choices.

To open the Projector Options dialog box, select the Create Projector command from the File menu, and choose the Options button (see fig. 4.5).

Create For: The Operating System Option

Director for Macintosh enables you to decide whether your projector runs on a Standard Macintosh, Power Macintosh Native, or All Macintosh models. If you select the option for All Macintosh models (or a fat-binary file), you should realize that the projector size will truly be "fat," or larger than the other two options, because it includes resources for both types of processors. Experiment with all three of these projector types to preview the size of the projector. When you select any of them, Director calculates the size of the projector in the Create Projector dialog box.

As noted earlier, Director for Windows enables you to create a 16-bit (Windows 3.x, Windows 95 Emulation) or a 32-bit (Windows 95, Windows NT) projector, but not both. If you intend to deliver to all three Windows platforms, you need to make two projectors. The installation software you use should then be able to detect which operating system is running and install one of the two projectors. Installer options are covered in the "Installers" section, later in this chapter.

Playback: Play Every Movie

If you select the Play Every Movie in the Playback options, Director plays back every movie you include in the play list. If this setting is not selected, Director plays only the first movie in the play list. If you are using a stub projector and include only one movie in the projector, you do not need to select this setting.

Playback: Animate in Background

The Animate in Background option tells Director to continue playing the movie if the user clicks outside the movie window. If you do not select this option, the movie stops playing when the user clicks outside the stage area.

Animate in Background is especially useful if used in conjunction with Lingo's open command to launch another application from Director. When Animate in Background is selected, the Director movie continues playing while the user launches another application. When the other application plays and later closes, Director still plays in the background. If Animate in Background is not selected, the Director animation is suspended when the other application launches, and resumes playing when it quits.

INSIDER TIP

When using the Animate in Background technique, loop the Director score when the other application launches. Otherwise, the movie continues running to the end.

If you would like the movie to loop in one frame, you can use a go to the frame loop in the script channel of that frame. If you would like to loop the entire animation, you can use a go to frame 1 loop in the Script channel of one of the last frames in the movie.

Options: Full Screen

When the user selects the Full Screen option, Director covers the area surrounding the stage with the color of the stage in frame 1. This is useful when the stage is smaller than the monitor and you want to cover the desktop behind the presentation.

In Director 4.0.4, the Full Screen option was available only with Windows. Macintosh users had to use a Macromedia XObject (Rear Window) or a commercial XObject (Finder Hider) for achieving this functionality. Since Director 5, Full Screen has been available for Macintosh as well as Windows.

Options: In a Window

The In a Window option is available in Director for Windows only. When selected, the Director stage displays in a normal window. It does not cover the desktop behind the stage, like the full-screen option, and it is not resizable.

Options: Show Title Bar

Show Title Bar is another projector option available in Director for Windows only. When the In a Window option is selected, Show Title Bar is available so that the window the stage occupies has a title bar. When the stage has a title bar, the window is movable.

Stage Size: Use Movie Settings and Match First Movie

The first two settings under Stage Size—Use Movie Settings and Match First Movie—are important when you're using settings for multiple movies. The projector follows those directions when it opens a new movie. If, for example, you would like to have the stage size for the movie change when new movies of a different size open, you should select the Use Movie Settings option. If you would like all movies to use the settings of the first movie, you should select the Match First Movie option.

Stage Size: Center

The Center option displays the stage in the center of the playback monitor. If your projector plays back in the top-left corner of the monitor, the problem most likely is that the Center option is not selected. You need to verify your projector's performance on a screen larger than the stage size.

Stage Size: Reset Monitor to Match Movie's Color Depth

The Reset Monitor to Match Movie's Color Depth option is available only on the Macintosh. (With Windows, you cannot explicitly change the color depth of the system; you need to select a different video driver and restart Windows.) When selected, this option changes the system setting for color depth in the monitor's Control Panel to match the movie's settings. The color depth of a Director movie is established by the bitmap cast member with the highest color depth.

LINGO LESSON

An alternative technique to resetting the monitor to match the movie's color depth in this dialog box is to do it with Lingo. Lingo enables you to set the color depth to whatever you like, then set it back when the movie is over. This way, the user's Macintosh monitor returns to the original settings when your movie is finished playing. The following is a sample handler to accomplish this:

```
on startMovie
global oldColor
--creates a global variable
put the colorDepth into oldColor
--puts the current colorDepth into the global variable
if the colorDepth <> 8 then
--checks if the colorDepth is < or > 8-bit
set the colorDepth to 8
--sets the colorDepth to 8-bit
end if
updateStage
end startMovie
on stopMovie
global oldColor
--calls the global variable from memory again
set the colorDepth to oldColor
--sets the colorDepth back to what it used to be
updateStage
end stopMovie
```

Media: Compress (Shockwave Format)

Select this projector option to compress the projector's movie date in the Shockwave format. As mentioned before in the discussion about the difference between .DXR and .DCR files, shocked files will be smaller than protected movies, but will take longer to load from the hard drive.

Xtras: Include Network Xtras

The Include Network Xtras option automatically includes the network Xtras needed for Network connectivity during playback. If you want to retrieve information from the Internet from the projector, you need to include the network Xtras, and you can do so with this checkbox.

Xtras: Check Movies for Xtras

If your movie uses Xtras, you need to distribute the Xtra with the projector for the Xtra functionality to be available to your movie. The Check Movies for Xtras projector option checks the Movie Xtras dialog box in the Modify menu for the Xtras you have used and includes them with the projector. Only Xtras you have used in the score are included in this dialog box. If you used a Lingo Xtra, you need to add it to the Movie Xtras dialog box. This option actually creates an Xtras folder for your projector with the appropriate Xtras in it.

Memory: Use System Temporary Memory

The option to Use System Temporary Memory is only available in Director for Macintosh, not Windows, because the two systems handle memory differently. When you select this option, Director takes advantage of available system memory when it uses up its own partition. If virtual memory is turned on, this option disables.

The Use System Temporary Memory option is available in both the Projector Options and the General Preferences of the Director for Macintosh application. It is helpful when Director needs more resources, but it also might slow down the system. If a user, or you, the developer, tries to launch another application in addition to Director, the system might run out of memory. Again, depending on what you are doing, whether your projector is running alone or with other applications, this option might or might not be what you want to use.

Deciding What to Include with Your Projector

It is easier to distribute a finished product in Director for Macintosh than it is for Director for Windows. This section covers the requirements for both platforms. This section also shows where to find the information you might need from Macromedia, Apple, and Microsoft for distribution of their products.

Two main issues must be considered when you set up your final production:

- ▶ The files necessary to run your production
- ▶ The licensing permission required for distributing those files

Deciding Which Files Are Necessary

Besides the projector file, you may need to include Director movies, linked media, and supporting files with your project. The list of what you need to distribute depends on the type of project you've created and what you've included in your Director project.

The Projector

First, include the projector file. If you have created a linear presentation, you may have a series of movies within the projector. If your project is interactive and offers the users random access to a series of files, the stub projector mentioned earlier can initiate a series of Director movies.

Director Movies

If your projector or main movie calls a Director movie, that Director movie needs to accompany the projector. These movies might be in the native .DIR format, the protected .DXR format, or the shocked .DCR format. Most developers create one large folder that contains the projector and a subfolder of all the Director movies outside of the projector that Lingo calls.

Director Casts

You need to distribute all externally linked casts in your Director movie with the final projector. Take into account the link to the original Director movie that references them. Be certain to test the final distribution members and their links in the final staging area. The staging area might be an external hard drive you'll use to burn a CD-ROM or a place on your hard drive where the project is contained in one large folder. Linked casts and media should all be contained in subdirectories of the Director movies that call to them.

Linked Media

All media that links to the Director production must accompany your Director production, preferably in the same folder as the projector. Many developers create another subfolder for media elements. You need to distribute any linked QuickTime, sound, and graphics files, and any media that you call to with Lingo along with your Director movie. QuickTime files are always linked to the Director movie, so you must distribute them along with the movies.

The LINGO.INI File in Windows

The first file a Director for Windows projector looks for when it launches is LINGO.INI. The LINGO.INI is designed to inform Director for Windows which Xtras, XObjects, or DLLs should be loaded when launching Director. You can find an example of a LINGO.INI file in the Director 6 directory. In Windows 95 and Windows NT, the text file is called Lingo. Open this file to view its contents.

You can use the LINGO.INI file for Windows at any time to give instructions to your Director for Windows projector. If, by chance, your Director for Windows projector comes across a LINGO.INI file from another Director production first, it follows those instructions instead. It is important, therefore, to include a text file called LINGO.INI in the same directory as your Director for Windows projector. You can create this file with any text editor and save it as LINGO.INI. Even if you distribute a blank file, you bypass troubles with other previously installed LINGO.INI files on the user's machine.

Xtras, XObjects, and DLLs

If you have used an Xtra, XObject, or DLL in your movie, it needs to accompany your projector as well. To check which Xtras are required by your movie, choose the Modify, Movie, Xtras menu. The Xtras that show in the Movie Xtras dialog box include those used in the score only. If you have used a Lingo Xtra, you should add it to this list through this dialog box.

The projector needs an Xtras folder to hold the Xtra, just like the Director application does. This is the only way it finds the Xtra. If you select the Check Movie for Xtras or Include Network Xtras options in the Projector Options dialog box, Director includes the Xtras you need for the movie and creates the Xtras folder for you.

If you did not create the Xtra or XObject yourself, you must obtain the author's permission to use and distribute it. Most Xtras, XObjects, and DLLs, such as the ones that ship with Director 6, come in a demo form. They all have ReadMe files with the developer's contact information and notes on licensing.

Fonts

If you want the font you use in your Director movie to appear the same on every playback machine, you have four choices:

▶ You can use a system font that you know is on the target machine.

▶ You can license the font from the font manufacturer and distribute it with your application along with installation instructions.

▶ You can convert the font to bitmap, so that it appears the same on every computer. By converting the font to a bitmap graphic, however, the font is not editable.

▶ You can use text cast members that use the rich text format (RTF). Text cast members are displayed as bitmaps at run time, so you don't need to worry about distributing the font used in that type of cast member. These cast members are still editable within Director, at authoring time, but for distribution, you won't need to worry about fonts.

Third-Party Resources

To play QuickTime for Macintosh or QuickTime for Windows, the computer must have the appropriate version of QuickTime installed. To play .AVI files on any machine, the computer must have Video for Windows installed. You need to distribute the run-time version of these system extensions to your end users if your Director project includes digital video files. The next section discusses ways to contact Apple and Microsoft about licensing their products.

Licensing Considerations

Licensing issues come into play when you want to distribute materials in part or in whole that other parties create. Content of your movie, as well as the software components that your movie uses, can be subject to licensing.

All software applications come with licensing agreements that specify the terms under which you can use and distribute the application. If you are unsure of any of the terms, contact the software manufacturer.

To distribute QuickTime for Macintosh, QuickTime for Windows, or any other Apple Macintosh product, contact Apple Software Licensing, at 512-919-2645. Both QuickTime for Macintosh and QuickTime for Windows are royalty-free, but you still need to contact Apple for complete information. On the web, you can access QuickTime information at `http://quicktime.apple.com/`.

To distribute Video for Windows, contact Microsoft. The Microsoft Video for Windows Development Kit contains a royalty-free licensing agreement. On the web, you can contact Microsoft at `http://www.microsoft.com/`.

For both QuickTime and Video for Windows, make certain to obtain the list of supporting files necessary to play back the version of the software you want to distribute. These lists are available from Apple and Microsoft, respectively.

Made with Macromedia

When you create a projector with Director for Macintosh or Windows, anything you create yourself belongs to you, such as your graphics, sounds, and scripts. Some parts of the projector still belong to Macromedia, too—mainly anything that enables the projector to run without Director.

The Macromedia licensing agreement enables you to distribute your projectors freely as long as you do not charge fees for them. If you want to distribute your projector for a fee, the licensing agreement is a little different.

You do not have to pay royalty to Macromedia for projectors you create with Director. You do, however, need to do the following:

▶ Sign a Macromedia licensing agreement

▶ Agree to include the Macromedia licensing considerations for final projects with the Macromedia logo both in your software and on your exterior packaging (see fig. 4.6)

▶ Agree to send two copies of your final product to Macromedia free of charge

Figure 4.6

The Made with Macromedia logo.

For the most up-to-date information on the Made with Macromedia program, visit Macromedia's web page at http://www.macromedia.com or call the Made with Macromedia FAQ hotline at 415-252-2171.

The latest version of the Made with Macromedia package, at the time of this publishing, can be found on the *Inside Macromedia Director 6 with Lingo* CD.

Distributing the Movie

The following sections list some of the most commonly used distribution means for Director productions. This does not cover Shockwave distribution, but more of the traditional, floppy disk and CD-ROM distribution information. For more information on Shockwave distribution, take a look at Part IV.

Depending on the scope of your project, you may be able to use a simple compression utility. If your project is large, you will most likely need an installation package.

Compressors

If your Director project is simple and the projector fits onto one floppy disk, you can distribute your movie yourself by copying the projector file onto the floppy. If your project exceeds the 1.44 MB limit of a floppy, you must compress it. Most Director projects are compressed with a third-party compression utility when distributing on floppies. If your project remains larger than 1.44 MB even after compressing it, compression utilities enable you to segment (on the Macintosh) or span (on Windows) the file into a number of sub-files that are then distributed across multiple floppy disks.

On the Macintosh, most developers use StuffIt Deluxe from Aladdin Systems. You can find contact information for Aladdin Systems in the next section. CompactPro is a shareware counterpart to StuffIt.

In Windows, developers use WinZIP or PKZip. Feedback from the Windows community indicates that end users are using more sophisticated installers. The next section covers commonly used installers.

Installers

Given the list of files you need to include with your Director projector, you most likely need to use an installation package to install your project on the end user's machine. The following are lists of the most common Macintosh and Windows installation packages.

Macintosh Installers

On the Macintosh, Aladdin Systems offers Installer Maker and StuffIt, mentioned previously. You can contact Aladdin at the following:

Aladdin Systems
165 Westridge Drive
Watsonville, CA 95076
408-761-6200
408-761-6206 (fax)
CompuServe: `75300.1666@compuserve.com`
AOL: `Aladdin@aol.com`

Another installation package used on the Macintosh is called Vice software.

The Macintosh installer that Macromedia uses for Director for Macintosh is InstallerVise by MindVision. You can contact MindVision at the following:

MindVision Software
840 South 30th Street, Suite C
PO Box 81886
Lincoln, NE 68510
CompuServe: `70253.1437@compuserve.com`
AOL: `MindVision@aol.com`
402-477-3269
402-477-1395 (fax)

For sales/licensing-related questions: `sales@mindvision.com`

For technical questions: `support@mindvision.com` or `winsupport@mindvision.com`

For product information: `info@mindvision.com`

Windows Installers

You can choose from many options when selecting a Windows installation program. Developers recommend many installers and often argue over which one is better. The following is a list of commonly used installers, along with company contact information. Depending on the scope of your project, you might prefer one over another.

▶ EDI Install Pro from Eschelon Development

EDI Install Pro
Eschelon Development
24-2979 Panorama Dr.
Coquitlam BC V3E 2W8, Canada
205-880-8702
CompuServe: `76625.1320@compuserve.com`
FTP: `ftp.halcyon.com\local\dsmith\inspro.exe`

▶ Freeman Installer by Freeman-Teresa Software

Freeman Installer
Freeman-Teresa Software
PO Box 712
Broadway NSW 2007
Australia
E-mail: tongk@arch.su.edu.au
Web: http://www.jumbo.com:80/util/win/install/
CompuServe: 100351.3364@compuserve.com

▶ InstallShield from Sterling Technologies

InstallShield
The Sterling Group
172 Old Mill Dr.
Schaumburg, IL 60193
1-800-3-SHIELD (1-800-374-4353)

▶ Installit by Helpful Programs, Inc.

Installit
Helpful Programs, Inc. (HPI)
600 Boulevard South, Suite 305
PO Box 16078
Huntsville, AL 35802
205-880-8782
800-448-4154
Web: http://www.instalit.com
FTP: ftp.instalit.com

▶ Setup Factory 3.0 by Indigo Rose Corporation

Setup Factory 3.0
Indigo Rose Corporation
PO Box 2281
Winnipeg, MB
Canada, R3C 4A6
800-665-9668
204-668-8180
204-661-6904 (fax)
E-mail: support@indigorose.mb.ca
Web: http://www.indigorose.mb.ca/indigo
FTP: ftp.indigorose.mb.ca/pub/indigorose

▶ Wise Installation System from Great Lakes Business Solutions

Wise Installation System
Great Lakes Business Solutions
39905 Lotzford, Suite 200
Canton, MI 48187
313-981-4970
313-981-9746 (fax)
Web: `http://www.glbs.com`
CompuServe: `go wiseinstall`

You can find demo files of many of these installation programs on Macromedia's CompuServe and AOL libraries, on their web site at `http://www.macromedia.com`, or at the online sites of the individual companies.

In Practice

Having read Chapters 2, 3, and 4 on preplanning, strategy, and distribution, you should be able to create your Director movies with foresight. It's better to know this information up front than to learn about it after you have finished your work only to find you have more work to do.

You have many more creative chapters ahead of you, beginning next, in Part II. After all, Director's creative side is its most fun.

The key advice you should remember from this chapter includes the following:

▶ Test early: Test all your media elements at the time you introduce them into your Director movie; create small movies; save your work often.

▶ Test often and on all your target machines.

▶ Test from a projector; this is the way to simulate what your audience experiences, and therefore is critically important. The Projector Options dialog box offers many choices for how the projector plays when launched.

▶ Define the minimum system requirements of your audience and test your project using those requirements, as well as on as many other representative systems as possible.

▶ Protect movies before you distribute them so that they can no longer be opened and edited in Director.

▶ Determine which files must be included for your Director project to run, and which licensing permission may be needed to distribute those files.

PART

Working with Director

Working with Director 6: Understanding the Metaphor

I once asked John "JT" Thompson, the lead Lingo engineer at Macromedia, what he would say about working with Director. He said, "Director is like a lived-in house. It has been reworked and reworked since 1985, and each new version has built upon the last. There are some hidden things, and many things remaining from past versions. With each version of Director, Macromedia has introduced a more standardized way of working."

Thompson also said to "sit back, relax, have a cup of tea." Start by reading others' advice on working with Director, such as this book, and by tapping into an online community. You'll quickly begin building your own approach to creating the most powerful multimedia applications for desktop computers.

This chapter describes how the basic Director windows work together, furnishes tips for using each of them, and teaches you how to use Lingo along the way. Specific topics covered include the following:

- ▶ The stage: what the audience sees
- ▶ The cast: behind the scenes
- ▶ The sprites
- ▶ The score
- ▶ Scriptless authoring
- ▶ Integrated Internet authoring
- ▶ Lingo
- ▶ Director references

Although this chapter touches on each of the main windows, it is largely an overview describing how they relate to one another. This chapter also points you to later chapters for more in-depth coverage of certain topics. For details on each window and its capabilities, also check under the Window menu and consult the Director documentation and the expanded, context-sensitive, online Help system.

If you're experienced with Director, this chapter will be a review, although it does cover how to use some of the features new to Director 6. If you've worked through the tutorials that come with Director and are still getting your feet wet, this chapter will clear up some of the concepts. If Director is new to you, this chapter will serve as background for the more advanced chapters that follow.

The Stage: What the Audience Sees

Everything the audience sees on the monitor in a Director movie occurs on the stage. The *stage* in Director serves a function parallel to that of a theatrical stage. Your characters enter and exit it and can say lines or dance to music on it. Keeping this theatrical stage metaphor in mind will help you understand how to work with Director.

When you first launch Director (see fig. 5.1), the three most important Director windows appear (after the splash screen): the Internal Cast, the score, and the Control Panel. If the Cast, score, and Control Panel windows aren't open after you launch Director, you can open them from the Window menu.

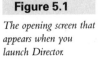

Figure 5.1

The opening screen that appears when you launch Director.

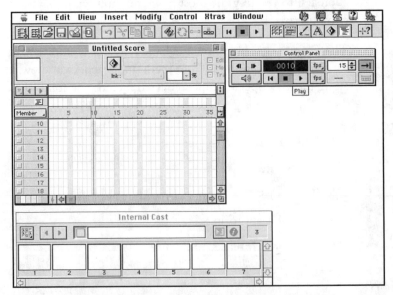

The white canvas in the background is the stage on which your movie takes place.

Setting the Stage Color

If you'd like to change the stage's color, you can do so in the Movie Properties dialog box (see fig. 5.2).

You can access the Movie Properties dialog box in Director 6 in three ways:

▶ Choose Modify, Movie, Properties.

▶ Press Command+Shift+D (Macintosh) or Ctrl+Shift+D (Windows).

▶ Control-click the stage on the Macintosh, or right-mouse click the stage in Windows 95, and choose "Movie Properties" from the pop-up menu.

In the Movie Properties dialog box, click on the white color swatch next to Stage Color setting (see fig. 5.2).

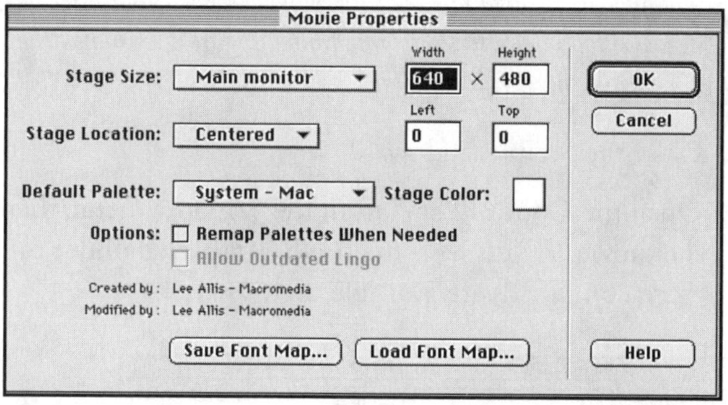

Figure 5.2

Use the Movie Properties dialog box to change the color of the stage as well as other movie settings.

After you click on the color swatch, a pop-up palette appears, and you can select a color for the stage from any of the 256 colors in the movie's active palette.

If you'd like to step on the gas and try out Lingo to change the color of the stage, use the following tutorial.

Using Lingo's stageColor Property

1. In Director, open a new movie by selecting File, New, Movie.

2. Open the score window and double-click in the Script channel of frame 2. (The Script channel is the channel above channel 1.)

3. Delete any text that appears in the Script window and type the following:

```
on enterFrame
  set the stageColor to random (256)
end
```

The preceding three lines set the stage color to a random color in the active 256-color palette each time the playback head enters that frame.

```
on exitFrame
  go to the frame
end
```

The preceding three lines tell the playback head that after leaving the frame it needs to loop back to that same frame. Figure 5.3 shows the sample script as it appears in the Script window.

4. Close the Script window.

5. Open the Control Panel from the Window menu, then rewind and play the movie. (If you have the toolbar displayed under the Window menu, these commands are available there as well.)

Figure 5.3

The sample script as it appears in the Script window.

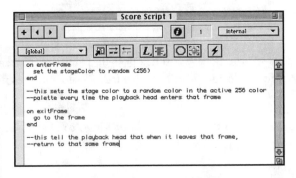

You will find a completed version of this movie on the accompanying *Inside Macromedia Director 6 with Lingo* CD. The movie, STAGECLR.DIR, can be found in the Chapter 5 folder.

Defining the Stage Size

One of the first steps as a Director author is defining the movie's stage size. You do this in the Movie Properties dialog box. Remember the theatrical stage metaphor? You can't set up the lighting and tell the characters where to go until the stage is defined. It's best to decide the stage size in the very beginning. Technically, if you draw animated characters to scale for a large stage and at the last minute decide that the movie should run with a smaller stage, it is difficult to automatically resize everything without a great deal of trouble.

Director opens with a default stage size of 640×480 pixels. This is a good setting if you're just trying to learn more about the product or if you're targeting a basic system. A typical multimedia presentation is authored for the standard monitor: 640×480 pixels with 256 colors.

Remember to consider your target audience from the very beginning. Will they have a 9- or 13-inch monitor? You can work with the stage size in two ways: You can make a project with the smallest stage size necessary, or you can design multiple versions of the project for different target systems. Regardless of the stage size, the horizontal dimensions must be divisible by 16 because of the way Director draws the stage internally.

Making Only One Project

If you intend to make only one version of the movie, you need to set the stage size to the smallest monitor dimensions that your intended audience uses. Cases for which you may need to make only one version include the following:

▶ Your project needs to be small enough to fit on a floppy disk

▶ You're authoring for the Internet

▶ You have limited time (most common reason)

Suppose that you're creating a CD-ROM title for mass market distribution. Your project team decides every school computer around the world—even those with 9-inch monitors—must be able to view your movie. You need to make the dimensions of your movie for the 9-inch monitor (512×342). If the 512×342 movie also is going to be played on monitors that exceed nine inches, you must cover the desktop area behind the movie before you distribute it.

You learned about setting up a projector for distribution in Chapter 4, "Delivering the Goods." Remember, the Full Screen projector option enables you to play the projector, while covering the desktop area behind the stage with the stage color of the first frame of your movie.

When you make one copy of your movie with the stage size set to the smallest dimensions necessary, the Full Screen option will fill the area behind the stage if the target monitor turns out to be larger.

Making Multiple Copies of the Same Project

If you decide to make more than one version of the same project, you can make both a 9-inch (512×342) and a 13-inch (640×480) movie, or more depending on the size of the monitors to be used. You might decide to design your production this way if you always want to have the Director stage occupy the entire monitor. In this case, you will need to make two completely separate movies or a series of movies. Doing so forces many extra steps because you must resize each bitmap to fit the proportions of the various stage sizes.

After you complete two (or more) projects, you can easily use Lingo to test for the monitor size and play one movie or another. The following tutorial shows you how to set up the Lingo test. This test runs on the assumption that you have already made two movies, one saved as SMALL.DIR and another saved as BIG.DIR.

Using Lingo to Test Monitor Size

1. Create a third movie and call it INTRO.DIR. Be certain that the INTRO.DIR movie's stage size is small enough to fit on any of the target monitors.

   This movie will use Lingo to call out and play one of the two movies, given the size of the monitor.

2. Under the Window menu, select Script window and type the following movie script:

```
on startMovie
  global monitorHeight, monitorWidth
  set monitorHeight = the stageTop + the stageBottom
  set monitorWidth = the stageLeft + the stageRight

  if monitorWidth < 640 then go to movie "small.dir"
    else
  go to movie "big.dir"
```

```
      end if

   end
```

The preceding code plays one of the two movies, depending on the monitor size. Line 5, for example, determines that when the monitor's width is less than 640, the SMALL.DIR movie will play. If the monitor width is greater than 640, the BIG.DIR movie will play.

3. In the Script channel of Channel 1, type the following Lingo script:

```
on exitFrame
    go to the frame
end
```

4. Save the movie.

5. Select the Create Projector command from the File menu and add INTRO.DIR to the projector list.

6. Click the Options button and select Full Screen in the Projector Options dialog box. This will fill the area behind the stage with the color of the stage.

7. Click the Create button.

8. Name the projector and choose Save.

The projector you created appears in the active directory or wherever you decide to save it. The projector first launches the INTRO.DIR movie. The Lingo you scripted determines the size of the monitor and plays one of the movies.

The Cast: Behind the Scenes

All the multimedia elements that are used in a Director movie are known collectively as the *cast* or *cast members*. To display the cast on the stage, Director works behind the scenes to access a database of cast members. As in a play or motion picture, cast members come in many shapes and sizes. In computer-generated movies, cast members include a number of computer-generated media elements, such as graphics, sounds, text, 3D files, digital videos, and other Director movies. Other types of cast members—such as custom palettes, behaviors, film loops, transitions, and scripts—are imported or generated while you are working in Director. These types of members might or might not be media elements, but you can access them from the Cast window (see fig. 5.4). Because you can access them from the Cast window, they still qualify as cast members.

The default cast is the Internal cast. Using multiple cast libraries, you might have additional internal or external casts. Take a look at Chapter 7, "Multiple Casts," for tips and techniques on using multiple casts in Director.

Figure 5.4

The Cast window is where all your cast members are stored.

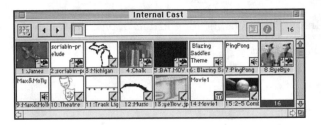

A Cast of Millions

Director 4 introduced the capability of including up to 32,000 cast members in each movie. Director 5 introduced the multiple cast feature in which multiple libraries of cast members are available to each file. Each cast is capable of containing up to 32,000 cast members. This means that you have virtually millions of possible cast members in each movie file.

By default, Director stores casts internally; hence the term, *internal casts*. If you want to create a new cast, select the Choose Cast button in the top-left corner of the Cast window. This opens the New Cast dialog box (see fig. 5.5), which enables you to specify whether the cast is internal or external.

Figure 5.5

The New Cast dialog box enables you to name the new cast and determine whether it is stored as an internal or external cast.

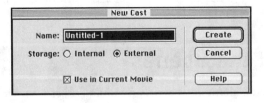

If you select the External option, Director automatically links the new cast to the current movie. By default, the Use in Current Movie option is selected for external casts. If you deselect this option, you can generate a cast in one Director movie for use in another Director movie, without ever using the cast in the first movie. One way you might use this feature is if you'd like to send a cast of updated graphics to everyone in your sales force. They could use this externally linked cast to change the content of their presentations on-the-fly with Lingo's set the fileName command.

You can share external casts between movies in Director 6 like you did in Director 5. For those of you jumping from Director 4 to 6, a shared external cast works the way a SHARED.DIR file did in Director 4. In Director 6, this file is called the SHARED.CST. Using multiple casts can be helpful to organize your cast members by type. You can have a cast of bitmaps, a cast of digital videos, and so on, and you can access all of them in the same file. You might organize graphics by resolution into multiple external casts so that the appropriate cast can be swapped into a movie depending on the resolution of the target audience's monitor.

To view the casts used in the active movie, select Modify, Movie, Casts to open the Movie Casts dialog box (see fig. 5.6).

Figure 5.6

Use the Movie Casts dialog box to view and modify the movie's casts.

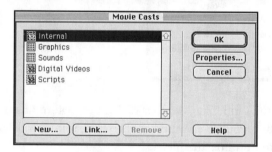

You can modify the movie's casts in this dialog box as well as view the names and types of all casts. The icon that looks like a director's chair indicates an internal cast and the "grid" icon signifies an external cast. For more information on working with multiple casts, refer to Chapter 7.

Tips on Using the Cast Window

Working in the Cast window is easy. You can drag and drop cast members in the window and organize them as you please. Director automatically updates the other cast member positions and all references to them in the movie. Director will not update your Lingo scripts to match the cast members you move, however, so be sure to use cast member names instead of numbers in your scripts.

You can drag and drop cast members directly onto the stage from the Cast window. You even can drag and drop cast members into the cast from the desktop. The Cast window is your reference for everything you create or import into your Director movie.

Finding Cast Members

You can find specific cast members by selecting Edit, Find, Cast Member. When you do, the Find Cast Member dialog box appears (see fig. 5.7).

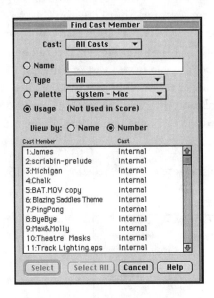

You often use the Find Cast Member dialog box before finalizing a project to find cast members you haven't used in the score. You then delete these unused cast members to optimize the file.

If you use Lingo to puppet sprites in your movie, those sprites might not appear anywhere in the score. One way to handle this is to set up an unused frame that contains all the puppeted sprites. That way, when you use the Find, Cast Member, Usage (Not Used in Score) commands, they will find those sprites not used in the movie and clear them from the cast. Puppets are discussed later in the section "Sprites and Lingo."

Sorting Cast Members

You can use the Sort window from the Modify menu to sort the cast members in the Cast window. To use the Sort window (see fig. 5.8), first select a range of cast members in the Cast window, and then select Modify, Sort.

Figure 5.8

Use the Sort window to sort the cast members in a particular cast.

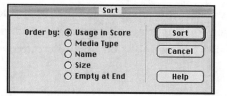

When you select Usage in Score in the Sort window, you optimize your movie for faster playback. This is especially important when you author for CD-ROM distribution. Sorting the cast by media type enables you to organize the cast. If you end up with a large internal cast with mixed media, you might first sort the internal cast by media type and take all the graphics, for example, into a cast of their own.

Previewing Cast Members

After you import cast members into a Director file, preview them from the Cast window—especially sound and digital video cast members (see Table 5.1).

Director is often used as an integrator of media elements that have been created or edited in another program, rather than as the tool for creating the media. For example, one team of people might create a set of cast members and then send it over a network or via an external medium to the Director author. Things can go wrong under such an arrangement, which is why previewing a cast member after it's imported is important.

Table 5.1

Previewing Cast Members

For	In the Cast Window, Do This
Graphics	Double-click on the cast member to preview it in the Paint window.
Sounds	Select the cast member and use the Information button or press Command+I (Macintosh) or Ctrl+I (Windows) to open the Sound Cast Member Properties dialog box. Click on the Play button to preview the sound.
Digital Video	Double-click on the cast member to launch the Video window and preview it. Use the Information button or press Command+I on the Mac, Ctrl+I in Windows to open the Digital Video Cast Member Properties dialog box. Make sure that Direct to Stage is turned on.

If the media element doesn't work properly in the Cast window, it won't work well in the movie either. You might need to return to the digital video editing, sound editing, or graphics editing tools you used to create the piece of content for further editing.

INSIDER TIP

If you double-click on the sound cast member, Director prompts you to launch an external sound editing program, such as SoundEdit 16. You can then edit the sound as necessary and return to Director with the freshly edited sound. You can set up this launch-and-edit feature for other cast members as well in the Editors Preference dialog box.

After you import or create a cast member, open the Cast Member Properties dialog box. This dialog box contains all the information on the cast member. You also can select special Director settings for cast members in these dialog boxes. For example, figure 5.9 shows the Cast Member Properties dialog box for a digital video cast member. This is where you will set up the way in which the digital video plays: Looped, Direct to Stage, with sound, and other options are available. Details on these and other specifications for digital video are covered in Chapter 12, "Digital Video: The Movie Within the Movie."

Figure 5.9

The Digital Video Cast Member Properties dialog box is where you select settings for the way in which the digital video will play.

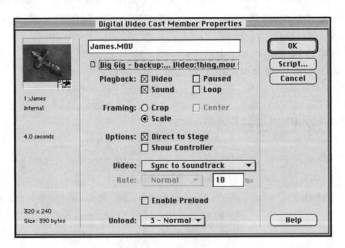

To open the Cast Member Properties dialog box, select the cast member in the Cast window, then do one of the following:

▶ Click on the blue "i," or Information, button in the window

▶ Press Command+I on the Mac, Ctrl+I in Windows

As you learn Director 6 you will want to experiment with different types of cast members to see the various options they provide.

Naming Cast Members

Naming your cast members after you import them is important. If you move them in the Cast window your Lingo scripts can find them if they are named. Your Lingo scripts generally should refer to a cast member by name and a sprite by number (sprites are explained in the next section). You can name a cast member in the Cast Member Properties dialog box, in the Cast window when it's selected, and many of the preview and editing windows. The initial member name of an imported file is the original name of that file on the hard disk.

If you run speed-critical Lingo scripts that refer to a cast member many times consecutively, you can enhance performance by using the number of the cast member rather than its name. This enhances your performance because Director accesses the cast member faster by number than by name. You can use `the number of member` Lingo function to find a cast member's number value, and then you can pass that value to your repeat loop, animated button, or other routine.

Sprites

A *sprite* is an instance of a cast member. When you drag a cast member onto the stage, you create a sprite that simply references that cast member in the Cast window.

A sprite can assume different shapes and sizes during a movie. These properties can change as the movie advances, still referencing the same, unchanged cast member in the Cast window. One cast member can be represented in many instances in the score, or sprite spans, yet still occupy only one cast position.

Each sprite occupies its own rectangular area on the stage and in its own span in the Director's score. The Director score keeps track of which cast member is on the stage and the sprite information for that cast member for each discrete moment of time in your movie.

A sequence of sprites, each reflecting a slight change in position or other characteristic from the preceding sprite, is viewed by Director's playback head to create animation.

Sprite-based animation is the key to Director's power. You can create keyframes within the span of the sprite in the score, in which each keyframe reflects a slight change in position from the previous keyframe. As the playback head advances through the score, Director updates what has changed from one frame to the next. This creates the sprite animation.

For example, think of an animated character walking across the stage. In the first frame of the animation, Director reads in the background bitmap and other things on the stage. As the character walks across the stage and the Director playback head advances to the next frame, it has to update only the small rectangular area of that one sprite. This way, Director can maintain a fast animation engine and a complete multimedia scene at the same time. Animation techniques are covered in detail in Chapter 6, "Director as an Animator."

Director supports the use of up to 120 sprites on the stage at any one time. The sprite's location is given by stage coordinates in relation to the top-left corner of the stage. Director's score keeps track of the sprite information at all times.

If you're having a hard time understanding the difference between a cast member and a sprite, think of, for example, a graphic picture of a tree. In the Cast window, you will have one copy of the tree. On the stage, you could have 10 of these trees to make a small grove. These 10 trees would be sprites on the stage, all referencing the same, single tree graphic in the Cast window. You don't need to have 10 tree cast members, only one that can be referenced multiple times on the stage and throughout the movie.

Sprite Spans

In Director 6, you will work with sprites differently than in previous versions of Director. In Director 5, a sprite occupied one cell in the score and you had to In-Between the sprite across the score for as long as you would like to see it on the stage. You would use the In-Between Linear and In-Between Special commands to create animations and actions on the stage over time.

Director 6 treats sprites as objects that span a period of time by default. When you drag a cast member to the stage, the sprite that is created occupies 28 frames, with each frame containing an identical instance of the sprite. You can change this default number in the Sprite Preferences dialog box.

You can drag the end frame of the sprite to extend or reduce the number of frames the sprite will occupy. You can add keyframes to the sprite to move them to create the animated movement of the sprite over time. You can even edit the keyframes directly on the stage.

The sprite object and everything about it—its location, behaviors, and properties—work as a whole for the length of time it is on the stage. Figure 5.10 shows two sprites in a Director score—Music and Michigan—each spanning 28 frames.

When you move a sprite on the stage, every instance of that sprite in the sprite span moves along with it. If you click on a cell in the score, the entire sprite you've selected is highlighted, not just one cell.

Figure 5.10

Sprite spans in the Director 6 score.

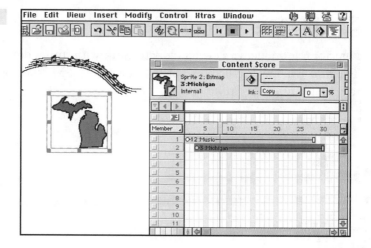

If you move this sprite in the score, you will move the entire sprite, not just one cell. If you want to edit the individual frames of a sprite, like you could in Director 5 and earlier, select the sprite on the stage and select Edit, Edit Sprite Frames. An edit with this mode selected will update each cell individually. To return it to a complete sprite, select a range of open cells and select Edit, Edit Entire Sprite. Using this selection, an edit will change the entire sprite span.

You can change the number of frames that make up a sprite span from 28 to any other number by using the Sprite Preferences dialog box (see fig. 5.11.) If you want to work with sprites the way you did in Director 5, change the preference for span duration to 1 frame.

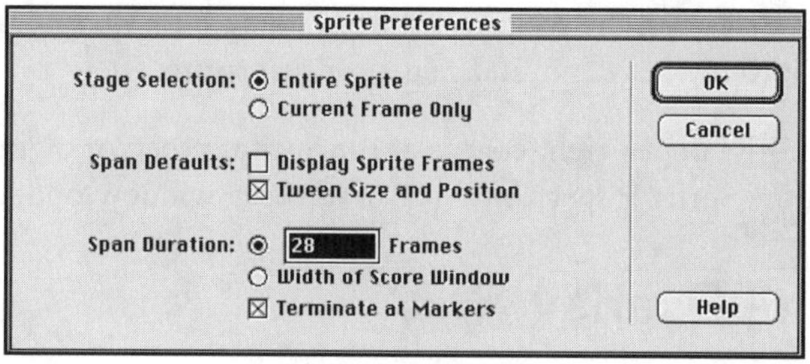

Figure 5.11

The Sprite Preferences dialog box enables you to choose the way sprites display on the stage.

You can use the Sprite Preferences to set up a variety of settings for the sprites on the stage. For a definition of each option, take a look at the online Help file that ships with Director 6.

Sprite Inspector

Director 6 introduces a new window to work with sprites directly on the stage. The new window is called the Sprite Inspector. To open the Sprite Inspector, select File, Inspector, Sprite (see fig. 5.12.)

Figure 5.12

The Sprite Inspector enables you to edit sprite properties directly on the stage.

The Sprite Inspector is useful for displaying and editing many of the commonly edited properties of a sprite. Select a sprite on the stage, and you will see all the information about that sprite. Say, for example, that you would like the span of a sprite in the score to last from frame 3 to 30. You can type these values into the Start and End values for that sprite.

Click in the upper-right corner of the Sprite Inspector's window to change the size of the Sprite Inspector to one of its three window options.

Sprite Overlay

Sprite Overlay is another feature introduced in Director 6 that makes working with sprites easier. With Sprite Overlay turned on, you can view useful sprite information in a small, transparent rectangle directly below the sprite on the stage (see fig. 5.13).

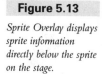

Figure 5.13

Sprite Overlay displays sprite information directly below the sprite on the stage.

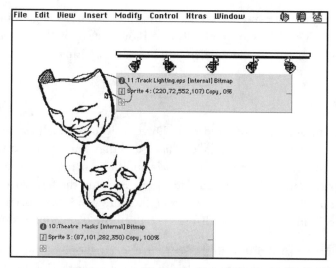

Using Sprite Overlay to dynamically display sprite information and the Sprite Inspector to edit the information, you can develop a rhythm to quickly edit sprites as you author.

You no longer need to open the Sprite Properties dialog box to edit many of the sprite properties. You can use Sprite Overlay and the Sprite Inspector together to edit sprites directly on the stage. If you need to open the Sprite Properties dialog box for other operations, you can quickly open it from the red information button in the Sprite Overlay. You can also open the Cast Member Properties dialog box and Behavior Inspector directly from Sprite Overlay.

To change the Sprite Overlay settings, open the Overlay Settings dialog box from the View, Sprite Overlay, Settings menu. You can choose to have Sprite Overlay displayed when you roll over a sprite, when you select it, or at all times. You can also change the color of the text in the Overlay display.

Sprites and Lingo

You typically use Lingo to examine or change the properties of a sprite as the audience interacts with a movie. For example, when the user clicks a button, you might change the properties of a sprite so that it looks like it's been pressed. You refer to these sprites by sprite number and change their properties in any way you want.

Chapter 16, "Lingo: The Basics," explains how you use Lingo to "puppet" a sprite and take control of it away from the score. You can use the Lingo commands to reference the score information and change it in any way you want. The analogy of the Hollywood sound stage or Broadway production shifts to a puppet show when you begin to use Lingo.

The Score

The most important window in Director is the score. It's similar to a spreadsheet—the columns are called *frames*, and they correspond to relative instances of time; the rows are called *channels*, and they correspond to types of content (sprites, Lingo script, audio, and so on). A cell in the score occupies one frame in one channel. Figure 5.14 shows the score window. A sprite occupies a series of cells in the score, and that score reflects the stage contents over time.

A sprite that is placed in the score may occupy one of the 120 sprite channels in the score window. Sprite 1 is in channel 1, sprite 17 is in channel 17, and so on. Because a cast member can be the source of multiple sprites, cast member 10 could be represented in sprite 1 and 17 simultaneously.

Figure 5.14

The score is where everything is controlled in the Director movie.

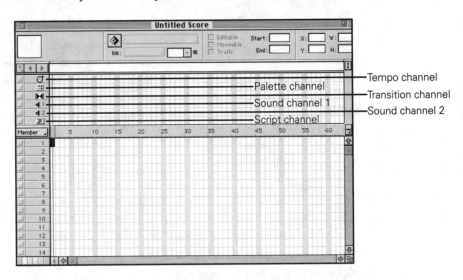

Director depicts what's happening on the stage by advancing across frames in the score. You can have an infinite number of frames in your movie. Each frame can represent a new scene in the movie or introduce an animation over time as the playback head advances.

By default, Director's playback head runs through the score until it reaches the end of a movie. You can develop a linear movie that has many frames, each representing a moment in time. You can also create an entire Director movie in one frame, in which case Lingo makes all necessary changes. You nearly always need to find a proper medium for your projects that falls between these two extremes. Chapter 16 covers how you can use Lingo to control which frames Director's playback head advances to in nonlinear, interactive projects.

The score is the element that has undergone the most changes in Director 6. In addition to the sprite changes mentioned previously, the score itself looks different. You can now open more than one score window at a time. You can have different score windows displaying various views of the same score information. You can drag and drop sprites from one score to another, zoom in and out to see other views of the score, and access the same information in the Sprite Inspector at the top of the score. The biggest change in the new score of Director 6 is the capability to have 120 sprite channels.

120 Sprite Channels

Every time you place a cast member on the stage, a sprite appears in a channel on the score. Likewise, every time you place a cast member in the score, it appears on the stage. The score contains 120 vertical sprite channels, allowing up to 120 visual sprites on the stage at one time.

This extension of the number of channels from 48 to 120 in Director 6 gives more flexibility and creativity to the authors. Be aware that using all 120 channels may take up much more memory than the 48 channels did in Director 5. If you use all or nearly all the channels, you'll want to test your movie early and make sure it performs to your satisfaction with the added media.

Ink Effects

The sprite channels are displayed incrementally in layers—channel 1 being in the background, channel 2 being on top of it, and so on. Ink effects are available in a pop-up menu in the score and also in the Sprite Inspector for creating layering effects among the vertical channels of the score. Director 6 ships with a nice ink effects lab in the tutorial files on the Director 6 CD that enables you to view the effects of each ink.

To apply an ink effect to a sprite on the stage, first select the sprite in the score and select one of the inks from the pop-up menu. One of the most commonly used ink effects is Background Transparent. Applying the Background Transparent ink effect wipes out the background color of the sprite. You can use this option to eliminate the white bounding box behind a bitmap image on the stage.

INSIDER TIP

Sometimes you might like to drop out a color other than white with the Background Transparent ink effect. To do so, select the sprite on the stage, and in the Tool Palette, select a different background color for that sprite. Background Transparent then removes whatever color you selected.

You also can change the sprite ink effect with Lingo during the movie. The following list presents the inks that are available through Lingo. The number before each effect is the number you will use when you assign an ink effect to a sprite with Lingo.

0:	Copy	9:	Mask
1:	Transparent	32:	Blend
2:	Reverse	33:	Add pin
3:	Ghost	34:	Add
4:	Not copy	35:	Subtract pin
5:	Not transparent	36:	Background Transparent
6:	Not reverse	37:	Lightest
7:	Not ghost	38:	Subtract
8:	Matte	39:	Darkest

The syntax for setting the ink of a sprite with Lingo is this:

```
set the ink of sprite 3 to 36
```

This example sets the ink of the sprite in channel 3 to Background Transparent.

The following tutorial shows you how to change ink effects with Lingo.

Changing Ink Effects with Lingo

To see how easy it is to use Lingo to set the ink of a sprite, open the INKS.DIR movie from the Chapter 5 folder of the Inside Macromedia Director 6 with Lingo *CD-ROM.*

1. Within Director, open the Control Panel and rewind and play the movie (see fig 5.15).

2. Click on the two buttons and notice how the sprites change. With Lingo, you are changing their ink effects.

Figure 5.15

The INKS.DIR movie on the Inside Director CD-ROM.

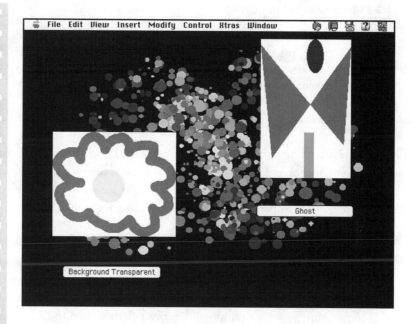

3. Stop the movie, open the Cast window and find cast member 6.

4. Double-click on cast member 6 and take a look at the score script (see fig. 5.16).

Figure 5.16

Score script to change the ink of a sprite to Background Transparent.

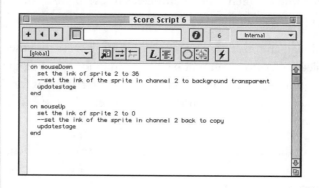

The script should read:

```
on mouseDown
    set the ink of sprite 2 to 36
    --set the ink of the sprite in channel 2 to background transparent
    updatestage
end
```

continues

```
on mouseUp
  set the ink of sprite 2 to 0
  --set the ink of the sprite in channel 2 back to copy
  updatestage
end
```

The preceding script sets the ink of sprite 2 to Background Transparent when the mouse is clicked down, and turns it back when the mouse is released. You could change the 36 in the second line of the script to any of the inks listed previously. Open cast member 7 to see the script that turns the ink effect to Ghost.

The Special Channels

In addition to the 120 sprite channels are six special channels that occupy the top rows in the Director score (refer back to fig. 5.14). You may use these to determine a movie's tempo and active palette, when to add transitions and sound, and when to use Lingo with specific frames of the score.

The Tempo, Palette, Transition, and Sound channels are perfect for linear, slideshow-type presentations. If you have a board meeting in two hours and you don't know which Lingo commands to use, these channels are perfect for setting up your controls.

If you design an interactive CD-ROM or kiosk that's supposed to have user-controlled navigation, you will be using Lingo for scripting the interactivity. In that case, you will also want to script the movie attributes for these upper channels of the score. The syntax is easy and enables the end user to interactively control the course of the movie at run time.

The rest of this section describes how you can use each of these special channels.

Tempo Channel

The Tempo channel is used to set up the tempo and establish tempo changes for the movie. You also can use certain Tempo dialog box settings to direct the Director movie to wait a specified amount of time for an event to happen on the system.

Figure 5.17 shows the events that Director will specifically wait for. Double-click in the Tempo channel of one of the frames to view the available options.

If you are familiar with previous versions of Director, you will notice a new addition to the Tempo channel. Director 6 enables you to set the score to wait for cue points in sounds and digital video files. This way, you can synchronize your animations with specific places in the soundtrack or places in the video.

Figure 5.17

Use the Tempo slider to establish a frames per second movie speed; use the Wait settings to have the movie wait in that frame until the specified event occurs.

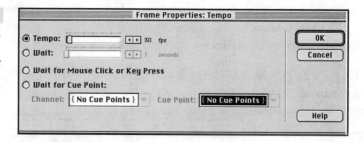

For more information on using this new feature, take a look at Chapter 11, "Sound: The Soundtrack."

Although the Wait settings in the Tempo channel are quick and easy controls you can set up in the score, you also can script these same Wait commands using Lingo.

Here is one example of writing a Lingo script to wait for a mouse click. You would place this script in the Script channel of the frame in which you would like the playback head to "wait."

```
on enterFrame
  if the mouseDown then
    go to the frame + 1
  end if
end
on exitFrame
  go to the frame
end
```

This way, if you offer the audience of the movie another way to exit the frame, the two Lingo scripts will work together. If you use the Tempo channel to set a wait and try to exit that wait with Lingo, you will confuse the playback head.

The Palette Channel

Palettes refer to a color look up table (CLUT) that graphics and a Director movie use to display colors on the monitor. A 256-color, or 8-bit, palette is the most commonly used in Director. 4-bit (16 color) and 1-bit (black-and-white) palettes are also available.

You use the Frame Properties: Palette dialog box to set up the active palette, make palette changes, and control color effects over time in the movie (see fig. 5.18). Double-click in one of the frames of the Palette channel to view the available settings in the Frame Properties: Palette dialog box.

Palette manipulation in Director might be new to you. If you need more information, Chapter 8, "Graphics: The Visuals," covers palettes in greater detail.

Figure 5.18

Use the Frame Properties: Palette dialog box to set up the active palette, palette changes, and color effects over time.

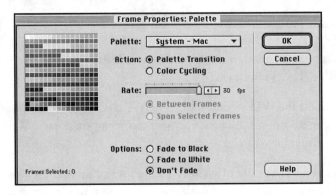

Color Depth

Palettes work hand-in-hand with your monitor's display settings; they must be set to match your monitor's color depth. On the Macintosh, you would set your monitor to 256 colors for 8-bit; you'd select a 256-color video driver in Windows.

An easy way to test for the active color depth of the monitor is to open the Message window (see fig. 5.19) and type the following script:

```
put the colorDepth
```

Press Return (or Enter) and the active color depth is returned to you.

Figure 5.19

Testing the color depth in the Message window.

The range of color depths depends on your system. Table 5.2 breaks down these possibilities.

Table 5.2

Range of Color Depths per System

Color Depth	Number of Colors
1-bit	black and white
2-bit	4 colors
4-bit	16 colors (VGA on Windows)
8-bit	256 colors (SVGA on Windows)
16-bit	32,768 colors (Thousands on the Macintosh)
24-bit	16,777,216 colors (Millions on the Macintosh)

Typically, you author Director movies for 8-bit environments—8-bit being the basic system today. Just like the size of the stage, minimum system capabilities becomes an issue again. You cannot, for example, display a 24-bit graphic in an 8-bit display with any success. If the machine you target has a limit of 256 colors, you need to author in 8-bit. You also must deal with palette issues, as well.

True color, or 24-bit, movies are available in Director 6 on both platforms—a breakthrough introduced in Director 5 when Director became a 32-bit native application. Playback in Director for Windows on Windows 3.1 is limited to 256 colors, but you can enjoy true color on Windows 95 and Windows NT.

You must think of that target 8-bit machine. Animation, combined with the system capabilities and the effects possible in Director, usually is best viewed in 256 colors if you are targeting a mass market. Palette transitions are ignored with more than 256 color screens, and performance is much faster with less information to process.

Switching Among Palettes

If you target an 8-bit environment and you scan 100 photographs to use in a Director movie, you must make sure that each photograph uses only 256 colors. You can use Photoshop, xRes, or your favorite graphics editing tool to create a custom palette for each graphic. Custom palettes estimate the closest 256 colors that an image uses. Because your target machine may have a 256 color display, and your scanned artwork may be 24-bit, or 16,777,216 colors, the image you display needs to be edited to use only 256 colors.

INSIDER TIP

> When you edit graphics, be sure to save them at 72 dots per inch (dpi). Director, when animating images across the screen, requires that they are 72 dpi, or screen resolution. If you happen to bring in an image with 300 dpi, or anything higher than 72 dpi, you'll notice that Director reduces the resolution to 72 dpi and dramatically shrinks the image's size. Chapter 8 covers working with graphics in more detail.

When you import a graphic that contains a custom palette into Director, a dialog box appears prompting you with a couple of options. One option is to import the graphic's palette as a cast member (see fig. 5.20). To ensure that the graphic uses the custom palette you've made for it, select this option, and make that palette cast member active in the palette channel of the score.

Figure 5.20

When importing an image with a palette that is not currently in the Director movie, you will be prompted with the Image Options dialog box.

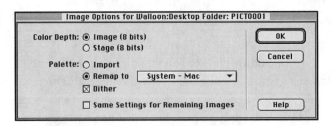

The second option you have for importing images is to remap the color depth and palette of the image to one of the palettes already within Director, a process sometimes called *auto remapping*. In auto remapping, Director replaces the image's colors with the most similar colors in a palette that you select from the pop-up menu. This can be done for images of all color depths. When you select the Dither option, Director blends the colors in the new palette you choose to approximate the original colors in the graphic.

Only one palette can be active on the monitor at a time; if you have multiple palettes in your movie, you need to switch among them while you work.

Director offers a couple options for dealing with multiple palettes. You can use the Palette channel's Fade to Black option or Fade to White option before displaying the next graphic. To avoid switching among palettes, many developers use editing tools from outside Director to make a common palette, or super palette. A *super palette* is a single, shared palette that is based on the colors found in all your movie images.

Tools that can help you create a super palette include the following:

▶ DeBabelizer from Equilibrium Technologies (Macintosh and Windows)

▶ Brenda (Windows)

After you create the super palette, you can activate it in the palette channel of the score for the entire movie. Applying the palette to frame 1 causes it to remain in effect for the entire movie. Alternatively, you can select it as the movie's default palette under Modify, Movie, Properties.

To change the palette dynamically using Lingo, you can use the `puppetPalette` command. When you puppet the palette, the palette you specify remains in effect until you use the `puppetPalette 0` command to turn it off. Director doesn't obey any more subsequent palette changes in the score as long as the puppet palette stays in effect.

If you would like to puppet a palette when you enter a specific frame, you would use the script:

```
on enterFrame
  puppetPalette "CustomPalette"
end
```

`"CustomPalette"` in this example is the name of the palette cast member.

Chapter 8 offers more information on using palettes in Director and Chapter 16 discusses puppets in detail.

The Transition Channel

The Transition channel enables you to set up the special effects among the scenes of your movie. For example, if you want to dissolve one scene into the next, set up the Dissolve, Pixels Fast transition in the frame of the score where you want it to take place. You usually can tell when a movie was created using Director because of its cool transitions. The Transition channel is easy to use, and if used properly, it can add the extra impact your movie or business presentation needs.

To set a transition in the score, first double-click in a cell in the Transition channel. The resultant Frame Properties: Transition dialog box contains a list of available categories and transitions (see fig. 5.21).

Figure 5.21

Use the Transition channel to create special effects for transitioning between scenes in your movies.

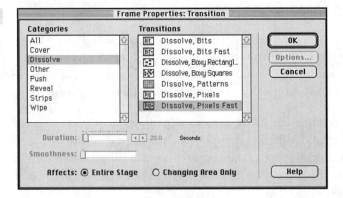

Director assigns transitions by category. Selecting categories such as cover, push, reveal, or wipe in the Categories scroll box gives you different sets of transitions in the Transitions scroll box. In turn, selecting different transitions in the Transitions scroll box offers different settings with which you can alter the transition. One setting might enable you to adjust duration, smoothness, and stage area of the transition, whereas another setting might enable you to change the transition's effects.

You can use transitions to add effects to the entire stage as you enter a new section of the movie. You can also apply them to only the part of the stage that changes as you enter a new frame. Applying a transition to the changing area enables you to highlight specific areas of the stage to add a special emphasis to just one part or another in your presentation. For example, you might create bulleted text to "push" on from the left, each line "pushing" on in each new frame.

Tips on Using the Transition Channel

Transitions are easy to use, but people often make a couple of common mistakes. These tips should help you avoid those mistakes.

▶ Set a transition in the frame to which the playback head is going, not from which it's leaving.

A transition occurs between frames, as the playback head enters a new frame. You might put a Dissolve Pixels Fast in the Transition channel of frame 3, for example, if you want the effect to occur when the movie reaches frame 3.

▶ Never loop or wait in a frame with a transition.

You might have the following loop set up in the score to loop in a particular frame:

```
on exitFrame
go to the frame
end
```

If you have a transition in this same frame, and you loop in that frame with the go to the frame loop above, the transition will repeat itself over and over. Doing so can cause performance problems and crazy visual disturbances.

Instead, create your loop sequence with two frames. Place the transition in the first frame of the sequence and use the go to the frame loop in the second frame.

▶ If elements on the stage drop out of a movie, turn off the transition in that frame and see whether the problem disappears.

▶ Transitions are memory- and processor-intensive. They are one of the most difficult tasks for the machine to complete. You might notice that the time a transition takes to execute increases significantly on a low-end system.

▶ Don't start a sound, test for mouse events, or try to apply palette effects in the same frame as a transition.

Transitions, like Lingo repeat loops, monopolize the processor, do their job, and get out. You cannot interrupt a transition with a mouse click. Let the transition occur and move on to the next scene.

▶ After you use a transition in the score, Director stores it in the cast. You now can reapply the same transition settings easily and share them with other movies in an external cast. Be sure to delete from the cast any transitions that you don't end up using in the score because they take up memory.

Transition Xtras

Using the Macromedia Open Architecture (MOA), third-party developers can create Transition Xtras to add to the library of built-in transitions. Chapter 21, "The Xtra Step," covers more about Transition Xtras and the Macromedia Open Architecture.

For a list of available Transition Xtras, take a look at Macromedia's web site: `http://www.macromedia.com`.

Two Sound Channels

Director provides two sound channels in the score, but you actually can play more than two sounds at a time. Director for Macintosh can support up to eight sound channels. And Director for Windows can combine multiple sounds into one with its built-in technology, MACROMIX.DLL. Chapter 11 covers sound techniques and cross-platform sound considerations in detail.

Before you can add sound to your movie, you must import sounds into Director's cast. The most commonly used file format for sound is the Audio Interchange File format (AIFF), which can play back on both Macintosh and Windows.

To use the two sound channels directly, double-click in the sound channel of the frame in which you would like to start the sound. The resultant Frame Properties: Sound dialog box (see fig. 5.22) contains a list of the sound cast members.

Figure 5.22

Use the Sound channel to assign sounds to a frame.

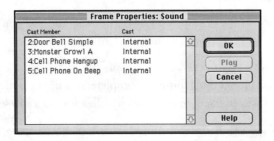

Selecting a sound in this list sets up the sound in that frame. You also can drag and drop a sound cast member from the Cast window to one of the two sound channels in the score.

If you use Lingo to control sounds, you can make a movie play a sound when a user clicks a button, as well as initiate a sound at a certain time during the movie. Using Lingo works better than using the score if you're playing the movie in a low-memory situation. If the sound is placed in the score, the sound might be purged from memory if memory runs low. If a sound is prompted by Lingo to play at a certain time, the sound has a better chance at playing successfully than a sound simply waiting in the score. Chapter 11 covers using Lingo with sounds.

Tips on Using the Sound Channels

The following are some tips for using the two sound channels in the Director score.

▶ Use sound channel 2 for background sounds. Reserve sound channel 1 for Lingo's `puppetSound` command.

▶ Avoid placing large sounds in frame 1 of your movie. Director loads the movie, its scripts, and other elements at that time. If possible, start the sounds after frame 1.

INSIDER TIP

After you set your sounds in the score, turn off the score's sound channel. One way to do this is to click on the square to the left of the channel. You'll want to turn the sound channel back on for testing, but while you continue to develop the movie, you won't have to hear the movie's sounds over and over.

The Script Channel

You use the Script channel (see fig. 5.23) to enter Lingo scripts that are in effect only while the playback head is in that particular frame. The scripts in the Script channel are called *score scripts*, but calling them *frame scripts* might be easier to remember because they're intended for events that take place specifically in that frame.

To enter scripts for a particular frame, double-click on the Script channel for that frame and type the script. By default, the Script channel contains an empty on `exitFrame` handler. The two primary handlers that any frame can have are the on `enterFrame` handler and the on `exitFrame` handler. A handler handles Lingo events. Lingo events and messages are covered in detail in Chapter 16.

Figure 5.23

Enter Lingo programming for a frame in the Script channel.

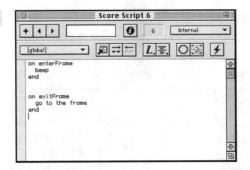

Director executes the on enterFrame handler when the playback head enters that frame. Likewise, it executes the on exitFrame handler when the playback head exits the frame. Every script in the Script channel can contain one, none, or both of these handlers. For example, if the tempo of your movie is set to 10 frames per second, the exitFrame message is received 1/10 second after the enterFrame message.

The Script channel is only one of four places where you put your Lingo scripts. To find out more about the Script channel and other places to put scripts, see Chapter 16.

Controlling the Playback Head with Lingo

The Director score settings are quick and easy to use, but you might have more control over your movie if you use Lingo to control the settings. (Never forget that you can do the same thing many different ways in Director. Part of your development as a Director author is finding which work best for you.) Chapter 16 begins the Lingo section of the text. Typically, when Director developers begin using Lingo and become familiar with it, they prefer to use Lingo exclusively. Using Lingo, you have complete control over the media you present in the movie and the memory Director uses to display that media, among many other things. Using Lingo, you may have control of any situation, whether or not you are there.

As you become more familiar with Director and begin to work on larger projects, you'll begin to use Lingo to control the course of the movie.

Looping with Lingo

With Lingo, you can set up loops to wait for a particular action to occur before enabling Director to advance to the next frame. With looping, Director cycles through one or a few frames for as much time as the user needs to view and interact with them. At the desired user interaction, the loop ends and Director proceeds to the next frame.

pause Versus go to the frame

The most important Lingo loop you should learn is as follows:

```
on exitFrame
go to the frame
end
```

The preceding handler also works if you use go the frame in the second line. Either way, it tells Director's playback head to go back to the beginning of the same frame when it exits that frame.

Users new to Lingo might learn the pause command and pause the Director playback head in that frame until the user clicks a button. Using pause, however, can cause problems because you can end up pausing other Director functions that should keep running.

A go to the frame loop enables animations, Movie in a Window, and user event processing to continue running while the movie continues to look paused to the audience.

You then can have a button with a script that executes the following to exit the loop:

```
on mouseUp
go to the frame + 1     --or "go to the frame – 1"
end
```

In the preceding code, note the text preceded by two hyphens in the second line. Any text with two hyphens in front of it in Script window is called commented text and will not execute. It's available so you can comment your code.

Memory is an important issue in multimedia. Learning to use Lingo successfully means knowing how to manage the way the cast of your movie is used in the score. Using Lingo to loop the playback head is the first step in controlling the score with Lingo. Chapter 17, "Managing Your Data," offers more information on memory management and using Lingo.

Scriptless Authoring

If you would like to loop in the score or create interactivity without using Lingo, you're in luck—Director 6 has a new way of authoring without scripting, and it's called the Behavior Inspector. Using the Behavior Inspector, you can assign behaviors to objects and frames with simple pull-down menus and no scripting.

To open the Behavior Inspector, select Window, Inspector, Behavior. You can also click on the Behavior Inspector icon in many other places: the Toolbar, within Sprite Overlay, the Sprite Inspector, even the top of the score (see fig. 5.24).

Figure 5.24

You can open the Behavior Inspector directly from the score, or in many other places.

Using the Built-In Behaviors

Director 6 ships with a large library of built-in behaviors. You can access these built-in behaviors in the Behavior Inspector and use them to create behavior cast members.

The following tutorial shows you how to use the Behavior Inspector to create a behavior that switches cast members on the stage. This is a common technique used to create realistic buttons. The first cast member is the button image, unpressed, to be switched with another cast member that looks like the button is being pressed. When you release the button, it switches back to the original image.

Using Built-In Behaviors to Create a Switch Cast Member Behavior

1. Open the BUTTON.DIR file in the Chapter 5 folder on the *Inside Macromedia Director 6 with Lingo* CD.

2. In Director, open the Behavior Inspector under Window, Inspector, Behavior.

3. In the top-left corner of Behavior Inspector, click on the + button and select New Behavior.

4. Name the behavior, for this example, "Switch".

5. In the middle section of the Behavior Inspector, select the Mouse Down event.

6. Then select a corresponding action for that event in the right side of the middle section. For this example, select the Sprite menu and the Change Cast Member option.

7. When the Specify Cast Member dialog box appears, select member 2 of castLib 1 and click OK.

8. In the Events category, select the Mouse Up event. This will then be the second event in this behavior.

9. In the Action category for this event, select the Sprite menu and the Change Cast Member option.

10. When the Specify Cast Member dialog box appears, select member 1 of castLib 1 and click OK.

A Switch behavior cast member is created in the cast. You can now drag and drop that behavior cast member onto any sprite on the stage. When you click on a sprite with that assigned behavior, it switches cast members with the one you selected. This is a common way of creating buttons in Director 6, without using any Lingo!

Editing the Built-In Behaviors

You can edit any of the behaviors created with the Behavior Inspector. When you create a behavior, the cast member that is created is actually a Lingo score script. You can edit this script at any time in the Script window or in the Behavior Inspector.

If you double-click on a behavior in the Cast window, the Behavior Inspector opens. If you select a behavior in the cast and click the script button at the top of the Cast window, you can edit it in the Script window.

You can also create your own behavior with Lingo. For more information on editing and creating your own behaviors with Lingo, take a look at Chapter 16.

Integrated Internet Authoring

In addition to alternative ways to create interactivity, Director 6 opens a new way to work with the Internet. You can dynamically link to the Internet in an authoring session in Director 6. Select File, Preferences, Network to open the Network Preferences dialog box to see the available settings (see fig. 5.25).

Figure 5.25

The Network Preferences dialog box enables you to set up the way in which Director connects to a network.

```
┌──────────────── Network Preferences ─────────────────┐
│ Preferred Browser:                   [ Browse... ]  [   OK   ] │
│ [Big Mac:Internet:Netscape Navigator™ 3.0        ]  [ Cancel ] │
│        Options: ⊠ Launch When Needed                │
│                                                      │
│     Cache Size: [10000]  Kb          [  Clear  ]    │
│  Check Documents: ⦿ Once Per Session                │
│                   ○ Every Time                      │
│                                                      │
│       Proxies: ○ No Proxies                         │
│                ⦿ Manual Configuration               │
│                                                      │
│                Location              Port           │
│        http: [                    ]  [      ]       │
│         ftp: [                    ]  [      ]  [  Help  ] │
└──────────────────────────────────────────────────────┘
```

The Network Preferences dialog box enables you to specify which browser to be launched when Director encounters a `gotoNetPage` command, the size of your cache, and how often Director checks cached documents against those on the server.

Lingo

Almost everything you can do in the score, you also can do using Lingo. When you're first starting to use Director, you learn about using the score to animate sprites, add sounds and digital video, and change cast members on the stage, but you can do all those using Lingo, too. The trick is to find an optimal combination of Lingo- and score-based management in your movie.

Many people say they know Director, but they have resisted learning Lingo because they anticipate a large learning curve. Although it's true that learning *everything* about Lingo entails a significant amount of time and committed effort, you don't need to know everything to make extremely good use of Lingo in your Director projects. You primarily use only a handful of Lingo terms. After you master these few terms, you are well on your way to high-quality Director work. Chapter 16 contains details on these essential Lingo terms.

Beyond the essential Lingo terms, Lingo becomes a robust scripting language. For serious programmers, it offers a complete interpretive language. Using Director with Lingo, you are virtually unlimited in what you can do. And if you can't accomplish what you want with Director and Lingo, you can use Lingo to communicate with C code compiled into Xtras. Xtras are overviewed later in this chapter.

Interactivity and Navigation

Lingo is essential to interactivity and navigation within a Director movie. *Interactivity* means just what it sounds like: the user interacts with the movie. Director combines multimedia elements, and you decide where they should appear on the stage in the score. After you decide where elements are placed on the stage, Lingo tells Director what to do when a particular event occurs, such as when the user clicks a button.

You can use Lingo to navigate around the Director score, navigate among Director movies, and launch other applications. The commands for this navigation are as easy as Play, Go, and Open. Examples of using these commands are covered in Chapter 16.

Special Effects

You can create special effects and feedback in your movie by using Lingo; this saves time in Director because you don't have to set up each new scene in the score. You can keep track of a user's path in a game you create that contains a maze, for example. If the user travels down the right corridor in the maze, you can play a particular sound, or you can switch the color of the stage on-the-fly. With Lingo you can initiate a transition, change the volume of a sound, or even quit the application.

Managing Media

Lingo provides many elements for managing the media in your Director movie. Director already has memory management built into it, but you might need to issue some explicit memory-management commands depending on what you include in your movie and the system on which you intend to run your movie. Some of these commands include Preload, Unload, and PreloadRAM.

You can use Lingo as a tool for testing the target machine and for testing the movie before you distribute it. Lingo is a powerful tool in a Director project, as well as other Director movies designed as testing modules. Examples of Lingo tools and managing media with Lingo are covered in Chapter 17.

Xtras

Director 5 introduced the Macromedia Open Architecture (MOA) as a way to extend functionality, even beyond what Lingo could do. As a result, you can use third-party C programming modules called Xtras to extend the capabilities of Director. Xtras are easy to use; currently available Xtras include the functionality for database connectivity, expanded printing, additional transitions, and more.

Xtras are an updated and expanded replacement of the XOjects used with previous versions of Director. Director 6 supports some XObjects, but most of the current XObject developers are working with Macromedia to update their XObjects for the Director Xtras architecture.

Director 6 also ships with an Xtras Development Kit (XDK), if you would like to develop these Xtras yourself. Chapter 21 covers Xtras and the Macromedia Open Architecture.

Using pre-existing Xtras is easy. After you put the Xtra in Director's Xtras folder or directory, it appears in the appropriate menu. Depending on the Xtra's function, it might appear in a number of the menus. If, for example, the Xtra creates a new cast member, it shows up in the Insert menu. If it doesn't fit into one of the menu categories, it appears in an Xtras menu.

To install an Xtra, drop it into a folder called Xtras in the Director application folder.

Projectors

As discussed in Chapter 4, after your movie is complete, you can save it as a projector. This projector can run on any machine that meets your movie's system requirements. The target machine doesn't need to have Director on it. The beauty of projectors is that the developer pays no royalty fees to Macromedia.

Remember that Director projectors are platform-specific. A Macintosh projector can play only on the Macintosh and a Windows projector can play only on Windows. To create the platform-specific projector, you must obtain the version of Director for each platform on which you want to distribute your movie.

You can put a number of movies in a projector and distribute only one file to your customer. For larger projects, however, placing in the projector one small file, which in turn calls to a number of smaller movies in the same folder or out on the CD, works better. This approach is a popular setup for creating hybrid CDs. You can have a CD-ROM with a Macintosh and Windows projector, each calling the same set of Director movies in a separate folder.

Depending on which media types your movie uses, you need to distribute certain files with the projector. On the Macintosh, your primary concern if you are using QuickTime movies is to install QuickTime on the target machine. See Chapter 4 if you need to review what to distribute with the Director projector.

Macromedia stopped thinking about charging a run-time royalty on all its products in 1994, at which time it introduced the Made with Macromedia program. Rather than a royalty fee, commercially distributed products require that you place the Made with Macromedia logo (see fig. 5.26) both on the packaging and also on the product.

Figure 5.26

Macromedia requires that you include the Made with Macromedia logo on the packaging and the product if you commercially distribute any products you create using Macromedia's products.

The Made with Macromedia logo and licensing information is easy to obtain on the *Inside Macromedia Director 6 with Lingo* CD-ROM or on the Macromedia web site at `http://www.macromedia.com`. Frequently asked questions can be answered at the Made with Macromedia FAQ voice mail: 415-252-2171. Chapter 4, "Delivering the Goods" and Appendix C, "Contacting Macromedia," cover additional information on the Made with Macromedia program.

Director References

Anytime you're working in Director and aren't sure what to do next, you have several options for finding additional help.

One option is Director's online Help system, which has undergone a complete overhaul and can help you considerably in Director 6. Check out the FAQs, the bookmarks you can set up, and the copy-text capabilities of the Help system. It is a preview of Macromedia's move toward comprehensive online documentation.

Using the Director Documentation

The Director documentation is another good option for finding help. If you haven't previously worked with Director, read the tutorials and examine the "Show Me" movies. The "Using Director" and "Learning Lingo" documentation are essential to read, and you should never write a line of Lingo without a "Lingo Dictionary" nearby. The online Help file contains all the "Lingo Dictionary" contents as well. The new Lingo terms in Director 6 are listed in Appendix B, "New Lingo Terms in Director 6."

In Practice

After having read this chapter, you no doubt have figured out that there is never just one way to do anything in Director. There is no single series of steps to take, or a formula for success, but there are tricks, techniques, and preferences that you develop as you go along. Borrow the best approaches from members of the Director community as you discover them in this book and elsewhere. And, when you build your own better mousetraps, you can return the favor by sharing your solutions.

This chapter was an overview of Director's features and how they work together. In the next chapter, you'll delve into detail on one of Director's most important functions: animation. Going forward, keep in mind the following:

▶ Set your stage size with your target audience in mind. If you're producing for a mass audience and want to make only one version of the movie, set the stage size to accommodate the smallest monitor dimensions your intended audience is likely to have.

▶ Sorting the cast by Usage in Score optimizes your movie for faster playback.

▶ Remember to preview imported cast members from the Cast window. Table 5.1 summarizes how to do so for graphics, sounds, and digital video. If the media element doesn't work well in the Cast window, it won't work well in the movie.

▶ Using all or nearly all 120 sprite channels in the Director score can be memory-intensive; test your movie early to make sure it performs well.

▶ Consider the target audience when setting color depth. The basic system today is an 8-bit environment (256 colors).

▶ Among the most important Lingo control you will want to use in your movies is the go to the frame loop. Using this instead of the pause command will enable the playback head to move and multimedia events to continue while waiting for user interaction.

▶ You can assign behaviors to objects and frames without scripting by using the Behavior Inspector, a new feature in Director 6.

▶ For help at any time, consult Director's documentation and the online Help system.

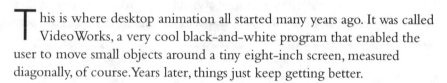

Jay Armstrong

chapter 6

Director as an Animator

This is where desktop animation all started many years ago. It was called VideoWorks, a very cool black-and-white program that enabled the user to move small objects around a tiny eight-inch screen, measured diagonally, of course. Years later, things just keep getting better.

Macromedia has added an arsenal of new features to Director 6. Throughout this chapter, you will find many step-by-step instructions to help get you up-to-speed in creating cool animation quickly. Also included are troubleshooting tips to help with some of the mistakes commonly made when creating animations in Director.

This chapter covers the following basic areas:

- ▶ Quick primer on animation principles
- ▶ How Director approaches animation
- ▶ Basic animation techniques
- ▶ Advanced animation techniques
- ▶ Troubleshooting

Quick Primer on Animation Principles

Animation is actually a trick being played on the eyes. The process of animation is achieved by presenting a series of images in rapid succession. These images are offset by a small amount from one frame to another to create the illusion of motion. As Director's playback head advances over the frames, you see movement on the stage; like magic, "animation" is created.

Whether you are creating animations for movies, videos, or computer presentations, all the information that the audience views is located in frames. The term *frames per second* (fps) is used to tell how fast a movie is being played. Basically, two different speeds for playback exist: 24 fps for motion pictures or film, and 30 fps for videotape.

The videotape category can be broken down even further into speeds and formats. The United States uses National Television Standards Committee (NTSC) format, which was developed in the early 1950s. The NTSC format runs at about 30 fps. Actually, the true speed of NTSC video is 29.97 fps. To avoid explaining the technical reasons for such a strange speed, however, this discussion rounds it off to 30 fps. The European standard is PAL (Phase Alternating Line), which runs at a speed closer to that of film at 25 fps. Director's playback head can travel at speeds ranging from one frame per second all the way up to 120 frames per second. With this wide range of speed settings, you can achieve just about any type of animation sequence.

Keep in mind the two basic ways of changing the speed of animation. One way, as just mentioned, is to change the speed settings for the playback head. A second way is to change the spacing of objects in adjacent frames with respect to one another. Objects placed closer together in adjacent frames move more slowly than objects spaced farther apart.

On the accompanying CD-ROM, open the file Speed Test from the Chapter 6 folder. When the animation is played, the file shows two balls moving across the stage. The speed of the animation is 15 fps for the entire movie sequence, and both balls move at 15 fps. Notice that the lower ball moves faster than the ball at the top, even though the movie stays at a constant 15 fps. Closer examination of the stopped file shows that the lower ball moves faster because the spacing of the top object in the frame is farther apart than the spacing of the lower object in the frame. When trying to adjust the speed of an animation, therefore, object placement can be just as important as playback speed.

How Director Approaches Animation

Animation occurs when Director advances the playback head over time and displays data contained in each frame to the screen. Sounds simple? It is, except that what happens from frame to frame is a little more complicated. As the playback head advances over time, it encounters frames, channels, sprites, tempo changes, transitions, sound cues, palettes, Lingo scripts, and a few more pieces of information. Considering each of these elements one at a time, the real complexity of animation becomes more apparent.

When a movie starts, Director first looks at the movie script. The movie script tells Director what to do at startup, during the playback, and when the movie stops. The startMovie handler can contain the color-depth settings for the monitor; it can adjust the volume of sound for the movie. It can do anything Lingo can do. As the playback head enters each frame, a list of up to 126 tasks must be followed before the playback head can advance to the next frame. These tasks, of course, correspond to the 126 channels in the score (see fig. 6.1).

Figure 6.1

The channels in the Score window.

Tempo Channel

Palette Channel

Sound Channels

Script Channel

120 Sprite Channels

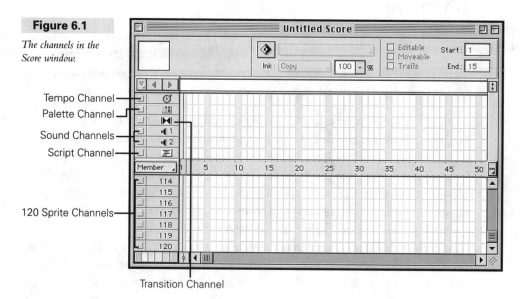

Transition Channel

Frames

Frames are viewed in the Score window. The first frame is located on the left side of the window. When you first open a new movie, the playback head, indicated in red on the screen, will be in frame 1 (see fig. 6.2). The frame numbers increase as the playback head travels to the right. The number of frames in a Director file has no limit, although you could get tired from scrolling millions of frames. The playback head indicates which frame is currently being shown on the stage. The Control Panel also displays the current frame number. A frame runs up and down the Score window as a vertical column. Each vertical frame column contains 120 channels of cast information and 6 channels of effects.

Figure 6.2

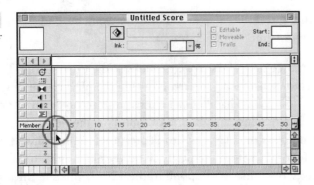

Channels

Channels are rows that run the entire length of a Director file. As the playback head passes over frames, all the channel layers affect the stage. The channel layers provide information about speed, palette settings, transitions, sounds, scripts, and sprite locations of cast members on the stage.

As the playback head enters a frame, the channels are executed in order, beginning from the top of the Score window, the Tempo channel, and continuing down to channel 126, the last of the channels. The order of the channels is important. Channel 1 is the first channel to be drawn on the stage, channel 2 is the second channel drawn on the stage, and so on. Sprites in higher numbered channels will be on top of sprites in lower numbered channels. In other words, channel 1 is located on the bottom of a stack visually and channel 120 is on top of the visual stack. Higher numbers equal higher sprites. The playback head then returns to the top of the next frame and travels down that frame's column of channels. This will happen for all the remaining frames of the movie.

Cells

A cell is the location in the Score window where a horizontal channel meets with a vertical frame. A cell can only contain one element at a time. The element can be one of many different things: a graphic, color palette, tempo setting, score script, sound, or transition. The key here is that the cell can contain only one item.

Sprites

As first mentioned in Chapter 5, "Working with Director 6: Understanding the Metaphor," a sprite is an instance of a cast member that has been placed on the stage. A sprite is not a cast member, but only the stage information pertaining to its cast member, such as which cast member it should be, the location on the stage, the location in regard to a previous frame, the ink effect, the blend amount, the visibility, and the script code.

Remember that Director 6 treats sequences of sprites as single objects, called *sprite spans*. You have the choice of editing and manipulating the span as a whole, or of breaking the span into its individual frames for frame-level editing. The default length of sprite spans is 28 frames. This setting can be adjusted in the Sprite Preferences dialog box under the File menu.

Each sprite span begins and ends with *keyframes*. These are frames where the user has defined attributes for the sprite by placing the sprite on the stage, or by entering attributes manually in Sprite Properties under the File menu. Director automatically calculates the sprite's attributes for frames between keyframes. You can add your own keyframes to a span by choosing Keyframe from the Insert menu.

WARNING

Because a cast member can be used hundreds of times throughout a movie, deleting a cast member might not be a good idea; removing a single cast member can remove hundreds of sprites with a single key press. The Delete key operates on the active or top-most window. Keep an eye on which window is active when deleting elements. A deletion in the Cast Member window deletes a cast member and all its sprites; a deletion in the Score window deletes only a single sprite.

Sprites are controlled by the Score window. The channels tell the sprites where they are and what color they should be and so on. This control can be taken away from the Score window and given to Lingo by turning the sprite into a puppet. A puppeted sprite can then be controlled by Lingo. To create a puppetSprite, use the following Lingo code:

```
puppetSprite 4, TRUE
```

or

```
set the puppet of sprite 4 to TRUE
```

This script sets the puppetSprite of the sprite in channel 4. The script can be placed in a movie script, a score script, or in a handler such as on mouseUp or on mouseDown. The puppeted sprite can now be moved to a new location by using locV and locH Lingo commands or changed to another cast member by using the memberNum command. The transparency of a sprite can be adjusted with the blend of sprite command. Remember to turn off the puppetSprite when finished by using the command <puppetSprite 4, FALSE>, or the sprite will behave very strangely when Score window changes are made later in the movie to the sprite in the fourth channel.

The Control Panel

To play back the animations on the stage, you can use the Control Panel. This small, easy-to-use panel has all the functions available to manipulate the playback head. Choose Control Panel from the Window menu or press Command+2 on the Mac, Ctrl+2 in Windows. Figure 6.3 shows all the Control Panel functions.

Figure 6.3

The Control Panel has all the functions available to manipulate the playback head.

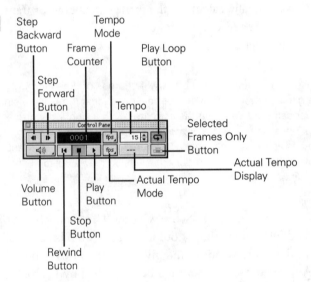

Starting at the top left of the panel, the functions are as follows:

▶ **Step Backward and Step Forward Buttons:** These two buttons will move the playback head forward or backward one frame. Holding down either button will quickly scan the movie in the corresponding direction.

▶ **The Frame Counter:** Displays the current position of the playback head. Entering a number in the frame counter and pressing Return advances you to that frame. Option-dragging the mouse in the frame counter moves the playback head quickly forward or backward.

▶ **Tempo Mode Pop-Up:** Determines how the Tempo is displayed. The choices are frames per second (fps) and seconds per frame (spf).

▶ **Tempo:** The area to the right of the Tempo Mode and left of the Loop Playback button. This is the assigned speed of the selected frame in either fps or spf. Entering a new Tempo into the field and pressing Return or clicking on the arrow buttons changes the Tempo.

▶ **Play Loop Button:** Sets the movie to play again after the last frame (down position) or to play only one time (up position).

▶ **Volume Button:** This pop-up menu sets the volume for the entire movie.

▶ **Rewind Button:** Rewinds the movie to frame 1. You can also select Rewind from the Control menu or press Command+Option+R on the Mac, Ctrl+Alt+R in Windows.

▶ **Stop Button:** Stops the movie on the current frame. Select Stop from the Control menu or press Command+. (period) on the Mac, Ctrl+. (period) in Windows.

▶ **Play Button:** Plays the movie from the current frame. Select Play from the Control menu or press Command+Option+P on the Mac, Ctrl+Alt+P in Windows.

▶ **Actual Tempo Mode:** This pop-up list sets the display mode of the Actual Tempo to the right of this setting. The choices are frames per second (fps), seconds per frame (spf), and Running Total and Estimated Total. Running Total is the elapsed time since the start of the movie. Estimated Total is a more accurate (although slower) calculation of elapsed time.

▶ **Actual Tempo Display:** This displays the actual tempo that Director is achieving in the current frame. Depending on how much activity is taking place on the stage, this could be less than the assigned tempo on slower machines. It will never exceed the assigned tempo.

▶ **Selected Frames Only Button:** Toggle this button on or off to set the movie to play only the selected frames in the Score window. A green line at the top of the Sprite channels indicates the selected frames. If the movie is looped, only the selected frames will play over and over.

Basic Animation Techniques

Building an animation from scratch is the best way to learn how Director deals with objects in motion. Much of the rest of this chapter consists of several step-by-step walkthroughs for creating basic animations. You will create just a few movies, but will revisit them throughout the chapter to explore various techniques and aspects of Director as an animator.

Bitmapped and Shape Elements

Any Director file can have two basic elements: bitmapped elements and shape elements. A *bitmapped* element is defined by an arrangement of pixels. A *shape* element is defined by geometrical relationships among its component parts.

All cast members that can be placed on the stage can be animated. Cast members can be imported from just about any application to become part of your Director animation. This includes scans, video captures, drawings, and clip art. Because Director has a built-in painting program, you will create your object within Director.

Bouncing balls are great for animation tutorials for a number of reasons. They are fun to watch, easy to control, and most of all, easy to replace later with real images. If you prefer to create a more complex image for this tutorial, feel free to do so; just keep the image small—about the size of a quarter. The new image will be a bitmapped graphic.

Creating a Bitmapped Element

1. Open a new Director file.

2. Close any open windows.

3. Save the file as Bounce Test.

4. Open the Paint window by choosing Window, Paint or press Command+5 on the Mac, Ctrl+5 in Windows.

5. When the Paint window opens, expand it to a larger working size.

6. In the Paint toolbar, select the Filled Ellipse tool (see fig. 6.4).

7. In the Foreground Color chip of the Color Selector, click and drag out to a color in the palette, and then release. The foreground color chip updates to this new color.

8. Press the Shift key and drag the mouse to create a circle about the size of a quarter. If you want to jazz up the image a little, add a small light-colored dot (created with the Paintbrush tool) to the ball for a highlight effect (see fig. 6.5).

Figure 6.4

Using the Filled Ellipse tool in the Paint window.

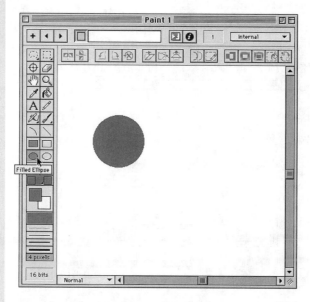

Figure 6.5

After creating a quarter-sized ball, add a highlight to it with the Paintbrush tool.

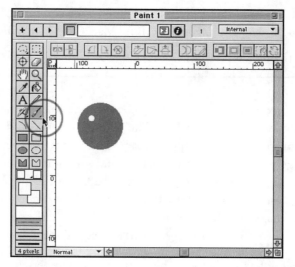

A couple of actions have taken place behind the scenes as the ball was being created. Figure 6.6 shows that the new ball artwork was added to cast member 1 and that a registration point was added to the center of the new artwork in the Paint window. The registration point can be seen by selecting the Registration Point tool in the Paint window's Tool palette. Registration points are set to the center of a new image by default.

continues

Creating a Bitmapped Element   continued

Figure 6.6

After the ball artwork is created in the Paint window, the artwork is added to the Cast Member window and registration point is added to the center of the artwork in the Paint window.

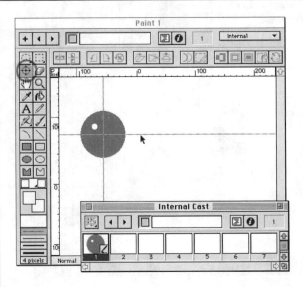

9. Close the Paint window and open the Tool palette from the Window menu or press Command+7 on the Mac, Ctrl+7 in Windows.

10. Save the file by pressing Command+S on the Mac, Ctrl+S in Windows.

The next object you create is a wall to bounce the ball against. This image is a shape created with the Tool palette. The difference between the wall shape and the ball bitmap is that a bitmapped image is created with several pixels. The size of the image is set at the time of creation and scaling up the image distorts the image with jagged stair-stepped pixels around the outside. A shape is an object that can be resized without distortion. Shapes animate more slowly than bitmapped images, but bitmaps use more RAM and disk space. Bitmapped images are best for motion; shapes work best as still images.

Another big difference between bitmapped cast members and shape cast members is that bitmapped cast members are created in the Paint window and are moved to the stage. Shapes are created directly on the stage. Both of these images appear in the Cast Member window as cast members after they are created.

Creating a Shape Element

1. Select the Filled Rectangle tool and draw a profile of a wall. Draw the wall shape directly on the stage in about the same size as shown in figure 6.7. Position your wall shape in the lower-right corner of your screen. You will bounce the ball off this wall.

Figure 6.7

Drawing a shape directly on the stage.

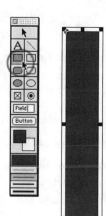

2. Close the Tool palette by pressing Command+7 on the Mac, Ctrl+7 in Windows.

3. Save the file by pressing Command+S on the Mac, Ctrl+S in Windows.

Recording Animations

Three examples are used to explain the steps of the animation process. Open the Score window from the Window menu or press Command+4 on the Mac, Ctrl+4 in Windows. In frames 1–28, channel 1 of the Score window, a span has been selected. This is the sprite span of the wall shape that was just created. The Display pop-up menu, located to the left of the frame number bar in the Score window, enables you to view your sprites in different ways in the Score window. Set the Display pop-up to Member for this part of the demo (see fig. 6.8). The options for the Display pop-up menu are as follows:

▶ **Member:** Shows the cast member of the sprite as a small pop-up window called a *data tip*. The default setting shows the number of the cast member followed by the name if there is room in the span. To change this setting so that the name of the cast member is displayed, select Cast from the Preferences sub-menu of the File menu and change the Label pop-up to Name.

▶ **Behavior:** Displays the behavior number associated with the sprite, if a script is attached.

▶ **Location:** Displays the horizontal and vertical coordinates of the sprite in the frame the cursor is in when over a particular sprite span.

▶ **Ink:** Displays the ink applied to the sprite span from the Ink pop-up menu to the right of the sprite thumbnail at the top of the Score window (see fig. 6.9).

▶ **Blend:** Displays the blend percentage as set in the Blend pop-up menu just to the right of the Ink menu in the Score or under Sprite Properties in the Modify menu.

▶ **Extended:** Displays the cast member number, the behavior, the location, the ink, the blend, as well as changes in the X and Y location. To customize the Extended Display options, select Score from the Preferences pop-up under the File menu.

Figure 6.8

The Display pop-up enables a sprite to be viewed different ways.

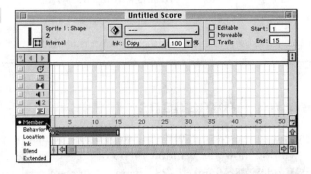

Figure 6.9

The applied ink effect can be seen on the sprites when the cast member Display pop-up is set to Ink.

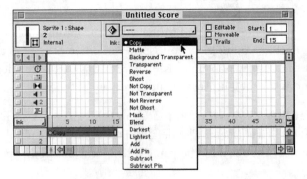

Like a tape recorder, Director can record all the moves on the stage and record them to the Score window. This technique is called *real-time recording*; it really is better for rough-draft animations because, as you will see, it is a little difficult to control. Later, however, you can do fine editing of the animation paths you create with real-time recording.

Real-Time Recording

1. Open the Score window and the Cast window. Position the windows so that they are neither blocking the stage area where you want the ball to move nor the wall sprite created earlier.

2. Select the ball cast member and drag it to the stage into the position where you want the recording to begin.

3. Click on the first keyframe of the ball's sprite span in channel 2 of the score to move the playback head into the first frame. Choose Real-Time Recording from the Control menu. This turns on Real-Time Recording for the selected sprite, the one you just created (see fig. 6.10).

Figure 6.10

The first keyframe of the ball's sprite is selected.

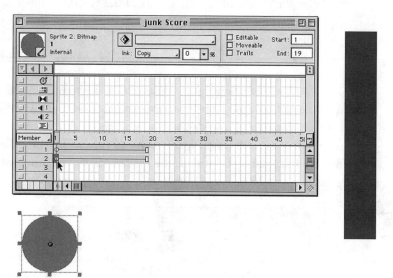

4. Using the mouse, click on the image of the cast member and drag it around the stage (see fig. 6.11). The playback head will move across the score as new keyframes are created in real time according to your movements.

5. To stop recording, release the mouse.

continues

Real-Time Recording continued

Figure 6.11

Dragging a cast member around the stage for a real-time recording session.

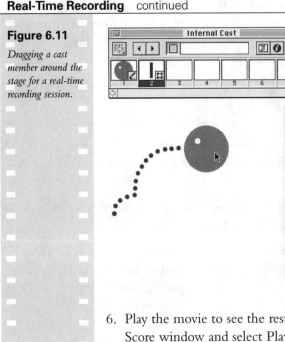

6. Play the movie to see the results of the real-time recording. Close the Score window and select Play from the Control menu or press Shift+Enter.

The real-time recording option created new keyframes in different locations of the Score window as the ball was dragged around the stage. If you rewind and play the movie, you'll notice that the wall disappears before the ball stops moving. To extend the wall sprite to fill all the frames the ball sprite is in, click on its end keyframe and stretch the sprite span by dragging it to the right (see fig. 6.12).

Figure 6.12

Because the wall sprite was located in the first frame of the real-time recording, the wall sprite was duplicated for the remainder of the frames.

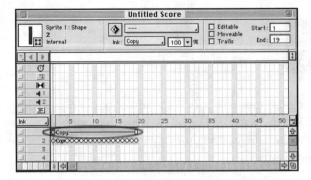

INSIDER TIP

Pressing Shift+Enter (not Return) closes all open windows and plays the movie. Pressing the Enter key again stops the movie and returns all the open windows.

In addition to Shift+Enter, which plays the movie and hides all windows, Command+Option+P on the Mac and Ctrl+Alt+P in Windows plays the movie without hiding windows.

An alternative to real-time recording is step recording. The only sprite needed to demonstrate step recording is the wall sprite in channel 1, frames 1–28. The remaining sprites need to be removed. The following tutorial shows the easiest way to remove unwanted sprites from the Score window.

Removing Unwanted Sprites

1. Click the number 2 in the beginning of channel 2 (see fig. 6.13). Don't click the gray square to the left of the channel number. Clicking the channel number selects all the sprites in that channel.

Figure 6.13

Clicking the channel number selects the entire channel.

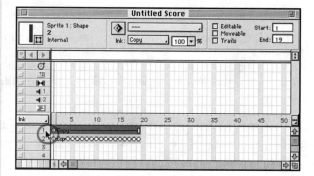

The gray square to the left of the channel numbers turns the channel's visibility on or off.

2. Press the Delete key on the keyboard or choose Clear Sprites from the Edit menu.

3. Click the number 1 in front of channel 1. This selects all of channel 1. The first frame needs to remain for the next demo and should not be removed.

4. To shorten the sprite span, click on its end keyframe in its last frame and drag it to the left to frame 2.

The real-time recording option can be somewhat inaccurate at times. Step recording is a little slower and can be much more accurate than setting up each frame and recording the frames one at a time.

Step Recording

1. Close the Score window by pressing Command+4 on the Mac, Ctrl+4 in Windows.

2. Open the Cast Member window by pressing Command+3 on the Mac, Ctrl+3 in Windows.

3. Drag cast member 1, the ball, out of the Cast Member window and on to the bottom-left corner of the stage. When the cast member is dragged on to the stage, its sprite appears and a span is placed in channel 2 of the Score window. Because channel 1 was occupied, any cast members moved to the stage will fill the channels in order.

   If the dragged out cast member were to be placed in channel 6 of frame 1, the blank cell in frame 1 of channel 6 would need to be selected before the drag was executed.

4. Close the Cast Member window by pressing Command+3 on the Mac, Ctrl+3 in Windows.

5. Open the Score window by pressing Command+4 on the Mac, Ctrl+4 in Windows.

6. To turn on step-recording, click on the first keyframe of the ball sprite span. Then choose Step-Recording from the Control menu. The red step-record arrow appears in front of channel 2.

7. Open the Control Panel by pressing Command+2 on the Mac, Ctrl+2 in Windows.

8. Either press the 3 key on the keypad (not the number 3 above the W and E keys on the keyboard) or click on the Step Forward button in the Control Panel to advance the playback ahead one frame. In Windows, press Ctrl+down arrow.

9. Move the ball to another position on the stage closer to the wall image. Do not click on the circle in the center of the ball. This moves the entire sprite, rather than the new keyframe you just created. Leave the wall where it is.

10. Repeat step 8 to continue the animation sequence for a total of 28 frames (see fig. 6.14).

Figure 6.14

Place the ball sprite close to these positions when creating the Step Record movie.

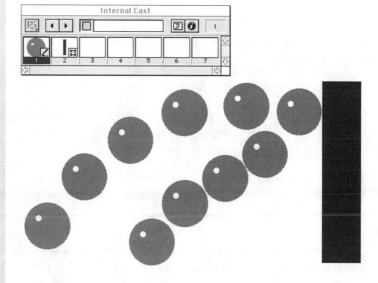

11. Rewind and play the movie to see the step-record animation.

If you want to make the animation shorter or longer than 28 frames, complete your step recording to the desired number of frames, and then stretch or shrink the wall sprite's span by clicking and dragging its end keyframe to the right or left to match the number of frames of your step recording.

Space to Time

The step recording option works well to create accurate animations. The only drawback to step recording is that you cannot see the animation sequence as it is being created. Using Space to Time, a sequence of sprites can be set up in a single animation frame. Then, Space to Time is applied and all the sprites in the single frame move out over multiple frames.

The following tutorial illustrates the use of Space to Time. The first steps show how to remove the unwanted sprites for this tutorial and leave the frame 1 sprites in channels 1 and 2.

Animating with Space to Time

1. Click on the area next to the channel number in channel 2.

2. Press the Delete key.

3. Rewind the movie (Command+Option+R on the Mac, Ctrl+Alt+R in Windows).

   First, the entire animation sequence needs to be built up in frame 1.

4. Choose Sprite Preferences from the File menu and set the Span Duration to one frame. This causes the sprites you drag on the stage to fill one frame rather than 28.

5. Close the Score window and open the Cast window.

6. Drag cast member number 1, the ball, to the lower-left corner of the stage.

   Because the ball is not changing color or shape, you will use the same cast member for the entire animation sequence.

7. Drag cast member number 1 again to the stage, above and to the right of the previous ball.

8. Repeat step 7, 11 more times until the stage looks something like it did in figure 6.14.

   Remember, for a more realistic-looking animation, sprites that need to move faster should be placed farther apart. Slower-moving sprites should be placed closer together.

   All the animation sequence is in frame 1 and is actually more like a still life than an animation, but the entire path of the ball can be seen as it hits the wall and bounces back to the ground. The process of cutting and pasting the sprites in the correct channels and frames would take a long time. To shorten this time, Macromedia has built in a function called Space to Time, which repositions sprites from consecutive channels, same frame and places them in the same channel, consecutive frames (see fig. 6.15).

9. Open the Score window (Command+4 on the Mac, Ctrl+4 in Windows).

10. Select channels 2–15 in frame 1 (the ball sequence) in the Score window.

Figure 6.15

Space to Time repositions sprites from a single frame to multiple frames over time.

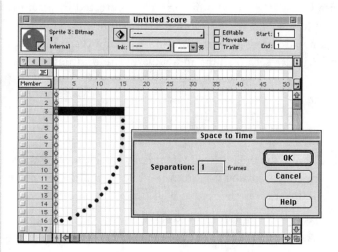

11. Select Space to Time from the Modify menu. A dialog box asking for input dealing with the separation of the moving sprites opens.

    The sprites need to be next to one another for this demo. A number of 1 in the Space to Time dialog box keeps the sprites together.

12. Enter 1 in the Space to Time dialog box and click on OK.

    The sprites in the channels of frame 1 jump into the frames of channel 2. The sequence now travels over time. But where is the wall? When the selection was made earlier, the wall sprite was not included. The wall sprite must be included in all the frames in the preceding sequence, not just the first two frames.

13. Click on the end keyframe of the wall sprite in channel 1 and drag it to the right to the last frame of the ball animation in frame 14. It will now remain on the stage in the same position through all the frames of the animation.

Sprite Tweening

Now it is time to bounce the ball on the wall a little differently. To do so, you use a function called *tweening*, in which Director automatically calculates the intermediate positions of a sprite for the frames between keyframes. The previous animation of a bouncing ball was created by placing all the sprites in the first frame. This time, a motion path will be created for the ball to follow. Keyframes are used along the motion path and tweening is applied to keep from having to set up all the individual sprite positions.

Animating by Tweening

Be certain that both the Cast and Score windows are open.

1. Change the default sprite span length back to 28 frames in the Sprite Preferences dialog box from the File menu. Be certain that Tween Size and Position is checked as well.

2. Delete the entire ball sprite from frame 2 by clicking on the area next to channel 2 and by pressing the Delete key.

3. Drag cast member 1, the ball, into the Score window to channel 2.

   The cast members dragged to the Score window appear in the aligned center on the stage.

4. On the stage, drag this newly placed ball to a position in the lower-left corner of the stage.

5. With the new sprite span still selected, move the playback head to frame 14 by clicking on the frame counter bar in the Score window. The playback head jumps to frame 14.

6. Choose Keyframe from the Insert menu. This places a new keyframe in frame 14 of the sprite span.

7. Drag the ball on the stage to the edge of the wall sprite. You have now defined a new location for the sprite in the new keyframe (see fig. 6.16).

8. Click on the last frame of the sprite in channel 2 of the score. This should be frame 28. Note that the span's last frame contains a rectangle icon. This indicates that no change in the sprite's position has occurred between the last frame and the immediately preceding keyframe. Again, choose Keyframe from the Insert menu.

Figure 6.16

*The second key-
frame in this
animation is
positioned against
the wall.*

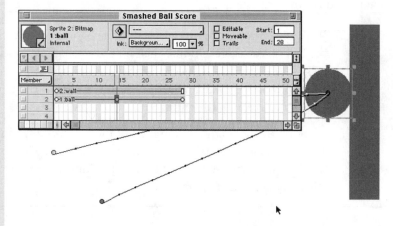

9. Drag the sprite on the stage to a position just to the right of its original starting position in frame 1.

Now you have set three separate keyframes in the sprite's span. Because you turned on Tween Size and Position in the sprite preferences, Director automatically calculated the intermediate positions of the sprite in the frames between the keyframes.

Just as the sprite's span appears in the score as a single object, the animation path that you just created can be viewed as a whole and edited.

Editing the Animation Path

1. Select the entire span in channel 2 of the score by clicking the middle of the span. Choose Show Paths from the Sprite Overlay pop-up menu in the View menu.

   Notice that the entire path of your animation becomes visible on the stage. Keyframes are represented in the path by small circles; other frames are even smaller squares. Using the Step Forward and Back buttons in the Control Panel, you can move the ball through the animation. The path may now be edited by moving it in its entirety or by adjusting the position of individual keyframes or adding new ones.

continues

Editing the Animation Path continued

2. With the entire sprite still selected in the Score window, click and drag the ball on the stage. Do not click on the small circle in the center of the ball. Notice that this moves the entire path on the stage. This way if you want to move the wall and the animation a little to the left, you can do it without re-creating the animation.

3. Click on the keyframe in frame 14 of the ball sprite span in channel 2 of the score. Then move the sprite on the stage by clicking and dragging the small circle in the center of the ball. This edits the position of only the currently selected keyframe.

Director does something useful when you move the positions of keyframes on the stage. It automatically adjusts the position of the sprite in all the other frames of its span. This enables you to do fine editing of the animation path quickly and easily. You can also add new keyframes anywhere you want to further control the complexity of the animation.

Director also enables you to control how the intermediate positions within a span are calculated and which properties of the sprite are taken into consideration during the tweening.

When you select Tweening from the Sprite pop-up in the Modify menu (Command+Shift+B on the Mac, Ctrl+Shift+B in Windows), the Sprite Tweening dialog box appears (see fig. 6.17).

Figure 6.17

The Sprite Tweening dialog box options.

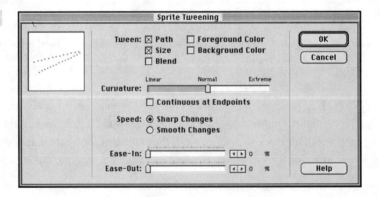

The Sprite Tweening dialog box options are as follows:

▶ **Curvature:** Adjusts how closely the tweened frames stay to the original placement of the keyframes. Moving the slider toward Linear makes the sprite move in straight lines from one keyframe position to the next. Moving it toward Normal makes the animation path more rounded. Extreme sends the sprite farther away from the linear path, an effect whose appearance varies with the original animation path.

▶ **Continuous at Endpoints:** Causes the curvature to apply to the beginning and end of the span, in addition to the middle. This is useful for circular animation paths.

▶ **Tween options:** Determine which attributes of the sprite are affected in the tween.

▶ **Speed:** Affects how quickly the sprite accelerates across the stage when it begins moving.

▶ **Ease-In/Ease-Out sliders:** Can be used to make fine adjustments to the speed of the newly created path at its beginning and end. Easing in makes the sprite accelerate more slowly at the start of the path. These options don't change the placement of the keyframes in the Score window, only the spacing of the new sprites.

The following exercise demonstrates editing animation paths on the stage.

Finalizing the Animation by Tweening

1. Choose settings you like in the Sprite Tweening dialog box, and click on the OK button.

   If the effect is not what you expected, choose Undo from the Edit menu and try again.

2. Save the movie as BOUNCE.DIR and play it to see the effects of In-Between Special applied to keyframes.

Modifying a Sprite on the Stage

Until now, sprites have been used as is on the stage to create an animation. This section deals with changing the actual sprites on the stage.

You will continue to use the same movie for this sprite-modifying tutorial. The movie should contain the bounce sequence of 28 frames.

A Visual Approach to Modifying Sprites

1. Open Bounce Movie on the accompanying CD if necessary.

2. Close the Cast window (Command+3 on the Mac, Ctrl+3 in Windows).

3. Open the Score window (Command+4 on the Mac, Ctrl+4 in Windows).

4. In the Score window, select only the middle keyframe of the ball sprite in frame 14.

   The effect that is going to be created will be the ball smashing against the wall.

5. Choose Tweening from the Sprite sub-menu in the Modify menu (Command+Shift+B on the Mac, Ctrl+Shift+B in Windows). Deselect Size in the Tween options. Click on OK.

6. Close the Score window, leaving the middle keyframe selected. Now you can see the ball touching the wall object on the stage.

   The ball is selected and is outlined in gray dots. The outline has handles on all four sides and corners.

7. With the mouse, click and drag the left-most handle toward the center of the ball. This makes the ball thinner. Release the mouse (see fig. 6.18).

Figure 6.18

Using the left handle to distort the ball.

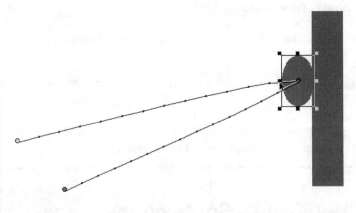

8. Next, use the handles at the top and bottom of the ball to expand it to make up for its lost volume. Actually, it just looks funnier this way (see fig. 6.19).

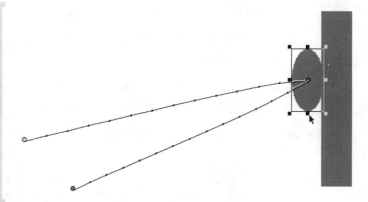

Figure 6.19

Using the top and bottom handles to distort the ball even more.

9. Save the movie as Smashed Ball and play the movie to see the effects of modifying sprites on the stage.

Modifying a Sprite by Number Input

The preceding tutorial used a visual approach. But what if the ball had to be smashed exactly in half? You might not get it just right. Sprites also can be modified by numbers and percents. The following tutorial demonstrates how to repair the ball and return it to its original size.

A Number-Input Approach to Modifying Sprites

1. Select the smashed ball keyframe in the Score window (frame 14).

2. Choose Modify, Sprite Properties.

   The Sprite Properties dialog box appears (see fig. 6.20).

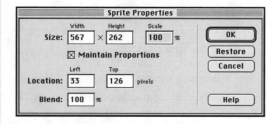

Figure 6.20

The Sprite Properties dialog box.

3. Select the Restore button to bring the ball back to its original shape.

continues

4. The ball's center position remains the same when restored. Use the left arrow key on the keyboard to return the ball to the correct position.

   In addition to the Restore button, the Sprite Properties dialog box offers the following modification choices for the stage element (not the cast member):

   ▶ **Size:** *An exact amount can be entered for both the height and width of the selected sprite.*

   ▶ **Scale:** *The selected sprite can be reduced or enlarged by a percentage. (Remember that a bitmapped object scaled up becomes jagged. A shape scales well either up or down.)*

   ▶ **Maintain Proportions check box:** *Keeps the left, right, top, and bottom proportions of the sprite equal.*

   ▶ **Location:** *These setting in pixels are the distance from the top and left sides of the stage. Use these boxes to exactly place a sprite on the stage.*

   ▶ **Blend:** *A sprite can have a transparency applied to it by setting a blend amount. A 50 percent blend displays a semitransparent sprite on the stage.*

   ▶ **Restore button:** *Closes the Sprite Properties dialog box and restores the sprite to its original size, the size of its cast member.*

Other Methods of Modifying a Sprite

Director 6 also has the following three ways to view and edit the attributes of sprites:

▶ Score window

▶ Sprite Inspector

▶ Acetate Layer (or Sprite Overlay)

The top of the Score window contains information on all the attributes of the sprite. Here you can quickly view and edit each of them.

In the Inspector's pop-up in the Window menu is the Sprite Inspector. The Sprite Inspector displays the same information found at the top of the Score window. Resize the Sprite Inspector to suit your screen space by clicking on its resize box at the top-right corner of the window (see fig. 6.21).

Figure 6.21

The Sprite Inspector.

The following sprite attributes are available in both the Score and Sprite Inspector windows:

► Cast member thumbnail

► Sprite channel: Cast member type

► Cast member number and name

► Cast name

► Assigned behaviors

► Ink

► Blend

► Editable: Whether field cast members are editable on the stage when the movie is playing

► Moveable: Whether the sprite is movable on the stage when the movie is playing

► Trails: Whether a movable sprite leaves impressions of itself behind on the stage when moved, creating a trails effect

► Start: The first frame of the sprite span

► End: The last frame of the span

► X: The distance of the sprite's registration point from the left side of the stage, in pixels

► Y: The distance of the sprite's registration point from the top of the stage, in pixels

► W: The width of the sprite, in pixels

▶ H: The height of the sprite, in pixels

▶ l: The distance of the left side of the sprite from the left side of the stage, in pixels

▶ r: The distance of the right side of the sprite from the left side of the stage, in pixels

▶ t: The distance of the top of the sprite from the top of the stage, in pixels

▶ b: The distance of the bottom of the sprite from the top of the stage, in pixels

The third way of viewing sprite characteristics is the Acetate Layer, or Sprite Overlay. It enables you to display a small window adjacent to individual sprites on the stage. Select Show Info from the Sprite Overlay pop-up in the View menu, and click on a sprite on the stage. The window contains channel, cast number and name, location, ink, blend, and behavior information. Buttons in the Sprite Overlay window give easy access to the appropriate dialog box for editing these attributes (see fig. 6.22).

Figure 6.22

The Sprite Overlay pop-up menu.

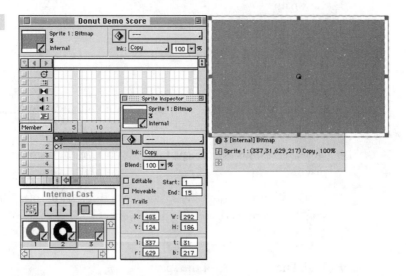

The Special Effect Channels

Above the sprite channels—the channels that contain all the visual elements—are the special effects channels. These six special channels control the speed, color, scene changes, sounds, and script executions of each of the frames in the movie. Double-clicking on any of the following special effect channel cells opens that setting for the frame. Each special channel also has a pull-down menu item in the Frame pop-up in the Modify menu. The following is a list of frame properties for each of the channels.

The Tempo Channel

With a cell selected in the Tempo channel, choose Frame Tempo from the Modify menu. This channel deals with time issues (see fig. 6.23). Each time the playback head enters a frame, the Tempo channel instructs the movie to use one of the following actions:

▶ **Tempo:** The playback speed of the movie. This speed can be seen in the Control Panel's Tempo display. The Tempo is set using frames per second (fps). The movie plays back at this set speed until another Tempo speed is encountered in a later frame. This speed is not a guarantee that the movie in fact plays at that speed; large moving or scaled images can cause the movie to play more slowly than the set Tempo speed.

▶ **Wait:** The playback head waits or stalls in this frame for the set amount of time. This wait setting is measured in seconds and ranges from 1–60 seconds.

▶ **Wait for Mouse Click or Key Press:** Without Lingo commands, the playback head waits until the mouse is clicked or a key is pressed on the keyboard. The function has its advantages over the Wait for Tempo setting previously described. When reading a screen of text, for instance, a two-second wait might not be long enough and five seconds might be too long. The Wait for Mouse Click or Key Press option enables the user to advance to the next frame at his own pace.

▶ **Wait for Cue Point:** When a sound is playing in the sound channel or a QuickTime video is playing in a sprite channel and the playback head enters a frame with a Wait for Cue Point tempo setting, the playback head stalls in the frame until the cue point is reached, and then moves on to the next frame. These cue points can be embedded in the sound or video file ahead of time, or you can just use the default end point of the file as the cue point. This causes the playback head to wait for the entire sound or video to play before moving on.

Figure 6.23

*The options of the
Frame Properties:
Tempo dialog box.*

The Palette Channel

With a cell selected in the Palette channel, select Palette from the Frame pop-up under the Modify menu. This channel sets up which color palette is to be used in the selected frame. Palettes also can be cycled. Only one palette per frame is allowed. Figure 6.24 shows the palette options.

Figure 6.24

*The options of the
Frame Properties:
Palette dialog box.*

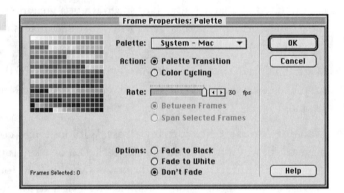

▶ **Palette pop-up menu:** Standard and custom 8-bit palettes can be chosen from this list. Custom palettes that are created or imported are stored as cast members.

▶ **Action: Palette Transition:** As the playback head moves from one frame to another, different palettes can be applied to each frame.

▶ **Action: Color Cycling:** Causes cast members with color gradients to cycle in a way that the color seems to move across the cast member.

▶ **Rate:** The palette rate is the time it takes for the palette to display. The rate is set in frames per second.

▶ **Between Frames:** The default setting for the Color Palette dialog box. Between Frames tells Director to change to a different palette after entering a frame.

▶ **Span Selected Frames:** If, in the Score window, more than one frame is selected, the Span Selected Frames radio button becomes available. The span selection allows the palette to change over the selected frames.

▶ **Options: Fade to Black:** The entire screen turns to black as the playback head enters the next frame in the Score. The rate slider sets the speed of the fade to black. A slow fade to black can make a dramatic effect in a project.

▶ **Options: Fade to White:** Same as the preceding Fade to Black setting, except the effect uses a white palette.

▶ **Options: Don't Fade:** This is the default. Believe it or not, this option won't do a fade.

Remember, palettes only operate in an 8-bit (256 color) environment. A palette effect is not be visible with a monitor set to anything other than 256 colors.

Transition Channel

A *transition* is a change in effect from one frame to the next. With a cell selected in the Transition channel, choose Frame Transition from the Modify menu. This channel affects the way in which incoming frames transition with the outgoing frames (see fig. 6.25).

Figure 6.25

The options of the Frame Properties: Transition dialog box.

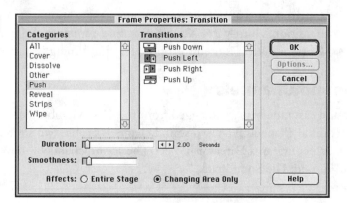

It is important to note that a transition is the effect from frame to frame, not image to image. In other words, two images cannot transition with two different effects in the same frame. Only one effect can be applied to a single frame.

The standard Director transition palette contains 52 transition effects. Third-party software developers can write custom transitions for the Transition channel in the form of Xtras. Xtras are discussed in Chapter 21, "The Xtra Step."

The upper portion of the Frame Properties dialog box is divided into halves. The left half contains the categories of transitions and the right half is an item-by-item list of the transitions in a selected category. The All item in the Categories side displays all the transitions available. The rest of the options in Frame Properties are as follows:

▶ **Duration:** Sets how long a transition takes to complete in hundredths of a second. Click on the right and left arrows from 0–30 seconds, or use the slider to adjust the duration.

▶ **Smoothness:** When set to the left, this executes a smooth transition. The slider set to the right executes a rough transition. Smoothness is like a group of pixels. A setting of smooth advances small increments of pixels throughout the transition. A setting of rough advances in large increments of pixels throughout the transition.

▶ **Affects: Entire Stage:** The entire stage area is included in the transition.

▶ **Affects: Changing Area Only:** Causes only the sprite that changes from frame to frame to be affected by the transition.

▶ **Options button:** Active only when modification can be made to the transition. Third-party Xtras enable fine-tuning to the transitions. The Options button is used to apply such fine-tuning.

Sound Channels

Sound cast members are dragged from the Cast Member window to either of the Sound channels. The two sound channels enable two sounds to be played simultaneously in a Director project. The sound channel is covered in Chapter 11, "Sound: The Soundtrack."

Script Channel

The Script channel is used to assign Lingo instructions to be executed in particular frames. Using the Script Channel is discussed in Chapter 16, "Lingo: The Basics."

Cast to Time

Another basic animation technique is Cast to Time. With it, Director can automatically place a sequence of related cast members on the stage. These cast members are placed over time with their registration points also aligned over time. The Director file named Pass Through, located in the Chapter 6 folder on the accompanying CD-ROM, is used to try out the Cast to Time feature of Director.

Pass Through is built of 15 individual cast members. All the cast members need to be moved to the stage to create an animation sequence. Cast to Time moves the cast members out to frames and automatically aligns them.

Animating with Cast to Time

1. Open the Pass Through file and close all open windows.

2. Open the Paint window.

   To view a quick flip-style animation in the Paint window, click and hold the Next Cast Member button to scan through the cast members.

3. Close the Paint window (Command+5 on the Mac, Ctrl+5 in Windows).

4. Open the Cast window (Command+3 on the Mac, Ctrl+3 in Windows).

5. Open the Score window (Command+4 on the Mac, Ctrl+4 in Windows).

   Set the window on the stage to match figure 6.26.

6. Set the sprite Span Duration to 1 frame in the Sprite Preferences dialog box.

7. In the Cast Member window, select cast member 1.

8. Hold the Shift key and select the last cast member—cast member 15—in the series. All the cast members are selected.

continues

Animating with Cast to Time   continued

Figure 6.26

*The window set up
for the Cast to
Time tutorial.*

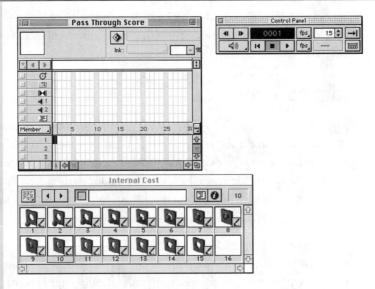

9. In the Score window, select channel 1, frame 1.

    This selected cell is the starting position for the sequence.

10. Select Cast to Time from the Modify menu.

    *The selected cast members are placed on the stage over time, in the same order as
    seen in the Cast Member window. These cast members are all aligned to one
    another, even though they are in different frames. Cast to Time places the entire
    sequence in the middle of the stage. To move the sequence, make certain that all the
    sprites in channel 1 are selected.*

11. With all the new keyframes selected in the Score window, click and drag
    the stage image to the upper-right corner of the stage.

12. Save and play the movie.

Reverse Sequence

To play the movie back and forth, Reverse Sequence is applied. Reverse
Sequence places selected sprites in their reverse order; in this case, it makes the
ball jump back through the block.

Animation in Reverse

1. Select the sprite span in channel 1 by clicking on it.

2. Select Copy from the Edit menu.

3. Select frame 16 in channel 1, the next empty frame.

4. Choose Paste Sprites from the Edit menu.

5. The pasted sprite in channel 1 should be selected. Choose Reverse Sequence from the Modify menu.

6. Play the movie.

   Make certain that the newly pasted sprite is selected before the Reverse Sequence command is given (see fig. 6.27).

Figure 6.27

Duplicating a Sprite in the score for a Reverse Sequence operation.

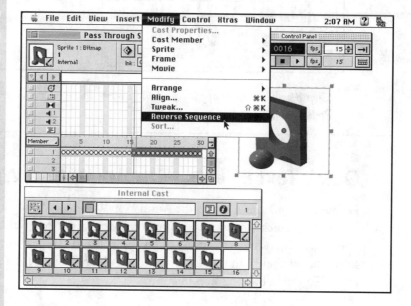

7. Select frame 16.

   The movie has two hesitations in it—one in frame 16 and one in frame 30. These frames are duplicates of frames 15 and 1 respectively. To remove the stalled frames, follow the next steps.

8. Choose Remove Frame from the Insert menu.

   When deleting frames, the frame the playback head is in is the frame that is removed (see fig. 6.28).

continues

Animation in Reverse   continued

Figure 6.28

When deleting frames, the frame the playback head is in is the frame that is removed.

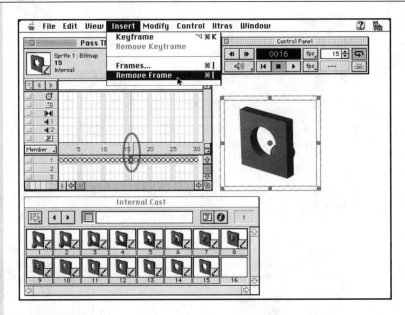

Step 8 should also be applied to the last frame in the movie to remove the other stalled frame.

Quick Text Effects with Animation Wizard

Located in the Xtras menu is the Animation Wizard, a Movie in a Window, for creating quick text effects. Animation Wizard contains four anti-aliased text effects. (Anti-aliasing is discussed in Chapters 8 and 10.) Just enter some text, select the attributes, and there you have it—rolling credits for a movie or text effects for a business presentation.

Using the Animation Wizard

1. Select a starting cell in the Score window. The Animation Wizard uses this cell as the starting point for any sprites it adds.

2. Choose Animation Wizard from the Xtras menu (see fig. 6.29).

Figure 6.29

Some of the many options available in the Animation Wizard.

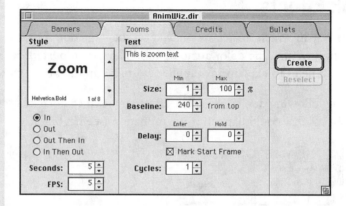

3. Select one of four text effects and adjust its attributes.

The following Animated text styles are available:

▶ **Banners:** Travels the text across the stage. The following options can be set: font style, direction of travel, sequence length, frames per second, placement on the stage, waiting period before entering the stage, and length of time to hold the banner in the middle of the stage.

▶ **Zooms:** Expands or contracts text on the stage. The following options can be set: font style, method of text movement, sequence length, frames per second, size of text when sequence starts and stops, placement on the stage, waiting period before entering the stage, length of time to hold the text in the middle of the stage, and number of times the zoom should repeat.

▶ **Credits:** Scrolling or fixed text is placed in the center of the stage. The following options can be set: font style, sequence length, frames per second, waiting period before entering the stage, and length of time to hold the text in the middle of the stage.

▶ **Bullets:** Moves text on to the stage one line at a time. The following options can be set: font style, bullet style, sequence length, frames per second, waiting period before entering the stage, and length of time to hold the text in the middle of the stage.

After the text has been entered and the settings are made, the Create button applies the text effect to the Score window at the position selected in step 1.

Ink Effects

The way in which sprites are viewed on the stage does not stop at their location. Setting the color attributes also plays an important role. The following tutorial helps to explain inks applied to sprites in the Score window.

In the following demo, sprite ink effects are used to correct a few visual problems that could happen in an animation (see fig. 6.30).

Figure 6.30

The Ink effect pop-up display in the Score window is used to change the way in which the sprite appears on the stage.

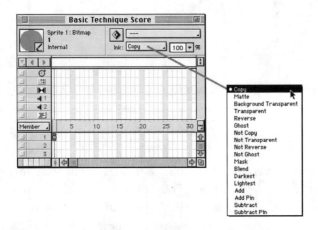

Using Ink Effects to Correct Visual Problems

1. Reset the span length to 15 in the Sprite Properties dialog box.

2. Open a new Director file.

3. Save and name the file Donut Demo.

4. Close all windows except the Paint window.

5. Select the Filled Ellipse tool.

6. In the foreground color selector, click and drag out a dark color, and then release. The foreground color chip changes to the selected color.

7. With the Shift key pressed, draw a medium-sized circle.

   The Shift key constrains the Drawing tool and keeps the shape circular. This newly drawn element is the outside of the donut.

8. To put a hole in the donut: In the foreground color selector, click and drag out to the white color chip (top-left corner) and release.

For this demonstration to work, the center of the donut must be white; a light gray color does not work.

9. Select the Filled Ellipse tool again and drag a smaller white circle over the center of the larger circle (see fig. 6.31).

Figure 6.31

With the white foreground color chip selected, draw a smaller circle in the middle of the larger circle to make a donut hole.

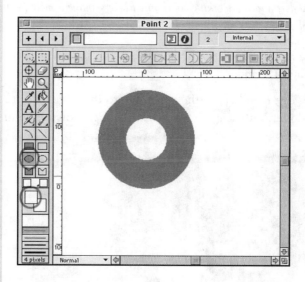

Placing the center correctly takes some practice. Don't worry if the hole is not in the center. Even donut makers miss from time to time. With the foreground color chip still set to white, add sprinkles to the donut.

10. Double-click on the Paintbrush tool and choose the small brush in the bottom-left corner. Click on OK.

11. With the Paintbrush, draw a few short lines on the solid part of the donut.

12. Save the file.

To demonstrate a visual problem, the donut must sit on top of a table.

13. Click on the New Cast Member button in the upper-left corner of the Paint window. This creates a new canvas for the table art.

14. Choose a bright color from the foreground color chip.

15. Select the Filled Rectangle tool and draw a rectangle about twice the size of the donut in the previous Paint window.

continues

Using Ink Effects to Correct Visual Problems continued

16. Close the Paint window (Command+5 on the Mac, Ctrl+5 in Windows).

17. Open the Score (Command+4 on the Mac, Ctrl+4 in Windows) and Cast (Command+3 on the Mac, Ctrl+3 in Windows) windows.

   To understand the workings of channel layers, make a mistake and then correct it by following these steps:

18. Drag cast member 1—the donut—to the stage. The sprite is placed in channel 1, frame 1.

19. Drag cast member 2—the tabletop—to the stage so that it overlaps half the donut. Your stage should look like that shown in figure 6.32.

Figure 6.32

The table sprite is above the donut sprite.

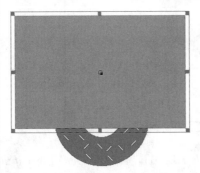

   Because you placed the donut on the layer below the table, you effectively placed the donut under the table. To change the order of the sprites, the tabletop could be cut and pasted to another place, then the donut could be cut and pasted into the table's original spot, and finally....Well, that's a hassle! Instead, use the arrange command. arrange moves selected sprites up or down channels, changing their layering order.

20. Select the tabletop, the sprite in channel 2, and then select Move Backward from the Arrange pop-up in the Modify menu (Command+down arrow on the Mac, Ctrl+down arrow in Windows) (see fig. 6.33).

   The tabletop moves up one channel (farther down the visual stack), and the donut is now on top, in channel 2.

   The problem with sprites is that they are created on a white canvas in the Paint window. Applying an ink effect to the sprites corrects the problem of white knockouts. A Matte ink effect is applied to change the white outside of the donut to clear, like acetate.

Figure 6.33

Choose Modify, Arrange, Move Backward to move the tabletop sprite underneath the donut sprite.

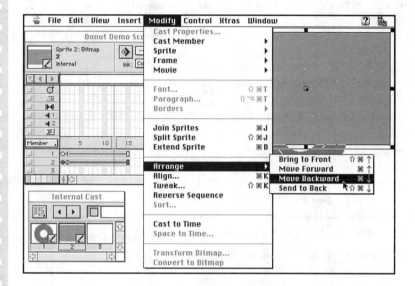

21. Drag the donut on the stage so that only half of the donut is on the table. The white knockout of the donut sprite can be seen in figure 6.34.

Figure 6.34

A white area of the donut sprite is visible with the ink effect set to Copy, the default setting.

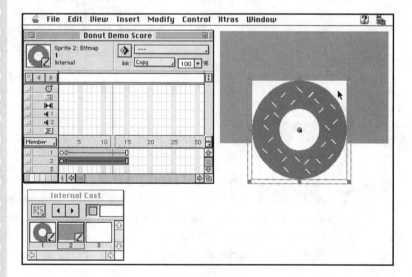

22. Select the sprite in channel 2, the donut.

23. In the Score window, select the Ink pop-up menu and choose Matte from the list.

continues

Using Ink Effects to Correct Visual Problems continued

The white edge is removed from the donut. The Matte ink effect changes any white pixel outside the sprite to clear.

To drop out the center of the donut, follow step 24.

24. In the Score window, select the Ink pop-up menu and choose Background Transparent from the list.

The center drops out. The Background Transparent ink effect changes any white pixel contained in the sprite to clear. The only problem is that the white sprinkles also are transparent.

Note that for step 20, the Move Forward command also could be applied to the donut sprite in channel 1, moving the donut in front of the tabletop.

Background Transparent ink will make any pixels that use the background color in the Tool palette transparent. In this case the background color was white, so all the white pixels are transparent. The problem of the transparent sprinkles can be fixed in two ways. The first way is to change the sprinkles to the light gray color in the Paint window. The light gray sprinkles will be visible. The second way to fix the problem of transparent whites is to mask them out. Masks are 1-bit, black-and-white cast members used to block pixels.

Creating a Mask

1. In the Cast window, move cast member 2, the table, to cast member 3 (see fig. 6.35).

This leaves an empty cast member in the second cast member position. Masks must be placed in a position that is one cast member to the right of the cast member to be masked. Because the donut is in cast position 1, the mask needs to be in cast position 2. In addition to being a 1-bit cast member, a mask must be the same size as the masked cast member.

2. Select cast member 1, the donut. Choose Duplicate from the Edit menu or press Command+D on the Mac, Ctrl+D in Windows to duplicate the donut to cast member 2.

This ensures that the mask is the correct size.

Figure 6.35

Moving cast member 2 to cast member 3.

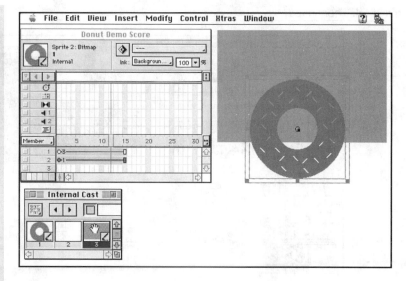

3. Double-click on the donut mask, cast member 2.

   The Paint window opens, showing the donut mask. The Paint bucket filled with black helps to set the correct color of the mask.

4. Set the foreground color chip to black.

5. With the Paint Bucket tool, click on the donut artwork to change it to black.

6. With the Paintbrush tool also set to black, paint the white sprinkles.

   The finished image is a black donut without sprinkles. The cast member looks black-and-white, but the palette is not. A 1-bit palette is needed for the mask to work.

7. To change the palette of the selected cast member: With the donut mask selected, cast member 2, choose Transform Bitmap from the Modify menu.

8. In the Transform Bitmap dialog box, set the Color Depth pop-up menu to 1 Bit and choose the remap colors option (see fig. 6.36). Select OK to the alert message about the undo for this command. You will receive an alert telling you the operation cannot be undone. Click on OK.

   The mask cast member is now the same size as the cast members to be masked and has a 1-bit palette. These are the two characteristics crucial to a cast member mask.

continues

Creating a Mask   continued

Figure 6.36

*Using the
Transform Bitmap
dialog box to
change the Color
Depth of the donut
mask.*

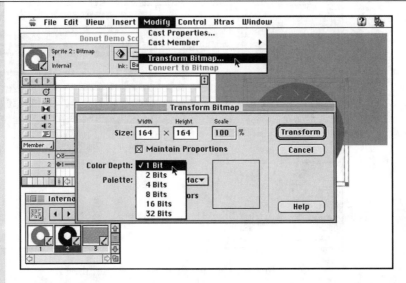

9. In the Score window, set the Ink effect pop–up menu for the donut sprite in channel 2, frame 1 to Mask.

    The black area of cast member 2 (the Mask) is blocking out the transparency of cast member 1 (the masked cast member).

10. Save the file (Command+S on the Mac, Ctrl+S in Windows).

The Ink pop–up menu contains 15 effects that can be applied to sprites in the Score window. Copy is the default ink setting. All the ink effects slow down an animation to some extent, especially Matte and Background. The effects are as follows:

▶ **Copy:** Displays the cast member as is. The rectangular bounding box of the image appears as white.

▶ **Matte:** Sets the white pixels within a bounding box of a sprite to transparent.

▶ **Background Transparent:** Sets all the white pixels within an image to transparent.

▶ **Transparent:** Makes all the colors in a sprite transparent.

▶ **Reverse:** Reverses all color in the sprite, sets white pixels to transparent.

▶ **Ghost:** Changes black to white and white to transparent. Works best on 1-bit cast members.

▶ **Not Copy/Not Transparent/Not Reversed/Not Ghost:** These ink effects are based on the immediately preceding four ink effects. First, a reverse effect is applied to all colors in the sprite and then the Copy, Transparent, Reverse, or Ghost ink effect (previously mentioned) is reapplied to the selected sprite.

▶ **Mask:** Uses the next cast member in the Cast window to block or unblock background colors. Rules for a Mask are as follows: must be the same size as the masked cast member, next cast member position in the cast window, and 1 bit.

▶ **Blend:** Applies a blend to the sprite. The amount used in the blend is set in Sprite Properties from the Modify menu.

▶ **Darkest:** Compares pixels of the foreground and background colors. The Darkest ink effect displays only the darkest pixel found in the background and foreground colors.

▶ **Lightest:** Compares pixels in the foreground and background colors. The Lightest ink effect displays only the lightest pixel found in the background and foreground colors.

▶ **Add:** Creates a new color. The values of the background and foreground colors are added to one another. The sprite displays the combined values. If the color value exceeds the maximum visible color, the color wraps around the color scale.

▶ **Add Pin:** The same as Add with the exception that if the color value exceeds the maximum visible color, the maximum color is used.

▶ **Subtract:** The opposite of Add with the exception that the minimum values are used. If the new value is less than the minimum visible color, the color wraps around the color scale from the top.

▶ **Subtract Pin:** The same as Subtract with the exception that if the color value is less than the minimum visible color, the minimum color is used.

The ink effects discussed in the preceding list can be confusing. The best way to understand the effects is to try each of them. The Copy, Matte, and Background Transparent ink effects are used 99.9 percent of the time. But you never know when a strange ink accident might be just the thing you need.

Editing in the Score Window

The score has to deal with many things such as spans, frames, channels, inks, and displays. The following are some useful things to know when editing in the Score window.

Span Selections

To select a sprite span, click on it. A darkened highlight indicates the selection.

To move a single span to another position, cut the selected sprite, then select a new position in the Score window, and paste.

To select a group of spans, click on the first span in the group, and then press the Shift key and click on the last span in the intended selection. Darkened highlights indicate the selections.

To move the group of spans, select and cut them. Then select a new position in the Score window and paste. The spans are pasted from this position and fill to the right until all are pasted. If a single cell is selected and six spans are pasted, the single cell is filled with the first span and then five more cells to the right of the single cell are filled with the remainder of the spans.

Drag-and-Drop Option

Spans can be moved around the stage without cutting and pasting. To select a span, click on it. To move the cell, click and drag it to another location in the Score window and release. A clutching hand cursor indicates the moving process (see fig. 6.37).

Figure 6.37

The Drag-and-Drop option enables the sprite to be moved around the Score window by clicking and dragging.

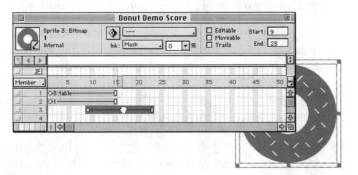

In addition to using Drag-and-Drop to move cells, pressing the Option key on the Mac, the Alt key in Windows, while dragging copies the cell to the new location.

To select a group of cells or spans, click a deselected cell and drag to select the remaining cells. The key to this selection is that the first cell is not already selected. If you try to select a group of cells with the first cell already selected, only the first cell will be moved.

Inserting and Deleting Frames

Cutting cells from a channel does not shorten a movie. This only removes images from a frame. To actually make the movie shorter, frames must be removed. The position of the playback head is important to the Delete Frame command. The frame where the playback head is located is the frame that will be removed when the Delete Frame command from the Insert menu is used.

The Insert menu's Frame command adds a frame, or many frames, to the movie. If any cells are located in the frame where the addition is to take place, the cells are duplicated and moved one frame to the right.

Color Coding Sprite Spans

When working with a 100-frame movie, the available cells for this movie are 100 frames multiplied by 126 channels, or 1,260 active cells. Trying to find a single sprite or cell in a group of more than 1,200 can take some time. Sprites can be colored for easier viewing and location. Moving elements might be blue, buttons might be red, and text media might be yellow. This makes spotting a sprite or group of sprites much easier.

To set the colors of sprite spans, select a span or range of spans, and then select a color from the cell color palette, indicated by the cursor in figure 6.38. The span is now color-coded. The color of the cell does not affect the sprite on the stage.

Figure 6.38

Select a range of cells and choose a cell color. Colored cells are easier to locate within the Score window.

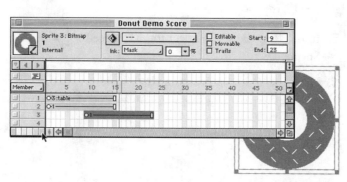

Advanced Animation Techniques

This section covers more advanced animation techniques using Director's built-in features such as film loops and the Cycling palette. In Director, many traditional animation techniques have been condensed to a few keystrokes and mouse clicks. This means more time spent being creative and less time spent repeating steps.

The tutorials begin by utilizing Auto Distort and film loops. Auto Distort is an Xtra that changes cast members and then applies the changes to multiple cast members to be used over time. Film loops are useful for creating such objects as flying birds and spinning tires on a car. A film loop is a sequence that repeats over and over and doesn't have to be baby-sat. Just place the looped cast member on the stage, and it will play through its loop, even in a single frame. Individual cast members from the loop don't have to be bothered with after a loop is made. The following tutorial enables you to make spinning clock hands.

Animating with Auto Distort

1. Open the Director file named Loop Demo located in the Chapter 6 folder on the accompanying CD-ROM.

2. Close all open windows, except the Cast window.

   The Cast Member window contains two cast members: a clock face and a single clock hand.

3. Double-click on cast member 2, the clock hand. The Paint window opens.

4. Close the Cast Member window.

   The first thing that needs to be done is to spin the clock hand cast member. Here, the single cast member will be duplicated into many positions by using Director's Auto Distort feature.

5. In the Paint window, select the Marquee tool with its option set to Shrink.

6. Drag a selection around the clock hand artwork. After releasing the mouse, the marquee snaps closely around the artwork (see fig. 6.39).

Figure 6.39

With the Marquee tool set to Shrink, drag a selection around the clock hand.

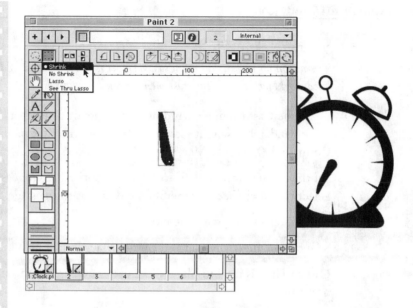

The clock hand needs to be rotated 360 degrees. The Paint window has a row of function keys for special effects. These effects are combined with Auto Distort to create a spinning loop cast member.

7. To spin the artwork: With the artwork selected, click on the Rotate Right button four times to rotate the hands 360 degrees. Don't deselect the artwork.

   The artwork is now in the process of distorting. Director knows the original position and the current position of the selected artwork.

8. Choose Auto Distort from the Xtras menu.

9. The Auto Distort dialog box displays, waiting for a number of new cast members to create. Enter 12 to create a total of 13 cast members. Click on Begin to create the new cast members (see fig. 6.40).

Figure 6.40

The Auto Distort dialog box.

continues

Animating with Auto Distort continued

10. Close the Paint window.

    The reason for making an extra cast member is to get the first and last positions lined up. Now, the duplicate cast member can be removed.

11. Open the Cast Member window and delete cast member 14, the last clock hand. Choose Cut Cast Member from the Edit menu or press Command+X on the Mac, Ctrl+X in Windows.

12. Set the default sprite length to 12 in the Sprite Preferences dialog box. Select the clock face cast member and drag it to the stage.

    This fills channel 1 with the clock face.

13. Save the movie (Command+S on the Mac, Ctrl+S in Windows).

    Cast to Time is used to place all 12 cast members on the stage, aligned over time.

14. Select all the clock hands in the Cast window by selecting the first clock hand, pressing the Shift key, and selecting the last clock hand.

15. Choose Cast to Time from the Modify menu. The Score window now shows a span of sprites in channels 1 and 2, the clock and hands. The Cast to Time automatically places all the cast members to the center of the stage.

16. Select the sprite span channel 2 of the Score window and set the ink effect to Matte.

    Step 19 accomplishes two things. Selecting the sprite span in channel 2 ensures that when the artwork on the stage moves, all 12 sprites move. The Matte ink effect removes the white area around the clock hands.

17. With the sprite span selected in channel 2, on the stage, drag the selected hand artwork to the center of the clock face (see fig. 6.41).

18. Save the movie, and then play it.

    The hands on the clock do not rotate correctly. They rotate from their own center and not the center of the clock. To recenter the hand without moving each sprite on stage, the registration point is changed in the Paint window.

Figure 6.41

Set the ink effect to Matte and reposition the clock hand to the center of the clock face.

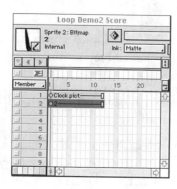

19. Open the Paint window and click on the Next Cast Member button until cast member 2, the vertical hand artwork, is selected.

    By default, the registration point is set to the physical center of the artwork.

20. To reposition the registration point on the artwork, select the Registration tool in the Paint window toolbox. Click on a new registration point on the white dot at the bottom of the artwork (see fig. 6.42).

Figure 6.42

Use the Registration tool in the Paint window to register paint images.

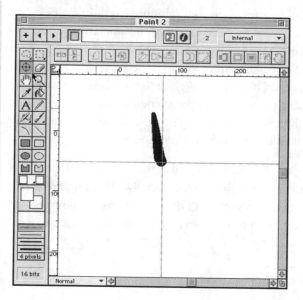

The white dot was added to the original cast member to help easily find the rotation point. This white dot can be filled in later if needed.

continues

Animating with Auto Distort   continued

21. In the Paint window, select the Next Cast Member button to advance to the next clock hand cast member and reposition the registration on this artwork.

22. Repeat step 21 until all the clock hands are registered. (Do not change the registration on the clock artwork.)

23. In the Score window, again select all sprites in channel 2. On the stage, drag the clock hand back to the center of the clock face, so that the registration point of the clock hands is in the center of the clock.

24. Close the Paint window and play the movie.

The hands now spin from the center of the clock face and only the registration points are moved to realign the sprites. Auto Distort has other options such as Skew, Warp, and Perspective. These options are applied in the same fashion as the rotate steps previously discussed.

The preceding tutorial created spinning hands of a clock. The animation could stay as is and would work okay until the animation sequence called for the clock to jump around as if it were ringing. The ringing animation would be more difficult to keep track of in the Score window because multiple cast members would have to be aligned to a moving object. A film loop enables all the hand cast members to be contained in a single cast member. Now when the clock jumps around, only a single cast member containing a series of events has to be handled by Director in the Score.

Film loops are easy to create, but sometimes it is difficult to understand why and when they are to be used. Generally, film loops are used when a repeating sequence is needed within a Director movie—a spinning tire on a car moving around the stage, a bird or birds flying around the stage, or hands spinning around a clock face.

Animating with Film Loops

1. With the Score window open, select the sprite span in channel 2, the spinning hands.

2. Be certain that the ink effect is set to Matte for all the sprites in channel 2.

   Ink effects must be applied to the sprite before the loop is made. Otherwise, the ink effect is locked into the looped cast member.

3. Open the Cast window. Arrange the cast and score in a way that you can see both.

4. Click and drag the sprite in channel 2 to an empty cast member slot.

5. The Create Film Loop dialog box appears (see fig. 6.43).

6. Name your new film loop.

Figure 6.43

Pasting sprites into the Cast Member window brings up the Create Film Loop dialog box.

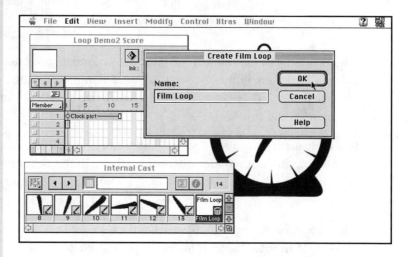

The Cast window sees 12 incoming sprites, but the Cast window only holds cast members. A film loop is a cast member, except that this loop cast member contains the location and cast numbers of the 12 sprites cut from channel 2.

7. Now that you've created the film loop, select the sprite span in score channel 2 and delete it. Again, do not delete the original cast members.

   The looped cast member must be placed back on the stage.

continues

Animating with Film Loops   continued

8. Make sure the playback head is in frame 1. Then drag the new film loop cast member to the stage and align it to the center of the clock face.

9. Save the movie and then play it.

   This fills in the remainder of the cell with the spinning hands.

The clock hands and face also could be made into another loop. Loops within loops are acceptable. To bounce the clock around the stage, only one sprite on the stage would have to be moved. This single sprite contains the clock and the spinning hand all in one place for easy movement around the stage.

WARNING

Never delete the original cast member used in the film loop. The film loop is using the originals to play back the loop. The original cast members can be modified; this modification appears in the film loop.

The final tutorial illustrates animating with color palettes. Animated color palettes work only within an 8–bit palette. The monitor on the computer must be changed to 256. Refer to your computer's user's guide for instructions on changing to 256 colors.

A color palette is a grid of 256 available colors. Swapping or moving colors within a palette can produce interesting effects. In the next tutorial, and by using color cycling, a toaster is made to look like it is becoming hotter over time.

The movie for this tutorial, Toaster Demo, is located on the accompanying CD-ROM in the Chapter 6 folder. To get started, copy the tutorial to the current computer. Open Toaster Demo from the hard disk and play it.

The movie contains all the cast members to make the movie except the palette to correctly animate the colors. In this tutorial, the toaster starts out as light blue, and as it heats, it turns more red. Color cycling is used to create this effect. You can also create the effect using different colored cast members, but this would take up a great deal more disk space. Color cycling only needs to add one cast member, a palette.

Animating with Color Cycling

1. Close all open windows.

2. Open the Color Palettes window (Command+Option+7 on the Mac, Ctrl+Alt+7 in Windows). See figure 6.44.

Figure 6.44

The Color Palettes window can be customized and stored in the Cast Member window.

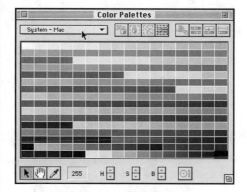

The toaster is currently light yellow. Light yellow is chip 1 in the color palette. First, the color of the toaster is changed to light blue. When you look at the color palette, you notice that a blue that is light enough is not available. You need to create a new color palette where the needed blue color chip will be created.

3. Double-click on chip 1 of the Color Palette window. The Color chooser appears. (Chip 1 is actually the pale yellow chip to the right of the white chip, which is actually Chip 0.)

4. Click and drag around the color wheel until you find a light blue (see fig. 6.45).

Figure 6.45

Selecting a light blue color from the Color Picker.

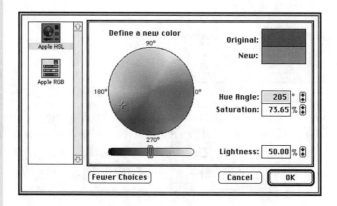

continues

Animating with Color Cycling continued

5. Click on OK in the Color chooser. An alert box appears.

   The System palette cannot be changed. When a change is made to the System palette, a duplicated palette is created.

   A name needs to be given to this new palette. The newly created palette appears in the Cast window as an internal cast member.

6. Name the palette Toaster palette.

   If the movie is played now, no change takes place. The movie is still using the default system palette.

7. To change to the new Toaster palette, open the Score and Cast Member windows.

8. Drag cast member 6, the Toaster palette, out of the Cast Member window and into the Score window, palette channel, frame 1 (see fig. 6.46).

Figure 6.46

Applying the Toaster palette to the Palette channel in the Score window.

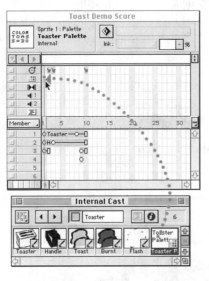

On the stage the toaster turns light blue. When working with the palette, Director worries about only one thing: the color of the chip in the cast member. Like a paint-by-number book, Director sees only the number of the cast member. If the palette being used has a yellow chip 1, the image is yellow; if the palette being used has a light blue chip 1, the image is light blue.

9. Save and play the movie.

To make the toaster change colors gradually is a little more difficult. The program has to be told to swap color in and out of the current palette. Color cycling is used to change color over time.

10. Close the Cast and Score windows.

11. Open the Color Palettes window. In the upper-left corner, select Toaster Palette Internal from the Palette pop-up menu (see fig. 6.47).

Figure 6.47

Selecting the Toaster palette in the Color Palette window.

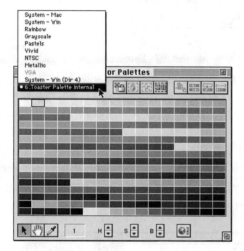

The color change that takes place is the toaster beginning as a light blue color and gradually growing more red as it appears to become hot. Using the color palette, a range of color is set up to display one after another, a cycle. First, the color has to be added to the color palette.

12. Double-click on chip 8 and change its color to a bright red. Click on OK. The first and last colors are now set.

13. To blend the two colors: With chip 8 selected, press Shift and click on chip 1, the light blue chip. All the chips in between are selected.

14. Choose the Blend button in the palette (see fig. 6.48).

continues

Animating with Color Cycling   continued

Figure 6.48

Selecting a range of color to In-Between in the Color Palettes window. The In-Between button is indicated by the cursor at the top of the palette.

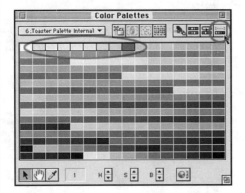

The light blue blends into the red. This blend can be as long or as short as needed. Be careful not to blend past the eighth color chip. The ninth color chip is used in the toast in cast member 3. Changing this chip also changes the light toast. Now that the palette is correct, the score has to know to cycle this toaster palette.

15. Close the Color Palettes window.

16. In the Score window, double-click on the Palette channel, frame 8. This frame is where the palette cycle occurs. The Frame Properties: Palette dialog box opens (see fig. 6.49).

Figure 6.49

Setting the Properties in the Frame Properties: Palette dialog box.

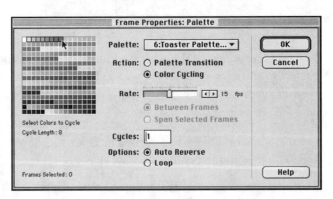

For the palette to cycle, a range of color chips must be selected.

17. Select the Color Cycling radio button.

18. In the Frame Properties: Palette dialog box, Choose Toaster Palette in the Palette pop-up menu. Click and drag over chips 1–8 in the chip mini-window as shown in figure 6.45. The cycle length at the bottom of the mini-window should be 8.

19. Set the Rate for the palette change; 15 frames per second is fine.

20. The effect occurs only one time. The Cycle number should be 1.

    To make the toaster heat up and cool down, a reverse must be applied.

21. Select the Auto Reverse radio button and click on OK.

22. Save and play the movie.

The toaster cast member changes colors without adding new cast members to the movie. The Palette options take time to understand, and a little planning ahead is also helpful. Moving color chips around a palette before artwork is created is much easier than trying to recolor artwork to match a modified palette.

Troubleshooting

The following sections cover what to look out for when beginning or working in Director.

Saving

A common saying is that if you save every two minutes, you can only lose two minutes of work; if you save every two hours, you can lose two hours of work. It is extremely important to save your work often. When working with a complex application such as Director, this becomes doubly important, because it can be difficult to remember what step you were on in a lengthy operation if your system crashes.

Some of the best times to save your work include the following:

▶ After you have opened a file and set up the parameters

▶ After you have entered a line or paragraph of text

▶ Before you print a document or run a movie

Scaled Sprites

The number one cause of a slow-playing Director movie is a scaled sprite. A scaled sprite is a cast member that has been imported from another application to the stage at a different size than its original size. Cast members should always be imported at their intended size. The playback head must travel through up to 126 channels of information (see the brief discussion on transitions later in this chapter). If in this lineup of information the playback head encounters a scaled sprite, the playback head literally calculates the differences in size and draws the object on the stage.

If you find that the sprite is the wrong size after importing, two things can be done to the cast member. First, return to the application and rework the master. (You did keep the master, didn't you?) Second, use Transform Bitmap from the Modify menu to resize the cast member (see fig. 6.50).

Figure 6.50

Use the Transform Bitmap dialog box to resize cast members.

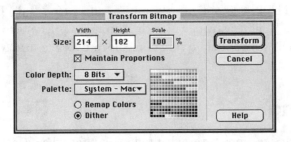

Transform Bitmap enables you to size the cast member in two ways: by percentage or by actual pixel size. If a sprite must be scaled, always scale down. In other words, import the image large and scale down on the stage. The image on the stage remains sharp, whereas an image scaled up becomes jagged and distorted.

Bit Depth

When creating images, it is important to choose a bit depth that allows for the amount of color detail you want as well as the amount of disk space you have available. Higher bit depths give more detail and use more disk space.

The monitor controls the show. When a new Director document is opened, the first thing Director does is check the monitor's *bit depth*—the number of colors that are displayed on the computer screen.

As an example of how the wrong bit depth can make things go awry, imagine that a client asks for a portfolio of quick color sketches and the portfolio has to be rather small to fit on leftover space on some type of removable media. You fire up Director and, as soon as you can, you create some nice illustrations, put them on-screen, and add Lingo scripts to navigate through the imagery.

Upon finishing the project and quitting Director, you find a file that is megabytes in size rather than kilobytes. Funny, the images weren't that big—only a few colors here and there. When you use Director again to investigate, you find that the monitor was set to millions of colors. The image that was to be small is actually many times the size it should have been.

This problem can be fixed by using Transform Bitmap from the Modify menu and changing the bit depth of the drawings. The only problem is that the 24-bit images dither. (*Dithering* is the process of replacing pixels in an image.) The incoming pixels are from a palette of fewer colors. The dither puts these limited colored pixels in small groups to try to match the colors in the original full-color image. A dithered image looks speckled compared to the original. If the monitor was set to the correct setting before launching Director, the images would have been created in the correct palette in the first place—without dithering the images.

Ink Effects

The ink effects applied to sprites can cause a slowdown in the playback speed. The Copy ink effect is the only ink effect that does not cause a slowdown in playback performance. The two inks that slow the playback the most are Matte and Background Transparent. If possible, fill the whole of a cast member with the color it passes over. If the image moves over different colored backgrounds, this technique does not work. A good rule of thumb is this: If the image doesn't move, it generally doesn't need an ink effect. The sprite in channel 1, the lowest layer, never needs an ink effect other than Copy. If an ink effect is applied to the background, even though no effect is seen, the computer processes the ink effect and slows the playback.

The Active Window

As people become more accustomed to applications, they tend to use keyboard shortcuts more and more. Just remember that in Director, cutting a cast member can remove many sprites. The Cast window and the Score window can be open at the same time, but only one of the windows can be active. The window with the title bar visible is the active window. Director does have a built-in safety: The program brings up an alert box if two or more cast members are being deleted.

Transitions

Each time the playback head enters a frame, 126 channels of information are passed to the stage. A *transition* is an effect from frame to frame. When transitioning from frame 5 to frame 6, the actual transition information occupies the transition channel of frame 6. The transition happens between frames 5 and 6 (see fig. 6.51).

Figure 6.51

A transition occurs between two frames. The playback head travels down one column of channels and then advances to the next frame and travels down that column of channels.

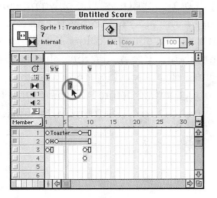

In Practice

Animation is at the heart of Director. Even people new to the tasks of animation can create professional and impressive animated presentations in a very short time by using Director's array of features and powerful engine. The next chapter examines another central feature of Director, one that makes rich, interesting animation possible: the cast, in particular, multiple casts.

Important facets of working with animation discussed in this chapter include the following:

▶ The speed of your animation can be changed in two ways: Change the speed settings for the playback head, or change the relative position of one object to the next in consecutive frames.

▶ Cast members can include bitmapped or shape elements. Bitmapped images are best for motion; shapes are best for still images.

▶ Real-time recording is effective for roughing out your animations and can be edited later for finer control and smoother final results.

▶ Step recording is slower but more accurate than real-time recording.

▶ Space to Time recording offers the accuracy of step recording and the convenience of seeing all the steps of the animation sequence as you create it.

▶ Tweening is an animation technique that combines quickness and accuracy. It relies on Director to calculate and draw positions of sprites in frames between keyframes.

▶ Cast to Time is an animation technique that automatically places a sequence of related cast members on the stage with their registration points also aligned over time.

▶ Use film loops to create events that occur repeatedly in your movie, such as a traffic light cycling through red, yellow, and green or a pattern of background traffic in a street scene.

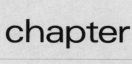

chapter 7

Kirk Keller

Multiple Casts

In keeping with the Director movie metaphor, you can think of casts as being the "cast" or group of performers in your multimedia production. Graphic, digital video and audio media as well as Lingo scripts and transitions are all represented as cast members in the Cast window. In the Cast window, the multimedia developer can get an overview of the elements that make up the multimedia production. The score serves as the script that tells your performers what to do when they get on the stage, and the Cast window can tell you what performers you have available for the production.

One sometimes-overlooked element of the Director Cast window is the capability to have more than one type of Cast window or library available for a movie. By looking at Cast windows as libraries or databases for the storage of your multimedia elements, you can see how they can be used to organize and reuse multimedia elements or to easily enable localization of multimedia projects.

Each Cast window in Director can be thought of as a cast library. If you needed to use more than one cast library in earlier versions of Director, you had to create a shared cast. Shared casts worked well for using the same cast member in different movies. Multiple cast files take this concept a great deal further. Now you can have, for example, a cast library of just navigational images, such as arrows, buttons, or icons. Sound files can be kept in a cast library of sounds. This helps you, the developer, to organize your media elements.

This chapter covers the use of the Cast Member window and multiple casts as follows:

- ▶ Overview of the cast windows
- ▶ Creating and using multiple casts
- ▶ Cast members and their properties
- ▶ Building a multiple cast project
- ▶ Using cast libraries for localization

An Overview of the Cast Window

Figure 7.1 shows the layout of the Cast window. Cast member files are stored on a hard disk. The Cast window is used to view the cast member files.

Figure 7.1

Director's Cast window.

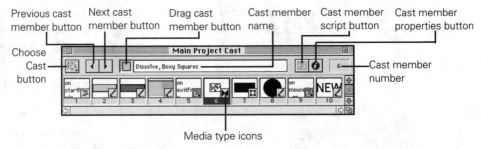

Media type icons

When working in the Windows environment, for cross-platform development or with web servers (for Shockwave applications), external libraries should be saved with a .CST extension. This is how Windows and MIME tables on web servers are able to recognize these files as Director cast libraries.

Following are the components of the Cast window:

- ▶ **Choose Cast button:** Press this button, located in the upper-left corner of the Cast window to bring up a pop-up menu of currently available internal and external cast files. A new Director movie shows only one cast file in this menu, the default internal cast file. Naturally, the menu grows as you add new cast files to the movie. Adding internal and external cast files is explained later in this chapter in the section "Creating and Using Multiple Casts."

▶ **Previous and Next Cast Member buttons:** These enable you to select cast members one at a time within a Cast window. Holding down one of these arrows enables you to scan through the Cast window very quickly.

▶ **Drag Cast Member button:** You can place a selected cast member onto the stage by using the Drag Cast Member button. To use this feature, select a cast member in the Cast window, and then press the Drag Cast Member button to drag the cast member out of the Cast window and on to the stage. You can then position the cast member on the stage. You can also use the Drag Cast Member button to drag a selected cast member to a cell in the Score window, thus creating a sprite. By default, this sprite is centered on the stage.

▶ **Cast Member Name:** The cast member's name appears to the right of the Drag Cast Member button. The name of an imported media element automatically appears in the name box of the cast member you select. You can change the name of a cast member you select by selecting and re-entering that name in the text box.

Even though Director's cast members can have the same name, you really don't want that. If two cast members share the same name and you use Lingo to call a cast member by that name, Director has no way of knowing which of the same-named cast members you want to call. The script chooses the first cast member with that name it comes across as it works its way through the cast library. (That is, the script always picks the cast member with the lowest cast number that has the correct name.)

▶ **Cast Member Script button:** This is the second button from the right in the Cast window. You use this button to open a selected cast member's script. If the selected cast does not have a cast script, opening this dialog box sets up an on mouseUp handler. Here, you can enter your Lingo script on the blank line between the on mouseUp and end statements (see fig. 7.2). A cast script is located inside the selected cast member.

Figure 7.2

Selecting the Cast Script button opens the Cast Script window. Here, Lingo code can be entered or modified.

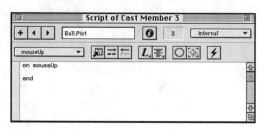

▶ **Cast Member Properties button:** This is the last button on the right of the Cast window and is covered in the section "Cast Members and Their Properties" later in this chapter (see fig. 7.3).

Figure 7.3

One of many Cast Member Property dialog boxes displays depending on which type of cast member you select.

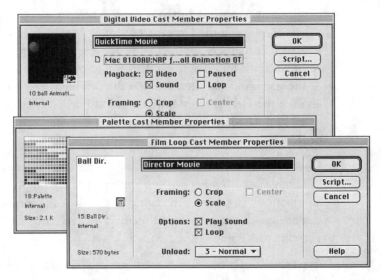

▶ **Cast Member Number:** The area in the upper-right corner of the Cast window is the number of the selected cast member. Double-clicking on this area launches an editor for the selected cast member if the element cannot be edited inside the Director movie. The launch editor is great for easily opening an application such as Macromedia SoundEdit 16 or other sound applications to make a quick modification to a sound cast member.

INSIDER TIP

To launch an application editor, double-click on a cast member that you cannot edit in Director, such as a sound file, or choose Launch External Editor from the Edit menu. If an editor has not been selected, a dialog box prompts you to search for the correct editor for that media type.

You can also set your preference for media editing packages in the Editors Preference dialog box in the File menu. This feature is new to Director 6. To set these preferences, choose Preferences, Editors from the File menu.

The cast members appear as icons in the Cast window. You can customize how the icons appear by choosing Preferences, Cast from the File menu (see fig. 7.4). Each Director movie can contain up to 32,000 cast members per cast library. The Cast Preferences dialog box enables you to set the number of cast members contained in each Cast window. You can also set the size of the thumbnail for each cast member in the Cast window.

Figure 7.4

*The Cast Preferences
dialog box.*

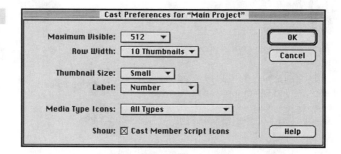

INSIDER TIP

Do not set the maximum visible setting to 32,000 if you use fewer than 512
cast members per window. Higher-than-needed numbers tend to slow down
both playback speed and load time.

The cast member preferences are as follows:

▶ **Maximum Visible:** Enables you to set how many cast members are seen
in a Cast window (512 to 32,000).

▶ **Row Width:** Limits how many cast members are visible from left to right
in the Cast window. A small number keeps you from having to scroll two
directions on a small monitor.

▶ **Thumbnail Size:** Adjusts the size of the cast member tile. If many of the
cast members need to be viewed, a setting of Small could be used,
although the resulting thumbnails might be difficult to see.

▶ **Label:** Cast members can be viewed by name, number, or both.

▶ **Media Type Icons:** Graphics icons displayed in the bottom of cast
member tiles can be turned on or off.

INSIDER TIP

Changes to the general appearance of the Cast window—such as thumbnail
size—affect only the active Cast window. If you open an unlinked Cast window
after changing the appearance of your internal Cast window, the unlinked Cast
window retains the default preference settings. You must change the remainder
of the Cast windows separately to apply the same settings.

Cast member icons contain media type icons in their lower corners to indicate
the type of cast member. In addition to showing the media type of the cast
member, these icons also show important information such as whether the
media for the cast member is linked to the movie or whether the cast member
has a Lingo script. Figure 7.5 shows the types of icons that you can view in a
cast member icon.

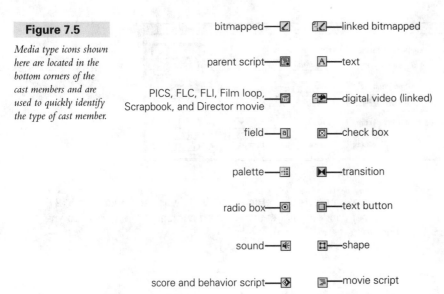

bitmapped——🗹   🗹——linked bitmapped

parent script——🖩   🅰——text

PICS, FLC, FLI, Film loop,
Scrapbook, and Director movie——🎞   📹——digital video (linked)

field——🗐   ☒——check box

palette——▦   🔀——transition

radio box——◉   ☐——text button

sound——🔊   🔲——shape

score and behavior script——◆   🗐——movie script

If you have used versions of Director earlier than version 6, you will notice some changes in the icons for Lingo cast members. Behaviors (a new script type in Director 6) and score Lingo cast members have a diamond-shaped icon. Movie scripts have the script icon that used to be associated with score-based Lingo. Parent scripts now have the script and black dot icon that used to be associated with movie and parent scripts.

Creating and Using Multiple Casts

You can have different casts libraries to organize the cast and hold different types of media or often-used media elements. Figure 7.6 shows an example of multiple Cast windows.

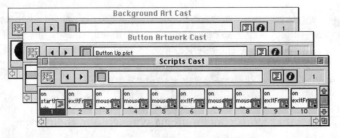

You can, for example, create a cast library of transitions. When you need a transition, you just drag the cast member from one Cast window to another Cast window (see fig. 7.7). If you are working with a server or with

Shockwave, you can have movies access external cast libraries through the use of aliases (on the Mac) or shortcuts (in Windows).

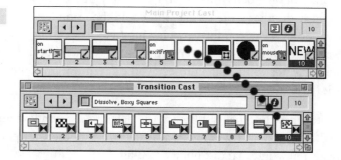

A Director movie can contain two types of cast member libraries: internal and external. *Internal libraries* are stored inside a Director document (for example, a movie, projector, or a Shockwave movie). These libraries tend to make the document file size larger, whereas an *external library* is stored outside the document, making for a smaller document. The drawback to an external cast member file is that the actual cast file needs to travel with the Director document. External cast member files act just like imported linked media.

The positive side to an external cast library is that the external library, like linked media, can be updated or modified outside the parent document. You can create a calendar in Director, for example, and save the file as a projector—a self contained application. Then each year, you can send a new external cast library with updated art and data to your users. All the user has to do is replace the old cast library with the new one. If the projector refers to a cast library on a web server, the user does not need to replace a cast library. Updating the cast library on the web server instantly enables any projector accessing that library to use the new media and scripts. All that is required to enable this updating of external casts is to either give the new external cast libraries the same name as the old cast libraries or use Lingo to set the file name of the cast library to that of the new cast library. This last technique is demonstrated later in this chapter in the section, "Using Cast Libraries for Localization."

Internal Cast Libraries

A Director movie can have an unlimited number of internal cast libraries. The benefit of using multiple internal cast libraries is that you can organize your media for quick reference.

One internal cast library can, for example, contain only background art. Another cast library can contain only buttons. Perhaps you could even add a cast library of only behaviors, so you can easily find them without getting them confused with other score scripts. You could then simultaneously open all these Cast windows on-screen for easy viewing (refer back to fig. 7.6). Director's drag-and-drop feature enables you to drag a cast member from one cast library to another. After you finish a project, you can remove unwanted cast member libraries from the movie.

To create a new internal cast library, the default Cast window must first be opened. After the Cast window is available, the Choose Cast pop-up menu to create a new internal cast library (see fig. 7.8).

Figure 7.8

Select New Cast in the Choose Cast pop-up menu to create a new cast library.

Creating a New Internal Cast Library

1. In the Cast window, press and hold the Choose Cast button to access the pop-up menu.

2. Select New Cast from the Choose Cast pop-up menu.

3. Name the new internal library.

4. Enable the Internal radio button (see fig. 7.9).

Figure 7.9

Setting up an internal cast member library.

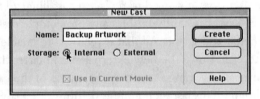

Another way to create a new internal cast library is to choose New, Cast from the File menu. Name the new cast library and enable the Internal radio button.

The new internal Cast window opens and the default Cast window closes. You can view the default window again by choosing the Choose Cast button pop-up menu and selecting the default library from the menu (see fig. 7.10).

Figure 7.10

*Opening a closed
default Cast window.*

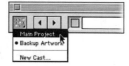

After you create an internal cast library, you cannot convert it to an external cast library. The internal cast library always remains part of the movie. The only way to delete an internal library is to remove it from the current Director movie. To remove an internal cast library, choose Movie, Casts from the Modify menu. Select the unwanted cast library and click on the Remove button. Before you do this, however, make certain that you have all the media out of the library that you want to use.

INSIDER TIP

To have a new or existing cast window open on top of the default Cast window (viewing both windows at the same time), hold down the Option key (Macintosh) or the Alt key (Windows) while choosing the Choose Cast pop-up menu. The Cast window you just opened is stacked on top of the first Cast window. You need to move this newly opened second window so that you can view both windows. To move the topmost window, click and drag the title bar of the top window to another location. Also, remember that only one Cast window can be active at a time. When you edit cast members in a paint or text modification window, be certain to know which Cast window is active. The selected cast member of the active window is the element to be modified.

External Cast Libraries

External cast libraries are stored outside the current Director movie and can be opened either as linked or unlinked libraries.

Linked External Cast Libraries

A linked cast library behaves the same as an internal cast library, except that it is stored outside the current movie and Director uses a path name to access it. Director needs to keep track only of the location of the linked external file. Figure 7.11 shows an external cast library in the same folder as the Director movie that uses it. The following tutorial explains how to create a linked external cast library.

Figure 7.11

The external cast member library named PAGEART.CST is stored outside the MCASTS1.DIR Director movie and is viewed as an independent file.

Creating a Linked External Cast Library

1. In the Cast Member window, press and hold the Choose Cast button to access the pop-up menu.

2. Select New Cast from the Choose Cast Member pop-up menu.

3. Name the new file.

4. Choose the External radio button (see fig. 7.12).

Figure 7.12

Creating a linked external cast member library.

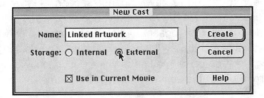

5. Make certain that the Use in Current Movie check box is enabled. Otherwise, the file won't be linked.

Another way to create an external cast file is to choose New, Cast from the File menu. Name the new cast file and choose the External radio button.

The new external Cast window opens and the default Cast window closes. You can view the default window again by selecting it in the Choose Cast pop-up menu.

Unlinked External Cast Libraries

The other type of external cast library is an unlinked external cast library. An unlinked external cast library has no ties or links to a Director movie. It is a free-standing file. Like a scrapbook or toolbox, you can drag media elements out of this type of cast library to the cast library of the current Director movie. An external unlinked cast library is easy to spot. When displayed, the framing of the Cast window appears darker in color than a normal Cast window.

You can create new unlinked external cast libraries by using one of three methods. Each method produces the same results; they are outlined in the next tutorial.

Creating an Unlinked External Cast Library

Method 1

1. Choose New, Cast from the File menu.

2. In the New Cast dialog box, enter the name of the new external file in the Name text box.

3. Enable the External radio button (see fig. 7.13).

Figure 7.13

Creating an unlinked external cast member library.

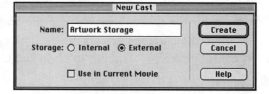

4. Disable the Use in Current Movie check box. If you leave this check box enabled, you end up with the new cast file being linked to the movie you are currently editing.

Method 2

1. Choose the Choose Cast pop-up menu of the active Cast window.

2. Select New Cast and name the new external file.

3. Enable the External radio button.

4. Disable the Use in Current Movie check box.

Method 3

1. Choose Movie, Casts from the Modify menu.

2. Click on the New button.

3. Name the new external file.

4. Enable the External radio button.

5. Disable the Use in Current Movie check box.

This unlinked cast library is saved independently of the current Director movie. You can store unlinked cast libraries on a local drive or on a server for easy access.

Before you can copy a media element from an unlinked external cast library to the current Director cast library, the unlinked cast library must be available to the current movie. It is not available through the Choose Cast pop-up menu because it is unlinked and has no ties to the current Director movie.

To open an unlinked cast library, choose Open, Cast from the File menu. In the file dialog box you can not only see Director movies, but external cast libraries as well. Select and open these external cast libraries as you would a Director movie.

After you open the unlinked cast file, you can copy the cast members and paste them into and out of the current Director movie's cast file. You can also link the unlinked cast library to the current Director movie. Linking an unlinked library is covered in the later exercise, "Linking an Unlinked Cast Library to the Current Project."

If you place an external cast library into the Director Xtras folder, you have a handy database from which you can drag often-used media elements and scripts into your Director movie. In fact, if you go to the Director Xtras menu, you will see that Macromedia has already done this with a library of Behaviors, Buttons, Widgets, and Palettes.

Use Director's drag-and-drop feature to drag a cast member from the unlinked Cast window into another Cast window of the current Director movie (see fig. 7.14). The media element remains in the unlinked file. The unlinked cast library remains unlinked. Your internal or linked cast library, however, now has a copy of the media element you just dragged and dropped.

Figure 7.14

Drag and drop to copy an unlinked cast member to the current Director movie.

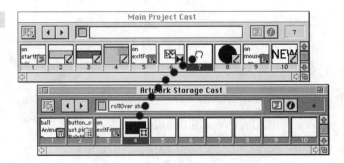

Sometimes you might want to link an unlinked library to the current Director movie. Suppose that you have an external cast library that contains several cast members that you know you will be using in your movie. Instead of copying all the cast members of the external library, it might be easier to link the external library to the movie.

In contrast to dragging a cast member from an unlinked Cast window to a linked Cast window, dragging a cast member from the unlinked Cast window to the stage or a cell in the score window of the current Director movie causes the unlinked library to link to the current movie (see fig. 7.15).

Figure 7.15

Dragging an unlinked cast member to a cell in the Score window links the cast member library to the current Director movie.

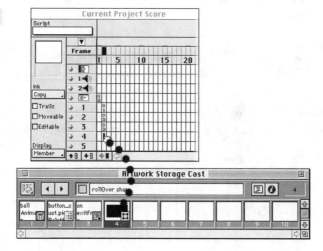

You can also link an unlinked cast library to the current movie by selecting Movie, Cast from the Modify menu. Choosing the Link button in the Movie Casts dialog box (see fig. 7.16) brings up a standard Find dialog box. After the correct library is selected, click on the Open button and the cast file is added as a linked cast library to the current movie.

Figure 7.16

An unlinked cast member library can be linked using the Movie Casts dialog box.

You can remove linked cast libraries from the current Director movie. While creating your movie, you might link several cast libraries. At a later point in time, however, you may want to reorganize the way that your media elements are stored. You may decide, for example, that instead of having an external library for movie scripts and another for score scripts, you want one linked library for all your scripts. If this is the case, then you will want to unlink one of the linked cast libraries.

Choosing Movie, Cast from the Modify menu opens a dialog box from which you can select the cast member file you want to remove from the current Director movie. An alert message appears, informing you of the consequences of removing this cast library.

Cast Members and Their Properties

Director 6 greatly increases the number of media file formats available for import on both the Macintosh and Windows. New file formats for both Windows and Macintosh versions of Director now support the following:

- ▶ .BMP
- ▶ .GIF
- ▶ .JPG (JPEG)
- ▶ .LRG (the Xres file format)
- ▶ Photoshop 3.0
- ▶ MacPaint
- ▶ .PNG
- ▶ .TIF (TIFF)
- ▶ .PIC (PICT)
- ▶ QuickTime
- ▶ .AIF (AIFF sound format)
- ▶ Shape
- ▶ Text
- ▶ Field
- ▶ Transition

- Color palettes
- Film loops
- Director casts and Director movies
- Sprite scripts and movie scripts

Director for Windows also supports the following file formats:

- Photo CD
- .PCX
- .WMF
- PostScript (PS)
- .FLC
- .FLI
- .WAV
- .AVI (Video for Windows)

Director for Macintosh supports the following additional file formats:

- PICS
- Scrapbook images

You can control the way these media elements behave in a Director movie through the Cast Member Properties dialog box of a cast member. The Cast Member Properties button is located in the upper-right corner of the Cast window. Choose the Cast Member Properties button of a selected Cast Member to open the dialog box for that type of cast member (see fig. 7.17).

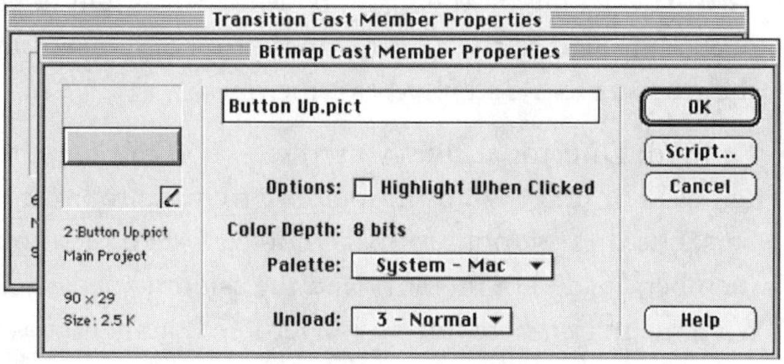

Figure 7.17

The Cast Member Properties dialog box of two cast members.

Property Options of Cast Members

The following is a quick tour of the cast member property options that most types of cast members have in common (see fig. 7.18). Later in the chapter, cast member types are considered with respect to the properties unique to each one. The shared cast member property options are as follows:

Thumbnail   Highlight options   Cast member name

Bitmap Cast Member Properties

computer.pict   OK

Options: ☐ Highlight When Clicked   Script...

Cancel

2 :computer.pict
Internal

Color Depth: 8 bits

64 × 64
Size : 4.0 K

Palette: [Grayscale ———]   Palette pop-up menu

Unload: [3 – Normal ▾]   Help

Cast member information   Unload pop-up menu

▶ **Thumbnail:** A small version of the selected cast member is shown on the upper left of the Properties dialog box.

▶ **Cast member information:** Located on the left side of the Properties dialog box. Here you can quickly view the cast member number and name, the type of palette in which the cast member is located, and the size in pixels and in kilobytes.

▶ **Cast member name:** For imported media, the name of the original file displays here. The name can be changed by entering new text. Cast members retain their names if moved to another location in the Cast window.

▶ **Script:** Clicking on the script button enables you to either view existing scripts attached to the cast member or create a new Lingo script to make the cast member a scripted cast member.

▶ **Unload:** Director enables you to set when cast members are to be removed or unloaded from memory to make room for other cast members. Use these settings to make Director keep the most-often used cast members loaded in memory and the seldom-used cast members unloaded from memory when you no longer need them. Following are the Unload options:

- ▶ **Normal:** This setting causes Director to unload this cast member first.

- ▶ **Next:** Cast members with this setting are removed from memory after the cast members set to normal are unloaded.

- ▶ **Last:** Cast members set to Last are unloaded from memory after the cast members set to Normal and Next.

- ▶ **Never:** Cast members with this setting are not removed from memory.

Properties Unique to Specific Cast Members

In addition to the properties described so far, many types of cast members have unique properties. This section examines each main category of cast members, focusing mostly on properties unique to that type.

Bitmapped Cast Member

As you saw in figure 7.18, bitmapped cast member properties include the shared options discussed previously. In addition, the Highlight and Palette options are available.

INSIDER TIP

You can use Lingo to access many of the properties of cast members examined in this chapter. This means that your Director movie can change many of these properties while the movie is running.

Consult the *Lingo Dictionary* for more information on the particular Lingo commands associated with various cast member properties.

Shape Cast Member

You use the Tools palette (Command+7 on the Macintosh, Ctrl+7 on Windows) to create a variety of shapes. In the Shape Cast Member Properties dialog box (see fig. 7.19), shapes can be changed (if necessary) to other shapes such as Oval, Rectangle, Rounded Rectangle, and Line. Shapes can also be filled or unfilled.

Shape cast members are useful because they are only 1-bit vectored graphics, which means that a shape cast member that covers the stage is very small in size. This small file size is critical when designing Shockwave movies—small file sizes make for small download times.

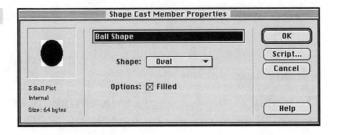

Figure 7.19

*The Shape Cast
Member Properties
dialog box.*

Film Loop Cast Members (PICS, FLC, FLI, Film Loop, Scrapbook, and Director Movie)

Although all the Film Loop cast members seem like very different types of cast members, they share one common feature. When imported to a Director movie, they consist of two items that take up at least two cast member positions. The first item is a container file. This file holds information about how the remaining parts of the file are to be used or placed in the Director movie. The second type of item is the actual media. Director treats PICS, FLC, FLI, Film Loop, Scrapbook, and Director movie cast member properties as Film Loop cast member properties. To make this more clear, observe the way that a PICS file is imported.

When a PICS file is imported, the item imported to the first cast member position is the container file. The next series of cast member positions are filled with the individual PICTS that make up the PICS animation.

Instead of having to place each individual PICT on the stage to create an animation, you need only place the container cast member on the stage at the desired location. When the movie is run, the container cast member swaps out, in sequence, each of the PICT images.

If you are in Windows and you import FLC or FLI animation files, the same process occurs. A container file is loaded along with each of the images in the animation file. The number of cast members required is determined by the number of frames in the animation.

PICS, FLC, and FLI files are often created in 3D animation programs. They provide an easy way to incorporate animation loops in Director. For more information on how to use this type of animation file in Director, see Chapter 9, "Adding the Third Dimension."

WARNING

Never delete the individual elements of a container type of File while in the Cast window. The container needs these files. Removing the single elements causes dropouts when you play the project.

Figure 7.20 shows the PICS cast member dialog box. The property options also enable you to create framing effects for a PICS cast member. These framing effects are also available with FLC, FLI, Scrapbook, and Film Loop cast members. The options are as follows:

- ▶ **Cropping:** Areas around the outside of the image are trimmed off. This does not affect the image.

- ▶ **Scaling:** Enables you to change the size of the image on the stage. This effect can distort the sprite from its original size.

- ▶ **Center:** Keeps the scaled or cropped image file centered inside its frame.

- ▶ **Sound:** If available, can be turned on or off.

- ▶ **Loop:** Enables the sound of an image, if available, to play over and over.

Figure 7.20

The PICS Cast Member Properties dialog box.

The property options for Film Loop, Scrapbook, and Director movie cast members enable you to create framing effects (see figs 7.21–7.23). The options for all three of these cast member types are the same as those for PICS, FLC, or FLI cast members.

Figure 7.21

The Film Loop Cast Member Properties dialog box.

Figure 7.22

The Scrapbook File Cast Member Properties dialog box.

Figure 7.23

The Director Movie Cast Member Properties dialog box.

Sound Cast Member

In addition to the basic information, such as cast name and file size, the attributes of the selected sound are displayed at the lower-left side of the dialog box. You can play the sound cast member from the Properties dialog box's Play button (see fig. 7.24).

Figure 7.24

The Sound Cast Member Properties dialog box.

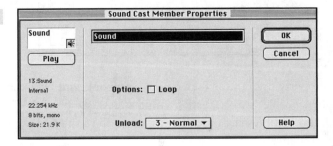

Selecting the Looped check box, located in the center of this dialog box, causes a sound to play over and over within a project.

In some sound-editing applications such as Macromedia's SoundEdit 16, a particular section of a sound sample can be set to loop. If this is done, that loop setting is used in Director.

Text Cast Member

Text cast members enable developers to add rich formatted text to a Director movie. Various font sizes and styles can be used without fear of whether the user will have correct fonts needed to display this text. The reason for this is that text cast members are converted by Director into bitmap images when the movie is run. This enables the developer to make regular text changes to the cast member until the movie is finished. Once finished, the movie converts this text into a graphic.

Properties options for text cast members are framing and anti-aliasing (see fig. 7.25).

Figure 7.25

The Text Cast Member Properties dialog box.

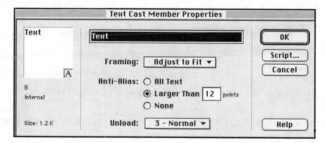

Framing

Framing refers to the way you draw text boxes on the stage. The following options are available within the Framing pop-up menu:

- ▶ **Adjust to fit:** Expands the text box as the user enters text.

- ▶ **Scrolling:** Presents the user with a scrollbar down the right side of the text box. By scrolling, large amounts of text can be read in a small amount of space.

- ▶ **Cropping:** Keeps the text box set to its original size—the text box does not expand when a user adds text to the cast member.

Anti-Aliasing

Anti-aliased text cast members render a smooth on-screen image, not a jagged one like you will find with field cast members. The process of anti-aliasing creates colored pixels around an object. A black letter, for example, will have a gray edge around it to anti-alias to a white background. A red letter on a white background will have a pink anti-aliased edge to smooth the letter on-screen. You can set the following anti-alias features:

▶ **All Text:** Sets all the text in the cast member to render smoothly on the stage regardless of size.

▶ **Text over a certain size:** This setting anti-aliases text over the indicated size only. Be careful. Small text can be very hard to read when smoothed on-screen. Generally, you should not anti-alias text under 11 points.

▶ **None:** No anti-aliasing is applied to this cast member's text on-screen, regardless of text size.

Field Cast Member

Field cast members are similar to text cast members. Both contain text that can be edited within Director. Field cast members, however, are saved as text when the movie is run. This means that during playback, the user can edit field cast members—either through user input or through Lingo.

Because field cast members remain as text and not as a bitmapped image during playback, field cast members cannot be anti-aliased in Director.

In general, text cast members are useful for creating screen banners or other text that is part of a screen display. The richness of the text cast member format and the capability to anti-alias text cast members makes it a good way to display quality text images.

Field cast members are useful in situations in which you need the user to input data while the movie is running or in which you need to search and retrieve data. Field cast members are useful for storing text information.

The field cast members deal with two areas: framing and options (see fig. 7.26).

Figure 7.26

The Field Cast Member Properties dialog box.

Framing

The following options are available within the Framing pop-up menu:

> ▶ **Adjust to Fit:** Expands the text box as the user enters text. Scrolling presents the user with a scrollbar down the right side of the text box.

> ▶ **Fixed:** Keeps the text box set to its original size and newly entered text continues down the text box unseen.

> ▶ **Scrolling:** Presents the user with a scrollbar down the right side of the text box. By scrolling, large amounts of text can be read in a small amount of space.

> ▶ **Limit to field size:** Keeps the text box set to its original size and ignores any newly entered text located outside the text box.

Options

The Options area of the field cast member properties deals more with the entering of data as opposed to the physical box configuration, with which framing deals.

> ▶ **Editable:** Enables the user to enter text as the project is running.

> ▶ **Word Wrap:** Causes text to return to the next line automatically. With Word Wrap off, the text continues past the right side of the text box until the user presses Return.

> ▶ **Tab to Next Field:** Advances the text entry point (if any) to the next editable text box.

You can use Lingo to access most of the settings in the Field Cast Member Property dialog box. For more information on how to control and use fields, see the discussion of text in Chapter 10, "Text: The Story."

Button Cast Member

You can create buttons either by using the Tool Palette (Command+7 on the Macintosh or Ctrl+7 in Windows) or by choosing one of the button types from the Insert, Control menu.

You can change cast member's properties for buttons in the Button Cast Member Properties dialog box (see fig. 7.27). The available choices are as follows:

> ▶ **Radio Button:** Radio buttons enable one item within a group of items to be selected true or false (ON or OFF).

▶ **Check Box:** Check boxes enable multiple items within a group to be selected true or false (ON or OFF).

▶ **Push Button:** Push buttons are used in a standard computer interface for OK, Apply, Cancel, and so on. Any text can be given to a push button in Director.

Figure 7.27

The Button Cast Member Properties dialog box.

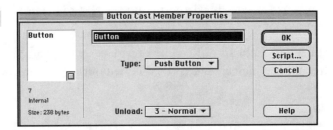

Text manipulation and search functions used on field cast members can also be used on the text for buttons as well. For more information on these functions, see the discussion of text in Chapter 10.

Palette Cast Member

For images that use an indexed color palette (in other words, images that are 8-bit or less), a palette cast member is associated with that image. This palette cast member contains the palette used to display the image.

You can change only the Name and Load properties of a Palette cast member (see fig. 7.28). However, you can affect the way in which a palette cast member is used in a Director movie in several ways.

Figure 7.28

The Palette Cast Member Properties dialog box.

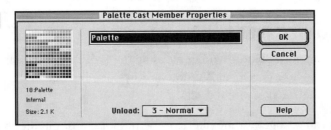

You can create a new palette for a cast member by choosing Insert, Media Element, Color Palette from the menu. This new palette cast member can then be modified. To modify the palette cast member, double click on the palette cast member in the Cast window. Doing so opens a Color Palettes window similar to the one shown in figure 7.29. This window enables you to rearrange colors in a number of ways.

Figure 7.29

The Color Palettes dialog box.

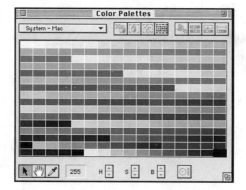

Palette cast members enable developers to more easily create images that are cross-platform in an 8-bit display environment.

Transition Cast Member

You can change only the Name and Load properties of a Transition cast member (see fig. 7.30). A transition Xtra might include options for a more customized look and information about the Transition Xtra cast member and its third-party developer.

Figure 7.30

The Transition Cast Member Properties dialog box.

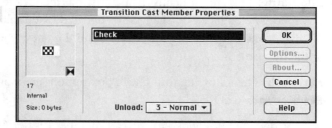

Digital Video Cast Member

Digital videos can be either QuickTime movies (on Macintosh or Windows) or AVI movies (in Windows). These are the files that provide high-quality video animation combined with sound.

The dialog box for the property of a digital video cast member is quite large (see fig. 7.31). You can give a considerable amount of control to a digital video within the Cast Member Property dialog box. In addition to the basic information, such as cast name and file size, the running time of the digital video you select appears at the left side of the dialog box.

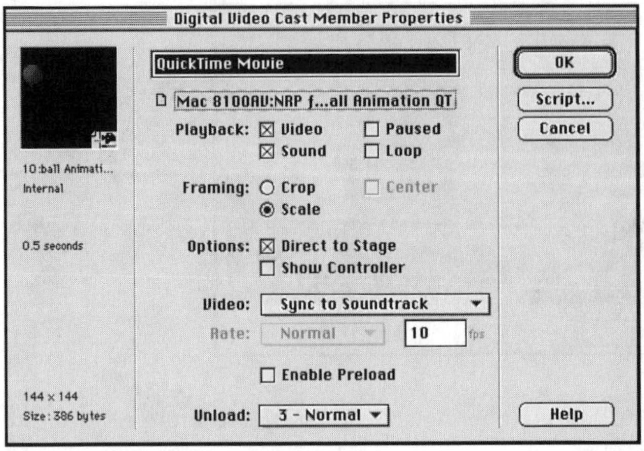

Figure 7.31

The Digital Video Cast Member Properties dialog box.

Figure 7.31

The Digital Video Cast Member Properties dialog box.

Remember that digital videos are always linked to a Director movie. When you transfer a Director project from place to place, the digital video must travel with the project.

The following options can be accessed in the Digital Video Cast Member Properties dialog box:

▶ **File name:** This area contains the path name (the location of the cast member). The path can be changed or updated by double-clicking on the file name box and selecting the movie again. The new path will be visible in the file name box.

▶ **Playback:** The following four check box options are available in the Playback Area set:

   ▶ **Video:** Sets the video of the cast member ON or OFF.

   ▶ **Sound:** Sets the sound of the cast member ON or OFF.

   ▶ **Paused:** Causes the movie to wait until either a Lingo script begins the video playback or, if it is available, the Play button is clicked on the controller.

   ▶ **Loop:** The digital video cast member will play over and over.

▶ **Framing:** The framing area of the digital video cast member properties adjusts how the user may manipulate the image on-screen.

   ▶ **Crop:** Areas around the outside of the image are trimmed off. This does not affect the image.

- ▶ **Scale:** Enables you to change the size of the digital video image on the stage. This effect can distort the sprite from its original size.

- ▶ **Center:** Keeps the scaled or cropped digital video centered inside its frame.

▶ **Options:** The Options check boxes deal with how the digital video cast member behaves with other sprites and user input on-screen. The available options are as follows:

- ▶ **Direct to Stage:** Using the Direct to Stage option of a digital video cast member enables the digital video to play more efficiently. When Direct to Stage is not selected, Director must, in addition to playing the digital video, calculate the effect of any other sprites that might overlap the video. If another sprite covers half the digital video, Director must calculate what the resulting image combining the digital video and overlapping will look like. By enabling the Direct to Stage property, Director plays the digital video directly to the stage without bothering to calculate the effect that any other graphic could have on the video. Because it can play the digital video without worrying about layering other elements in front of the digital video, Director can more effectively deal with playing the frames of the digital video.

- ▶ **Show Controller:** QuickTime digital videos have an additional movie controller that can be enabled if the Direct to Stage option is enabled. This controller enables the user to start, stop, pause, and step the movie forward and backward within a running project by displaying a control bar at the bottom of the digital video cast member.

▶ **Video:** The video options adjust how the digital video cast member plays back on-screen. The options are as follows:

- ▶ **Sync to Soundtrack:** This option plays the video and its contained sound at normal speed.

- ▶ **Play Every Frame (No Sound):** In normal playback of a digital video, frames are dropped to keep up with the sound, a normal occurrence for a slower computer. Play Every Frame plays every frame of the video, but no sound is heard. The video can now be played at different speeds. Normal is the speed of the video at time of capture. Maximum plays the video as fast as the computer is capable. Fixed enables you to set how fast the video plays back (to the maximum).

▶ **Enable Preload:** The last check box for the digital video property options, Enable Preload, is used to load the selected digital video into memory all at one time. By default, digital videos load in small chunks for playback on all configurations of machines. This Enable Preload setting really speeds up the playback speed of the digital video movie.

The rest of the properties for digital video cast members are those common to all cast member types, as discussed earlier.

For more information on digital video cast members, see Chapter 12, "Digital Video: The Movie Within the Movie."

INSIDER TIP

Scaling is not the best thing to do with a digital video. Always try to retain a digital video's original proportions. This is very important for option viewing. Not only does scaling make the movie look bad, it also slows the computer's performance.

Script Cast Member

Within the properties of a Script cast member, you can change the type of script to a sprite script, movie script, or parent script (see fig. 7.32). These categories of scripts are explained in Chapter 16, "Lingo: The Basics."

Figure 7.32

The Script Cast Member Properties dialog box.

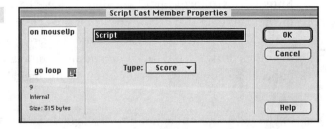

Building a Multiple Cast Project

The fastest way to learn Director 6 is to experience it. In this section, several tutorials walk you through the process of building an interactive project. The project uses multiple cast files, both internal and external, linked and unlinked. This project shows the convenience of using multiple cast files to quickly assemble interactive media projects.

You can find the demo for this exercise on the accompanying CD in the Chapter 7 folder.

INSIDER TIP

You might have heard this caveat many times before, but it always bears repeating: *Remember to save your work often.* If you save every two minutes, you can lose only two minutes of work. If you save every two hours, however, you can lose two hours of work.

First, copy the Chapter 7 folder from the CD to your hard disk.

Open the Chapter 7 folder and look at its contents. It should look like figure 7.33. The directory contains three Director movies: MCASTS1.DIR, MCASTS2.DIR, and LOCAL.DIR. The directory also contains two cast libraries and a "localize" directory that contains three cast libraries.

Figure 7.33

The contents of the Chapter 7 CD folder.

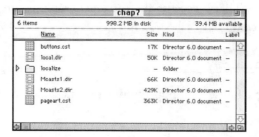

The MCASTS2.DIR movie is a finished version of the movie you are going to create from the MCASTS1.DIR movie.

Creating the Default Internal Cast Window

1. Open the file MCASTS1.DIR (the unfinished movie).

2. To open the score window, choose Score from the Window menu (Command+4 on Macintosh, Ctrl+4 in Windows).

   This score contains three frame markers, a go to the frame *script used three times and three text cast members associated with each of the three marker frames. The* go to the frame *script keeps the playback head from continuing to the next frame or marker until it is instructed to do so. The frame markers have been spaced apart to give some visual separation. The movie would play no differently if the markers were located one frame apart or one hundred frames apart.*

3. To open the Cast window, choose Cast from the Window menu (Command+3 on Macintosh, Ctrl+3 in Windows).

continues

Creating the Default Internal Cast Window   continued

4. To name the Default Internal Cast File, choose Cast Properties from the Modify menu.

5. Name the internal cast file "main content." Media elements will be added to this empty "main content" Cast window from other Cast windows.

6. To save the movie, choose Save from the File menu (Command+S on Macintosh, Ctrl+S in Windows).

You might notice that the go to the frame script does not appear in the main content cast library. That is because this movie is keeping score scripts in a separate internal cast library called Scripts.

Viewing the Scripts Internal Cast Library

1. Choose the Choose Cast pop-up menu of the active Cast window.

2. Select Scripts.

   You should now see the Scripts internal cast library with its one Script cast member.

Now it is time to add graphics to this movie by using a library of backgrounds and buttons that you have available. The advantage to having external libraries like this is that media and scripts placed in these external libraries can be used in other projects.

Adding Internal and External Cast Members

1. Choose Open from the File menu.

2. In the Open dialog box, select the PAGEART.CST cast.

   The PAGEART.CST cast library opens on top of the current cast member library. The color of the PAGEART.CST window is dark gray to identify it as an unlinked library. Make certain that main content internal cast library is visible (if it is not, follow the steps you took to view the Scripts library). Drag the PAGEART.CST Cast window to another location so that you can more easily view both windows. You are going to copy the two background images from the PAGEART.CST library to the main content internal cast library.

3. Drag the blue background (cast member 1) from the PAGEART.CST library to the cast 4 position of the main content cast library.

4. Drag the red background (cast member 2) from the PAGEART.CST library to the cast 5 position of the main content cast library.

5. Close the PAGEART.CST library by clicking on the Close Window button for the cast library window.

6. Make certain that the score to the movie is open (Command+4 on Macintosh, Ctrl+4 in Windows). Make certain that you have your sprite preferences in Director set so that the span duration for new sprites is only one frame. Otherwise, your score will look—and may behave—differently than the finished MCASTS2.DIR movie.

7. Drag the blue background (cast member 4) to channel 1 in frames 1, 10, and 20 (see fig. 7.34). Notice that by dragging the background on to the score, the image automatically centers on the stage.

Figure 7.34

Dragging the blue background from the Cast window to the score.

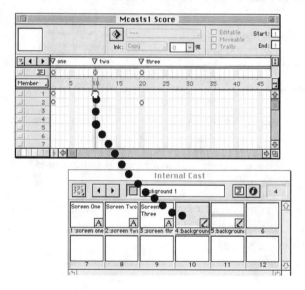

8. Drag the red background (cast member 4) to channel 2 in frames 1, 10, and 20 and align the red background bar so that it runs along the bottom of the stage in frames 1, 10, and 20.

Notice that a duplicate cast member is created in the main content cast library. Duplicate cast members are created when you drag a cast member from or to an unlinked cast library to a linked cast library.

You now have your background graphics for this movie. You still need some buttons, however, to help you navigate through the movie. Use the BUTTONS.CST cast library for your set of buttons in this movie.

Linking an Unlinked Cast Library to the Current Project

1. Open the cast library named BUTTONS.CST. Choose Open from the File menu and select BUTTONS.CST.

2. Drag the next button (cast member 1) to the lower-right corner of the stage in frame 1.

3. An alert dialog box appears stating that the BUTTONS.CST library is not yet linked. Choose to link the cast to the movie and click on the OK button (see fig. 7.35). (Notice that the cast library is already named Buttons.)

Figure 7.35

The Link Options dialog box for linking cast libraries or copying cast members.

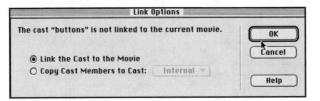

4. Follow steps 1 and 2 for the previous button (cast member 2), placing it in the lower-left corner of the stage in frame 1.

5. Using the score, copy and paste the previous and next buttons in frames 10 and 20.

6. This is a good time to save your work. From File, choose Save All. This action ensures that all changes to both internal and open external cast libraries are saved.

When you link the buttons library, notice that the Cast window changes from a dark gray to the color of a linked Cast window.

To make a cast window active, select the window. You can also select windows by choosing Cast from the Windows menu. You can try this now by selecting and closing the Buttons cast library from the previous tutorial.

To reopen an attached external cast file, choose Buttons from the Choose Cast pop-up menu in the current Cast window (see fig. 7.36). The Cast library reopens.

Figure 7.36

Reopening a closed cast library by using the Choose Cast pop-up menu.

Although your buttons are on the stage, they don't really do anything yet. You need to add behaviors to these buttons. To keep your behaviors from getting mixed up with your other scripts, keep them in a Behaviors cast library. A new internal cast library will be created to store incoming behaviors for the current project.

Creating an Additional Internal Cast Library

1. Select New Cast from the Choose Cast pop-up menu.

2. In the New Cast's dialog box, name the new cast library Behaviors.

3. Because you want this new cast library to be internal, enable the Internal radio button (see fig. 7.37).

Figure 7.37

Creating a new Cast library to hold behaviors.

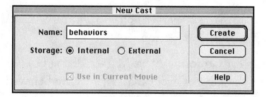

An internal cast library is part of the Director movie and cannot be viewed or selected on the hard drive the way you can an external cast library.

Macromedia ships Director with an external cast library of behaviors in the Xtras menu. You will copy two of these behaviors to your new internal Behaviors cast library.

Opening a Cast Library in the Xtras Menu

1. Select Behavior Library from the Xtras menu. This action opens the Macromedia Behaviors cast library.

2. Find the two behaviors: go to the next marker and go to the previous marker. They will be fairly easy to find because their cast member names are "go to the next marker" and "go to the previous marker."

continues

Opening a Cast Library in the Xtras Menu   continued

3. Drag each of these behaviors into the first two cast member positions of the internal Behaviors cast library.

4. Close the Behavior library's unlinked external cast library.

If you have general scripts, palettes, or other graphic elements that you use in most of your projects, you can store them in an external cast library and place the libraries in the Xtras directory of Director. Then you can easily access them through the Xtras menu.

To complete this sample project, you need to add these behaviors to your buttons.

Adding Behaviors to Cast Members

1. Move the playback head to frame 1 so that the Next and Previous buttons are visible on the stage.

2. Drag the go to the next marker behavior from the Cast window to the stage on top of the Next button.

3. A Parameters for Go to the Next Marker dialog box will appear asking you to name the kind of event that triggers the behavior. Choose MouseUp from the menu. That activates the behavior when you click and release the Next button.

   Although you won't see anything happen, you have just placed the behavior into the score for the channel that holds the Next button.

4. Repeat Steps 1–3 for frames 10 and 20. Then follow the same procedures for the Previous button and the go to the previous marker behavior.

5. Save your project, rewind it, and play it. If you click on the Previous and Next buttons, you should move to and from frames 1, 10, and 20.

Maybe during the production of the project, an unlinked cast file is linked and then needs to be removed. You will notice that there is an internal library of graphics, called Graphics, that you have not used at all. You might as well get rid of the internal cast library.

WARNING

Removing a cast library can be very dangerous if cast members are being used in the current movie. The cast members must first be transferred to another linked or internal cast library before removing the unwanted cast library. Removing a cast member library from a Director project also removes its corresponding sprites from the Score window. Removing a cast member library could remove hundreds of active sprites.

Unlinking the Linked Cast Member Library

1. Select Movie, Cast from the Modify menu.

2. In the Movie Casts dialog box, select the Graphics cast library.

3. Select the Remove button.

   An alert box appears, explaining the consequences of removing a cast with references to a movie. Because the cast member media was never used in the project, this alert box can be ignored. Also, if this were an external library and changes were made to the outgoing cast library, Director asks whether the cast library should be saved to disk.

4. Click on the OK button to remove the library.

5. Save your work.

   The cast library is now unlinked from the current movie and the Cast window closes.

Using Cast Libraries for Localization

Although unlinked external cast libraries are useful as databases for often-used media elements, linked external cast libraries can be used to easily localize software.

Localization of software refers to the tailoring of the operation graphics or text of software to a particular group of users. The most common type of localization is the release of software with Japanese, French, or German versions. Each version functions in the same manner. Some of the graphics and text are changed to enable greater ease of use by a user group.

Localization need not be restricted to considerations in language, however. Suppose that you are to create a kiosk application that gives directions to visitors in an amusement park. There will be 10 kiosks located at different locations. Depending on the location, the typical "you are here" maps will be different. Also the park owners might want a different color scheme for each of the kiosk locations.

One way to build the application is to build 10 different applications, keep track of which one got installed on which computer, and make certain that the park never switches the location of the kiosks.

A better solution, however, is to build one application with external cast libraries used for localization. The developer first identifies the items that change from location to location. These are maps and possibly background images. These items are then placed in external cast libraries. All these external cast libraries are installed on all kiosks.

After the kiosks are installed at their locations, a simple Director script can be run to set the active external cast for that location. This means that any of the kiosks can be used in any other location by changing the external cast library being used by the application.

To make this point better understood, open the LOCAL.DIR movie in the Chapter 7 directory on the accompanying CD.

If you run this movie, you will see a very simple three screen movie about Kirk Keller, similar to that shown in figure 7.38. Stop the movie and open the Cast window (Command+3 on Macintosh, Ctrl+3 in Windows). If you look at the Choose Cast pop-up menu in the Cast window, you see a series of internal casts similar to those in MCASTS2.DIR. In addition, you see a Localization library. Open this library.

Figure 7.38

A screenshot of the LOCAL.DIR movie localized for Kirk.

Five cast members are in the Localization library. These are media items particular to Kirk Keller. The Localization library is a linked external cast library called KIRK.CST, stored in the Localize directory.

Changing the Localization Library with Lingo

1. With the LOCAL.DIR movie open, open the Message window by selecting Message from the Window menu.

2. In the Message window type the line:

   ```
   localize "skippy"
   ```

3. Close the Message window.

Now look at the stage of the movie. It looks like the movie shown in figure 7.39. It has a color background and different buttons. Instead of seeing media associated with Kirk, you see media created by Skippy. Stop the movie and look again at the Localization library. Notice that it no longer has the media it did before. What has happened? The file that was linked as the Localization cast library has been changed from KIRK.CST to SKIPPY.CST.

Figure 7.39

A screenshot of the LOCAL.DIR movie localized for Skippy.

Changing the Localization Library in Director

1. Choose Cast Properties from the Modify menu. You can see that the file name for the Localization cast library is SKIPPY.CST.

2. Click on the file name shown in the Cast Properties dialog box.

continues

Changing the Localization Library in Director   continued

3. In the Find File dialog box, go into the Localize directory and select the KIRK.CST cast library.

4. Click on the OK button.

You should now have the old Localization library back.

When you typed in the Message window, you called a Lingo event handler stored in the Scripts cast library in cast member 1. The localize handler is as follows:

```
-- This handler will load the appropriate localized library.
on localize castlibrary
    if the machineType = 256 then
        set dirchar = "/"
    else
        set dirchar = ":"
    end if
    set the filename of castlib "localization" = the pathname &
    ➥"localize"&dirchar&castlibrary
```

The handler takes the name you type and then looks in the Localize directory for that cast library name. It then sets the file name of the Localization cast library to that file.

Notice that you did not have to type "KIRK.CST" in the localize handler, but just "KIRK". This is because Director recognizes the .CST extension and can call the handler without the extension.

The cast libraries used for localization need not be limited to those found on your hard drive or CD. With Director 6, cast libraries can be downloaded from the Internet. All that is needed is a web server to store the cast libraries and a connection to the Internet for the computer running the Director application. The web server must have the .CST file type added to its current MIME type table. For more information on this, see Chapter 14, "Creating Shockwave Movies."

Getting a Cast Library from the Internet

1. If you do not have the LOCAL.DIR movie open, open it again.

2. Make sure that your computer has a network connection to the Internet. If you typically dial up your access with a modem connection, do so now.

3. With the movie running, open the Message window, type the following command, and press Return:

```
set the filename of castlib "localization" = "http://www.grommett.com/
➥chap7/net.cst"
```

At this point, Director attempts to download this cast library from the Internet. If your computer is connected to the Internet with a T1 line, this should be rather quick. The library is 30K in size so with a 28.8 baud modem connection, it should take about 15 seconds.

4. Navigate through the movie to view the new media elements available through this Internet delivered cast library.

If you would like to try placing your own cast library on a web server, the cast library you just downloaded from the Internet is also available in the Localize directory. It is called NET.CST.

The possibilities for using external cast libraries are endless. You could build an application that uses cast libraries on a local hard drive or on a web server, based on user preference. If a user is running Windows, the application could load a directory of AVI files rather than QuickTime files.

When using external cast libraries for localization, however, you do need to be careful and plan ahead. Follow these steps:

▶ Determine which elements of the application need to be localized.

▶ Move those elements to a linked external cast.

▶ Use this external cast as a template for the creation of new localization cast libraries.

▶ Make certain to keep the order and naming of cast members the same in all localization cast libraries.

In Practice

Multiple cast member libraries can speed up the production time of a project. Scrolling around a Cast window with hundreds of elements can take quite a lot of time. Breaking the cast elements into smaller groups using multiple casts is much easier. Also, as projects are created, the cast library can be continually updated with new elements and shared with other members of a project team or network.

This chapter completes Part II of this book, covering the structure of Director and the basics of working with it. The next chapter, "Graphics: The Visuals," begins Part III, which looks at each of the major multimedia components of Director on a chapter-by-chapter basis.

When working with casts, keep in mind these practical approaches:

▶ Consider whether internal or external cast libraries are more appropriate for your project. Advantages of external cast libraries include the fact that they do not increase the size of your project and they can be updated outside the parent movie. The disadvantage is that they must be kept in a place where the Director movie can find them. If external cast libraries are placed in the wrong directory when distributed with a Director application, the application is not able to find and load them.

▶ Consider using multiple internal libraries, organized by purpose, so that they are easier to find and manage.

▶ Use the Unload option in the Properties dialog box for cast members to manage memory. Set the option to unload seldom-used cast members when you no longer need them.

▶ Use linked external cast libraries for localization—tailoring of a project to various users.

▶ External cast libraries need not be distributed on CD or diskette. Applications made in Director can access cast libraries on a web server. For this to work, the web server must support the .CST MIME type and the computer running the application must have a connection to the Internet.

PART

Director's Multimedia
Components

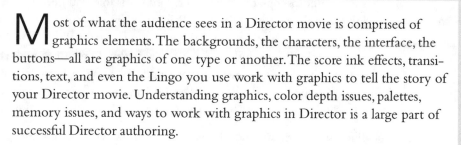

chapter **8**

Jay Armstrong

Graphics: The Visuals

Most of what the audience sees in a Director movie is comprised of graphics elements. The backgrounds, the characters, the interface, the buttons—all are graphics of one type or another. The score ink effects, transitions, text, and even the Lingo you use work with graphics to tell the story of your Director movie. Understanding graphics, color depth issues, palettes, memory issues, and ways to work with graphics in Director is a large part of successful Director authoring.

Director has a built-in paint program for creating and editing graphics—the Paint window. This chapter explores basic graphics concepts, importing graphics into Director, and ways in which Director works with graphics.

Topics covered in this chapter include the following:

- ▶ Director and Photoshop
- ▶ Bitmapped graphics and palettes
- ▶ Importing graphics into Director
- ▶ Graphics sources
- ▶ Director 6 and graphics
- ▶ The Paint window
- ▶ Photoshop-compatible filter support
- ▶ Onion skinning

Director and Photoshop

Adobe Photoshop is the standard graphics editing tool on the market today. Most Director users are well-versed in Photoshop. Macromedia also has its own image-editing tool, xRes, which is distributed with the Director Multimedia Studio. xRes is marketed as a companion to Photoshop for quick editing of high-resolution images. No matter what other editing tools you like to use, at one point or another, you will need to use Photoshop, and possibly xRes, to create artwork for your Director movie.

Some people try to compare Director's Paint window to Photoshop. They ask why they should use Director's simple Paint window when powerful programs such as Photoshop are available. The answer is that you need the best tool for the job. You will use both. Director's Paint window is simple and easy for those new to creating computer graphics; the learning curve for Photoshop is much steeper. By using the Paint window, you can stay within Director to make a basic edit or create a simple graphic, without exiting to Photoshop. Just select the cast member, open the Paint window, make the changes, and away you go. Making the same changes in Photoshop takes a great deal longer to accomplish.

Photoshop users and most Director users know why they choose to use Photoshop. While Director's Paint window works well for creating simple sharp edges and creating artwork for animations, Photoshop provides specialized functions such as image layers, special effects, and anti-aliasing. If you were to scan hundreds of images for a Director movie, you would first edit those scans in Photoshop before bringing them into Director. Director is often used as a media-integrator rather than a media-creator for graphics, digital videos, and sounds.

Bitmapped Graphics and Palettes

All elements created in the Paint window or imported from an image editing application are bitmapped graphics—"just a bunch of pixels." A *pixel* is the smallest element that can be viewed on-screen. These pixels are clustered in groups to create areas of color—your graphics.

The colors used in a graphic with an 8-bit color depth and below are contained in palettes. A *palette* is a table of colors stored in the computer color look up table (CLUT). These tables can be as small as 1 bit.

▶ A 1-bit palette contains only black-and-white pixels.

▶ A 4-bit palette contains 16 colors. On the Macintosh, you can customize these 16 colors. In Windows, you can only use one 16-color palette, the

Microsoft VGA palette. If you are making your Director movie for a 4-bit machine and intend to distribute it cross-platform, you will want to use the Windows VGA palette.

▶ An 8-bit color palette contains 256 colors. This palette contains black, white, a small range of grays, and a general selection of basic colors. You can customize an 8-bit palette on both the Macintosh and Windows. Director ships with a number of built-in 8-bit palettes. You also can import custom 8-bit palettes into your Director movie with images that use them, or on their own in the standard palette format (PAL). They are then stored as cast members.

▶ The 16-bit, or thousands of colors, color depth contains 65,536 colors. This color depth was created to closely match the color values of a normal television set. This color depth does not have a palette associated with it.

▶ The 24/32-bit, or millions of colors, color depth contains 16,777,216 colors. This is the maximum numbers of colors that can be viewed on a computer monitor. This number is actually overkill because a person with normal vision can only perceive about nine million colors. This color depth does not have a palette associated with it.

NOTE

The notation 24/32 may seem a bit odd. The 32 refers to total bits of information—24 bits for everyday colors and 8 bits that deal with alpha channel information or other special effects. You can't, however, work in 24 bits; when someone says 24-bit he is actually referring to a 32-bit resolution.

In deciding what color depth to use, keep in mind that the fewer colors used in the images, the faster your animation plays. Director has a lot to keep track of in addition to color at any given moment: Each frame in a movie can contain up to 120 channels of graphics information, and Director can run up to 120 frames per second. Not only does Director have to deal with showing 120 channels, 120 times per second, but it also has to dispose of the information. This process is taxing on machines of any speed. For these reasons, when designing your graphics, always try to create and work with them in the smallest color depth.

If you edit an image to an 8-bit palette or less, it uses either one of the system palettes or its own custom palette. The problem is that monitors set to 8-bit color can only display one palette at a time, so everything on the stage must use the same palette. Switching between palettes and managing multiple palettes can be difficult in large projects. Chapter 5, "Working with Director 6:

Understanding the Metaphor," mentions several techniques for dealing with multiple palettes, including developing an aggregate palette with the colors used by all of your images, using Fade to Black or Fade to White, and using Lingo's puppetPalette command.

Importing Graphics into Director

One of the new features of Director 6 is support for more bitmapped image formats in addition to the files used by Director 5. Those image formats include the following:

- ▶ **BMP:** A common Windows graphic format.
- ▶ **GIF:** A format originally used by CompuServe known as the Graphic Interchange Format.
- ▶ **JPEG:** Defined by the Joint Photographers Experts Group as a high-quality compressed image format.
- ▶ **LRG:** The native format of Macromedia's xRes image editor.
- ▶ **Photoshop:** The native format of Adobe Photoshop.
- ▶ **MacPaint:** An older Macintosh image format.
- ▶ **PNG:** Portable Network Graphics format.
- ▶ **PICT:** Originally defined for the Apple Lisa computer, now a standard Macintosh image format.
- ▶ **Targa:** Also known as the .TGA format. Targa was the name of the Truevision graphics card that first used the .TGA format.
- ▶ **TIFF:** Tag Image File Format.
- ▶ **PAL:** The standard Windows 8-bit palette format.
- ▶ **Microsoft Palette:** Microsoft's own palette format.

Director supports these new formats via Xtras. Director's Xtras folder contains an Xtra for each image format that Director 6 supports. This support enables the addition of new formats without an entirely new version of Director. (For more information on Xtras, see Chapter 21, "The Xtra Step.")

Director for Windows imports a number of graphics file formats in addition to those in the preceding list. These formats are Photo CD, Windows Metafile, .PCX (an older DOS image format), and PostScript files. Upon import,

Director gives you the choice of handling the file internally so that both Macintosh and Windows can read it, or of retaining the image's native format data for use by external image editors that may be launched from within Director.

Many people wonder why Director doesn't accept Encapsulated PostScript (EPS) files. Actually, Director 6 for Windows can import EPS and retain the original file data. Director 6 for Macintosh cannot, although this may change in future revisions. EPS is used for printing to PostScript printers at varying resolutions without losing quality.

The three things to remember when creating and importing graphics— regardless of the application in which they were created—are anti-aliasing, resolution, and bit depth.

Anti-Aliasing

Anti-aliasing refers to a group of computer techniques used to blend or blur the jagged edges of bitmapped graphics. Anti-aliasing is applied to cure the problem of jagged edges and make bitmapped elements look more like continuous photographic images. Unfortunately, the cure sometimes causes other problems: An anti-aliased graphic has a fuzzy edge surrounding it.

Assume, for example, that you create a circle graphic in Photoshop. The circle is red with a white background. If you look closely at the graphic, the edge on the circle is comprised of pink pixels where the circle touches the white background. This is the anti-aliased edge. Save the file as a PICT and import it into Director.

If the red cast member is placed on to the stage with a white background, the pink edge blends into the Director background with no problem. But if you create a black background, things are going to change a little. The pink anti-aliased edge of the red circle glows pink against the black background, creating a halo.

If the red circle/white background is not going to move during your movie, you might not notice the halo. But if the circle is to move about your stage and pass over other sprites of different colors, the halo will become more noticeable.

To avoid the halo when working in a painting program such as Photoshop, be certain to turn off the anti-aliased features of the tool you are using. If the graphic has already been created, use a selection tool with its anti-aliased or feathering features turned off before copying or cutting and pasting it into Director.

To edit the halo effect within Director, you can use the Switch Color tool in the Paint window. The Switch Color tool is helpful in removing unwanted pixels from an 8-bit graphic. With it, you can select the unwanted colors within an exact area and swap them with pixels of another color, including white. The Switch Color tool is covered in more detail later in the Paint Window section of this chapter.

INSIDER TIP

Another way to avoid the halo effect is to create a hard-edged image in Director's Paint window "from scratch," rather than importing an anti-aliased graphic. A colored circle, for example, is extremely simple to create in Paint. Most of your images, however, will be more complicated than a circle. For something as complex as a human body or face or a company logo, you need to create the image or scan it from elsewhere, and work on the halo effect in Photoshop before importing the image into Director.

Resolution

One of the joys of using Director is finding out how many ways something can be done. People try to solve problems in so many ways, and even though some of these solutions don't work, it is still great to witness all of them. Most instructors wish they had a dollar for every time they have heard this one: "I saved the file at 144 dpi so that it would look better, but the file comes in too big. Why?"

Saving a file at 144 dpi will not make the file twice as good, only twice its actual size. A 2×2-inch image saved at 144 dpi in a paint program *always* imports as a 4×4-inch image in a Director file. To understand the reason why, you need to understand the relationship between resolution and image size.

Image Size

A Director movie is an on-screen, multimedia experience and works in screen resolution only, or 72 dots per inch (dpi). The phrase "dots per inch" comes from the printing world and refers to the sharpness of an image. Lower-dpi images look poorly focused when printed, and higher-dpi images look razor-sharp. When you think of the monitor always being 72 dpi, this means that if the image on the monitor were printed out on paper at 72 dpi, it would look poorly focused. This is also why diagonal lines on-screen often look slightly jagged.

Monitors with a lower resolutions display larger pixels (fewer *pixels* per inch) and monitors with a higher resolution display smaller pixels (more pixels per inch). A file set to 640×480 pixels, therefore, stays the same dimensions in pixels, but those pixels, and thus the image will be smaller or larger depending on the monitor's resolution setting. In other words, an image that is 640×480 pixels will fill the entire screen when it is also set to 640×480 resolution, but will only fill the center 50 percent of the screen if it were set to twice that resolution (1280×960).

The resolution of a Director file is *always* 72 dpi—not 72 dpi for graphics and 300 dpi for photographs. Photographers, graphic designers, and film people have the most trouble with this concept. They are accustomed to thinking in terms of a variety of dpi settings, 600 to 1200 dpi for high-end printers such as Iris and Splashes, and 150 lpi (lines per inch) linescreens for printing presses at the local print shop. To them, 72-dpi images are low-resolution images. But because monitors are 72 dpi, that's the standard to know and love. In fact, images saved at 72 dpi look great for computer presentations.

When changing an image size, the application doing the scaling must add or remove pixels to the image.

When enlarging an image, the computer looks at two adjoining pixels and creates a new one to match the original two. This made-up pixel causes the image to look out of focus. When reducing an image, the program removes pixels and the image stays fairly sharp.

The moral of the story: Try to scan, create, edit, and save the image at the size it will be used in the presentation if possible. Reducing an image is generally acceptable, but enlarging an image is going to present a problem.

Color Mode

One major concern of a Director author is the file size of the Director movie. Graphics are what make the file size larger.

One trick to cutting down on the size of graphic cast members is a technique you can use in Photoshop or xRes. When editing an image, make certain that you save the image in Indexed Color mode. Typically, your image is in RGB mode when it is scanned or acquired elsewhere. One graphic could take up more than 500 KB. In Photoshop, if you save the image in Indexed Color mode, one indexed color replaces the R (red), G (green), and B (blue) color values associated with each pixel. The file size of the image reduces from 500 KB to 77 KB with a single command.

Color Depth

The *color depth* is the amount of color available in a graphic file. It is not the amount of color used to make the graphic, but rather, the number of choices of available colors in the palette, or the range of colors. You could, for example, draw a black-and-white happy face picture. Even though the artwork is black and white, the color depth of the file could be 24/32 bits (millions of colors).

Figure 8.1 shows the bitmap cast member properties of two identical files, one saved in 1 bit (black and white), the other file saved in 24/32 bit (millions of colors.) The 1-bit image is 2.4 KB in size; the 24/32 bit image is 75 KB—a substantial difference. This difference could be critical when trying to develop a project that has to fit on a floppy or when you have a CD too full to place just two more small images on. When importing an image from another program, such as Photoshop, the image should have its color depth set before the import takes place.

Figure 8.1

The same cast member imported with two different color depths and their subsequent kilobyte differences.

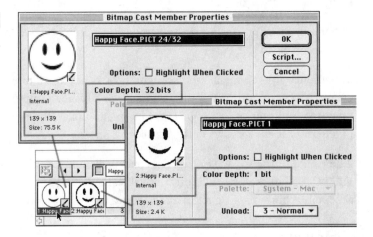

Director 6 supports the editing of multiple color depths in the Paint window. This means that your monitor can be set to millions of colors and you can edit in 256 colors, or vice versa. When finished, you can open another graphic of a different color depth and edit that graphic as well, without switching the resolution of your monitor or the graphic.

Working in multiple color depths adds flexibility to the Director editing session. When an image is imported into Director and the image color depth does not match the project's stage color depth, Director asks how to import the image (see fig. 8.2). The color-depth mismatch alert box provides added control over the way each image is handled. You can save hours of switching between tools and re-editing graphics with this capability. You can either keep the image as is or sample it up or down to match the project's color depth.

Figure 8.2

The import options for an incoming image that does not match the screen depth of the current project.

INSIDER TIP

The project bit depth is the setting of the monitor in the Macintosh's Monitors control panel in the System folder (see fig. 8.3). On Windows machines, the Display control panel is used. Anytime an image is imported, Director checks the settings of the monitor and gives you the option of the bit depth that the incoming image can be—either the setting of the incoming image or the setting of the monitor.

Even though Director is capable of converting one bit depth to another, this task is best handled by the program that created the graphic.

Figure 8.3

The monitor settings in the Monitors control panel.

Graphic Sources

Besides creating your own graphics for a Director project, you can use graphics from at least two other sources: scanned images and stock photography and imagery.

Scanned Images

Assume, for example, that you are not too keen on painting or drawing or that you would like to use a group of photographs you have shot. Media elements don't have to be drawings; scanned images can be imported as well. Scans, too, are bitmapped images. Layered photos with text effects overlaid can make an impressive presentation. A scanned image can be helpful for digitizing your company logo. A black-and-white cartoon could be scanned and then electronically colored.

Because a scan is a bitmapped image, the image can be modified just like any other image, using filters and effect options. Consider this example of a creative use of scanned images. A student needed a woodgrain pattern for an interactive project. After rolling his computer table over to a heavy pitted wooden door and hitting the scan button, he quickly held the scanner up to the door and scanned the surface. Not only did the project turn out well, but the story that goes along with the project always causes a second look at the file.

INSIDER TIP

Scan photographs at a resolution of 100 dpi. Previously in this chapter, it was discussed that 72 dpi is the correct resolution, but for the best-looking scans, scan the photo at a resolution of 100 dpi. Set the scanner to scale the image to the size it will be in the project. Save the scan and import the file into Photoshop. In Photoshop, select Image Size from the Image menu and change the resolution to 72 dpi. Scanned photos look better when the resolution is modified in Photoshop as opposed to setting the scanner to scan at 72 dpi. Scanning at higher than 100 dpi does not produce a discernible gain in image quality.

Stock Photography and Clip Art

If you don't like to draw or paint and you don't have a scanner, many services, such as Image Club Digital stock photography from Adobe, provide stock photography. Here you can buy a CD full of images such as sunsets, skies, weather, or textured backgrounds. Image Club offers dozens of CDs from which to choose. Each disk contains approximately 100 ready-to-use images that can be easily copied and pasted into your project. Remember to adhere to applicable copyright agreements for each image.

If you are looking for clip art, you will find volumes of clip art CD-ROMs in any software store. Be certain to check the licensing agreements on the clip art before using it in a Director movie you intend to distribute. Many companies publish royalty-free clip art you can use.

Director 6 and Graphics

Following is a list of how Director uses graphics and all cast members. This list is a review for experienced users, but some of the terminology has been changed with Director 6. When working with graphics and other media elements, it is often necessary to review the basic functionality of Director. This way, when lost in your Lingo code, you can remember where you are and to what you are referring. For those of you new to Director, the following can be a good way to learn how Director works.

1. When a graphic is created or imported into Director it becomes a cast member.

2. Cast members are stored in the Cast window. (Basically, the Cast window is a database of all the media elements used in the movie.)

3. For Director to use these media elements, the cast members are placed on the stage.

4. When a cast member is placed on the stage, it appears as a sprite in the Score window.

5. A sprite on the stage also appears as a span across cells in the Score window (see fig. 8.4). The main terminology change in Director 6 has to do with the way sprites are represented in the score. Sprites that occupy more than one frame of a given channel are said to "span" those frames and are called *spans*.

Figure 8.4

In the Score window, cells are where frames and channels meet.

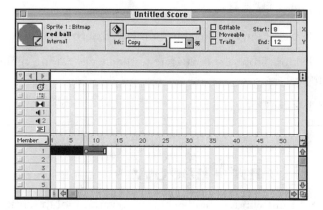

6. Animation is achieved by adding and removing graphics from cells and advancing the playback head at a high speed.

Director 6 offers a major new feature: the capability not only to import a variety of image formats, but also to launch the image editor of your choice for each format by double-clicking on the cast member in the Cast window. When you specify an editor for an image format in the Editors Preferences dialog box, Director retains the data used by that editor to define layers and other special characteristics (see fig. 8.5). When the user launches the external editor, Director sends the original image data to the editor, enabling characteristics to remain intact and editable. This integration can save lots of time that would otherwise be spent re-importing files after each change or update. The following tutorial shows how to choose an image editor for a particular format.

Figure 8.5

The Editors Preferences dialog box.

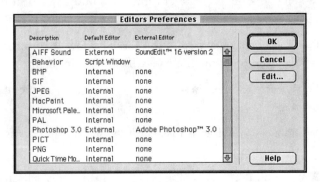

Selecting and Opening an Image Editor

1. Select Editors from the Preferences pop-up menu in the File menu.

2. Click on the format for which you want to define an editor in the scrolling list.

3. Click on Edit, and then click on Use External Editor.

4. Click on Browse and navigate to the image-editing application you want to use.

5. Click on Open and then on OK.

The Director 6 Paint Window

Director's Paint window has become a powerful tool for creating and editing media for animation. It includes an extensive tool palette and function buttons, manageable text options, rulers, unlimited filters, and onion skinning (see fig. 8.6). These features have given Director authors reason for using the Paint window much more often for media creation and editing. This section covers all the Paint window's features, giving you a solid background in the functionality of each part of the Paint window.

Figure 8.6

Director's Paint window.

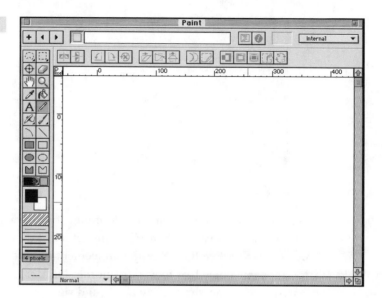

This section covers the following features of Director's Paint window:

- ▶ Tool palette
- ▶ Gradient selector area
- ▶ Color selection chips
- ▶ Pattern selector area
- ▶ Line weight settings
- ▶ Paint ruler
- ▶ Effects toolbar
- ▶ Cast information

Tool Palette

The following sections describe Director 6's Paint tools. The best way to understand the selection tools is to experiment with each one. You might want to have a sample image on-screen and try applying each tool to it as you read the descriptions. Note that if an arrow appears in the lower-right corner of a tool, you can click on the tool to display a pop-up list of options (see fig. 8.7).

Figure 8.7

The Paint window tool palette.

Selection Tools

The two selection tools, the Lasso and the Marquee tool, offer you a choice of seven selection options between them. Clicking either of these tools invokes a pop-up menu selection (see fig. 8.8). After an element or part of an element is selected, it can be cut, copied, or moved to another location on the canvas. After you make a selection, the up, down, left, and right arrows on the keyboard move the selection one pixel in that arrow's direction.

Figure 8.8

Seven pop-up options are available between the Marquee and Lasso selection tools.

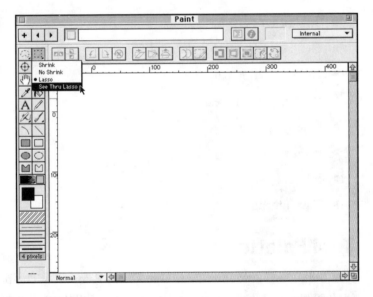

The seven options available with the Marquee and Lasso selection tools are as follows:

▶ **Marquee, Shrink:** On selection of an element, the selection marquee shrinks up to the outside edges of the artwork to create a rectangular selection. All white pixels contained within this selection are seen as opaque white.

▶ **Marquee, No Shrink:** On selection of an element, the selection marquee remains in the dragged position as a rectangular selection. All white pixels contained within this selection are seen as opaque white.

▶ **Marquee, Lasso:** On selection of an element, the color of the pixel where the drag was started and all same-colored touching pixels are ignored. All other colors within the selection are selected within a flat-sided selection. All white pixels contained within this selection are seen as opaque white.

▶ **Marquee, See Thru Lasso:** This option behaves the same as Marquee, Lasso except all white pixels contained within this selection are seen as transparent (no value).

▶ **Lasso, No Shrink:** The area drawn with the Lasso tool retains its shape and selects all its content. All white pixels contained within this selection are seen as opaque white.

▶ **Lasso, Lasso:** On selection of an element, the color of the pixel where the drag was started and all same-colored touching pixels are ignored. All other colors within the selection are selected within the drawn area. All white pixels contained within this selection are seen as opaque white.

▶ **Lasso, See Thru Lasso:** This option behaves the same as Lasso, Lasso, except that all white pixels contained within this selected area are seen as transparent (no value).

INSIDER TIP

Have you ever tried to select one colored item inside of another in Photoshop? It's not an easy task in Photoshop, but with Director's selection tools, the process is easy. Using either selection tool, with its pop-up option set to Lasso, drag around an object of one color within another colored object and release. Like magic, you have a selected color within another.

Registration Point Tool

A *registration point* is a set position within a cast member. By default, the registration point is set to the center of a newly created, imported, or pasted cast member, but you can change the position of the registration point (see fig. 8.9). Either way, the registration point is used to align the cast member with other cast members on the stage.

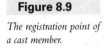

Figure 8.9

The registration point of a cast member.

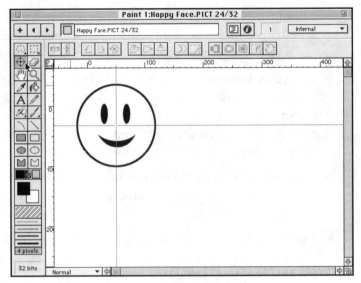

To create the spinning hands of a clock, for example, you need to create multiple clock hand sprites, each showing a different position relative to the clock face. To align each sprite for animation purposes, the registration point is placed at the pivot point of each of the clock hand cast members. Note that the pivot point in this case is not the default, center position of the cast member. Then, the Cast to Time command in the Score menu aligns all the hands to a central location on the stage. See Chapter 6, "Director as an Animator" for further explanation of this process. If you move a registration point from its default position, you can reset it to the center of a cast member by double-clicking on the Registration tool.

Eraser Tool

This one-size-fits-all tool does one thing—it gets rid of whatever it has drawn over. Actually, it changes the colors it touches on the canvas to white. Double-clicking on the Eraser tool removes all the art contained on the canvas, not just the viewable area.

INSIDER TIP

For erasing a relatively broad area, the block shape of the Eraser tool works well. But for erasing fine lines or even individual pixels, the Paintbrush tool or another small-tipped tool set to white is easier to work with than the Eraser tool.

Hand Tool

The Hand tool is used to move around artwork in the Paint window. As you use the Hand tool, the scroll bars at the top and right sides of the Paint window update to show where the artwork is in relation to the window frame.

INSIDER TIP

Pressing the spacebar invokes the Hand tool even with another tool selected in the Tool palette. This enables you to quickly move selections in the Paint window without switching tools. For obvious reasons, this technique does not work if the Text tool is selected.

It is possible to temporarily lose artwork in the Paint window, however, by dragging the artwork beyond the top or side rulers. Such positioning puts the artwork in a no-man's-land until the Paint window is closed and reopened or the Next or Previous cast member buttons are used to return to the lost cast member.

Zoom Tool

To get a closer look at your artwork, use the Zoom tool (magnifying glass). Starting at the actual size of the image, the Zoom tool doubles the magnification for each click of the mouse, up to 800 percent. Clicking on the upper-right actual size mini-window returns you to actual size. The Zoom features can also be accessed by using the Zoom submenu from the View menu.

INSIDER TIP

Another way to zoom is by pressing the Command key (Ctrl Key on Windows) and clicking the mouse. Pressing the Command or Ctrl and Shift keys while clicking the mouse zooms out from the artwork. These shortcuts help you to get a better look at your artwork without changing tools in the palette.

People new to the computer sometimes don't understand the difference between scale and magnify. The Zoom tool only changes the magnification of your view—the way you look at the artwork. The actual size of the artwork is not changed when you zoom in or out on an image. To change actual size, you must scale your artwork using the Transform Bitmap dialog box under the Modify menu, which allows you to actually resize a cast member. This is best reserved for scaling graphics downward.

Eyedropper Tool

The Eyedropper tool is a handy tool used to pick up a color used in a piece of art. The color under the eyedropper at the time of the mouse click is placed into the Foreground Color chip. This color becomes selected in the foreground color selector, enabling it to be used when creating new graphics elements.

Pressing the Option key while clicking on a colored pixel with the Eyedropper tool fills the Gradient destination color chip with the color under the clicked cursor (see fig. 8.10).

Figure 8.10

Clicking on a color with the Eyedropper tool while pressing the Option key causes the Gradient destination color chip to change.

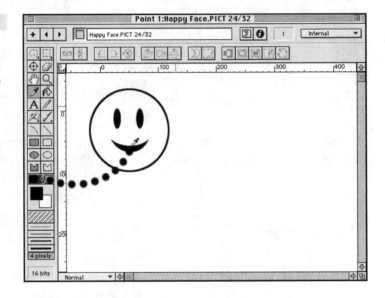

Paint Bucket Tool

Use the Paint Bucket tool to pour a color on to the canvas. First, select a color from the Foreground color chip, and click on the Paint Bucket tool. Then click on a pixel within the artwork; the pixel and all the pixels that touch it and have the same color change to the selected Foreground Color chip's color.

INSIDER TIP

The *hot spot* or *target spot* of the Paint Bucket tool is the tip of the pouring paint. Be careful: This hot spot is only three pixels in size and it is sometimes difficult to select the right pixel. Zooming in might help, or you might need to Undo if you click on the wrong pixel.

Text Tool

The Text tool is used to enter bitmapped text into the Paint window. Clicking on an area in the paint canvas with the Text tool creates a text box; here you can enter text from the keyboard to fill the selected area. As long as the box is active, the text can be modified.

With the text box active, double-click on the Text tool in the Tool palette and the Font dialog box appears (see fig. 8.11). Here, all the attributes of the text inside the active text box—such as font, size, and color—can be modified. Click on an area away from the active text box or select another tool from the Tool palette to deselect the text box.

The text entered into the Paint window is only text until it is deselected, at which point it becomes a bitmapped graphic. Be certain that the spelling is correct before deselecting the text.

Pencil Tool

One of the many great things about the Director Paint window is the simplicity of the tools. The Pencil tool draws only a one-pixel-thick line in the color of the Foreground Color chip. The word "only" used in the preceding sentence is not intended to be derogatory! Drawing a one-pixel line in Photoshop can be accomplished, but the line weight has to be set, the anti-aliasing has to be turned off, and the transparency has to be checked—not to mention a handful of other settings. Director enables you to draw a line, plain and simple.

Pressing the Shift key and dragging a pencil line constrains the line to a horizontal or vertical direction. The Pencil tool does not have a snap-to function; the Shift key must be depressed before the drag is started. Pressing the Shift key after the line is started yields no effect.

Air Brush Tool

The effect the Air Brush tool creates, at first, might not look like paint being sprayed out of an air brush. To get a very smooth spray, the pixels must be smoothed out or anti-aliased, something you generally don't want to do in a Director animation. The Air Brush tool can create some fun patterns despite its limitations. This tool has five fixed settings, ranging from small to large, and a custom setting dialog box to set up your own air brush pattern (see fig. 8.12). Click on the Air Brush tool to activate the pop-up menu. Choose Settings (or double-click on the Air Brush tool) to open the Air Brush Settings dialog box.

Figure 8.12

The Air Brush tool has five presets and a custom settings dialog box.

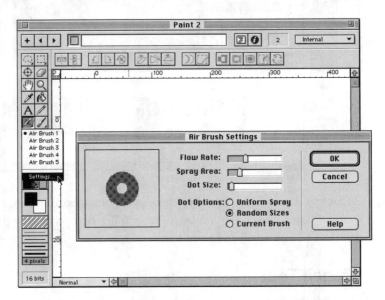

The following settings are available for the Air Brush tool.

- ▶ **Flow Rate:** How fast the paint comes out of the gun. The higher the setting, the more quickly the paint dots come out of the gun.

- ▶ **Spray Area:** How much area the dots can cover for each click of the mouse. If the mouse was to be clicked and held in one place for a period of time, the paint dots would fill the entire spray area.

- ▶ **Dot Size:** Size of the paint dots that hit the canvas.

Brush Options:

- ▶ **Uniform Spray:** Sprays an even amount of paint from the tool.

- ▶ **Random Sizes:** Paints dot of random sizes.

- ▶ **Current Brush:** Sets the paint dot to the shape of the Paintbrush tool. Double-click on the Brush tool to set this option.

Brush Tool

The Brush tool is for freehand drawing; it draws in the color of the Foreground Color chip. You can preset up to five brushes in the Paint window at any one time. Click on the Brush tool to select one of the five brushes. To adjust the settings for a brush, first select the brush you want to alter, and then select Settings from the list or double-click on the Brush tool. In figure 8.13, Brush 1 has been selected, and Settings has been selected to open up the Brush Settings dialog box.

Figure 8.13

The Brush tool has five presets and a dialog box which allows you to choose between standard and custom settings.

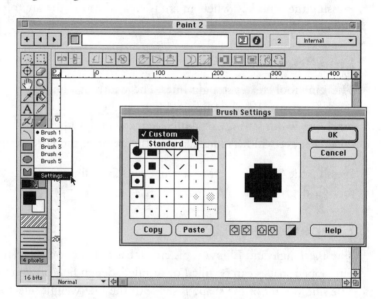

In the Brush Settings dialog box, you can choose one of the preset Standard brush tips. As shown in figure 8.13, these brush tips appear in a box on the left in the dialog box. You can also access the brush tips by clicking on the pop-up menu at the top of the dialog box to customize one of the Standard settings.

The palette of Standard brush settings is fully customizable via the Custom Brush Settings. With the Custom Brush Settings open, select an area outside the dialog box and a black-and-white image of what is under the cursor will be placed in the custom brush creation canvas, shown in the right-side box of the Brush Settings dialog box in figure 8.13.

Within the Custom Brush Settings dialog box, pixels can be added or removed from the enlarged brush creation canvas on the right of the dialog box. Pixels can be shuffled up, down, right, and left one pixel by using the move arrow buttons below the brush creation canvas. The pixels in the blown-up area can also be swapped or inverted: white to black or black to white. In addition, brushes can be copied to or from the clipboard.

Arc Tool

The Arc tool draws an arched line on the canvas the thickness of the line set in the line weight selection area of the Tool palette. The color of the line is the same as the Foreground Color chip.

Pressing the Shift key when an arc is created causes the arc to constrain to a circular radius.

Line Tool

The Line tool creates straight lines. The width of a line in the Paint window can be between 1 and 64 pixels. Click on the default one-, two-, and three-pixel line width settings, or double-click on the Other Line Width setting to select a larger width. A line takes on the color of the Foreground Color chip.

Pressing the Shift key before starting to draw a line causes the line to constrain to a 45-degree angle.

Shape Tools

The Rectangle and Ellipse tools create basic shapes on the canvas. These bitmapped shapes can be filled or unfilled, depending on which tool you select. The line weight of the shape is set with the line weight selectors and the fill color is set with the Foreground Color chip.

Pressing the Shift key as the bitmapped rectangle or ellipse is being created constrains the shape to square or circular, respectively.

The Polygon tools create both filled and outlined polygons. Each click you make on the Paint window with the Polygon tool becomes a corner of the desired shape. The shape can be finished by either double-clicking to close the shape or by clicking on the last position over the top of the first position.

Gradient Colors Settings

This cluster of three boxes sets the behavior of a gradient fill (see fig. 8.14).

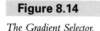

Figure 8.14

The Gradient Selector.

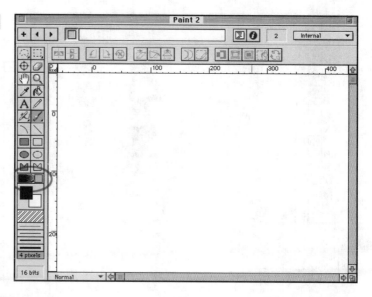

The box on the left sets the start color for the gradient. The box on the right sets the destination color for the gradient. The pop-up menu box in the middle sets the style of the gradient effect. Figure 8.15 shows the many combinations of gradations.

Figure 8.15

The many options of the Gradient Settings dialog box.

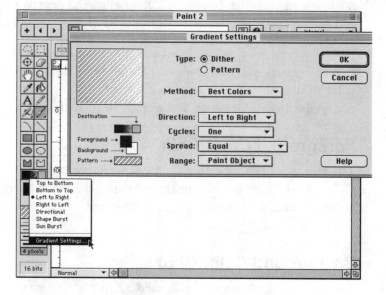

To set one of the tools in the Tool palette to fill with this gradient effect, choose a tool in the Tool palette, set the Paint window ink effect to Gradient, and either create a new element or recolor an existing element with a gradient fill (see fig. 8.16).

Figure 8.16

Setting the Paint Bucket to fill with a gradient fill.

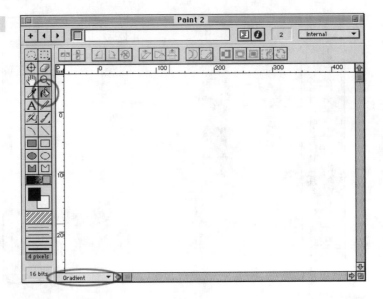

Color Selection Chips

Clicking on the mouse over the Foreground or Background Color chips pops up a selection of 256 colors. White is always the top-left chip and black is in the lower-right corner. To choose a color, click and drag to a preferred color and release. The color chip changes to this newly selected color.

Director's Paint window can draw from any of the 256 colors in the active palette. Corrections can be made to a 16- or 24-bit image in Director's Paint window, but only with its palette of 256 colors. If more colors are needed to correct the image, you must edit the image in another image editing application.

Foreground Color Chip

The Foreground Color chip is on the top left, overlapping the Background Color chip beneath it. The Foreground Color chip most often is used to set the colors of items, such as fills, lines, text color, and start location for a graduated fill effect.

Background Color Chip

The Background Color chip is located below and to the right of the Foreground Color chip. The Background Color chip is used in conjunction with the Pattern tool just below the color chip selection tools. Patterns are two colors. The background color chip is the background for the pattern. Note that as you change the background color selection, the background of the patterns in the pattern selector area change.

Pattern Selector Area

Patterns add texture to the fill of an image. Pattern styles in the Paint window range from very little to a lot of the background color showing through the foreground color. The pattern selector is helpful in creating a color effect when a limited color palette has to be used. The pattern selector has many options.

Patterns

Clicking and holding the pattern selector displays the Selector menu. Choose from a palette of 56 patterns and 8 tiles (see fig. 8.17). The pattern style with its corresponding foreground and background color is shown in the pattern selector. As the foreground and background color chips change, the pattern selector updates to show the new pattern colors. Custom patterns can be created by selecting Pattern Settings from the bottom of the pattern selector pop-up menu. The Pattern Settings dialog box enables the use and creation of custom and standard patterns.

Figure 8.17

The many choices of patterns in the Pattern selector.

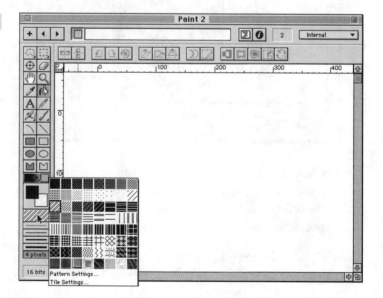

Tiles

Tiles are located on the bottom row of the pattern selector pop-up menu. You can select from eight colored tiles or define your own. Tiles are perfect when authoring for the Internet, where file size is an issue. They are 1 bit and take up little disk space.

Tiles are used as repeatable patterns for fills. The following tutorial shows how to create your own tile pattern.

Creating a Custom Tile

1. Create an image you would like to use for the tile and make it a cast member.

2. Choose Tile Settings from the pattern selector pop-up menu.

3. In the Tile Settings dialog box, select Cast Member for the source and click on the arrow keys until you find the cast member you created (see fig. 8.18).

Figure 8.18

The Tile Settings dialog box enables you to create custom tiles.

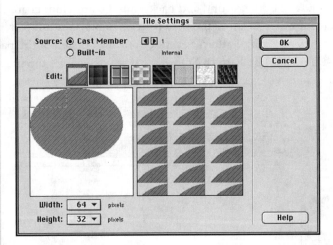

4. Click on the image to define the area for the tile. You can adjust the width and height of the selection in the pop-up menus at the bottom of the dialog box. You can also move the selection area to select a different area of the cast member. Click on OK.

5. Choose the tile you created from the Pattern Selector in the Paint window.

6. Click the filled ellipse tool and drag out an oval. It should be filled with the pattern you just created.

The new tile you create replaces one of the default tiles. If you delete the cast member you used for the tile, the tile is removed from the Tile palette and replaced with the default tile.

Line Weight Settings

Select from one of the four preset line weights in the Paint window. The line weight is applied to any nonfilled element created in the window. Double-click on the fifth button in this series, the "Other" Line Width button, to open the Paint Window Preferences dialog box. Here, you can define the line width from 1 to 64 pixels (see fig. 8.19). The "Other" Line Width setting retains its setting until you change it in the Paint Window Preferences again.

Figure 8.19

To preset a heavy line in the Paint window, double-click on the "Other" Line Width button and adjust the line's thickness in the Paint Window Preferences dialog box.

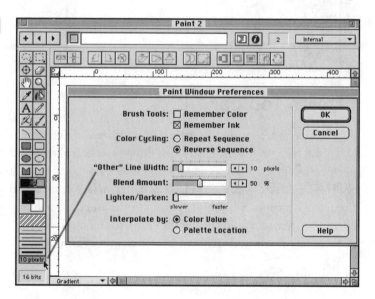

Paint Ruler

With the Paint window open and active, choose Rulers from the View menu to activate the Paint window rulers. Click on the upper-left corner where the rulers meet to change the type of measurements. The display changes between Inches, Centimeters, and Pixels. To assist in accurate editing, dotted lines follow your mouse on both the Rulers as you move it around the Paint window (see fig 8.20).

Figure 8.20

Turning on the Paint Window Rulers.

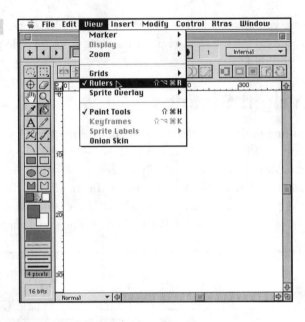

Effects Toolbar

All the effects are located in their own toolbar in Director 6's Paint window. With the click of a button, you can flip an image, rotate it, warp it, apply perspective, invert it, darken and lighten its colors, and much more (see fig. 8.21). The effects become available when a valid selection is made with one of the selection tools. A button is grayed out if an effect will not work with the current selection. The smoothing button, for example, is only available when an 8-bit object is selected; 16- and 24-bit elements cannot be smoothed.

Having the effects in a toolbar gives you quick access to them and automatic feedback to the effect you make.

▶ **Flip:** The grouped Flip Horizontal and Flip Vertical tools flip a selected element across a horizontal or vertical axis.

▶ **Rotate:** Selected elements can be rotated 90 degrees clockwise or counterclockwise. The Free rotate tool enables the selected element to rotate freely around its center. The selection places handles on each of the element's corners. Drag these handles to a new position to produce the rotation.

Figure 8.21

The Paint window toolbar holds all the effects tools.

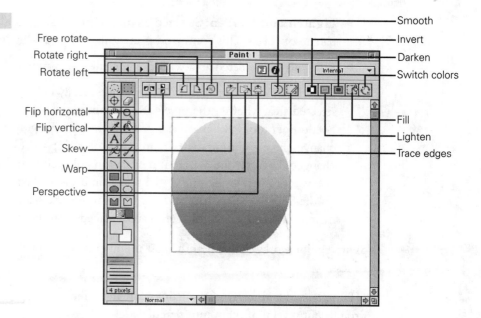

▶ **Distort:** The next three buttons can create interesting effects. The Skew tool skews selected elements by slanting the sides of an element equally, leaving the top and bottom of the element perpendicular to one another. The Warp tool enables handles of the selected element to be pulled around to create a smashed or twisted effect. Last, the Perspective tool shrinks or expands the edges of the selected element to give the illusion of depth.

▶ **Smooth:** This enables smoothing of pixels within a selected area of artwork. The smoothing effect functions only when the bit depth of the cast member is set to 8 bits.

▶ **Trace Edges:** This creates a new 1-pixel thick line around the edges of the original pixels of the artwork, leaving the original pixels white.

The last group of buttons in the effects toolbar deals more with the color of a selection rather than the shape or orientation of it.

▶ **Invert:** When clicked on, Invert causes the selection to change its black pixels to white and white pixels to black. Colors in the active 8-bit palette flip to the opposite side of the palette. To see the exact place a color occupies in a palette, open the Color Palettes window from the Window menu. If an image has a color depth higher than 8 bit, the Invert button replaces the colors with their RGB complement colors.

▶ **Lighten and Darken:** Selected elements grow lighter or darker in its palette of colors. This command is unavailable in a 16-bit color space.

▶ **Fill:** Fills any selected area with the current foreground color or pattern.

▶ **Switch Colors:** Changes the color of identically colored pixels in a selected area, whether the pixels are touching each other or not. Use the Eyedropper tool to click on the color within the image you want to change, thereby setting the Foreground Color chip to color to be changed. Then set the Gradient destination color chip to the new color you want to use. Using one of the selection tools, make a selection. Click on the Switch Colors tool and any pixels inside the selected area that match the foreground color chip are replaced with the destination color.

Switch color works only when the cast member is set to a palette of 256 colors or less.

Having considered many of the Paint tools and effects individually, now it is time to put several of them into practice.

Applying Paint Tools and Effects

To try out the previous effects, follow these steps:

1. Launch Director 6 and open the Paint window by pressing Command+5 on the Macintosh or Ctrl+5 on Windows.

2. Select the Air Brush tool to the left of the Brush tool (see fig. 8.22).

3. Select Cycle from the inks at the bottom of the Paint window.

4. Choose a wide range of colors for the start and end colors of the Gradient Colors and spray ink in the window.

5. Double-click on the Marquee tool. Doing so selects the entire bitmap.

   If you would like to erase the entire image in the Paint window, press the Delete key after you have selected it with the Marquee tool, or double-click on the Eraser tool.

6. In the Paint window toolbar, click on the Invert button. Flip the image with the Flip Horizontal or Flip Vertical button, warp it, and darken it.

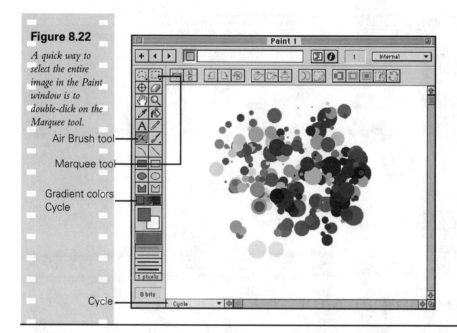

Figure 8.22

A quick way to select the entire image in the Paint window is to double-click on the Marquee tool.

Air Brush tool

Marquee tool

Gradient colors
Cycle

Cycle

Congratulations! You have successfully made programmer art. Now you are ready to apply these same effects to the real art for your project.

Cast Information

To help you work with multiple casts, Director 6's Paint window displays the cast of which the active graphic is a part in the top-right corner of the window (see fig. 8.23).

To create a graphic for another cast, make certain that cast is selected in the Cast pop-up menu of the Paint window. Then, any new graphics cast member you create is placed in that cast. Of course, the cast must already exist before you can select it in the pop-up menu. For information on creating a new cast and on multiple casts, refer to Chapter 7, "Multiple Casts."

To view the bitmap members of a particular cast one-by-one in the Paint window, make certain that the cast you are interested in is active in the Cast pop-up menu. If you would like to display the graphics of a different cast, choose that cast from the pop-up menu and one of the graphics in the new cast appears.

Figure 8.23

The top of the Paint window helps keep track of which cast you are working with by displaying the current cast name.

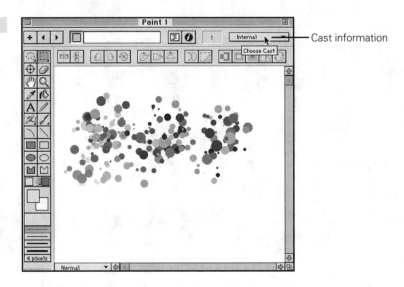

Cast information

Photoshop-Compatible Filter Support

An important element of Director's Paint window is its Photoshop-compatible filter support. Filters are effects that can be applied to image data. When the effect is applied, the image is said to have been filtered. The Macromedia Open Architecture (MOA) enables Director to open its architecture to third-party Photoshop-compatible filters. Hundreds of filters are available on the market, including the following:

▶ Andromeda's Series 1 Circular Multiple Images and Series 2 Three D Filter

▶ The Human Software Company, Inc.'s Squizz

▶ MetaTools Inc.'s Kai's Power Tools

▶ Multimedia Marketing GmbH's HoloDozo

▶ Xaos Tools' Paint Alchemy, Terrazzo, and TypeCaster

The filters are accessed by the Photoshop Filters Xtra, which communicates to Director through MOA. Filter support enables developers to update, edit, and create special effects directly in the Paint window.

Installing Photoshop-Compatible Filters

To have a Photoshop-compatible filter appear in Director 6's Xtras menu, Director must first find it or a reference to it in its Xtras folder.

Place the filter, an alias to the filter, or a folder of filters in the Xtras folder in the Director 6 folder.

When you create an alias to the filters, you are able to store the filters where you currently have them stored on your hard drive. You may make an alias of the Filter folder in the Photoshop program's Plug-in folder, for example, to make all the filters available in Director.

After you place the filter or an alias to the filter in the appropriate place, launch Director. If Director was running when you set up the Xtras folder, you must quit Director and relaunch it. Director reads the filters or other Xtras and places them in the appropriate menu.

If the filters you install do not show up in Director, you might be missing the Photoshop Filters Xtra. After Director is properly installed, you should find this Xtra in the Director Xtras folder. If you do not find this Xtra in the correct place, reinstall Director.

To find out about Xtras in more detail, see Chapter 21, "The Xtra Step."

Applying Photoshop-Compatible Filters

Third-party image filters for use with Director 6 offer a variety of controls and effects. Within Director, you can use one of three primary commands: the `Filter Bitmap` command, the `Recent Filter` command, or the `Auto Filter` command. This section describes how the filters and the new commands work together.

To apply a filter to a graphic cast member, select the cast member either in the Cast window or the Paint window. If you select the cast member in the Cast window, the effect you choose is applied to the entire cast member. Applying a filter to a bitmap from the Cast window also enables you to simultaneously apply the same effect to a range of cast members.

You usually apply a Photoshop-compatible filter in the Paint window. The Paint window enables you to use the Marquee or Lasso tools to select part or all of the image to which you want to apply the filter effect. In contrast to the Cast window selection, the Paint window enables you to view the area you will affect before and after you apply an effect, zoom in on specific areas, and use the other Paint window tools.

Filter Bitmap Command

To apply a Photoshop-compatible filter to a single bitmap member or a series of bitmap members, use the `Filter Bitmap` command. The Filter Bitmap command is available in Director 6's Xtras menu. To activate the command, you must select either the Paint window or a bitmap in the Cast window. The images to which you apply filters might be scanned images, work created by your art department, art you created in the Paint window, and so on. The following tutorial walks you through the creation of specialized text in the Paint window.

Using the Filter Bitmap to Create Specialized Text

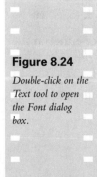

To step through this example, you must have the desired Photoshop-compatible filter installed in the correct place. For information on installing Photoshop-compatible filters, see the previous section.

1. Launch Director 6 and open the Paint window by choosing Paint from the Window menu or pressing Command+5.

2. In the Movie Properties dialog box, under the Modify menu, set the stage color to black.

3. Double-click on the Text tool in the Paint window (see fig. 8.24).

Figure 8.24

Double-click on the Text tool to open the Font dialog box.

Text Tool

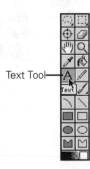

4. In the Font dialog box, select a font, size, style, and color for your text. This example uses Monaco, 36 points, bold, and pink (see fig. 8.25).

Figure 8.25

The Font dialog box is where text is defined in the Paint window.

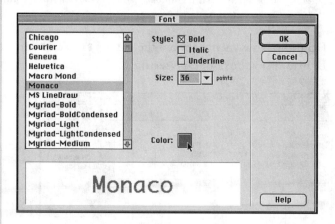

5. Click on OK.

6. Next, click somewhere on the Paint window and type **Director 6 Filters!** (see fig. 8.26).

Figure 8.26

Creating specialized text in the Paint window.

7. Select the Marquee tool and draw a box well outside the words you typed.

   Make certain that the Marquee tool is set to No Shrink mode so that you are able to make this selection.

continues

Using the Filter Bitmap to Create Specialized Text continued

You might be tempted to just double-click on the Marquee tool to select the entire graphic, but be aware that a number of filters grow the image dimensions. A tightly fitting selection will "clip" the filtered image.

8. From the Xtras menu, choose the `Filter Bitmap` command. The Filter Bitmap dialog box appears (see fig. 8.27).

Figure 8.27

The Filter Bitmap dialog box displays the filters installed on your machine that are available to Director.

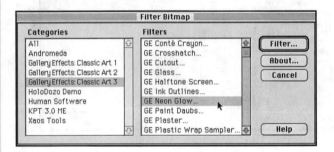

9. Select the desired filter and click on the Filter button. The Preview dialog box appears (see fig. 8.28). In this example, the neon glow effect has been chosen.

Figure 8.28

The Preview dialog box for filters enables you to adjust the filter settings and preview the before and after effects of the filter.

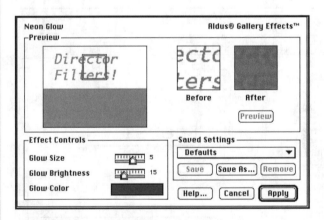

You return to the Paint window with the filter applied to the marqueed region.

11. Now, drag the filtered text on to the stage. Apply score ink effects such as Ghost and Not Copy to it against a non-white background to see the various looks you can achieve (see fig. 8.29).

Figure 8.29

The results of the Smudge filter from Kai's Power Tools.

 INSIDER TIP

> Repeating the last effect applied in the Paint window is easy: Use the Repeat command in the Edit menu, or press Command+Y. To pick from several previously used filters, use the Recent Filters command, described in the next section.

Recent Filters Command

After you use a particular filter, Director places it into the Recent Filters submenu of the Xtras menu. This way, you can apply the same effect at a later time without resetting the effect.

To use the Recent Filters command, select all or part of the graphic in the Paint window to which you want to apply the filter. Alternatively, if you know you want to apply a filter to the entire bitmap, you can apply it to the cast member in the Cast window instead.

Whether you use the Paint window or the Cast window, to select a filter from the Recent Filters list, Director launches the filter Preview dialog box for that filter. The Recent Filters command opens the filter you used before with the same settings. You can click on the Apply button to apply the filter the same way as before or adjust the settings in this dialog box before you reapply the effect.

Auto Filter Command

In addition to the Filter Bitmap command, Director 6 introduces the Auto Filter command for creating filter animations across a series of images. You can apply a filter effect to a series of images already created or tell Director how many cast members you would like it to generate with the interpolated effect. All you have to do is adjust the filter parameters for the start and end positions of the animation and tell Director how many cast members to generate between the positions.

Not all filters support the Auto Filter command. If the filter you are using supports this feature, it appears in the Auto Filter dialog box.

The next tutorial demonstrates the creation of a filter animation.

Creating a Filter Animation

1. Select a bitmap cast member in the Cast window or double-click on a bitmap cast member in the Cast window to open it in the Paint window.

   Make certain not to select anything in the Paint window. As this book goes to press, the Auto Filter *command can only be applied to the entire image, and applied in the Paint window, only if nothing is selected.*

2. Choose the Auto Filter command from the Xtras menu. The Auto Filter dialog box appears (see fig. 8.30).

Figure 8.30

The Auto Filter command enables you to animate filter effects over a series of cast members.

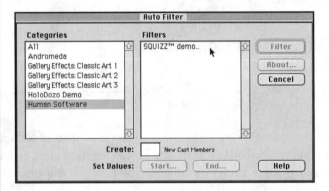

3. Select the filter you want to apply and click on the Start button in the Set Values settings.

4. In the filter Preview dialog box, select the settings you want for the initial image in the animation and click on the Apply button.

5. In the Auto Filter dialog box, click on the End button. Next, select the settings you want to finish with and then click on Apply.

6. You will again be returned to the Auto Filter dialog box. Type the number of New Cast Members you want to generate in the animation and click on the Filter button.

   A progress bar appears as Director creates a new series of cast members.

7. After the effect is complete, cycle through each image in the Paint window to preview the animation by clicking on the right and left arrow buttons.

   If the effect was not what you expected or if the filter animation did not work, take a look at the later section, "Tips on Working with Filters."

After your filter animation is complete, use the Cast to Time feature to bring that series of cast members to the stage. Cast to Time tells Director to place the images in subsequent frames, one right after the other when the animation plays.

INSIDER TIP

> Before you bring an animation to the stage, make certain that the registration point for each image is in the same place. An easy way to do this is to open the Paint window with the first image in the animation. Double-click on the Registration tool and Director sets the registration point to the center of that image. Repeat this step for all the images, and they all register at the same location. Assuming the center is the best place for the registration point, this will align all the images perfectly.

To apply the Cast to Time command, first select the first cell in the score that you would like the series of cast members to occupy. Then select the range of cast members in the Cast window; from the Modify menu, choose Cast to Time. Rewind and play the movie. Looping Director's score in the Control Panel enables you to view the entire animation.

After you have created this animation, you might want to create a film loop or export it to a QuickTime movie. Using the QuickTime technology, rather than using full-bitmapped animations, enables you to compress the animation and link it to the Director movie. When exporting to QuickTime, establish the desired QuickTime movie dimensions before exporting. Repeat the Cast to Time sequence described previously, and export to QuickTime from Director's File menu. The QuickTime file can then be imported into your main Director movie as a cast member.

For more information on QuickTime, refer to Chapter 12, "Digital Video: The Movie within the Movie." For information on creating a film loop, refer to Chapter 6, "Director as an Animator."

Tips on Working with Filters

If the effect you selected does not work or you experience trouble when working with Photoshop-compatible filters and Director 6, try doing one of the following:

▶ Allocate more memory to Director when you work with filters. Some filters take more memory than you might expect. You should compensate for the processing and memory needed for the cast members you generate with the Auto Filter command.

> ▶ If your machine freezes when you are working with filters, restart your machine. Before you launch Director again, find the Director 6 Preferences and Director 6 Xtra Cache files in the Preferences folder of your System folder and throw them away. Now when you launch Director, these files are rewritten for you. Make certain that you read the Read Me files for each of the filters before you use them. Many need specific system and extension requirements to run. You must have QuickDraw 3D installed on your PowerPC, for example, to use the HoloDozo filters.

> ▶ If the `Auto Filter` command generates the number of cast members you specify, but no effect is applied to the new cast members, make certain that you have nothing selected in the Paint window before using the `Auto Filter` command. Future versions of Director might support applying the `Auto Filter` command to only part of an image, but version 6 does not.

Onion Skinning

The final feature of the Paint window that this discussion considers is onion skinning. *Onion skinning* enables animators to create score animations completely within Director's Paint window. It allows you to see multiple cast members overlayed on top of one another in the Paint window at the same time.

Onion skinning takes its name from the traditional animation technique of using thin "onion skin" paper to create movie animations. The images on the sheets underneath the top sheet show through, so the artist can use them as references in drawing the next cell in the animation sequence. Similarly, Director's Paint window displays, for reference purposes, the cast members that appear before and after the one being created. The user can quickly create cast members for animations built by replacing one cast member with another in adjacent frames of the Score, much like a traditional flip-book. This feature drastically improves an artist's productivity within Director and control over the creative process.

The accompanying CD contains three movies created with onion skinning. These were made by Mark Shepherd, the Director engineer at Macromedia who is responsible for the onion skinning technology. You will find Mark's movies in the Chapter 8 folder on the CD. Take a look at all three movies before you experiment with onion skinning.

The following sections and tutorials illustrate the onion skinning tools by using Mark Shepherd's movies as examples.

Enabling Onion Skinning

You access the onion skin feature from the View menu in the Paint window. Try it now: First open the BLAH.DIR movie in the Mark Shepherd folder located in the Chapter 8 folder on the accompanying CD (see fig. 8.31). Then open the Paint window and choose Onion Skin from the View menu. The Onion Skin floating toolbar appears (see fig. 8.32). Do not close the BLAH.DIR movie; you will use it in the next section.

Figure 8.31

Mark Shepherd's BLAH.DIR movie was created using onion skinning.

Figure 8.32

The Onion Skin tool enables creation of score animations within Director's Paint window.

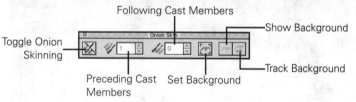

With the Paint window open, you can toggle the Toggle Onion Skinning button to enable or disable onion-skinning. When enabled, dimmed images of cast members preceding or following the active cast member in the Cast appear in the Paint window's drawing area as you create the new cast member. To turn off those reference images, toggle the Toggle Onion Skinning button to the off state.

Preceding and Following Cast Members Settings

To determine which cast members display along with the current cast member in the Paint window, adjust the Preceding Cast Members and Following Cast Members settings.

The Preceding Cast Members setting indicates how many cast members, from cast positions immediately preceding the position of the active image, will blend into the current image in the Paint window. The following Cast Members setting indicates how many cast members, from cast positions immediately following the position of the current image, will display in the Paint window. Cast members farther away from the active image appear dimmer than ones closer to the image.

Setting and Viewing Preceding Cast Members

1. With the BLAH.DIR movie open, make cast member 2 active in the Paint window.

2. The Onion Skin toolbar should still be open, but if not, open it again from the View menu and click on the Toggle Onion Skinning button.

3. Type **1** in the Preceding Cast Members setting to see how Mark used the previous cast member to create the new one that makes the man look like he is talking (see fig. 8.33).

Figure 8.33

Director's Paint window, displaying a previous cast member as you create a new one in the animation.

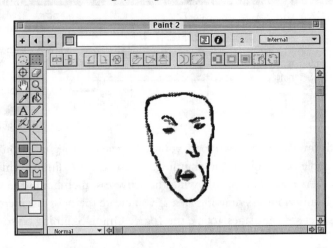

If you cycle through the remaining images in the Paint window, you see the entire animation.

4. Press Command+1 on the Macintosh or Ctrl+1 on Windows to close all the windows or select Stage from the Window menu. Then rewind and play the movie to see the final effect.

Creating Keyframes

The basic advantage of the Onion Skinning tool is the capability to view other images while you create new keyframes in an animation. For the following tutorial, you create a new movie—use the example of drawing an animation of the moon waxing from crescent to full. You import or draw the first cast member as the crescent moon. To create subsequent phases of the moon by using onion skinning, follow the next tutorial.

Creating a Keyframe with Onion Skinning

1. Open the MOON.DIR file in the Chapter 8 folder on the accompanying CD. Select the initial cast member in the Paint window.

2. Open the Onion Skin tool from the View menu.

3. Click on the Toggle Onion Skinning button on the Onion Skin toolbar and set the Preceding Cast Members setting to 1. Make certain that the other settings are disabled or set to 0.

4. Click on the + button in the Paint window.

   You should now see a dimmed version of the original cast member.

5. Create the second version of the character, a new moon phase.

6. Press the + button again and continue to create new moon cast members until you have a full moon.

7. In the Sprite Preferences dialog box under the File menu, set the Sprite Span Duration to 1 frame.

8. Place the cast members in channel 1 of the score in sequential order to create the animation of the moon becoming full.

The next section demonstrates how easy it is to use onion skinning to create an element in an animation in-between two extremes already created.

Creating Animations

Open the SNAKE.DIR movie in the Mark Shepherd folder from the Chapter 8 folder on the accompanying CD and play the animation. This example demonstrates the creation of an entire animated movie with the help of onion skinning (see fig. 8.34).

Figure 8.34

With Onion Skinning enabled, you can view the entire snake animation within the Paint window.

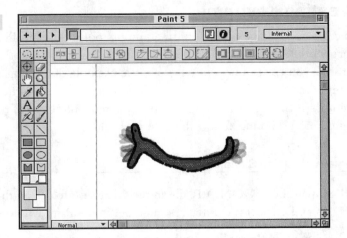

Step through the Paint window to preview the animation. By adjusting the onion skinning settings for Previous and Following Cast Members, you see how helpful it is to view other keyframes in an animation while creating a new character.

Now try it yourself. Open a movie you are working on, or create a new movie. After you create the extreme keyframes, you can use the Preceding and Following Cast Members settings to view the key images when creating the in-between states of the animations. The following tutorial illustrates one way to create an in-between version of two extreme keyframes by using onion skinning.

Animating with Keyframes in Onion Skinning

1. In a new movie, open the Paint window and select Onion Skin from the View menu.

2. Click on the Toggle Onion Skinning button so that it is depressed and turn off all other settings if they are not already off.

3. In the Cast window, drag the two key images to cast positions 1 and 3.

4. To open cast member 1 in the Paint window, select it in the Cast window and double-click on it to make it active in the Paint window.

5. Click on the + button in the Paint window.

   If you leave the Cast window open beside the Paint window, you notice that Director creates a new graphic cast member in cast position 2.

6. From the Onion Skin toolbar, set both the Preceding and Following Cast Members settings to 1.

7. Now you can draw a new version of the cast member as an in-between version of the two extremes as the two extremes display dimly in the same canvas.

Creating Special Effects with Paint Window Inks

Use the Onion Skinning tool along with the Paint window inks to create special effects on the graphics you are currently using.

Using Reveal Ink with Onion Skinning

1. Import a scanned image or graphic into Director and make it active in the Paint window.

2. Open the Onion Skin toolbar from the View menu, and click on the Toggle Onion Skinning button.

3. Set the Preceding Cast Members setting to 1 and set everything else to 0 or disabled.

4. With your image active in the Paint window, click on the + button in the Paint window. A new painting canvas appears with a dimmed version of the first image in the background.

5. Select the Paintbrush tool and the Reveal ink effect.

6. Brush part of the preceding image to create a new, partial image of the original.

You have created a new cast member—a copy of part of the image. You can use the score ink effects to layer that partial image as a mask on top of the original.

Background Settings

The Onion Skin toolbar has three background settings, as shown previously in figure 8.32: Set Background, Show Background, and Track Background.

Set Background and Show Background

To set a particular cast member as the background for other images, select the Set Background button in the Onion Skin toolbar. The active cast member displaying in the Paint window becomes the background reference cast member, and remains so unless you actively set a different background. Unlike the Preceding and Following Cast Members option, the background selected with Set Background can be any cast position; it is not restricted to the cast positions immediately preceding and following the active cast member. The Show Background button is a toggle to show or hide the background image.

Director remembers the background image you set and can display it behind any subsequent images. To set an alternative cast member as the background cast member, click on the Set Background button again with the new cast member active in the Paint window. Practical uses for Set Background and Show Background are discussed next.

Drawing Images to Scale

The background settings are useful for creating new cast members in relation to the background you will later have on the stage. You can use the Sprite Properties scaling feature after the images are on the stage, but you generate higher-quality images if you first create them to scale in the Paint window.

Like many Director authors, you might create a custom interface or main menu in which your audience navigates to and from various scenes in the production. If you display the interface image as a background in the Paint window, you can create buttons to scale directly in the Paint window. This can all be done before you place anything on the stage.

Setting the Scene

Perhaps you would like to create an animation with characters drawn to scale in relation to one another while the background is active. Use the Preceding and Following Cast Members settings and toggle the Show Background setting to view the entire scene in the Paint window. You can then cycle to a new cast position and work on another active image.

Using Track Background

The Track Background setting is useful when you want to use different images as a series of backgrounds behind a series of foreground images. A good example might be to create an animated character giving a walking tour through various European cities.

To begin, you might have a series of scanned photographs, each of a different European city. The Track Background feature enables you to cycle through the background images as you create a new version of the foreground image, or, in this case, a character. The following tutorial gives an example of using Track Background.

Creating a Series of Cast Members with Track Background

1. If you have a series of images you would like to use as a series of backgrounds, import them into a new Director movie. You can also use the MOON2.DIR file in the Chapter 8 folder of the CD-ROM.

2. In the Cast window, make certain that the backgrounds you want to use are in adjacent cast positions.

   The Track Background feature of onion skinning only follows along a series of images if they are in consecutive order in the cast.

3. Select Onion Skin from the View menu and click on the Toggle Onion Skinning button of the Onion Skin toolbar. Make certain that all other settings are set to 0 or disabled.

4. Open the first cast member you would like to track as a background in the Paint window. In MOON2.DIR this will be cast member 1.

5. From the Onion Skin toolbar, click on the Set Background button. Click on the + button in the Paint window in anticipation of creating a new cast member in the foreground of the Paint window. You will create the new cast member in step 7 (see fig. 8.35).

continues

Creating a Series of Cast Members with Track Background continued

Figure 8.35

Setting the background image when using onion-skinning.

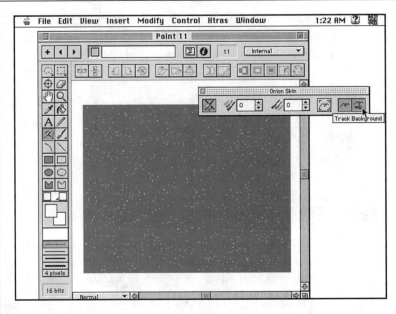

6. Click on the Show Background button to display the background cast member you set and click on the Track Background button (see fig. 8.36).

Figure 8.36

Click on Track Background to use sequential cast members as backgrounds for each new cast member in the Paint window.

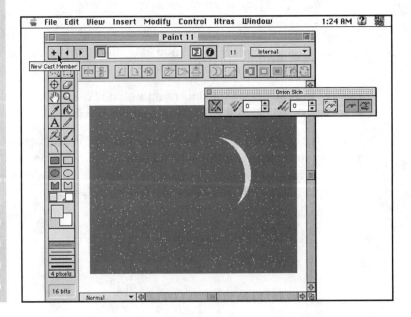

7. Draw your initial foreground cast member. If you are using MOON2.DIR, draw a crescent moon.

8. Click on the + button in the Paint window again to create another new bitmap cast member. The Paint window becomes empty, except that the next background in the series appears as the background for the new cast member. You then can draw a new version of the foreground character (see fig 8.37).

Figure 8.37

Click on the + button to add the next new cast member.

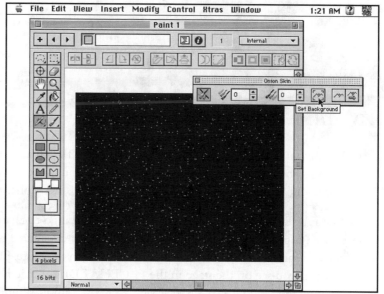

The number of cast members you can create in a series is limitless. Repeat step 8 until you finish your series of cast members.

Onion Skinning with Lingo

For a good example of combining onion skinning with Lingo, open Mark Shepherd's FACEHAT.DIR movie. You will find it in the Mark Shepherd folder in the Chapter 8 folder on the accompanying CD. Open the movie, and then rewind and play it (see fig. 8.38).

Figure 8.38

Mark Shepherd's FACEHAT.DIR movie is a great example of combining animations created with onion skinning and Lingo.

When you play the movie, roll your mouse over the character and notice the cast members change and follow the mouse as you move it. Check the script cast members in the Cast window to see how this was done.

The FACEHAT.DIR movie demonstrates using Lingo to change the memberNum of sprite property. This way the cast member that occupies a particular sprite channel can be changed with Lingo rather than in the score. Each different cast member you see on the stage in the FACEHAT.DIR movie is being placed there by using the Lingo set the memberNum of sprite. Onion-skinning was used to create the cast members and Lingo is being used to increment between them.

Notice that the color of the faces change as well. This is also being accomplished through Lingo by using the forecolor of sprite property. By using the Lingo set the forecolor of sprite, the color can be changed without creating an elaborate and potentially unwieldy score. See Chapters 16–20 for more discussion of Lingo's possibilities.

In Practice

This chapter described how to use the most common media element used in Director—the graphics. It has touched on graphics concepts and some techniques in third-party image editing tools necessary to understand when working with graphics in Director. For more information on the third-party tools discussed, check out the books dedicated to those products.

Given the pervasiveness of graphics in Director projects, it won't surprise you to learn that the next chapter continues with this topic, focusing on three-dimensional graphics. Many of the variables that affect the quality of two-dimensional graphics, as discussed in this chapter, also affect three-dimensional graphics. In preparation for Chapter 9, and for all your work with graphics in Director, keep in mind these practical considerations:

▶ Director's Paint window is best for creating art used for animations. Its tools provide specialized functions for this purpose. High-resolution image editing is best accomplished in a dedicated graphics-editing application.

▶ To avoid the halo effect sometimes associated with anti-aliasing, turn off the anti-aliased features of the graphics editing tools you will be using. To edit an existing halo, try the Switch Color tool in the Paint window to "remove" unwanted pixels by changing them to another color.

▶ The resolution of a Director file is always 72 dpi. For nonphotographic images, try to scan, create, edit, and save them at 72 dpi. If you must resize, it is better to start too large and reduce to 72 dpi than to start too small and enlarge to 72 dpi.

▶ For photographic images, best results are obtained by scanning at 100 dpi and then changing the resolution to 72 dpi with Photoshop's Image Size function.

▶ To minimize file size of graphic cast members, use Photoshop or xRes's Indexed Color mode to save the image.

▶ When importing an image from another program, set the bit depth before the import takes places and remember: The higher the bit depth, the larger the memory requirements and performance implications for your movie.

▶ You can apply a Photoshop-compatible filter in either the Cast window or the Paint window, but the Paint window gives you more flexibility. In Paint, you can select all or part of the image, view it before and after filter effects are applied, zoom in on specific areas, and use other Paint window tools.

▶ Allocate more memory to Director when you work with filters to compensate for the additional processing and memory requirements they often entail.

▶ In Director's significant toolbox of animation techniques, onion-skinning is another useful tool, available through the Paint window.

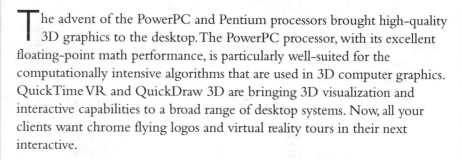

chapter **9**

David Miller

Adding the Third Dimension

The advent of the PowerPC and Pentium processors brought high-quality 3D graphics to the desktop. The PowerPC processor, with its excellent floating-point math performance, is particularly well-suited for the computationally intensive algorithms that are used in 3D computer graphics. QuickTime VR and QuickDraw 3D are bringing 3D visualization and interactive capabilities to a broad range of desktop systems. Now, all your clients want chrome flying logos and virtual reality tours in their next interactive.

This chapter discusses the creation of 3D graphics and animations for your Director projects. This chapter is not meant to replace reading the manual of your 3D program. It provides a brief overview of the 3D design process for beginners, tips on integrating 3D graphics and animation into Director, and ways to add interactivity to 3D animations. This chapter discusses the use of relatively inexpensive desktop 3D graphics software with a special emphasis on Extreme 3D—the 3D modeling, animation, and rendering component of the Macromedia's Director Multimedia Studio. Examples will illustrate how to use QuickDraw 3D and QuickTime VR with Director.

This chapter covers the following topics:

- ▶ Using 3D graphics
- ▶ 3D tools
- ▶ Creating 3D graphics
- ▶ Using 2D programs to create 3D effects
- ▶ 3D interfaces, backgrounds, and objects

► 3D animation

► Using QuickDraw 3D

► Using QuickTime VR

Using 3D Graphics

When you create a 2D drawing of a 3D object, you use your illustration skills and imagination to give the image depth and realism. When you create the same object in a 3D program, it exists within a fully realized 3D world and the computer calculates the perspective, shadows, reflections, atmospheric effects, and object overlap. The computer does a lot of the work for you, enabling you to experiment with your illustration.

After a 3D world is created, it is the ultimate reusable graphic asset. You can re-create it with different perspective and lighting for other projects. You can use objects in the 3D world over and over again in various contexts. In some respects, the creation of 3D graphics is similar to sculpture, photography, videography, set design, and stage design in that you work with composition, lighting, and 3D objects in a controlled 3D environment. But you never have to strike the set; it always exists inside your computer, ready to be changed or reused whenever you need it.

Many 3D programs create 3D animations. Three-dimensional animation has many advantages over traditional 2D cell animation. To animate and rotate objects over time, 3D programs use keyframe or time-based animation, similar to keyframe animation in the Director score, but more powerful. Extreme 3D enables you to animate almost every editable parameter, including shape, position, texture, lighting, camera view, motion paths, and so on. After you set up your keyframes, the computer automatically generates the intermediate frames.

Three-dimensional programs also make it easier to provide alternate views of a scene or object for the user. You can simulate real-world, dynamic processes and illustrate complex motions with 3D animation. 3D graphics make the spatial and functional relationships of objects and interfaces more clear. Navigable 3D worlds provide visualization of 3D environments that are impossible or dangerous to see in the real world.

High-quality 3D graphics and animation on the desktop are subject to the same limitations on playback and file size as 2D graphics and animations. Creating 3D graphics means investing time and equipment. 3D programs have a steep learning curve, but intuitive interfaces, such as Extreme 3D's, are making it easier. The creation of 3D content takes longer than creating the same content elements in 2D. Final rendering of a long, complex 3D animation can tie up computer resources for hours and even days.

3D Tools

This section discusses some of the hardware and software that you need to create 3D graphics. The advent of faster processors, consumer-level hardware acceleration, and system-level 3D support on desktop computers is changing the 3D landscape. Some of the information provided here might be dated by the time you read it. Keep tabs on recent trade magazines for the latest information. Trade magazines that cover 3D issues include *PCWeek*, *PCWorld*, *Digital Video*, *PC Graphics and Video*, *3D Design*, *MacWeek*, *MacUser*, *MacWorld*, *New Media*, and *3D Artist*.

System Requirements

Three-dimensional graphics programs require a lot of RAM. The more complex your models and animations and the more texture maps you use, the more RAM you need. You may want to have other programs, such as Photoshop, open while you work in your 3D program; doing so makes further demands on RAM. You also might want to leave room to expand your system's RAM to accommodate changing memory requirements. In short, get as much RAM as you can afford. Most 3D programs perform best with at least 16–20 MB of RAM for the program, although complex models may require more. A machine with 32–64 MB of total RAM makes a serviceable 3D graphics workstation, and workstations with greater than 200 MB of RAM are not unusual.

Your CPU should be as fast as possible. Many 3D programs for the Macintosh are PowerPC-native and are typically optimized for the PowerPC chip. If you have an older Macintosh, make sure it has an FPU, or floating-point unit. Pentium Pro systems running Windows NT are becoming popular desktop-based 3D graphics workstations for 32-bit programs, such as Autodesk's 3D Studio MAX.

Consider purchasing a 3D accelerator board. Many companies sell low-cost 3D accelerator boards for desktop systems. Unfortunately, comparing the performance of boards can be difficult. Reviews in unbiased trade magazines can be helpful. Consider the video-out capabilities of your system if you want to output animations to videotape.

You'll also need ample disk space. As a rule of thumb, a 1 MB 3D animation easily generates 10 MB of intermediate and scratch files.

3D Software

The 3D design process involves several tasks. These tasks include modeling, animating, rendering, and compositing. 3D software programs handle one or more of these tasks. You may need to use more than one program to create your 3D graphics.

Extreme 3D is the integrated modeling, animation, and rendering program that is part of the Macromedia Multimedia Studio. It's a capable and relatively inexpensive package for desktop multimedia. Extreme 3D provides CAD-accurate, spline-based modeling with an easy-to-use, intuitive interface. Figure 9.1 illustrates this interface. You can animate just about any editable parameter by using keyframe and time-based animation. The Extreme 3D file format is compatible across Macintosh and Windows systems and comes with a built-in, cross-platform, production-quality, distributed renderer. The tutorials and tips in this chapter use Extreme 3D, but the same concepts are applicable to other 3D programs.

Even if you use an integrated 3D program, such as Extreme 3D or Strata StudioPro, you may want to exchange files among various 3D and 2D programs during the production process. On the Macintosh, it's easy to exchange files among programs. Be sure that the 3D program you choose is able to export animations as QuickTime movies, as a sequence of numbered PICT files, or as PICs. Your 3D program should support DXF import/export. DXF is a common, though limited, format used to exchange 3D models among programs. EPS or EPSF import enables you to import 2D Bézier curves and graphics from FreeHand and Illustrator. TARGA and TIFF are useful cross-platform image formats. 3DMF (3D Metafile or QuickDraw 3D format) import/export is a useful cross-platform format with viewers for Macintosh,

Windows, and the web. Virtual Reality Modeling Language (VRML) export enables you to put 3D graphics on the web. Table 9.1 is a listing of file types, extensions, and descriptions for importing text and graphics on the web.

Figure 9.1

Extreme 3D interface.

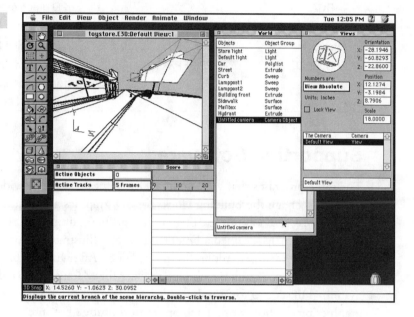

Table 9.1

Program Names Followed by Their Extension and Function

File Type	Extension	Function
QuickTime	.MOV, .QT	Cross-platform digital video and animation format
Audio Video	.AVI	Windows digital video format Interleave
DXF	.DXF	ASCII-based 3D format
3D Studio	.3DS	Autodesk's 3D Studio format
3D Meta-File	.3DMF, .3MF	Cross-platform QuickDraw 3D format
VRML	.WRL	Virtual Reality Modeling Language for the web
TIFF	.TIF	2D graphics format

continues

Table 9.1	continued	
Program Names Followed by Their Extension and Function		
File Type	**Extension**	**Function**
TARGA	.TGA	2D graphics format
PICT	.PICT, .PIC	2D graphics format
Bitmap	.BMP	2D graphics format
EPS, EPSF	.EPS, .EPSF	Encapsulated PostScript; 2D format for programs such as FreeHand and Illustrator

Supporting Software

The same programs that you use for 2D graphics and digital video editing can be used to create the building blocks for 3D graphics and texture maps, to post-process and composite 3D graphics for final output, and to add effects to 3D animations. Macromedia FreeHand, Adobe Illustrator, Adobe Photoshop, Fractal Design Painter, Adobe Premiere, Adobe After Effects for Macintosh, Avid Videoshop, Equilibrium's DeBabelizer for Macintosh/Windows, and Inset Systems' HiJaak Pro for Windows all provide supporting functions in 3D graphics production work. Each program is unique but integral for multi-dimensional graphics:

▶ Use FreeHand and Illustrator to create 2D profiles for importing into your 3D program and to use in 3D modeling.

▶ Photoshop and Painter add dimensionality to 2D images and provide many useful image editing and compositing features. Painter is a powerful paint program that emulates natural media, such as oil, paint, and charcoal. Painter also includes 2D animation features, such as onion skinning, and support for animation formats, such as QuickTime. Premiere is a QuickTime-based, digital video editing program.

▶ After Effects is a digital video and animation post-processing tool that supports alpha channels for compositing and has powerful keyframe and time-based animation controls. After Effects also provides effects such as motion blur and fully editable Bézier curve motion paths with sub-pixel positioning. Final Effects is a series of plug-ins for After Effects that includes a particle animation system for special effects such as rain, fire, smoke, and explosions. Painter, Premiere, and After Effects export compositions as a sequence of PICT files or as QuickTime movies.

▶ Equilibrium's DeBabelizer saves time whenever you do any kind of animation work. DeBabelizer is an essential tool for batch processing animation files and creating optimal palettes. You can automate repetitive processes by using a macro utility such as QuicKeys. Daystar Digital's free Photomatic utility automates many Photoshop processes. You can download Photomatic from `http://www.daystar.com/`.

QuickDraw 3D

Apple Computer's QuickDraw 3D (QD3D) is a software-based, 3D system extension for Macintosh and Windows 95/NT computers. QD3D provides real-time, workstation-quality rendering while delivering interactivity and animation of 3D graphics on PowerPC and Pentium-class PCs.

Users don't need to add accelerators or peripherals to existing systems to use QD3D, but QD3D supports hardware accelerators and peripherals when they are present. QD3D consists of system extensions, user interface, and programming toolkits for MacOS and Windows 95/NT, and a cross-platform file format called 3DMF. Apple Computer, Netscape Communications, and Silicon Graphics have agreed to incorporate the 3DMF format into the next generation VRML that provides interactive 3D graphics on the web.

QD3D for Macintosh requires the following:

▶ A PowerPC Macintosh

▶ System 7.1.2 or later

▶ 16 MB of RAM

▶ QD3D system extensions

QD3D for Microsoft Windows requires the following:

▶ A Pentium-class machine

▶ Windows 95/NT

▶ 16 MB of RAM

▶ 16- or 24-bit display card

▶ QD3D system extensions

3D MetaFile or 3DMF is the file format for QuickDraw 3D models. Many 3D programs support this format including Extreme 3D version 2, Strata Studio Pro, and Specular Infini-D. Add interactive QuickDraw 3D content to Mac and Windows Director projectors by using the free cross-platform QD3D Xtra for Director available on Macromedia's web site. With the QD3D Xtra you can import 3DMF files into the Director Cast. The QD3D Xtra provides real-time 3D interactivity and rendering from within Director as long as the QD3D system extension is installed on the playback machine. Later sections in this chapter describe how to create 3DMF models and how to add them to your Director projects.

Check out `http://product.info.apple.com/qd3d/QD3D.HTML` for all the latest developments and free downloads of the software and development kits.

For the latest on the availability of QD3D Xtras for Director, check out `http://www.macromedia.com/`.

QuickTime VR

QuickTime VR (QTVR) is a cross-platform "virtual reality" technology from Apple Computer. With QTVR movies, users of QuickTime-capable Macintosh and Windows systems can interact and navigate through 3D environments on their computers. QTVR movies are special QuickTime movies that enable users to move through 3D environments, pick up and manipulate 3D objects, and activate hot spots embedded in the 3D scene. Interaction is with a mouse and keyboard. Users don't need high-end workstations, special headsets, goggles, or other peripherals. QTVR movies are characterized by high-quality, photographic images, fast playback, and small file-size. Although QTVR is optimized for photographic images, it also works with computer-generated images. Sometimes QTVR is called photographic VR to indicate that the source of the VR image is often more than one photograph and this differentiates it from other kinds of VR technologies such as VRML, which is based on three-dimensional geometric models.

You'll need a QuickTime-capable Macintosh or Windows computer to view QTVR movies. The minimum system requirements for the Macintosh include:

▶ 68030, 25 MHz processor

▶ 8 MB of RAM

▶ QuickTime 2.0

▶ System 7.1

▶ 8-bit video

▶ A QTVR-capable playback application

The minimum system requirements needed to view QTVR movies with Windows include:

▶ 386SX, 33 MHz processor

▶ 8 MB of RAM

▶ QuickTime 2.0 for Windows

▶ Windows 3.1

▶ 8-bit video

▶ A QTVR-capable playback application

You can download free samples of a QTVR player for Macintosh and Windows systems and sample QTVR movies from Apple Computer's web site at `http://qtvr.quicktime.apple.com`. You can add cross-platform, QTVR playback, and Lingo control to Director by using freely distributed Xtras for both Macintosh and Windows.

A section and tutorial later in this chapter describe how to create simple QTVR movies on a Macintosh with free authoring tools distributed from Apple Computer's web site and includes instructions on how to incorporate them into Director projectors for both Macintosh and Windows by using the free QTVR Xtra, also from Apple. Authoring tools for Windows may also be available by the time you read this.

Creating more complex navigable QTVR movies requires the QTVR Authoring Tools Suite for Macintosh from Apple Computer or Nodester from Panimation:

`http://www.panimation.com/`

For more information, contact Apple Computer or visit Apple's web site at the following address:

`http://qtvr.quicktime.apple.com/`

RealVR

RealVR is a virtual reality multimedia technology from RealSpace (recently bought by Live Picture) that combines photographic VR (similar to QTVR) with VRML 2.0, video, and audio playback. RealVR enables you to create a 3D multimedia environment for disk-based playback, CD-ROMs, the web, and hybrid CDs. Authoring tools, including a free converter for QTVR movies, are provided by RealSpace/Live Picture at the following address:

`http://www.rlspace.com/`

You can add RealVR multimedia to your Director project with the RealVR Xtra. For playback on Macintosh you will need the following:

▶ Power Macintosh

▶ MacOS 7.5 or greater

▶ 12 MB RAM

▶ 16-bit color display

For playback on a PC you will need the following:

▶ Pentium class processor

▶ Windows 95 or NT

▶ 12 MB RAM

▶ 16-bit color display

▶ QuickTime for Windows to view QuickTime movies

Plug-In Filters

Director 6 supports Adobe Photoshop plug-in filters. The Director 6 CD ships with several plug-in filters that enable you to add 3D effects to your graphics from within Director. Some plug-ins require the QD3D system extension. To use these plug-ins within Director, install them with the included installer program. To apply a plug-in to a bitmap cast member in Director, select the cast member in the Cast window, choose Filter Bitmap from the Xtras menu, and select the desired plug-in from the Filter Bitmap dialog box.

Creating 3D Graphics

As you make the move from computer-based 2D illustration to 3D graphics and animation, the change can be daunting at first because it involves a different way of creating computer graphics. The creation of 3D graphics is an iterative process that involves several tasks.

▶ In the modeling step, you create the basic structure of your objects and place them in a 3D world.

▶ In the animating step, you typically assign keyframe positions to objects along a timeline. The computer generates intermediate frames between keyframes—a process called *tweening*—to simulate motion in your 3D world. Tweening does all the work of creating perspective, lighting, shadows, and environmental effects. This step is similar to keyframe animating in the Director score, only more powerful.

▶ In the rendering step, the computer paints your 3D world based on the lighting, material properties, and camera views you created. Material properties define an object's color, texture, and surface properties. Lights and atmospheric effects define the environment of your world.

▶ Often, the final step is to merge or composite 3D graphics with other graphics elements by using programs such as Photoshop, DeBabelizer, Director, After Effects, or Premiere.

Designing a 3D world isn't a simple, linear, step-by-step process. It usually involves alternating between modeling and animation; even performing test renderings at different stages to see whether all the various aspects of your world look just right. Performing a final, high-quality render might take many minutes, hours, or even days. The following sections provide more detail on the process and provide tips on how you can create 3D graphics and animations for Director.

The 3D World

In 2D programs, such as FreeHand and Director, the screen is divided into an X and Y, 2D coordinate system. You might be familiar with FreeHand, which enables you to set precise X and Y values for the positioning and alignment of objects. 3D programs add a third dimension to this coordinate system. The third axis, or Z-axis, extends into the computer screen. Programs such as Extreme 3D enable CAD-accurate positioning and alignment within the 3D coordinate system.

Viewing your 3D world through a window on the computer screen gives you the editable capability of having parameters, such as perspective and orientation. At first, you may feel disoriented as you construct your 3D world. Become familiar with the way you change and edit View Parameters in your 3D program. In the beginning, it may be easiest to stick with a set of default views such as Front, Back, Top, Right, and so on—if your program provides them.

The camera is a special object. It can be manipulated like any other 3D object or it can be used to take "snapshots" of your 3D world. The view you use to edit your 3D world can be the same view as the camera view, but it doesn't have to be. Camera position and look-at points are animated to provide panning, dollying, tracking, zooming, and fly-throughs.

Modeling

Modeling is the process by which you construct your 3D objects and create the basic structure of your 3D world. (Both the objects and the world are often referred to by the general term *model*.) Many 3D programs provide a set of primitive shapes, such as a cube, a sphere, and a cone, from which you can create more complex models. Most 3D programs provide a rich set of tools to construct 3D models from 2D profiles. The tool set usually includes Extrusion, Lathe, Sweep, and Skin (loft) tools. Extreme 3D models are built up from true Bézier curves, similar to paths in FreeHand and Illustrator. In Extreme 3D, you can edit and animate models at the vertex or point level to create complex organic shapes.

Positioning objects in your 3D world by using the mouse or by entering 3D coordinates with programs such as Extreme 3D enables you to place an object at precise points in your 3D world. It sometimes can be difficult to tell exactly where your object is within the 3D coordinate system. When first creating an object, you might want to align it to the $(0, 0, 0)$ point in your world and then move it at right angles along the X, Y, and Z axes to get a feel for how an object is oriented in the 3D space.

Animating

You create animation through a sequence of still images or frames that are played rapidly in succession so that the eye is fooled into perceiving continuous motion. 3D programs with animation capabilities typically use a keyframe-based timeline similar to the score in Director to create animations. The computer calculates all the intermediate frames between keyframes. In Extreme 3D, you can animate almost every editable property, including texture maps and individual vertices or control points. Motion paths are fully editable curves as well.

The Material World

To make your 3D world look realistic, assign different material properties to objects, and create lights and atmospheric effects. Materials can be procedural-based or texture map-based, as described in following sections. Lights can mimic sunlight, spotlights, or other types of lights.

Lights and Shadows

The lighting in a 3D world is similar to the lighting of a stage or movie set in the real world except that you can place lights anywhere in 3D space, and you can easily change the properties of each light, such as color or dustiness. Light sources in 3D programs include distant lights, spotlights, and ambient light. *Distant lights* simulate the sun and throw parallel light rays. *Spotlights* are typically cone-shaped lights that focus on specific points. *Ambient light* is the global, environmental light that suffuses your scene from all directions.

Lighting in the 3D world doesn't have to follow the laws of physics. You can have lights that don't cast shadows. Anyone who has done photographic, stage, or film lighting can appreciate this feature. Lights can even have negative intensity; that is, you can take light out of an area instead of illuminating it.

Procedural Textures and Texture Maps

The appearance of the surface of your 3D objects depends on the materials of which they are made and the lighting and environment of your 3D world. Texture mapping and procedural textures are two common ways to simulate materials for your objects.

Texture mapping is the process of applying a bitmap image, such as a PICT file, to a 3D surface. At the simplest level, texture mapping is similar to stretching a decal or placing a label on the surface of an object. You can animate textures, tile textures, and project and place textures with different orientations to create interesting texture maps. You can simulate surface roughness, lighting effects, and transparency settings with texture maps. You can overlay several texture maps on the same surface. Some programs even support QuickTime movies as texture maps.

Procedural textures use mathematical equations to generate surface properties. Because procedural textures are mathematical calculations, they don't require as much disk space or memory as texture maps. They also are resolution-independent. You can get close to an object with a procedural texture and the texture won't become pixellated. Because procedural textures extend through an object, you can carve into objects and still see the texture. Procedural textures can take a long time to render and sometimes require much tweaking to look realistic. Bryce is a 3D program that uses procedural textures extensively to re-create natural forms and textures.

Rendering

Rendering is the process by which the computer generates an image based on all the material properties, positions, lights, and models that you have in your 3D world. The following list describes several rendering methods. Naturally, the highest-quality methods take the longest time to render:

- ▶ **Bounding box rendering:** This type of rendering represents 3D objects as boxes that enclose each object. This method is the fastest and is used to show the basic positions of objects.

- ▶ **Wireframe rendering:** This method represents the underlying structure of 3D objects as a grid of interconnected lines and is commonly used for interactive rendering of animations.

- ▶ **Flat-shading method:** Flat shading renders objects with faceted polygons.

- ▶ **Gourand shading:** Gourand shading provides semi-realistic shading and smoothness and is a good intermediate-quality rendering method for test renders during modeling.

▶ **Phong shading and ray-tracing:** These are the highest-quality render methods, take the longest time, and are generally used for final output. Of the two, ray-tracing takes the longest time, because each pixel is calculated based on the simulated light rays from every light source, including reflections.

Interactive rendering is the rendering used to display your 3D world on the screen while you work on it. You want the screen display to be fast, but you also want enough information to be able to create your model and see what you're doing. Many programs use the wireframe rendering method for interactive rendering.

Extreme 3D provides fast interactive rendering. In Extreme 3D you can assign objects different render modes. This feature can save time during interactive rendering. If you want to see detail in one object but only want to see the rough positions of other objects in a scene, for example, it saves considerable time. QD3D also provides system-level support for fast interactive rendering within any program that supports QD3D interactive rendering, such as Director, SimpleText, or Extreme 3D.

At several stages in your project you might run high-quality test renderings by using final output settings. Most programs can render high-quality test renderings to the screen instead of to disk. You might want to render selected keyframes at the highest possible setting to make sure your 3D world is shaping up the way you want. You also can render short but critical parts of animations to see what they look like at the final output settings.

Final rendering at high-quality settings usually takes a long time. Many programs enable you to distribute rendering across multiple machines on a network. With several machines rendering different pieces of the file simultaneously, the total render time can be significantly reduced. Extreme 3D has a built-in distributed renderer.

You also might want to render images at larger sizes and higher color depths than needed for a particular project. Then reduce size and color depth during post-processing using programs such as Photoshop, DeBabelizer, or After Effects. It is easier to produce high-quality images at varying dimensions if you start with a large dimension and reduce the size to fit. Consider rendering against a solid color background to make compositing easier.

Compositing

Compositing is the process of merging, or layering, separate graphic elements into a single image or animation. Sometimes it is better to render 3D objects and animations separately and then composite them together in a dedicated tool. In Director, for example, several simultaneous small animations generally have better playback performance than one large animation that takes up the entire screen. Using After Effects, Photoshop, Premiere, or Director to composite separate 2D and 3D graphic elements against different 2D backgrounds enables you to reuse the graphics elements in different projects. Compositing enables you to add different backgrounds, change motion paths, or add and delete individual elements, without having to rerender the entire scene. Also, you might want to render one object at a higher level of detail and quality (and corresponding longer render time) compared to other objects in a scene. You could then composite the high-detail and low-detail objects to save rendering time.

If you plan to composite your 3D graphics, render them with an alpha channel. An *alpha channel* is an invisible, 8-bit, grayscale image that most 3D programs create automatically when you render for final output. An alpha channel is useful for compositing in such programs as After Effects and Photoshop. Use the alpha channel for masking, transparency, and selection. A file has an alpha channel if it has a color depth of millions+ or 32 bits (24 bits plus an 8-bit alpha channel).

INSIDER TIP

> To load the alpha channel as a selection in Photoshop, choose the alpha channel (typically channel 4) with the Select, Load Selection command.

You will probably use several tools for compositing. Although Director supports layering, it doesn't support alpha channels except with third-party Xtras such as AlphaMania. Thus, you will probably composite graphics in other programs such as Photoshop, Premiere, or After Effects and then import the finished composition into Director.

Using 2D Programs to Create 3D Effects

You don't need a dedicated 3D program to add dimensionality to 2D graphics. Many 2D graphics programs provide ways to add shadows, surface textures, and extrusions to 2D graphics. This section teaches you how to use 2D programs to create 3D effects and textures.

Adding Dimensionality to 2D Graphics

In Photoshop and Painter, you can paint in shadows and highlights by hand using tools such as Dodge, Burn, or Airbrush. You also can use several techniques to add drop shadows to objects. If you add drop shadows, consider creating them on a separate layer in Photoshop or Painter. Then you can composite and animate them in a compositing program or in Director as separate sprites if necessary.

Painter has a rich set of lighting effects that adds dimensionality to graphics. You can use the Apply Surface Texture command in Painter to texturize your graphics and to add dimension to type. Photoshop also has lighting effects. The use of lighting effects with grayscale images to create 3D graphics is described in the next section.

Grayscale Bump Maps

Both Photoshop and Painter use grayscale images to create 3D surface textures and lighting effects. The idea is simple. To create a textured 3D surface, these programs interpret the white areas of a grayscale image to be the "bumps" or raised areas of the surface. The black areas of the grayscale image correspond to the *pits*, or the lowest points of the surface. Gray areas have intermediate heights depending on the gray level. Grayscale images used in this way are sometimes called *grayscale bump maps* or *height fields*. Adding lighting effects to an image with a grayscale bump map shades the image based on the "bumps" in the grayscale bump map. This effect is similar in some respects to the emboss filter, but is more powerful. You can use this feature to create intricate, detailed surface textures. You also can use this feature to create 3D interface objects, such as buttons.

In Photoshop, you can use the Filter, Render, Lighting Effects command and any grayscale image to create quick 3D textures and surfaces (see fig. 9.2). You can texturize and emboss any image by using a grayscale version of the image in conjunction with the Filter, Render, Lighting Effects command. In Photoshop, to create a grayscale image from any other image or channel with the maximum image options and control use the Image, Calculations command. If the transitions between gray values are too sharp, add blur to smooth out the grayscale image.

Figure 9.2

The upper image is the grayscale bump map used to create the lower image with Photoshop's Lighting Effects filter.

Creating Textures

A texture map is a bitmap that you apply to the surface of your 3D object, such as a decal or a coat of paint. Painter, Photoshop, Extreme 3D, and most 3D programs come with libraries of textures. You can use dedicated texture creation programs or Painter and Photoshop to create original texture maps for your 3D models. Any bitmap can become a texture map. Instead of creating intricate detail in a 3D model, draw the detailed look you want in a 2D program importing it as a texture map into the 3D program. Sometimes, adding a little noise to texture maps in Photoshop gives them a less sharp-edged, computer-generated look. Other ways to create real world texture maps include scanning and video capture.

Creating 2D Bézier Curve Profiles

Extreme 3D provides spline-based drawing tools, similar to tools in FreeHand and Illustrator, that create 2D curves or profiles. Various 3D object tools turn your 2D profiles into 3D objects. It is sometimes easier to create 2D profiles directly in FreeHand or Illustrator with their rich toolset for creating 2D curves. Then import the 2D curves into Extreme 3D. Extreme 3D 2.0 imports FreeHand 4.0, 5.0, and 7.x files directly. If you're using FreeHand 7 files you will have the added advantage of drag and drop from FreeHand to Extreme 3D.

Extreme 3D imports FreeHand 4.0 or 5.x files directly. It also imports 2D files saved in EPSF format. Extreme 3D creates profiles from the Bézier curves in your 2D files. It ignores such elements as the fill patterns and bitmaps in your 2D drawing.

If you create your 2D profiles in FreeHand, here are some tips for using FreeHand with Extreme 3D:

▶ Before you save your FreeHand file for import into Extreme 3D, choose the Document Inspector and drag your page to the lower-left corner of the pasteboard.

▶ After you import your FreeHand file into Extreme 3D, choose the View, Fit to Window command to see the profiles in the Extreme 3D workspace.

▶ Align the profiles in the workspace by choosing the Object, Align command.

▶ If the sharp corners of your 2D profiles look rounded in Extreme 3D, press B while you manipulate the handles of the corner points. Pressing B breaks the point handles and enables you to create sharp corners in your profiles.

Faking 3D in Director

Director provides some built-in tools that help produce the illusion of depth. These tools won't replace a dedicated 2D or 3D graphics program, but they do provide a quick way to simulate a third dimension on a flat computer screen.

To distort a bitmap so that it looks like it's being viewed in perspective, you can use the Perspective tool in the Paint window.

1. Select the bitmap with the rectangular Marquee tool.

2. Click the perspective tool button in the Paint window toolbar.

3. Drag the handles of the selection rectangle to squish the bitmap so that it looks like it's receding toward a vanishing point.

Another way to produce the illusion of depth is to lighten or darken bitmaps that are farther away from the viewer in the 3D world. To lighten or darken bitmaps, choose the Lighten or Darken button in the toolbar of the Paint window.

To produce the illusion of a sprite or bitmap moving into a 3D space and getting smaller and farther away from the viewer, use the Scaling command with the Auto Distort command.

Because Director 6 supports Photoshop plug-in filters, you can use your 3D plug-ins on Director bitmaps. The *Inside Macromedia Director 6 with Lingo* CD comes with several Photoshop plug-ins and Director Xtras for you to try out, such as HoloDozo (which requires QuickDraw 3D) and Xaos Tools' TypeCaster for 3D type.

3D Interfaces, Backgrounds, and Objects in Director

Adding 3D elements to Director is as simple as adding 2D bitmaps and involves many of the same issues, such as file size and palette optimization. Bitmaps are discussed in Chapter 8, "Graphics: The Visuals." You can look at adding 3D elements to Director in several ways. You can create a background or interface in a 3D program, for example, and composite 2D graphics on top of it. You can create a background or interface in a 2D program, and use Director to composite 3D elements on top. The key to integrating 3D elements in Director is to composite the various 2D and 3D graphic elements as seamlessly and in as stylistically consistent a way as possible, even though the elements are created in different programs.

3D Interface Design

Chiseled gray buttons and dialog boxes are commonplace in user interfaces. Just look at the standard Macromedia User interface. 3D graphics and textures appeal to the tactile sense and enhance the feeling that you are directly manipulating objects on the computer screen. A well-designed 3D user interface is logically organized and gives a clear visual impression of interface functions.

3D user interface design uses the same principles as 2D user interface design. 3D interfaces have the tendency to accentuate bad interface design. Design carefully! Keep in mind the following points as you design:

▶ When you create 3D interfaces, don't overpower the content with sumptuous textures.

▶ Don't compete with the dimensionality of other 3D elements on the screen. Detailed 3D interfaces will compete visually with 3D content.

▶ Restrict the height of 3D interface objects to two or three levels of depth.

▶ Avoid closely packed, chiseled buttons that create distracting grids.

▶ Subdue the tonal range of shadows and highlights in the interface. Just a few tenths of a percent difference in the gray values of shadows and highlights is enough to give the impression of a third dimension.

▶ Depending on the type of interface you are designing, keep the shadows and light sources consistent across your interface.

▶ Use parallel lighting (distant lights in Extreme 3D) to reduce banding, especially if you need to restrict your interface to a few colors.

▶ Use numeric positioning of objects to ensure consistent placement.

Use 2D programs, such as Photoshop, or 3D programs to create your interface elements. Draw your interface as 2D Bézier curves in FreeHand, for example, leaving holes for the content. Then, import the curves into Extreme 3D and extrude them slightly. Another way to create intricate, molded interfaces is to use a grayscale bump map with the Filter, Render, Lighting Effects command in Photoshop, as discussed previously.

3D Backgrounds

An easy way to add a third dimension to your Director project is to use a 3D background over which you can composite graphics and animations. A 3D background can be as simple as a picture frame for a QuickTime movie or as complex as a fully realized stage set for a character animation. By creating your background as a model in a 3D program, it's easy to change perspective, lighting, and atmospheric effects—even render different parts of the scene separately.

The following list provides a few basic techniques and tips to keep in mind:

▶ Set up an interesting perspective for your background by using the camera and view parameters in the 3D program.

▶ Avoid flat surfaces parallel to the computer screen. Dramatic, low-angle lighting and shadows add a sense of depth.

▶ Consider rendering your background model in foreground, middle-ground, and background layers in E3D. Then, use Photoshop to composite them.

▶ A simple technique, such as adding a slight Gaussian Blur to the background layer using Photoshop's Gaussian Blur filter, creates a sense of depth in a scene.

▶ Most important, make sure your background doesn't compete visually with the content and interface and that it has a graphic style similar to the rest of the project.

3D Objects

When you composite 3D elements that are rendered separately, it's important that they have stylistic consistency so that the elements don't look out of place. Here are some guidelines:

▶ All elements should be lighted from the same directions so that shadows fall consistently. The lights should be of similar intensity and color.

▶ Global environment settings, such as ambient light and fog, should be the same in your rendered 3D graphics, unless you are designing for a particular effect. Use similar colors and surface properties to give your graphics stylistic unity.

▶ Before you start rendering, determine the layering order of your 3D graphics in Director and plan your compositing accordingly.

At the outset, decide how you will composite shadows in Director. Will you composite shadows against the background with the 3D object or animate shadows on a separate layer or channel? Shadows aren't sharp-edged; actually, they are blurry. Merging them realistically with the background can be challenging. See the later sections on anti-aliasing for ways to handle the blurry edges of shadows and other images. You can render shadows with the 3D object, render shadows against the actual background bitmap, render shadows as a separate object, paint shadows later as a separate layer in Photoshop, or paint them directly on the background with the Photoshop Airbrush tool.

Often, it's a good idea to render your 3D images with larger dimensions than you need. Resize the image to the dimensions you want for your Director project. The quality of resized graphics is better if you start with a large graphic and reduce the size, rather than start with a small graphic and increase the size.

Most 3D programs render images at a color depth of 24 bits. So, you'll need to reduce the color depth to use them in an 8-bit Director project.

A common problem with reducing color depth in 3D graphics, however, is that a smooth gradient, such as a smooth, shadowed surface, becomes banded when it's reduced from 24 bits to 8 bits. Before you reduce the color depth, use Photoshop to add a small amount of noise to smooth gradients and to see whether it helps reduce banding. You also can render the image in your 3D program at a color depth of 8 bits.

Anti-Aliasing

Anti-aliasing uses different techniques to blend or blur the jagged edges of computer generated (pixel-based) imagery. Anti-aliasing helps computer imagery look more like a continuous-tone photograph. You can perform one of these anti-aliasing techniques by choosing the Director Paint window. Use the jagged circle you just created and scale it 25 percent by using the Transform Bitmap command. Now, use the Transform Bitmap again and scale the image up by 400 percent. The edges of the circle are now blurred. If the circle you created is dark-colored, drag the circle onto a dark-colored stage and set the ink type to Background Transparent or Matte. A halo of anti-aliased pixels surrounds the circle (see fig. 9.3.)

NOTE

To see aliasing, draw a circle in the Director Paint window and zoom in. The edge of the circle isn't smooth, but jagged. Aliasing is an indication of computer-generated imagery.

Figure 9.3

Aliased and anti-aliased graphics.

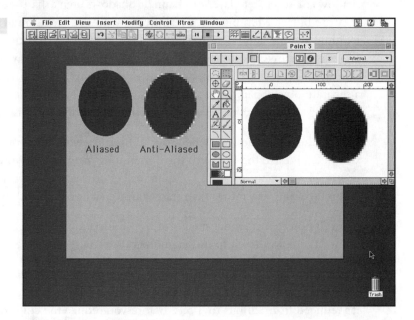

Anti-aliasing generally makes computer-generated imagery appear more realistic, but it has the disadvantage of taking up a lot of computer time and resources to render and display. Fortunately, in most 3D programs you can control the amount of anti-aliasing in your renders.

Be sure you render your anti-aliased images with an alpha channel. Alpha channels are used in such programs as Photoshop and After Effects to composite anti-aliased images against varying backgrounds without creating a halo. After compositing your anti-aliased images, you can import the composited bitmap into Director.

Director is a hard-edged world because it doesn't support alpha channels. If you plan to composite irregularly shaped, computer-generated imagery in Director, choose a way to deal with the dreaded anti-alias fringe or halo. The Alphamania Xtra from MediaLab enables anti-aliasing in real-time for Director projects. Find out more at the following address:

```
http://www.macromedia.com/software/xtras/director/medialab.html
```

Resolving Anti-Aliasing Problems

Several problems have been associated with anti-aliased graphics, such as anti-alias fringe, a large time cost, Director's lack of support for alpha channels, and so on. This section discusses ways to remove anti-alias fringes from graphics for use in Director or other ways to use anti-aliased graphics in Director. The technique you use depends on the particular graphic, its shape and color, the background involved, production values of your project, and time constraints.

One way to work around the problems of using anti-aliased graphics in Director is to render the image without anti-aliasing at the cost of realistic-looking imagery. Fortunately, a couple techniques enable you to process anti-aliased graphics for use in the Director cast.

In Photoshop, several ways exist to remove anti-aliased edges from objects. Most techniques involve modifying the selection outline around the object, and then copying and pasting into new files or against new backgrounds.

If you use these processes on a sequence of PICT files in an animation, preserve the registration points when you copy and paste. After you have the selection outline the way you want it, but before you paste the selection into a new file:

1. Press the Shift key while the Selection tool is still active.

2. Add two small rectangular selections in the upper-left and lower-right corners of the image. This ensures that the image's original size is preserved.

3. Now, when you copy and paste the selection into a new graphics file or into the Director cast you will have preserved the original dimensions, and thus, the original registration point of the graphic.

If the file has an alpha channel that corresponds to the object's edges, you can use the Threshold command to modify the alpha channel and to create a selection outline that removes the anti-aliased edges.

The following tutorial shows you how to utilize the Threshold command in Photoshop to create an alpha channel to use as a selection. You can use this selection to remove the anti-alias fringe from a graphics element. After you have the selection the way you want it, you can copy and paste the graphic into the Director cast.

Handling Anti-Aliasing in Photoshop: The Threshold Command

1. Select the alpha channel in the Photoshop Layers palette.

2. Choose Image, Map, Threshold and adjust the slider so that the white area shrinks.

3. Select the RGB channel in the Layers palette and load the alpha channel as a selection.

4. Repeat this process until you have a clean-edged selection outline.

5. Copy and paste the object into the Director cast or into another Photoshop file for further processing.

The tutorial that follows discusses another technique for removing anti-aliased fringes in Photoshop.

Handling Anti-Aliasing in Photoshop: Modify, Contract

1. Select the object by doing one of the following:

    ▶ Loading the alpha channel

    ▶ Using the Magic Wand tool

    ▶ Using the Color Range command

    ▶ Painting the selection mask in QuickMask mode

2. When the Selection outline is the way you want it, choose Modify, Contract from the Select menu with a value of 1 pixel. This command shrinks your selection outline by one pixel and removes most of the anti-aliased halo.

3. After you remove the anti-aliasing to your satisfaction, copy and paste the object into the Director cast or into another Photoshop file for compositing.

Here is another Photoshop technique you can use with floating selections. After you paste an object into a new file (while it's still a floating selection) use the Select, Matting, Remove White Matte; Select, Matting, Remove Black Matte; or Select, Matting, Defringe commands to remove extraneous pixels that you rendered against a white, black, or a colored background, respectively.

Another way to handle anti-aliasing is to render your 3D graphics against a neutral, solid-color background. If the tonal values and colors of your Director background are similar, such as all dark grays and blues, try to render the object against a solid-color background in your 3D program. The solid-color background should be in the mid-range of the tonal values and colors of the Director background. A medium gray, solid-color background, for example, works well if your Director background contains a range of different grays.

You also can render the image against the actual background that you'll be using in Director. In Extreme 3D, for instance, you can import any PICT file to use as a background for your 3D world. This technique can provide the highest quality seamless compositing, but also can require a lot of work, render time, and planning.

3D Animation

Three-dimensional animation can be more than adding morphing chrome logos to your interactive project. 3D animation can provide visualization of complex objects and environments and illustrate dynamic processes. By adding interactivity to 3D animations, you can create navigable virtual reality experiences.

General Considerations

The use of 3D animations involves the same issues as 2D animations. As always, plan ahead for 3D graphics. Before you begin rendering in your 3D program, make sure you understand how the animation fits into the Director project and how the animations interact with and overlay other graphic elements.

Animation Formats

Animation formats for 3D animations are the same as for 2D animations—PICs, Director film loops, imported Director movies, sequences of frames in the main movie, sequences of frames in a MIAW, or QuickTime. If you want to add interactivity to animations, create them as a sequence of separate PICT files, as QuickTime movies, or as 3DMF (QuickDraw 3D) files. QuickTime and QuickDraw 3D provide many benefits including compressed files, built-in interactivity, and many useful Lingo commands for controlling playback. In addition, a QuickTime movie or QuickDraw 3D model takes up only a single cast slot or sprite channel and usually animates much faster than a sequence of bitmaps. Decide at the outset how you will layer and composite 3D objects in Director and plan your rendering accordingly.

If you want to add interactivity, you'll probably want to output your animation as a sequence of separate PICT files, as a QuickTime movie, or as a 3DMF file. Users will need the QuickTime system extension to view QuickTime movies and the QuickDraw 3D system extension to view 3DMF models. QuickDraw 3D provides the most sophisticated built-in interactivity of all these options, enabling the user to directly manipulate 3D models with the mouse in real-time. Large PICT files may animate slowly, but are supported natively; test your animation on target playback systems.

The same issues regarding importing and playback performance of 2D animation and digital video apply to 3D. See Chapter 6, "Director as an Animator," for a discussion of animation in Director; see Chapter 12, "Digital Video: The Movie Within the Movie," for a discussion of use of digital video and QuickTime.

Compositing and Post-Processing Animation

All the compositing and post-processing issues for static 3D graphics also apply to 3D animation, except that they are multiplied by the number of animation frames.

You can use the symmetry of your 3D object to reduce the render time and the number of separate frames and cast members in your animation. If you want to rotate the letter "A" 360 degrees about its vertical axis, for example, you only need to rotate it through 180 degrees because of the mirror-plane symmetry along the vertical axis.

Determine the layering order of your 3D graphics in the Director score before you start rendering and plan your compositing accordingly. Animated 3D graphics look more realistic if they throw shadows across background graphics. This is because the shadows change shape as the element animates and they fall on different surfaces and objects. Plan from the start how to composite animated shadows. Sometimes you can get by with using a simple drop shadow in a separate channel in the Director score that moves with the object.

As you post-process separate animation frames, you might want to preserve the original size of each frame to preserve its registration points. Outline each frame with a solid line or paint small, solid-color squares in the upper-left and lower-right corners of the image. When you import these graphics into the Director cast, the original size and registration points are preserved. Remove these marks after you've set up the animation in the Director score. Crop your frames to reduce file size as the last step—after the animation is set up in Director—so that you don't lose your registration points.

Color depth reduction of 3D animations can cause banding of smooth gradients and pixel drift of dithered patterns. The quality of a color-depth reduction depends on the particular palette and the colors you use in the 3D world. Sometimes, adding a small amount of noise in Photoshop before you reduce the color depth helps.

Large areas of flat, solid-color in animations also can have annoying pixel drift when dithered to 8-bit color. Avoid dithering solid-color areas when you reduce color depth. It's a good idea to output a short test animation at your final render settings and run a test color-depth reduction to see how the 24-bit animation looks at 8 bits. Consider creating an 8-bit super palette in Equilibrium's DeBabelizer. A *super palette* is based on the colors found in a range of different images, such as frames in an animation. The super palette uses different algorithms to optimize the appearance of graphics within a limited range of colors. After you create the super palette, you can use DeBabelizer to batch dither all the graphics to that palette.

Animated 3D Objects

Animated 3D objects can add appeal to your Director project. Animation in a 3D interface can make it easier to understand and use. A 3D animation can provide alternate views of a complex structure, such as a sculpture, a human heart, or a flower.

One way to provide multiple views of a complex object is to show the object rotating about an axis.

Object Rotation in Extreme 3D

1. Select the object you want to rotate.

2. Select a keyframe for the end of the animation. The number of frames for a full-circle rotation depends on the requirements of your project. Thirty-six frames generally provides a smooth rotation, but you might be able to get by with fewer frames.

3. Choose the Animate, Auto Rotate command in Extreme 3D and specify a rotation angle of 360 degrees for a full-circle rotation. You might want to rotate about the object's Y axis (vertical axis), but it depends on how your 3D world and your object axes are set up.

4. Extreme 3D automatically creates an animation of the object rotating 360 degrees about its center point on the axis you specify.

5. Now render the animation to disk as a QuickTime movie or a sequence of numbered PICT files.

If the object swings out of view or doesn't rotate the way you want it to, you might need to move the object's center point. To line up the object's center point with the axis of rotation, use the Object Center tool. Another trick is to link the object to a construction point you place on the axis of rotation. Then, use the Auto Rotate command to rotate the construction point. The object appears to rotate or orbit around the construction point.

You can output your animation as a QuickTime movie or a sequence of PICT images. You can then add interactivity with Lingo, enabling the user to rotate the object to the right or to the left. The movie HEART.DIR on the accompanying CD demonstrates one way to do this with an animation output as a sequence of PICT frames. See the Lingo handlers in this movie for an example.

Probably the easiest way to add interactive 3D models to Director, in terms of authoring, is to use QuickDraw 3D and output your models in the 3DMF format. Extreme 3D version 2 and other 3D programs support 3DMF output. QD3D provides interactivity and fast, software-based rendering of objects saved in 3DMF format. With the QD3D Xtra and the QD3D system extension you can add fully interactive, rendered 3D objects to the Director cast and use them from within Director.

A QTVR object movie is a special QuickTime movie format for 3D objects that enables you to manipulate and rotate photographic-quality objects in real-time on average desktop PCs. Use QTVR if the objects you want to represent are real-world objects such as sculptures or archeological artifacts. You create a QTVR object of a real-world object by taking a series of photographs of the object from many different angles. Creating photographs of an object for use in creating a QTVR object movie usually requires special equipment, such as a turntable, on which to place the object that you are photographing. You can also create QTVR objects from 3D models by using the 3D camera to take "snapshots" of the model from different angles and saving each snapshot as a PICT file.

The QTVR Object Tool available free at Apple Computer's web site enables you to create object movies from sequences of photographs or PICT files. Documentation with the tool explains how to create a series of photographs or PICT files that you can use to create a QTVR object movie. You can also embed QTVR objects in standard QTVR scenes or panoramas, but you will need the QTVR Authoring Tools Suite to do this. Use the QTVR Xtra and QuickTime extension to view and interact with QTVR movies in Director on both Mac and Windows.

Creating a QuickDraw 3D Object

A QuickDraw 3D object is a 3D model saved in the 3DMF format. Extreme 3D and other 3D programs will save models in this format. You can save 3DMF files as binary files or ASCII files. The format you choose depends on your playback engine or platform (for example the web or Windows), but the QuickDraw 3D Xtra will read both formats. Test playback on your target systems to make sure the files are being read correctly. Binary files usually are smaller than their ASCII counterparts and are probably better for web-based playback. To export a 3DMF format file in Extreme 3D choose Export, Binary 3D Metafile or Export, Text 3D Metafile from the File menu.

Tips for reducing the file size of 3DMF models in Extreme 3D include the following:

- ▶ Avoid using texture maps.
- ▶ Use primitive, basic objects such as spheres, cubes, and cones.
- ▶ Reduce the quality settings in the "Adaptive Smoothing…" or "Uniform Smoothing…" dialog boxes under the Render menu.

Adding a QuickDraw 3D Object to Director

The QuickDraw 3D Xtra gives a wide range of interactivity and display options that you can access at author-time from a tabbed dialog box or that you can control at the sprite level via Lingo (see fig. 9.4). You will need the QuickDraw 3D extension for Mac and Windows available free from Apple Computer to author and view QD3D models and use the QD3D Xtra. Your users will also need this extension to view 3DMF models.

Figure 9.4

QuickDraw 3D Xtra.

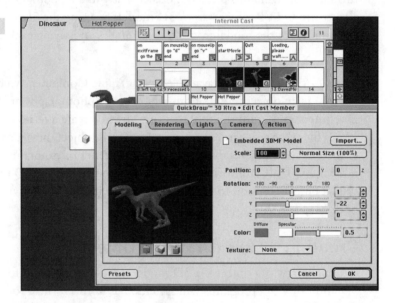

Using the QD3D Xtra is incredibly easy. After you drag the QD3D Xtra to your Xtras folder in the Director directory, launch Director and choose Modify Element, QuickDraw 3D Model from the Insert menu and choose a 3DMF model to insert. Double-click on the QD3D cast member to display the Cast Member Properties dialog box. You can use this dialog box to set a wide range of initial properties for the object, such as scale, rotation, surface properties, enabling direct manipulation of the object with the mouse and drag-and-drop features. The Xtra comes with excellent documentation. See the QD3D Xtra that comes with Director 6 for more details. As with all Director Xtras, you will also need to distribute the Xtra with the final project as is mentioned in Chapter 21, "The Xtra Step."

Navigable Environments

One of the most useful applications of 3D animation is to provide visualization of 3D environments that are impossible or too expensive to see in the real world. Adding interactivity enables the user to explore the 3D world by using the computer keyboard and mouse. Interactive controls typically provide the capability to turn left or right, and move forward and backward within the 3D world.

QuickTime VR, the cross-platform virtual reality extension of QuickTime, provides photographic-quality imagery, sophisticated navigation features, embedded hot spots, and the capability to pick up and manipulate objects within the 3D scene. QuickTime VR movies are special QuickTime movies created with the QTVR Authoring Kit or free QTVR Authoring tools from Apple Computer or Nodester from Panimation.

The animation features of most 3D programs enable you to create navigable environments fairly easily. You can typically create animations for navigable environments by animating the camera in the 3D world:

▶ To simulate a panoramic effect in a 3D world, rotate the camera about its center point.

▶ To simulate a walk-through or fly-through in the 3D world, animate the camera along a prescribed path.

▶ You also can create animations with multiple panoramic views and multiple motion paths for a more immersive, virtual reality-type experience.

With some planning and a little work, you can create navigable 3D environments with Lingo in Director. The file PANORAMA.DIR in the Chapter 9 folder on the accompanying CD provides an example of one way to implement a simple panning effect entirely in Lingo. If you have the QTVR Authoring Tools Suite, you can create QuickTime VR movies and play them back in Director with a full range of interactivity using XCMDs, XObjects, or Xtras.

Panoramas and Fly-Throughs

A *panorama* is a wide, typically 360-degree view of a 3D world as seen from a single spot. This spot is sometimes called a *node*. Some 3D programs, such as

Bryce, have a special panorama rendering mode that automatically creates 360-degree views of a 3D scene. By showing various pieces of the panorama, you can simulate the act of standing at the node and looking around in different directions in your 3D world. In other programs, such as Extreme 3D, you can place the camera at the node, rotate it 360 degrees, and create PICT-file animations or a QuickTime movie. Playing the animation simulates turning a full circle while standing in a single spot.

The Director movie PANORAMA.DIR in the Chapter 9 folder on the accompanying CD is an example of using Lingo to produce an interactive panoramic effect. Open the cast window and take a look at the scripts used to produce this effect.

Walk-throughs and fly-throughs simulate the act of moving through a 3D environment. If you render the fly-through as a QuickTime movie, you can use QuickTime's built-in controls or Lingo's digital video commands to move back and forth along the predefined path. Chapter 12, "Digital Video: The Movie Within the Movie," discusses the use of Lingo and digital video in Director. You also can render the animation as a sequence of PICTs, import them into the cast, and use the Cast to Time command to create the fly-through animation in the Director score. You then can add interactivity by using Lingo.

Creating Fly-Throughs in Extreme 3D

Walk-throughs and fly-throughs are easy to create in Extreme 3D. You can turn any spline curve into a motion path for your camera. You also can use keyframe animation to animate the camera.

Using Keyframe Animation to Create a Fly-Through

1. Open the Views browser and create a series of keyframe views or establishing shots.

2. Create a view for the beginning of the fly-through, the end of the fly-through, and any intermediate steps, such as turns.

3. When you're finished, set the current frame to 0 in the Animation Control window.

4. Select the view that is the starting point of your fly-through in the Views browser.

5. Choose View, Align Camera, To View.

6. Change the current frame to the next keyframe and select the second view from the Views browser.

7. Choose View, Align Camera, To View again. Repeat this with every view until you reach the end of your fly-through.

8. From the Views browser, select the Camera view and play back the animation. If it looks OK, render the animation to disk.

Creating Animations in POV-Ray

POV-Ray is an incredible 3D ray-tracer. Ray-tracing is a computationally intensive (that means slow) but high-quality type of rendering. Ray-tracing excels at creating photorealistic lighting effects, such as reflections and refractions. POV-Ray is based on David Buck's original ray tracer, DKB-Trace, and has been developed and maintained over the years by a group of hard-working, volunteer programmers. It is available free on the Internet at the following URL:

http://www.povray.org/

Currently, version 3 of POV-Ray is available for DOS, Windows 3.1, Linux, SunOS, Unix, PowerMac, and Macintosh 68K systems.

A large collection of software related to POV-Ray exists, including modelers, viewers, utility programs, scene files, and rendered images. Many of these are available at the POV-Ray web site and on the Ray-Trace! CD-ROM from Walnut Creek. You can check out some of the contents of the CD at the following:

http://www.povray.org/pov-cdrom/

An updated version of the POV-Ray CD-ROM for version 3 may be available by the time you read this.

POV is a rendering engine only. Figure 9.5 shows an example image included in the POV-Ray distribution. You create 3D objects and worlds by using a text-based scene description language. You can also use one of several shareware modelers and conversion utilities to convert or create models for rendering in POV-Ray.

Figure 9.5

POV-Ray image and scene description file.

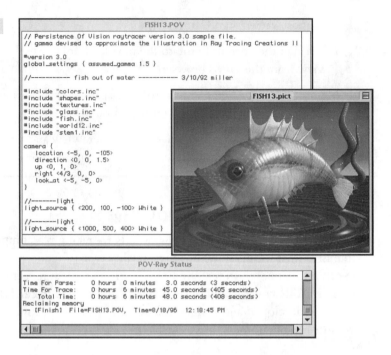

An excellent FAQ for POV-Ray beginners can be found at the following address:

http://www.whoville.com/pov-ray/faq/

The instructions that describe a POV-Ray image are stored in a text file. The file contains commands and parameters in the POV-Ray scene description language that tell the POV-Ray renderer how to render your scene. These commands tell the renderer about the geometry of objects, surface properties, lighting and many other things. Instructions and parameters are usually grouped within curly braces. For example,

```
object {
   Cube
   scale <10000, 1, 500>
   translate -25*y
}
```

tells the POV-Ray to render a box-shaped object that is scaled along the X, Y, and Z axes and moved or translated 25 units along the Y-axis. All objects are initially created at the 0,0,0 point of the 3D world.

The commands

```
object {
   Cube
   scale <10000, 1, 500>
   translate -25*y

   texture {
      pigment { color red 0.0 green 0.07 blue 0.0 }
}
```

tell the renderer to give the box a greenish color.

The command

```
light_source { <200, 100, -100> White }
```

adds a white light source to the scene at the indicated coordinates. You will see similar commands when you look at VRML worlds.

The POV-Ray scene description language contains many useful features to help you create beautiful imagery and animations. It is beyond the scope of this chapter to describe the features of this language. But to give you an idea of the capabilities of POV-Ray, this section will look at one of the most useful features for animations—the "clock" variable.

By using the clock variable you can animate a property over time. The clock variable is a number that is incremented by a set amount in each animation frame. You can set the initial and final values of the clock variable in the animation preferences dialog box. The clock variable can be added to, multiplied by, subtracted from, or otherwise used to modify any numeric property in your scene. First, you must set up your POV-Ray scene to render a sequence of animation frames.

Rendering Animation Frames with POV-Ray

1. Choose Preferences, File Rendering… from the Edit menu.

2. Choose Animation from the Settings for: pop-up menu (see fig. 9.6).

3. Check the Turn on "clock" animation check box.

4. Enter a total number of frames for the animation in the Final: Frame Number box.

continues

Rendering Animation Frames with POV-Ray   continued

Figure 9.6

Animation settings in POV-RAY.

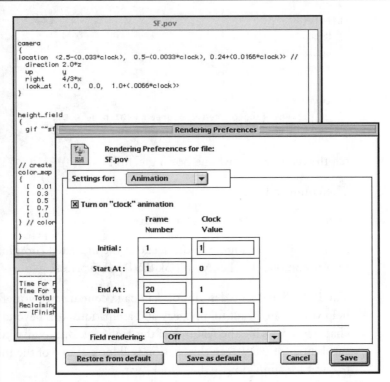

5. You can also specify a restricted range of frames to animate in the Start At: and End At: settings if you want to render only a part of the total animation.

6. Enter an initial value for the Clock value. This value is the initial value of the clock variable in the first frame.

7. Enter a final value for the Clock value. This value is the final value of the clock variable in the last frame.

   In each frame, the clock variable will be incremented by the following:

$$\frac{(\text{The Final Clock Value} - \text{The Initial Clock Value})}{\text{The Number of Frames}}$$

8. Click Save.

Now you can use the clock value to animate properties over time. The clock variable will be incremented in each frame. To create a fly-through animation, for example, you can add the clock value to the values for camera location and camera look-at point in the scene description file. The following code, for example, creates a camera that flys-through your scene:

```
camera
{
location  <2.5-(0.33*clock),  0.5-(0.0033*clock), 0.24+(0.0166*clock)>
  direction 2.0*z
  up        y
  right     4/3*x
  look_at   <1.0,  0.0,  1.0+(.0066*clock)>
}
```

The factors `(0.33*clock)`, `(0.0033*clock)`, `(0.0166*clock)`, `(.0066*clock)` are added to the camera's location parameters and look-at point. The values of these factors will change in each frame with the changing clock variable and move the camera through the scene.

When creating animations in POV-Ray, it's often useful to define keyframes and perform test renders at the keyframes. Then, divide the animation into smaller pieces with starting and ending points defined by keyframes. Use the keyframe values of the parameters that you want to animate and calculate the clock values. Figure 9.7 shows the camera's settings and accompanying picture.

Figure 9.7

Fly-through animation in POV-Ray.

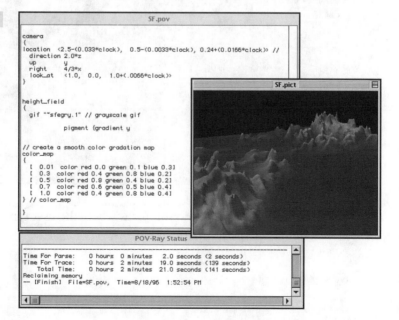

Views, Nodes, and Meshes

But what if you want to do more than just fly along a single path? How do you give the user the ability to look around, change directions and otherwise navigate through the scene? You can invest in QTVR authoring tools from Apple and production equipment, or you can use your 3D program to create views and animated motion paths, and use Lingo to control the navigation.

Creating a fully navigable 3D environment requires some planning. You use the concept of a *node*, a spot where the user can stop and look around, as well as the concept of a *motion path*, a defined route that the user can take to move between nodes in your 3D world. Basically, you break down the navigation you want into nodes and motion paths, and map them out as animations in your 3D program.

1. Map out the motion paths in your 3D world. You might want to render your world from a bird's-eye view and sketch the possible motion paths (see fig. 9.8).

Figure 9.8

Bird's-eye view of a 3D world with nodes.

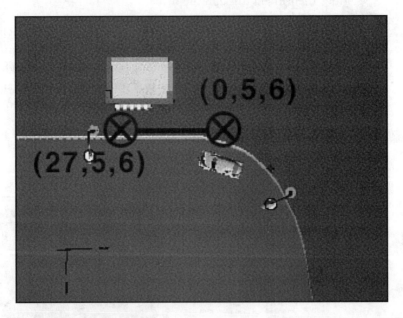

2. Select places along the motion paths where the user can stop and look around. These places are the nodes.

3. Decide how many views the user has at each node. It might, for example, be possible to just have four views at 90-degree angles (forward, backward, left, and right). If you have only one motion path, the user can move forward and backward along the motion path at each node.

4. If you want the user to be able to move throughout your 3D world, you'll have to decide which directions the user is able to move at each node, such as right, left, up, down, right 30 degrees, and so on. Then, you can create more motion paths extending from that node.

5. As you add more motion paths, you quickly create a network of interconnected motion paths. This network is sometimes called a mesh.

A *mesh* consists of a web of nodes and motion paths in two or three dimensions. Strands of the mesh are the motion paths the user follows to navigate through your environment. To provide a navigable 3D environment, create animations that simulate looking around at each node and animations that simulate moving between nodes along each path.

▶ For planning animations and Lingo control, use a naming convention for nodes and views. For nodes, you can use the X, Y, Z coordinates of the node in 3D space, for example (1, 2, 1). For the views, you can use the cardinal positions, for example N, E, W, S, NNE, NE, ENE, and so on.

▶ Planning your camera shots and node positions on a spreadsheet is helpful (see fig 9.9). You can plan each keyframe or all frames. One way to organize the spreadsheet is to have each row represent the frame or keyframe that you want to specify. In the columns of the spreadsheet enter the X, Y, Z coordinates of the node, the camera position and look-at point for each view, and the names of the nodes you can travel to from each view.

▶ Set the units of your 3D world to reflect the node structure so that the nodal coordinates fall on integers.

▶ Plan the number of animation frames for each view and motion path.

▶ If you have more than three or four nodes, you might want to create a navigable QuickTime movie.

Figure 9.9

Spreadsheet to set up a navigable QuickTime movie.

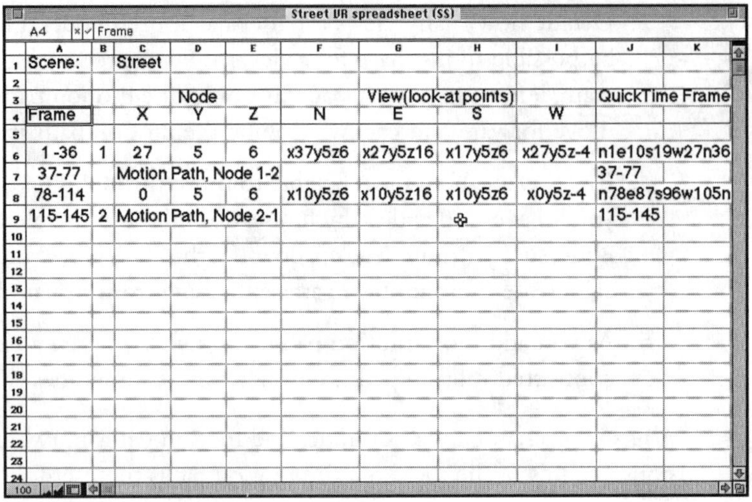

	A	B	C	D	E	F	G	H	I	J	K
1	Scene:		Street								
2											
3				Node				View(look-at points)		QuickTime Frame	
4	Frame		X	Y	Z	N	E	S	W		
5											
6	1-36	1	27	5	6	x37y5z6	x27y5z16	x17y5z6	x27y5z-4	n1e10s19w27n36	
7	37-77		Motion Path, Node 1-2							37-77	
8	78-114		0	5	6	x10y5z6	x10y5z16	x10y5z6	x0y5z-4	n78e87s96w105n	
9	115-145	2	Motion Path, Node 2-1							115-145	

▶ In a QuickTime movie, you create navigation by jumping to a frame using Lingo's digital video commands and playing a selected range of frames that simulate moving between nodes or looking around at the node. Chapter 12 teaches you about controlling QuickTime with Lingo.

▶ In your spreadsheet, include a column for the number or range of QuickTime frames for each view and motion path.

QTVR

QTVR provides high-quality photographic 3D imagery, compressed files, and built-in navigation and interactivity of 3D worlds on average desktop PCs. You can create simple panoramas and 3D object movies by using free authoring tools or more complex navigable environments by using the QTVR Authoring Tools Suite from Apple Computer. To create complex navigable environments, you still have to map out your 3D world with a mesh of motion paths and nodes and then create the views at each node, but QTVR handles compiling it into a single file and automatically provides the navigation controls. Look for this process to become easier as the technology matures. To create QTVR movies for playback from Director, you need the QTVR Authoring Tool Suite or the free QTVR Authoring Tools. Check out availability and pricing at the following:

```
http://qtvr.quicktime.apple.com.
```

The rest of this chapter shows you how to create simple QTVR movies and incorporate them into Director projects by using freely available tools and Xtras. To create more complicated QTVR movies with multiple hot spots and multiple navigation paths, you will need to invest in the QuickTime VR Authoring tools and special camera rigs.

You can also download the QTVR Xtra from Apple at the following:

```
http://qtvr.quicktime.apple.com/dev/tool.html
```

Other QTVR tools and advanced authoring information can also be found there.

To create a QTVR panorama you need the following:

▶ A panoramic PICT file, which is a wide-angle view of a scene that is specially warped and distorted for use in QTVR panoramas. You can create a panoramic PICT file in a 3D graphics programs such as MetaTools' Bryce, Strata Studio Pro, or POV-Ray or use a special panoramic photographic camera to take panoramic pictures of real-world scenes.

▶ The free Make QTVR Panorama tool from Apple Computer is available on this book's CD or at the following address:

```
http://qtvr.quicktime.apple.com/
```

▶ A Macintosh running System 7 or later, QuickTime 2.0 or later, and enough memory to load the source PICT, plus 2 MB.

Currently, you need a Macintosh to author QTVR movies, but you can create panoramic PICTs on Macintosh or Windows machines.

The next two tutorials show you how to create a panoramic PICT file in MetaTool's Bryce (see fig. 9.10) and in POV-Ray (see fig. 9.11), respectively. Both are cross-platform 3D programs. After you have a PICT file, the next tutorial will show you how to turn it into a QTVR movie, and the final discussion will show you how to integrate this movie into your Director project.

Creating a Panoramic Image in Bryce

1. Make sure your camera is level. Double-click on the ball with the cross on it on the left side of the Bryce interface screen. In the Camera dialog box, under the Angle settings, enter 0 for X settings and 0 for Y settings.

2. Choose Document Set-up under the File menu. Select QTVR panorama and click the check mark.

3. Choose the Render Options menu by clicking on the downward pointing arrow next to the rendering control balls and select the 360 Panorama option in the Render Options menu.

4. Choose Render to Disk under the File menu. Select 72 dpi and check the Auto-rotate option. Click the check mark.

5. Save the file as a PICT file.

Figure 9.10

Rendered panorama in Bryce.

Creating a Panoramic Image in POV-Ray

1. Set up the camera in your scene description file. The following is a fragment of the POV-Ray scene description language that will set up a camera to render a panoramic image from QuickTime VR:

```
camera { // Creates a 360 degree camera view for a QTVR panorama
cylinder 1
right  1*x up      4*y
vertically angle 360
location  <0.0, 0.0, 0.0> look_at   <0.0, 0.0, 1.0>
}
```

2. Choose Preferences, File Rendering... from the Edit menu.

3. Choose Output Size from the Settings for: pop-up menu.

4. Enter dimensions for the rendered image.

   As mentioned previously, the width of the panoramic image in pixels should be evenly divisible by four and the height should be evenly divisible by 96. Try 576×384 for low-resolution renders or 2016×756 for high resolution renders.

5. Choose Start Rendering from the Render menu.

6. After completion you will have a panoramic graphic suitable for use in QTVR.

   Eduard Schwan has provided a sample POV-Ray scene description file for QuickTime VR in the Scenes:QuickTimeVR! folder contained within with the POV-Ray 3 distribution.

Figure 9.11

Panoramic image rendered in POV-Ray.

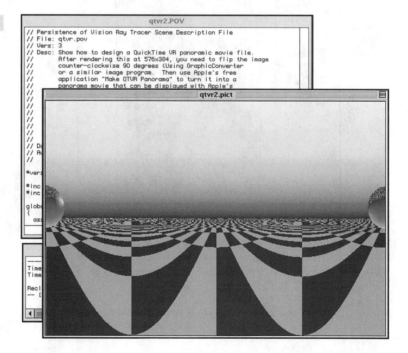

After you have the panoramic PICT, you can convert it to a QuickTime VR panorama.

Creating a QTVR Movie with the Make QTVR Panorama Tool

You can get the free QTVR Panorama tool from the following:

```
http://qtvr.quicktime.apple.com/
```

1. Rotate the PICT 90 degrees counterclockwise so that the bottom of the image is to the right, in an image processing program such as Photoshop (see fig. 9.12).

Figure 9.12

Rotated panorama in Photoshop.

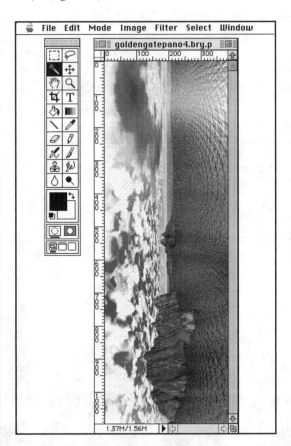

2. Start the Make QTVR Panorama tool and open the PICT that you want to convert or drag-and-drop the PICT file to the Make QTVR Panorama icon.

3. Change the dimensions of the movie to the dimensions you will use in your Director project, such as 240×180 or 160×120.

The default compression settings work pretty well. Greater compression will improve playback on CD-ROMs or the web at the expense of image quality.

Figure 9.13

The Settings dialog box in the Make QTVR Panorama tool.

gldngate.p

Source PICT: *Daedalus:Desktop Fol...ion:ch5 figs:gldngate.p*

Compression Settings... *Cinepak High (75)*

Tile Movie: *Daedalus:Desktop Fold...:ch5 figs:gldngate.p.tile* Set...

View Size: width: 240 height: 180

Default Horizontal Pan: 0.0 *(0 to 360)*

Default Vertical Pan: 0.0 *(~-45 to +45)*

Default Zoom: 0.0 *(enter 0 for default)*

QTVR Movie: *Daedalus:Desktop Fold...ch5 figs:gldngate.p.snm* Set...

Make Default Cancel Create

4. Choose Create. The PICT is saved as a QuickTime VR panorama.

QTVR Xtra

Now you have a QTVR panorama movie. The rest of this discussion will show you how to use the new, QTVR Xtra to incorporate the QTVR movie into a Director project. The QTVR Xtra for both Macintosh and Windows is available from the following URL:

http://qtvr.quicktime.apple.com/

The QTVR Xtra that is available now is a Lingo Xtra. The Xtra provides the Lingo commands to open and control QTVR movies in Director (see fig. 9.13). By the time you read this, a QTVR Asset Xtra, similar to the QD3D Xtra, may be available. A QTVR Asset Xtra will enable you, among other things, to insert QTVR movies into the cast by using the Insert, Media Element menu.

Figure 9.14

Using the QTVR Xtra.

Keep in mind the following points while using the QTVR Xtra:

▶ QTVR movie files are external to Director.

▶ QTVR movie files should be flattened for cross-platform compatibility. For information about flattening QuickTime movies, see Chapter 12.

▶ Lingo Parameters and return values of QTVR functions are passed as strings.

▶ Properties persist—for example, the HotSpotType property returns the value of the last HotSpot type that the mouse was over, whether the mouse is currently over it or not. The extensive documentation that comes with the QTVR Xtra describes all the different properties.

▶ The order in which you invoke a series of certain QTVR commands is important. See the documentation accompanying the QTVR Xtra for details.

▶ Cursor feedback may be inconsistent in Director. See the documentation for details.

Incorporating a QTVR movie into Director by using the QTVR Xtra can be a little tricky. To provide interactivity for a QTVR movie you will have to periodically test to see if the cursor is over the QTVR movie and explicitly pass control to the QTVR Xtra. Typically, the steps you will take to add a QTVR movie in Director are as follows:

1. Create a transparent rectangular sprite in the space on the Director stage that you want to place the QTVR movie.

2. Use the `QTVROpen` Lingo command to open the QTVR movie at this location.

3. Use Director's `rollOver` command to test if the cursor is over the rectangular sprite that is underneath the QTVR movie.

4. Use the `QTVRMouseOver` and `QTVRIdle` Lingo commands to provide interactivity for the QTVR movie.

The file QTVRSTUB.DIR in this book's Chapter 9 folder on the accompanying CD-ROM is a bare bones example of integrating a QTVR movie in Director with the minimum Lingo you will need to provide interactivity. The file TESTBED.DIR provided by Apple Computer is a full-featured example that illustrates the full range and functionality of the QTVR Xtra.

In Practice

3D graphics can add interest to an otherwise "flat" Director project. 3D graphics and textures appeal to the tactile sense and enhance the feeling that you are directly manipulating objects on the computer screen. This chapter and the previous one covered the graphical aspects of your Director project. The next chapter proceeds to another critical multimedia component—text.

▶ You don't always need a 3D program to get good 3D effects. Know what your 2D programs are capable of with respect to creating 3D effects and use them when appropriate.

▶ Consider whether there are compelling advantages to 3D presentation for the information that you're trying to communicate. Certain content—complex objects, dynamic processes, real-world environments that are difficult or expensive to reach—often benefit from 3D presentation.

▶ 3D user interfaces tend to accentuate bad design. Design carefully.

▶ Get familiar with tools that make it easier to incorporate 3D graphics and animation into Director projects. In Director 6, Photoshop plug-in filters are used directly on cast members. 3D filter effects can be animated within Director. Extreme 3D is a powerful yet easy-to-use 3D program that ships as part of the Director Multimedia Studio.

▶ New cast and Lingo Xtras enable you to integrate QuickTime VR and QuickDraw 3D scenes and objects with a full range of powerful interactive and rendering features.

Text: The Story

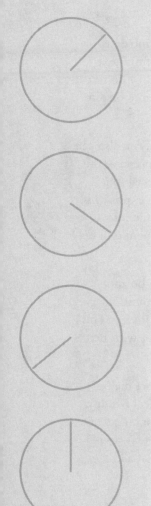

With the capability to incorporate video, audio, and graphics in multimedia applications in Director, it is often easy to overlook the powerful features that Director offers for the manipulation of text.

Some of the techniques discussed in this chapter depend on an extensive use of Lingo. Although the Lingo examples in this chapter are carefully explained, if you are not yet familiar with Lingo you might want to look at Chapter 16, "Lingo: The Basics" before looking at the Lingo coding in this chapter.

This chapter covers the following topics:

- ▶ Differences between types of text formats
- ▶ Designing for change with text cast members and fields
- ▶ Using text fields for advanced concepts
- ▶ Using FileIO for retrieval and storage of text files

Differences Between Text Fields, Rich Text, and Bitmapped Text

Most experienced Director users understand the difference between cast members that are bitmapped text and those that are traditionally considered text. Traditional text items in computer programs contain textual information such as word count or which lines contain what words. This textual information can be searched by word and usually even edited by word or letter.

Bitmapped text is a bitmapped image of what was at one time text information. When text becomes bitmapped, it contains none of the text information (such as words or sentences) that it did as text. It is now just a graphics image. This means that it is impossible to do to bitmapped images of text such things as search for a particular word or make changes to fonts or styles.

With Director 5 and 6, the two types of text items are as follows: field cast members that were available in earlier versions of Director, and text cast members (or rich text). This chapter refers to these two text types as text cast members and field members (or just "fields").

Text Cast Members

Text cast members become bitmapped images when the Director movie is running. As bitmapped images, they can retain the look you want from text that appears in multimedia applications: They can be anti-aliased; they do not require font information on the host computer, so they look the same on any machine; and they animate quickly.

Text cast members enable paragraph formatting and definable tabs. You also can import Rich Text Format (RTF) files into text cast members and preserve the format of these files. Suppose that you create a document with special font styling or format in a word processor such as WordPerfect. You can export this file as an RTF (Rich Text Format) file and then import that RTF file into a text cast member. The special font styling and format of the document will be preserved in the text cast member.

Another advantage of text cast members is that the text image can be anti-aliased. Anti-aliasing blends the edges of an image with the background image and thus creates a smooth integration of the text and background images. This is more attractive in appearance than the jagged appearance you get with text in field cast members.

The anti-aliasing feature of text cast members is set in the Properties dialog box for text cast members. If you select a text cast member and select Modify, Cast Member, Properties, you find the properties that can be set for a text cast member (figure 10.1). The three options are to either anti-alias all text, anti-alias only text larger than a specified font size, or anti-alias no text at all.

Figure 10.1

The Properties dialog box for text cast members.

Text cast members, however, have two serious drawbacks: They cannot be edited outside the Director authoring environment and, thus, cannot be edited when a Director movie is made into a finished product. To make changes to a text member, you must open the movie inside Director and edit the text member. Also, text cast members cannot be used to keep text information, such as words, because this information is lost when the multimedia application is made into a finished product. You cannot do word searches in a text member, for example. This is because the text cast member stores the text as a bitmapped image. It becomes a graphic like any other image.

Field Members

Field members are cast members used to store what has been traditionally considered to be text. Field members contain text information, and because of this, they can be searched for particular words. These words or characters can even be edited.

The obvious advantage of field members is that they can be used to store and retrieve text information such as names, pages of documents or other text items. Fields can be used to hold data, temporary values, Lingo commands, or even to act as dynamic menus for user input.

The disadvantage of field members, however, is that their display is dependent on the fonts available on the computer being used. If field members are created with an unusual font, they appear differently on computers that do not have that font.

Also, field members cannot be anti-aliased like text cast members can be. Because of this, they look less attractive than text cast members in a finished product.

Both field and text cast members have their place in multimedia applications. The rest of this chapter examines how both text cast members and field cast members work and how they can be effectively used to enable rapid development of applications and to enable last-minute changes to the production of an application.

Understanding the Usefulness of Text and Field Cast Members

To appreciate the usefulness of text and field cast members, it's necessary to briefly examine a problem they help fix: how to easily make changes to a multimedia application while it is still being created.

Changes to a project after development has begun are almost inevitable. These changes affect every aspect of development—from personnel assignments to available budgets and customer satisfaction. Steve McConnell's book, *Rapid Development*, suggests that changes to a project during development can increase the cost of a project by a factor ranging from 50 to 200.

Typically, you have two ways to deal with changes to a project after it has begun. One is to develop strategies that minimize the chances that changes will be introduced to a project. Although doing this is helpful to the developer, it does not enable the developer to be responsive to customer demands.

Another way to deal with changes in a project is to develop practices that more easily accommodate changes in a project. Suppose that instead of building your screen graphics—complete with text—in a paint program, you used Director's text cast members for the screen text. If any changes had to be made to the text, you could make these changes without having to re-create the entire screen graphic.

Suppose that instead of scattering the Lingo code that controls the navigation of your Director application, you control the navigation of your application from one script. If you had to make last-minute changes to navigation, you could do so easily.

Text cast members and field cast members do much more than display text. They are powerful tools that can enable you to create sophisticated multimedia applications as well as facilitate changes during the design, production, and revision of these multimedia applications.

Using Text Cast Members for Changes to Screen Titles or Text

Although text cast members cannot be changed in finished products, they can be changed in the Director authoring environment. The obvious advantage to this is that screen titles or other screen text can be quickly added to an application and then later edited as decisions on fonts, styles, or content are made.

Text cast members were first made available in Director 5. Extensive use of text cast members was sometimes hampered, however, by Director 5's limit of 48 sprite channels. In a situation where a developer runs out of available sprite channels, screen text is usually the first item to be incorporated into the main screen graphic. The problem with this solution, however, is that to edit screen text that has been incorporated into the main screen graphic, the entire screen graphic must be loaded into a paint program and redone (because the text and background are now one image).

With the availability of 120 sprite channels in Director 6, developers now have more "working room" and, thus, are in a better position to keep screen text as separate cast members. This means that screen text can be kept separate from the main screen background image. These text members can be easily edited inside Director without altering the background image used as the main screen image.

In general, multimedia applications present information in a number of ways. A CD-ROM on aircraft, for example, may give users a choice of sorting aircraft by geographic location, name, nomenclature, or use. Regardless of how the information is presented, the basic information about each aircraft remains the same.

The most efficient way to develop a CD-ROM application such as the one just described is to place all important information about the aircraft in a central database. This database could then be queried, sorted, and presented in a number of ways. The capability to search the text in this database is a key component, so it would need to be stored in a field member.

After the screens were developed for presenting information for one aircraft, you would know that the screens would work for all aircraft you add to the database.

If last-minute changes were made to the information about the aircraft in the CD-ROM application, you would need to make changes to the database only.

INSIDER TIP

Keep in mind when using field members as a database that fields can only hold 32 KB of text—the amount of text that can be stored in a field member is limited.

If you find that the data in your application is larger than 32 KB, you might consider storing parts of the data in different fields. A better approach for databases of this size is a database Xtra.

Excellent Xtras for Director are available that enable applications to use database files. One of these Xtras is the FileFlex Xtra that comes with Director.

Using Chunk Expressions in Text Searches

To understand how Director can search and retrieve text from fields, it is important to understand how Lingo commands deal with "chunk expressions."

The term *chunk expressions* refers to "chunks" of text. This text may exist in a number of places:

▶ A field member

▶ A variable

▶ The text that is created from any of the three button types from Director's toolbar

▶ A script member or script of any cast member

Text can be divided into chunks in a number of ways. Lingo can look at chunks of text (from the smallest to the largest type of chunk) in terms of the following:

▶ The number of characters

▶ The number of words

▶ The number of items

▶ The number of lines

▶ The entire text

What makes chunk expressions so useful is that they can be used in combination to get specific information about the text of a member. Consider the following text in a field called "autos":

```
the red car,the orange car,the brown truck
```

Using Lingo, you can find the information presented in Table 10.1 about the text of the field, "autos".

Table 10.1

Information Obtained with Lingo's Chunk Expression Commands

Lingo	Result
`put field "autos"`	the red car, the orange car, the brown truck
`put the number of lines of field "autos"`	1
`put the number of words of line 1 of field "autos"`	9
`put the number of items of line 1 of field "autos"`	3
`put the number of words of item 1 of line 1 of field "autos"`	3
`put word 2 of item 1 of line 1 of field "autos"`	red
`put the number of chars of word 2 of item 1 of line 1 of field "autos"`	3
`put chars 1 of word 2 of item 1 of line 1 of field "autos"`	r

A number of combinations of Lingo can be used to get specific information about any member that contains text. If you are dealing with a variable called "autos" rather than a field, you can still search the text in the same way. The only difference is that instead of instructing Lingo to look in field "autos", you instruct Lingo to look at autos. If the variable contained the following text:

```
the red car,the orange car,the brown truck
```

the Lingo in Table 10.2 yields the following results:

Table 10.2

Results from Using Lingo's Chunk Expressions on a Variable

Lingo	Result
`put autos`	the red car, the orange car, the brown truck
`put the number of lines of autos`	1
`put the number of words of autos`	9
`put the number of items of line 1 of autos`	3

Notice that because you have only one line of information in both the field and the variable, it doesn't matter whether you include the command to look in line 1. Another thing to notice is that variables, just like fields, can have more than one line of text. Lines of text are separated by a RETURN (or line feed). This is an important point. It comes up later in this chapter when you look at the `last_marker` handler in the movie navigation example.

Searching and Retrieving Text from Fields

The aircraft CD-ROM example can also demonstrate how fields can be useful for holding values and data. It serves as a launch point to discuss basic principles for using fields.

Assume that you have been asked to build a simple application that displays an image of an aircraft along with some basic information about it. The application would enable users to select aircraft either by their name or country of origin. One catch is that you will not get the information on all the aircraft until near the end of your production cycle.

By using fields, you can develop a prototype with all the features you want, even before getting all the information on the aircraft.

Building the Field Database

Begin by making a database containing basic information you have about the aircraft. This information follows the basic format:

```
nomenclature,image,name,country,type,engine
```

At this point, you should look in the directory on the accompanying CD-ROM and copy the Planes directory to your hard drive. In this directory, you will find the AIRCRAFT1.DIR movie. Open this in Director to see how you can use this data.

In the first frame of the movie is a sample data field called "aircraft data" that contains the following three lines:

```
F-15C,f15c.jpg,Eagle,USA,fighter jet,twin engine
P-51D,p51d.jpg,Mustang,USA,propeller fighter,single engine
P-38J,p38j.jpg,Lightning,USA,propeller fighter,twin engine
```

These lines serve as sample data for development purposes. Each line of this field has six items. The items are separated by a comma as the item delimiter.

The first item is the nomenclature of the aircraft, the second item is the name of its image file, and so on.

A choices field and a Search by Nomenclature button also appear on the stage (see fig. 10.2).

Figure 10.2

The movie AIRCRAFT1.DIR, with the data field, nomenclature search button, and choices field.

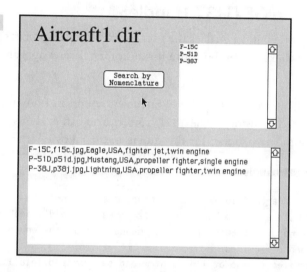

Aircraft1.dir

```
F-15C
P-51D
P-38J
```

Search by
Nomenclature

```
F-15C,f15c.jpg,Eagle,USA,fighter jet,twin engine
P-51D,p51d.jpg,Mustang,USA,propeller fighter,single engine
P-38J,p38j.jpg,Lightning,USA,propeller fighter,twin engine
```

INSIDER TIP

The comma is the default character used to separate (or delimit) items in a field. Sometimes, however, you may want to change this, such as when your items themselves contain commas.

The character used by Director to delimit items can be read and set by the `item delimiter` Lingo command.

To set the character that separates items to a colon, use the following command in your `startMovie` handler.

`set the itemdelimiter = ":"`

Remember, however, that the colon will remain the delimiter for all fields in the Director application until you set a new delimiter.

In the final product, of course, you probably would not want to see the database as it is displayed here. At this point, however, it enables you to keep track of what is going on.

You want the user to be able to click on a series of buttons to display a list of aircraft either by nomenclature or by name.

Director enables you to search fields by character, word, item, or line. Because you are dealing with data in which each part of a record contains more than one word (for example, an aircraft may be a "fighter jet" or "propeller fighter"), you must use items separated by commas.

Using the GETLIST Handler

Currently, one button enables the user to search by an aircraft's nomenclature. If the user clicks on this button, a list of nomenclatures appears in the "choices" field.

The search and retrieval by the Nomenclature button (shown in figure 10.2) is accomplished by using the GETLIST handler. You can find this handler and the rest of the movie handlers for this movie in the "movie" script cast member.

The GETLIST handler looks like this:

```
on GETLIST searchfield, wordno, itemno, destinationfield
   repeat with a = 1 to (the number of lines in field searchfield)
     -- if wordno is zero, then that means we pull the whole item
     if wordno = 0 then
        put item itemno of line a of field searchfield into line a of field
        ➥destinationfield
     else
        put word wordno of item itemno of line a of field searchfield into
        ➥line a of field destinationfield
     end if
   end repeat
end
```

Take the time to examine each line of this handler. The handler accepts the following parameters:

- ▶ **searchfield:** The field being searched

- ▶ **wordno:** The number of the word being searched

- ▶ **itemno:** The number of the item being searched

- ▶ **destinationfield:** The field in which you want the resulting list displayed

For now you just want to search whole items, so you can ignore the wordno parameter. To get the handler to ignore the wordno parameter, enter a zero value for it.

If you want to get a list of all the nomenclatures in the "aircraft data" field (which is item 1) and place the resulting list in the "choices" field, call the GETLIST handler and pass it the following parameters:

```
GETLIST "aircraft data",0,1,"choices"
```

The first line of the handler begins a loop that goes through all the lines of the field being searched. If you have passed a zero value for wordno, it knows that you want to list the entire item and not just particular words in that item. Depending on the value of wordno, the handler places either a word from an item or the entire item in a line of the field that displays the resulting list.

With this generic handler, searching by name, nomenclature, or any other word or item is simple. Use this handler to build another search button—one that searches and lists aircraft by their type.

Adding a Search by Type Button

1. With the AIRCRAFT1.DIR movie open, open Director's Tool Palette by pressing Command+7 (for the Windows version of Director, use the Ctrl key rather than the Command key for all key shortcuts).

2. Choose the Button tool.

3. On the stage, create a button and enter **Search by Type** for its text.

4. Open the Cast window (Command+3) and select this new button.

5. Open a Script window for this member by clicking on the Script button.

6. You want the script to list all the aircraft types in the database (item 5), so you need to create the following button script:

```
on mouseDown
  --First, clear out the "choices" field
  delete field "choices"
  --Now search the database
  GETLIST "aircraft data",0,5,"choices"
end
```

7. Now close the Script window, run the script, and click on the new button that you created.

   A list of aircraft types should appear in the "choices" field. Your movie should look like the one shown in figure 10.3.

continues

Adding a Search by Type Button   continued

Figure 10.3

AIRCRAFT1.DIR with the new Search by Type button.

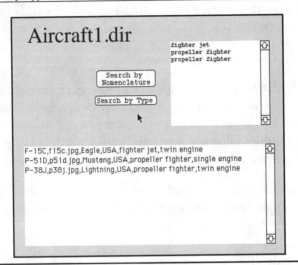

Using the SORTLIST Handler

From the preceding tutorial, one problem you may immediately notice is that the types or nomenclatures are not displayed in alphabetical order in the "choices" field. Another problem is that duplicate aircraft types are listed. Two propeller fighters are in the database, so "propeller fighter" is listed twice. You can fix both of these problems with the SORTLIST handler.

The SORTLIST handler takes the information from a field, sorts it alphabetically, and removes duplicate listings. The SORTLIST handler Lingo is as follows:

```
SORTLIST searchField
  -- create temporary list
  set templist = []
  -- put the items into a list for sorting
  repeat with a = 1 to (the number of lines in field searchField)
    addAt templist, a, (line a of field searchField)
  end repeat
  -- sort the list
  sort templist
  -- put the items back in the field
  delete field searchField
  -- If the item in the list is empty, we don't put it in.
  if getAt(templist, 1) = "" then
    set b = 1
  else
    put getAt(templist, 1) into line 1 of field searchField
    set b = 2
```

```
    end if
  repeat with a = 2 to count(templist)
    if getAt(templist,a) <> getAt(templist,a-1) then
      put getAt(templist,a) into line b of field searchField
      set b = b + 1
    end if
  end repeat
end
```

The SORTLIST handler accepts the following parameter:

▶ **searchField:** The field being sorted

The SORTLIST handler puts the lines of the field into a temporary list and uses Director's sort command to sort that list. The elements of the list are then placed back into the field. This handler also does two other things. It is possible that the GETLIST handler could return an empty string. An example would be to list the second word of the first item where one record does not have a second word for the first item. The SORTLIST handler checks for empty strings and drops them out of the list.

The SORTLIST handler also checks for duplication of an item before adding it to the field. That way, if you display types of aircraft and more than one propeller fighter is in the database, "propeller fighter" appears only one time.

The SORTLIST handler can be called from the various search button scripts. The modified script for the Search by Type button looks like this:

```
on mouseDown
  --First, clear out the "choices" field
  delete field "choices"
  --Now search the database
  GETLIST "aircraft data",0,5,"choices"
  SORTLIST "Choices"
end
```

Now as you click on each of the search buttons, the available choices are listed in the "choices" field without duplicates and in alphabetical order.

Notice that the "choices" field redraws twice—one time with the list and then again with the sorting. Because this looks unattractive, you should have both the GETLIST and SORTLIST output their information to a field not displayed on the stage. When the handlers are finished, add one last line to the search button script that copies the content of this off-stage field to the "choices" field. Do that now.

Adding a Sorting Feature to AIRCRAFT1.DIR

1. Open the Cast window (Command+3).

2. Select the "choices" field.

3. Copy this field (Command+C).

4. Select an empty cast member and paste a new field (Command+V).

5. Name this field "choices off stage".

   The "choices off stage" *will be the field you use to build new lists of information. After the new list is built and sorted, its entire contents will be moved into the* "choices" *field.*

6. Go to the Search by Type button and open its Script window.

7. Change its script to the following:

```
on mouseDown
  -- first, clear out the "choices off stage" field
  delete field "choices off stage"
  -- Now search the database
  GETLIST "aircraft data",0,5,"choices off stage"
  SORTLIST "choices off stage"
  -- Now that we're finished with our search,
  -- we'll put it on the stage.
  put the text of field "choices off stage" into field "choices"
end
```

Now the Search by Type button works with the "choices off stage" *field and, when finished, copies the final text to the* "choices" *field.*

Run the application and see how the display works. Click on the Search by Nomenclature button to compare its display method to the one you have just made. Go ahead and update the Search by Nomenclature button script as well. If you could not get the example to work correctly, open the finished example movie, AIRCRAFT2.DIR, to see how the scripts should work (see figure 10.4).

Figure 10.4

The AIRCRAFT2.DIR movie shows the finished product.

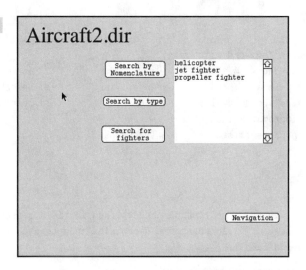

Using the GETLINE Handler

It is great to be able to list items in your database, but you also need to display the entire record for a particular aircraft. This means that when a user selects one of the items in the "choices" field, the application needs to figure out which database records have this item. That is what the GETLINE handler is meant to do.

If you click on the Search by Nomenclature button, the GETLIST handler lists the nomenclature of the aircraft in the "choices" field. The user can now click on a particular aircraft in the "choices" field and get the rest of the information about that particular aircraft. The GETLINE handler finds out which line of the "aircraft data" has information that matches the item on which the user has clicked.

The GETLINE handler enables you to find a line that matches a particular word, item, or string within a line. For what you are doing here, you are only interested in finding a line with an item that matches what the user clicked on in the "choices" field. Because of this, you need only examine the first line and last nine lines of the handler in this example:

```
on GETLINE searchfield,wordno,itemno,thingtomatch
  set templist = []
  -- search for item match
  if wordno = 0 and itemno <> 0 then
    repeat with a = 1 to (the number of lines in field searchfield)
      if item itemno of line a of field searchfield = thingtomatch then
        append templist, a
```

```
        end if
      end repeat
      -- search for word match
    else if wordno <> 0 then
      repeat with a = 1 to (the number of lines in field searchfield)
        if word wordno of item itemno of line a of field searchfield =
        ➡thingtomatch then
          append templist, a
        end if
      end repeat
    else
      -- search for line match
      repeat with a = 1 to (the number of lines in field searchfield)
        if line a of field searchfield contains thingtomatch then
          append templist, a
        end if
      end repeat
    end if
    return templist
end
```

The GETLINE handler accepts the following parameters:

▶ **searchfield:** The field being searched

▶ **wordno:** The number of the word being searched

▶ **itemno:** The number of the item being searched

▶ **thingtomatch:** The word or item to match

The GETLINE sets up a temporary list that keeps the number of the lines that fit the match criteria. This list returns when the handler completely goes through the field being searched.

If you want to find out which lines of the field "aircraft data" contain "F15-C" as their first item, call the GETLINE handler with the following parameters:

```
GETLINE "aircraft data",0,1,"F15-C"
```

If you want to find each line that contains "F15-C" anywhere on the line, call the GETLINE handler with the following parameters:

```
GETLINE "aircraft data",0,0,"F15-C"
```

With the GETLINE handler understood, look at the cast script of the "choices" field.

```
on mouseDown
  -- We first make sure the user isn't using the scrollbar.
  if the mouseline = -1 then exit
  -- If not, then we capture the line number the user clicked.
  put line (the mouseline) of field "choices" into field "search item"
  -- We clear out the field we're going to use to display the record
  delete field "results"
  -- Now we call the GETLINE handler to search the database
  GETLINE "aircraft data",0,0,(the text of field "search item")
  put the result into MATCHLINE
  -- We might get more than one match.
  -- For each record, we want to list the information and
  -- a list of aircraft images.
  delete field "image choices"
  repeat with c = 1 to count(MATCHLINE)
    put item 1 of line getAt(MATCHLINE, c) of field "aircraft data" & RETURN
    ➥after field "image choices"
    repeat with a = 2 to (the number of items in line getAt(MATCHLINE, c) of
    ➥field "aircraft data")
      put item a of line getAt(MATCHLINE, c) of field "aircraft data" &
      ➥RETURN after field "results"
    end repeat
    put "---" & RETURN after field "results"
  end repeat
-- Get rid of the those empty lines at the end of the fields created by
-- those last RETURNS
  delete the last line of field "image choices"
  delete the last line of field "results"
  go "record"
end
```

The cast script is a mouseDown handler, so it executes when the user clicks on the "choices" field. The first line checks to make certain that the user has not clicked on the scrollbar. The second line puts the line the user has selected in the "search item" field. This field acts as a global variable for the program.

The handler now clears the "results" field to prepare it for new results. The GETLINE handler is called and told to search the "aircraft data" field for the lines that contain a match to the text found in the "search item" field. The number of the lines that contain the match are returned from the GETLINE handler and placed in the MATCHLINE list. The mouseDown handler then finds the number of items in the matching lines of data and places each item on a separate line in the "results" field. This is done for each element in the MATCHLINE list with three dashes separating each matching line of data.

One of the database elements is the name of an image file for the aircraft. You will want an extra field displayed to give you a choice for displaying that image. Because of this, you will have the script for the "choices" field also put the first item of the chosen records into another field for "image choices".

With the text retrieval finished, you have the application go to another frame of the movie to display information on the records you have chosen.

You now have a fully functional simple database. The advantages of this approach are many. One is that you can rapidly prototype a multimedia application even if your customer is not yet certain of the exact nature of his data. Suppose that you need to add a new record to the aircraft data. Simply add a new line such as this:

```
HH-65,hh65.jpg,Dauphin,France,helicopter,twin turbine
```

In fact, go ahead and do this now. Open the "aircraft data" field and type this line into the field. Close the field and run the program. See how the new record works perfectly with the application?

Not only can you add records at the last minute, but you can also edit information. Open the "aircraft data" field again. Now for the second item of each line, add this URL to the file name:

```
http://www.grommett.com/planes/
```

A line in the field should look something like this now:

```
HH-65,http://www.grommett.com/planes/hh65.jpg,Dauphin,France,helicopter,twin
➥turbine
```

Make certain that your computer is connected to the Internet, then run the program. Notice that the photos you are getting are coming from a web server rather than from the CD-ROM or hard drive of your computer.

By using fields as a database, adding information to the database becomes as simple as copying and pasting the text into the field from a word processor or using Director's FileIO Xtra to bring an ASCII file into the field.

Performing Multileveled Searches

In the aircraft database, the "search item" field is used as a variable that the GETLINE handler uses. The "choices" field is also used as a list generated on-the-fly while the application is being used. Fields can be used in this manner to create complex multilevel searches.

Altering Fonts in Fields

You may have noticed while working with the AIRCRAFT1.DIR movie that the font and style of the text in fields varied depending on the setting. In the finished aircraft database movie, fonts should be consistent. Open the AIRCRAFT2.DIR movie and run it. Notice that the text of the fields remains consistent. This is because Lingo scripts format the text in fields. This feature of fields can be useful as long as the developer is aware of its limitations.

The font, style, size, and color of a field can be set with the `font of member`, `fontstyle of member`, `fontsize of member`, and `forecolor of member` Lingo commands. Although the `backcolor of the field` cast member can be set with the `backcolor of member` command, it can only be called with a reference to the entire field cast member and not a reference to a particular word or line of the field cast member. These commands (with the exception of the `backcolor of member` command) can affect not only the entire field, but also a line, word, or character of that field. You can write Lingo code, for example, that will change the second word of the third line of the field "choices" to font size 12 by executing the following Lingo code:

```
set the fontsize of word 2 of line 3 of field "choices" = 12
```

Run the AIRCRAFT2.DIR movie and click on the Search for fighters button. Then click on "fighters" in the "choices" field to display the matching records.

Notice that three records match. Furthermore, when you click on one of the aircraft images to display, notice that the information about that aircraft appears in bold type as shown in figure 10.5.

Figure 10.5

The displayed aircraft has its information in bold type.

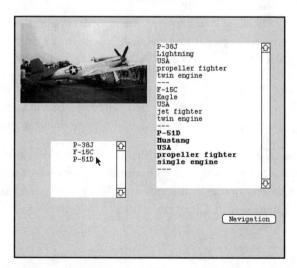

Part of the mouseDown script effects the bold for the "image choices" field. That part of the script is as follows:

```
-- Change the font of the "results" field
set the fontstyle of field "results" = "plain"
set a = 1
repeat while a < the number of lines in field "results"
  if line a of field "results" = field "search item" then
    set st = a
    repeat while line a of field "results" <> "---"
      set a = a + 1
    end repeat
    set ed = a
    exit repeat
  else
    set a = a + 1
  end if
end repeat
set the fontstyle of line st to ed of field "results" = "bold"
```

The script first changes the style of the entire field to plain in case something was bold from a previous display request. The script then finds the first and last line of the information about the aircraft being displayed and simultaneously sets this entire set of lines to bold (making for a more clean update of the screen).

With a little effort, you can come up with a number of ways to use this feature to spice up an otherwise dull display of text.

Mapping Fonts Between Platforms

After you have finished building your multimedia application with its various uses of text, you need to ensure that it will look similar on both Macintosh and Windows platforms.

With text cast members, this is not a problem. Because Director turns text cast members into bitmap images of the text when the movie is made, these bitmap images will look the same on both Macintosh and Windows platforms.

Field cast members, however, are a different story. Field cast members always depend on the fonts available in a computer's system software to display the proper font. If a particular font is not available in the system software, the Director application will substitute another font—sometimes with undesirable results.

This font substitution problem has two solutions. The first solution isto distribute the fonts you used when designing the fields with your application. If you do this, however, remember that you must include fonts that can be installed on both Windows and Macintosh platforms. Also remember that the distribution of fonts is covered by copyright laws.

The second solution is to use fonts that are standard on most computer systems. If you do this, however, you need to take into account that standard fonts found on a Macintosh and Windows machine are different. You can account for this difference by using the FONTMAP.TXT file.

The FONTMAP.TXT file lists how fonts are to be substituted depending on the platform being used. When you execute a Director application the application looks for a font map called FONTMAP.TXT in the same directory as the application. If no font map exists, the application executes in a normal fashion. If it does exist, however, the Director application will use information in the FONTMAP.TXT file to determine the fonts that should be used. A Director application, for example, might be created on the Macintosh platform and use the Helvetica font in a field cast member. Many Windows machines, however, do not have a Helvetica font. Instead they have a similar-looking font called Arial. When this application is run on a Windows machine, the font map determines the Arial font should be used in place of the unavailable Helvetica font.

A FONTMAP.TXT file can be found in the same directory as your Director authoring software. This file contains mappings for standard Mac and Windows fonts. Additional font mappings can be added to this font map file. You can then distribute a copy of this FONTMAP.TXT file in the same directory as your finished Director application. When the application is launched, it will look at the font map file to see the substitutions it should make if it is asked to display a font unavailable in the system software.

Navigation Within the Application

You have seen how fields can be used to enable last minute changes to be made in terms of information presented to the user, text displays, and even location of media files. Now look at the way fields can help a developer design navigation within an application that can be easily updated or modified.

Navigation within Director requires some type of Lingo command such as "go to frame 5" or "go to frame "main" of movie "title". When designing for change, the developer must keep in mind that the number of navigation options in the application and where these options go may change during the course of production.

An application may begin the production phase as one Director movie. At this point, navigation choices can be controlled by telling Director to go to a frame designated by a marker. As the application is developed, however, it might be necessary to break the application into several movies. With the appropriate planning, this kind of change can be done with little effort.

The aircraft example demonstrates how fields can be used to create a database. Fields can also act as a database of possible Lingo navigation commands to be executed by the Director application. To demonstrate this use of fields, you will introduce another movie to the aircraft application—a navigation map Movie in a Window.

Executing Data from Fields

The navigation movie is the MAP.DIR movie. It is called from the aircraft movie as a MIAW (Movie in a Window). The MAP.DIR movie is generic enough that minor changes to its graphics and fields enable you to modify it for your own navigation tool. The MAP.DIR movie being used for navigation is shown in figure 10.6.

Figure 10.6

The MAP.DIR MIAW used for navigation.

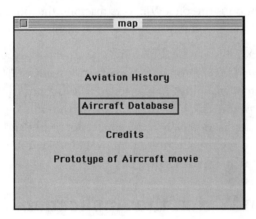

When the MAP.DIR movie is called from the stage, it presents the user with a navigation map. This map lists all areas of interest in the project and highlights the current location of the user with a red outline. If the user clicks on a new area of interest, the MAP.DIR movie tells the stage to go to that frame or movie.

The MAP.DIR movie tells the stage to use the `last_marker` handler in the MAP.DIR movie to find out which area of the movie the stage is currently in. You will return to the `last_marker` handler a little later.

The name of the area the stage is displaying is also the name of the marker placed at the beginning of this area. The three possible areas of interest in the AIRCRAFT2.DIR movie are main, credits, and history. This information, along with the name of the movie that called it (obtained by the `moviename` function) gives the MAP.DIR movie the basic information it needs to navigate.

Navigation is determined by two fields: the `"location"` and `"movies"` fields. The `"location"` field is used to highlight the user's location on the navigation map. The `"movies"` field is used to navigate to the item the user selects from the navigation map.

The text in the `"location"` field is as follows:

```
aircraft2    history     7
aircraft2    main        8
aircraft2    credits     9
aircraft1    main        10
```

The text in the `"movies"` field is as follows:

```
nothing
tell the stage to go to frame "history" of movie "aircraft2"
tell the stage to go to frame "main" of movie "aircraft2"
tell the stage to go to frame "credits" of movie "aircraft2"
tell the stage to go to movie "aircraft1"
```

The `"location"` field lists every possible location from which the user may be calling the navigation map. Each line contains three words. The first word refers to the movie where the user is located. The second word is the name of an area or marker in the movie. The third line is the number of the sprite that can highlight this location on the navigational map. If you look at the text in the `"location"` field, you can see that the red box that would highlight `"credits"` is located in sprite channel 9 of the map movie. If the user opens the MAP.DIR movie while in the `"credits"` area of the AIRCRAFT2.DIR movie, the sprite in channel 9 will be made visible.

The highlight of the current location is done in the `MARK_LOCATION` handler.

```
on MARK_LOCATION
  tell the stage to set SCREEN = last_marker()
  tell the stage to set MNAME = the movieName
  -- slice off the .DIR or .DXR extension
  SLICE_EXTENSION mname
  put the result into mname
```

```
repeat with a = 1 to (the number of lines in field "location")
  -- we check against the field that has the names of the movies and the
  -- appropriate sprite numbers associated with them.
  if MNAME = word 1 of line a of field "location" then
    if SCREEN = word 2 of line a of field "location" then
      set the ink of sprite value(word 3 of line a of field "location") = 36
      exit repeat
    end if
  end if
end repeat
updateStage
end
```

The handler gets the name of the movie that called it from the `moviename` Lingo function. After removing the .DIR extension, it looks for a match between this name and the first word of each line in the `"location"` field. If it finds a match, the handler then checks the second word of the line to see whether it matches the value in the `"SCREEN"` variable. If it finds a match, it then looks at the third word of that line to determine which sprite it needs to make visible (via an ink effect) on the navigational map. If the user is, for example, in the history area of the AIRCRAFT2.DIR movie, the MAP.DIR movie would go through the procedure illustrated in figure 10.7.

Figure 10.7

An illustration of how the MAP.DIR movie displays a user's location in an application.

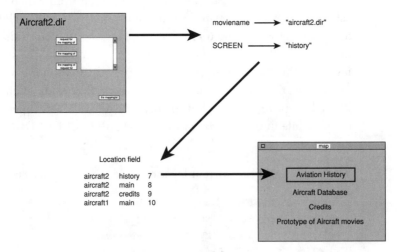

Using the do Command

When the user clicks on an area, the movie calls one button script.

```
on mouseDown
  repeat with a = 2 to 4
    if rollover(a) then
      do line a of field "MOVIES"
      updateStage
      exit repeat
    end if
  end repeat
  tell the stage to close window "MAP"
end
```

This mouseDown handler first checks to see which sprite has been clicked. These sprites are in channels 2 through 5. The "movies" field contains possible movie commands in lines 2 through 5. If the user clicks on sprite 2 (which is over the "history" icon), this handler uses the do command to execute the second line of the "movies" field. In this case, the handler, via the do command, issues the following Lingo command.

```
tell the stage to go to frame "history" of movie "aircraft2"
```

If, during the production process, the location of "history" changes, all that is needed to correct the navigational map is to change this line of text and the line of text in the "location" field that determines where the user goes when he clicks on the "history" hotspot in the map movie.

Creating Templates for do Commands

Fields not only can hold text data to be executed with the do command, but they can also hold rules or templates for the execution of this command. One example of this use of fields is the last_marker handler in the MAP.DIR movie.

The last_marker handler is designed to return the label of the marker associated with the screen the stage movie is currently displaying (see fig. 10.8).

Figure 10.8

The score of the AIRCRAFT2.DIR movie is designed so that the different screens of the application (main, record, credits, and so on) have a marker and label associated with them.

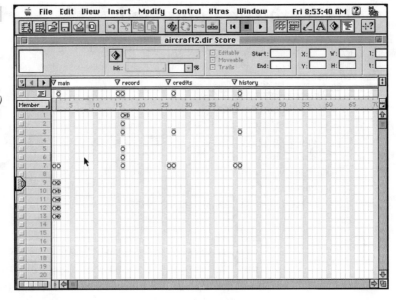

The Lingo script for the handler is as follows:

```
on last_marker
  set labelFrame = EMPTY
  put the labelList into LL
  repeat with i = 1 to the number of lines of LL
    put line i of LL into LB
    do "put string(label(" && QUOTE & LB & QUOTE &&") ) into labelFrame"
    if labelFrame = marker(0) then return LB
  end repeat
end
```

The handler uses Director's `labelList` function to get a list of all labels used in the stage movie. This list is then put into the `LL` variable. The text in the `LL` variable contains line feeds between each of the listed labels so that each label is listed on its own line. To see this, progress with the following tutorial.

Looking at Lines of Information in the labelList

1. Open the AIRCRAFT2.DIR movie.

2. Open the Message window.

3. In the Message window, type **global test_var**.

4. In the Message window, type **put the labelList into test_var**.

At this point, the list of labels for the movie is in the variable test_var.

5. In the Message window, type **put test_var**.

In the Message window, you should see the following display:

```
-- Welcome to Director --
global test_var
put the labelList into test_var
put test_var
-- "main
record
credits
history
"
```

The test_var variable contains the name of each label with a line feed (or RETURN character in Lingo). Now do the following:

6. In the Message window, type **put line 2 of test_var**.

You should get the following display of text:

```
put line 2 of test_var
-- "record"
```

Variables can contain more than one line of text. You can search and retrieve information in variables just as you have in fields.

The last_marker handler steps through each line of the LL variable and determines whether the label on that line is the closest to the user's location in the movie.

Normally, if you wanted to find out at which frame number a marker with a particular label was located, you would type the following Lingo command:

```
put string(label( "history" ) ) into labelFrame
```

This would put a string with a frame number into the "labelFrame" label. The problem here is that you cannot know ahead of time the marker name for which you want to look. You don't know whether it will be "history", "credits", or some other label name.

You cannot just use a variable because the Lingo command used to identify label frames requires the label name to be in quotation marks. You must, therefore, somehow use a variable, yet put it into quotation marks. This is where the do command comes into play.

You create a template for the do command. Take the current label being checked and put it into the LB variable. Then place quotation marks around it.

```
do "put string(label(" && QUOTE & LB & QUOTE &&") ) into labelframe"
```

If the user is in the "history" section of the movie, this template would construct the following line:

```
do "put string(label( "history" ) ) into labelframe"
```

By using the QUOTE commands, you are able to create a Lingo command that puts the LB variable into quotation marks. This Lingo command is then executed by the application.

You can see how fields can be used to easily create very complex applications. At this point, you have created an application that uses a database to choose and display graphics and information. In addition, you have created a sophisticated navigation tool that can be used in Director applications.

The examples you have seen only scratch the surface of what can be done with text in Director. Many other features can be added to the Director application by using field cast members.

Using Fields for Other Advanced Concepts

In addition to designing navigation and database tools that can be easily changed, fields can be useful for a number of other applications. These include reading and writing text to files, special types of user entry of information, and manipulation of Lingo scripts.

Using the FileIO Xtra

Director comes with an Xtra that enables you to read and write text files in a Director application. If you look in the planes directory you copied previously from the CD in this chapter, you will find the FILEIO.DIR movie. This movie uses the FileIO Xtra to read and write text to a file. If you open and run this movie, you should see the application shown in figure 10.9.

Figure 10.9

The FILEIO.DIR movie.

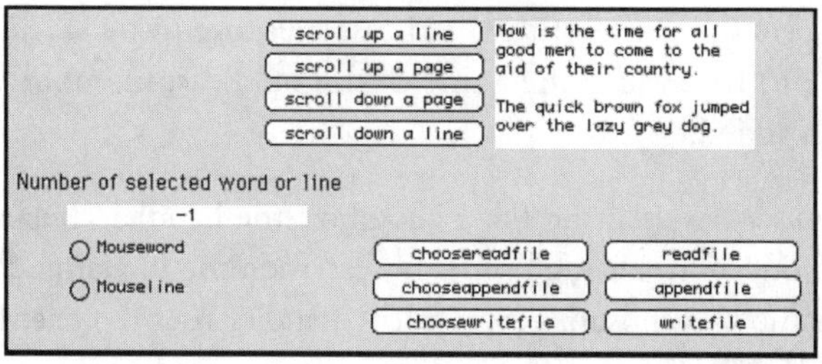

The FILEIO.DIR movie has six buttons that can be used to read or write a text file. The heart of all these buttons is Lingo script that uses the FileIO Xtra. The choosewritefile button, for example, calls the following `chooseWriteFile` handler:

```
on chooseWriteFile destcast
  global gWriteObject                              -- Make variable for fileio
                                                   -- instance global
  set gWriteObject = new(xtra "fileio")            -- Create a new instance of
                                                   -- the fileio xtra
  -- set the filename to the name of the file to save
  -- We set the title of the dialog box to "save file" and filename
  -- We set the default name under which to save the file to
  -- the cast member name with ".txt" after it.
  set filename = displaySave(gWriteObject, "Save file"&&destcast,
➥destcast&".txt")
  if fileName = "" then                            -- Did the user cancel the
                                                   -- write?
    alert "save cancelled"
  else
    createFile(gWriteObject, filename)             -- Attempt to create the
                                                   -- file
    openFile(gWriteObject, fileName, 2)            -- Open the file in mode 2
                                                   -- (write only)
    put the text of field destcast into thetext    -- Get the text to write to
                                                   -- file
    writeString (gWriteObject, thetext)            -- Write file
  end if
  closeFile(gWriteObject)                          -- Close the file
  set gWriteObject = 0                             -- dispose of the fileio
                                                   -- instance
end
```

The `displaySave` command is used to open a File dialog box that enables the user to select the file to write. In this handler the `displaySave` command is set up to display the name of the field cast member to be saved. The default name of the file to be saved is the name of the field cast member with a .TXT file extension added.

After the user has used the File dialog box, the handler checks whether the user cancelled out of the dialog box. If he has, then the filename chosen will be empty. If a file name was chosen, however, the handler uses the createFile command to create a file with the chosen file name. If one already exists, then a user prompt asks whether the file is to be replaced. The file is then opened in write-only mode and written to with the writeSting command. Then the file is closed and the FileIO instance is disposed by setting the instance variable to zero.

Compare the chooseWriteFile handler to the following chooseReadFile handler:

```
on chooseReadFile destcast
  global gReadObject                          -- Make variable for fileio
                                              -- instance global
  set gReadObject = new(xtra "fileio")        -- Create a new instance of
                                              -- the fileio xtra
  set filename = displayOpen(gReadObject)     -- Find the name of the
                                              -- file to open
  if fileName = "" then                       -- Did the user cancel the
                                              -- write?

    alert "read cancelled"
  else
    openFile(gReadObject, fileName, 1)        -- Open the file in mode
                                              -- 1 (read only)
    put readFile(gReadObject) into field destcast -- Read file & put string
                                              -- into field "test"
  end if
  closeFile(gReadObject)                      -- Close the file
  set gReadObject = 0                         -- Dispose of the fileio
                                              -- instance
end
```

The only real differences between the two handlers is that the chooseReadFile handler uses the displayOpen command to obtain a file's file name to open and the openFile command opens the file for reading only (mode = 1). This handler also checks to determine whether the user cancelled the Open File dialog box. If a file name is selected by the user, however, a readFile command is used to read the file and place the text of the file into a field cast member.

Sometimes you may not want to merely write to a file but, instead, want to append text to that file. This can be done by modifying the `chooseWriteFile` handler as follows:

```
on chooseAppendFile destcast
   global gWriteObject                             -- Make variable for fileio
                                                   -- instance global
   set gWriteObject = new(xtra "fileio")           -- Create a new instance of
                                                   -- the fileio xtra
   -- set the filename to the name of the file to save
   -- We set the title of the dialog box to "save file" and filename
   -- We set the default name under which to save the file to
   -- the cast member name with ".txt" after it.
   set filename = displaySave(gWriteObject, "Save file"&&destcast,
destcast&".txt")

   if fileName = "" then                           -- Did the user cancel the
                                                   -- write?
      alert "save cancelled"
   else
      -- If you don't want the computer to prompt the user on whether to
      -- replace the file, then get rid of the next line. This, however, is
      -- not advised since the createFile is a handy way to make sure a file
      -- exists to write to.
      createFile(gWriteObject, filename)           -- Attempt to create the
                                                   -- file
      openFile(gWriteObject, fileName, 2)          -- Open the file in mode 2
                                                   -- (write only)
      set flength = getLength(gWriteObject)        -- get the length of the
                                                   -- open file
      setPosition(gWriteObject, flength)           -- set the file position to
                                                   -- the EOF
      put the text of field destcast into thetext  -- Get the text to write to
                                                   -- file
      writeString (gWriteObject, thetext)          -- Write to file, beginning
                                                   -- at current EOF
   end if
   closeFile(gWriteObject)                         -- Close the file
   set gWriteObject = 0                            -- dispose of the fileio
                                                   -- instance
end
```

The `chooseReadFile` handler is like the `chooseWriteFile` handler in every way except one. Before the `writeString` command is executed, the `getLength` command is used to determine the end of the file being written. The `setPosition` command is then used to tell the FileIO Xtra to begin writing to the file at its end. When the `writeString` command is executed, it appends the text to the end of the file.

If you do not want or need the user to pick the file to read or write, you can simply pass the file name directly to the handler and not use the `displayOpen` or `displaySave` commands. The following `ReadFile`, `WriteFile`, and `AppendFile` handlers do this.

```
-- you must call the filename with full pathname
on Readfile filename, destcast
  global gReadObject                            -- Make variable for fileio
                                                -- instance global
  set gReadObject = new(xtra "fileio")          -- Create a new instance of
                                                -- the fileio xtra
  openFile(gReadObject, fileName, 1)            -- Open the file in mode 1
                                                -- (read only)
  if status(gReadObject) <> 0 then              -- Check to make sure a
                                                -- file got read
    alert "Error:"&&error(gReadObject, status(gReadObject))
  else
    put readFile(gReadObject) into field "test" -- Read file and put string
                                                -- into field "test"
  end if
  closeFile(gReadObject)                        -- Close the file
  set gReadObject = 0                           -- Dispose of the fileio
                                                -- instance
end


--

-- You must call the filename with full pathname
on WriteFile castfrom, filename
  global gWriteObject                           -- Make variable for fileio
                                                -- instance global
  set gWriteObject = new(xtra "fileio")         -- Create a new instance of
                                                -- the fileio xtra
  createFile(gWriteObject, filename)            -- Attempt to create the
                                                -- file
  openFile(gWriteObject, fileName, 2)           -- Open the file in mode 2
                                                -- (write only)
```

```
    put the text of field castfrom into thetext    -- Get the text to write to
                                                    -- file
    writeString (gWriteObject, thetext)            -- Write file
    closeFile(gWriteObject)                         -- Close the file
    set gWriteObject = 0                            -- Dispose of the fileio
                                                    -- instance
end


--


-- You need to call the filename with the full pathname
on AppendFile castfrom, filename
    global gWriteObject                             -- Make variable for fileio
                                                    -- instance global
    set gWriteObject = new(xtra "fileio")          -- Create a new instance of
                                                    -- the fileio Xtra
    openFile(gWriteObject, fileName, 2)            -- Open the file in mode 2
                                                    -- (write only)
    set flength = getLength(gWriteObject)          -- Get the length of the open
                                                    -- file
    setPosition(gWriteObject, flength)            -- Set the file position to
                                                    -- the EOF
    put the text of field castfrom into thetext   -- Get the text to write to
                                                    -- file
    writeString (gWriteObject, thetext)            -- Write to file, begining at
                                                    -- current EOF
    closeFile(gWriteObject)                         -- Close the file
    set gWriteObject = 0                            -- Dispose of the fileio
                                                    -- instance
end
```

These handlers work in the same fashion as their related handlers that open a File dialog box. The difference is that the file name is passed directly to the readFile or writeString command. Because of this, no checking is done to determine whether the user has actually selected a file.

For the readFile or writeString commands to work, however, they must have a complete file pathname to the file to be read or written.

The handlers in the FILEIO.DIR movie can be used in any movie in which you want to read or write a text file or append text to an existing text file. They can all be found in the movie Lingo script cast member.

Using the mouseLine and mouseWord Commands

One Lingo command used in the AIRCRAFT2.DIR movie was the `mouseLine` command. This command can be used to determine what line number of a field cast member was clicked on by the mouse. You can see an example of this in the FILEIO.DIR movie. If you run the movie and click in the large scrolling field, you will see the number of the line of text you clicked on displayed. If you select the `mouseWord` command from the radio buttons on the left, the number of each word in the large text field you click on will be displayed in the field to the left.

If you click on the scrolling bar of the large text field, you will see that this click displays a −1 for both the `mouseLine` and `mouseWord` commands. If you look at the Lingo used to in the AIRCRAFT2.DIR movie you will see that it first checks to see whether the user has clicked on a scrolling bar before trying to pull information from its database.

The Lingo script that uses the `mouseWord` and `mouseLine` commands can be found in the cast script for the `"test"` field.

Using the scrollByLine and scrollByPage Commands

If you want to eliminate the slightly unsightly scrolling bar that is displayed on scrollable field cast members, you can use the `scrollByLine` or `scrollByPage` commands.

If you look at the score for the FILEIO.DIR movie, you will notice that sprite 16 is not visible. If you click on the visibility button for sprite 16, you will see that sprite 16 is a gray box that covers the scrolling bar of the scrolling field. You can use the scrolling control buttons to the left of the display to control the scrolling of the field, however.

Make sure that enough text is in the field to enable it to scroll. Then run the movie and click on the scroll buttons. As you can see, they can scroll the field quite easily.

The command to scroll the field up a line is the following:

```
scrollByLine member "test", -1
```

The command to scroll the field down a line is the following:

```
scrollByLine member "test", 1
```

At first these commands may seem backward, but they are not. If you want to scroll down a line, that means that you want to go further down the field. This means that the number of the lines you will be displaying in the field is higher in number. If you scroll down a line, the top line displayed will be line 2 of the field instead of line 1. Because of this, you `scrollByLine` with a positive number.

The `scrollByPage` command is called in the same way as the `scrollByLine` c mmand. To jump down a page, you use a positive number (with t

e numbers here referring to sections of the field—pages—displayed at a time in the field).

The Lingo scripts used to control the scrolling in the FILEIO.DIR movie can be found in the cast scripts for each of the different scroll buttons.

Inserting Characters into a Field

Some situations arise when you do not want to display exactly what the user types into a field. If you allow only five digits for a zip code field, for example, you may want the program to beep and refuse any input after the fifth digit. Or perhaps the field is a password field and you want to display asterisks in the field rather than the password characters. You can control the content of the field by checking the key or keycode with each key press and appending the character to the field yourself. After you append the character to the field, you also must reposition the text cursor at the end of the line. The following script, originally written by Gretchen Macdowall in *Inside Macromedia Director 5 with Lingo*, could be placed in the frame where you a have a password entry you do not want displayed:

```
on keydown
    global realPassword
    -- save the characters the user is typing in realPassword
    put realPassword & the key into realPassword
show asterisks in the field
put field "Password" & "*" into field "Password"
set le = length(field "Password")
-- set the selEnd at one character after the field
-- set the selStart at two characters after the field
```

```
-- this is a round-about way of getting the text cursor
-- to display at the end of the field
set the selEnd = le + 1
set the selStart = le + 2
end
```

This handler is called when the user presses any key. A global variable, "realPassword", is used to record all the characters the user types. Instead of these characters being displayed in a field, an asterisk is added to the Password field for each character typed.

Because you are using Lingo to put characters into the field, a trick using the select text commands in Director is used to keep the cursor for the field at the end of the row of asterisks.

This handler is a good example of how information the user types can be stored in one area—in this case a variable—while Lingo places characters in a field. To use this handler for password entry, you need to have a button added to the application so that when the user enters the password, he can click the button and have additional Lingo check the validity of the password.

Treating Lingo Scripts Like Fields

The do command demonstrates how fields can hold Lingo commands. You can also exchange data between fields and Lingo or search Lingo like you would a field or variable.

You can search the existing Lingo in the movie in much the same way you have been searching fields. One example is the LIST_HANDLERS handler.

```
on LIST_HANDLERS
  set tempvar = EMPTY
  repeat with a = 1 to the number of castMembers
    -- Does the cast member have lingo?
    if the scripttext of cast a > 0 then
      -- Search each line and see if a line
      -- starts a handler (i.e., it starts with "on ")
      repeat with b = 1 to the number of lines of the scripttext of cast a
        if word 1 of line b of the scripttext of cast a = "on" then
          put word 2 of line b of the scripttext of cast a & return after
          ➥tempvar
        end if
      end repeat
    end if
```

```
   end repeat
   return tempvar
end
```

The LIST_HANDLERS handler is actually pretty simple for what it does. You know that any handler has to begin with the word "on". The handler name is the second word on the line.

With this in mind, the LIST_HANDLERS handler first gets a number of the last member in the cast window. It then steps through each possible cast number to see whether it has Lingo script. If it does, the handler then steps through each line of the Lingo script to see whether the first word is "on". If it is, it places the second word into the tempvar variable. Each handler name is kept on a separate line by placing a RETURN character after it. The multiline variable is then returned.

Give the handler a try. Do the following:

Using the LIST_HANDLERS Handler to List Handlers in the AIRCRAFT2.DIR Movie

---

1. Open the AIRCRAFT2.DIR movie.

2. Open the "movie" movie script member and type the Lingo script for the LIST HANDLERS handler exactly as it appears in this chapter.

3. Using the Tool Palette, create a new field member and call it "list of handlers".

4. Open the Message window in Director and type the following command:

```
put LIST_HANDLER ()
```

You should get a message display that looks something like this:

```
put list_handlers ()
-- "startmovie
GETLIST
SORTLIST
GETLINE
LIST_HANDLERS
mouseDown
exitFrame
mouseDown
mouseDown
exitFrame
```

continues

Using the LIST_HANDLERS Handler to List Handlers in the AIRCRAFT2.DIR Movie   continued

```
mouseDown
mouseDown
mouseDown
"
```

With the other data search and retrieval techniques covered in this chapter, you can build your own development handlers that look for particular handlers, change the font color or style of particular Lingo scripts, or a number of other operations.

In Practice

When effectively used, fields enable a developer to rapidly design a product that facilitates easy changes to the location of linked media, navigation, and data presented to the user. Keep in mind the following applications of text cast members and field members:

▶ Use Director's extensive search and retrieval of text through Lingo, to easily make changes to fields or find information about all text and scripts used in an application.

▶ The FileIO Xtra enables you to build Director applications that can read and write text files.

▶ The mouseWord and mouseLine commands enable you to determine the words or lines on which a user has clicked.

▶ The text cast member enables you to add anti-aliased text to your screen graphics. This text can easily be edited in Director. Using text cast members enables you to make changes in screen graphics text without having to re-create all your screen graphics.

▶ By using the font style commands in Lingo, you can change the font, size, or other attributes of text displayed in field cast members.

▶ By using the FONTMAP.TXT file, you can make sure that field cast members have their fonts displayed correctly whether the application is played on a Macintosh or Windows machine.

Text is one of the most fundamental components of multimedia. With this chapter and the previous two chapters, you now have a solid background in graphics and text in Director. The next chapter looks at another important ingredient in your multimedia mix: sound.

chapter 11

Matt Davis

Sound: The Soundtrack

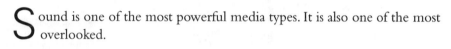

S ound is one of the most powerful media types. It is also one of the most overlooked.

This chapter explores the procedure of using sound in your Director movies. Sound is almost too broad a label, because the many subdivisions are as different from one another as a graph is from a "talking head" video.

Sound includes dialog, voice-over, music (theme and incidental), atmospheric sound, spot sound effects, special effects, and so on. Interactive multimedia brings requirements beyond those of traditional cinematography to sound, such as navigation sounds, ambient tracks, button sounds, and identity stings.

Sound is an integral part of cinema and television—a dominant and long-established form of multimedia. Only recently has sound become an integral part of interactive multimedia, thanks to a standardization of hardware modules. The Macintosh platform has had sound capabilities from the start, although the PC platform was the first to make 16-bit audio generally available. Today, virtually all domestic and business machines are capable of high-fidelity stereo sound output, even if their speakers are smaller than a transistor radio's.

Many problems associated with sound can be worked around; others can be avoided by careful authoring procedures. This chapter focuses on solving and avoiding such problems. It also touches on other challenges that are not as easy to resolve, but which may, over time, be addressed by new products and updates.

The CD that accompanies this book includes example sound files in different formats, along with Director movies to demonstrate the methods and Lingo involved.

This chapter focuses on the following areas:

▶ Introduction to digital audio

▶ File formats

▶ Technical choices

▶ Sources of audio

▶ SoundEdit 16 and SoundForge

▶ Other software tools

▶ Handling audio in Director

▶ Techniques for recording audio

▶ Troubleshooting

▶ Creative aspects of sound

Introduction to Digital Audio

People sense sound through minute changes in air pressure. The *amplitude* (or loudness) of a sound is governed by the amount of pressure change, and the pitch of a sound is controlled by the frequency of pressure waves (see fig. 11.1). Most importantly, note that we sense sound as an analog medium—there are no digital steps to sound. The human ear can distinguish sound frequencies between 150–15,000 Hz (or 15 kHz). Natural variations occur from person to person, but the limit—due to the way the ear is constructed—is approximately 20 kHz.

Figure 11.1

Sound waves.

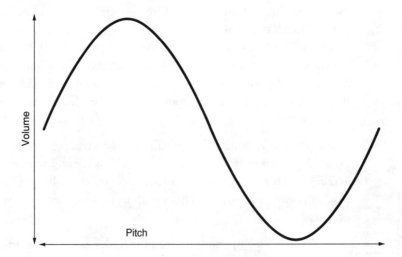

Early sound recordings using wax cylinders were directly analog, in that the constantly changing air pressure waves were directly related to the undulations in the wax cylinder: An artist would shout in a horn to make a flexible disk at the horn's end resonate with the pressure waves produced by the vocal chords of the artist. A needle attached to the disk would etch the vibrations into a wax cylinder. The process could be reversed, where the groove in the wax cylinder could reproduce the vibrations via a needle attached to the disk, which would be amplified by the horn. This method is by no means perfect, but astonishing results could be obtained with little sophistication.

In contrast to analog recordings, digital sound must be comprised of entities that are either on or off. To digitize sound, the incoming sound wave must be regularly sampled, and the pressure must be measured and recorded. This process is similar to digitizing a photograph, in which the picture is divided into regular areas (pixels) and measured for brightness.

The rate at which audio is sampled is like the resolution of a scanned image, which defines how many samples will be taken in a given time or space. The sample rate defines the *clarity* (the detail of the sound wave) of the recorded sound. More samples allow more detail, which means shorter wavelengths (high pitch sounds) can be recorded. Natural sounds contain a wide range of frequencies from low to high; thus, the capability to record high-pitched sounds adds to the clarity of the overall sound.

Examples of common sample rates include 44.1 kHz, 22.05 kHz, and 11.025 kHz. The depth at which the samples are measured is like the color depth of a scan—256 colors (8 bit), thousands of colors (16 bit), and millions of colors (32 bit). Digital audio can be sampled at 16 bits per sample or 8 bits per sample. Lower bit depths are unacceptable and unpleasant to listen to due to the lack of clarity.

Bit depth controls the signal-to-noise ratio, measured in decibels (dB), and refers to the number of times the quietest sound must be amplified to match the loudest sound. Again, an analogy to graphics is useful: In a grayscale TIFF file, the darkest pixel must be ramped up 255 times to make it white, whereas the darkest pixel in a 4-bit picture that contains only 16 colors must be ramped only 15 steps to reach the maximum. Similarly, an 8-bit sound sample has 256 steps from the quietest sound to the loudest sound. A 16-bit sample contains more than 65,000 steps. Thus, bit depth controls the *dynamics* of the sound— the differences between loud and quiet. With 65,000 steps from quiet to loud, the ear cannot perceive any stepping (just as the eye cannot perceive any stepping in a 24-bit picture). An 8-bit sound, with only 256 steps from quiet to loud, does not contain enough information to fool the ear, and we perceive the stepped sound as sounding artificial (similar to an undithered 8-bit photo).

The relationship between sample rate and sample depth can be varied to accommodate differing quality and playback requirements. A 11.025 kHz audio file, for example, that uses 8 bits will sound like a scratchy telephone line. The same rate used with 16 bits improves the dynamics of the sound but not the clarity. The 8-bit file, however, requires half the storage space that a 16-bit file does. The best results will come from using the highest sample rate with the largest bit depth, which creates the largest file size. This is the familiar trade-off between quality and memory requirements, which applies to many aspects of multimedia and computer work in general.

The analog-to-digital conversion process is a vital step. As with all digital media, it is essential to obtain as clean and complete a sample as possible—scanning in a higher resolution than will be required, even if the sound will be played back at a lower rate. As with scanned photographs and digital video, it is advisable to work with high-quality originals and to digitize them at the highest quality you can. Downsampling should always be the final step (if required).

Figure 11.2

Sampling an analog sound wave at different rates.

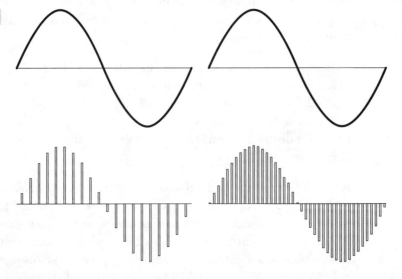

When the sound wave is recorded, the analog nature of the sound pressure waves is sampled. When played back, the samples are used to reconstruct the sound wave. Figure 11.2 shows the results of sampling an analog sound wave at two different rates. Note that neither digitized wave is identical to the analog wave, but that the lower resolution wave looks significantly different from the original. The digital-to-analog conversion has created an *artifact*—a difference in data between the digitized copy and the analog original. The artifact is evidenced by the sharp transition from sample to sample, and makes the sound seem hollow, dry, or metallic.

File Formats

Two broad categories of sound are used with Director: internal sounds, which are imported into the cast and become integral with the file, and external sounds, which are linked to a cast while remaining external to the Director movie or cast file. All audio will be imported as a file of some sort, except for sounds that are recorded from within Director using rudimentary controls.

Just as many digital file formats exist for photographs (.PICT, .TIFF, .TGA, .GIF, and so on), the same is true for digital audio. Some formats are standardized cross-platform formats, others are specialized formats with added features but with limitations in use.

Director supports a number of sound file formats, either directly or by using Xtras: .AIFF (Audio Interchange File Format), .WAV, System 7 Sound (on the Macintosh), QuickTime, Video for Windows, .MIDI, and .SWA (ShockWave Audio).

Unfortunately, not all sound files are compatible on Macintosh and Windows computers, and some formats don't support certain bit depths or sampling frequencies.

INSIDER TIP

> Sound cards for Windows require certain sampling frequencies, which tend to be multiples of the Audio CD standard 44.1 kHz. A sampling frequency of 24 kHz is acceptable for a Macintosh, but will not be playable on a PC—use 22.05 kHz and sidestep the problem altogether. Unfortunately, Macintosh software tends to refer to this as 22 kHz (rounding off the .05 Hz). Avoid the more esoteric sampling frequencies on the Macintosh unless you have a specific reason to use them—for example, some professional digital audio tape (DAT) recordings are sampled at 48 kHz.

Sound file format is a concern when initially importing the sound into Director, or when the sound is used as an external linked member. After a sound file has been imported into an internal sound member, that sound will be compatible with both the Mac and PC. The following sections introduce you to the most widely used digital audio files.

AIFF

Audio Interchange File Format (AIFF or sometimes Audio IFF) is the work-horse of the digital music industry. It is most favored by the multimedia industry because of its universal standard. AIFF files can be played on Windows, Macintosh, and some specialized platforms (such as Amiga and 3D0). A variant of AIFF, AIFF-C (or simply AIFC), denotes compression.

The Interactive Multimedia Association (IMA) introduced an analog to digital "pulse code modulation" (ADPCM) compression algorithm capable of squeez-ing 16-bit music into one-quarter the disc space to obtain near-CD quality. Today, IMA compression has recently been supported on both Windows and Macintosh. The two classes of IMA compression are known by their *compression ratio*—the difference in size between the uncompressed and compressed files. A compression ratio of 2:1 IMA is slightly higher quality than 4:1, but both are close to full Audio CD quality. Note that IMA works with 16-bit files only.

WAV

WAV (or Wave) is the standard Windows file format for sound, and is analogous to the Macintosh System 7 sound. WAV is widely supported by Windows applications, and is useable on a Macintosh with QuickTime 2.5 or later. Director 6 supports WAV directly on Windows and via the WAVE Import Export Xtra on the Macintosh. You also can convert WAV files to AIFF files (or System 7 Sound) with the MoviePlayer application, which is included with QuickTime. With MoviePlayer you can listen to WAV files in the Import dialog box by using a QuickTime controller (see fig. 11.3).

Figure 11.3

The Sound Import dialog box (Macintosh).

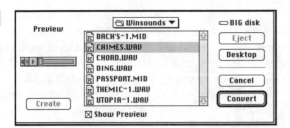

System 7 Sound

System 7 Sound is the Macintosh sound file format. Macintosh aficionados may like to know that a System 7 Sound is in fact an SND resource in a document wrapper, which means that you can see it in the Finder, play it by double-clicking the file, and use it as a system alert sound (a beep). Virtually no support exists for the System 7 sound on platforms other than Macintosh, so this format should be fully imported into Director for cross-platform projects, or converted from System 7 sound to WAV on the Macintosh using SoundEdit and transported in WAV format if bringing it onto a PC.

Digital Video Sound

Apple's QuickTime and Microsoft's Video for Windows are formats that are usually associated with digital video movies. Sound-only movies are commonly used when long segments of audio are required with random access in Director. Digital Video Sound format enables you to use Lingo to fast-forward or jump to a part of the audio and play from that designated point. You can also use Lingo to pause the score's playback head at certain specified points, while still enabling the audio to continue, which is a great way to obtain tight, sprite-to-audio, synchronization for animation.

MIDI

Musical Instrument Digital Interface (MIDI) is a universal standardized computer language developed for manufacturers of digital music equipment and music software. MIDI is not a sound file, but instead lists what notes to play and when to play them. MIDI requires a sound generator such as a synthesizer or sampler—hardware sometimes built into a PC sound card. QuickTime 2.5 for Macintosh and Windows, however, includes a software synthesizer, enabling you to hear MIDI files without the need for extra hardware.

Because MIDI is based on notes and timing, three interesting characteristics make MIDI special:

▶ MIDI files are very small, because they contain a list of notes to play, not the sound of the notes playing.

▶ Playing a MIDI file at double or half speed alters the tempo but does not alter the pitch (unlike other sound formats).

▶ MIDI files contain a list of instruments that are recommended, but if they are not available on the user's machine, substitutes can be switched or patched in. This is at the control of the author or the end user.

Director can use MIDI directly via QuickTime. With the use of third-party Xtras, Director can control the patching (switching) of MIDI sounds, and even control external devices using MIDI. However, MIDI is most useful as a method of replaying long segments of music from small files—20 minutes of Bach can be represented as a 500K MIDI file.

SWA (ShockWave Audio)

ShockWave Xtras and Plug-ins enable direct-delivery of multimedia over a network by using Internet protocols, and specifically address the biggest constraint of network delivery—limited bandwidth. ShockWave Audio is a mechanism that, like QuickTime, incorporates a file format that can begin before the file has downloaded completely. What sets ShockWave Audio apart from QuickTime is the wide range of compression available—from 4:1 to 128:1, enabling a 16-bit mono file to be played back over the Internet and received on a 14.4 Kbaud modem.

Because of the processing power and complex math required to achieve these extreme compression rates, the authoring of SWA files is limited to Power Macintosh computers and Pentium machines running Windows 95 or Windows NT (via a special Xtra for Director, as SoundEdit 16 is currently unavailable for Windows).

SWA files can be used within Director when authoring ShockWave movies, but the compression is achieved at the cost of audio quality. SWA provides remarkable results in extremely limited bandwidth, but for the sake of outright quality, QuickTime audio or similar uncompressed audio should be used where bandwidth allows for large files (for example, CD-ROM, hard disk, or a local Ethernet).

RealAudio

RealAudio (.ra) files perform a similar function to ShockWave Audio, but require a helper application rather than a plug-in. This places dominance on the audio as a separate entity rather than as an integral part of a page. (Progressive Networks also makes its SDK available on its web site. Using their SDK you can create ShockWave movies to play back RealAudio audio across the web.)

RealAudio can also be broadcast, so that a continuous live feed appears, rather than a sequence of discrete files. Progressive Networks' RealAudio client-server software system enables Internet and online users equipped with conventional multimedia personal computers and voice-grade telephone lines to browse, select, and play back audio or audio-based multimedia content on demand, in real time. Playback in real time is a breakthrough for audio over the Internet because typical download times of audio, using conventional online delivery methods, are five times longer than the actual program. The listener would have to wait 25 minutes, for example, before listening to just five minutes of audio.

Other File Formats

The adoption of Internet protocols, and specifically the dominance of the World Wide Web, has introduced the Macintosh and Windows communities to two formats common to the server world: μ-Law (pronounced "mew-law"—a 2:1 compressed 16-bit format) and .AU. Both can be opened and converted by QuickTime 2.5 and later, but they are not directly supported by Director.

A variety of specialist file formats exist, such as .VOC (associated with SoundBlaster cards for the PC), .MOD (from the Amiga platform) and so on. Most of these formats predate the AIFF standard.

MACE is a compression system, not a format. It only supports 8-bit sound and is only available on Macintosh hardware. Similarly, MPEG (another compression system covered in more detail in Chapter 12, "Digital Video: The Movie Within the Movie") can be used as an audio format, but is limited to hardware and requires special equipment to compress files.

Technical Choices

When planning and developing your audio requirements, you have three fundamental technical choices: bit depth, frequency, and whether to treat the files as internal or external. As is so often the case, the decisions you make will involve trade-offs between quality, hardware requirements, and speed of access.

High-quality means extra demands on hardware. In the past, an 8-bit, 22 kHz, mono audio sample was considered optimal quality. Today, higher quality is feasible and often expected by audiences. The same file, however, as a 16-bit 44.1 kHz stereo file is eight times larger! The computer may be able to deal with the moment-by-moment requirements, but practical implications for the physical location of such a file do exist, and compression is often needed to keep storage requirements in check.

An audio file stored on disk will take longer to access than an audio file in RAM. Three options exist: Keep the audio file linked but separate and stream from disk; keep the audio file linked but separate and preload the member before playing; or fully import the audio file for compatibility or security.

Bit Depth

The bit-depth resolution of a sound establishes its dynamic range, or signal-to-noise ratio measured in decibels (dB). Sounds that are 8 bit have a maximum signal-to-noise ratio of 48 dB. This is similar to a cheap cassette recorder. 16-bit sounds have a maximum signal-to-noise ratio of 96 dB—better than the highest-quality analog tape recorder.

Most multimedia assets are acquired at the highest possible quality as master files and then resampled to the final bit depth after editing. In the past, limited hardware required 8-bit graphics and sound, but 16 bit is slowly taking over. Although there is no loss in quality during the digital audio editing process, the sound quality will never get better than the original recording. Even if the final sound format will be 8 bit, it is recommended to record and edit 16-bit sound files and convert to 8 bit when you're finished. If acquiring in 8 bit is unavoidable, pay close attention to sound levels. Sound that is 8 bit does include a fair amount of noise and hiss.

Despite the noise, 8-bit audio remains popular. The main reason is compatibility, although this issue will decrease because most computers manufactured in the past two years are compatible with 16-bit sound. The other reason 8-bit sound is popular is file size, which also affects the speed at which files can be loaded into RAM. Professional-quality CD sound is sampled and stored at 16 bits, 44.100 kHz. Storage of one minute of stereo digital audio consumes roughly 10 MB of disc space. If you resample this audio to 8 bits, you cut the disc space in half, while retaining most of the clarity perceived on speakers commonly found on PCs. If loading or size is the issue, you can apply further steps.

Frequency

Although the best quality is undoubtedly from 44.100 kHz audio, it is difficult to use this frequency for playback in average machines because it takes too long to load into RAM. Professional developers still prefer 22.050 kHz because it has low noise level on built-in speakers, lots of high frequency response for clarity, loads fairly quickly into RAM, and is generally compatible with a wide range of computers. The average computer can process this sound and still enable loading of additional cast members from a CD-ROM without too long of a wait—if the file is a single audio track (mono rather than stereo).

Remember, stereo files are two single audio files joined together—they are twice as large and take twice the time to load. It is best to use small mono files for internal sounds. Large, high-fidelity stereo files are usually external sounds that are streamed from disk.

The 11.025 kHz audio files are falling into disuse with the new compression techniques that are available. At 11.025 kHz, sound is scratchy and of poorer quality than the lowest quality built-in speakers. Speech can sometimes sound like the person has a lisp. The background noise and hiss is objectionable on good, high-fidelity sound systems.

Use the following guidelines when sampling or resampling audio for multimedia.

▶ **5.564 kHz:** Poor quality, speech only—intended for voice annotations rather than multimedia. *Voice annotations* are sound files attached to documents intended for comments, memos and so on. The file sizes are very small (suitable for floppy disks and slow networks), but the quality is less than a pocket dictation machine.

▶ **7.418 kHz:** The lowest recommended quality for speech (Macintosh only). Very small file sizes, although ShockWave Audio can provide similar sizes in powerful machines.

▶ **11.025 kHz (CD):** A good choice for playback on older Windows and Macintosh computers. Some distortion and background noise (equivalent to a telephone line). Use for low-quality music or medium-quality speech.

▶ **11.127 kHz:** This was the original standard frequency for older Macintosh computers. New Macs have adopted the IBM 11.025 kHz frequency. This frequency (11.127) is not recommended if you are producing a cross-platform production. Some PC sound cards will not play this frequency.

▶ **22.050 kHz:** The most popular choice for Macintosh and Windows. Good quality music and narration, similar to a strong AM radio broadcast.

▶ **22.225 kHz:** The old, high-quality Macintosh standard. Suffers compatibility problems on Windows machines.

▶ **44.100 kHz:** Standard compact disc (CD) audio rate.

Internal and External Sound Files

When you import a sound file into Director, you must decide whether the sound will become an internal or external sound cast member. Figure 11.4 shows the cast window with an internal and an external sound member.

Figure 11.4

An ellipsis in the member icon indicates that a file is linked. This can be seen on the left, for the UTOPIA~1 cast member.

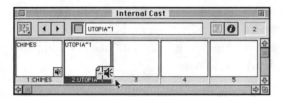

Internal sounds are saved as data inside the Director movie. This makes the audio file hidden and secure when the movie is protected. Some audio suppliers such as music libraries require that you hide the sound file from users to prevent unauthorized copying of the material they provide. Internal sounds cannot be spooled from disk. The entire sound member will be loaded into RAM before playback. Internal sound members are best reserved for short sounds.

External files remain outside the Director movie, although Director 6 offers the option to include file header information that tells Director how big the file is. The file header is important for streaming files over slow networks, because without this information, Director will check the entire file before it starts playback. Setting the standard information is shown in figure 11.5. As with all linked media, remember to keep the linked files within a common folder hierarchy.

Figure 11.5

The Import Files dialog box with an Options pop-up menu.

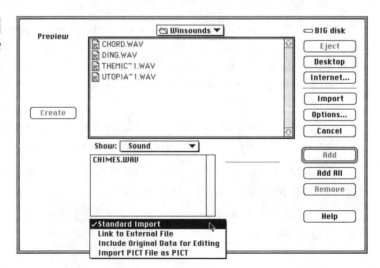

The type and purpose of the sound are strong indicators of whether the file should be stored internally or externally.

A good example of internal audio is *spot effects*—sound effects that cater to button actions and other such activities. For rapid access, spot sound effect files must be stored in RAM. Looped audio files also must load into RAM for optimum smoothness. Sounds that must occur at a precise time during an animation—sometimes referred to as *hits* or *stings*—need to be in RAM. It still takes time to load these sounds into RAM; thus, 8-bit sound is a popular choice if the order of playback for sound files is not known. An example is a looped sound of ambient noise (such as traffic, wind, water lapping) in a Myst or DOOM style game. As the user chooses a new room or area to explore, a 10 or 20 second loop can be loaded in a couple of seconds.

Long pieces of music and narration that spool from the hard disk or CD-ROM are frequently too large to load into RAM and instead must be played back directly from the disk. These must be external to the Director movie. If the audio is streaming from a CD-ROM, a wait time is involved because the playback head of the CD searches for the data files. If additional graphics must be loaded at the same time, serious problems can occur, such as sluggish performance and even sound dropouts. The CD-ROM's playback head has to move to different parts of the disc to search for graphics and audio. Still, this data flow can be managed, for example, by managing the size of the audio files via changing the bit depth and frequency or by explicitly preloading graphics before streaming audio starts.

INSIDER TIP

If you name a movie MAIN.DIR, save your narrated audio files with the names MAINNAR1.AIF, MAINNAR2.AIF, and so on. By using this naming procedure you will keep your Director and audio files close to each other on the disk when you copy the data and sound files to another disk or CD-ROM.

The files are usually copied in alphabetical order, unless specified otherwise by your CD-ROM authoring software. This will speed Director's performance because the files that are linked to a particular movie can be found by the CD-ROM drive almost immediately.

Avoid creating large audio files and importing them into the Director movie. Director or the Projector will attempt to load the sound file entirely into RAM, halting playback while it does so, and possibly causing problems by unloading other members from RAM. If you must import a long audio segment into a movie rather than linking it, consider splitting the file into subsections. A narration can be split into files containing just a paragraph, or even just a sentence. A music loop followed by a sting (a short musical phrase usually associated with an introduction or ending) means that the loop can continue for as many iterations as you want until "ending" it with the sting. Remember to set the loop property in the Sound Cast Member Properties dialog box (see fig. 11.6).

Figure 11.6

Make sure the Loop box is selected in the Sound Cast Member Properties dialog box. If it is not selected, the loop points are ignored.

External files provide more flexibility with sound formats, are more efficient with RAM, and make Director movies quicker to save and load. The downside is that external sound files are accessible to the user, are sensitive to physical location, and may require file name concessions for Windows 3.x compatibility.

Sources of Audio

The next step after using the simple controls to record sound on your computer seems to leap straight into the world of professional audio production. Compression gates, high impedance line drivers, and spectral EQ and PFL buttons are from a different world, but are faithfully replicated in sound recording software.

If you are a graphics artist who has little experience with audio, fear not. The world of sound design is a lot simpler than you think. An entire industry exists to support you, and great audio tools—such as SoundEdit 16 and SoundForge—enable you to create your own material.

Almost all computers for sale today have the built-in capability to record sound at 16 bits, either from a microphone or tape deck, or by converting CD-audio tracks from discs placed in the CD-ROM drive.

WARNING

Input devices can be divided into two categories: Mic and Line. *Mic*, short for microphone, accepts relatively low level signals produced by microphones that are amplified many times to reach a standard level, known as *Line* level. Because of the amplification used for microphone inputs, be sure to check that you connect microphones to a Mic input and other devices such as tape decks to a Line input. If you connect a Line level device into a Mic input you may damage the circuits of your equipment, blow your speakers, or blow your eardrums if you're wearing headphones.

Some Macintosh computers with a single input require a special microphone jack that is longer than normal to switch on the pre-amp. Other Macs, and most PCs, have separate inputs for Line and Mic. Most pre-amp circuits contain damping to avoid serious damage, but even if a line input into the microphone socket doesn't blow anything, the signal will be severely distorted.

Voice-Over

Voice-over refers to a spoken accompaniment to visual material, in which the speaker is not seen (unlike narration). This can be the simplest and quickest form of audio. All it requires is that a microphone be plugged into the computer (some monitors and notebook computers include built-in microphones). This, however, will generate mediocre results because such features are designed only for audio notes.

Microphones come in all sorts of configurations and price points. For example, using the microphone supplied with a Hi-8 camcorder with your computer will give better results than using the microphone that came with the computer. A professional tie-clip microphone will give even better results, but such microphones cost the same as a mid-range word processor.

Tips on achieving high-quality voice-over recording are covered later in this chapter.

Library Music/SFX

A wide range of stock music has been available on audio CD for the past several years. Video, film, and multimedia production companies often license music and sound effects libraries.

Professional libraries usually provide CDs to producers free or at a minimal cost. The music is licensed on a per use basis, and priced according to audience size, repetitions, and so on. Other music libraries provide the CDs at a high initial cost, but the music is provided royalty-free.

The range of material available is vast, from world music to pastiche, and orchestral to indie. The choices can be overwhelming. Like stock photography, library music has a long history but is constantly refreshed.

As with music, some sound effects libraries come with a buy-out license enabling you to use the music or sound effects for as long as you want and on as many titles as you want. Others require you to pay an annual fee (the CDs are updated on a subscription basis).

Both music and sound effects are supplied as audio CDs. Thanks to the universal adoption of CD-ROM and their compatibility with *Red Book audio* (the term used to refer to the format of an audio CD), it is simple to convert CD-audio tracks into an audio file useable by Director. MoviePlayer, SoundEdit 16, and SoundForge all perform this function. The Red Book audio file is directly translated into a file format such as AIFF or QuickTime, rather than requiring the digital CD to be converted to an analog signal and redigitized (with a subsequent loss of quality).

Music Programmers and Session Musicians

When a budget allows, or when the title demands, you can commission music specifically for a project.

The most common reason for composing and recording music specifically for a title is so that the needs of interactivity can be taken into consideration. If music must be synchronized with a game player's activities, the traditional linear structure of a composition is broken. The music must be written so that a passage of music can last four bars or forty. *Segues*, or musical transitions, are especially valuable to interactive multimedia but are hardly catered to in library music.

Another important advantage of working directly with musicians is to arrange music tracks in a manner that is loop-friendly. Bridging between percussion tracks (the drum break fills, for example) can be tricky with one programming style, a cinch with another.

The Internet

The Internet holds a great collection of interesting sound effects. Tread carefully: the laws of copyright are routinely ignored by much of the community. Usually the files are of extremely poor quality and of dubious origin. However, demos from commercial organizations, independent musicians and new or breaking bands can be found. The Net is one of the riskiest sources of such material, but it may be the best way to find something unique.

Commercial CDs

Record store CDs from known artists are often the inspiration for a particular sound or feel. The ease with which it is possible to convert a track to an .AIF file, chop out a loop, and place it in a Director movie is inversely proportional to the ease in obtaining the permission to do so.

It's interesting to note that for some special uses, the cost of licensing a passage of an existing recording is often more than reasonable. The complication comes in obtaining the correct permission for use. Using *samples* (in the music industry's sense—a couple of bars of music or a line of a vocal) in recent times has eased the process, but often it is difficult for multimedia to define audience size or the number of times or copies for which the music will be used—the key factors in the minds of publishers.

As with obtaining rights to video, it is advisable to obtain the necessary rights before production for a better bargaining position. Using first and asking later is illegal.

SoundEdit 16 and SoundForge

Macromedia's sound editing application, SoundEdit 16—and its Windows counterpart, SoundForge—is a necessity for all developers who need to prepare sound files for Director productions. Either application can be seen in two ways: as a creation tool to modify sounds and create new effects, and as a utility to ensure clean sound in the correct format.

In its creative role, SoundEdit 16 can meet the need for a specific but un-available sound—an explosion, for example. Real explosions are rather uninteresting—just big bangs. The art of cinematic explosions involves using many different little sounds made to sound bigger by slowing them down and then carefully montaging the sounds into a single performance. SoundEdit 16 enables variable pitch bending, mixing of multiple tracks, stereo imaging, and more.

INSIDER TIP

What would a teddy bear two meters tall sound like if it could talk?

A talking teddy bear was required for an information kiosk. Obviously, it had to be a big fat voice, deep, but not threatening and gravelly—this was an enthusiastic teddy bear, not a horror film trailer.

The voice-over was first recorded with the artist speaking in a natural tone of voice, but unnaturally quickly. When played back, the voice was the right tone, but the pronunciation sounded slurred—the artist couldn't talk that fast.

The solution was to take a straight recording within SoundEdit. The Pitchbend filter dropped the voice by almost an octave, and the tempo control was used to speed the results. Because the tempo control does not affect pitch, the result was that pronunciation sounded very natural.

SoundEdit 16 has the capability to record sound by using the Macintosh's built-in audio capabilities. SoundEdit 16 can then resample the sound to various frequencies and bit depths, add effects, edit unwanted portions of the audio, convert to different file formats, mix stereo files to mono, and most important for Director users, it has the capability to add cue markers and create loop points (see fig. 11.7).

Figure 11.7

SoundEdit 16 Edit window with loop points.

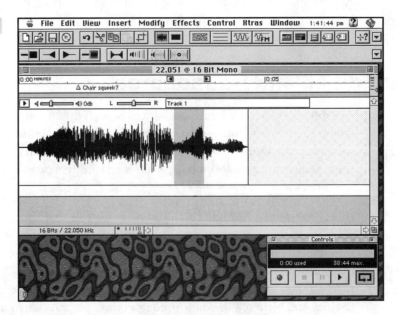

Loop points are markers inside the AIF file that tell Director where to begin and end in a piece of imported audio that has its loop box checked. Rather than looping the entire file, the sound plays from the beginning on the first loop, then when the end loop point is passed, the playback begins again from the start of the loop. This continues until the sound is stopped, or switched to another sound file.

With correctly set loop points, you can repeat or loop a bar of music within a sound file so seamlessly that it sounds like a long verse, bridge, or chorus of a song. You can loop sound effects such as crickets to create an ambiance of background sounds. The loop points function saves disk space and creates an interesting opportunity to use the first section of a sound file as the introduction to the looped section.

New to Director 6 are cue points. *Cue points* are named markers within an AIF file that are similar to markers within the Director score window. Cue points greatly assist the synchronization of score-based animation to a sound file. For example, the `cuePassed` event handler can cause a score-based animation that is running slowly to jump to a relevant frame. The following code shows how `cuePassed` works:

```
-- when a sound with a cuepoint named "Bang!" in channel 2
-- passes the cue point, an event is called, and picked up
-- by the following handler, which ensures that it coincides
-- with a point in the score labeled "explosion":
on cuePassed channel, number, name
  -- these three parameters can now be checked to see if
  -- the name is "Bang!" and to react to it.
  if name = "Bang!" then go to frame "explosion"
end
```

The addition of cue points enables Director 6 movies to emulate digital video recovery techniques if picture and sound lose synchronization due to, for example, increased disk activity. Dropping frames of animation is less noticeable than modifying the sound, and it is more likely that pictures will lag behind sound due to the extra processing involved.

Cue points are useful for issuing events that handlers can respond to. The key feature is the compatability to create a specific named event associated with a moment of sound that can be tracked and acted upon with the `cuePassed` handler.

A member can be checked for cue points within it, either by gathering the names of the markers with the `cuePointNames` property, or by the times (in milliseconds) with the `cuePointTimes` property. If a cue point is not named, Lingo returns an empty string.

The following exercise demonstrates the use of cue points in a sound file to control a film loop in the score. The Director movie—named BUBBLES.DIR—is included on the CD-ROM that accompanies this book. The bubbles movie represents a sea floor, while an ambient soundtrack plays. The soundtrack has an occasional "rising bubble" sound, which we want to ensure coincides with an animation of a rising air bubble while other things happen on the stage.

Cue Points in Use

1. Play the movie BUBBLE.DIR and note the behavior of the rising bubble. It rises in synch with the ambient sound. Change the tempo setting to 30 fps; although the bubble rises quickly, it only begins to rise when the sound begins.

2. In SoundEdit, open BUBBLE.AIF. Toward the end of the sound is an upward-pointing triangle labeled Bubble, which marks the beginning of the rising scale of the sound. Select a point earlier in the sound—at the two second point, for example.

3. Choose Cue Point from the Insert menu, and type a name for the cue point. The dialog box enables you to enter a precise time if necessary, using a variety of time units. In this case, precision is not required, so click OK to insert the cue point.

4. Save the file under a new name, using the AIFF file type. Only AIFF and QuickTime movies can contain cue points. Import this file into the BUBBLE.DIR movie. Remember to check the cast member properties and ensure that the sound loops.

5. With your new sound selected in the Cast window, switch to the score window and select the sound in channel 1. From the Edit menu, select Exchange Cast Members.

6. Play the movie again. Note that two bubbles rise each time the sound loops. Open the Script window and look for the movie script. The script follows:

```
on startMovie
  puppetSprite 2, TRUE
  sound fadeIn 1, 3 * 60
end
```

```
on stopMovie
  puppetSprite 2, FALSE
end

on cuePassed
  set the locH of sprite 2 to random(512)
  set the member of sprite 2 to "bubble"
  updateStage
  set the member of sprite 2 to "bubble trail"
  updateStage
end
```

7. The `startMovie` handler sets up channel 2 for the bubbles and fades the sound over three seconds. The `stopMovie` handler resets the channel as a matter of courtesy. The majority of the work is done by the third handler.

8. Each time a cue point occurs in the sound channel, an event is sent out which is picked up by the `on cuePassed` handler. The sprite is moved to a new position, switched from the film loop to a stationary cast member, and the changes made by issuing an `updateStage` command. The sprite is then changed back to the film loop to reset the film loop to the beginning again, using the `updateStage` command to confirm the change.

Cue points enable you to do things that were difficult if not impossible to do before. A sound can be looped a specific number of times, for example, or the same movie can react to different soundtracks.

Another feature of SoundEdit 16 version 2.0 includes the capability to batch process audio files. If you want to convert 200 AIFF files to IBM PC WAVE files, for example, SoundEdit 16 works unattended, automatically opening, converting, and then saving the new files.

SoundEdit 16 edits the audio portion of QuickTime video, including the *interleaved* formats such as CinePak. The CinePak compression format (discussed in Chapter 12) combines video and audio tracks into one stream. This combination of video and audio tracks is called *interleaving* and enables smooth playback from single-speed drives. SoundEdit 16 strips out the audio track for editing, and then replaces the original interleaved track when complete.

Software Tools

Macromedia SoundEdit (for Macintosh) and SoundForge (for Windows) are not the only tools available for manipulating audio.

Another element of Director Studio for Macintosh is Macromedia Deck II (see fig. 11.8). Deck is essentially a digital multitrack studio. Although aimed at music production, Deck's capability to quickly shuffle sound clips and play many tracks simultaneously make it a great layering tool. Deck is unlike SoundEdit 16 in that almost all its editing is non-destructive—cropping the beginning and end of a sound file does not remove the audio from the original file.

Figure 11.8

A typical Deck II session.

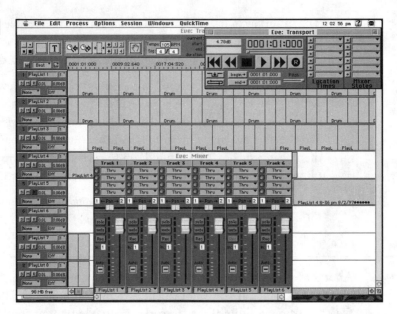

Many similar solutions exist for Windows computers, although these solutions require additional hardware and high performance disk drives.

Professional music applications include Cubase Audio, which includes some of the disk recording features of Deck II. Cubase combines these features with MIDI sequencing to create a total music production environment. MIDI is to music what Director is to animation.

Apple's QuickTime MoviePlayer 2.5 (with authoring extensions) is a more down-to-earth example of a great utility. More than a simple movie player, MoviePlayer can import CD audio files, select and preview a portion of a CD track, and convert it into either a QuickTime movie or to an AIFF format (see fig. 11.9).

Figure 11.9

*The Audio CD Import
Options dialog box.*

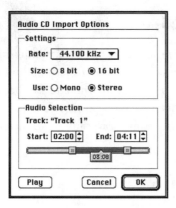

Other tricks QuickTime can perform include editing movies, opening MIDI files, assigning instruments to the MIDI tracks, translating MIDI files into AIFF files, adding text tracks, adding copyright information to QT files, and setting parameters such as cache hints and poster frames. QuickTime is discussed in more detail in Chapter 12.

SoundConverter is a utility from Apple that can change the sampling frequencies and formats of sound files. Although applications such as SoundEdit perform this function, SoundConverter is available free of charge, takes up little room, and has modest hardware requirements.

SoundEffects is a powerful shareware sound editor. Its strength resides in its capability to apply many digital effects to recorded sounds. The effects are plug-in modules—you can enhance the program by adding new modules as they become available. Not only can SoundEffects change sounds in many ways through its variety of effects, but it also can handle multichannel sounds, sampled at any rate up to 64 kHz and with any sample size between 1 and 32 bits. Recording rate and sample size are only limited by your Macintosh or your sound input device.

Optical Media's Disc to Disc program is a good tool to have in your tool chest when you need to convert many Red Book audio files for playback in Director. The Disc to Disc program enables you to select several songs or portions of songs from a CD, and then automatically batch process the audio to the format that you request.

Handling Audio in Director

Incorporating sound into your production can be accomplished in a variety of ways. Every Lingo programmer will have a preferred method that depends on his particular style of authoring. This section will address the many options that are available. Each method has its pros and cons. The correct mix that gives you fast performance and high-fidelity sound can only be found through experimentation.

Sounds in the Score

Director has two sound channels in the score. The Macintosh and Windows versions of the sound channels may look similar, but they are different in the way that the internal architecture of the two platforms handle and mix sounds together.

Most users who are new to Director attempt to stay away from Lingo commands that trigger audio files. By using the two audio channels in the score, you can drag-and-drop audio cast members into the sound channel cells. When the playback head reaches a frame containing a sound file, Director plays that sound. If the same frame contains both a sound in channel 1 and a sound in channel 2, Director mixes the sounds. The sounds will play simultaneously as long as they are not both linked files. The drive cannot read from two places on the drive at once when spooling the audio. Nothing, however, will stop you from having one channel spool from disk while playing a sound file that has been imported into the cast and will therefore play from RAM in the other channel.

Generally speaking, most programmers prefer to use channel 2 for music and narration. These audio files may be linked-to-file and played directly from the disk. Channel 1 is then used for internal sounds that are stored in RAM.

If you want the sound to play while you load a new movie, the sound must be internal (not linked-to-file), and you must place the sound in the same channel in both the movie you are starting from and the movie you are going to.

Alternatively, you can play a sound while loading a new movie by using Lingo to use a puppetSound.

Playing a sound file while a new Director movie loads was a common workaround when the entire movie and all the cast had to be loaded into memory before continuing. These intermission breaks are rarely needed with the `preload cast when needed` cast property, but keeping a smooth soundtrack between movies still requires this technique.

puppetSound

Quite often a situation arises in which music is playing in the background and users push a button to go to a different movie or a different scene in the movie that they are currently playing. Users need some type of immediate feedback to know that the computer recognizes their selection, and this is a good opportunity to use a `puppetSound` within the `mouseDown` handler.

To accomplish this, attach the following handler script to the button:

```
on mouseDown
  puppetSound "thunk"
  -- button actions
  updateStage
end
```

The preceding command causes the cast member that is named `"thunk"` to play immediately from RAM in sound channel 1 when the user clicks the mouse. This sound must be an internal sound. If you have audio playing in the score in sound channel 1, that sound stops and the sound called `"thunk"` plays in its place. Therefore, make sure you reserve sound channel 1 for `puppetSounds` when you plan to use this method of mixing sounds interactively. After you take control of sound channel 1 with `puppetSounds`, sound channel 1 is no longer available for use in the score until you apply the Lingo command `puppetSound 0`. This can be handled by a `mouseUp` handler in the same script:

```
on mouseUp
  puppetSound 0
end
```

The `0` function returns sound channel 1 to its original state and cancels any current `puppetSound` when the mouse is released. If sound was playing in sound channel 1 before the mouse was clicked, the sound returns and this channel is now under control of the score's playback head.

INSIDER TIP

In Lingo terms, `puppetSound` is just like `puppetSprite`—it takes control of the score in that area, and therefore, declaring `puppetSound 0` is analogous to declaring `puppetSprite x, FALSE`.

When you have a lot of noisy buttons, however, things can go awry if a button fails to catch a `mouseUp` event (for example, the user clicks on a button, then drags away from the area before releasing the mouse). In this instance, you can call `puppetSound 0` immediately before calling `puppetSound "MyClickSound"`. Remember to call a final `puppetSound 0` when you're through.

sound playFile

Use the Lingo command `sound playFile` to call and play an audio file that was not imported as a Director cast member. This function is opposite to `puppetSound` in that sounds must be external to the cast and linked. Make sure that the audio file (preferably AIFF) and the Director movie file are in the same folder to avoid having to use path names.

The primary use of `sound playFile` is to access audio tracks in addition to the two represented in the score. There is a limit to the number of audio channels, and each platform is different. The requirements for each platform follow:

▶ Six additional audio channels are available on Macintosh and Power Macintosh computers to make a total of 8 channels.

▶ Two additional channels are available to PCs with the MACROMIX.DLL installed. MACROMIX.DLL is installed with Director for Windows, but if you create a Projector, check that this file is part of the projector package if you intend to use more than the two score channels.

▶ Windows PCs with Windows 95 and QuickTime for Windows 2.5 or later have six additional channels for a total of eight, although QuickTime for Windows 2.5 is required for playback.

Now take a look at an example of the ways to use `sound playFile`.

Look for the file SOUND.DIR in the Chapter 12 folder on the CD-ROM that accompanies this book. Open it and perform the following steps.

A series of ten 3D PICS files that produce a spinning globe sit in 10 frames of one channel and loop over the 10 frames. We want to have this globe speak to you when you click the mouse. Looped background music also is playing as the globe is spinning.

The internal looped music is set in sound channel 2. It is set in 11 frames, which are located directly above the animated sprite channels. As the playback head loops over and over in these frames, the globe spins and the music plays continuously.

The 10 sprite cells that contain the world animation have a score script attached to them.

The Lingo script reads as follows:

```
on mouseUp
    sound playFile 1, "narrate.aif"
end
```

When the globe is clicked, the animation continues to spin; the background music keeps playing; and the narration that resides on the disk, NARRATE.AIF, plays in channel 1, along with the music and spinning globe. Notice that the audio file NARRATE.AIF is in the same folder as the movie file. If this is not possible in your production, you must supply a path name, such as the following:

```
on mouseUp
     sound playFile 1, the pathName && "/audio/" & "narrate.aif"
end
```

Digital Video Sounds

Digital video need not contain digital video! Audio-only movies were once very useful to keep audio in step with the playback head in the score.

Without cue points described earlier, obtaining a precise synchronization for audio to animation could be difficult because of the various playback performances of computers.

A QuickTime or AVI movie can be imported into the score as a sprite rather than an audio track, and the audio is controlled using the movieTime and movieRate controls. The disadvantage of using a digital video file instead of cue markers is that you must find out when your cue points occur and then work out the relative position of that point from the beginning of the digital video file in ticks (1/60th of a second).

On the other hand, a digital video audio track can be played back at full speed, half speed, or even backward. If you are looking for maximum control rather than ease of cueing, a digital video sound is very flexible.

Another feature of QuickTime available to the Macintosh (and to QuickTime for Windows 95 version 2.5 and later) is multiple sound tracks. This is useful for multiple language narration, in which a single control mechanism and one file can cater for many different languages simply by enabling or disabling tracks in a single movie.

A common use of multiple tracks on Macintosh titles is to simulate a recording studio by enabling many tracks and altering the volume of each one independently under user control.

Digital video control is covered in detail in Chapter 12.

Controlling the Volume

You can use Lingo to control the overall volume of the computer, fade audio in and out, and adjust the volume of individual sound channels.

Computer Volume

The volume level of your computer is controlled by a property called `soundLevel`. `soundLevel` is defined as a value from 0–7, in which 0 gives no sound and 7 is the maximum sound. Using Lingo to control the volume in this method is the same as changing the volume slider in the Sound control panel.

The following Lingo `mouseUp` button script turns up the volume of the computer to full:

```
on mouseUp
   set the soundLevel to 7
end
```

To turn down the sound to half volume, use the following script:

```
on mouseUp
   set the soundLevel to 4
end
```

The `soundLevel` is a system property—if your Director movie sets the sound level to 0, alert sounds and other sounds will be muted. As with changing the color depth of the monitor, if you must change the `soundLevel`, be courteous and store the level it was set to when your movie started. When the user quits or closes your movie, restore the `soundLevel` to the original setting.

Channel Volume

To adjust the volume of an individual channel, use the `volume of sound` property. Set a value for the volume; 0 is silent and 255 is the maximum.

The following script turns the volume of sound channel 1 to half volume:

```
on exit Frame
    set the volume of sound 1 to 127
end
```

To control the volume of a digital video sound, the word sprite is used instead of sound. The script turns the volume of the digital video cast member in sprite channel 10 to half volume.

```
on exitFrame
    the volume of sprite 10 to 127
end
```

You can picture the relationship between `soundLevel` and the `volume of sound` as the volume knob on an amplifier and a fader on a mixing desk. `soundLevel` affects everything, even the computer operating system. Because there are only six levels and silence, `soundLevel` is unsuitable for fine audio control. The `volume of sound` command affects only one channel at a time, but offers very fine control.

To perform a smooth fade on many channels at once, use the `Fade` command.

Fade

To fade in the sounds in the score, use the following handler, which is in the score script. Place the following Lingo in the frame before the sound starts:

```
on exit Frame
    sound fadeIn 1, 1 * 60
    sound fadeIn 2, 1 * 60
end
```

The audio in sound channels 1 and 2 fades in, in one second. `sound fadeIn 1` specifies channel 1. `1 * 60` is the time (one second), measured in 60 ticks per second. This is channel-specific and you can independently fade the sound channels in and out over different periods of time.

To fade out the sound:

```
on exitFrame
   sound fadeOut 1, 2 * 60
   sound fadeOut 2, 4 * 60
end
```

The audio fades out in sound channels 1 and 2. Channel 1 fades to silence over two seconds and channel 2 fades to silence in four seconds.

To combine the various forms of Lingo associated with the sound, take a look at the BUTTONS.DIR movie included in the Chapter 11 folder on the accompanying CD and also shown in figure 11.10. This simple movie includes a button that plays a music track while depressed. On release the music stops, but on subsequent pressing, the track takes off from where it stopped. Note that the button sounds are internal cast member movies, and that the music is a digital video member which is set to loop and start in a paused state.

Figure 11.10

The Noisy Buttons example, with both internal and external sound members. Note the alternative pair of buttons.

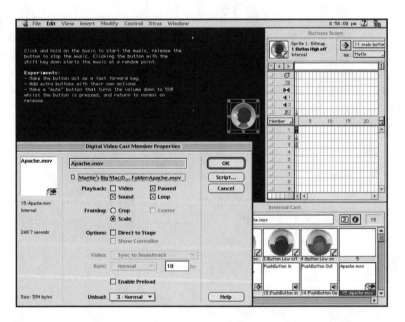

As well as starting and stopping the audio track, the button makes a different sound on being pressed than it does when released. The hard work in the movie is done by a generic button script that combines `mouseUp` and `mouseDown` actions. As before, the script below is cross referenced to the steps that follow in the next exercise:

```
-- Button handler (Step 1)
global tempChannel

on mouseDown
  if the shiftDown then set the movieTime of sprite 2
➡to random(200*60)
  -- (Step 2)
  put the clickOn into tempChannel
  -- (Step 3)
  puppetSound 0
  puppetSound "PushButton In"
  updateStage
  -- (Step 4)
  puppetSprite tempChannel, TRUE
  set the memberNum of sprite tempChannel to
➡the memberNum of sprite tempChannel + 1
  updateStage
  -- (Step 5)
  -- pass to handler
  GenericButtonHandler tempChannel
  -- (Step 6)
  set the movieRate of sprite 2 to 1
end

on mouseUp
  -- (Step 7)
  set the movieRate of sprite 2 to 0
  -- (Step 8)
  puppetSound 0
  puppetSound "PushButton out"
  puppetSprite tempChannel, FALSE
  -- (Step 9)
  updateStage
end
```

Noisy Buttons

1. The script is designed to work on many different sprites, so we use a global variable to remember which button the user has clicked via the channel in which it resides.

2. Establish the channel of the clicked sprite and store it.

3. If a button has been clicked or other sounds are active, stop them immediately, because the next sound should occur as soon as possible.

continues

Noisy Buttons continued

PuppetSound 0 cancels all puppeted sounds and the next line plays the PushButton In sound. This is followed by the UpdateStage command to ensure that the sound plays immediately.

4. The next part of the script takes control of the channel and momentarily switches the member to its neighbor (buttons in this movie are stored in pairs for convenience). Another UpdateStage is called to display the results on-screen.

5. Now that the artwork has changed and the sound has been made, the main purpose of the button can be undertaken. Because this is a generic handler, it should be passed to another handler with the channel number by adding genericButtonHandler. tempChannel needs to be enabled so that the genericButtonHandler knows which button was pressed by the channel it was in.

6. Set the QuickTime audio only movie in channel 2 to play back at normal speed using the movieRate property. For fun, try the values 0.5, 2, and −1 here.

7. Now that the button has been released, the QuickTime movie is stopped by setting the movieRate to zero.

8. The same process of events to play the button sound is put into action, shutting off any puppetSounds that may be playing in preparation for the sound you want to play on cue with the restoration of the button artwork.

9. The updateStage call refreshes the screen and plays the sound. If actions or processes take place between the puppetSound and the puppetSprite (as in the previous instance) each event is given its own updateStage to ensure that they weren't delayed.

10. Try adapting the script so that the music begins to play, and the button acts as a fast forward control. Alternatively, make the button act as a partial mute control, reducing the volume by 50 percent.

The second line in the mouseDown handler is a small Easter egg to skip to a random part of the music. Other things you may want to try include dragging another button from the cast to the stage and applying the same script to it, or swapping a low button for a high button. As the script and handlers try to avoid specific reference to a particular member, you can add multiple buttons that have corresponding actions in genericButtonHandler.

Please note that the button handling in this example is a quick and dirty method. A more robust solution should check for and handle situations such as users clicking on a button and dragging with it before releasing the mouse.

Techniques for Recording Audio

The best sound samples are obtained from clean originals. Professionally recorded material will come from soundproofed studios with a high-end kit. With some creative ingenuity, however, you can obtain high-quality results on modest equipment.

Separate Sounds

Clean recordings contain only the subject—a voice-over does not include the sound of a vacuum cleaner, and vice versa. If a voice-over is required over the sound of a vacuum cleaner, the two are recorded separately and mixed.

When two or more sounds need to be mixed, the relative volumes of the sounds often need to be carefully designed to match what the human ear is used to hearing. The human ear has a wide dynamic range—the difference between the quietest and the loudest sounds it can hear is far wider than any recording and playback equipment can emulate. If, for example, a door slam and footsteps are to be heard simultaneously, it is necessary to make the door slam quieter and the footsteps louder. This is achieved by recording each sound group separately and at their individual correct levels. (In cinema, footsteps are so commonly required to occur simultaneously with other sounds that the industry has special *footstep artists*—also known as *foley artists*.)

Recording Environment

The primary requirement for the recording environment is to obtain a quiet space that is free from hard surfaces that lead to echoes or reverberation—*reverberation* is essentially lots of small quick echoes. It is the reverberation of sound that tells us how big the space is that the sound occurred in. By achieving a "dry" sound (no reverberation), we can place the object in any sized container from a closet, which is the size of most voice-over booths, to the Super Bowl and beyond by adding reverberation.

INSIDER TIP

You can add reverberation and echo, but it is difficult to take it away. If you try to record a quiet personal voice-over in the quietest unoccupied room in your office, it will sound like it's coming from inside a refrigerator—such reverberant surroundings are described as *wet*. In such circumstances, it is highly advisable to drape yourself and the microphone in a heavy coat or blanket to absorb the extra reverberation.

Modulating reverberation is one way of providing a sense of scale to the scene. Another important way is by positioning the microphone close to or away from the subject. This is analogous to the camera techniques of the close-up, mid-shot, and long shot. Sound recording is no different. We are accustomed to seeing a presenter speaking louder in a long shot, and in quieter tones when in a close-up. If the roles are reversed, the effect can be upsetting.

INSIDER TIP

A familiar segue between narrative voice-over and in-shot presenter is to shoot the presenter in long shot, but keep a tie-clip microphone close to his mouth. The visual "joke" is established by zooming in on the presenter, whom we have assumed is part of the background.

A close microphone effect with dry or no reverberation establishes intimacy. A close microphone effect with reverberation establishes looming claustrophobia. Conversely, a distant microphone effect with dry reverberation creates a feeling of the vast outdoors, space and distance, whereas a distant microphone with reverberation creates the sense of an individual or object isolated within a large structure. These examples may seem melodramatic, but they are part of our experience of sound.

Trim Loops

Some sound loops contain a little thump on each iteration. This spoils the illusion of smooth and contiguous sound; the thump seems louder than the rest of the sound file.

To prevent this, looped sounds need to have loop points that start and end in the same part of a wave cycle. If you magnify a sound in an application, such as SoundEdit 16, you can see the sound wave oscillate between the zero point. Figure 11.11 shows correctly aligned waves.

Figure 11.11

Correctly aligned sound loop waves.

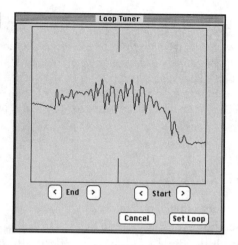

The loop should be started and ended as the line crosses the zero point heading in the same direction. Anything else will confuse the digital side and cause the analog circuitry to thump. Figure 11.12 shows an example of edits that are liable to cause thumps or clicks.

Figure 11.12

Incorrectly aligned sound loop waves.

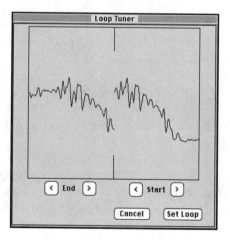

SoundEdit 16 includes a loop tuner Xtra for the purpose of starting and ending loop points in the same part of a wave cycle. This task can also be accomplished by visual inspection with much the same result.

INSIDER TIP

I prefer working visually, because the loop tuner forces me to work at a degree of magnification in which the relationship between the waves and what is heard is lost. With less magnification, you can see the start of a different note or a loud sound. This is helpful because a loop point is best a fraction before a large transition, rather than on a specific region worked out by timing exactly four beats. A few milliseconds can be added or removed to ensure the correct length of the loop.

Monitor Your Sound

It is important to consider where your material will be played—will it be in the quiet of someone's home or in the noise of a mall? Will it be played with high-quality speakers, or the dime-sized speaker underneath the hard disk?

Do not rely on huge, warm, swirly bass sounds being reproduced on small speakers. The smaller the speaker, the worse the bass response. High-pitched sound, however, carries far better than low frequency sound; medium and high frequency sound will work better than bass in a noisy environment.

High-pitched sound includes *toppy* sound, which means that it lacks bass frequencies, and *sibilant* sound, which refers to the hissy and percussive voice sounds in words such as "system" and "teach."

Kiosks in noisy malls also benefit from a *gated* sound, which means that a distinct transition is made between quiet and loud. This refers to an audio gate, a process that will fade any sound under a certain threshold. This is useful to remove a noisy background.

If an audio gate is overused, it can make the sound feel *gappy*, which refers to the silence between words and phrases, or sound effects). This silence helps punctuate through the hum of noisy surroundings, but sounds completely wrong in a quiet office.

Another important measure is to listen to your audio on the type of equipment on which it will be played.

Do not try to mix sound while wearing headphones if your final sound is going to be played on loudspeakers. Headphones have entirely different characteristics than speakers. Similarly, do not use hi-fi speakers to mix sound to be used for internal computer speakers. It's worse than color balancing scans on an LCD screen, then playing them back on an ordinary monitor.

Close the door, work odd hours, but check and recheck on your target equipment!

Location Sound

Location sound can be divided into two types: the stuff you want, and the stuff you don't want. The latter category includes distracting sounds, general hum, and wind noise. Context is everything. The hiss of wind over a microphone may be appropriate if you are evoking an outdoor scene of a desolate landscape, but is objectionable when recording an interview or impromptu voice-over.

Choosing the correct equipment is important in moderating location sound. Microphones are sensitive devices, and are often fitted with an acoustically transparent windshield—often a spherical wire mesh screen. This is enough to avoid or greatly disrupt the popping sound, which can result from a close microphone technique, but not enough to deal with outdoor wind.

The *rifle microphone* is more popularly known as the *hairy sausage* because this is what it resembles. It is often used by outdoor television crews. The fluffy acoustic shield wrapped over a metal cage disrupts much of the wind blast associated with outdoor shoots without cutting down the higher frequencies from the sound source. The narrow beam of the long, thin, microphone inside cuts out extraneous sounds that strike it from the side. Best results are obtained by either holding the microphone low and pointing it up to a sound source, or by holding it high and pointing it down onto the source—whichever sounds best.

After you have managed to cut out as much of the location sound as possible and have obtained clean and well-balanced recordings, you'll need some *atmos*—a carefully recorded sound of the location. Atmos is used to avoid *dead air*—unnatural gaps in sound—and to patch up any problems with the recording, such as the need to blend two takes together. In addition, any item that may be featured in any way should also be isolated and recorded (for example, vehicles arriving, clocks chiming, animals reacting, crowds applauding). Digital audio tape (DAT) is cheap, reshoots aren't.

Editing Narration

Voice-overs will require editing. Minor irritations such as chair squeaks, page rustles, and background noise will require removal, as will the inevitable stumble on words and phrases.

INSIDER TIP

If you're new to narration, print your lines in a large font, and mark punctuation (vocal punctuation) with a red pen. Include smiley faces, exclamation marks, and slow-down spirals. Write the first line on the next page at the bottom of the previous page. Bend the top-left and bottom-right corners of each page up so that you can pick them up quietly. Use stiff paper. Practice silly faces before and after each take to stretch your face—otherwise, you'll be tense and begin to mumble. Try to stand up and face the microphone unless you want intimacy. On a stumble, give it a beat, then pick up the sentence again. If you keep stumbling, rewrite it—forced practice makes it sound suspicious. Have a toothbrush handy and take time out for a scrub if you begin to hear clicking and smacking sounds caused by dehydration.

Useful edit points in narration occur immediately after the speaker inhales. Other, trickier points occur at the threshold of percussive and sibilant sounds made when speaking consonants. Sibilant sounds are difficult to edit because the voice changes in character after these sounds in proportion to the force of the consonant. Breathing must be watched, because too much enthusiastic editing can make passages sound unnatural or even surreal. Where possible, try to edit around punctuation. Remember to include some breath sounds for a natural effect.

Troubleshooting

Testing on various computers is a must if you plan to release your production to other users. Your product may work flawlessly on your computer and it may fail on others. If you encounter a problem, try to discover first whether it is a hardware malfunction. If other titles work, you know the problem is with the software.

No Sound

Are your speakers still plugged in? The tiny miniature phone jacks that supply sound input and output can become disconnected by accident, and cheaper cards can make it difficult to know if the plug is properly seated. If you connect your Power Macintosh to a hi-fi setup, is the correct input selected?

Is the volume on the computer turned off? The Macintosh will blink the menu bar when the sound is set to zero and a system beep is called for.

Are your headphones plugged in? This will disconnect your speakers.

Macintosh users should make sure that you and your end-users have installed the latest versions of Sound Manager. At the time of this writing, the latest version of Sound Manager was version 3.1, which enables the playback of 16-bit sound files. You can get this update free from Apple or an Apple dealer. You will need a license from Apple to distribute Sound Manager to your end-users.

Windows users can always download the latest drivers for their sound cards from the manufacturers of the card.

Intermittent Sound

Intermittent sound demonstrates that the system is able to create sound, but is unable to keep up with the demand due to other activity within the system. The usual culprit is unnecessary disk activity.

Macintosh users should try turning off virtual memory in the Control Panel. Director uses its own memory management protocols, and conflicts can occur.

Stay away from RAM Doubler and similar products. Once again, Director is a RAM-intensive application and it is best to stay away from any system INIT that optimizes RAM use.

Is the movie trying to play two audio files that are linked to file at the same time? Remember that the drive's pickup head cannot be at two places at once.

Loud Hum

If you are going to be digitizing sound, make sure your equipment is properly grounded. If you have a microphone mixer, keep it away from the computer. Quite often, the motors in fans and hard drives will create a hum if placed too near to the input transistors of microphone mixers. Overly long microphone cables piled over voltage transformers (that is, tungsten halogen lights or uninterruptable power supplies) can create hum. The cable acts as an aerial that picks up the alternating current at around 60 Hz.

Another cause of very loud hum is a fault in an audio cable. This may simply be an incorrectly seated plug on some audio equipment. Turn down the volume and replug it. If this fails to solve it, the connections at either end may be damaged. If the connection is damaged, the only way to get around the hum is to replace the cable.

Distortion

When recording sound, make sure that none of the sound channels are being driven to excessive high levels (in the red). A limiter is a good thing to rent or purchase when processing sound. It limits the amount of sound from the microphone, while keeping the volume up loud without overloading your computer's input amplifiers. Other esoterica to look out for are compressors, which both limit the high-level sounds and amplify quiet passages for a thicker more intense sound. A thick, intense sound is synonymous with high-energy delivery, but useful for smoothing out a hesitant speaker.

WARNING

> Distortion in analog equipment is an annoyance, but when a digital signal hits the red, it is capped, producing a pronounced thump in the sound. Because momentary overloads are so noticeable, most recording software includes automatic gain control—fine for voice annotation or dictation software, but lacking fine control. Use the Levels window in SoundEdit.

Noise

Noise has two types: the kind outside the computer or made by the hard disk on your desk, and the kind that is generated in the quantum mechanics of modern circuitry. The first category can be countered with sensible studio or microphone techniques. As for the latter, a level of noise will inevitably be within any system. Using high-quality masters and attention to correct levels will keep noise to a minimum.

If that once-in-a-lifetime recording does have a freeway in the background, noise gates (described earlier in the chapter) can alleviate the problem by tracking the main sound amplitude and making the peripheral noise quieter. This can either be hardware (high-quality results and very quick to set up) or software (far cheaper but requires quite a bit of fiddling to obtain good results). Used too aggressively, this technique creates odd-sounding results, but it can correct some cases of irritating noise.

Authoring Mac and Windows Hybrid CD-ROM Titles

Use AIFF audio files where possible because they play on both Windows and Macintosh platforms without the need for extra software.

If you use QuickTime digital video sound files, make sure that the Windows computer has QuickTime for Windows installed or QuickTime for Windows on your CD-ROM. QuickTime for Windows is free from Apple. You will still need to obtain a license to distribute it (see Chapter 4, "Delivering the Goods"), but it's just a formality. QuickTime for Windows is included with Director.

INSIDER TIP

Strange things can happen on Windows PCs when you go to a new movie. Sometimes the sound from the previous movie just keeps playing over your new movie. Test your movies in progress on both computer platforms.

The following Lingo in the movie script will stop the preceding audio from playing over your new audio.

```
on StartMovie
    if soundBusy(1) then sound stop 1
end startMovie
```

Creative Aspects of Audio

Sound has always struggled for equal treatment with pictures in video and cinema. The audio component has so much to offer the creative process. Consider one of the most dynamic forms of multimedia, the music video: The sound comes first. The audio suggests the visual and leads it throughout. The capability to conjure up moods and atmospheres has long been understood by radio producers (without the budgetary constraints of the cinema industry). Sound surrounds us. We expect sound as feedback. Think about the sound of buttons, the grate or swish of transitions…

As an experiment, I created a simple but pretty graph animation for a business presentation. Without sound, it was a graph. With an audible whoosh or two, it was an elegant illustration. With some cartoon sound effects, it made people laugh out loud and it broke the ice nicely. Pop quiz: What does a pie chart sound like?

Interactive pictures need interactive sound. The linear progression of verse to chorus to verse of traditional pop music doesn't fit the browsing hierarchical layers of interactive media—opportunities in ambient soundtracks exist where music exists in layers that can be traversed in many directions. Melody is often defined as pitch over time. In interactive multimedia, time is a variable rather than the fixed metronome in a musical performance.

Select an anthem in advance and let your imagination experience the mood of the song. Letting a musical soundtrack drive your production will have a definite effect on your Lingo scripting, which is certainly one of the most important aspects of creating multimedia.

If you are working in a team situation, play the music to the members of your group in the preplanning stages. You will be surprised at their creativeness when they hear and feel the emotions the music creates. Ideas for animation jump out at you when you hear sparkles in the melody. Your choices of color, text styles, and size will flow and harmonize with the production. Then, when all the elements are brought together, the job of programming the Lingo that keeps the production in sync is fun and creative. A good Lingo programmer can be compared to the conductor of a live orchestra in a Broadway musical.

Productions that feature narration instead of music probably will have the opportunity (and hard drive space) to produce quality, 8- or 16-bit, 22.050 kHz audio files. If pictures or animation are to accompany the narration, you may have to first record the narration and then have the art department create the graphics. After these artists hear the tone, accent, and manner of the voice, images with style and content suddenly pop into their heads.

Use sound—put the *multi* back into multimedia!

In Practice

If at the beginning of this chapter you thought of multimedia primarily in terms of visual components, hopefully, by now it is clear that audio and visual are equally important. The next chapter returns to the visual component: digital video. Like audio, digital video must be imported into Director; you will find certain analogies between the two.

As you begin to author movies in Director keep in mind the central practical aspects of audio:

▶ Bit depth affects the dynamics of your sound file—the gradations between softest and loudest sounds. Sample rate affects the clarity of the sound, the range of pitches that can be distinguished.

▶ Your particular choices of bit depth, sample rate, and whether your sound file is stored internally or externally have practical implications for quality, speed of access, and hardware requirements.

▶ When authoring for cross-platform playback, balance the features of file formats with their capabilities to work on both platforms—AIFF remains a solid choice, and QuickTime also offers useful features.

▶ The general practice for channel allocation is to use channel 1 for internal sound files and channel 2 for linked sound files.

▶ Optimizing synchronization between audio and animation may be approached in several different ways, including cue points, `movieTime`, and loop markers. The one that works best will vary depending on the particulars of your project.

▶ Separating sounds, eliminating reverberation in the recording environment, trimming loops, anticipating the playback environment for your project, eliminating unwanted location sound, and editing narration are critical quality-control techniques for recording audio. Start with high-quality material and work with it. If you need to compress the material, do so at the last stage.

▶ Plan for sound early in the production process, and look out for innovative opportunities.

Digital Video: The Movie Within the Movie

Digital video is reputed to be a dark subject, full of folklore, secret tricks, and many pitfalls to catch the unwary. It continues to provoke common complaints such as stuttering video clips, clips that suddenly fall silent, flashes of color, video not appearing when bidden, and an assortment of minor ills.

Fortunately, Director provides a great deal of control over this powerful medium, far beyond the capability to display a "talking head" video clip. Director is a valuable digital video creation tool, also. The superior layering controls and ruthless optimization for on-screen use are invaluable to the world of digital video. Conversely, digital video can play back prerecorded Director animation where Director may slow considerably—especially in high pixel depth (16-bit and 24-bit screens) and complex layering situations.

Director is not, however, a digital video editing application. Editing digital video is done better by specialist applications, and this chapter covers several of them.

A list of the major topics covered in this chapter follows:

- ▶ Introduction to digital video
- ▶ Digital video formats
- ▶ Technical choices
- ▶ Sources for video content

▶ Techniques for optimizing digital video

▶ Hardware and software tools

▶ Handling digital video in Director

▶ Helper applications

Digital video can appear problematic, difficult to work with, and ultimately disappointing. It needn't be so. Digital video combines two distinct worlds with interests that often conflict. This chapter, therefore, contains a lot of theory and background information. These background concepts are important because most pitfalls associated with digital video lie outside Director.

Introduction to Digital Video

The term digital video is a bit misleading, because it need not be video at all. Digital video can—and frequently does—encompass sequences of speech, text, images, and music.

Furthermore, digital video is a blanket term that covers more than the files on your hard disk. Remember that the many features of digital video can be isolated and used in their own right. In the spirit of *Saturday Night Live*, you could say of digital video, "It's a floor wax, and hey, it's a great dessert topping too!"

Using digital video in a Director movie can solve several problems:

▶ Digital video in a Director movie can solve complex sprite animation problems, for example, by removing the performance hit of using many layers with many ink effects.

▶ Digital video can solve timing problems by synchronizing sprite animation with audio on a variety of machines.

▶ Digital video can help in asset management, with, for example, a collection of photographic images stored in a single QuickTime movie.

▶ Digital video incorporates compression, enabling 288 minutes of CD-quality stereo sound on a CD-ROM instead of 72 minutes of standard CD audio.

Digital video and Director may end up showing similar things, but their approach is different. Director's method is careful moment-by-moment direction and control (think of a puppeteer). A digital video is the finished performance—a movie of the puppetry.

Two foundations of digital video must be understood: time and compression.

Time-Based Media

Time is central to the underlying plot of digital video, because the original requirement was that a series of pictures be synchronized to an audio signal and remain in synch from the second frame to the very last hour.

This behavior differs from Director. Director plays every frame of its sprite animations; a very common occurrence is slower playback speed on a computer that is less powerful than the developer's system. A sequence that plays for 10 seconds on one system may take 15 or 20 seconds on a slower system. All frames are seen, but the action occurs more slowly.

Digital video, on the other hand, normally gives priority to timing: To play back a one-minute video on a slower system, digital video resorts to skipping (dropping) picture frames as needed to maintain the predefined timing of the soundtrack. Some describe the behavior as *sound priority*, that is, the soundtrack of a digital video—short of total overload—plays normally, with no loss of quality, while the video sometimes stutters and jerks to "keep up" with the music or speech.

Sometimes, video must take priority. A complex 3D animation might be ruined by a dropped frame. To make the digital video stop dropping frames and adopt the normal Director behavior, open the Member Information panel for your digital video member and check the Direct to Stage and Play Every Frame options. This disables the soundtrack, however.

A time-based media is composed of more than gluing pictures to sound. Digital video formats, such as QuickTime, can keep text and music (stored as *Musical Instrument Digital Interface*—MIDI—described in Chapter 11, "Sound: The Soundtrack") together in a single file. This means that lyrics to a song can be stored in the movie and made to appear and disappear depending on the notes being played. The advantage of this method over simply calculating the number of seconds from the start of a song is that the lyrics are still synchronized if the music is played at half speed, or *any* speed.

Digital video is an addition to the operating system of your computer, rather than a feature of Director. This means that a digital video can have a different frame rate to your movie. A 30 frame per second (fps) digital video animation from a 3D package can play at 30 fps even if your Director movie is playing back at 15 fps. The two time bases are independent but can be linked or controlled separately.

Digital video is based on time and is good at synchronization but is not limited to a single time base: it can be real time (as in sound to video), metronome time (such as MIDI), or frame time (similar to Director).

Compression

Compression is the other fundamental concept behind digital video. If a picture is worth a thousand words, then an animation could be worth around a thousand pictures! In fact, this is precisely what animation is—hundreds, thousands, perhaps hundreds of thousands of pictures, each faithfully recorded in high resolution, taking up storage space. The vast amount of data and high data rates associated with animation underscore the importance of compression to digital video.

Consider the following as an example of the need for compression in digital video: The US video standard, *NTSC* (*National Television Standard Committee*), is known as a 525-line system, of which 480 are used for pictures. The 4:3 ratio means 640 pixels across each row. If you multiply 480 by 640 and then multiply that by 3 (for Red, Green, and Blue), the number of bytes required to store just one frame of NTSC video can be worked out.

The number of bytes required for a 24-bit bitmap image of a single frame of NTSC is 0.9 MB of memory. The NTSC TV system displays 29.97 frames per second. As you watch the television, you are seeing about 26.9 MB of raw data flash past per second, and this does not include sound.

These statistics are impressive because they represent the volume of data your digitizer board handles at the start of the pipeline. It is also the sort of data volume written to D1 videotape used in high-end video and film production.

The bottom line is that if you want video on your computer, you're going to have to cheat. Today's average personal computer is not capable of moving 32 MB of data per second from its disk drive to the screen, which would be required to play a "raw" full-sized video stream. High-end desktop computers achieve 4 MB per second, but most digital video is played from a CD-ROM between 300–900 KB per second, and from the Internet between 1–5 KB per second.

The number of bytes that can be transferred per second is commonly referred to as *bandwidth*, but is also known as data rate. Data rate is covered in detail later in this chapter.

The magic of digital video is the clever data compression schemes devised to reduce the volume of the data stream to a manageable rate. Data compression schemes can employ temporal or spatial algorithms (or both), and can be characterized as lossy or lossless.

Temporal (Delta Change) Compression

Visualize a traditional animation of a ball bouncing across the frame as depicted in figure 12.1. The difference between the first frame and the second frame is small. Rather than drawing frame 1 onto the screen, and then drawing frame 2, it would be quicker to redraw only the area that changed between frames 1 and 2. The same principle can be applied to the differences between frames 2 and 3, and so on.

Figure 12.1

Recording only the changes between frames.

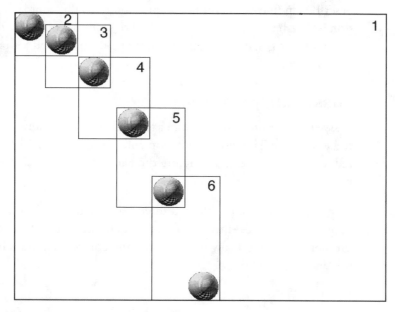

The *delta change* or *temporal* compression method records the changes between frames, rather than the frames themselves. Remarkable savings can be achieved in certain circumstances. But this method of compression is not perfect for every situation—for example, when you are panning or zooming, the whole scene changes from frame to frame!

Spatial Compression

Spatial compression methods record changes between areas of a single frame. The "talking head" against a white background, for example, can be described, row by row, as sequences of pixels by color, with a stretch of gray pixels (hair) being interrupted by a stretch of white pixels (background). Spatial compression achieves its efficiency by recording the places where the data changes. This particular example represents a specific category of spatial compression called *run-length encoding*. By recording consecutive runs of colors, you can achieve high reductions in the amount of data needing to be stored in representing clean simple areas. In complex areas of detail, however, run-length encoding is inefficient.

An alternative method to run-length encoding is color space models, edge detection, and sharpening algorithms to analyze an image. In this way, large spaces of similar tone are described in sparse detail, and areas of contrast are described in fine detail. JPEG compression takes this approach. JPEG compression is designed to work with 16-bit (thousands of colors) or 24-bit (millions of colors) images. Run-length encoding tends to be used for pictures with limited colors—8 bits (256 colors) or less.

Lossy Compression

Lossy compression is so named because information is quite literally lost, never to be retrieved. The lost information and lower quality are offset by remarkable reduction in file size and therefore the bandwidth required to play the file back.

Compression can be classified in three ways: frame size, bandwidth (or, more accurately, data rate—the number of bytes transferred per second) and compression ratio (how many times smaller the compressed file is in comparison to the uncompressed file).

Compression ratios vary according to use: 3:1 for broadcast television production, 12:1 for industrial video, 45:1 for CD-ROM. Alternatively, the size of a single video frame in kilobytes can range from 300 KB for a broadcast system, 75 KB for industrial, and 20 KB for CD-ROM.

The reduction of the data rate with lossy compression is significant; compression ratios on the order of 100:1 are commonplace. Lossy compression is the only possible method of delivery of live-action footage in digital video.

The amount of compression is a variable under your control. Some levels of compression govern what can be ignored and what should be recorded in both the frame-by-frame basis (delta or temporal compression), and others deal with the detail within the frame (spatial compression, also referred to as "q" or "quality").

Lossy compression introduces artifacts to an image. An *artifact* is something in the image that wasn't there before, such as a by-product of compression. As the amount of compression increases and the files decrease in size, the artifacts become more severe. The artifacts start revealing themselves as a slight loss of clarity, leading to finely shaded areas becoming blotchy. At high compression rates, areas of subtle detail, such as smudges on a painted wall, are lost and become blotchy masses. Details and edges are picked out with aggressive image sharpening effects such as "ringing" (see fig. 12.2).

Figure 12.2

The effects of lossy compression.

Imagine that lossy compression is like instant coffee: A handful of beans can be reduced to a teaspoonful of powder (achieving remarkable compression) that can be almost instantly turned into a cup of coffee (superb decompression). It provides most of the key properties that the original did (it looks like coffee, tastes like coffee, and so on), but it cannot be reverse-engineered (it isn't quite like fresh coffee—the full range of subtle flavor cannot be reconstituted).You, the author/coffee brewer, should retain—and ideally work with—original material (coffee beans) stored in the next category of compression: lossless.

Lossless Compression

As the name suggests, the *lossless* compression method reduces the file size without losing any information from the original file. Quality is preserved at all times, and no matter how many processes the material goes through, a lossless compression scheme faithfully retains all the detail with which your material started.

The drawback is that the reduction in file size is generally not sufficient for most playback systems. Although files can sometimes be reduced to as little as a tenth of their original size (10:1), a more typical space saving is 50 percent. This may seem like a lot, but it relates to a ratio of only 2:1, and if the original files are very large, this method is suitable for archive material and special cases only.

Data Rates

The rate at which data can be manipulated by a playback machine is subject to restrictions and bottlenecks throughout the computer system. By decreasing the amount of data, compression schemes help mitigate the restrictions. Limited RAM is a common restriction; also, a backlog often results due to the rate at which data is transferred from storage device to processor—or from RAM to the screen, for example.

The nature of CD-ROMs is another source of data bottlenecks for digital video. The original CD-ROM drives spun their disc 150 revolutions per minute, which means approximately 150 KB from the disc every second. Although it was theoretically possible that a CD-ROM drive could deliver 150 KB per second, it turned out to be unlikely for a number of reasons. Both then and now, the data isn't necessarily accessed in sequential order and time is spent moving the disc head to new locations. Furthermore, the computer needs time to decompress the data after it is read from the disc, and more time to display the data.

Although the theoretical maximum transfer rate was 150 KB per second, it became advisable to assume that—with everything else happening in the computer—you could only hope to get two thirds of that. One hundred kilobytes per second is not much.

Since then, of course, we have seen the speed of CD-ROM drives increase to ten times the original speed, which certainly offsets some of CD-ROM's inherent data bottlenecks. These rates will increase even more in the future with DVD (see Table 12.1). *DVD*, or *Digital Video Disk*, promises a standard spin speed equal to a 9" CD-ROM drive. It is inevitable that this speed will be progressively doubled.

Table 12.1

CD-ROM Performance Rate Specs: The Reality

Speed	Theoretical Rate	Maximum Rate	Safe Rate
x1	150 KB/sec.	100 KB/sec.	90 KB/sec.
x2	300 KB/sec.	200 KB/sec.	180 KB/sec.
x4	600 KB/sec.	400 KB/sec.	360 KB/sec.
x8	1200 KB/sec.	900 KB/sec.	720 KB/sec.
x10	1500 KB/sec.	1000 KB/sec.	900 KB/sec.
x12	1800 KB/sec.	1200 KB/sec.	1080 KB/sec.

The preceding table shows the conservative end of digital video data rates for the original single-speed drives, the double-speed drives that dominated the market from 1993 to 1995, and the sequentially faster drives that took over after that time.

Keep in mind that data rates are not the only factor affecting performance of digital video on CD-ROM. CD-ROM drives often spin down if they are not accessed for a period. Faster CD-ROM drives can take *longer* to spin up to speed than the slower drives. Access time (moving the reading head from place to place) and the way your files are laid out on the CD-ROM are important too, regardless of their spin speed.

Although the size, frames per second, and compression method of a digital video cast member dictate the range of the playback rate, it is possible to improve the rate by choosing an optimal compression amount given the power of the processor and the speed of the CD-ROM.

A more powerful processor can decompress a frame more quickly, and therefore you can increase the data rate. A faster CD-ROM drive means less compression is required. These balances represent fine-tuning, which pays dividends in controlled situations such as kiosks. Improvements beyond the "safe" rates in Table 12.1 can only be achieved by individual machine setup, rather than the average for a particular class of machine.

INSIDER TIP

To meet the data rate limitations of the worst case target system, adjust the movie dimensions, frame rate, compressor type, and compression quality. Beyond the choice of compressor, the biggest improvements are made by reducing the dimensions of the movie.

Some authoring tools and utilities automatically adjust compression quality and keyframe rate to achieve a specified bandwidth. Reducing the number of frames per second helps a great deal. Beyond these controls, check the media prioritization tip in Chapter 11.

Digital Video Formats

By now it should be clear that compression is a central issue for digital video. Having considered it in the abstract, this chapter now turns to the practicalities of compression formats. Several standard formats exist, namely QuickTime from Apple Computer, Video for Windows from Microsoft, and MPEG from the Motion Picture Experts Group.

Over the past few years, these three main offerings have settled into their respective niches. Your decision about which one to use should be based on feature set, platform or operating system choice, and the reason for delivering content.

QuickTime

QuickTime, developed by Apple Computer, Inc., was released in December of 1991. Based on CD-ROM technology, at the time of release QuickTime was capable of providing the traditional "postage stamp" movies (120,160 pixels) that would play at 12 fps (frames per second). Today, if you take the same machinery and replace the old QuickTime with the new, it offers up to 320×240 pixel movies at 12 fps, or 240×180 pixel movies at up to 30 fps. That's the same equipment as in 1993—Mac IIvx, 030, 8 MB of RAM.

On today's equipment—a Power Macintosh or Pentium, for example— QuickTime movies can measure 640×480 pixels and play at a super-smooth 30 frames per second from a quad-speed CD-ROM drive without hardware assistance.

Full screen used to mean 640×480 pixels, but today it is difficult to purchase a computer with less than 800×600. The new standard screen, at 50 percent larger, has had a negative impact on the performance of full screen QuickTime movies (even with Pentium and PowerPC chips). The alternative is to create your movie for less than full screen and put up with a big border.

If your Director work is destined for low- to mid-range LCD projectors—many still don't support 800×600— you'll need to work at 640×480 anyway.

Along with compressed video and audio, QuickTime 2.5 (Mac) and 3.0 (Mac and Windows) provides access to MPEG material—including the "White Book" MPEG-1 standard streams found on CD-i disks. MIDI is also built into QuickTime and covered in Chapter 11. The important thing for you to remember as a Director developer is that MPEG and MIDI material can be controlled the same way that other video elements are, using the same Lingo.

QuickTime is a very cross-platform technology. Not satisfied with MacOS, Windows 3.x, and Windows 95, QuickTime is moving into Unix—notably the Sun and SGI platforms used in high-end Internet server applications and in television and film. Even a solution for OS/2 is available—should you feel so inclined. The wide applicability of QuickTime is one of its major advantages. Along with Shockwave, QuickTime is one of the top five Windows web browser plug-ins installed. QuickTime is also common in PC entertainment titles.

As QuickTime (QT) grew to encompass sprites, MIDI, QuickDraw 3D, and so on, it came to be officially referred to as the QuickTime Media Layer (QTML). QTML includes QuickTime VR, QuickDraw 3D, QuickDraw GX (a font and drawing mechanism), scripting, and basic interactivity—currently considered as separate entities.

Previously, QuickTime creation was a Mac-only affair. Applications that created QuickTime movies on the PC used to write data in the Video for Windows (VfW) format and put a QuickTime wrapper around it. Features found on the Macintosh, such as multiple tracks of a similar type, were not possible on the PC.

QuickTime 3.0 achieves parity for both Macintosh and Windows. This is a significant achievement, because it requires a Windows version of SoundManager 3 (the Macintosh sound technology) and even a significant amount of QuickDraw (the Macintosh graphics technology) to be brought to the 32-bit Windows systems such as 95 and NT. Note that it is unlikely that this will be achievable on the 16-bit Windows systems.

WARNING

> Versions of QuickTime prior to 3.0 have some important differences between the Macintosh and Windows platforms. Windows files are limited to one video track and one audio track. No MIDI or text tracks are available.

Although QuickTime is now considered part of the Macintosh system software, it is not so common on the Windows platform. To distribute the QuickTime components with your application, you must obtain a license from Apple Computer.

Your first step in licensing is to contact Apple's licensing department with your contact details, postal address, and the software you want to license. For QuickTime, it's expedient to license for Macintosh and PC platforms regardless of actual destination. This will soon be extended to cover various flavors of Unix.

The traditional method of contacting the Apple licensing department is via their generic e-mail address at SW.LICENSE@apple.com. For the most up-to-date information on Apple's software licensing, check their web site at http://quicktime.apple.com/dev/lic.html. Alternatively, call them directly at 512-919-2645, or fax them at 512-919-2120.

Apple sends you copies of the license agreement that you must complete and return. When the papers are processed, Apple returns a copy for your records and includes the official QuickTime logo artwork for packaging. The mammoth signing session needs to only be done once for QuickTime. As you release additional products requiring QuickTime, fax the details of your product to the legal department at Apple using the form provided. Similarly, the same agreement has covered revisions to QuickTime, requiring little or no action from you should a new version of QuickTime be released.

Among your obligations as a licensee, a few interesting points are noteworthy. Don't just provide the system extension or DLLs as provided on the Apple web sites and on the QuickTime Software Development Kit (SDK). You should include all the components for a QuickTime install.

The proper installation includes the simple player application and Apple's own software license agreement. Similarly, when providing QuickTime for Windows, the safest option is to include the installation provided by Apple. If you intend to write your own Installer, be sure to read and follow the guidelines in your QuickTime Licensing Agreement.

Video for Windows and ActiveMovie

Microsoft's counterpart to Apple's QuickTime is Video for Windows (VfW), which handles the Audio Video Interleave files known as AVI files. Director for Windows can use either QuickTime for Windows or VfW. For the sake of efficiency, cross-platform projects developed on the Macintosh generally employ QuickTime for Windows for their Windows incarnation, in which case QuickTime for Windows has to be included with the project.

VfW is ideal in Windows-only titles because almost every system will have VfW installed. VfW is part of Windows 95 and Windows 3.1.1, but was optional on Windows 3.1.

WARNING

Although almost all Windows machines will have VfW installed, you may need to install your choice of "codec" because only a limited selection is supplied as standard. Codecs are examined in detail in the next section.

ActiveMovie is an ActiveX module that extends VfW and the AVI file format with features such as multiple soundtracks, scriptability, and time-based controls. Although the feature set is not as comprehensive or widespread as the QuickTime Media Layer, it is strongly supported in corporate development.

Director has direct Lingo support for the QuickTime Media Layer, but not ActiveMovie.

 INSIDER TIP

Macintosh-based developers of corporate solutions for Windows (such as presentations, kiosks, and demonstrations) are often faced with the client's requirement to use AVI rather than QuickTime. This can be worked around by using QuickTime tools to generate the digital video assets, and converting them to AVI by using Microsoft tools. Note that QuickTime compressors such as "video" and "animation" must be recompressed with the Microsoft Video and Microsoft RLE components (available as a Macintosh plug-in to QuickTime). CinePak, on the other hand, is part of both AVI and QuickTime.

To distribute VfW, you need to obtain a license from Microsoft. As with QuickTime, this does not involve a licensing fee.

Unlike the QuickTime licensing process, however, you must be a part of the Microsoft Developer Network (membership must be at Level 2). This membership includes the right to distribute the VfW mechanism in your products. Chapter 4, "Delivering the Goods," covers the process of contacting Microsoft.

MPEG

MPEG has been associated with the holy grail of computer video—Full Screen, Full Motion Video (FSFMV)—having stolen this crown from Digital Video Interactive (DVI).

It is the first scheme sophisticated enough to play quality full-screen video and high-fidelity sound from a single-speed CD-ROM. It is quite impressive that all this information can be squeezed into the same space used by the original audio-only compact disc. Highly sophisticated mathematics are used to accomplish this—not only on the video but also to compress the audio. All this calculation can't be handled by the average personal computer. As a rule, hardware is required for playback in the form of an MPEG card.

MPEG, like QT and VfW, is a mechanism that contains a number of variations. MPEG has two broad categories, each with subtle variations for size: MPEG-1 (with a sub-variant MPEG-1.5), and MPEG-2. MPEG-1 is a tightly controlled standard designed for a high degree of compatibility; frame size, frame rate, pixel shape, keyframes, and interleaving are all fixed. MPEG-1.5 provided more flexibility and combinations. MPEG-2 is designed for the higher data rates of newer equipment and is more open, with almost the same control as QT and VfW. Commercially available MPEG digitization cards are designed for MPEG-2.

In the Windows camp, MPEG has found favor with the authors of kiosks because, with the author's control over hardware, it delivers FSFMV without fail and at a quality level exceeding that of most VHS machines. MPEG has not made a great impression on the Mac camp due to its reliance on hardware previously unavailable for Macintosh.

Digitizing video for MPEG-1 playback is a black art. The best quality requires frame-by-frame compression. This involves a computer-controlled VCR (usually a professional-quality format) outputting a single frame to video circuitry to clean the image. Each frame is then analyzed by the computer, with reference to the previous frame, and the results stored. Good MPEG digitization requires specialized (and expensive) equipment.

MPEG is by no means perfect. Unlike the software compression methods, MPEG implementations on the 16-bit Windows platform can require a change of screen mode, resulting in an "all or nothing" capability. That is, the digital video can either monopolize the entire screen or be entirely absent, but cannot share the screen with other elements. The Director stage will disappear for the duration of the MPEG video.

MPEG is not directly recognized by Director. Windows 3.x projects tend to utilize Machine Control Interface (MCI) commands, although Xtras are now available for Windows 95 and 3.x. The higher end Power Macintosh computers can handle MPEG files as if they were QuickTimes movies with special QuickTime extensions.

M-JPEG

Not to be confused with MPEG, *M-JPEG* (Motion JPEG) uses the high-quality compression from the Joint Photographic Experts Group, and accelerates it to be able to work with video signals. As a result, M-JPEG has the capability to both digitize and deliver high-quality video. Like MPEG, M-JPEG is reliant on special hardware, but unlike MPEG, M-JPEG is not designed to work with a CD-ROM. In fact, most M-JPEG solutions require high-speed AV drives to both record and play back video.

The cost of an M-JPEG card is far higher than an MPEG-1 playback card, and about the same as an MPEG-2 card, but a fraction of the cost of the equipment required to digitize MPEG-1. Today, M-JPEG is the popular choice for digitizing and mastering video, even if it's destined for CD-ROM or Internet playback using a software decompression system. On one hand it delivers high quality when reliant on the special hardware (that is, for broadcast TV use). On the other hand, the digital video production process is sped up when using the hardware to accelerate the tedious compression process in preparation for CD-ROM playback.

Technical Choices

In addition to choosing a digital video format for final distribution, you need to make a number of other technical choices for your product. Before delving into practical demonstrations of digital video, it is necessary to overview these basic technical considerations for digital video.

Basics of Video Capture

The digital video community uses the word *grab* to refer to the process of acquiring, scanning, or digitizing a video image or sequence. You grab some video just as you scan a picture. An alternate term is *video capture*.

Digitizing (grabbing) video shares many principles with scanning artwork. If you are digitizing material from videotape, you should endeavor to grab at the highest quality achievable to capture a complete unadulterated copy of the video sequence. You must be able to record every frame without wasting a fraction of a second in unnecessary compression. *Bandwidth-dependent compression* (that is, compressing to a specific data flow such as 230 KB per second) should be a final step rather than an intermediate one.

Remember that video is just another media source—like scans from a flat-bed scanner. It is sensible practice to scan pictures at 300 dpi in 24 bit, performing all scaling and balancing operations on this large file. Only then would you resample or scale to 72 dpi at 8 bits. Never the other way around!

Grabbing video is similar. Aim for as much quality as you can get with your equipment. The resultant movies are virtually unplayable without hardware assistance—this is a very good sign! It shows that far more information is recorded than can be displayed in real time. Like a 24-bit picture on an 8-bit system, this file looks bad and is far too large and unwieldy for everyday use, but you need its content—which equates to quality—for editing.

Grab video with as little compression as your hard disk space can manage, and elect to "post compress" with applications such as FusionRecorder. QuickTime choices include Component or None, but these require a fast hard disk and a powerful processor. For modest equipment, try Apple Video (set to high). On the other hand, best results are obtained from disk arrays and one of the M-JPEG variants with hardware assistance.

Although the end product may be played by using a software decompressor, such as CinePak, the capture and editing may all be done by a hardware compressor-based system, such as VideoVision Studio, using high-speed hard disk arrays (see the "Tools" section later in this chapter). Although the M-JPEG compression used by these systems is not lossless, the quality is superior to virtually all lossy software compressors. These systems also enable you to edit image sizes greater than the end product. This helps to preserve the quality until the final preparation step when the video is compressed with a software compressor such as CinePak while being scaled down to the final size.

One exception to the "grab big, reduce later" rule is step-frame (or frame-by-frame) grabbing from video-disk players under computer control, in which case the video (usually a finished entity requiring no further editing) can be digitized at a leisurely pace by a slow computer, as in the case of high-quality MPEG described earlier in this chapter.

Having obtained your high-quality material, it is important to preserve it during the editing process. When the assembly is complete, export the results as a stand-alone movie, correctly scaled, with the compression regime you require. Be prepared for a long wait.

Compression Schemes

For "quick-and-dirty" projects or prototypes, you may want to capture and compress the video all at once. Be aware that software-based compressors are asymmetrical—that is, it takes more time to compress the video than play it back. Some highly asymmetrical compressors, such as CinePak, are not practical for real-time compression while capturing. Others, such as Apple Video, can compress while digitizing with a fast enough computer system.

It is important to compress to a lossy codec such as CinePak only when your edit is complete. (A *codec* is a tool comprised of both a *co*mpression method and a *de*compression method.) Compression is a lengthy process and involves great computational power. The more compression required, the more power required in the computer. CinePak, for example, can be described as a 140:1 compressor. On average, every minute of video it decompresses requires 140 minutes or longer to compress. Note that the ratio expressed here is the compression *time*, not the file size compression.

Other codecs do not offer as much compression but are faster. When you're working to meet deadlines you need to keep in mind this fundamental trade-off between compression amount and time required. The role call of the most-used codecs could run as follows:

► CinePak and Indeo

► Apple Video and Microsoft Video

► Animation

► YUV (Component)

► Graphics

► Sprite

CinePak and Indeo

CinePak and Indeo are 24-bit codecs, but when displayed on an 8-bit screen, they dither to the palette they find in operation (usually the system palette).

INSIDER TIP

CinePak and Indeo can have a color palette that should override the current palette, but this is ignored by Director. Director uses the palette it finds in the palette channel and, therefore, affects the palette designed for the movie.

If this causes problems, Xtras and XObjects such as QTpaletteFix can fix it. An easier alternative is to save your digital video as 24 bit or color (not 256 colors) and let Director force palettes you have created with DeBabelizer or Photoshop, or even from Director.

CinePak also works well in 16 bit.

Both CinePak and Indeo tend to be very lossy. CinePak was originally referred to as Apple Compact Video, but in subsequent revisions has become universally known as CinePak. The Indeo format includes a hardware-assisted version that can be used for digitization in real time from tape, but its real strength is in software playback in limited bandwidth situations, such as from CD-ROMs.

In the "software-only" form, neither are suitable as a master format, and they introduce artifacts that degrade quality quickly over edit generations.

When used at the highest quality settings, CinePak achieves good quality for hard disk playback, although compression is still a lengthy process, taking 80 times the length of the video clip.

INSIDER TIP

It is important to include keyframes with these codecs. Too few or no keyframes significantly increase compression time and lead to unmanageably high data rates and poor quality. Keyframes are described in detail later in this chapter.

Apple Video and Microsoft Video

Apple Video and Microsoft Video are codecs that are optimized for a 16-bit color space or an 8-bit grayscale space. They do not record actual colors in a Color Look Up Table (CLUT); they simply record color information as a separate, compressible signal to the luminance signal.

WARNING

Apple Video and Microsoft Video can be used on an 8-bit (256 color) screen, but, unlike CinePak and Indeo, are not optimized for dithering down the colors. This results in a bigger performance penalty for running on an 8-bit monitor.

Unlike CinePak and Indeo, Apple Video and Microsoft Video compress video quickly—perhaps only a half second per frame. They can compress video in a 4:1 to 10:1 ratio, and the highest quality settings approach lossless compression—albeit at the expense of bandwidth. If you're working with fast equipment, but without the luxury of time or hardware acceleration, these codecs provide a good compromise.

Both Apple Video and Microsoft Video work well with Director output when the animation codec cannot achieve the required bandwidth.

Animation

Animation is a lossless compressor, good for archiving computer-generated (rendered) material. The Animation codec works at all color depths, including the Thousands+ and Millions+ depths, where the plus signs imply *alpha* or *matte* channels (also known as linear key signals to the video fraternity). *Matte* is a term held over from the film world. It used to be a picture painted on a sheet of glass, but in terms of digital video, it is the same as an "alpha channel"—a grayscale image "behind" the color image that makes a movie "transparent" in the matte channel's black areas, solid in the matte's white areas, and translucent in the gray areas.

Animation's modest compression is obtained through recording changes in frame—a method similar to, but more advanced than, the PICS or FLI formats.

INSIDER TIP

> If you're using the Animation codec as a delivery format, remember that it primarily records the changes between frames. Therefore, to obtain smooth results, a higher frame rate is better than a slower frame rate—especially if you elect to use the Play Every Frame method.

Component (YUV)

Component video is another 24-bit codec. It is not intended as a playback codec (without hardware assistance). As an acquisition format, Component achieves superior quality with modest compression.

More importantly, Component understands the finer points of video, including fields as opposed to frames, and the 29.97 actual frame rate of NTSC. To elaborate, video has two interlinked fields rather than a frame as such. The first field has all the odd rows and scan lines, and the second field has all the even lines. With 29.97 frames per second, this leads to some complex hiccups, which the Component format copes with—unlike, for example, Apple Video.

Component is also known as *YUV*, which is a professional video term to describe how color information is recorded. A full color image is split into a brightness channel (Y) and two color channels (U and V), and these three components are recorded simultaneously and recombined into a single *composite* signal for playback or transmission. Semi-professional equipment has a simpler method where the U and V are combined as C, known as Y/C.

Component records no composite video artifacts—such as blurring and smearing—from component sources, such as Betacam; this results in higher image quality than those based on composite (and even Y/C) video.

The Component codec is good as a master format and for archival uses. This codec makes an efficient editing format for FSFMV with appropriate hardware, although hardware-assisted M-JPEG formats tend to be more popular outside the broadcast industry.

Graphics Codec

Graphics works best in palletized environments (8 bits or less). The Graphics codec is a lossless compressor optimized for quick decompression of run-length encoded graphics.

INSIDER TIP

> QuickTime is modular in construction. Graphics can include translators and compressors; therefore, extra plug-ins for QuickTime now support GIF, Photoshop, and so on. Some of these formats are directly supported by Director, but newer or specialist formats can be provided for by QT acting as a "wrapper."

Sprite Codec

QuickTime's Sprite codec has been part of QuickTime for some time now, but very few applications could generate the files; therefore, movies have not been common. Unlike other codecs, Sprite is not concerned with compression.

The main difference between QuickTime sprites and a Director stage is that QuickTime sprite movies are scalable with little degradation of performance and quality. A 640×480 stage can be exported and then scaled to 1024×768. Similarly, conversion of color depth is handled by QuickTime; a 16-bit movie can play back on an 8-bit monitor.

Presentations created in Director can be exported in Sprite format and played back with a simple player rather than the full Director projector, played back full size on any resolution screen.

As this book was being written, an Xtra for Director 5 is available, though a version for Director 6 should follow.

Video Dimensions

Certain tools associated with digital video—especially lossy compressors—are optimized, that is, they assume that certain conditions are met to perform "as advertised." Video dimensions are among the conditions that must meet a certain expectation. Your video dimensions must take into consideration a "magic number."

Throughout this chapter, numerically gifted readers probably noticed a preponderance of numbers that share a common link. These numbers are usually divisible by 8, sometimes by 16, but in almost all circumstances, are divisible by 4. A digital video must subscribe to a magic number according to the depth of the monitor on which it is playing. Both its size and position on-screen in relation to the top-left corner of that screen must be cleanly divisible by that magic number (see Table 12.2).

Table 12.2

Examples of Optimized Dimensions for Digital Video

Monitor Depth	Magic Number	Examples
4	16	160×120, 256×192
8	8	248×186, 240×176 (not 240×180!)
16	4	108×456

Interestingly, 240×180—one of the common digital video movie sizes—is legal for a 16-bit screen, but illegal for an 8-bit screen (it is not cleanly divisible by 8), where it can lead to poor performance, such as dropped frames. If you have a movie that measures 240×180 and is likely to end up on an 8-bit screen, it should be cropped (now) to 240×176. When you lose two pixels each from the top and bottom of the video, it makes a big difference!

If in doubt, make 8 your magic number and ensure that both the dimensions of your digital video and the position coordinates are cleanly divisible by it.

Remember, to enjoy the benefits of performance gain, both the location (with respect to the monitor, not the stage) and the size of the movie must be cleanly divisible by the magic number.

The magic number rule isn't actually an all-powerful route to digital nirvana, but it can help a great deal in critical situations such as CD-ROM work. The biggest benefits from using magic numbers occurs on slower equipment.

The magic numbers stem from the division of the movie into squares and treating each region as a special case. You can see this happening on CinePak movies in 8-bit, where the checkering is very apparent. If you don't use magic numbers, the areas aren't square, forcing the digital video mechanism to do more math and therefore degrade performance.

Keyframes

Also known as *iFrames* in some codecs and compression systems, a *keyframe* is a full-frame image that the codec works from when deciding what has changed from frame to frame. Keyframes are inserted periodically throughout a movie, usually once a second or every 15 frames.

The importance of keyframes can be illustrated in this example. A digital video of an interview shows a standard digital video controller, enabling the user to stop and start the video, and drag the control bar. If the codec records the changes between frames, to scroll backward, the digital video system would have to scuttle back to the beginning of the video and track forward to the point selected by the user—a lengthy and messy procedure. By inserting keyframes every 15 frames, the playback point is never more than 15 frames away from a full frame from which to work out the image. This saves time and processing power.

Keyframes are a central part of most codecs, especially CinePak and Indeo. It is easy to overlook the control in compression options, because good results are regularly achieved by automatically using one keyframe per second—but room for experimentation exists. The more keyframes you use, the more stable the movie; the fewer keyframes you use, the better the data rate. Be certain to include at least a few keyframes—at the very least, one keyframe every five seconds.

Adding too many keyframes pushes the data rate up (possibly beyond the constraints of a CD-ROM drive) because the savings afforded by delta compression are lost. But in a fast-moving video clip (action, dance, "punk" camerawork, and so forth), delta compression has little to work on; every frame is somewhat different anyway. In this case, a higher keyframe rate—two times a second (every seven frames if the movie was 15 fps)—helps the quality tremendously.

Conversely, using too few keyframes (or none at all) has the disk head hunting for the nearest keyframe if it has to drop a frame, often causing it to drop the keyframe too, and thus the movie falls apart. Too few keyframes make skipping around in the movie a lengthy process.

In general, one keyframe per second remains the safest option, but keep these questions in mind:

- ▶ Will the video be used with a controller? If not, you can ease up on the keyframes for more bandwidth.

- ▶ Will the video be stepped frame-by-frame in both directions? If so, you need each frame to be a keyframe.

- ▶ Will the video run backward? If you want a shuttle effect, a keyframe every second works well.

Controller movies prefer a keyframe every 0.5–3 seconds, depending on the kind of movie (fast action means more keyframes; head shot means less keyframes).

Illustrative movies (where the movie will be browsed frame by frame—a slow motion car crash, for example) prefer more keyframes—every half second or more.

Keyframes are used for showing a movie that runs backward (rewinds). With a 15 fps movie that lasts 20 seconds, jumping from the end to the beginning plays the keyframes at about 4 fps, lasting about five seconds. If you want the movie to play smoothly backward and forward, the logical method is to make every frame a keyframe. Don't do this—you'll lose all the benefits of temporal compression! Cheat! Make two movies—the second version being a reversed copy of the normal one that appears to go backward when playing forward. Some Lingo programming and coinciding frame calculation may be required for interactive controlled movies.

INSIDER TIP

If no sound is associated with a movie, switch on "play every frame." If sound is required, you can synchronize an audio file in RAM (such as a fully imported sound member) to the video either by checking the `movieTime` property and using the `puppetSound` command to start the audio on cue, or by using cuePoints inserted into the digital video in SoundEdit. The `movieTime` property and cue points are discussed later in this chapter.

Note, however, that using separate files for sound and video applies to sounds in RAM. Playing a QuickTime movie and a spooled sound file (such as an AIFF) is not a good idea—especially on the CD-ROM. The disk head must skip between two physical locations on the disk, spending more time in skipping from point to point than reading the two files.

Slideshow movies have been a useful way to incorporate a large number of pictures that must be displayed in all color depths. They consist of a sequence of pictures, each picture being in one frame of the movie. The digital video software handles the compression (and, therefore, the speed at which it can be read from the storage device), dithers the 24-bit image, and fits it to the palette in use if the monitor is set to 8-bit or less.

Slideshow movies require 60 frames per second and 60 keyframes per second to work properly. Because the movies are not intended to be played, alternative codecs such as JPEG can be used. These provide higher quality in still images than the codecs used for motion.

To conclude, careful use of keyframes is essential. Be prepared to experiment.

Additional Tracks

For both Macintosh and Windows 95, QuickTime 3.0 handles four distinct track types within Director, which are identified within Director by the four symbol types: #Video, #Audio, #Text, and #Music. The latter refers to the MIDI tracks that can access the musical instruments built into the QuickTime mechanism. Prior to 3.0, QuickTime for Windows did not support multiple tracks, MIDI, or text.

Under the MacOS operating system (and Windows 95/NT with QTW 3.0), QuickTime defines a file format that can include a time track with many separate items linked to it, not just one of each type. Audio tracks are possible for multiple languages, for example, or a single movie can contain 15 songs on separate MIDI tracks.

The concept of multiple non-video tracks was part of the original QuickTime 1.0 but has taken time to filter into common use, due in part to the lack of easy access to tracks other than video and audio. Because Director 6 facilitates access to other tracks, the following sections overview the track types found in QuickTime.

Video Tracks

Windows users prior to QTW 3.0 can access one video track per QuickTime movie. MacOS users, however, can include multiple video tracks and switch between them.

Why would you want more than one video track in a movie? One example is in the simulation of a TV studio with four cameras. The user can cut between cameras stored on separate video tracks and listen to the production talkback while mixing the actors voices with sound effects and music.

QuickTime contains the facilities to store the result as a *dependency* movie, which contains pointers to other movies from within its data fork; therefore, it takes up little space.

The Lingo command `trackEnabled` within Director 6 enables MacOS users to select which video track to use at playback.

Audio Tracks

QuickTime's audio tracks can contain audio data at any sampling rate (11 kHz, 22.05 kHz, 48 kHz, and so on) and compression method (IMA, MACE, and so on). In the MacOS environment, you can selectively switch on or off multiple soundtracks stored within a QuickTime movie. The method is described later in this chapter.

INSIDER TIP

The MacOS is relatively relaxed about the sample frequency, but many PC sound cards require certain frequencies. These are multiples of the CD standard 44.1 kHz. Be sure to check, and use 44.1, 22.05, or 11.025 for safety.

You can synchronize multiple audio tracks to a single video track. The user can access the audio tracks on-the-fly, for example, to hear multiple language translations of a group discussion. The process of remixing a piece of music uses this method. Another, less glamorous use may be multiple descriptions of a single event, such as a road crash. Further detail on audio tracks is covered in Chapter 11.

Multiple audio tracks require sound mixing, which is looked after by the Sound Manager on the Macintosh and the QTW 3.0 software on Windows 95/NT. Before QTW 3.0 and Video for Windows, however, both Windows platforms had access to only one digital video audio track at a time. Director provides multichannel capability on the PC with the Macromix library, but Macromix handles sound members rather than audio tracks within a digital video file.

Text Tracks

The traditional role of the text track has been to provide subtitles to pop videos and, with the MIDI track below, karaoke movies complete with synchronized text highlights. Now that the text track is accessible to the Director user, it can store Lingo data or handlers.

An example might be an observation test. A video is shown, and the user must spot clues and identify key characters. Text tracks hold the names of characters that are in the scene, a track per character. At any point in time, the video can be interrogated by Lingo to see which characters are in the scene. In a long movie, users can find character entrances and exits using a simple text search facility.

Another example is a digital video of a presenter, who has accompanying graphics prepared in a Director movie. By inserting the name of a slide as a text track in the presenter's video, Director can call up the correct slide as the digital video plays. If the user decides to skip a few minutes, the slides in the Director movie can keep up by simply querying the text track and going to a labeled frame corresponding to the text in the text track.

By attaching handlers or lists to specific parts of a video, you can allow users to react to time-oriented media with time-specific data. Because this data is manipulated at the same time as the video, audio, and MIDI data, a great deal of control is delegated to the QuickTime mechanics, leaving Director to handle the moment-by-moment interface requirements and ideally increasing responsiveness.

Text tracks have sample points over time, where a string of up to 32 KB of text can be stored. Although a paragraph, for example, can be stored in one frame, the next frame can be the same thing (and therefore continue the same sample point), or it can contain a full movieScript, or it can contain nothing at all.

To access the text, you can find the next or previous sample point from a given position within a movie—set with the movieTime if necessary—with the `trackPreviousSampleTime` and `trackNextSampleTime` properties, respectively. Manipulating text tracks is difficult to explain and understand in the abstract; this chapter concludes with a tutorial to walk you through a sample text track application.

Tools to build, edit, and create text tracks in QuickTime movies are supplied on the QuickTime SDK, available from the Apple Programmers and Developers Association (APDA). Macintosh users, however, can experiment with text tracks by creating them with SimpleText and MoviePlayer.

Music Tracks

The QuickTime music track provides an opportunity to provide a soundtrack in the MIDI format. The music track plays either instrument sound samples that come in the QuickTime Musical Instruments extension or special instruments created by the developer. Unlike traditional MIDI solutions, QuickTime's MIDI track does not require hardware—it is a software-only solution that can use hardware *if available*.

The main feature of the music track is its minuscule size in comparison to a digitized audio file. MIDI does not record the sound of music. It concentrates on the note-by-note dynamics and passes responsibility of instrument selection to a synthesizer, producing the instrument sound. In QuickTime, this is under developer control, too. You can lock the choice of instrument to your specific choice or, with the aid of an Xtra, pass the choice of instrument on to the user, thereby opening up wide opportunities for creativity—or abuse.

The QuickTime musical instruments have included a subset of the 128 standard instruments (licensed from Roland, a manufacturer of MIDI keyboards). The full General MIDI instrument set is coming in future versions of QuickTime.

If you are developing for a kiosk or have full control over your playback hardware (for example, presentations), keep in mind that it is possible to create your own "instrument" samples, including properly multisampled instruments, all at CD quality if you want (at the expense of RAM). Alternatively, rather than using the internal synthesizer, QuickTime music tracks can be switched to function as part of an Open MIDI System (OMS) by connecting to external equipment via a MIDI interface on the serial port. Note that the Director developer is still dealing with a QuickTime movie!

Originally, the QuickTime Musical Instruments extension contained the MIDI instruments, which could pose problems to developers wanting to provide their own sounds on the user's machine. Instruments can now be stored as part of the QuickTime movie.

Tools for converting standard MIDI files and for creating instruments are available on the new QuickTime SDK mentioned earlier.

Factors in Effective Compression

This section could be titled, "What Hurts Compression and How to Fix It." So far we've considered optimizing compression largely from a delivery standpoint—using the correct size, the correct color depth, and the correct codec. This section covers optimizing compression from an origination standpoint.

To obtain the best performance from digital video, certain situations should be avoided. Due to the way many compressors work, defects and artifacts that are present in low-quality originals are emphasized and accentuated rather than glossed over. This means that a digital video movie with poor image quality also achieves poor performance.

The following conditions are guaranteed to adversely affect performance:

- ▶ Noisy video
- ▶ Pans and zooms
- ▶ Hand-held shots
- ▶ Lighting effects
- ▶ Video dropouts
- ▶ Composite video
- ▶ Over-optimistic compression settings
- ▶ Wrong compressor
- ▶ Fragmented media on disk

Noisy Video

Avoid TV "snow" from poor reception of broadcast material or from electrical interference. Some video cameras are fitted with a "gain" control for poor lighting conditions. When used, this amplifies noise inherent in the camera system. Obscure sources of noise include long wavelength colors (such as reds). Avoid deep red objects shot on VHS.

Codecs, such as CinePak, work by looking for broad areas of little change and compressing them, while also seeking areas of high contrast (such as edges) and emphasizing them. Thus, every speck of noise is carefully and faithfully reproduced, and every edge of every speck is tastefully enhanced, which wastes bandwidth and makes the movie hard to compress.

INSIDER TIP

When confronted with noisy sources, remember to grab big and apply a gentle Gaussian Blur (such as the "Despeckle" filter). Before editing continues, try cropping the edges of a video where those smudgy, flickering tracking errors that are painful to digitize are found.

Pans and Zooms

Though legitimately part of the techniques of television, pans and zooms in digital video guarantee every pixel is changing from frame to frame unless they are performed against a studio *cyclorama*, a professional-quality backcloth.

On the higher end of the camcorder market, controls are offered for "shutter" speed. Use the slow shutter setting—probably indicated for dim light. Alternatively, switch on image stabilization to get a light blur on moving objects (motion blur). This is easier to digitize.

If you must pan or zoom, do so slowly, using plain background if possible. If you must pan, try to obtain a "fluid head" for your tripod. If you need to zoom, remember the curse of the camcorder: tromboning. *Tromboning* is repeated zooming in and out, a cinematic style seen on home movies around the world.

INSIDER TIP

Treat zooms and pans as a special effect. Rather than zooming in on a subject, pick up the camera and place it closer to the subject. Whenever possible, shoot scenes twice, from different angles, rather than darting back and forth.

An example is the ad hoc interview. It is tempting to start your shot tight on the interviewer for the introduction, zoom out to show the interviewee, and then zoom in to the interviewee. Then if the interviewer asks a new question, you do a quick pan (possibly a sneaky zoom out) to catch it. It looks dreadful!

Instead, shoot the interview first, keeping on the subject. Then shoot your "establishing shot." The interviewee will be more relaxed now that the interview portion of the shoot is over. With the subject free to go, the interviewer can repeat the questions into thin air for the benefit of the camera. Remember to include "reaction shots"—also known as *noddies,* for obvious reasons— because these shots can be used to cover a multitude of sins (or to chop an overlong answer).

Hand-Held Shots

Hand-held shots should be justified. If you can't use a tripod, can you use a monopod? Is there any way of supporting the camera steadily? Digital video performance is degraded by hand-held shots; each movement or unintentional jiggle is like a mini-pan.

Use image stabilization if your camera has this feature. If not, lean against a wall or steady the camera on a sturdy object. It helps to rest the camcorder on a small cushion or beanbag both to protect the camera and to help you align it.

Alternatively, consider begging for or borrowing a SteadyCam.

INSIDER TIP

You can emulate a SteadyCam in an emergency. Mount a camcorder onto a photographic tripod. Keep the legs folded up and fully extend the center post. Grasp the tripod under the pan and tilt the head. Hold it away from your body with your elbow bent. Try to keep it steady, but resist the temptation to tuck your elbow into your body. It is tiring and you may develop some interesting muscles, but the results are surprisingly good.

Lighting Effects

Moving lights cast moving shadows. These may affect the entire image between frames, making it difficult to compress. Contrast lighting can aggravate things—lots of edges for CinePak to investigate. This slows compression, too. Fluorescent lights (strip lights) pulse with the alternating current. This means that you may experience beating, where the lights appear to fade up and down every second or so.

Flashes—from photographers' cameras, or lightning, for example—create two large jumps between frames—from standard to bright, and then from bright to standard. This means double trouble from the compression viewpoint.

Aside from the technical constraints, consider lighting in general. Highlights and shadows lend shape to your subject, not just rendering it visible.

A rule of thumb in lighting is to use *three-point lighting*. This consists of a strong "key" light that both illuminates and casts shadows on the subject, placed to one side of the camera, and pointed at the subject. On the other side of the subject, a softer light fills the shadows from the key (alternatively, a large reflector can be used such as a board painted white or a commercial silvered reflector such as Lastrolite). Finally, a spotlight is placed above and behind the subject out of shot of the camera, known as a back- or rim-light. This separates the subject from the background.

Video Dropouts

Video dropouts can be as bad as noise. *Dropouts* are big blips on the screen that are caused by bits of magnetic material literally dropping off the tape. Like flashes, dropouts present double trouble as their entry and exit are recorded, and their edges are accentuated by a lossy compressor. The playback of a digital video containing a "carefully digitized" dropout may balk (the software will not know that it's an error), causing dropped frames or a gap in sound. Due to the interleaving of sound and video, something has to give.

INSIDER TIP

> How much use is too much for videotapes? Tapes that contain more than a dozen plays or tapes that are used in many machines should probably be left on the shelf. The better the condition of your tape, the less likely it is for your tape to experience dropouts.

Composite Video

Composite video is always difficult because of the natural behavior of intense colors—especially reds—and the strange color effects caused by regular patterns of dark and light, known as *cross color* or *strobing*. A Y/C output (also known as S-VHS) helps to remove some—but not all—of these artifacts.

One magic box that you should consider is the *TimeBase Corrector* (TBC). Although a TBC can appear to be an expensive luxury (costing more than a camcorder), it dramatically improves the quality of your video source by acting as a "laundry" to the video coming in from the tape before dispatching it neatly ironed to your digitization hardware. Although the full use of TBCs cannot be covered in this chapter, it earns its keep in a busy studio.

INSIDER TIP

> Many industrial and virtually all broadcast videotape recorders (VTRs) have a TBC built in, such is their necessity in professional video. It is a feature worth looking for.

Over-Optimistic Compression Settings

Getting a movie compressor to compress a full-screen, full-motion video of hand-held VHS footage to 150 KB per second takes a long time and will probably make the compressor drop most of your frames to compress it to the specified data rate. Choose reasonable compression settings for your project.

Using the tables and guides to file sizes that are presented earlier in this chapter will help you map realistic digital video sizes and target data rates.

INSIDER TIP

> Sometimes the best settings can sound counter-intuitive. For example, if you have a movie that you want to have full screen on a powerful system and quarter screen on a lesser computer, it is easier to produce a 640×480 movie and halve the size on the stage for the lesser machine rather than double the size on the powerful machine. It is easier for the small machine to drop un-wanted data than it is for the larger machine to double it up.

The Wrong Compressor

This chapter has repeatedly recommended working with material in a high-quality format from acquisition all the way through to the production process. The resulting file will be big and unwieldy, but all the information it contains is required.

No matter how high-quality the source material, however, using CinePak during the editing process or Graphics on a photograph does not render desirable results. Use the correct compression tool for the job as outlined in Table 12.3:

Table 12.3

Examples of Codec Choices

Subject	Right Codec	Wrong Codec	Reason
3D render	Animation 24+	Apple Video	Quality loss
Rough edit	Video	CinePak	Wastes time
24-bit photograph	JPEG	Graphics	Not for 24 bit
Screenshot	Graphics	JPEG	Lossy
Final video edit	CinePak	Video	Not as good
Director movie	Animation 16	Animation 24+	Improper depth

Fragmented Media on Disk

Although not strictly a compression problem, the effects of fragmented media on disk can look similar.

When a file is stored on a disk, it doesn't necessarily get stored in a contiguous line of bits (like a track on a record). The filing system of the computer often splits the file into little bits so that it can fit a large file into several small holes. When the computer needs to read in the file, it consults a directory on the disk that contains a list of the physical locations of the fragments of the file and reads them back in the correct order. The file, therefore, is *fragmented*.

Digital video files are extremely sensitive to file fragmentation during playback. Time taken by the disk to consult the directory and find the next fragment is time not spent on reading and decompressing the video—resulting in dropped frames. When coupled with low-quality material or over-optimistic compression settings, the movie may simply die. It will appear to stop playing back as the time taken to catch up extends beyond the time left to play.

Some CD-creation applications defragment files when creating the "image" files they use to burn the CD, but many simple packages do not. It is strongly recommended that you run a defragmentation utility in such circumstances.

File fragmentation should not be confused with media prioritization. Media prioritization is concerned with optimizing the physical location of files on a disk. This is also extremely important for CD-ROM work. Chapter 11 includes tips on achieving media prioritization.

Sources of Digital Video Content

It's good to know the technicalities of your digital video delivery mechanism, but exactly what do you show? Where does all this stuff originate?

You easily can create your own digital video with Director by exporting it as a digital video file. Remember that back before QuickTime, Director—known then as VideoWorks—started life as an animation tool, creating movie files for applications such as HyperCard.

The main sources of digital video include (in rough order of increasing cost):

▶ Director movies

▶ Clipmedia (or multimedia clip art)

▶ Videotape you shoot yourself

▶ Library material

▶ Videotape shot for you

▶ Broadcast material

Note that "videotape you shoot yourself" could mean using anything from a camcorder to a fully equipped, outside-broadcast truck.

Director Movies

Macromedia Director is an excellent tool for creating animation-oriented digital video content. The frame-based metaphor and the superb control of sprites enable careful and structured composition of digital video movies.

To create successful digital video files from your Director movies, consider the limitations and methods of digital video. Unlike Director's "movie loops," digital video members tend to be constrained to a rectangular area. If you want your animation to occur on your Director background, you must pre-matte the animation onto the designated area of the background in a separate application, such as Premiere. This method is described later in the chapter in the section, "Adding Transitions with Premiere."

WARNING

Certain caveats apply to exporting digital video from Director.

Transitions do not export well, if at all. This is because Director's transitions are created in a way that QuickTime cannot see. Transitions can be replaced in a digital video editing package.

Sounds do not export. Replace sounds either in a digital video editing package or in SoundEdit or SoundForge.

Recording It Yourself

The do-it-yourself attitude is a grand subject. It can cover activities from the recording of a simple "hello world" voiceover with a computer's built-in microphone to a three-month shoot on 35 mm cine film, complete with a cast of thousands. Most people settle on the happy medium of a high-end consumer (increasingly known as *prosumer*) Hi-8 or S-VHS camcorder complete with image stabilization and S-Video connectors. If budget or status allows, Betacam equipment assures a significant boost in the quality of the end product. Conversely, using VHS equipment saves cash, but generously contributes to the time and trouble bills.

Aside from the mere technical considerations, remember that by writing, producing, and shooting your own content, you can bypass a great deal of hassle and expense over negotiations with asset providers and buying of rights to existing material. You may find yourself in the enviable position of being your own content provider or "asset owner."

If you plan to use your own content, the primary objective is to create material with the highest quality possible. Content quality is up to you. You can use a checklist approach for technical quality.

Assuming that your assets are from real life, shoot on the highest quality format possible. The dream-team list would follow as such:

▶ D1

▶ Digibeta

▶ BetaCam or C format one-inch tape

▶ JVC DVT

▶ Hi-8 or Hi-band U-Matic

▶ S-VHS or Video-8

▶ Somebody else's Video-8 or S-VHS

▶ VHS, but only under extreme duress!

If you really must use VHS, at least ensure that your VHS equipment is clean and the machine is new and well maintained.

INSIDER TIP

> One-inch tape and U-Matic are falling into disuse with the new digital tape formats. D4 and the new Digital Cassette video systems are taking the higher end.

When shooting your own material, remember to check your legal position. Ensure that you obtain the correct permissions when shooting testimonials or vox-pops. *Vox-pops* (short for *vox populii*—"the voice of the people") commonly involve popping down to the local mall and shoving a microphone under the nose of a member of the public to obtain an opinion. Talk to the mall folks first. Ensure that all your interviewees know the purpose of the shoot and that you get their permission.

Obtaining Video from Elsewhere

When buying material, keep in mind two major categories. These categories tend to represent the two extremes of the cost scale.

- ▶ Clipmedia (clip art)

- ▶ Pre-existing material (such as TV shows and library material)

Clipmedia material is created with the express purpose of being used repeatedly. Often this material is offered as "royalty-free"—note this does not mean "copyright free"—in that after you have purchased the material, you may use it in any manner you choose, usually with the exception of inclusion into a similar clipmedia product.

As with all clip material, the content is likely to be generic, follow a set theme, and be designed for use on low-end machines. Unlike PostScript clip art, however, it is usually provided "as is," with little scope for customization. What you see is what you get, and if what you get is not quite right, it can be frustrating if not impossible to edit. Often, the trade-off for the relatively low cost of clipmedia is not getting exactly what you want.

Clipmedia is one of the cheapest forms of obtaining digital video, however, and often can provide material that would not be cost effective to use any other way. An example is Apple's QuickClips. QuickClips includes comic bursts of 1950s information films and B movies to create what can only be described as "video punctuation marks."

QuickClips does not, however, include anything as famous or widely recognized as the original "I'll be back" clip from *The Terminator*. If you really want to use a famous clip of film, you have no other choice than to obtain the right to use existing footage.

Licensing pre-existing material involves expense, which may be considerable in the example of licensing a famous film clip. Furthermore, artists' contracts may mean that you need their permission in addition to the owner's permission.

On one hand, the right to use a clip of a commercial may be given free of charge. If, however, the content is likely to add credence to your project, work with a lawyer and a negotiator. Talk to agents.

INSIDER TIP

A golden rule is to never start using uncleared material and then seek clearance. Get clearance first for a better bargaining position. Obtaining clearance is the most difficult, expensive method of obtaining digital video assets, but you may get exactly what you want, and it could very well be central to the success of your project.

Unlike clipmedia, licensed material is rarely supplied predigitized, and although a choice of formats may be offered, AVI or QuickTime tends not to be one of them. Remember to budget for digitization on top of licensing costs. The benefit of doing your own digitization of licensed material is that you are in control of the quality. If you used the "Really, what was it?" clip from Apple's QuickClips, you are limited to its 160×120 size and 8-bit sound. This was leading edge three years ago but is impractical today. If you had digitized it yourself (after having negotiated with the film's publishers), you would be able to use the full-screen version and IMA 16-bit sound available today.

Techniques for Optimizing Digital Video

Having decided to create your own material, what can you do to ensure a smooth-running, high-quality digital video movie? The answer depends on the type of material you want to use: traditional video (existing footage); the vox-pop or testimonial style video (usually an interview scene); a presenter or studio shoot; or computer-generated material from 3D software or from Director itself.

Live Footage and Testimonials

The majority of material in this category can be labeled as the "talking head." Like most broad terms, it includes everything from the established professional presenter to the impromptu interview with, for example, Mom coming out of the store with the kids in tow. The two sides to this material are the technology and the content. Content is subjective, and is not covered here. The following list acts as a guide to the technical aspects of generating digitally friendly video:

▶ Use a tripod. Tripods need to be heavy. Make a tripod heavy by hanging your kit bag from the center post. If you want to raise the camera, try to use the leg extensions rather than the center post.

▶ When shooting a predominantly vertical shot (such as a talking head), turn the video camera on its side as you would a stills camera. This might seem silly, but remember that you can rotate it in your video editing package later.

▶ Watch for distracting backgrounds. Backgrounds can be detailed, but should not move if compression is an issue (as it usually is). Beware of trees on windy days, as well as busy streets.

Although this chapter is not about the techniques of shooting video, the following list includes a few more pointers:

▶ If the subject isn't a seasoned presenter, he will not be comfortable looking directly into the camera. Have the subject talk to someone to the left or right of the camera to avoid the "furtive, darting eyes" of someone trying to remember what comes next. Frame the shot so that the nose is centered and just a bit higher than the middle of the screen. On the Director stage, if the head is looking to your left, place the movie to your right, giving your subject space to look into.

▶ Remember that videotape is cheap. Shoot everything and shoot it well. You will not be digitizing it all. Sometimes, those "by-the-way" comments are just what you want—even if they're wanted in a completely different section or project.

▶ By keeping the tape rolling, you can often get a far better performance from a subject who isn't used to the shiny end of a camera. Shouting "cut" may be good therapy for the director, but leads to more takes than doing a "keep-going" smile of encouragement. Factual presentations now use the "American Cut"—a quick dissolve between two takes without the cut-away to the presenter. The cheekily named "American Cut" has now become the video representation of ellipses (…).

Color Separation Overlay (ChromaKey)

Color separation overlay used to be the province of television studios and film special effects departments, but now is a feature in $400 digital video editing applications, such as Premiere. *Color Separation Overlay* (CSO) is the generic name for the ubiquitous "blue-screen" method, but many know it by the brand name—ChromaKey. (Others include Ultimatte and Digimatte.) The basic procedure of replacing a background color with another image source is the process of CSO.

CSO solves many scenic problems and is an established technique for a wide variety of situations—from flying superheroes to simply combining live action with computer graphics. This latter category is of utmost interest to the Director user—whether it's for weather maps or dramatic effect.

Good CSO is slightly better than some blue paper tacked to a wall. The trick is in even lighting—and lots of it. For this, you'll need space. The number of lights used generates a lot of heat, so good ventilation is important.

At least two lights are required for the background alone—probably four (see fig. 12.3). Blue paper tends to be trickier to light than blue felt, because paper is in fact quite shiny and picks up highlights. Note that if you use felt, it is a good idea to use the flame-retardant or flame-proof material.

Check for *hotspots* (abnormally bright areas) on the backdrop. Although a light meter is customary in these circumstances, you can sometimes get away with a squint test.

Arrange your scene so that the distance between the subject and the background is twice the distance between the camera and the subject. The real intention is to keep the subject as far away from the background as possible.

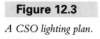

Figure 12.3

A CSO lighting plan.

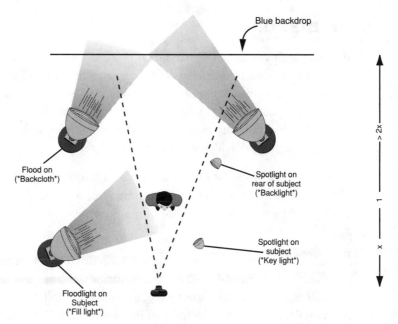

Due to the amount of light shining onto the background, some of the light bounces back, illuminating the subject with a blue wash of light. This causes horrible fuzzy edges in which the CSO works only partially. To make doubly sure that no blue light spills onto the subject, pour more light onto the back of the subject—this is known as a *backlight*—and then balance your subject's *key light* (the spotlight on the subject) and *fill light* (the floodlight on the subject) accordingly, watching for shadows on the background.

It's handy to have your video digitizing computer wired to the camera to preview results. To help ensure clear images, check the background for hot spots by grabbing just the background and use the Equalize command in an application such as Photoshop to show where the hot spots—and "black holes"—are located.

Blue creates the sharpest outline with composite video equipment. (It uses a higher frequency than red or yellow and therefore achieves better resolution.) Blue is the most common choice because it is an "alien" color that contrasts well with all types of skin and hair color, but it is not the only color for CSO. Green is sometimes preferable to blue light for contrast, because blue is a popular clothing color.

Animation

Working with animation-based digital video is a lot less time consuming than working with analog video. By definition, such material is generated digitally, and the content does not suffer from "pollution," such as noise from tape or artifacts from conversion to digital. Animation is "cosmetically perfect," so to speak, and raises the threshold of what is achievable in terms of frame rate and the area that a digital video can occupy on the stage.

Although 320×240 at 12 fps is a theoretical limit for video via a double-speed CD-ROM in a home computer, the same setup may be able to achieve 20 fps at 320×320 by using a clean, computer-generated source untouched by analog dirt.

Digital video is not restricted to the 4:3 ratio of your television screen or computer monitor. A 640×120 movie contains the same amount of pixels as a 320×240 movie, therefore giving the appearance of full-screen animation. For an example, check out the Pond presentation on the CD-ROM that accompanies this book. This movie is discussed in detail with other examples of digital video in Director later in this chapter.

Tools

As far as tools go, this chapter has repeatedly mentioned digital video editing software such as Premiere. This section discusses Premiere and briefly covers several other types of hardware and software tools. The hardware discussed is digitization hardware. Several types of basic software are also covered. The discussions of software are pertinent to digital video in the general sense. When used in conjunction with Director, however, some applications change slightly in their approach. The section titled "Helper Applications," later in this chapter, revisits this software in the context of Director.

Digitizing Hardware

The Macintosh digitizing hardware comes in two varieties: built-in (as in the AV class machines and most high-end Power Macintoshes) and third-party digitization cards.

All PCs require third-party digitization cards, although there is an extraordinarily wide range from which to choose.

Built-In Video (Macintosh Only)

The AV class Macs, starting with the Quadra 840 AV and Centris 660 AV, have video and audio digitization built into the hardware. Both composite and S-Video inputs are provided and are capable of coping with digitizing a 240×180 window at 12–15 fps with the built-in disk drive. With clean material and a lean system folder, 320×240 can be achieved, but should not be relied upon.

The Power Macintosh AV systems can cope with larger window sizes and higher frame rates, but FSFMV is still difficult to digitize.

The AV hardware in Macintosh systems is not limited to video grabbing. A little-known feature enables the mixing of live video with Macintosh graphics in a method similar to CSO.

Mac Graphics Over Live Video

An AV Macintosh can overlay graphics onto a video signal with the monitor set to 8 bits. A 640×480 monitor works best. Connect a video source to the Mac.

1. In the Finder, launch Director. Switch back to the Finder from the Application menu. Now launch either the Apple Video Player or Video Monitor application, and select the large size or full screen option. You should see your video playing. Switch back to Director.

2. Set the stage to the darkest green of the system palette via the Movie Properties dialog box.

3. You should now see your video playing on the stage.

4. If the video freezes, switch from Director to the Video Player and back again. The video freezes are due to Director drawing windows. Once in playback mode, the video plays normally.

Digitization Cards

If you want to digitize video that fills the screen at more than 15 fps, it is best to get a specialized card to do so.

Digitization cards exist for every budget—from the entry level (but very effective) Video Spigot to the broadcast-quality Targa 2000 and Media 100 systems.

WARNING

Pixels in the computer world are square. Pixels in the world of digital television are *not* square, but rectangular—they are wider than they are high. This is part of the CCIR-01 specification.

This anomaly affects only high-end cards designed around the professional CCIR-601 format, and these tend to be the base of digital video editing systems.

Check with your supplier to make sure that your choice of card vendor supports square pixels; otherwise, the grabbed video will be distorted on your (square pixel) monitor.

A low-end card will cost about the same as a camcorder. High-end cards are in the family car budget. With both solutions, a very large hard disk is obligatory. When working with video hardware, use AV class or *nonthermo resetting* hard disks. Ordinary disks take a rest from their usual chores occasionally and recalibrate themselves. If you happen to be recording video at that time, the effect is disastrous. AV drives do not need recalibration.

If your demands are for broadcast quality, an AV drive is not enough. You need a RAID (Redundant Array of Inexpensive Disks). Two hard disks (sometimes four) are controlled by a special card so that they work as one unit. This enables data to be written at a sustained 10 MB per second or more.

If you need to back up the raw digitized material, the only cost-effective way is to budget for a Digital Linear Tape (DLT) drive, too.

Digitizing Software

Digitizing cards usually come with their own software or a limited version of commercial software that has been customized to their product. Computers with built-in video digitization facilities also come with a simple application to grab video.

These applications tend to have just one job in mind—to get video into your system. Functions such as editing and fine control over compression are not addressed.

Digitization software should offer a flexible frame rate, a flexible movie size (including a variable aspect ratio, not just 4:3), a choice of sampling rates for audio, and the capability to record directly to disk or RAM and compress afterward (for a better frame rate). Some control over brightness and contrast is offered at this stage, but this is where a TimeBase Corrector comes in handy.

Think of digitizing software as the equivalent to a scanner plug-in. Rather than devoting processor power and RAM to fancy functions, it is devoted to only one job: getting the entire video/audio and nothing more.

Some board manufacturers create their software (or versions of their software) to work as a plug-in with applications such as Adobe Premiere.

Editing Software

Three broad categories of editing software are available: those suited to mixing traditional analog footage, such as Premiere; those that are oriented to compositing digitally created material, such as After Effects; and a catch-all special effects group that includes filter sets, such as Boris Effects, and transitions, such as Morph.

Editing software for analog footage blends techniques of film editing with the terminology of video editing. Such software offers asset management to handle the large number of clips in a full edit. Such applications are suited to putting together a 10-minute interview rather than a 10-second promo sting.

If your requirements are to matte a ray-traced 3D animation over a sequence of stills with a feathered drop shadow, the editing moves beyond assembly into the realm of *compositing*, which is the domain of applications such as Adobe After Effects.

Features to be found in a compositing application are similar to a paint application on one hand: high-quality interpolation of pixels (in scaling and rotation operations) and exemplary anti-aliasing throughout the many layers of graphics. On the other hand, the features are similar to Director: layer control, trajectory control over time, tweening, and so on.

The major difference between applications such as After Effects and Director is that After Effects is not a real-time application. The movies it creates require rendering in addition to the compression stage.

The special effects category of editing applications covers the world of effects packages—some of which blur the line between application and plug-in, such as Boris Effects. Others, such as Morph, resolutely remain a one-trick pony—be it ever such a good trick.

INSIDER TIP

> Morphing software has thrown off its "flavor of the month" mantle, but it should still be a part of your tool kit. Morphing can be used for tricks such as color replacement, matching illustration to photograph, and creating a non-looping sequence loop such as clouds, water, or flags. It helps 2D animation break into 3D—for example, sliding a face from profile to full face. It also continues to morph and caricature, of course (no longer a special effect!).

Utilities

Microsoft and Apple publish Software Development Kits (SDKs) which include many specialist utilities that are not publicly available. Such SDKs are worthwhile for the professional author, although there are third-party alternatives available from the World Wide Web.

The best source of QuickTime-oriented utilities is the QuickTime SDK. The SDK contains applets to perform tricks such as adding text tracks from documents, burning text onto the screen, converting MIDI files from PC formats, setting copyright information, and so on. Buried deep in the CD are special "cleaning" applications that ensure your movies have the correct number of keyframes and that the poster frame is set correctly. Many of these applications are also available—at no cost—on the seeding and beta disks available to Apple developers. Others are available via the Internet. The SDK, however, comes with full documentation, whereas the developer disk and Internet versions are unsupported.

Handling Digital Video in Director

Digital video is a resource-hungry media, as is Director. It is remarkable how the two get along so well, considering that both are busily doing low-level tasks with the screen, each with strict adherence to their own, sometimes conflicting, time bases.

Planning a Movie Within a Movie

The single largest constraint in the use of digital video with Director is the target playback platform. It is possible to achieve full-screen, full-motion video within a Power Macintosh computer or a Windows machine with an MPEG card of the correct type correctly installed. But unless you can guarantee these conditions, your authoring platform is likely to be far more powerful than the playback platform.

When planning your use of digital video, set a target platform and adhere to it strictly. Have a representative of your target platform available, remembering the Director user's mantra of "Test Early, Test Often, Test on All Target Platforms."

Examples: Digital Video and Director

The following three examples refer to projects that are on the CD-ROM that accompanies this book. The projects are in the Chapter 12 folder. It is a good idea to check out the projects before reading further or trying to follow along with the tutorial.

Pond deals with simple control of digital video via Lingo, Ellipse describes the process of "matting" a digital video onto a background, and Micons explores using the text track.

Pond: Controlling Digital Video with Lingo

Pond is a presentation template that depicts a water and pearl motif, in which each presentation slide is punctuated with a rising pearl that hovers throughout the slide's duration as water ripples beneath it.

The animation, created in Specular Infini-D, comprises 45 frames of animation in a single movie measuring 480×128 pixels. The animation is divided into three parts: 15 frames of rising pearl, 15 frames of floating pearl, and 15 frames of exiting pearl. The ripples on the pond are synchronized with these three stages, and if frame accuracy is achieved, the animation should appear seamless.

Clearly, if each frame were imported into Director, complex frame handling would be required to achieve the seamless transition among the three states. More than 2 MB of RAM would be needed just for the animated motif, and a slice of the available computing power would be devoted to that task only. As it stands, this movie will play in a 486 class machine with 8 MB RAM.

The score contains three simple Lingo handlers to perform the following three tasks as follows:

▶ Between slides, the digital movie can run freely. It is given enough time to display at least 16 frames of the video, then check the digital video and prepare it to enter a holding pattern:

```
-- Set things up for the loop
on exitFrame
  if the movieTime of sprite 2 > 132 then
    go to the frame
  end if
end
```

▶ As a slide builds up and text appears, the first script checks the movieTime of the pearl video, "catches" the pearl at the top of the screen, and holds it there by "opening" the movie into frames 16–30:

```
-- Building up the slide
on exitFrame
  if the movieTime of sprite 2 > 132 then
    go to the frame
  end if
end
```

▶ The third script performs a similar function but allows time for a mouse or key event to interrupt and move the playback head onward:

```
-- Pause for slide
on exitFrame
  if the movieTime of Sprite 2 > 112 then
    set the movieTime of Sprite 2 to 60
  end if
  -- catch a click for the next slide
  if the mouseDown then
    cursor -1
    go to the frame + 1
  else
    go to the frame
  end if
end
```

> ▶ This script enables the movie to escape from the 16–30 loop and into frames 31–45, but as soon as the loop is exited, the handler enables the score to take over and the movie "runs free" until the playback head hits the next build-up.

The entire process can be bound into one large Lingo handler, but this template was originally designed for use by Director users with little or no Lingo experience.

The QuickTime video in this example was originally saved in the QuickTime animation format set at 24 bits at the highest quality. To achieve the required bandwidth to play back on a humble Windows machine, it was compressed using CinePak at a quality and spatial setting of 50.

Ellipse: Matting a Digital Video Cast Member

This example uses Premiere to composite a video onto a background from a Director project.

Sample files are provided in the Ellipse folder inside the Chapter 12 folder of the accompanying CD-ROM. Besides the finished movie and digital video file, the original rendered animation with a matte channel is included in the subfolder.

The goal is to place a rendered animation (in this case, a spinning globe) created in Infini-D at a size of 240×176 onto a full-screen background. The problem is that the animated globe is rendered with a matte (or alpha) channel. You want the globe to sit cleanly on the sky background, cut out from its current black background using the matte. The animation should be centered horizontally and in the upper part of the screen.

A third application is required, capable of using the matte channel to composite the globe on the background. In addition, you need a portion of the background where the digital video sits.

Pixel accuracy is needed to get the final composite video sprite to seamlessly superimpose on the Director background. It helps to have a calculator and some aspirin ready. Before the process begins, calculate the location and dimensions of the final digital video. Sketching the layout is helpful (see fig. 12.4).

The coordinates to which you want to refer are in the top-left corner of your digital video in relation to the stage. These coordinates are X and Y.

The movie you want to matte measures 240 pixels horizontally and 176 pixels vertically. These dimensions are known as X1 and Y1.

The stage measures 640×480, and dimensions are known as X2 and Y2. All three sets of coordinates and their relative positions are shown in figure 12.4. Therefore:

$$X=((X2–X1)\div2)$$
$$Y=(Y2\div2)–((Y2\div2)–Y1)$$

Figure 12.4

Diagrams are better than equations.

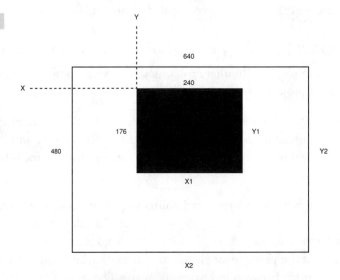

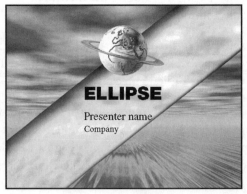

You need to isolate the portion of the background between X and Y and X1 and Y1, which is the area between the stage coordinates 200, 64 and 440, 240. As you can see, catch-all equations are tempting to suggest, but diagrams and doodles are a great help in sorting the relationships between numbers!

Matting a Digital Video Cast Member

1. In Director, select all the items in the frame on which you want the digital video movie to sit, and use the tweak window to type a negative value of X and Y. That means moving everything up by 64 pixels (–64) and to the left by 200 pixels (–200).

2. Now set the stage size of your Director movie to that of the digital video (in this case, 240×176). This has isolated the exact area that is covered by the digital video movie.

3. Choose Export from the File menu, and choose This Frame as PICT.

4. You can now quit Director and launch your video editing application, such as Premiere.

5. In Premiere, set the Project size and output movie to that of your render. In this case, the size is 240×176, which is probably not in the list of predefined project sizes.

6. Import the exported portion of background and the QuickTime movie.

7. Matte the movie over the background by placing the background in Channel A and the animation in the overlay channel. Drag the background end point to match the animation.

8. Select the animation and choose Transparency from the Effects menu. In this case, the movie has an Alpha channel; choose this option from the pop-up menu and click on the OK button.

9. You now can make a movie by choosing Make Movie from the Make menu. Choose the following options: Whole Movie, QuickTime Movie, with the compression settings set to Apple Video with a Quality of 50 at 15 fps and a keyframe every 15 frames.

10. Press the Option key while dragging the Quality slider to set the Temporal quality (the delta change settings—how much needs to change to register movement). Use a spatial setting of 75 (see fig. 12.5).

continues

Matting a Digital Video Cast Member   continued

Note that the control over temporal settings can be accessed only when the keyframe option is checked. Also, notice that the Director QuickTime Options dialog box does not have this control. To compress a Director movie with a lossy codec, export it from Director using the Animation codec and recompress it in Premiere or a compression utility such as Apple's ConvertToMoov or MovieCleaner from Terran Interactive.

Figure 12.5

Temporal compression settings are not accessible in Director 6.

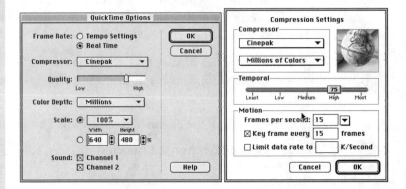

11. After you set the compression settings and the format, select a location and a name for the movie. A sensible location is in the same folder as your Director movie.

12. When this is complete, quit Premiere and relaunch Director with the movie on which you require the digital video animation.

13. Import the movie by choosing Import from the File menu or pressing Command+R on the Mac, Ctrl+R in Windows. Choose Digital Video from the pop-up menu. Locate your newly created digital video file from the standard file dialog box.

14. In the Cast window, select the digital video member, and click on the Information button to set the attributes of the digital video.

    For best results and the highest performance for this kind of member, choose Direct to Stage, Loop, and Play Every Frame. Turn off the Sound property because this movie does not use sound.

15. In the Score window, locate the frame in which you want the animation to appear. From the Cast window, drag the digital video onto the stage.

16. Position the movie by using the Sprite Inspector or Sprite Properties dialog box (Ctrl+click (Mac) or Right-click (Win) the digital video and choose Sprite Properties from the pop-up menu).

17. Enter the X and Y coordinates (in this case 200 and 64) and press Enter. The digital video sprite is now positioned correctly, ensuring that the "magic numbers" are used.

An important point to keep in mind is that animation is sensitive to the area of movement. Full-screen movement in digital video should be avoided. The worst case for a codec, for example, is four small sprites that chase around the edges of the screen. Here, delta change compression would render every frame entirely different. Sprite-based animation, such as the Director score-based animation, is much more effective. Digital video can help out, but it isn't a panacea.

Micons: Using Director to Create a Composite Digital Video

This example demonstrates the use of Director to create a digital video for use within a different Director movie to reduce complexity of the score and increase performance. It also demonstrates the loading of small digital video files into RAM so that several can play simultaneously.

The term *micon*, or motion icon, was coined in 1989 by its inventor, Hans Peter Brøndmo. Micons are small, self-contained animations that represent an object or concept much as a traditional icon does. In fact, due to their ubiquity, many people group this class of interface element into the generic button category.

Micons are captivating items, bringing life to otherwise static choice screens and providing encouragement to interaction. Micons, however, pose an interesting challenge for the Director developer.

Consider the screenshot of the "micon" example shown in figure 12.6. This is from a typical kiosk application, designed to run from a hard disk in relatively cheap equipment. If you want to try the example supplied, copy the Micon folder from the Chapter 12 folder on the accompanying CD-ROM to your hard disk first, and be sure to set your monitor to thousands of colors. Note that this movie is used as an illustration only, so the buttons will not work.

Figure 12.6

Multiple digital video members on the stage.

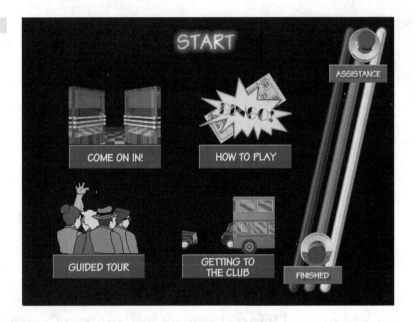

Four distinct animations are built from a combination of traditional Director (sprite) animation and 3D animation. If it were done with bitmap sprites, each member would need to be present in RAM for every frame of all the animations. This applies to animation in the score, in a movie loop, or as a Director movie imported into the cast. In this case, using digital video avoids that burden on RAM and helps performance a great deal.

Each micon was created separately in Director from original material and a diverse set of applications. The bus, for example, was drawn in Deneba Canvas and colorized in Director. The taxi was drawn by hand in Photoshop, where the vibrations were added with the Wave filter.

For each micon, the digital video size is established by setting the stage size to 160×120, which offers a good balance between size and performance. When the design is complete, the movie is exported using the Animation codec and brought into the main movie as a digital video member.

Note the way each micon has a unique duration. The animations slip in and out of synchronization with each other, obscuring the loop points. To do this with manual score animation is virtually impossible; to do it with Lingo is possible if the performance hit of up to 120 puppetSprites and their control is acceptable. Another alternative would be to import one Director movie into another, but in these circumstances, doing so would add to the already complex matting going on, further degrading performance.

Using digital video, the overwhelming complexity of managing numerous animation channels is reduced to a single frame containing four sprites. The Lingo programmer needs only to look after button handling and branching options; the digital video looks after the animation.

Of course, it's not quite that simple. First, the micons are set to play every frame—Director never drops a frame, and thus never loses synchronization between the micons. Second, due in part to their small size and looped nature, the digital video micons—when memory permits—load into RAM. This is very important. Third, the micons all want to spool off disk at the same time.

WARNING

> The first *pass* where each animation plays for the first time before looping) will be slow as each frame of each digital video is loaded into RAM. Performance improves thereafter. It is inappropriate to load large digital video files into RAM.

Remember to pay attention to the physical location of the digital video assets on your disk. In the case of playing four QuickTime movies simultaneously from disk, the files should be positioned close together. Playing from RAM is no longer a problem, but the first pass is from disk and therefore slow. Media prioritization helps speed progress on the first pass.

INSIDER TIP

> Most disks and CD-ROM drives have caches and "read-ahead" buffers. These items are of use to kiosk developers, who have direct control over the playback platform. A correctly sized cache also can help prevent trips from the read head's current position to directory tables in the center of the disk to pick up the next location point.

Importing and Exporting Digital Video Cast Members

Due to the relatively large size of digital video, all digital video members are imported into Director as linked members. This means that the digital video remains external to your Director movie.

Remember that with linked assets such as pictures, sounds, and digital video, the Director movie refers to that asset with nothing more than a path name. To ensure proper operation of linked members consider the following:

▶ Ensure that you include all linked assets in addition to your projector, as well as Director movies if not built into the projector.

▶ Try to keep the same file hierarchy when you move the completed project to another part of a hard disk or another disk entirely. This is part of asset management, but there is plenty of room to trip up.

▶ If your projector, Director files, and digital video movies all reside in one folder, the proper hierarchy is simple to achieve. If, however, your digital video movies are kept on another disk from the Director files that call to them, care must be taken in planning the hierarchy. Consider, for example, a presentation stored on a hard disk that also uses video material stored on CD-ROM. Planning the hierarchy frequently requires the use of full path names and scanning connected drives.

▶ When protecting movies (converting from a .DIR format to the impenetrable .DXR format or the minuscule DCR format), Director does a final check of the internally held path names to your digital video. Beware: This helpful trick has a nasty sting to it; if you protect movies to another location and move them back, Director (Windows) is unable to find the digital video files, despite being in the same place as the original files (see the following warning). To avoid this, make note of the movies' locations before protecting them and then move the .DIR files that need to be converted out of their hierarchy. Select the destination in the Protect Movies dialog box as the location from which the movies originally came.

WARNING

Do not send movies somewhere else to be protected and then manually move them back. All connections to your linked assets will be broken.

Actually, a Macintosh projector will probably survive the broken links. A Windows projector, on the other hand, will display dialog boxes asking for the location of your linked files. Remember to move your movies out of the hierarchy and "protect" them back in again. The Director online community hears of this disaster about once a month. You have been warned.

Color Depth

As described earlier in this chapter, most of the digital video codecs are designed to work in high color depths (thousands of colors), but some are designed for paletted environments (256 colors or 8 bit).

Since the introduction of Director 5, the use of 16-bit and 24-bit stages is no longer the exclusive realm of the Macintosh community. Director 5 opened high-color depth to the world of Windows, thus removing the biggest source of anguish at a stroke.

INSIDER TIP

> High-color depth stages (movies requiring thousands or millions of colors) are available only for 32-bit projectors (for Windows 95 and Windows NT). 16-bit and 24-bit color is *not* available for Windows 3.11 and earlier.

Codecs such as CinePak, Microsoft Video 1, Apple Video, and Indeo are all optimized for a 16-bit environment. If writing to an 8-bit display, the digital video system software performs on-the-fly, dithering to the palette currently assigned to the stage, with resulting performance degradation. This is due to the extra "dither" processing required. (Any palette stored in the digital video member is disregarded by Director.)

Common Problems

Some common problems with digital video in Director include disappointing performance, movies persisting on-screen too long, and a few tears caused when transporting digital video from Macintosh to Windows.

Logically, a digital video movie playing in a simple player application and the same movie playing from within Director, even with Director's Direct To Stage option set, will be slightly different in terms of maximum performance. The poorer performance occurs because more things are going on at the same time in Director. Although the CD-ROM drive imposes a limit on the data transfer rate, the processor must divide its time between decompressing and displaying that data, and running your projector or Director itself. As mentioned earlier in this section, playing 24-bit digital video in an 8-bit environment requires an extra computational process and more RAM in which to perform it.

The first step in curing performance ills is to check magic numbers (refer to Table 12.2 earlier in this chapter). The position of the digital video on the stage may need to be altered or the movie itself might not conform to the magic number rule. If conforming to the magic number does not solve the problem, the solution may be to recompress the movie with slightly more pessimistic settings, or investigate workarounds, such as cropping the movie slightly.

Testing often reveals an artifact of using digital video that can faze the uninitiated: persistence, associated with using the Direct To Stage property.

The symptoms of persistence are easy to spot. Director plays the digital video as normal. When set to jump to a new frame without the digital video on the stage, an image from the movie remains. The image is obliterated if sprites pass over the area or a transition occurs. Colloquially speaking, digital video hangs around, bumping into things.

This effect happens because Direct To Stage cuts a hole in the Director stage and hands control of this area to the digital video mechanism, such as QuickTime. When the movie has finished, Director cannot tell that the area needs to be refreshed. To prevent a mess, you should make the stage redraw itself immediately following your use of digital video by using one of the following methods:

▶ Replacing the digital video sprite with an invisible draw rectangle

▶ Adding `Set the stageColor to the stage Color` to the frame script following the digital video

▶ Adding a full stage transition effect to the following frame—setting the transition time to the minimum and the chunk size to the maximum

▶ Writing a handler that sets the visible of sprite X to FALSE (in which X is the channel that contains the video) and calls `updateStage`

Finally, several performance issues are associated with peculiarities of QuickTime and associated applications. One problem is difficulty in getting a QT movie to play on a non-Macintosh machine.

INSIDER TIP

When porting from Macintosh, QuickTime for Windows lets Director know what is happening. A comprehensive listing of error codes and their meanings is available from the Macromedia web site at `http://www.macromedia.com`. Search for Technote 3110TN.TXL.

If your Mac QuickTime video doesn't work with QuickTime for Windows, flattening and forks may be the cause. *Flattening* means making the movie self-contained, so that it doesn't point to any other movies. For a Macintosh QuickTime movie to play on a non-Macintosh computer, it must be flattened and then have the header information taken out of the resource fork and integrated into the data fork (that is, made single-forked). Figure 12.7 shows the layout of a QuickTime movie in the three stages: unflattened, flattened, and single fork.

Figure 12.7

Digital video file structures.

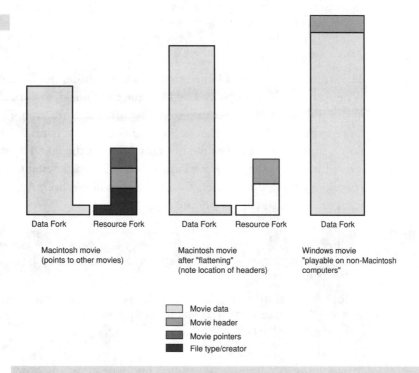

Data Fork   Resource Fork

Macintosh movie
(points to other movies)

Data Fork   Resource Fork

Macintosh movie
after "flattening"
(note location of headers)

Data Fork

Windows movie
"playable on non-Macintosh
computers"

Movie data
Movie header
Movie pointers
File type/creator

INSIDER TIP

A movie can be comprised of nothing but pointers to other movies, meaning that the pointer movie is minute—5 KB or so. Making a movie entirely of pointers to other movies enables the simulation of video editing with the capability to save many versions without clogging up the hard disk. This is limited to the Macintosh with versions of QuickTime prior to 3.0. If you move the movie of pointers onto a different system, however, it cannot play because the source movies are not available.

Confusion arises because in some helper applications, the term *flattening* is used imprecisely to mean "playable on a non–Macintosh computer" instead of "self-contained." So, in some applications (such as MoviePlayer), both "Make movie self contained" and "Playable on non–Apple computers" check boxes might have to be set, whereas others (such as FlattenMovie) do both in one simple step.

WARNING

Another common cause of not being able to play your QT movie on a non-Macintosh machine is that you may have used a special Mac codec that isn't installed on the Windows machine, although this is more likely when converting from AVI to QuickTime.

The structure of a QuickTime movie leads to another performance issue. When a movie is encountered by Director, the QuickTime mechanism spools to the end of the file to pick up some important information. This can take quite a while with a long movie. From QuickTime version 2.2, this information is stored at the head of the file, rather than at the end. Digital video created with versions of QuickTime prior to 2.2 may benefit from this minor "tweak" by using the ConvertToMoov tool available from Apple's web site or from the `www.quicktime.org` home page.

INSIDER TIP

QuickTime movies, like Director 6 movies, can now be *streamed* over the Internet. As soon as enough data arrives to display the movie, you can begin to play or manipulate it.

To make a QuickTime movie streamable, it must be streamlined by passing it through an application called Movie Streamliner (available from the Apple QuickTime web pages).

In conclusion, a flattened movie does not depend on any other movies. A movie that is playable on non–Macintosh computers does not depend on any other movies and keeps the header information and the movie information in one fork.

Existing Lingo Controls

Director 6 doesn't contain new Lingo for digital video, though some improvements have been made to the Lingo dictionary for the more obscure references.

movieRate

The `movieRate` property is the equivalent of your VCR buttons. Setting the `movieRate` to 0 stops it; setting it to 1 plays it forward at normal speed; setting it to 2 plays the movie forward at double speed. If you set it to −2, Director will attempt to play it backward at double speed.

movieTime

The `movieTime` property is similar to a VCR's tape counter or timecode track, with the added bonus of being able to set the property, which will instantaneously move the playback head to that point, achieving random access. The key thing to remember is that the `movieTime` has nothing to do with frames per second. `movieTime`—measured in ticks—is the standard Director time unit. One second contains 60 ticks. Therefore, to make a movie jump to a point that is 37 seconds from the beginning of the movie, set the `movieTime` as follows:

```
set the movieTime of sprite X to (37 * 60)
```

For fairly loose timing, the preceding example is fine. When dealing with digital video generated by animation software and replayed as a "play every frame" movie, however, you want to refer to individual frames rather than the movie time per second. Knowledge of the exact frames per second setting is required, so that if you want to remain looping in the middle third of a 45-frame movie (frames 16–30), and you know that the movie is created with 15 fps, the ticks per second divided by frames per second will give the number of ticks per frame (60÷15=4 ticks per frame); therefore, the code reads as follows:

```
on exitFrame
if the movieTime of sprite X > (4 * 30) then
set the movieTime of sprite X to (4 * 16)
end if
end
```

New Lingo Controls

Rather than act as a second copy of the *Lingo Dictionary*, the following sections represent a few of the high spots. Director's online help includes a short section on this Lingo control of digital video. Much of the online help concentrates on reading the properties of a digital video member, but the excitement is in the access to digital video "tracks." If you work on cross-platform or Windows-only projects, please bear in mind the caveats regarding multiple track types noted earlier in this chapter.

digitalVideoTimescale

The `digitalVideoTimeScale` sets the scale factor used by Lingo when reading and setting `movieTime` properties. By default it is 60. Setting the `digitalVideoTimeScale` to 1 enables you to deal with QT times in round seconds; setting it to `timeScale` of a member gives the highest possible resolution. Normally the QT times are truncated to the nearest 1/60 second.

The `digitalVideoTimescale` does not tell you the frames per second of a member. If you need to obtain the frames per second of a member, the `frameRate` of member X is the way you would expect to determine the normal rate. Unfortunately it is only a valid number when the member's Play Every Frame and Fixed Rate properties are set. Here's a way you *can* discern the frameRate of a digital video (with the variable `timeunits`):

If the digital video is known to be at first frame—by setting the `movietime` = 0, for example—the timeunits per frame = `trackNextSampleTime`(sprite 1,1).

If the digital video is set somewhere in the middle of its duration—
the timeunits per frame = `trackNextSampleTime` (sprite 1,1)–
`trackPreviousSampleTime`(sprite 1,1).

trackType

The `trackType` property enables you to inquire about the specific content type in a particular track of a digital video member or a sprite of it on the stage (differing only in the way it is addressed). Also, it returns the type in the form of a symbol from the track types available: #video, #sound, #text, and #music—MIDI data.

The following example puts the track details of a digital video member on the stage into the message window.

```
on checkMemberTracks whichVideoSprite
-- this puts the track details of a digital video
-- member on stage into the Message window.
-- Remember to pass the sprite number!
put the memberNum of sprite whichVideoSprite into targetMember
put trackCount(member targetMember) into howMany
put "Sprite" && whichVideoSprite && ", member "& targetMember
repeat with i = 1 to howMany
put "track" && i && trackType(member targetMember, i)
end repeat
put RETURN
end
```

trackText

The trackText property extracts the text string that is present in the text track at the given movieTime. The text need not be visible on the movie (it might be disabled with the trackEnabled property), so when used in conjunction with the following Lingo properties and the movieTime, you can progress through a digital video member and assemble a list of text strings to enable text searches of a video clip.

trackNextSampleTime and trackPreviousSampleTime

The trackNextSampleTime and trackPreviousSampleTime properties navigate between "events" in tracks such as the text track. Each sample combines a string of text with an *in-point* (when the text appears) and an *out-point* (when the text disappears), so that you can locate adjacent text pages by examining the track next/previous sample times.

trackNextKeyTime and trackPreviousKeyTime

The trackNextKeyTime and trackPreviousKeyTime Lingo properties find your choice of the keyframe closest to current frame within a digital video member, which should provide a clean image and a convenient mid-movie starting point. Note that QuickTime movies that have passed through applications such as MovieShop (described in the next section) might have additional keyframes added at irregular intervals.

Helper Applications

Director is an excellent playback platform tool for digital video, and it plays a valuable creation role. Although you may not need many helper applications, however, Director is neither designed nor suitable for video editing.

Compressing Video with MovieShop and Movie Cleaner

MovieShop has been around since the earliest days of QuickTime. Early in the history of QuickTime, MovieShop was the only "industrial strength" movie analysis and compression tool. Behind a fearsome interface, MovieShop constantly processed a movie to make it play back at a certain bandwidth by varying spatial and temporal compression on a frame-by-frame basis, inserting keyframes where necessary.

Today, MovieShop is used by a diminishing "die-hard" clique of developers, because many people have discovered Movie Cleaner from Terran Interactive.

Movie Cleaner provides the functionality of MovieShop and adds a raft of extra functions and enhancements that make it an essential utility. Movie Cleaner comes in two versions: a $15 shareware "lite" version available from the Terran web site (www.Terran-Int.com) and a $200 "pro" version that adds batch process, Power Macintosh acceleration, and specialized features such as filters for "talking head" video.

ConvertToMoov, available on the QuickTime FAQ web site, http://www.quicktimeFAQ.org, is another multifunctional tool that works very well. It is more of a power user's tool than Movie Cleaner, but makes concessions to ease of use (unlike MovieShop).

Adding Transitions with Premiere

Due to the intense optimization required for real-time smooth effects, Director's transitions are barely supported in digital video export. A workaround is required.

Exporting a Director movie to digital video is not a real-time thing. Each frame is created, snapped, compressed, and then recorded. You can simulate transitions with complex score animation that, although not working in real-time, end up looking better than the original transitions. Still, this is a painstaking exercise. Why not cheat?

By exporting the animation from Director in chunks of digital video and bringing them into Premiere, you can use many of the unique transitions that are a part of the basic Premiere package or experiment further with third-party extensions such as the TransJammer effects.

In the end, the best results come from compromise: simple wipes and transitions that cover the entire stage are created in Premiere, and transitions such as "reveal" and "push" are re-created with sprite animation.

Synchronizing Sound with SoundEdit

Director does not export its soundtracks in digital video movies. Remember that Director's design emphasis is on real-time animation performance—its export function is somewhat limited.

SoundEdit 16 (Mac) and SoundForge (Windows), included as part of the Director Multimedia Studio, cover virtually all the features needed in a multimedia sound tool. In addition, SoundEdit's capability to synchronize sound with digital video has been enhanced for this very purpose.

Creating Text Tracks with MoviePlayer

With the launch of QuickTime for Windows 3.0, Windows applications will soon be able to take advantage of text tracks.

Macintosh users with System 7.5 or later can start experimenting with text tracks immediately. You can create and edit text tracks with two applications that are likely to be on everyone's Mac: SimpleText and MoviePlayer 2.1 or later (with the authoring plug-ins available from the QuickTime home page and the QuickTime SDK). Create your text in SimpleText, using the Return key to separate each line of text. Subtitles should be kept short.

Creating Text Tracks with MoviePlayer

1. In MoviePlayer, open a QuickTime movie.

2. Choose Get Info from the Movie menu (see fig. 12.8).

Figure 12.8

Options available with the Authoring Extensions.

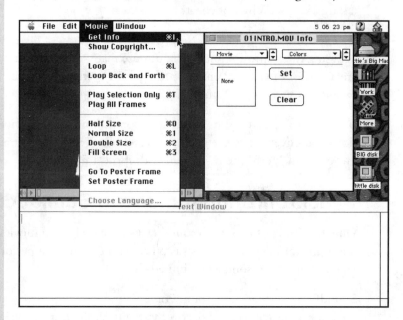

3. Switch back to the Finder and launch SimpleText. You may want to arrange the windows as shown in figure 12.8 so that you can see MoviePlayer's Info window, the Movie window, and your SimpleText document at the same time.

4. Type a sentence of text in SimpleText, select it, and drag the text over the movie. The movie border should highlight. A new text track is placed in the movie (see fig. 12.9).

   If the movie border does not highlight, you must install the drag-and-drop extension available from the Apple web site or magazine cover disks, or upgrade to System 7.5 or later.

5. Click on the movie window and rewind the movie to show the new text as a full frame. Notice that the left pop-up menu in the Info window now includes a text track. Choose this track (see fig. 12.10).

Figure 12.9

Drag text onto the movie.

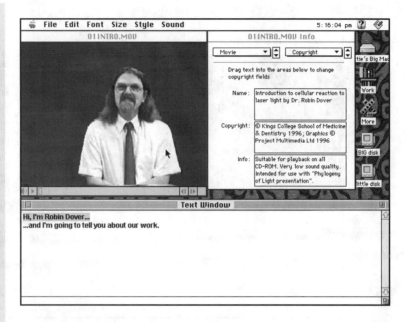

Figure 12.10

Select the newly created Text Track.

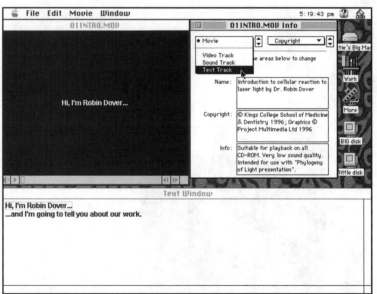

6. In the right-hand pop-up menu, choose the Text Replace option. You can click on the arrows to the right of the pop-up if you want (see fig. 12.11).

continues

Creating Text Tracks with MoviePlayer continued

Figure 12.11

Select the Text Replace option.

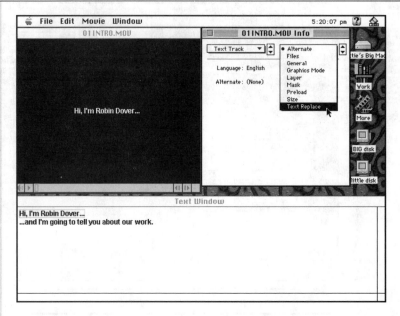

7. Drag the same text from SimpleText to the area marked Drag Style Here. The text area in the QuickTime movie now shrinks to the size of the text. Note that you can change the font, size, and style of the text in SimpleText and repeat the drag to change your subtitle style (see fig. 12.12).

Figure 12.12

Drag-and-drop styles and text.

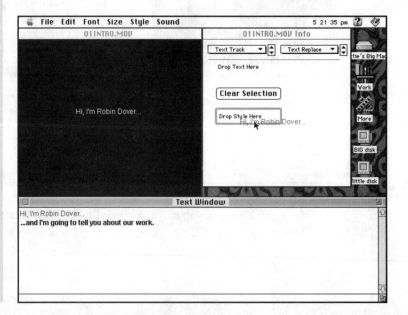

8. The subtitle window is traditionally at the bottom of the frame, so it needs to be moved. Choose Size from the Info window of MoviePlayer and click the Adjust button (see fig. 12.13). Drag the area to the bottom of the screen, click the Done button, and switch to Text Replace in the right-hand pop-up menu.

Figure 12.13

Adjust the area that the text occupies.

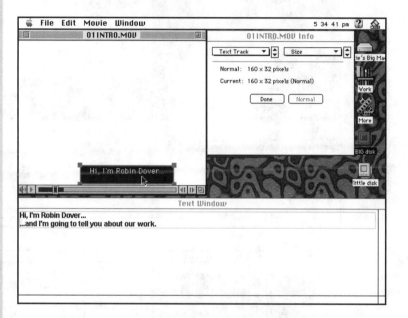

9. In the Movie window, select a portion of the movie to place the text over. Drag the control bar to the start point, and while pressing the Shift key, drag the control bar to the end point (see fig. 12.14).

10. Switch to SimpleText. Select the line of text that you want to insert and drag it to the area in MoviePlayer's Info window marked Drop Text Here. The text is now put into the text track of your movie. Note that if you drag more text to the MoviePlayer display window, an additional text track will be created (see fig. 12.15).

11. Continue to add your text by selecting the timespan in MoviePlayer, then dragging the text into the Drop Text Here area in the Info window. If you make a mistake, select the timespan and click the Clear Selection button (see fig. 12.16).

continues

Creating Text Tracks with MoviePlayer continued

Figure 12.14

Use the Shift key to set in and out points in one action.

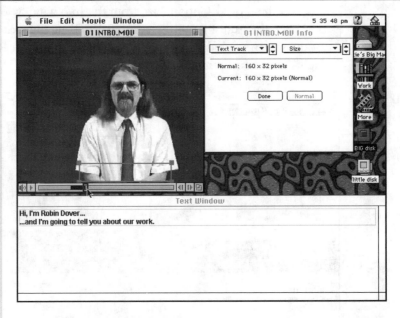

Figure 12.15

Dropped text is displayed during the highlighted time.

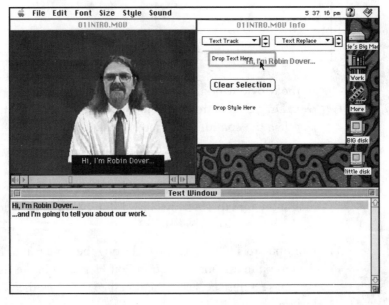

Figure 12.16

Select a timespan and choose Clear from the Edit menu to remove text.

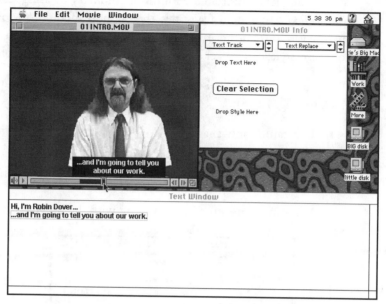

12. Save your movie, import it into Director, and admire (see fig. 12.17).

Figure 12.17

The finished movie in situ.

When you feel comfortable with this method, try creating an entire SimpleText document of subtitles, then import them into MoviePlayer. Clicking the Options button in the Import dialog box enables you to directly set the font, size, style, color, background color, alignment, and size properties.

The Import dialog box also enables access to some special features of the text track (see fig. 12.18):

▶ Text can be anti-aliased

▶ Text can be keyed (a transparent background)

▶ Text can be hidden

▶ Text can be prevented from scaling with the movie

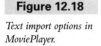

Figure 12.18

Text import options in MoviePlayer.

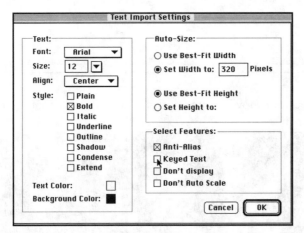

In Practice

This chapter concludes the portion of this book devoted to multimedia components that can be utilized in Director. Although it has certain additional complexities associated with it, digital video is just another one of these multimedia components. Remember that digital video is a useful container for all types of media. Exploit the time-oriented nature and the superb compression. Keep in mind the following practicalities of working with digital video:

▶ Plan for the end user's system configuration, especially the data rate.

▶ Ensure that your digital video dimensions and stage positions are divisible by the magic numbers—use 8 as a magic number when in doubt.

▶ Defragment your hard disk and prioritize media when possible.

▶ Use the best quality originals. Try to obtain the master tape if presented with a VHS. If you only have a VHS camcorder, record live action directly to hard disk.

▶ Grab large, grab more, reduce later.

▶ Use applications such as Movie Cleaner to compress your digital video.

▶ Watch cross-platform issues. Remember to test early, test often, test on your target platform.

▶ Micons: Use Director-created digital video to exceed speed and composition limits and simplify the use of the Score.

▶ Watch out with transitions: If creating digital video with Director, do not rely on transitions and sound; use Director for the animations; add them later.

▶ Read the Technotes: 3110TN.TXL Tech note (from `http://www.macromedia.com`) that outlines the error codes for digital video in Director. This exhaustive list should be stuck to your wall within easy reach. It serves as a quick check on what went wrong or as an overview of what can go wrong.

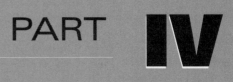

PART IV

Multimedia on the Web with Director and Shockwave

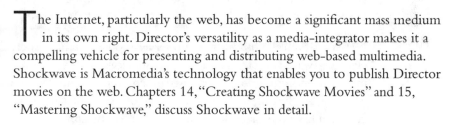

chapter 13

David Miller

Designing Multimedia for the Web

The Internet, particularly the web, has become a significant mass medium in its own right. Director's versatility as a media-integrator makes it a compelling vehicle for presenting and distributing web-based multimedia. Shockwave is Macromedia's technology that enables you to publish Director movies on the web. Chapters 14, "Creating Shockwave Movies" and 15, "Mastering Shockwave," discuss Shockwave in detail.

Shockwave for Director 6 is just one of several ways to add multimedia to web pages. As a multimedia developer, you probably have other tools in your toolkit that you can use to deliver web multimedia. What you use depends on the goal of your web site, what you are trying to communicate, the nature of your target audience, and the hardware/software limitations of both client and servers. This chapter, therefore, sets aside for the moment the close examination of Director and turns instead to some of the more general issues and tools pertinent to web-based multimedia. This chapter covers the following topics:

▶ An overview of TCP/IP-based networks

▶ Challenges to delivering web-based multimedia

▶ Management of web-based multimedia challenges

▶ Reasons to use the web and multimedia

▶ Mechanisms for delivering multimedia on the web

▶ HTML for multimedia

▶ Client-side scripting

▶ Project planning and design considerations

This chapter does not require specialized knowledge about the web, but it does assume a basic knowledge of the web and HTML. It is geared to first time users who are just getting started creating web sites with Shockwave or other rich content, and it is geared to established webmasters wanting to learn about web-based multimedia. Of course, a single chapter cannot give you a comprehensive understanding of multimedia on the web. For that, you should consult a reference dedicated to the topic, such as *Web Multimedia Development* from New Riders.

Overview of TCP/IP-Based Networks

Delivering multimedia Director products on networks presents a unique set of challenges when compared to delivery via CD-ROM or disk.

Networks typically follow a client/server model. Clients—such as web browsers, Net-aware Director projectors, or Shockwave movies—make requests for information from servers. Requests are commonly initiated by users, for example, by clicking on a hypertext link or using the `GetNetText` Net Lingo command. Servers listen for requests and take the appropriate actions, such as delivering a web page. With third-party Xtras such as XtraNet you can even create your own servers in Director!

Communication between clients and servers on the web and the Internet is based on TCP/IP. *TCP/IP* stands for Transmission Control Protocol and Internet Protocol. Several protocols are built on top of TCP/IP-based networks including the HyperText Transfer Protocol (HTTP), which you use when you click on a hypertext link in a web browser. Another common protocol is File Transfer Protocol (FTP). Uniform Resource Locators (URLs) are used as a generalized way to address different TCP/IP-based services such as addressing web pages with HTTP or files with FTP. HyperText Markup Language (HTML) is used to format and hyperlink web pages and other Internet resources. And this is only the first course in an alphabet soup of networking acronyms!

Data on the Internet is transferred in packets, which are discrete little chunks of data. Each little chunk contains the address of its destination and instructions on how to assemble the data when it arrives at its destination. It is up to the client machine receiving the data to make certain that all the packets that arrive are assembled into the correct file, web page, graphic, or other element. Packet-based data can cause problems for time-synchronized multimedia because all the pieces may arrive at the client machine at different times.

Organizations and enterprise departments are increasingly using web browsers as front-ends of organization-wide information systems. In such a configuration, information systems are hosted by web servers on internal, TCP/IP-based Local Area Networks (LANs). These internal networks are commonly called *intranets*. Bandwidth on intranets is significantly greater than the global Internet, and application of web-based multimedia on intranets has great potential.

For security reasons, intranets are commonly behind firewalls. A *firewall* is specialized software running on a machine that sits between the internal intranet and the rest of the Internet. The firewall filters the traffic between the intranet and the rest of the global Internet to prevent certain data from getting in or out. Firewalls can cause problems for multimedia data, blocking its transfer in some cases. Thus, it may be difficult to access pages outside your organization that contain multimedia elements that must be downloaded to local disk. Talk with your network administrator to see the traffic types allowed through your firewall.

Challenges to Delivering Multimedia on the Web

The biggest roadblock to delivering multimedia on the web is the time it takes to download rich, multimedia content over slow network lines. This roadblock has led some to refer to the web as the World Wide Wait. Although the speed and processing power of the local computer sometimes affect multimedia display capabilities (such as for JPEG compression or video playback from hard disk), the main limiting factor for multimedia on the web is the long download times of large multimedia files.

With so much hype surrounding the web and multimedia, it is easy to see how people expect full-screen, full-motion, TV-quality, interactive multimedia streaming off web pages. The reality, of course, is much less.

Two Kinds of Web Users

People connect to the web in different ways. For the purposes of delivering multimedia content, you can look at web users as falling into two groups:

- ▶ Those who connect via modems at 28.8 Kbps or less
- ▶ Those who connect at higher speeds, typically 56 Kbps or higher

The first group is typically home users. They are often paying per minute charges for Internet and web access. As a multimedia developer, you must factor the time and money issues facing an audience into your project design. They want to access your content as quickly as possible because time is money.

The second group is typical of corporate or university intranets. This group often has web access subsidized by their company or school. Users in this group typically reside on a shared LAN; thus, moving large multimedia files to individual workstations impacts performance of the network for all users on the local network. Like home users, they too are interested in obtaining multimedia content as efficiently as possible. Again, you must factor this into your project design and implementation.

Bandwidth and Other Limitations

Multimedia producers often look at the data transfer rate for a particular system as the major limiting factor in the kinds of multimedia content and quality of multimedia content that they can deliver. *Data transfer rate,* or *data rate,* is the amount of information transferred to the user's display per unit time. It is typically measured in kilo*bytes* per second, or KB/s. Data rates are usually limited by the user's hardware. Data rates for multimedia playback from CD-ROM are typically in the range of 100–200 KB/s.

When authoring for the web, data transfer rate has a broader meaning: *Bandwidth* refers to the amount of data that can be transferred down a wire or connection per unit time. It is typically measured in kilo*bits* per second, or Kbps. The rates 28.8 and 56 Kbps, mentioned previously as typical home and corporate connection rates respectively, are measures of bandwidth. Modems enable a maximum bandwidth of about 33.6 Kbps on phone lines. In reality, accessing the Internet can be much slower because many users are still connecting at 14.4 Kbps or less. This decreased rate could be due to phone lines that are old and "noisy" (thus limiting maximum bandwidth), or networks that might be congested—further slowing down transfer.

Table 13.1 compares data rate and bandwidth for several network connection methods. The bandwidth on an ISDN connection ranges from about 64–128 Kbps. Users on LANs typically have bandwidth in the same general range. On shared LANs, such as TCP/IP-based intranets, this available bandwidth is divided between multiple users.

Table 13.1

Comparison of Connection Rates

Connection	Data Rate (KB/s)	Bandwidth(Kbps)
14.4 modem	1.6	14.4
Single line ISDN	8.2	65.5
T1	192	1536
CD-ROM	150	1200
TV	27000	216000

Bandwidth has several implications for multimedia on the web:

▶ Multimedia is largely a "wait for it to download and then play it" experience. New features such as "streaming" Shockwave and "FastStart" QuickTime improve the user experience considerably by enabling media to begin playback before the entire media file is downloaded. Still, the media must be delivered to the user's machine, which takes time and is subject to the vicissitudes of the Internet.

▶ To achieve data rates comparable to CD-ROM over current modems, streaming technologies must achieve compression ratios that are 10 to 100 times what they are for CD-ROM.

▶ Internal networks have the bandwidth necessary for the delivery of many types of multimedia, although many still have less bandwidth than a slow CD-ROM.

In addition to bandwidth, other factors that can degrade delivery of multimedia on the global Internet are the saturation of the Internet backbones or main trunk lines and many of the performance and bottleneck issues related to the explosive growth of the Internet. Congested network lines that slow downloading web pages and the inability to connect to overcrowded sites are becoming increasingly common. Not all these problems are related to moving large multimedia files around the Net, but multimedia does tax the limits of the current infrastructure as more people log on and start streaming video or downloading 1 MB Shockwave movies.

Management of Web-Based Multimedia Challenges

If you develop a multimedia web site, be kind to the Net and its bandwidth. Hopefully some of the tips in this book will help you effectively use multimedia on the web without chasing away your users or adding to the general Internet gridlock with long downloads.

Download and Play

The multimedia element must be completely downloaded to the user's local hard drive before it can be viewed. Thus, a top priority for multimedia content providers is keeping file sizes to a minimum to reduce the download time. Keeping file sizes small usually means a reduction in media quality, such as fewer colors in graphics or a slower frame rate for animation. It is up to the multimedia author to balance the trade-off between file size and quality.

Streaming

Streaming is the continuous delivery of time-based media—such as animation, audio, or video—to a user's machine in real time. The user doesn't have to wait for the file to be completely downloaded before viewing the content. Multimedia can be streamed in real time, such as during an audio or video-conference, or pre-existing files can be streamed from a server. In Director 6, for example, you can create your Shockwave movie, place it on a server, and have the first few frames download rapidly for viewing by a user, while the rest of the file is downloaded from the server in the background.

Streaming can be tricky to implement. The Internet was not designed for the delivery of continuous, synchronized, time-based data. Internet data is packet-based, which means it is delivered asynchronously in discontinuous chunks. You don't know when each discrete chunk will arrive at its destination. It will get there whenever it can, bouncing around the Net looking for the best path. Interruptions in the continuous data stream can cause stutters and gaps during playback of animation.

Most streaming technology uses proprietary data formats and buffering systems to implement continuous playback. RealAudio and RealVideo from Progressive Networks uses streaming of precompressed files. Audio and video-conferencing on the web uses real-time streaming data formats. QuickTime movies can use the FastStart feature available in many QuickTime authoring tools, and Streaming QuickTime may be available by the time you read this.

Director 6 enables you to create Shockwave movies that provide streaming playback. See Chapter 14 for a description on authoring streaming Shockwave movies.

Compression

One way to deal with limited bandwidth on networks is to compress files for transport. It is up to the client software to decompress the files for viewing.

Director 6 provides compression of movie files. Shockwave compression creates files optimized for network playback. This compression is the same kind of compression used by the AfterBurner Xtra in previous versions of Director. These files typically have the .DCR file name extension. You create .DCR files in the Director authoring environment by choosing Save and Compact from the File menu and then Save as Shockwave movie from the File menu. .DCR files can be played back in web browsers using the Shockwave plug-in or a projector. .DCR files are the most highly compressed format for Director movies, but they must be decompressed during playback, which may affect performance at run time. If file size is not an issue, save the Director movie in .DXR format. A .DXR file is larger than a .DCR file, but playback is faster because the playback engine does not have to decompress the file.

Caching

Caching is another way to deal with limited bandwidth. A *cache* is a special folder or directory that is typically on a local hard disk or CD-ROM, although it could also be on a local server.

You may be familiar with the Netscape Navigator disk cache. The Navigator *disk cache* is where web pages and embedded media are downloaded when you click on a hypertext link. This type of cache must be write-enabled so that downloaded files can be stored for later retrieval. After the files are downloaded to the cache, they do not have to be reloaded again if the user revisits the web page. Instead, the files are loaded rapidly from the local disk cache.

Another kind of cache is a *static cache*, such as a CD-ROM. In this type of cache, the files are all provided on a write-protected directory, folder, or volume. The multimedia client or browser knows the location of this local cache and can load files as needed.

Shockwave for Director 6 uses the web browser cache for its cache. You can use the Net Lingo command `preLoadNetThing` to load files into the browser cache. You can also preinstall files in the Plug-in support folder. These files are accessible to your Shockwave movie. See Chapters 14 and 15 for a discussion of these features. LiveCD is a caching mechanism developed by Netscape for CDs. By the time you read this, an Xtra may be available to enable LiveCD features from Shockwave.

Net-aware projectors in Director 6 automatically create their own special support folder for preferences, downloaded Xtras, and linked media if the projector is on a write-enabled volume. You can also create and manage your own cache by using the `downLoadNetThing` command. See Chapters 14 and 15 for more on this Net Lingo command. Consult Macromedia's documentation for the most up-to-date information. Appendix C, "Contacting Macromedia," presents ways to reach Macromedia.

In the authoring environment, the cache options are set in the Network Preferences dialog box.

Web Publishing: Advantages and Disadvantages

Many organizations and individuals are rushing to publish material on web-based intranets and the global Internet. Web publishing has many advantages, including the following:

- ▶ 24-hour global access
- ▶ Cross-platform delivery
- ▶ Associative linking (hypertext and hypermedia)
- ▶ Easy to add interactivity
- ▶ Easy to update
- ▶ Easy access (if you have a computer on the Net)

Advantages of putting multimedia on the web include the following:

- ▶ Offers all the advantages of other web-based media
- ▶ Engages multiple senses, provides reinforcement and feedback
- ▶ Illustrates some concepts better, such as dynamic processes or visual information

▶ Can communicate more effectively than plain text

▶ Offers dynamic content that is visually engaging

▶ Multimedia cues and information design can help make abstract information spaces concrete and usable

▶ Provides a "hook" that makes a site stand out from the babel of the web and makes users want to return

▶ Browsers provide a cross-platform interface and multimedia authoring environment

Disadvantages include the following:

▶ Bandwidth limitations

▶ Slow networks

▶ HTML is a primitive page layout language

▶ Interactivity and multimedia support and playback on the web are still limited compared to other media, such as CD-ROMs

▶ Copyright and intellectual property issues

Mechanisms for Delivering Multimedia on the Web

The mechanisms for delivering multimedia on the web are changing rapidly. Besides the familiar multimedia in web browsers, new easy-to-use development tools for Java and the new Internet features integrated into Director 6 are enabling the rapid creation of custom, multimedia clients for the web.

Hybrid CD-ROMs represent a clever compromise mechanism for multimedia on the web. They contain large media files on a local CD, but access time-sensitive, low bandwidth media, such as text files containing the latest pricing information for a product, over the Internet.

Push technology is touted as a new way to deliver customized multimedia information services to users' desktops.

Push technology is, in many implementations, a timed "pull." For example, PointCast, a popular push client/server product, automatically and periodically updates content channels available from a server, such as stocks, news, and sports within its custom desktop client.

Two companies that provide these services and that also support Shockwave are Marimba with its Castanet tuner application and Intermind with its Communicator application. You can reach these companies' home pages with the following URLs:

- ▶ **Marimba:** `http://www.marimba.com/`

- ▶ **Intermind:** `http://www.intermind.com/`

A detailed discussion of hybrid CD-ROM and push technology as multimedia venues is beyond the scope of this book. The rest of this chapter focuses on delivery of multimedia in web browsers.

Multimedia in Web Browsers

Web browsers display multimedia content in three basic ways:

- ▶ Native inline

- ▶ Helper applications

- ▶ Inline via external code modules such as plug-ins, Java applets, or ActiveX controls

Native inline media can be displayed directly in the web page without any additional programs or viewers. All graphical browsers natively support .GIF graphics. Some natively support .JPEG graphics and other media types as well.

Until recently, helper applications were the standard way to view multimedia content on the web. Displaying non-native multimedia by using helper applications is compatible with nearly all browsers. Multimedia content is downloaded to the client hard disk and then displayed in a separate player application, such as MoviePlayer or PLAYER.EXE in the case of QuickTime video.

Inline display can be achieved with external code modules such as Netscape-compatible plug-ins or Java applets. These external "mini-programs" enable you to play back multimedia content directly on the web page. These features appeared in web browsers beginning with Netscape Navigator 2. Several multimedia plug-ins are automatically installed with Netscape Navigator 3.

In addition to displaying multimedia content, web browsers have evolved to the point where they can be used as multimedia authoring and integration tools in their own right, providing a consistent cross-platform interface to multimedia information.

The next section discusses the way in which browsers provide sophisticated multimedia playback, such as playing Shockwave movies within a web page, by using the Internet MIME protocol.

MIME

MIME stands for Multipurpose Internet Mail Extensions. It was originally developed to send multimedia content such as graphics, audio, and video via e-mail. MIME includes a standardized way to identify and characterize multimedia content. It has been integrated into the HTTP protocol (the main communications protocol used by web servers). Browsers use MIME to determine whether a file can be displayed as native or inline, or whether a plug-in or helper application must be called.

To serve Shockwave movies in a web browser, you must set up your web server to recognize the Shockwave MIME type. You can use the `NetMIME()` Lingo command to determine the MIME type of media on the Internet from within Director.

By the time you read this, you may be able to use the `APPLET` tag to embed Shockwave movies. Shockwave movies then play back on any Java-enabled browser. This feature uses the `SHOCKWAVEPLUGIN.CLASS` Java "wrapper" installed with Shockwave and eliminates the need for setting up MIME types. Visit Macromedia's web site for the latest updates on this feature.

MIME Types and Sub-Types

Every document, graphic, and multimedia file on the web can be characterized by a MIME type and sub-type. The MIME type `text` and sub-type `plain`, for example, indicate an ASCII text file. MIME types and sub-types are commonly written like so: `text/plain`. An HTML document has the MIME type and sub-type of `text/html`. A .GIF file has the type `image/gif`. Browsers and web servers use the MIME type and sub-type to determine the way to process multimedia data.

File Name Extensions

The most common way to distinguish computer files with different MIME types is to use standardized file name extensions. Each web server contains a large table that associates a particular file name extension with a particular MIME type. All HTML files on a particular server will have the .HTML extension, for example, and will be associated with MIME type `text/html`. Or, all .JPEG files on the server will have a file name extension of .JPG or .JPEG and be associated with the MIME type `image/jpeg`.

How Browsers Use MIME Types

When a browser requests a file named BANNER.GIF, for example, the web server looks up the file name extension in its MIME type table, determines that the file is a .GIF file, and then sends the MIME type information back to the browser. The browser then determines the appropriate action, such as displaying the .GIF inline or launching a helper application or plug-in.

All web browsers can display content of MIME type `text/plain` and `text/html`. In addition, most graphical browsers can display inline images of type `image/gif` —that is, images in .GIF format, and sometimes `image/jpeg` (images in .JPEG format).

Server Setup

Each web server must be set up to handle different MIME types. Multiple file name extensions can be associated with the same MIME type. Files with file name extensions of .QT and .MOV, for example, are commonly associated with the MIME type `video/quicktime`.

If you are serving multimedia content from a web site, you must make certain of the following:

▶ Your multimedia files have the correct file name extensions.

▶ The server has been set up to associate these extensions with a particular MIME type.

Most web authoring tools come with information about file name extensions and MIME types for their particular media type. Shockwave for Director files, for example, can have file name extensions of .DCR, .DXR, and .DIR and are associated with type `application/x-director`. Consult your web server documentation or web server administrator for information about configuring the web server for different MIME types.

Helper Applications

Helper applications (apps) are a way for web browsers to display or otherwise process MIME types and multimedia content that they cannot display natively.

To display a QuickTime video, for example, browsers don't need to include special display capabilities for viewing video. Instead they can launch a separate viewing application on the local client machine (see fig. 13.1). This separate application handles display of the video. Helper applications were developed as an extensible way to provide rich, multimedia content on the web without having to build viewing capabilities for myriad multimedia data types directly into the web browser. Helper applications are used less frequently today to provide multimedia content than they once were. Increasingly, inline display methods are replacing helper applications.

Figure 13.1

Helper application used in lieu of an inline plug-in.

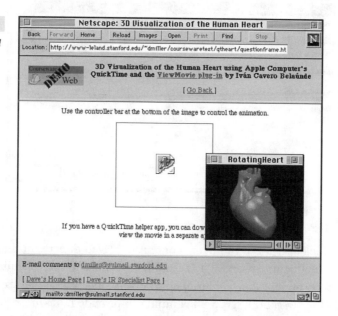

Drawbacks of Helper Applications

A drawback of helper applications is that media is displayed in a separate, disconnected window. No integration occurs between information in the page and the helper application. Also, users must have the appropriate helper application on their machines, configure their machines properly to use this application, and have the system resources to support a helper application.

Browser Setup

Browsers, using a MIME type association table, know which helper application to launch. This table is usually configured in a web browser preference setting (see fig. 13.2). Some settings in this table are preconfigured, but usually the user must manually associate a particular helper application with a particular MIME type. When a web server tells a Windows browser that data of type `video/quicktime` is coming down the wire, for example, the browser knows to launch the program PLAYER.EXE.

Figure 13.2

Setting up helper applications in Netscape.

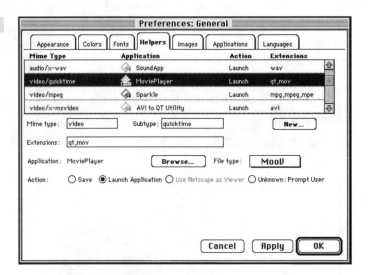

Inline Multimedia

Inline multimedia is multimedia content displayed directly in the web page along with the document text. The capability to display inline graphics as .GIF files has been present in graphical web browsers since 1993. Netscape Navigator and other web browsers are beginning to provide built-in or native support for other inline graphics and multimedia file types. With the release of Netscape Navigator 3, the Netscape web browser provides out-of-the-box support for several multimedia data types and has become a formidable media integration and multimedia authoring tool in its own right.

The first generation of inline multimedia is used in much the same way as inline .GIFs. The multimedia is displayed inline, in the web page, and the user often has the option of using standard controllers—such as Play and Pause buttons—to control playback. The second generation of inline multimedia is providing more sophisticated media integration and the sharing of information between multimedia elements, the HTML document, Java, JavaScript, the web server, and other resources on the web.

Plug-Ins

The Netscape plug-in architecture is one method of displaying inline multimedia content via external code modules. It enables developers to extend the functionality of the Netscape web browser (see fig. 13.3). Other major browsers such as MSIE (Microsoft Internet Explorer) also support Netscape plug-ins. Plug-ins enable the display of interactive animations, VRML (Virtual Reality Modeling Language) worlds, QuickTime media, Macromedia Director files, Authorware courses, FreeHand vector graphics, Adobe Acrobat digital documents, and many other data types.

Figure 13.3

Embedded QuickTime video using plug-ins.

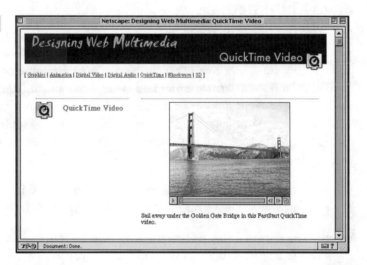

Plug-ins must be downloaded and installed by users. Future versions of Netscape Navigator will automatically download plug-ins as needed. Besides supporting standard .GIF, .GIF animation, and .JPEG image formats, Netscape Navigator 3 ships with several integrated plug-ins (so the user doesn't have to download or configure anything), providing out-of-the-box support for following inline media:

- ▶ QuickTime and QTVR media for Macs and Windows

- ▶ Video for Windows (AVI) on Windows machines

- ▶ AIFF, WAV, AU, digital audio, and MIDI sound

- ▶ Virtual Reality Modeling Language (VRML)

- ▶ Java applets

OLE/ActiveX

ActiveX is Microsoft's component software architecture for the web, and is based on OLE (Object Linking and Embedding). It is similar in spirit to Netscape plug-ins, and it can also be used in other software that supports ActiveX. The external OLE/ActiveX modules are called *controls*. OLE/ActiveX is natively supported in Windows 95 and Windows NT versions of MSIE 3, the browser by Microsoft. Netscape Navigator support is provided via a Netscape plug-in that plays the ActiveX control as if it were a plug-in.

Java Multimedia

Java is an object-oriented, cross-platform programming language developed by Sun Microsystems. Java is commonly touted as a way to add multimedia to web pages. At this time, however, other tools such as QuickTime, Shockwave, GIF animation, and so on, enable easier and faster development, higher-quality media, broader client support, and smaller file sizes than Java-based multimedia. This may change in the coming year with the addition of sophisticated multimedia features to Java, such as QuickTime integration and the maturation of Java development tools.

Java programs on the web, called *applets,* can be embedded in web pages just like plug-ins and ActiveX controls using the APPLET HTML tag.

By the time you read this, a Director Xtra may be available that enables you to embed Java applets in Shockwave movies. Also, you may be able to use QuickTime multimedia services within Java applets by using forthcoming tools from Apple Computer and Sun Microsystems.

Client-Side Scripting

Client-side scripting is a way for plug-ins, ActiveX controls, and Java applets to communicate with each other and with the run-time browser. Client-side scripting enables web authors to tightly integrate multimedia elements on a web page and provide features previously restricted to server-side scripts written in languages such as Perl or C. Features provided by client-side scripting include image maps, dynamic images, forms validation, testing of the user's machines for presence of plug-ins, and the capability to share data between plug-ins and Java applets.

JavaScript is the scripting language used by Netscape Navigator. Most, but not all, JavaScript features are supported in Microsoft Internet Explorer. VBScript is Microsoft's scripting language based on Visual Basic. It is only supported by MSIE.

HTML for Multimedia

This section provides an overview of the HTML tags that you use to embed multimedia objects in your web pages. This section shows you how to accomplish the following:

▶ Provide rich content such as sound and digital video with the HREF tag

▶ Use the IMG tag to provide inline graphics

▶ Use the EMBED tag to embed inline multimedia in Netscape Navigator 2 or later

▶ Use MSIE tags to embed inline multimedia

▶ Use these HTML tags so that your multimedia web pages load faster and can be viewed by both Navigator and MSIE

The EMBED tag is used by Netscape to embed multimedia elements that require Netscape plug-ins to display. Beginning with Netscape 3, many multimedia plug-ins are automatically installed with Navigator, eliminating your worries about users having the appropriate plug-ins. (See the previous section, "Plug-Ins," for a list of media types supported as of this writing.)

In addition to some overlap with Netscape tags, Microsoft Internet Explorer supports a different set of multimedia tags, which are supported in Microsoft Internet Explorer only. Microsoft's plug-in architecture, OLE/ActiveX, is only supported in MSIE for Windows 95 and Windows NT. Microsoft Internet Explorer 3 also supports most Netscape plug-ins. Tags that MSIE supports are discussed in a following section.

In addition to existing tags, the draft HTML 3.2 standard contains a new tag called the OBJECT tag. The OBJECT tag specs, current as of this writing, are described later in this chapter in the section entitled, "OBJECT Tag."

Table 13.2 lists browser support for multimedia tags:

Browser Support for Multimedia Tags

Feature	Netscape 2	MSIE 2	Netscape 3	MSIE 3
Plug-ins	Yes	Mac only*	Yes	Yes*
ActiveX	No	No	No	Windows 95/NT only
EMBED tag	Yes	Mac-only	Yes	Yes*
MSIE tags	No	Yes	No	Yes
OBJECT tag	No	No	No	Windows 95/NT only

Not all features were supported as of this writing. Be certain to test with the latest version.

HREF and Helper Applications

The simplest way to provide multimedia content on your site is to link to the content files by using the HREF tag. The HREF tag is compatible with most browsers, but requires the following:

▶ The user must have an appropriate helper application

▶ The user must configure the browser to use the helper application correctly

Clicking on a link initiates download of the media file. After the file has been completely downloaded, the browser automatically launches a helper application to display the media. Your browser knows which helper application to launch based on the file name extension of the data. If your browser is asked to display a file with the .MOV extension, it realizes that it is a QuickTime movie and automatically opens the file with SimpleText or PLAYER.EXE.

The following sample of HTML code creates a link to a QuickTime movie:

```
<A HREF="MyQTMovie.mov"> QuickTime movie </A>
```

"MyQTMovie.mov" is the path name to the QuickTime movie file on the web server. In this case, the QuickTime movie file is in the same directory as the HTML document. Note the .MOV extension on the file name. The file name of your media must have the appropriate extension for it to launch the helper application. Table 13.3 lists common file types and their file name extensions.

Table 13.3

File Types and Their File Name Extensions

File Type	Extension
plain text	.TXT
HTML document	.HTML
GIF image	.GIF
TIFF image	.TIFF
X Bitmap image	.XBM
JPEG image	.JPG or .JPEG
PostScript file	.PS
AIFF audio file	.AIFF
AU audio file	.AU
WAV audio file	.WAV
MIDI sound file	.MID
QuickTime movie	.MOV
MPEG movie	.MPEG or .MPG
VfW movie	.AVI
VRML	.WRL
Shockwave	.DCR

Configuring Helper Applications

As stated previously, to receive multimedia by using helper applications, the user must correctly set up the browser. To configure a helper application for QuickTime, for example, the user must tell the browser that files ending in .MOV and .QT have the MIME type VIDEO/QUICKTIME and should be launched by an appropriate QuickTime player application such as SimpleText, MoviePlayer, or PLAYER.EXE, depending on which system the user has.

Netscape Navigator comes configured for playing many types of multimedia content. Navigator 2 comes configured for many common helper applications, and Navigator 3 comes with several multimedia plug-ins. Browsers have different procedures to configure helper applications (refer to fig. 13.2). The following tutorial shows you how to set up a helper application for QuickTime content in Navigator 2. The process is similar in other browsers and for other multimedia types.

Configuring a Browser for a Helper Application

1. In Netscape, choose Options, General Preferences/Helpers.

2. Type the Mime type **video**.

3. Type the Mime sub-type **quicktime**.

4. Type the extension **.qt, mov**.

5. Set the Action to Launch Application.

6. Click on Browse, and select the application you want to use to display and play back QuickTime content, such as MoviePlayer or SimpleText on a Macintosh or PLAYER.EXE on Windows.

7. Close the Preferences panel of Netscape, close Netscape, then, restart Netscape.

Obtaining Helper Applications

You can find general information about helper applications at the following URL:

```
http://home.netscape.com/assist/helper_apps/index.html
```

Helper applications for Macintosh systems can be found at the following URLs:

Info-Mac HyperArchive
```
http://hyperarchive.lcs.mit.edu/HyperArchive.html
```

University of Michigan Archives
```
http://www-personal.umich.edu/~sdamask/umich-mirrors/
```

University of Texas Mac Archive
```
http://wwwhost.ots.utexas.edu/mac/
```

Netscape
```
http://home.netscape.com/assist/helper_apps/mac_helpers.html
```

Helper applications for Unix systems can be found at the following URLs:

NCSA
```
ftp://ftp.ncsa.uiuc.edu/Mosaic/Unix/viewers/
```

Netscape
```
http://home.netscape.com/assist/helper_apps/unix_helpers.html
```

Helper applications for Windows systems can be found at the following URLs:

Stroud's Consummate Winsock List

```
http://www.frontiernet.net/cwsapps/inx2.html
```

Netscape

```
http://home.netscape.com/assist/helper_apps/windows_helpers.html
```

IMG: HTML for Graphics

Graphics are the most common multimedia element on the web. Inline .GIFs were the first multimedia element supported in graphical browsers. .JPEGs and Progressive .JPEGs are supported by Netscape browsers and will probably be supported in other browsers in the future.

Inline graphics are embedded in HTML documents using the IMG tag. The IMG tag requires an SRC attribute that is an URL to the source graphic in quotes. The source graphic should have a file name with an appropriate extension such as .GIF. The graphic will be displayed "inline" or directly in the web page. The IMG tag is supported by all graphical browsers. The IMG tag also has many other attributes to control the appearance of the graphic. These attributes are discussed in the following sections.

The IMG tag is also used by Microsoft Internet Explorer to embed multimedia content. This use of the IMG tag is only recognized by Microsoft Internet Explorer. Microsoft Internet Explorer's use of the IMG tag to embed other types of multimedia is discussed in a separate section.

ALIGN

The ALIGN attribute of the IMG tag has three values:

- ▶ TOP
- ▶ MIDDLE
- ▶ BOTTOM

and is written as follows:

```
<IMG SRC="myGreatGraphic.gif" ALIGN = TOP>
```

This attribute aligns the current line of text to the top, middle, or bottom of the image. The default behavior is alignment to the bottom of the image.

ALT

The ALT attribute enables you to display alternate text if certain events such as the following occur:

▶ Browsers are text-only

▶ Images have been turned off

▶ Images can't load for some other reason

The ALT attribute is written as follows:

```
<IMG SRC="myGreatGraphic.gif" ALT= "You're missing my fabulous graphic!">
```

Include an ALT attribute with all your IMG tags so that users get an idea of what they are missing. The alternate text acts as a link if the image is also a link.

Image Maps

Clickable image maps are a common way to provide navigation on the web. Image maps can be implemented in two ways:

▶ Server-side image maps

▶ Client-side image maps

Server-side image maps require a special program on the server. Client-side image maps, on the other hand, can be created entirely within an HTML document and are processed on the client. Client-side image maps were introduced in Netscape 2 and are supported in the latest versions of Microsoft Internet Explorer. They may eventually be added to the evolving HTML standard.

Server-Side Image Maps

Server-side image maps use a program on the server to convert mouse-clicks to URLs. To implement a server-side image map you need the following three parts:

▶ A program on the server that translates the location of the mouse click into an URL and loads it into the browser. This program is typically called "imagemap" and is found in the cgi-bin directory.

▶ An image map graphic.

▶ A text-based map definition file that contains pixel coordinates of clickable regions on the graphic and the URLs that correspond to each clickable region.

The HTML for embedding a server-side image map typically looks something like the following:

```
<A HREF = "http://www.server.com/cgi-bin/imagemap/myImageMap.map"><IMG SRC=
➥"myImageMap.gif" BORDER=0 ISMAP></A>
```

in which:

▶ `myImageMap.gif` is the name of the image map graphic.

▶ `http://www.server.com/cgi-bin/imagemap` is the location of the image map program.

▶ `myImageMap.map` is the name of the text-based map definition file that contains coordinates of clickable regions and associated URLs.

▶ The `ISMAP` attribute tells the server the graphic is an image map.

Image maps are implemented differently depending on the server. Typically, the differences are in the path to the image map program (`http://www.server.com/cgi-bin/imagemap`, in this case) and the way to specify the location of the text-based map file. Check with your server documentation to see how server-side image maps are implemented on your system.

Client-Side Image Maps

Client-side image maps, in many ways, are easier to set up and implement than server-side image maps. You don't need special access to the server or a special server-based image map program. The processing of mouse clicks is performed by the browser. Another benefit of client-side image maps is that you can target frames that have URLs in client-side image maps. That is, an image map in one frame can change the content of another frame. At this time, only Netscape 2 and later versions support client-side image maps, but new versions of Microsoft Internet Explorer will support it, and client-side image maps may be added to the emerging HTML 3.2 standard.

You define the clickable regions or hotspots for the image map in an HTML document within the <MAP></MAP> tag. Usually, web authors embed this tag within the HTML document that contains the map, but it can be in any

HTML document that can be referenced with an URL. A sample HTML for the MAP tag that defines hotspots for a navigation image map follows:

```
<MAP NAME="navigation_map">
<AREA SHAPE="RECT" COORDS="0,0,30,76" HREF = "index.html">
<AREA SHAPE="RECT" COORDS="0,77,30,149" HREF = "dmdesign1.html">
<AREA SHAPE="RECT" COORDS="0,150,30,221" HREF = "webmedia1.html">
<AREA SHAPE="RECT" COORDS="0,222,30,294" HREF = "sciedu1.html">
<AREA SHAPE="RECT" COORDS="0,295,30,370" HREF = "mus1.html">
</MAP>
```

If your hotspots are all rectangular, you can omit the SHAPE="RECT" attribute, which is the default. You can also have circular hotspots by using the CIRCLE attributes. Circles are defined by three numbers that specify the horizontal and vertical coordinates of the center of the circle and its radius in pixels. You can also specify arbitrary polygonal hotspots by using the POLY attribute, in which coordinates are vertices of the polygon.

You turn an image into a client-side image map by adding the USEMAP attribute to an IMG tag. The value of the USEMAP is an URL or anchor to the HTML document that contains a map hotspot definition within the <MAP></MAP> tags. You reference the map definition with the value of the NAME attribute that you specified in the MAP tag. In the preceding example, the name is "navigation_map". To reference a map definition in the same file as the image map, prepend the name with a "#". For example, this HTML:

```
<IMG SRC="../images/maps/map1.gif" USEMAP="#navigation_map">
```

references the map definition named "#navigation_map" contained within <MAP></MAP> tags within the same HTML file as the image map.

NOTE

You should review Netscape's documentation on client-side image maps and other Navigator HTML extensions. You can find documentation at http:// home.netscape.com/assist/net_sites/html_extensions_3.html.

You can also mix tags for client-side and server-side image maps, as in the following example:

```
<A HREF = "/cgi-bin/imagemap/myMapDefinitionFile.map"><IMG SRC=
➡"myImageMap.gif" USEMAP = "#navigation_map" ISMAP></A>
```

If a browser supports client-side image maps, the client-side map runs. If a browser doesn't support client-side image maps, the browser ignores those tags and the server-side version runs.

Drawbacks of Image Maps

Clickable image maps tend to be overused on the web. Image maps are useful for real maps, such as the map of a city showing locations of different tourist attractions. These tourist attractions can then be clickable links to pages about the attraction. Another use might be for complex, two-dimensional information distributions (such as an organizational chart). Clickable image maps have many drawbacks, including the following:

▶ Large image maps can take a long time to download.

▶ Unlike hypertext navigation, image maps do not provide feedback on which sites have been visited and which links are active.

▶ Users may have images turned off. If they do, and only image maps are available for navigation, users won't be able to navigate anywhere. To prevent this, be certain to provide alternate, text-based navigation.

▶ The performance of server-side image maps is dependent on the server load and how fast the server can run the map script. On busy or slow servers, map processing can be slow. Also, different implementations of image maps means server-side image maps are not portable to other servers. In contrast, client-side image maps are processed by the browser, don't require server intervention, and are portable.

Faking Image Maps with Tables

You can fake an image map by embedding graphics in HTML table cells and making them clickable by adding an HREF tag. In some cases, a few small graphics may load faster than one large graphic. Following is sample HTML:

```
<TABLE BORDER = 0 CELLPADDING = 0 CELLSPACING = 0>
<TR>
<TD><A HREF = "home.html"><IMG WIDTH=150 HEIGHT=67 BORDER = 0 SRC =
➥"home.gif" ALT = ""></A>
</TD>
<TD><A HREF = "section.html"><IMG WIDTH=150 HEIGHT=67 BORDER = 0 SRC =
➥"section.gif" ALT = ""></A></TD>
<TD><A HREF = "where.html"><IMG WIDTH=150 HEIGHT=67 BORDER = 0 SRC =
➥"location.gif" ALT = ""></A>
</TD>
```

```
<TD><A HREF = "whatsnew.html"><IMG WIDTH=150 HEIGHT=67 BORDER = 0 SRC =
➡"new.gif" ALT = ""></A>
</TD>
</TR>
</table>
```

This HTML creates a table in which the table cells are completely filled with a clickable graphic. Make certain that the BORDER, CELLPADDING, and CELLSPACING attributes are all set to 0 so that no spaces show between your graphics.

Netscape Navigator Extensions to the IMG Tag

This section describes Netscape extensions to the IMG tag that are supported in Navigator 2 or later. Many of these are so useful that they have been supported by other browsers and may be adopted in the next HTML standard.

LOWSRC

The LOWSRC attribute enables you to specify another graphic file that downloads first and displays before the graphic file that is specified in the SRC attribute. You can use LOWSRC to download a low-resolution, low color-depth version of your SRC file that will download and display quickly. As the main SRC graphic downloads, it is displayed over the LOWSRC graphic. LOWSRC is commonly used to display a 1-bit, black-and-white version of a larger color graphic. The 1-bit graphic downloads fast and then the color graphic is displayed. The overall impression is of a snappy download with the color graphic being poured into the black-and-white version. You can also use the LOWSRC attribute to perform simple two-frame animation. The LOWSRC graphic is not displayed if the SRC graphic is in the disk or memory cache. If a user visits your site twice in a session, therefore, the LOWSRC graphic probably does not display the second time.

HTML for the LOWSRC attribute looks like this:

```
<IMG LOWSRC = "myTeenyGraphic.gif" SRC="myGreatGraphic.gif" ALT= "Logo
➡Graphic">
```

WIDTH and HEIGHT

The WIDTH and HEIGHT attributes specify the dimensions of your graphic or embedded multimedia element. They are used by Netscape 2 and Microsoft Internet Explorer 3 and later to lay out text around an image before the image is downloaded. HTML for WIDTH and HEIGHT is written as follows:

```
<IMG SRC="myGreatGraphic.gif" ALT= "Logo Graphic"  WIDTH = 160 HEIGHT = 120>
```

Use WIDTH and HEIGHT attributes to speed the download of the text on your web page and to help give the impression of snappy response time. Early versions of Netscape plug-ins required these attributes in all graphics and multimedia elements for the plug-in to work properly.

You can use the WIDTH and HEIGHT attributes to scale an image, but you can get better results scaling images in a graphics program. You can also give the HEIGHT and WIDTH as percentage values of the browser window, but browsers other than Netscape Navigator, such as Microsoft Internet Explorer, interpret these as pixel values.

BORDER

The BORDER attribute enables you to put a simple black border or frame around a graphic. If you use a graphic in conjunction with the HREF tag, you can turn off the border by setting the BORDER = 0. An example of this follows:

```
<A HREF = "anotherwebPage.html"><IMG SRC="myLink.gif" ALT= "A link somewhere
➥else" BORDER = 0></A>
```

Alignment Extensions

Netscape has introduced several alignment extensions for inline graphics. Probably the most useful of these are the following:

▶ ALIGN=LEFT

▶ ALIGN=RIGHT

▶ HSPACE

▶ VSPACE

The ALIGN=LEFT and ALIGN=RIGHT values align a graphic to the left or right margins of the page, respectively. You can use the HSPACE and VSPACE attributes to control the white space around a graphic. For example:

```
<IMG SRC="myGreat.gif" ALT= "A really great graphic" ALIGN = RIGHT HSPACE =
➥16>
```

aligns the graphic to the right edge of the web page and gives 16 pixels of horizontal, space around the graphic before text is displayed.

Netscape has also introduced the following new values for the ALIGN attribute:

▶ **ALIGN = ABSBOTTOM:** Aligns the bottom of the graphic with the bottom of the line

▶ **ALIGN = ABSMIDDLE:** Aligns the middle of the graphic with the middle of the line

▶ **ALIGN = TEXTTOP:** Aligns the graphic with the top of the text

HTML for Netscape Plug-Ins

Much of the inline multimedia content on the web is implemented with Netscape plug-ins. One drawback of using plug-ins is that users must download the appropriate plug-in and place it in Navigator's Plug-ins folder before they can view multimedia content. Fortunately, several plug-ins are automatically installed with Netscape Navigator 3, as listed earlier in this chapter.

Beginning with Netscape Communicator 4 and Microsoft Internet Explorer 4, Shockwave will also be bundled with browsers and will be part of the standard install.

LiveConnect is Netscape's term for the integration of plug-ins, Java applets, JavaScript functions, and your web page. LiveConnect enables the creation of more dynamic, interactive web pages. You can use a JavaScript function, for example, to set the start frame of an embedded video based on user input at run time. Netscape plug-ins need to be rewritten to support the LiveConnect features. Several of the plug-ins included with Netscape Navigator 3 are LiveConnect-enabled. Shockwave for Director 6 provides extensive support for LiveConnect.

EMBED

To embed plug-in media in a web page, use the EMBED tag. Netscape Navigator 2 and later recognizes this tag. Following is sample HTML:

```
<EMBED SRC="mymovie.dcr" WIDTH=175 HEIGHT=135 >
```

The value of the SRC attribute is the URL to the media element, similar to the SRC tag for IMG (graphic) elements. Be certain that the file name in your SRC tag has the appropriate file name extension for the media type. In this example, the extension .DCR indicates a Shockwave animation.

Microsoft Internet Explorer 2 for Windows does not support the EMBED tag or Netscape plug-ins. Microsoft Internet Explorer 2 for Macintosh, however, does support the EMBED tag and displays most Netscape plug-ins—although some features may not be supported, such as network extensions to Shockwave.

Microsoft Internet Explorer 3 for both Mac and Windows supports most Netscape plug-ins and the EMBED tag.

WIDTH and HEIGHT for Multimedia

The WIDTH and HEIGHT attributes are used in very much the same way for multimedia as for graphics. They are the dimensions of your embedded multimedia element and are used by Netscape 2 and later versions to lay out text around an embedded element before that element is downloaded. An example of how to use these attributes follows:

```
<EMBED SRC="myQuickTimeMovie.mov" WIDTH = 160 HEIGHT = 120>
```

As mentioned earlier, using the WIDTH and HEIGHT attributes is a great way to speed download of the text on your web page in browsers that support it. Remember that some Netscape plug-ins require these attributes in all graphics and multimedia elements for them to be drawn properly within the page.

PLUGINSPAGE

Include the PLUGINSPAGE parameter for users who may not have the necessary plug-in installed. The PLUGINSPAGE parameter directs web browsers without the necessary plug-in to a web page where they can download the appropriate plug-in. The value of the PLUGINSPAGE parameter is a fully qualified URL, in quotes, in which the user can download the appropriate plug-in. Following is sample HTML code:

```
<EMBED SRC="myQT.mov" HEIGHT=144 WIDTH=160 PLUGINSPAGE = "http://
➥quicktime.apple.com/qt/sw/sw.html" >
```

NOEMBED

Unfortunately, the ALT attribute does not work with the EMBED tag as of this writing. To provide alternate content in browsers that do not recognize the EMBED tag, such as Microsoft Internet Explorer 2 on Windows, use the NOEMBED tag.

Microsoft Internet Explorer 3 supports some Netscape plug-ins. In some cases, when Microsoft Internet Explorer encounters a web page with an EMBED tag, it displays a gray rectangle in place of the multimedia element referenced by the

EMBED tag. Microsoft Internet Explorer 3 does not load the necessary Netscape plug-in, but instead prompts the user to download an alternate ActiveX control.

Providing Alternate Content

Even though Navigator is still the most popular browser, not all your audience will be using it, and those who are using it may not have multimedia plug-ins installed on their machines.

To provide alternate multimedia content for these users, follow these guidelines:

▶ For browsers that don't support the EMBED tag, use the NOEMBED tag to provide alternate content.

▶ Always use the PLUGINSPAGE parameter of the EMBED tag to point users to an URL where they can download the appropriate plug-in.

▶ For users who have helper applications correctly configured, provide a link to your movie with the HREF tag.

Following is sample HTML code that implements all these suggestions. This example uses QuickTime multimedia content, but this technique works for other multimedia data types that use Netscape plug-ins.

```
<EMBED SRC="MyQT.mov" HEIGHT=144 WIDTH=160 PLUGINSPAGE = "http://
➥quicktime.apple.com/qt/sw/sw.html"> <NOEMBED>
<IMG SRC="MyQTFrame.gif" HEIGHT=120 WIDTH=160>
```

If you do not have the QuickTime plug-in, but have a QuickTime helper application, click on the following link to view the QuickTime movie.

```
</NOEMBED>
```

View the <A HREF="MyQT.mov"> QuickTime movie </A> if you have your browser set up with the correct helper application.

Browsers that don't support the EMBED tag display the file MYQTFRAME.GIF and also enable the user to view the original QuickTime file if they have a helper application. In browsers that *do* support the EMBED tag, but in which the user lacks a plug-in to play QuickTime, the user can still see the content by using a helper application.

Microsoft Internet Explorer 2 and later versions use the DYNSRC attribute with the IMG tag to embed AVI movies and VRML worlds in a web page. Following is sample HTML that implements alternate content for Microsoft Internet Explorer 2 for Windows. This example uses QuickTime multimedia content, but the technique also works for other multimedia data types that use Netscape plug-ins.

```
<EMBED SRC="MyQT.mov" HEIGHT=144 WIDTH=160 PLUGINSPAGE = "http://
➥quicktime.apple.com/qt/sw/sw.html">
<NOEMBED>
<IMG SRC="MyQTFrame.gif"  DYNSRC = "MyQT.avi" HEIGHT=120 WIDTH=160>
```

If you do not have the QuickTime plug-in, but have a QuickTime helper application, click on the following link to view the movie:

```
</NOEMBED>
```

You can also view the original `<A HREF="MyQT.mov">` `QuickTime movie` `</A>` if you have your browser set up with the correct helper application.

On Windows versions of Microsoft Internet Explorer 2, this HTML plays an alternate AVI movie and enables users to view the original QuickTime file if they have a helper application. Other browsers that don't support the EMBED and don't support the Microsoft DYNSRC tag display the file MYQTFRAME.GIF and also enable the user to view the original QuickTime file if they have a helper application.

On the Macintosh version of Microsoft Internet Explorer 2, the browser attempts to load the appropriate Netscape plug-in, if present. Otherwise, it shows an error message. The user can click on the link `<A HREF="MyQT.mov">` `QuickTime movie` `</A>`, and Microsoft Internet Explorer 2 and later versions download the QuickTime file and play it in a separate, floating window without the need of a helper application. Other media types are played or viewed by helper applications if the browser has been configured correctly.

The section, "Multimedia Extensions for Microsoft Internet Explorer," in this chapter provides more detail on the multimedia tags used by Microsoft's browsers.

Netscape, OLE, and the EMBED Tag

On Windows 95 and Windows NT systems, if a plug-in is not present to handle the media type encountered in the EMBED tag, Netscape 2 and later versions play multimedia as an embedded OLE object within the browser page. Navigator uses OLE associations set up in the Windows 95 file type association registry.

Editing the File Associations for OLE

1. Launch Windows Explorer.

2. Choose View, Options.

3. Click on File Types.

4. To add a new type, click on the New Type... button.

5. To edit an existing type, select a registered file type and click on the Edit... button.

The OLE object is displayed within the dimensions specified in the WIDTH and HEIGHT attributes of the EMBED tag. If the application used to display the object has a controller, such as MPLAYER.EXE for AVI files, the media is scaled to make room for the controller. If playback of media as an OLE object is a possibility, test your page to see whether unpredictable interactions or behaviors occur. This is mainly an issue with Navigator 2, because Navigator 3 has built-in support for the most popular multimedia types.

Using OLE/ActiveX Controls in Netscape

OLE/ActiveX controls are alternate ways to embed multimedia content in web pages. At this time, the only browser that supports OLE/ActiveX controls natively is Microsoft Internet Explorer 3 for Windows 95 and Windows NT. Other platforms and browsers may be supported by the time you read this.

Although Netscape Navigator does not natively support OLE/ActiveX controls, you can add OLE/ActiveX capabilities to Navigator 2 and later versions by using a Netscape plug-in with the EMBED tag.

Two plug-ins, NCompass from NCompass Labs and OpenScape from OneWave Inc., enable you to embed OLE/ActiveX controls. To find the latest information on these plug-ins, check out the following addresses:

NCompass

http://www.ncompasslabs.com/

OnWave Inc.

http://www.busweb.com/

Multimedia Extensions for Microsoft Internet Explorer

Microsoft Internet Explorer for Windows 2 and later versions use the IMG tag and BGSOUND tag to embed multimedia elements in an HTML document. These tags are only recognized by Microsoft browsers.

In Microsoft Internet Explorer 3 for Windows 95 and Windows NT, OLE/ActiveX controls are embedded in HTML documents by using the OBJECT tag. Using the OBJECT tag to embed OLE/ActiveX controls is discussed in the next section.

To embed Video for Windows (AVI) files or VRML worlds in an HTML document for the Microsoft Internet Explorer browsers, use the DYNSRC attribute on Windows systems.

The following sample shows how the DYNSRC attribute is used:

```
<IMG SRC="MyMovieFrame.gif"  DYNSRC = "MyMovie.avi" HEIGHT=120 WIDTH=160>
```

The BGSOUND tag can be used to embed WAV and MIDI files in an HTML page that will be played back on Microsoft browsers. The syntax is as follows:

```
<BGSOUND SRC="MyTune.mid"  >
```

Note that Microsoft Internet Explorer 2 for Windows does not recognize the EMBED tag or Netscape plug-ins. However, Microsoft Internet Explorer 2 for Macintosh *does* recognize the EMBED tag and *does* display most Netscape plug-ins. Some features of individual plug-ins may not be supported, however, such as network extensions to Shockwave.

Microsoft Internet Explorer 3 supports most Netscape plug-ins and recognizes the EMBED tag.

Embedding OLE/ActiveX Controls

OLE/ActiveX controls are similar to Netscape plug-ins and perform similar functions within Microsoft Internet Explorer. In addition, they can be used in other applications that support OLE technology. Currently, OLE/ActiveX components are only supported in Microsoft Internet Explorer 3 for Windows 95 and Windows NT. Other platforms may be supported by the time you read this.

Several ActiveX controls are included in Microsoft Internet Explorer 3 for Windows 95:

- ▶ Chart
- ▶ Label
- ▶ New Item
- ▶ Preloader
- ▶ Timer

OLE/ActiveX controls are embedded in HTML documents by using the OBJECT tag. Here is an example of using the OBJECT tag to embed an OLE/ActiveX control:

```
<OBJECT
ID=clock1
CLASSID="clsid:663C8FEF-1EF9-11CF-A3DB-080036F12502"
DATA="http://www.company.com/ole/activex/clock.stm">
<IMG SRC=clock.gif ALT="A clock">
</OBJECT>
```

The CLASSID attribute uses the clsid:URL scheme to specify the ActiveX class identifier. See the documentation for your ActiveX control to see how to implement this attribute. The IMG tag provides alternate content in case the user does not have ActiveX display capabilities. You can also use the EMBED tag within the OBJECT tag to provide content for Netscape plug-ins and ActiveX controls. The following code uses the EMBED tag within the OBJECT tag:

```
<OBJECT
ID=clock1
CLASSID="clsid:663C8FEF-1EF9-11CF-A3DB-080036F12502"
DATA="http://www.company.com/ole/activex/clock.stm">
<EMBED SRC="MyClockQT.mov" HEIGHT=144 WIDTH=160 PLUGINSPAGE = "http://
➥quicktime.apple.com/qt/sw/sw.html">
</OBJECT>
```

Be certain to test this HTML in your target browsers to make sure both EMBED and OBJECT tags are displayed correctly.

For all the latest information on authoring for Microsoft browsers visit:

http://www.microsoft.com/workshop/

Embedding Java Applets

Java programs are called *applets*. You embed Java applets in an HTML page by using the <APPLET></APPLET> tag. The APPLET tag takes the following required attributes:

▶ CODE is the file name of the applet.

▶ WIDTH and HEIGHT are the dimensions of the applet in pixels.

Sample HTML looks like this:

```
<APPLET CODE  = myJavaApplet.class WIDTH = 160 HEIGHT=120></APPLET>
```

The following attributes are optional:

▶ CODEBASE is the path name to the applet specified in the CODE attribute.

▶ ALIGN takes values of TOP, MIDDLE, and BOTTOM and aligns text similar to the IMG tag.

▶ ALT enables you to provide alternate text if the user does not have a Java-enabled browser or if he has disabled Java.

The <PARAM> tag is used to pass applet-specific parameters to the Java applet. It is used as follows:

```
<APPLET CODE  = myJavaAnimationApplet.class WIDTH = 160 HEIGHT=120>
<PARAM NAME=frame VALUE = "animationFrame1.gif">
</APPLET>
```

To provide alternate content for users who do not have a Java-enabled browser or have disabled Java, you can use the ALT attribute. You can also put alternate HTML code within the APPLET tag, as follows:

```
<APPLET CODE  = myJavaAnimationApplet.class CODEBASE = WIDTH = 160
➥HEIGHT=120>
```

```
<PARAM NAME=frame VALUE = "animationFrame1.gif">
<H3>This page contains a Java-based animation.</H3>
You need a <A HREF http://www.javasoft.com>Java</A>-enabled browser to view
➥this animation.
</APPLET>
```

INSIDER TIP

> To find out the latest about Java, check out this site:
>
> `http://www.javasoft.com/`

By the time you read this you may be able to use the APPLET tag to embed Shockwave movies. Shockwave movies will then play back on any Java-enabled browser. This feature uses the SHOCKWAVEPLUGIN.CLASS Java "wrapper" installed with Shockwave and eliminates the need for setting up MIME types.

OBJECT Tag

The OBJECT tag is a new HTML tag proposed by the World Wide Web Consortium (W3 Consortium), a non-profit group formed to establish standards for the web. The OBJECT tag is proposed as a way to standardize the embedding of multimedia content in web pages. At the time of this writing, the OBJECT tag was only supported in Microsoft Internet Explorer 3 for Windows 95 and Windows NT for the embedding of OLE/ActiveX controls.

Following is an example of the proposed OBJECT tag syntax for embedding a Shockwave movie:

```
<OBJECT DATA=myShockwave.dcr
TYPE="application/x-director"
WIDTH=288 HEIGHT=200>
<IMG SRC=myShockwave.gif ALT="A cool Shockwave movie">
</OBJECT>
```

The IMG tag provides alternate content in case the user does not have Shockwave display capabilities.

To find out the latest about the OBJECT tag, visit:

`http://www.w3.org/pub/WWW/TR/WD-object#object`

To find out about the evolving HTML 3.2 specs, visit:

`http://www.w3.org/`

Using OBJECT and EMBED Together

The following HTML shows how to support multiple browsers. This syntax displays your Shockwave movie in Netscape 2.x or 3.x, or Microsoft Internet Explorer 3 on most platforms and provides alternate content for browsers that do not support these tags:

```
<OBJECT ID="ShockwaveMovie"
CLASSID="CLSID:166B1BCA-3F9C-11CF-8075-444553540000"
CODEBASE="http://www.macromedia.com/..."
WIDTH=160 HEIGHT=120
    >
<PARAM NAME="swURL" VALUE="myShockwaveMovie.dcr">
<EMBED SRC="myShockwaveMovie.dcr"  PLUGINSPAGE = "http://www.macromedia.com/"
➥WIDTH=160 HEIGHT=120>
</EMBED>
<NOEMBED>
<IMG SRC="NoShock.gif" ALT="Get the Shockwave plugin to see this cool
➥animation" WIDTH=160 HEIGHT=120 ALT="A Shockwave Movie">
</NOEMBED>
</OBJECT>
```

The following code enables you to display a Java applet if the Shockwave plug-in or ActiveX control is not present.

```
<OBJECT ID="ShockwaveMovie"
CLASSID="CLSID:166B1BCA-3F9C-11B -7·w5-444553540000"
CODEBASE="http://www.macromedia.com/..."
WIDTH=160 HEIGHT=120
   >
<PARAM NAME="swURL" VALUE="myShockwaveMovie.dcr">
<EMBED SRC="myShockwaveMovie.dcr"
WIDTH=160 HEIGHT=120  PLUGINSPAGE = "http://www.macromedia.com/">
</EMBED>
<NOEMBED>
<IMG SRC="NoShock.gif" ALT="Get the Shockwave plugin to see this cool
➥animation" WIDTH=160 HEIGHT=120>
</NOEMBED>
<APPLET CODE="AnimationApplet"
WIDTH=160 HEIGHT=120>
<IMG SRC="NoApplet.gif" ALT="A Java applet"
WIDTH=160 HEIGHT=120>
</APPLET>
</OBJECT>
```

Client-Side Scripting

One of the most exciting new features incorporated in Navigator 3 and Microsoft Internet Explorer 3 is the addition of client-side scripting capabilities. Client-side scripting is implemented with JavaScript on Navigator 2, Navigator 3 for Mac and Windows, and Microsoft Internet Explorer 3 for Windows, and with VBScript (Visual Basic Script) on Microsoft Internet Explorer 3 (see Table 13.4). Client-side scripting enables you to create dynamic documents, enhance interactivity, perform forms validation, and share information between plug-ins, applets, and other page elements. In general, client-side scripting enables you to perform operations that previously were restricted to scripts and programs written in programming languages such as Perl and C that resided on servers. Shockwave for Director 6 is tightly integrated with the browser scripting environment in both Netscape Navigator 3 and Microsoft Internet Explorer 3.

Table 13.4

Client-Side Scripting Support

	Navigator 2	Navigator 3	MSIE2	MSIE 3
JavaScript	Yes	Yes	No	Yes*
VBScript	No	No	No	Yes

Windows only

You embed scripts directly in an HTML document by using the <SCRIPT></SCRIPT> tag, as follows:

```
<SCRIPT LANGUAGE = "JavaScript"
<!-- Your script goes here-->
</SCRIPT>
```

For more information on JavaScript, visit the following URLs:

```
http://home.netscape.com/eng/mozilla/2.0/handbook/javascript/
index.html
```

```
http://home.netscape.com/eng/mozilla/3.0/handbook/javascript/
index.html
```

```
http://home.netscape.com/comprod/products/navigator/version_2.0/
script/script_info/index.html
```

```
http://www.gamelan.com/
```

For more information on VBScript, visit:

```
http://www.microsoft.com/workshop/
```

Shockwave for Director 6, discussed in detail in Chapters 14 and 15, has extensive support for client-side scripting in Navigator and Microsoft Internet Explorer.

Dynamic Graphics Using JavaScript 1.1

JavaScript is an "object-oriented" scripting language, similar to the Parent/ Child objects in Lingo. It is beyond the scope of this section to discuss the object model of JavaScript in detail. (See the book *Web Multimedia Development* for a description of JavaScript's object model and Chapter 20 of this book, "Object-Oriented Programming in Director," for a description of the Lingo object model.) This chapter just briefly examines sample code.

The version of JavaScript implemented in Netscape Navigator 3 is version 1.1. A new object added to JavaScript 1.1 is the image object. image objects contain the characteristics of graphics referenced by the IMG tag in an HTML document. image objects are properties of the document object. You can refer to them by using the dot syntax (document.myImage, for example).

Images have several properties. Some properties you are already familiar with as attributes to the IMG tag, such as SRC, HEIGHT, and WIDTH. For image objects, you access these properties with the dot syntax (document.myImage.src, for example). New properties have also been defined for image objects. New properties are specified in custom attributes of the IMG tag. You can use the image object to create JavaSript animations (see fig. 13.4).

Figure 13.4

JavaScript animation.

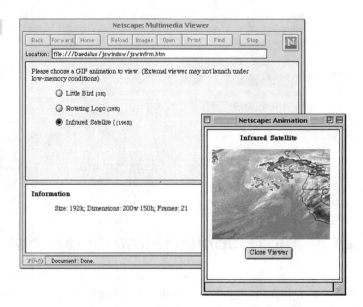

The following sample HTML code has new custom attributes:

```
<IMG NAME="dynamicImage" SRC="image0.gif" WIDTH = 119 HEIGHT = 68
ALT="Dynamic Gif" onLoad="setTimeout('changeGif()', secondsToWait)">
```

The custom attribute NAME is the name of the image. You can use this name to refer to the image from other JavaScript statements ("*document*.dynamicImage", for example). Images can also have event handlers. The preceding example shows an onLoad event handler that executes when the image loads in the browser window.

The following tutorial outlines how to create a "dynamic billboard" by using the new image object.

Creating a Dynamic Billboard with JavaScript

1. Put this script within the HEAD tag of your document:

```
<SCRIPT LANGUAGE = "JavaScript">
var secondsToWait = 1000*1   //number of milliseconds between changes
var imageNum = 1     //index number of first image
var imageMax = 3     //number of images
// Create an array and load it with images
myImages = new Array()
```

```
for(i = 1; i < (imageMax + 1); i++) {
myImages[i] = new Image()
myImages[i].src = "image" + i + ".gif"
    }
// Function that changes images
function changeGif() {
document.dynamicImage.src = myImages[imageNum].src
imageNum++
if(imageNum > imageMax) {
imageNum = 1
    }
}
</SCRIPT>
```

The function changeGif *changes the graphic named* dynamicImage *after the time specified in* secondsToWait *has passed.*

Next you want to customize the function changeGif.

2. To add your own graphics, the graphics must be named like this:

   image1.gif

   image2.gif

   up to the number specified in imageMax. The graphics must be in the same directory as the HTML document that contains this script.

3. In this example, images are displayed for one second, and then changed. To change the number of seconds that each image is displayed, change the *secondsToWait* variable. To have each graphic display for 30 seconds, for example, type:

```
var secondsToWait = 1000*30   //number of milliseconds between changes
```

4. To change the number of graphics that display, change the *imageMax* variable to the total number of images.

5. To create a dynamic image in the HTML document, set the onLoad event handler of that image to setTimeout('changeGif()', *secondsToWait*).

   The function setTimeout *is a built-in JavaScript function. The* setTimeout *function calls the* changeGif *function after* secondsToWait *seconds have passed. This function is reset every time you load a new image.*

A complete HTML listing follows.

```
<HTML>
<HEAD>
<TITLE>Dynamic Graphics with JavaScript</TITLE>
<SCRIPT LANGUAGE = "JavaScript">
var secondsToWait = 1000*1  //number of seconds between changes
var imageNum = 1     //index number of first image
var imageMax = 3     //number of images
// Create an array and load it with images
myImages = new Array()
for(i = 1; i < (imageMax + 1); i++) {
myImages[i] = new Image()
myImages[i].src = "image" + i + ".gif"
    }
// Function that changes images
function changeGif() {
document.dynamicImage.src = myImages[imageNum].src
imageNum++
if(imageNum > imageMax) {
imageNum = 1
   }
}
</SCRIPT>
</HEAD>
<BODY BGCOLOR="ffffe0">
<CENTER>
<TABLE>
<TR>
<TD BGCOLOR = "3399ff">
<FONT COLOR = "ffffe0" SIZE = +2> Dynamic Graphics Using JavaScript</Font>
</TD>
</TR>
</TABLE>
<P>
<IMG NAME="dynamicImage" SRC="image0.gif" WIDTH = 119 HEIGHT = 68
ALT="Dynamic Gif" onLoad="setTimeout('changeGif()', secondsToWait)">
<P>
This graphic changes every second.
</CENTER>
</BODY>
</BODY>
</HTML>
```

Scripting Navigator Plug-Ins

LiveConnect is Netscape's name for its client-side scripting environment that enables you to integrate and communicate with Java applets, JavaScript, and Navigator plug-ins. You can control plug-ins and applets from JavaScript, for example, or enable Java applets to access data in a plug-in.

As of this writing, much of the LiveConnect functionality has just been incorporated in the Navigator browser, and most plug-ins and Java applets must be recompiled to take advantage of LiveConnect. Shockwave for Director 6 has extensive support for LiveConnect features.

For the latest information, visit these sites:

```
http://home.netscape.com/comprod/products/navigator/version_3.0/
connect/
```

```
http://home.netscape.com/eng/mozilla/3.0/handbook/plugins/index.html
```

```
http://home.netscape.com/eng/mozilla/3.0/handbook/javascript/
index.html?moja
```

To view a showcase of LiveConnect-enabled applications, visit:

```
http://home.netscape.com/comprod/products/navigator/version_3.0/
connect/lc-showcase.html
```

To find out the latest about the LiveConnect implementation in Netscape Navigator's bundled plug-ins, check out:

```
http://home.netscape.com/comprod/products/navigator/version_3.0/
developer/mojava.html
```

```
http://home.netscape.com/comprod/products/navigator/version_3.0/
developer/newplug.html
```

LiveConnect and JavaScript

To use LiveConnect in conjunction with JavaScript to script, the plug-in must be programmed using the LiveConnect application programming interfaces. Netscape's bundled plug-ins, LiveAudio, LiveVideo, and Live3D, are LiveConnect-enabled, as is Shockwave for Director 6. The following are LiveConnect-enabled plug-ins:

Shockwave for Director 6
```
http://www.macromedia.com/
```

Flash 1.1: Interactive Animation Viewer
```
http://www.macromedia.com/
```

Tumbleweed Envoy Plug-In: Digital Document Viewer
```
http://www.tumbleweed.com/
```

Jamba: Java Development
```
http://www.aimtech.com/
```

Koan: Audio Player
```
http://www.sseyo.com/
```

mBed: Multimedia Viewer
```
http://www.mbed.com/
```

PointPlus: PowerPoint Presentation Viewer
```
http://www.net-scene.com/
```

The second requirement for LiveConnect to work in conjunction with JavaScript is that Java and JavaScript must both be enabled under Options, Network Preferences, Languages preferences settings.

LiveConnect-enabled plug-ins have a custom NAME attribute specified in the EMBED tag. For example:

```
<EMBED SRC="hello.aif" NAME="greetings" AUTOSTART = TRUE>
```

You can then reference this embedded media type from JavaScript by its NAME attribute, for example:

```
document.greetings.play()
```

You can also reference plug-ins from JavaScript by using the new embeds array object. The plug-in for the first EMBED tag in a document is referenced as document.embeds[0], the second as document.embeds[1], and so on.

Some plug-ins enable you to create special functions called *callbacks*, which are similar to event handlers. See the documentation for each plug-in for details on how to use callbacks.

As of this writing, many LiveConnect features were not available. Visit the previously mentioned Netscape web sites for the latest information.

The following section shows how to use LiveConnect with LiveAudio, and Chapters 14 and 15 discuss using the LiveConnect features of Shockwave.

Using LiveConnect to Fade Background Audio

The following code uses LiveConnect commands to fade a LiveAudio background sound after a specific length of time by using the JavaScript setTimeOut function:

```
""<HTML>
<HEAD>
<TITLE>Fading Out LiveAudio Background Sounds</TITLE>
</HEAD>
<BODY>
<EMBED SRC="hum.aif" NAME=greetings AUTOSTART = TRUE HIDDEN=TRUE>
<SCRIPT LANGUAGE = "JavaScript">
window.setTimeout('document. embeds["greetings"].fade_from_to(100,0)',1000)
</SCRIPT>
</BODY>
</HTML>
```

The HTML code within the EMBED tag embeds an AIFF audio file in a web page. Following are LiveAudio attributes to the EMBED tag:

- ▶ **NAME:** Assigns a name to the plug-in media so that it can be referred to in LiveConnect JavaScript statements

- ▶ **AUTOSTART:** Is set to TRUE so that the sound file starts playing automatically

- ▶ **HIDDEN:** Hides the standard LiveAudio controller

The JavaScript statement:

```
window.setTimeout('document.embeds["greetings"].fade_from_to(100,0)',1000)
```

uses the built-in JavaScript function setTimeOut to fade out the LiveAudio sound after a specified length of time. You have seen the setTimeOut function used to create a dynamic billboard of changing graphics in a previous example. In this example, the setTimeOut function takes the following two parameters:

- ▶ The first parameter to setTimeOut is the function that automatically runs after a specified length of time. The function:

```
document.embeds["greetings"].fade_from_to(100,0)
```

uses the new `embeds` object in JavaScript 1.1 to reference the LiveAudio media. The method `fade_from_to(100,0)` is a new feature of LiveConnect-enabled LiveAudio plug-ins. This method fades out or fades in the LiveAudio sound. The method takes two parameters. These parameters are integer values in percent of sound volume of the starting point of the fade and the ending point of the fade. In this example, the fade starts at 100 percent volume and fades out to zero percent volume.

▶ The second parameter to the `setTimeOut` function specifies the time in milliseconds that will pass before the function specified in the first parameter is called. In this example, one second will pass and then the `fade_from_to` method will be called.

VBScript and OLE/ActiveX Scripting

VBScript is a client-side scripting language developed for Internet Explorer by Microsoft. It is a subset of Visual Basic. At this time, VBScript is available only in Microsoft Internet Explorer 3 for Windows 95 and NT. More platforms should be supported by the time you read this.

VBScript performs similar functions to JavaScript and LiveConnect. VBScript enables you to create HTML documents on-the-fly and communicate between the HTML document, OLE/ActiveX controls, and Java applets.

VBScript syntax is similar to JavaScript. It may become an important part of a web author's toolkit because of the numerous existing Visual Basic applications that can be repurposed for the web. At this time, it is still a nascent technology and is not supported in any browsers other than Internet Explorer 3 for Windows 95 and NT.

For all the latest information on VBScript, visit:

```
http://www.microsoft.com/
```

VBScript enables you to create custom functions that are similar to JavaScript functions. VBScript functions are called *subroutines*. To create subroutines, you use the VBScript keyword `SUB` in much the same way as you use the JavaScript keyword `function`. For example:

```
SUB showAlert
alert "A VBScript alert"
END SUB
```

defines a VBScript subroutine `showAlert` that you can call from other VBScripts in your HTML document.

VBScript Event Handlers

VBScript also supports event handlers, similar to JavaScript event handlers. If you have previously defined the `"showAlert"` subroutine, the following HTML calls the subroutine `"showAlert"` when the user clicks on the hyperlink:

```
<A HREF="http://myserver.net/somedoc.html" onClick="showAlert"> A
➥hyperlink.</A>
```

Custom HTML Documents with VBScript

VBScript enables you to create custom HTML documents on-the-fly based on a user's environment. The following is an example that creates an HTML document depending on the time of day:

```
<HTML>
<HEAD>
<TITLE>Dynamic Documents with VBScript</TITLE>
<SCRIPT LANGUAGE="VBScript">
<!--
If Hour(time) < 12 then
document.write('A morning document');
Else
document.write('An afternoon document'');
End If
-->
</SCRIPT>
</HEAD>
<BODY>
</BODY>
</HTML>
```

The comment tags hide the VBScript statements enclosed within the SCRIPT tag from browsers that don't support VBScript, such as Netscape Navigator and Internet Explorer 2.

Project Planning and Design

The discussion so far in this chapter has focused on implementation details—the mechanics of embedding multimedia content for web presentation. The planning and design process is equally important, however, and occupies a good deal of your time and effort before and after implementation.

This section provides an overview of ways to maximize the effectiveness and performance of your multimedia web pages.

Your application of the advice given here depends on the goals of your web site, your audience, and their connection speed. If your main audience is modem users connecting at 14.4 Kbps, you will design pages differently than if your audience is entirely on a campus intranet connecting at Ethernet speeds. Many factors outside your control, such as network traffic and server load, also affect performance.

Content Design

Like any communication format, web multimedia can be more or less effective depending on the quality of its design. Perhaps the first and most important design question to ask yourself is whether the multimedia you are planning truly adds value to the overall communication goals of the page.

Web multimedia is an exciting new area in web content, but don't use it just for the sake of using it. When .GIF animation support was added to the major browsers, animated .GIFs danced on every web page, taking over the browser status bar, and distracting users from reading text.

Ask yourself the following questions: "What value does this multimedia element add to my web page? Does it add to the visual impact? What is the effect on download time? What is the multimedia element trying to communicate? Can this be more effectively communicated some other way?"

Other aspects of good content design concern the individual elements of your multimedia presentation and how well they work together, both aesthetically and practically. In developing multimedia elements for the web, be certain to address the following issues:

▶ Will the background of your multimedia element match the background of your page?

▶ Does the size of the multimedia element fit within the page layout grids you have set up?

▶ Will other elements on the page, such as text, graphic identity elements, and navigational controls, also fit on the page?

▶ Is the multimedia element rendered in the 216 color, cross-platform browser palette? This palette is included with Director 6. If the multimedia element asserts a custom palette on 8-bit or 256 color displays, colors in the rest of the web page and in the rest of the user's display may change unpredictably or contain dithering artifacts.

▶ Do you have conflicting palettes between graphics and multimedia elements? You may have created adaptive or custom palettes to maximize the appearance of individual graphic elements. When all the elements are included on the same page the total number of colors used will exceed 256, the limit of 8-bit displays. You may want to design all graphical page elements to a common palette.

▶ Do you have competing multimedia elements, such as two looping animations that distract the user and diffuse the focus of your page?

▶ Do you have multiple sounds playing? Are the sounds loud, looping, or annoying in any way?

▶ Does the multimedia element fit within the visual context of the page or is it obtrusive and distracting? Are palettes and graphics styles similar between page elements and multimedia elements? Consider integrating graphics elements from the page into the Shockwave movie or other multimedia element to reinforce stylistic unity and context.

User Control and Preferences

Another important component of project planning and design is anticipation of how users of your web multimedia can interact with and control it.

Users like to feel in control of the computer. When you add multimedia to your web page, you may want to do the following:

▶ Provide ways for users to stop or pause looping animations and looping sounds

▶ Control sound volume

▶ Control playback and media manipulation with the standard controllers provided by such media as QuickTime and Shockwave for FreeHand

▶ Provide sophisticated interactivity with Shockwave for Director/Authorware, Toolbook, IconAuthor, CelAnimator, WebPainter, Java applets, or OLE/ActiveX controls

▶ Allow the user to control time-based media (see fig. 13.5)

Figure 13.5

Standard QuickTime controller for embedded multimedia.

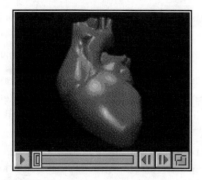

Show Sizes and Download Times

A hyperlink to a multimedia-rich page should give users some indication of what to expect if they click on that link. Will clicking a link initiate a potentially long download that will tie up the computer for many minutes? Warn users before they commit to a large download. Give your users some idea about the download time before they click on a link or go to a media-intensive page. One way to do this is to indicate the size in kilobytes and the estimated download time next to each link. Include the media size in KB and the estimated download time over 14.4 modems (about one second per kilobyte). You can include this information in a smaller relative type size by using the SIZE attribute of the FONT tag. For example:

```
<FONT SIZE = -2> 107 KB (about 1.5 minutes on a 14.4 modem)</FONT>
```

Shockwave for Director 6 enables you to stream Shockwave movies from the server. Playback begins before the file is completely downloaded. Thus the apparent download time is reduced. You may still want to show file sizes and indicate that the user is downloading a streaming file.

Thumbnails

Another way to provide a hint of what a long media download provides is to create a small, low-bandwidth thumbnail graphic of a larger file such as a large 24-bit graphic or long QuickTime movie.

You can also create short clips of video or animation. Before downloading a 500 KB QuickTime movie, for example, you could provide a small three or four frame .GIF animation. This animation will play on Netscape 2 or later and MSIE 3 or later, and give the user a taste of the real movie.

Provide Low-Bandwidth Alternate Content

Provide alternate content for browsers that don't support multimedia features or for users who don't want to download the multimedia. Provide a single frame from a QuickTime movie as a .GIF, or provide a text description of the media element. Provide text-only pages for text-based browsers. Use LOWSRC with the IMG tag to download a 1-bit, black-and-white image first and then download the full color graphic over it.

You could provide alternate pages of low-bandwidth content or provide two versions of a media element—a very short 8-bit video clip and longer 16-bit clip accessible from a low-bandwidth entry page, for example.

Users may have image loading turned off to improve response time. Use the ALT parameter of the IMG tag to provide text describing a graphic's purpose or content. This text also provides an alternate text-based link if the graphic is a button or link.

It is not a good idea to rely on graphical elements to provide all the essential information or navigation for your site. The most important information on your page should be included in the page's text. If you use an image map for navigation, remember to also include text-based navigation links.

Provide Helper Application Support

If you embed a multimedia element directly in a web page, and the multimedia element also has helper application support, you can provide a direct link to the media element. This way, users who don't have the necessary plug-in or browser and don't want to spend the time downloading and installing can still view the media if they have their helper applications set up correctly.

Provide External Links to Helper Applications and Plug-Ins

Your multimedia web page may require helper applications or plug-ins that the user does not have. Provide links to places on the web where they can find the necessary programs. The following section on HTML shows how to use the PLUGINSPAGE attribute with the EMBED tag to point users' browsers to appropriate download sites.

Provide Low-Bandwidth Entry Points

One way to shield users from large downloads is to provide an entry-point page or a table of contents page before going to a media-rich part of your site. You can display thumbnails, indicate download times, and provide links to plug-ins and helper applications from this single low-bandwidth page.

Performance

The interplay between file size and download time is a critical aspect of your web multimedia's performance. You can do many things to manage file size and download time.

Less Is Fast

The first step in speeding download time is reducing the total size of each web page. Every byte counts. Never pass up the opportunity to shave a byte off a graphic or text. Be precise and concise in your text copy. Add graphics only if they add value. Typical users may only wait 6–10 seconds or so for a page to download.

Reduce the total amount of text on a page. Provide text in small, screen-size chunks that download fast. Most users don't want to scroll through a lot of text. Most users probably won't read a lot of text on a web page anyway, instead scanning text quickly for key words and interesting links.

Reduce the total number of inline graphics and multimedia elements. When you are serving multimedia content, it is important to remember that each file, inline graphic, and multimedia element embedded in your HTML document requires a separate, independent connection to the server. An HTML document with ten separate inline graphics requires ten separate connections to the HTTP server to retrieve each file.

If you want to include multiple graphics, consider referencing the same graphic several times. The browser can retrieve the file from the disk or memory cache without opening another connection to the server.

Examine each frame in your video and animation. What are the essential elements you want to communicate? Pare down the video or animation to the scenes with the most impact. Think of it as a movie trailer or a six second reel for a client. Only show your best stuff. Do you really have to fade from black at the beginning and fade to black at the end? Put video credits and video text within the text of the web page.

Performance Checklist

To keep media files to the smallest size possible and minimize the time it takes to image and display a web page, consider the following checklist of issues:

- ▶ Reduce the dimensions of large media files. The dimensions of multimedia elements should be the smallest possible.

- ▶ Reduce your palette to the 216-color, cross-platform browser palette.

- ▶ Reduce the palette to as few colors as possible.

- ▶ Use .GIFs for solid color graphics such as logos and illustrations.

- ▶ Interlace .GIFs.

- ▶ Use .JPEG for continuous-tone, photographic imagery. This is a general rule of thumb for .JPEG usage. Your mileage may vary depending on the type of image you have and its size.

- ▶ Use Progressive .JPEG. (But remember that not all browsers support progressive .JPEG.)

- ▶ Use HEIGHT and WIDTH parameters on all IMG and EMBED tags, because they help the web page text appear more quickly on the screen.

- ▶ Edit video and animation.

- ▶ Compress video. Use a high-quality video source with minimal visual noise because it compresses better. Compression trade-offs can be easily compared by using expert tools such as Terran Interactive's Movie Cleaner Pro and web Motion plug-in.

- ▶ Use a Maximum Mono, 8-bit, 11 kHz Digital Audio.

- ▶ Use MIDI.

Make the Most Frequently Accessed Pages Small

What is the usage pattern for your site? Examine the usage statistics or task-flow diagrams for your site and determine which are the most frequently accessed pages. Make these pages the smallest pages on your site.

Your main, top-level page will probably be accessed most frequently. Entry points to second-level content areas will also be accessed frequently. The main, top-level pages and entry point pages should be the most compact pages on your site—under 30 KB is a good rule of thumb.

Use Local Storage

Another way to improve performance is to place bandwidth-hungry media—such as video and large graphics—on a local storage medium such as CD-ROM, cache, or hard disk. This either requires an installation procedure or that the user download the media and place it in a predetermined cache or directory.

Using the same graphics repeatedly at a site means that they will only need to be downloaded one time; subsequently, they are loaded from the user's disk or memory cache.

Testing

The testing advice covered in the early chapters of this book applies to Director projects on the web as well as other venues. In addition, you should keep in mind a couple of web-specific aspects of testing.

If you embed your multimedia element within a table cell or frame, be certain to test it on multiple platforms and browsers. Some first generation plug-ins crash when embedded in tables or frames.

Does your multimedia element—such as a Shockwave animation or Java applet—take over the processor on the local machine so that all interactivity or other processor activity on the computer grinds to a halt? If so, you must find another solution. Test your pages under low memory and slow processor speeds to see whether your page is usable on minimum systems.

If you have more than one multimedia element on a page, are the elements competing for system resources (trying to play back two sounds at the same time on a Windows machine, for example)? Using multiple media elements in general—such as two sounds, three .GIF animations, and a VRML world—can overload processors and the user's ability to view your site.

In Practice

With the advent of Netscape plug-ins, OLE/ActiveX controls such as Shockwave, and Java applets, multimedia objects can be embedded directly in web pages. From a layout and presentation perspective, this is a big improvement over the disconnected floating windows provided by helper applications. But it does present its own presentation issues, including the questions of how to integrate the multimedia element with the rest of the page, and how to give the user control of the media and provide a user-friendly experience.

This chapter established some general principles for effective web multimedia. The next chapter turns toward exploring Director's role in developing and integrating information for distribution over networks.

Keep in mind the following important approaches for working with multimedia on the web:

► Minimizing download time is one of the most important things you can do to ensure good performance. Methods for minimizing download time include keeping file sizes to a minimum, taking advantage of streaming technologies, compressing files, and using cache.

► Avoid gratuitous media. Add multimedia content only if it adds clear value.

► Design for a diverse audience: Users have different browsers, different bandwidth capabilities, different fee arrangements, and different reasons for accessing your product. Showing sizes and download times and offering alternate content are not just courtesies, but often necessities.

► One way to support multiple browsers is to use the OBJECT and EMBED tags in conjunction with one another.

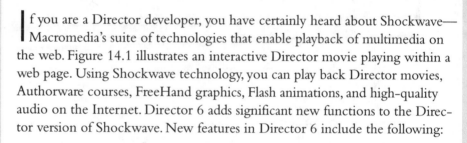

chapter **14**

David Miller

Creating Shockwave Movies

If you are a Director developer, you have certainly heard about Shockwave—Macromedia's suite of technologies that enable playback of multimedia on the web. Figure 14.1 illustrates an interactive Director movie playing within a web page. Using Shockwave technology, you can play back Director movies, Authorware courses, FreeHand graphics, Flash animations, and high-quality audio on the Internet. Director 6 adds significant new functions to the Director version of Shockwave. New features in Director 6 include the following:

▶ Shockwave integration in the authoring environment

▶ Integration of desktop and Internet, including the capability to link to Internet-based content

▶ Streaming playback

▶ Increased integration with browser scripting environments such as JavaScript

▶ "Shocked," Net-aware projectors

This chapter and Chapter 15, "Mastering Shockwave," get you started if you have never developed Shockwave movies. If you have created Shockwave movies in previous versions of Director, this chapter identifies and explains the new features. Macromedia is constantly updating Shockwave functionality and features. To find out the latest, visit Macromedia's web site at the following address:

```
http://www.macromedia.com/
```

Figure 14.1

Interactive graphing of mathematical functions in Shockwave.

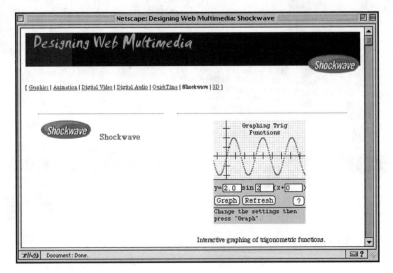

This chapter covers the following topics:

▶ Authoring on the Internet

▶ Creating Shockwave movies

▶ Creating low-bandwidth content

▶ Streaming playback

▶ Xtras in Net-aware projectors and Shockwave movies

A note on terminology is needed at this point. *Shockwave* generally refers to the range of Macromedia technologies that enable playback of various kinds of Macromedia-produced media on the Internet. Because of the new Internet features, Shockwave has taken on an expanded meaning compared to earlier versions. In the following sections, Shockwave is generally used to refer to the playback of Director movies in a web browser. The term *Net-aware projector* is used to refer to Director projectors that incorporate Shockwave Internet technologies. Hopefully, this is not too confusing and the meaning throughout this chapter will be clear from context.

Authoring on the Internet

If you have developed web-based Shockwave movies in Director 5, you have probably been frustrated with the lack of Shockwave support in the Director authoring environment. Good news! With Director 6, Shockwave is fully integrated in the authoring environment. Shockwave integration in authoring means that you can make network calls while authoring and even link to Internet-based content during authoring or playback.

This section discusses the integrated Internet features in the Director authoring environment. These new features fall into two main categories:

▶ The capability to use Shockwave features and Net Lingo while authoring

▶ Integration of the Internet into the desktop file system

Be aware that some network features behave slightly different whether they are invoked in the authoring environment, web browser, or Net-aware projector.

Setting Up Internet Authoring Preferences

You set up your author-time preferences in the Network Preferences dialog box (see fig. 14.2). Some of these preferences also affect the performance of Net-aware projectors. Shockwave in web browsers generally uses the network preferences set up in the web browser by the user.

To set up network preferences, choose File, Preferences, Network. A dialog box with several options appears.

Figure 14.2

The Network Preferences dialog box.

Preferred Browser specifies the browser to launch with the GoToNetPage Lingo command. Be certain that the Launch When Needed option is enabled if you use GoToNetPage.

Net-aware projectors retain this setting during run-time calls to GoToNetPage. Based on the preferences that are set, one of the following occurs:

▶ If preferred browser is enabled, and a path to a browser is specified, Net-aware projectors attempt to launch the browser with the URL specified in GoToNetPage.

▶ If preferred browser is enabled, but no path is specified, Net-aware projectors use the default browser specified in the Windows Registry or Internet Config on a Mac.

▶ If no default browser exists, Net-aware projectors ask the user to specify a browser for viewing web pages.

Proxy servers are commonly used on intranets protected behind a firewall. Proxy servers provide a filtering mechanism between the internal intranet and the external Internet. The proxy server options within the Network Preferences dialog box enable you to set up Shockwave to interact with local proxy servers during authoring. If you want, you can have your Shockwave movie retain these settings at run time. You can also set these parameters via Lingo.

The Cache options specify cache settings during authoring and within Net-aware projectors. Shockwave in a web browser uses the settings specified in the web browser.

Authoring with Internet-Based Content

In Director 6, the Internet is part of the file system. When a network connection is present, standard file open and import dialog boxes contain a button labeled Internet. Clicking on this button brings up a dialog box where you type in a fully qualified or absolute URL to a file on the Internet. You can import media directly into the Director cast so that it is saved internally with your Director movie. You can also link to the external media, the same way that you link to other external media on a local disk, such as digital video files.

You can link to most types of media that Director supports internally—for example, text, various graphics formats, digital audio, other Director movies, and external casts. New import formats include .BMP, .GIF, .JPEG, .LRG (xRes), Photoshop 3.0, MacPaint, .PNG, .TIF, and .PICT graphics formats.

As of this writing, the media must be on an HTTP or FTP server (that is, URLs that begin with an http:// or ftp:// protocol specifier), and you must provide a fully qualified URL to the media.

Importing Internet Content into the Cast

1. Choose Import from the File menu (see fig. 14.3).

Figure 14.3

The Import dialog box with Internet options.

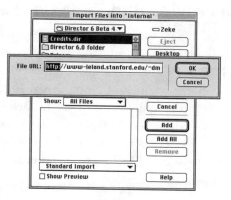

2. Click on the Internet button.

3. Enter the absolute URL to the content in the dialog box.

Linking to External Files on the Internet

You can also link to external media at a location on the Internet in authoring mode and at run time. The media remains external to the Director file. Director imports the media from the specified Internet location the first time the movie runs.

To link to external media on the Internet, choose Link to External File from the Media pop-up at the bottom of the Import dialog box.

If you have experience using the Internet or a web browser, or creating web sites or other TCP/IP applications, you realize that network operations sometimes fail. What do you do if your linked external content cannot be downloaded at run time? Included in the file BEHAVIOR.CST that shipped with Director is a Net Show Proxy behavior. Use this behavior to display an alternative cast member if a linked cast member is not available.

Movies playing in web browsers do not require the special Net Xtras to use linked Internet-based content. Net-aware projectors *will* require these Xtras to retrieve media from the Internet during playback. To include these Xtras automatically, turn on Include Network Xtras in the Projector Options dialog box when you create your projector. A subsequent section, "Xtras in Net-Aware Projectors and Shockwave Movies," discusses using Net Xtras.

Using Lingo to Provide Run-Time Content Linking

In addition to content linking by using the standard file open and import dialog boxes, you can use Lingo to import and link to content. In fact, you can use an URL to an HTTP or FTP server in just about every place in Lingo that accepts a file path name. Some commands in web-based Shockwave movies accept relative URLs, but most require absolute URLs. Before you use an URL in Lingo, such as the `file name of member` or `ImportFileInto`, you should use `PreLoadNetThing`, with movies playing in a web browser. Alternatively, use `DownLoadNetThing`, with Net-aware projectors, to first download the content and then test whether the download succeeded.

Perhaps you want to change the cast members of your movie based on user input or the day of the month or to update a game with new media. You can put the updated media on a web server. Then users of your Director application on client machines can access the media when needed.

In a Net-aware projector, for example, the Lingo:

```
set gDLNewCastID = DownLoadNetThing("http://www.myWebServer.com/
➥0697Cast.cst", the applicationPath&"0697Cast.cst")
```

downloads the file `0697Cast.cst`, a cast library of new, time-dependent media, into the same folder as the Director application. The Director application must be on a write-enabled volume for this to work. The following Lingo loops in a frame until the new cast downloads successfully and then sets the file name of a cast library to the downloaded file.

```
if NetDone(gDLNewCastID) then
  if NetError (gDLNewCastID) = "OK" then
    set the fileName of castLib "CastOfTheMonth" = the
    ➥applicationPath&"0697Cast.cst"
  end if
else
  go the frame
end if
```

Using URLs in Director

Keep in mind the following limitations on using URLs in Director:

▶ In the URL Import dialog, URLs must be 256 characters or less.

▶ In Lingo commands such as `the filename of member`, URLs must also be 256 characters or less.

▶ URLs used in Net Lingo, such as `GetNetText`, can be longer than 256 characters.

▶ Net Lingo called within the Shockwave web browser plug-in generally can accept a relative URL. The URL is relative to the Net location of the Shockwave movie, not the Net location of the HTML file containing the `EMBED` tag for the movie (for a discussion of embedding Shockwave movies in web pages see Chapter 15).

▶ If the relative URL points to a file nested several directories deep, it may not work.

In addition, Internet Explorer 3 handles relative URLs a little differently than Netscape Navigator. You must prepend a "./" before the relative URL. If the following call was in a Shockwave movie:

```
GetNetText "./someTextFile.txt"
```

it would retrieve the file `someTextFile.txt` that is in the same directory on the web server as the Shockwave movie.

You also can open HTML files in a web browser by using the `GoToNetPage` Net Lingo command. The HTML files can be local to the Director application or on the Internet. To use `GoToNetPage` from a Net-aware projector on a CD-ROM and to open an HTML file that is also on the CD-ROM, follow these steps:

1. Make certain that the Preferred Browser and Browser Launching is enabled in the Network Preferences dialog box, as discussed previously.

2. Use the syntax `GoToNetPage "file:///myLocalHTMLFile.html"` to specify the URL.

The following Lingo commands do *not* accept URLs:

▶ openResFile, closeResFile, showResFile

▶ openXlib, closeXlib, showXlib

▶ save castLib

▶ saveMovie

▶ getNthFilenameInFolder(<folderPath>, <fileNumber>)

▶ the searchPaths

Caches

Caching at author-time is set in the Network Preferences dialog box.

When playing in a web browser, Shockwave movies use the browser's cache and cache management facilities. The Lingo command PreLoadNetThing loads the specified URL into the browser's cache. Be aware that preloading provides no guarantee that the preloaded media will actually be present. The browser or the user can flush the cache at any time.

Creating Shockwave Movies

Shockwave creates files optimized for network playback. These files are compressed for fast download over a network. Compressed Shockwave files typically have the .DCR file name extension.

You create .DCR files in the Director authoring environment by choosing Save as Shockwave Movie from the File menu. .DCR files can be played back in web browsers by using the Shockwave plug-in, or they can also be played from a projector.

.DCR files are the most highly compressed format for Director movies, but they must be decompressed during playback. Because they are decompressed at playback, .DCR files may have slower performance at run time. If file size is not an issue, save the Director movie in .DXR format. The file size is larger than a .DCR file, but playback is faster because the playback engine does not have to decompress the file.

The digital media that make up your movie contribute the most to file size, especially digital video, bitmaps, and digital audio. Digital video must be external to your movie and compressed separately. See Chapter 12, "Digital Video: The Movie Within the Movie," for details on compressing digital video. Bitmaps are compressed automatically when you create a .DCR file. Generally, bitmaps that contain large areas of solid color compress the most. Also, Macromedia recommends using 1-bit or 8-bit graphics to maximize compression. See the following section, "Creating Low-Bandwidth Content," for details on creating graphics for Shockwave movies.

Audio compression is handled by Macromedia's powerful Shockwave for Audio, which is built into Director 6. Shockwave for Audio provides high-quality audio compression with compression ratios up to 176:1. You can use Shockwave for Audio compression in Director 6 movies in two different ways: You can compress internal sounds by using Shockwave for Audio compression, or you can link to external compressed sounds that stream on playback.

Think small when creating Shockwave movies—or just about any multimedia —for the web. Create compact files that can be downloaded quickly over slow, sometimes overloaded, network connections. You can do a lot in under 10 KB. This chapter provides tips on how to create small movies.

Keep in mind a few basic optimization techniques and restrictions when creating Shockwave movies. First, remember the value of streaming. Also, remember that some Director features, discussed in Chapter 15, are disabled in Shockwave for playback in a web browser. For security reasons, most of the Lingo commands that provide access to the client hard disk, file system, or operating system have been disabled. In contrast, Net-aware projectors can have the full range of Director functionality.

To create Shockwave movies for playback on the web, follow these steps:

1. Create the Director movie.

2. Compress the embedded audio, if any exists, with the Shockwave for Audio Settings under the Xtras menu.

3. Choose Save as Shockwave Movie from the File menu.

4. Integrate the movie into an HTML document by using the EMBED tag for the Netscape Navigator plug-in or OBJECT tag for the ActiveX control. For example:

```
<EMBED SRC = "myShockingMovie.dcr" WIDTH = 160 HEIGHT = 120 PLUGINSPAGE
➥ = "http://www.macromedia.com/shockwave/">
```

See Chapter 15 for details on using the EMBED and OBJECT tags.

Figure 14.4 illustrates a Shockwave movie embedded in a web page.

Figure 14.4

Graphical display of real-time, Internet-based data using Shockwave.

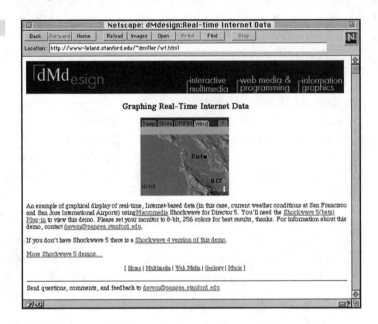

5. Upload the HTML document and converted movie. Be certain that the movie is uploaded as a raw, binary file. The web server must be configured to associate files with the .DCR extension to the MIME type application/x- director.

To create a Net-aware, stand-alone projector, follow these basic steps:

1. Choose Create Projector from the File menu.

2. In the Create Projector dialog box, choose Options.

3. Check Include Network Xtras.

To compress internal audio present within your Director movie, choose Shockwave for Audio Settings from the Xtras menu and click on the Enabled option. If you use Shockwave for Audio compression on your internal audio, be aware of the following:

▶ Compression is not performed until you choose Save as Shockwave movie from the File menu.

▶ All internal sounds (except IMA compressed sound) are compressed.

▶ Cue points (discussed in Chapter 11, "Sound: The Soundtrack") are not recognized.

You can also link to external Shockwave for Audio files that stream on playback. Chapter 11 and the next section provide details on creating Shockwave for Audio files, compression/quality trade-offs, and using Shockwave for Audio on the Internet.

Streaming Shockwave

Streaming is the capability to download the first part of a time-based media file, such as a Director movie, and begin playback fairly quickly, while the rest of the file downloads in the background. Chapter 13, "Designing Multimedia for the Web," discusses streaming media on the Internet in general terms. Streaming playback is one of the most important new features in Director 6. It enables a much better user experience for Shockwave movies on the web.

You will generally use Director 6's streaming playback features with large Shockwave movies playing in a web browser. Small movies—less then 10–20 KB, for example—may not benefit much from streaming playback, but it depends on the particular movie.

Creating a Streaming Shockwave Movie

1. Choose Modify, Movie, Playback. You will be presented with the dialog box shown in figure 14.5.

Figure 14.5

Options for streaming Shockwave.

2. To turn streaming on, select Use Media As Available or Show Placeholders.

3. To set the number of frames that must be present on local disk before the movie starts playing, select Pre-Fetch and specify the number of frames.

The following possible options are available for movie playback:

▶ **Wait for All Media – No streaming:** Downloads the entire movie before playing.

▶ **Use Media As Available – Movies:** Streams and plays without available media, if that has not been downloaded. When media becomes available, the media is displayed.

▶ **Show Placeholders – Movie:** Streams same as the preceding item, except bounding boxes are displayed until downloaded media becomes available.

The movie does not stream during playback; the entire movie downloads before it begins playing if:

▶ The movie was created in Director 4

▶ The movie was created in Director 5

▶ Wait for All Media is checked in the Movie Playback Properties dialog box

If you have created a streaming movie, the various parts of the movie download in the following order:

1. Score

2. Scripts

3. Shapes created from the Tool palette

4. Cast member properties

5. Scripts, shapes, and cast member properties from external casts

6. Xtras required by the movie

7. Cast member media (bitmaps, audio, text, and so on) found in the frames specified with the Pre-Fetch option

Use the Pre-Fetch option in the Movie Playback Properties dialog box to specify the number of initial frames that must be downloaded before the movie begins playing. By creating your movie with an initial "attract loop" or simple animation, you can loop on this initial animation while waiting for the rest of the movie to download. Test the `frameReady` and `mediaReady of member` Lingo properties to make sure that certain parts of your movie are downloaded before playing.

Streaming playback changes the behavior of some Lingo commands. `preloadMember` or `preLoad`, for example, has no effect if the data is not on disk and the `idleLoadMode` is set to zero. To determine whether media has arrived on local disk, use the `frameReady` and `mediaReady of member` Lingo commands. The commands that are affected are still being determined as of this writing.

Support Folders and Preferences

Support folders enable a preset place or "sandbox" that you can use to store Xtras and external casts between sessions, or to receive downloaded media that you want to have available to your movie. You can also use these special folders to write preferences files as a way to preserve state across sessions.

Many of the support folder features for Net-aware projectors have not been finalized as of this writing.

Shockwave Plug-In Support Folder

The Shockwave support folder is a special folder on the client hard disk that can be used for external files, such as linked QuickTime movies or digital audio, Xtras, XObjects, and external casts.

A drawback of the support folder is that users must download external files separately from the Shockwave movie and also must make certain that these external files are in the correct folder/directory on their hard drive. Possible uses of the support folder include support for online services or CD-ROM/ Internet hybrids. An installer on the CD-ROM or online service software can automatically place external media, such as QuickTime movies that take a long time to download, in the Shockwave support folder. Then, when the user accesses Shockwave movies on the Internet, the external files in the support folder are available to the Shockwave movie. Table 14.1 shows the name and location of the support folder.

Table 14.1

Name and Location of Shockwave Support Folder

Platform	Support Folder	Location
68K Mac	NP-Mac68K-Dir-Shockwave folder	Plug-ins folder in the Netscape Navigator folder
PPC Mac	NP-MacPPC-Dir-Shockwave folder	Plug-ins folder in the Netscape Navigator folder
Win 3.1	NP16DSW	C:\NETSCAPE\PLUGINS directory
Win 95	NP32DSW	C:\Program Files\ Netscape\Navigator\ Program\Plugins directory

During authoring, place the external file in the same folder as the Director movie. When you call an external file from your Shockwave movie, Shockwave automatically searches the special support folder on the client hard disk.

Use the following Lingo commands to access files in the support folder:

▶ openXLib

▶ closeXLib

▶ open castlib x

See Chapter 15 for a list of Lingo commands that do not work with external media under Shockwave in a web browser.

Open a Lingo Xtra or XObject in the startMovie handler:

```
on startMovie
   global gXtra
   if objectP(gXtra) then gXtra(mDispose)
   openXlib "NeatoXtra"
   set gXtra = NeatoXtra(mNew)
end startMovie
```

Close the Lingo Xtra or XObject when you are finished using it. To be certain that you do not forget and to free up memory, include the following code in the stopMovie handler:

```
on stopMovie
   global gXtra
   if objectP(gXtra) then gXtra(mDispose)
   closeXlib "NeatoXtra"
end stopMovie
```

During authoring, place the Xtra or external cast in the same folder/directory as your movie file. During playback, the Xtra or external cast must be in the appropriate Shockwave support folder on the client machine.

Shockwave Plug-In Preferences

With Shockwave for Director 6, you can save user data across sessions by using a Preferences file in the special Shockwave support folder. You write to and read from this Preferences file using the following Lingo commands:

▶ `setPref prefFileName, prefValue`

▶ `getPref(prefFileName)`

The file name of the Preferences file (the `prefFileName` parameter in the preceding examples) must be a valid file name. Restrict this name to the 8.3 DOS file-naming conventions for compatibility with all systems.

When you first use the `setPref` command within your Shockwave movie, the file is automatically created in the local Shockwave support folder. For testing purposes in the authoring environment, these commands use the cache settings in the Network Preferences dialog box.

For example:

```
setPref gamepref.txt, score1:456
```

creates the file `gamepref.txt` in the Shockwave support folder of the local hard disk and appends the string `score1:456`.

This function `getPref(prefFileName)` returns the content of the file named `prefFileName` that is present in the special Shockwave support folder. If the file does not exist, `getPref` returns void. For example:

```
set myPrefText = getPref("gamepref.txt")
```

loads the variable `myPrefText` with the contents of the text file `"gamepref.txt"` in the special Shockwave support folder.

Projector Preferences Folder

The first time a projector is run on a write-enabled volume, it creates a special folder in the same folder as the projector. This special folder can be used to store preferences or other data. You also can use this folder to download media or other content. You can access this folder from Lingo commands that take path name parameters and with the FileIO Xtra.

Xtras in Net-Aware Projectors and Shockwave Movies

As of this writing, the files shown in Table 14.2 must be in your Xtras folder for network functions to work at author-time, but this information may change by the time you read this. You can find out which Xtras are needed for network functions by checking out the XTRAINFO.TXT file installed with Director. Lines with the type property of #net are needed for network features to work.

Table 14.2

Files Required for Network Functions During Authoring

Platform	Xtras and Support Files
68K Mac	Netlingo, Netfile
PPC Mac	Netlingo, Netfile, Ineturl, NetManage Winsock Lib
Win 3.1	Netlingo, Netfile, Ineturl
Win 95/NT	Netlingo, Netfile, Ineturl

To create a Net-aware projector, you must include the appropriate Network Xtras from Table 14.2 within your projector. The following tutorial outlines how to do so.

Including Network Xtras for a Net-Aware Project

1. Choose Create Projector from the File menu.

2. In the Create Projector dialog box, choose Options.

3. Check Include Network Xtras.

You can include other Xtras within your projector in a similar fashion. See Chapter 21, "The Xtra Step," for details.

To use Xtras with Shockwave movies that play in web browsers, you must have users manually install Xtras in the Shockwave Support folder in the browser's plug-ins folder or provide an installer that accomplishes this task.

Creating Low-Bandwidth Content

The following techniques should help you create small, compact movies that won't take long to download over the Internet.

Text

Director 6 has two types of text-based cast members:

▶ "rich text" or just "text"

▶ field text

Recall from Chapter 10, "Text: The Story," that rich text contains many of the same formatting options you have in a word processing program. In addition, rich text can be anti-aliased against its background so that it looks good on-screen. Rich text has access to fonts on the authoring machine. It is fully editable in the authoring environment, but cannot be edited in a projector or Shockwave movie. When you create a projector or compress your movie for the web, rich text is converted to a bitmap. Because rich text is converted to a bitmap, it can take up a lot of space. To create rich text, use the Text tool in the Tool Palette or the Text window.

Field text has more limited formatting options than rich text. It is not anti-aliased. Field text can be edited in the authoring environment. Unlike rich text, however, field text can also be edited by users in a projector or Shockwave movie. You make field text editable by selecting the Editable check box in the score, selecting the Editable check box in the Cast Member Property dialog box, or by using the Lingo `editable of sprite` command.

Field text uses much less disk space than rich text or other bitmapped text; thus it is especially useful for Shockwave movies. Field text uses the fonts available on the playback machine. It is probably safest to stick with the standard fonts that come with most Macintosh and Windows systems such as Times, Helvetica, Geneva, and Courier on Macintosh, or Arial, Courier New, and Times New Roman on Windows. To create field text, use the Field tool on the Tool Palette or choose Field from the Control submenu on the Insert menu.

The contents of fields can be changed while a Shockwave movie runs. Fields are a good way to provide status and help bars for users. Field text can be used for animated text effects. Many field text properties, such as size and color, can be set by Lingo. For example:

```
set the fontSize of member "myFieldText" = 18
```

changes the point size of the text in cast member `"myFieldText"` to 18.

Fonts on different systems have different kerning and leading. Shockwave maps fonts on one system to a similar font on another, but text kerning and leading will probably be different. Be certain to view your Shockwave movie on multiple systems.

Shockwave uses the file FONTMAP.TXT, included with your Director installation, when mapping cross-platform fonts. This file is automatically included with your Shockwave movie. If your Shockwave movie does not contain fonts, you can use a resource editor to delete FONTMAP.TXT from your Shockwave movie to reduce file size.

You can also create bitmaps of text in the Director Paint window or import bitmaps of text from programs such as Photoshop.

1-Bit Graphics

One way to keep your file size small is to use bitmap graphics that have 1-bit color depth. To convert graphics to 1-bit in Director, select the cast member in the Cast window and choose Transform Bitmap from the Modify menu. Then, choose 1-bit from the Color Depth pop-up menu.

You can also use an image processing program such as DeBabelizer or Photoshop to convert graphics to 1-bit.

In Director, 1-bit graphics consist of two colors: a foreground color and background color. You can change the forecolor and backcolor of sprites on the stage by selecting the sprite and then clicking on the color chips in the Tool Palette. This action brings up a 256-color pop-up palette from which you can choose another color for the foreground or background.

You can also change the foreground color and background color of graphics by using the Lingo commands `forecolor of sprite` and `backcolor of sprite`. On 8-bit systems, the 256 possible colors are referenced by a number between 0 and 255. For example:

```
set the forecolor of sprite 10 to random(255)
```

sets the forecolor of the sprite in channel 12 to a random color between 1 and 255 in the currently active palette. To change the foreground color and background color of Field text, use the Lingo commands `forecolor of member` and `backcolor of member`.

The trails effect leaves a copy of a graphic behind as it moves across the stage, as if the graphic were a paint brush. Trails can be a low overhead way to add multiple copies of a graphic to the stage or to paint large areas of color. Activate the trails effect by selecting the Trails check box in the score. A drawback of trails is that trails are not repainted if the user covers and then uncovers the Shockwave movie with another window.

Vector-Based Graphics

Vector-based graphics are different from bitmap graphics in that the computer stores vector-based graphics as a mathematical formula rather than a collection of pixels. Thus vector-based graphics are small in size and very useful for creating web-based animations.

Director 6 comes with a limited set of vector-based graphics tools. In Director 6, vector-based graphics are called *shapes*. Shapes include lines, ovals, rectangles, and rounded rectangles. You access shapes from the Tool Palette. Use the Tool Palette buttons to change the type, line size, fill pattern, and color of shapes.

Macromedia Flash is a new vector-based animation tool that has recently been added to the Shockwave toolkit. Using Flash or another animation tool, such as Totally Hip's WebPainter, is a good way to create high-quality, low-bandwidth animations, assuming they don't require the complex interactivity available in Director-based Shockwave.

New Lingo commands enable you to change the type of shape, fill, patterns, and line size of Shape cast members from Lingo. For example:

```
set the lineSize of sprite 10 = 4
```

sets the line size of the shape sprite in channel 10 to 4 pixels.

```
set the filled of member "myCircle" = TRUE
set the pattern of member "myCircle" = 1
```

fills the shape cast "myCircle" with a solid color pattern.

Ink Effects

Ink effects are an easy way to create interesting visual effects with graphics without creating extra cast members. Ink effects control the way pixels in a 1-bit graphic are composited with underlying pixels. Some ink effects are processor-intensive and can slow screen redraw (see the Director 6 documentation for details). Generally, ink effects lower in the Ink Effects pop-up menu are more processor-intensive. Access the Ink Effects pop-up menu from the Score window, the Paint window, or press the Command key on the Macintosh or the Ctrl key on Windows and select a sprite on the stage. Text cast members support only Copy, Background Transparent, and Blend inks.

Tiles

Tiling is an efficient way to build backgrounds and create patterns in Director movies. Tiling takes a small bitmap, for example 16×16 pixels in size, and repeats it over and over to fill up a much larger space. You can use 1-bit graphics as tiles for even greater file size optimization.

You access the Tile Settings from the Pattern Fill button on the Tool Palette (beneath the color chips) or in the Paint window. You define a tile pattern by choosing a rectangular region of any bitmap cast member.

You can define multiple tiles from the same bitmap. Tiles can be any rectangular size. It is probably best to stick with rectangles with pixel dimensions divisible by 16.

After it is created, a tile can be used to fill a bitmap or vector-based shape.

Palettes and Colors

Your movie will probably play back on an 8-bit display. For playback on the web, it is probably best to create 8-bit Shockwave movies. If you author in 16-bit or 24-bit, you can change the color depth of your Director movie by changing your monitor's color depth and then saving the movie.

The color in your 8-bit movie will be mapped to the currently active browser palette unless you specify otherwise with the PALETTE parameter in the EMBED tag. This means that colors in your animation that are not in the browser palette will be dithered to colors in the browser palette, which might make some of your graphics look speckled. Netscape Navigator and Internet Explorer use a slightly different palette on Macintosh and Windows systems. These palettes share 216 colors. These 216 shared, non-dithered, cross-platform colors are the same colors as the middle 216 colors of the Macintosh system palette. If you use these colors, you can be assured that your graphics will not be dithered. A big drawback of this palette is its limited range of grays. If you are not using custom palettes and want to provide the highest degree of cross-platform, palette compatibility, you should probably stick to these colors. Director 6 includes a special Netscape web palette within the PALETTES.CST file in the Xtras menu.

INSIDER TIP

See Chapter 13 of this book or the book *Web Multimedia Development*, also by New Riders Publishing, for details on using web palettes.

You can embed a custom palette in your Shockwave movie and force the browser to use this palette by using the PALETTE attribute within the EMBED tag. See the Net Lingo guide for the HTML syntax. Set PALETTE = FOREGROUND to assert a custom Shockwave palette. A custom palette shifts all the colors in the rest of the display, which can be disorienting for some users. Also, if the user jumps to a new page, the palette may not get reset. Internet Explorer does *not* support the PALETTE attribute at this time.

If you use the Lingo commands the `forecolor of sprite` for bitmaps and the `forecolor of member` for Field text, the palette index number used to reference a specific color might differ among systems. These colors might not display accurately on 16-bit and 24-bit displays.

To set the background color of your Shockwave movie so that it matches the background color of your HTML document, choose Movie/Properties from the Modify menu, and select a color for the background on the dialog box.

Sound

Shockwave movies are an easy way to add sound to a web page. The Shockwave for Audio Xtra enables you to compress sounds embedded in Director, or to create external, streamable audio files by using SoundEdit for the Macintosh. These files are called .SWA files for Shockwave Audio.

To play sounds in a Director movie, add them to the sound channels in the Director score, just like you add other cast members. Alternatively, you can use the Lingo `puppetSound` command to play sound cast members. You can also link to streaming Shockwave for Audio files that reside on a web server and that play back in your Shockwave movie for the web or Net-aware projector. The tutorial in Chapter 15 on creating Shockwave movies discusses incorporating external, streamable Shockwave files.

If you don't use SWA compressed sounds, try to keep your sounds to 11 kHz mono, 8-bit or below. For sounds such as button clicks, you may get by with as little as 8 kHz. Test sounds with low sampling rates on different systems to see whether the quality is acceptable. To loop sounds, set the Looped Property in the Sound Cast Properties dialog box.

Endlessly looping sounds can be annoying, so provide a way for users to stop the sound. For example:

```
on mouseDown
 if soundBusy(1) then sound stop 1
end
```

stops the sound playing in sound channel 1 when the user clicks the mouse.

Instead of using a sound editor to create fade ins and fade outs, use the Lingo commands `sound fadeIn` and `sound fadeOut`. By using Lingo for fades you can reduce the total size of your sound file, for example, by using a small looping sound. Use the Lingo command `the volume of sound` to set the volume of a sound relative to the overall sound level of the user's machine.

Shockwave for Audio Xtra

Shockwave for Audio Xtras are part of the Shockwave, SoundEdit, and Director distribution from Macromedia. The Shockwave for Audio Xtras enable you to:

▶ Compress embedded audio in Director

▶ Create specially formatted streaming audio files with SoundEdit on a Macintosh

▶ Play back streaming audio from Shockwave movies

No special server is required to play back audio. Audio plays back from a Shockwave movie only. Compression ratios for audio are up to 176:1. Playback rates are as low as 8 Kbps, which enables playback even over slow modem connections.

Shockwave for Audio Xtras consists of several components for authoring and playback. In most cases, playback Xtras automatically install in the correct places on your hard drive when you run the Shockwave installer. The authoring Xtras also automatically install when you install Director and SoundEdit. Tables 14.3–14.5 list Xtras and locations.

Note that the Xtras in Table 14.3 must be in your Director 6 Xtras folder. The Xtras in Table 14.4 must be in SoundEdit 16's Xtras folder. Finally, the Xtras in Table 14.5 must be in a special Shockwave folder within your Netscape Plug-Ins folder.

Table 14.3

Shockwave for Audio Xtras for Authoring in Director

Macintosh	Windows
SWA Compression Xtra	SWACmpr.x32
SWA Settings (DIR) Xtra	SWASttng.x32
SWA Streaming Xtra*	SWA Streaming Xtra*

A copy of these Xtras must also be in the special Shockwave folder within your Netscape Plug-Ins folder.

Table 14.4

Shockwave for Audio Xtras for Authoring in SoundEdit 16

Macintosh	Windows
SWA Export Xtra	Not available
SWA Settings (SE) Xtra	Not available

Table 14.5

Shockwave for Audio Xtras for Playback in Netscape Navigator

Macintosh	Windows
SWA Decompression Xtra	SWADCmpr.x32
SWA Streaming Xtra	SWA Streaming Xtra

The Shockwave for Audio Xtra for Director enables you to save settings for audio compression of sounds embedded within your Director movie. Compression works best on audio sampled at 16-bit, 22 kHz, or higher.

The following exercise provides detailed steps on using SWA in Director.

Compressing Embedded Audio Files for Shockwave Movies in Director

1. Choose Shockwave for Audio Settings under the Xtras menu (see fig. 14.6).

Figure 14.6

Shockwave for Audio Settings in Director.

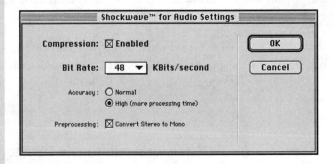

2. Check the Enabled check box

3. Choose the bit rate in KBits/second from the Bit Rate pop-up menu.

   A high bit rate produces larger files of higher quality. A low bit rate produces a small file of lower quality. If your movie will be played back by modem users, choose 32 KBits/second. This setting is the lowest setting possible within Director. The Shockwave for Audio Xtra for SoundEdit 16 enables setting a bit rate as low as 8 KBits/second for external streaming audio files. If processing time is not an issue, choose the High option.

4. Check the Convert Stereo to Mono check box if the bit rate is greater than 32 and you want to convert a stereo file to mono.

   Most users will probably have only mono playback anyway. If you are playing back audio over an intranet in a music lab, for example, where you know that users have stereo playback, do not check this box.

5. Choose OK.

Using Shockwave for Audio with SoundEdit 16

Shockwave for Audio Xtras for SoundEdit 16 automatically install when you install the latest version of SoundEdit 16. Refer to Tables 14.3–14.5 for a list of the names and install locations of these Xtras. You can also obtain the Xtras from Macromedia's web site.

You can create SWA files on Windows within Director for Windows with the help of the Shockwave Audio Xtra for Director, available at the following address:

http://www.macromedia.com/support/director/how/shock/director_devtools.html.

Streamable audio files are highly compressed digital audio files that can be played back by a Shockwave movie or projector. Streamable .SWA files can reside on a web server and are external to the Shockwave movie that plays them. They are referenced from the Shockwave movie via a valid URL.

Before exporting an SWA audio file, do the following:

▶ Use audio sampled at 16-bit, 22.050 kHz or 44.100 kHz. Macromedia recommends upsampling 11 kHz source files to 22.050 kHz. 11 kHz stereo source files are automatically converted to mono in all cases.

▶ You may want to experiment with equalization settings. Filtering frequencies in the 4 kHz to 8 kHz range (high frequencies) may improve quality. The following exercise shows you how.

▶ If your audio fill is in stereo, convert the file to mono. Most users probably won't have stereo playback capabilities. The .SWA Export Xtra automatically converts a file to mono if you choose a bit rate of 32 KBits/second or less.

Filtering Frequencies in SoundEdit 16

1. Select the area of the sound sample you want to filter.

2. Choose Equalizer under the Effects menu (see fig. 14.7).

continues

Filtering Frequencies in SoundEdit 16   continued

Figure 14.7

Equalizer in SoundEdit 16.

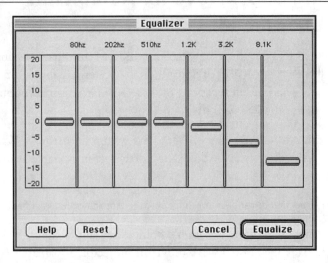

3. The rightmost two sliders affect the high frequencies. Move these sliders down to filter out some of the high frequency range.

Now you are ready to export your finished audiofile.

Exporting a Sound File with SWA Export Xtra

1. Close SoundEdit 16's Levels palette when exporting SWA files.

2. Choose Shockwave for Audio Settings from the Xtras menu to configure the compression options (see fig. 14.8).

Figure 14.8

Shockwave for Audio settings in SoundEdit 16.

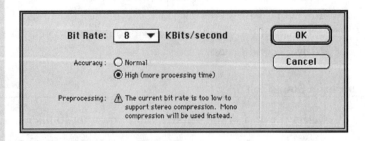

3. Select the bit rate (KBits/second) you want from the Bit Rate drop-down menu.

   Lower bit rates produce lower quality files that are streamable over modems. Higher bit rates produce higher quality files that are streamable over fast connections, such

as a corporate or university intranet; however, these higher quality files break up over slower connections.

4. Click on OK.

5. Choose Export under the File menu.

6. Choose .SWA File from the Export Type drop-down menu.

7. Make certain that the file name has the .SWA file name extension. Give the file a name that follows the file-naming conventions of your web server.

As discussed in step 3 of the preceding tutorial, you must consider optimization issues when choosing a bit rate for a sound file. The bit rate you choose depends on the following:

▶ The connection speed of your users.

▶ The characteristics of your sound file. Voice and narration audio files, for example, can generally be played back at lower bit rates without perceived loss of quality. Music, however, requires higher bit rates. Table 14.6 summarizes recommended bit rates for various connection speeds.

Table 14.6

Recommended Bit Rates for Representative Connection Speeds

Bit Rate	Connection Speed
8 KBps	14.4 modem connections, typical home user
16 KBps	28.8 modem connections
32–56 KBps	ISDN lines
64–128 KBps	T1 delivery, corporate or university intranet

Using IMA-Compressed Sounds in Shockwave Movies

The Interactive Multimedia Association (IMA) defined an audio compression standard that, prior to Shockwave for Audio, was one of the most popular ways to provide high-quality compressed audio in Director. You may already have a lot of sound files that are compressed in this format. Or you may want to use this format because of playback or compatibility issues for your target audience and platform.

You can use IMA-compressed sounds in Shockwave. At this time, however, they can only be imported in the Macintosh authoring environment—although they will play back on Windows. The following tutorial outlines how to create an IMA-compressed sound on a Mac from a sound-only QuickTime movie in MoviePlayer.

Creating IMA-Compressed Sound

1. Choose Export from the File menu.

2. Select Sound To AIFF.

3. Click on Options.

4. Select IMA 4:1 for compressor.

5. Select a sampling rate of 11.025, and Mono.

If you have SoundEdit 16, you can also export IMA compressed sounds.

General Shockwave Authoring Tips

This section contains miscellaneous tips for Shockwave authors.

▶ Use the Cast Member Properties dialog box to see the size of your cast members in kilobytes. Find out the total size of several cast members by selecting them all in the Cast window and then choosing Cast Member/ Properties from the Modify menu. You can also access the cast properties by pressing Ctrl on Macintosh or the right mouse button in Windows and clicking on a sprite on the stage.

▶ Use small size cast members and then use the Sprite Properties dialog box to resize the sprite on the stage. Access the Sprite Properties dialog box by choosing Sprite/Properties from the Modify menu or by pressing Ctrl on Macintosh or the right mouse button in Windows and clicking on a sprite on the stage. You can also use this dialog box to set keyframe properties for animating sprites over time. Animating sprite sizes can be processor-intensive, slowing down screen redraw, and tying up the user's machine—so use judiciously and test on your target machine.

▶ Avoid long repeat loops that tie up the processor. Instead, loop on a frame.

▶ Use the Lingo `Halt` command to stop your movie when it is finished playing, and thereby ensure that your movie does not eat up processor cycles after it finishes playing.

▶ Transitions, such as Dissolve, and ink effects can be processor-intensive, slowing down screen redraw and tying up the user's machine.

▶ Sprite locations are given relative to the stage. The Lingo commands `stageRight`, `stageLeft`, and so on are given in absolute coordinates, relative to the monitor.

▶ Putting Shockwave movies inside table cells, especially nested table cells, tends to crash browsers.

▶ To test your Shockwave movie on a Macintosh, drag and drop the .DCR file on the Netscape browser window. To test your Shockwave movies on a PC, hold the Alt key while choosing File, Open File, which will show the .DCR file type in the Open dialog box.

In Practice

This chapter gets you started creating Shockwave movies in Director. After reading this chapter you should be able to:

▶ Use Shockwave features during authoring

▶ Link to Internet-based content at author time and run time

▶ Create Shockwave movies for web browsers

▶ Create stand-alone Net-aware projectors

▶ Create and optimize Shockwave for Audio

▶ Create Shockwave movies with low-bandwidth content, optimized for the Internet

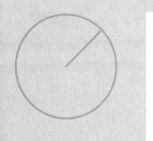

chapter **15**

David Miller

Mastering Shockwave

The last chapter provided information on many of the new Internet features in Director 6. This chapter provides more advanced tips and tricks for creating Director movies for Shockwave playback in a web browser (see fig. 15.1) or Net-aware projectors that incorporate Shockwave network functions.

This chapter covers the following topics:

- ▶ Browser support

- ▶ Using the Shockwave Netscape plug-in

- ▶ Using the Shockwave ActiveX control

- ▶ Shockwave for browsers that do not have the Shockwave plug-in installed

- ▶ Using CGI with Shockwave

- ▶ Creating dynamic content, custom, user-defined attributes, and Shockwave streaming audio

Figure 15.1

An interactive, 3D Shockwave movie playing in a web page.

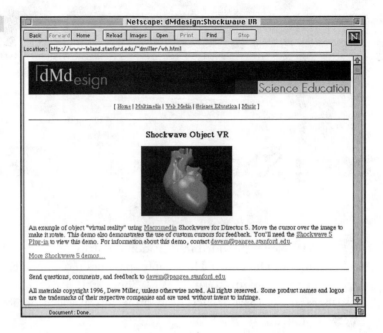

Browser Support

Currently, Shockwave for Director is supported in Netscape Navigator 2 and later for Macintosh, Windows 3.1, Windows 95, and Windows NT, and is partially supported in Microsoft Internet Explorer (MSIE) 2 for Macintosh and fully supported in MSIE 3. The Shockwave plug-in is included with Netscape's PowerPack 2 add-ons for the Navigator browser and is also available free from Macromedia's web site at:

`http://www.macromedia.com/Tools/Shockwave/index.html`

Shockwave for Director is also an ActiveX control for Windows 95 and Windows NT versions of MSIE 3. Macromedia has announced Shockwave bundling deals with Microsoft Internet Explorer 3, America Online, CompuServe, and Apple Computer's Internet Connection Kit.

Table 15.1 lists browser support for Shockwave at the time of this writing.

Table 15.1

Browser Support for Shockwave

Feature	Netscape 2	MSIE 2	Netscape 3	MSIE 3
Shockwave Plug-in	Yes	Mac-only, No NetLingo	Yes	Yes
Shockwave ActiveX	No	No	No	Windows 95/ NT only

Not all features may be supported.

Shockwave makes large demands on memory and disk space. The recommended minimum setting for web browser RAM is 10 MB and the recommended cache size is 10 MB.

For a list of Director features that are disabled in Shockwave for web browsers, turn to the later section "Security Features."

Using the Shockwave Netscape Plug-In

Chapter 13, "Designing Multimedia for the Web," provides extensive documentation on using Netscape plug-ins in HTML documents. This chapter, therefore, only briefly overviews this topic. In general, to embed a Shockwave movie in your HTML document, use HTML as follows:

```
<EMBED SRC="MyShock.dcr" HEIGHT=144 WIDTH=160 PLUGINSPAGE = "http://
➥www.macromedia.com/">
<NOEMBED>
<IMG SRC="MyShockFrame.gif" HEIGHT=120 WIDTH=160></NOEMBED>
```

The preceding code both embeds your movie and provides alternate content in case the user does not have a Netscape browser.

A following section, "Using OBJECT and EMBED Together," explains the HTML code you can use to support multiple browsers, including Internet Explorer. A subsequent section in this chapter, "Shockwave Unplugged," explains what to do if your users do not have the Shockwave plug-in installed.

Using the Shockwave ActiveX Control

The Shockwave for Director ActiveX Control is an ActiveX control for Internet Explorer 3. At this time, the Shockwave ActiveX Control works in MSIE 3 on Windows 95 and NT systems only. Support for Windows 3.1 and Macintosh may be available by the time you read this. If an application supports embedding ActiveX controls in its documents, you can use the ActiveX control to embed Shockwave movies in these documents.

To embed ActiveX controls in your HTML document, use the OBJECT tag. The OBJECT tag can take various attributes or parameters.

Reportedly, the Shockwave ActiveX Control recognizes Shockwave movies embedded within HTML documents by using either the OBJECT tag or the EMBED tag.

One advantage of the Shockwave ActiveX Control is the capability to provide automatic version control and downloading. This feature is provided with the CODEBASE parameter.

The following sample OBJECT tag is for a movie named MYSHOCK.DCR:

```
<OBJECT CLASSID="clsid:166B1BCA-3F9C-11CF-8075-444553540000"
CODEBASE="//active.macromedia.com/director/sw.cab#version=5,0,1,54"
WIDTH="320" HEIGHT="240" NAME="Shockwave" ID="logoshck">
<PARAM NAME="SRC" VALUE="myShock.dcr"></OBJECT>
```

The CLASSID parameter specifies the universal class identifier for the Shockwave ActiveX Control. It must be as follows:

```
CLASSID="clsid:166B1BCA-3F9C-11CF-8075-444553540000"
```

The CODEBASE parameter is similar to the PLUGINSPAGE attribute of the EMBED tag. The CODEBASE parameter to the OBJECT tag specifies where the Shockwave for Director ActiveX Control can be obtained if the user doesn't have it already installed in the browser or has an older version installed. Check Macromedia's web page for the latest version of the ActiveX control.

The WIDTH and HEIGHT parameters have their usual values. The ID parameter provides a name with which to refer to the Shockwave movie from other parts of the HTML document.

The PARAM tag enables the setting of various parameters. You must specify a source URL with the NAME parameter. The NAME="SRC" parameter tells the browser where to find the Shockwave movie to display in the web page. You can also provide additional parameters, such as:

```
<PARAM NAME="BGCOLOR" VALUE=#FFFFFF>
```

to set the background color to white, and

```
<PARAM NAME="PALETTE" VALUE="foreground">
```

to assert a custom palette.

The Shockwave plug-in for Netscape Navigator supports user-defined custom attributes in the EMBED tag (see previous discussion). Unfortunately, these attributes are not recognized by the Shockwave ActiveX Control. The Shockwave ActiveX Control only recognizes external parameters with specific predefined names within the OBJECT tag. The Director 6 manuals specify the names recognized. You can access these specific-named parameters from within your Shockwave Director movie by using the same Lingo functions you use to access custom attributes:

```
externalParamValue(ParamNameInQuotesOrNumber)

externalParamName(ParamNameInQuotesOrNumber)

externalParamCount()
```

If, for example, you used the previously listed OBJECT tag syntax to embed a file in a web page, the Lingo:

```
put externalParamValue("SRC") into field "paramDisplay"
```

puts the text MYSHOCK.DCR into field "paramDisplay".

For the complete list of predefined parameters recognized by the Shockwave ActiveX Control, see the Director 6 manuals.

Using OBJECT and EMBED Together

Chapter 13 provides more detail on using the OBJECT and EMBED tags. The following HTML shows how to support multiple browsers. This syntax displays your Shockwave movie in Netscape 2.x, Netscape 3.x, or Microsoft Internet Explorer 3 on most platforms and provides alternate content for browsers that do not support these tags:

```
<OBJECT ID="ShockwaveMovie"
CLASSID="CLSID:166B1BCA-3F9C-11CF-8075-444553540000"
CODEBASE="http://www.macromedia.com/..."
WIDTH=160 HEIGHT=120
    >
<PARAM NAME="swURL" VALUE="myShockwaveMovie.dcr">
<EMBED SRC="myShockwaveMovie.dcr" PLUGINSPAGE = "http://www.macromedia.com/"
➥WIDTH=160 HEIGHT=120>
</EMBED>
<NOEMBED>
<IMG SRC="NoShock.gif" ALT="Get the Shockwave plugin to see this cool
➥animation" WIDTH=160 HEIGHT=120 ALT="A Shockwave Movie">
</NOEMBED>
</OBJECT>
```

The following code enables you to display a Java applet if the Shockwave plug-in or ActiveX control is not present.

```
<OBJECT ID="ShockwaveMovie"
CLASSID="CLSID:166B1BCA-3F9C-11CF-8075-444553540000"
CODEBASE="http://www.macromedia.com/..."
WIDTH=160 HEIGHT=120
    >
<PARAM NAME="swURL" VALUE="myShockwaveMovie.dcr">
<EMBED SRC="myShockwaveMovie.dcr"
WIDTH=160 HEIGHT=120  PLUGINSPAGE = "http://www.macromedia.com/">
</EMBED>
<NOEMBED>
<IMG SRC="NoShock.gif" ALT="Get the Shockwave plugin to see this cool
➥animation" WIDTH=160 HEIGHT=120>
</NOEMBED>
<APPLET CODE="AnimationApplet"
WIDTH=160  HEIGHT=120>
<IMG SRC="NoApplet.gif" ALT="A Java applet"
WIDTH=160 HEIGHT=120>
</APPLET>
</OBJECT>
```

Shockwave Unplugged

Chances are, some browsers that hit your page will not have the Shockwave plug-in installed. In Netscape Navigator 2 or compatible browsers, a broken icon appears if the Shockwave plug-in is not present. At the very least, if you provide Shockwave content on your site, you should provide a link to the Macromedia Shockwave page at:

```
http://www.macromedia.com/shockwave/
```

so that users can download the plug-in for their system.

You also can use the PLUGINSPAGE parameter in the EMBED tag to automatically point users' browsers to the Shockwave download page. For example:

```
<EMBED SRC="myShockWave.dcr" WIDTH= 160 HEIGHT= 120  PLUGINSPAGE= "http://
➡www.macromedia.com/shockwave/ ">
```

Using Shockwave and the <META> Tag

You also can use Shockwave and Lingo network extensions to detect the presence of the Shockwave plug-in and automatically send the browser to a Shockwave-enabled page if the plug-in is present. If the plug-in is not detected, the <META> tag sends the user to an alternate, non-Shockwave page. This method was used by Macromedia on its home page.

Using the <META> Tag

1. Create a small Shockwave movie that contains the gotoNetPage command in a frame script; for example:

   ```
   gotoNetPage "myShockwaveEnabledPage.html"
   ```

   The page specified in the gotoNetPage command is your Shockwave-enabled page. In this case, "myShockwaveEnabledPage.html".

2. Embed this movie in an HTML document.

3. Place the following HTML between the <HEAD></HEAD> tags of your HTML document:

   ```
   <META HTTP-EQUIV=REFRESH CONTENT="20; URL=myNonShockedPage.html">
   ```

When a user loads the HTML document in the preceding tutorial, the Shockwave movie loads and sends the browser to the Shockwave-enabled page if the user has Shockwave installed. If the user does not have Shockwave, the broken plug-in icon appears. If you use the PLUGINSPAGE parameter described earlier, the user has the choice to go to a page to download the plug-in. The

HTML in the <META> tag automatically sends the user to the non-Shockwave page after 20 seconds.

Using Tiny Shockwave Movies

A variation on the preceding technique uses a small Shockwave movie.

1. Create a small Shockwave movie (1-by-1 pixel in size, for example) that contains the gotoNetPage command in a frame script, such as:

   ```
   gotoNetPage "myShockwaveEnabledPage.html"
   ```

2. Embed the Shockwave movie in a web page.

When a user loads this HTML document, the Shockwave movie loads and sends the browser to the Shockwave-enabled page, if the user has Shockwave installed. If the user doesn't have Shockwave, the user won't see the broken icon, because the movie is too small to display it, and the EMBED tag should be ignored by the user's browser.

JavaScript Workaround for Netscape 2 and Later

The following JavaScript workaround is a variation on sample code from Macromedia's *Shockwave Developer's Guide*, and it is designed to provide a solution for the no-plug-in problem for the most number of browsers. Here's what it does: In Netscape 2-compatible browsers, the broken plug-in icon displays when no Shockwave plug-in is present and the PLUGINSPAGE parameter automatically points the user to a download site. In browsers that do not support Netscape-compatible plug-ins, it usually displays the HTML between the NOEMBED tags.

```
<script language="JavaScript">
    <!-- hide this script tag's contents from old browsers
    document.write ( '<EMBED SRC="myShockWave.dcr" WIDTH= 160 HEIGHT=
    ➡120  ' );
    document.write ( ' PLUGINSPAGE= "http://www.macromedia.com/shockwave/
    ➡">'  );
    <!--done hiding from old browsers -->
</script>
<NOEMBED>
    <IMG SRC="noPlugin.gif">
</NOEMBED>
```

Using JavaScript 1.1 to Detect the Shockwave Plug-In

This example shows how to use some of the new features of JavaScript 1.1 to determine whether a user has installed a particular plug-in. At this time, this example works in Netscape Navigator 3 and later only.

The function described here uses the `mimeTypes` property of the built-in `Navigator` object. When passed a valid MIME type and sub-type, this function does the following:

▶ Returns 1 if Navigator recognizes the MIME type and has an enabled plug-in to handle it.

▶ Returns 0 if Navigator recognizes the MIME type, but does *not* have an enabled plug-in to handle it—if the MIME type is handled by a helper app, for example.

▶ Returns −1 if Navigator does *not* recognize the MIME type.

Here is the function:

```
<SCRIPT LANGUAGE="JavaScript">
function CheckForPlugin (myMime)
{
hasMimeType = navigator.mimeTypes[myMime]
if (hasMimeType)
{
   // The MimeType is recognized by Navigator, now determine if there is a
   ➥plug-in present
  hasPlugin = hasMimeType.enabledPlugin
  if (hasPlugin)
      // Plug-in is present
      return 1
   else
      // No plug-in, but the MIME type is recognized so, maybe a helper app
      ➥is set up
      return 0
}
else
{
   // MIME type not recognized
   return -1
}
```

```
} //end function
</SCRIPT>
```

The function has one parameter, myMIME. This parameter is a quoted text string that is the MIME type and sub-type of the media type in which you are interested—for example, "application/x-director" for the Shockwave plug-in or "video/quicktime" for QuickTime.

The line

```
hasMimeType = navigator.mimeTypes[myMime]
```

checks to see whether the MIME type is registered with the Navigator object and stores the results in the hasMimeType variable.

If the MIME type is recognized, the line

```
hasPlugin = hasMimeType.enabledPlugin
```

checks whether this MIME type has an enabled plug-in associated with it. If it does, the function returns 1. If the MIME type is recognized but does *not* have an associated enabled plug-in, the function returns 0. If the MIME type is *not* recognized, the function returns −1.

Use this function with the document.write method to create an HTML document at run time based on the user's browser environment. If the CheckForPlugin function is present within the HEAD tag of an HTML document, for example, the following code within the BODY tag creates custom content based on the return value of the CheckForPlugin function:

```
<SCRIPT LANGUAGE="JavaScript">
if (CheckForPlugin ("application/x-director")==1) document.write("You have
➥the Plug-in!")
if (CheckForPlugin ("application/x-director")==0) document.write("You have
➥the Helper App!")
if (CheckForPlugin ("application/x-director")==-1) document.write("Get
➥Plugged!")
</SCRIPT>
```

In practice, you would put appropriate HTML code with the document.write method for each possibility. The complete listing follows here.

```
<HTML>
<HEAD>
```

```
<TITLE>Checking for Plug-ins with JavaScript</TITLE>
<SCRIPT LANGUAGE="JavaScript">
function CheckForPlugin (myMime)
{
hasMimeType = navigator.mimeTypes[myMime]
if (hasMimeType)
{
   // The MimeType is recognized by Navigator, now determine if there is a
   ➥plug-in present
   hasPlugin = hasMimeType.enabledPlugin
   if (hasPlugin)
    // Plug-in is present
    return 1
   else
      // No plug-in, but the MIME type is recognized so, maybe a helper app
      ➥is set up
      return 0
}
else
{
   // MIME type not recognized
   return -1
}
} //end function
</SCRIPT>
</HEAD>
<BODY>
<SCRIPT LANGUAGE="JavaScript">
if (CheckForPlugin ("application/x-director")==1) document.write("You have
➥the Plug-in!")
if (CheckForPlugin ("application/x-director")==0) document.write("You have
➥the Helper App!")
if (CheckForPlugin ("application/x-director")==-1) document.write("Get
➥Plugged!")
</SCRIPT>
</BODY>
</HTML>
```

Using CGI with Shockwave

Common Gateway Interface (CGI) is by far the most common way to exchange information between servers and clients on the web. CGI scripts are
commonly written in a scripting language called PERL.

You can use the Net Lingo commands `GetNetText` and `GoToNetPage` to invoke a CGI script and to send data to a CGI script. Both commands use the `GET` method to send data to the CGI script.

You can invoke a CGI script as follows:

```
GetNetText ("http://www.myServer.com/cgi-bin/CGIscript.cgi")
set myResult = NetTextResult()
```

where `CGIscript.cgi` is a CGI script present on your web server and `myResult` contains the data returned from the CGI script.

If the CGI script accepts data, you encode it as follows:

```
GetNetText ("http://www.myServer.com/cgi-bin/
CGIscript.cgi?name1=value1&name2=value2")
```

where the string following the question mark contains name/value pairs of different variables that the CGI script is expecting and their constituent values, separated by ampersands.

It is beyond the scope of this chapter to go into the details of CGI scripting.

INSIDER TIP

For a great archive of ready-to-use CGI scripts see Matt's Script Archive at the following address:

`http://worldwidemart.com/scripts/`

Net-Aware Projectors

Besides creating the familiar Shockwave movies for the web, with Director 6 you can also create stand-alone, Net-aware projectors. Net-aware projectors have much of the same functionality of a Shockwave movie playing in a web browser—without requiring a web browser, plug-in, or ActiveX control. In addition, Net-aware projectors have many features that are disabled in the plug-in, such as the capability to read and write files from a disk. Net-aware projectors enable you to create custom, task-specific Internet clients and hybrid applications.

A Net-aware application is an application that can contain a mix of CD-ROM, disk-based, and Internet features. Director 6 provides Internet functionality within "Net-aware projectors," that have many of the same Internet features as a movie playing in a web browser. Authors can also leverage off of web browsers to provide Internet features.

The possibilities for Net-aware applications include the following:

▶ Running a Director projector from disk or CD-ROM and accessing time-sensitive information on the Internet, such as stock quotes or price lists

▶ Linking to external casts and media on the Internet from disk or CD-ROM to provide updates for a game or catalog

▶ Linking to content on a local disk or CD-ROM from a Shockwave movie playing in a web browser

▶ Using a web browser as a navigational shell to browse materials on CD-ROM, local hard disk, or the Net

▶ Distributing a web site on CD to users who may not have a Net connection

With additional third-party Xtras such as Allegiant Marionet (`http://www.allegiant.com/`) or Human Code's Xtranet (`http://www.gmatter.com/`), you can create peer-to-peer chat applications, custom news readers, and multiplayer games.

Net Lingo Guide

Net Lingo consists of extensions to the Lingo scripting language and enables you to make asynchronous network calls. *Asynchronous* means that the Net Lingo function or command does not return results immediately, but your movie can continue running and processing other events while you wait for the results of the Net Lingo call.

Your Shockwave movie can use the network extensions to Lingo to branch to another Shockwave movie anywhere on the web or to load web pages in a browser. You can also use Lingo network extensions to retrieve content on the Internet or create richly interactive control bars or navigational panels that load HTML documents into separate frames.

This section provides a guide to the most commonly used Net Lingo, including the new features in Director 6, along with code that you can use in your projects. If you are unfamiliar with Lingo's syntax and usage, details of this section will make more sense to you after you read Chapter 16, "Lingo: The Basics."

Net Lingo commands behave slightly differently depending on whether the commands are invoked in the authoring environment, within a web browser, or in a Net-aware projector. Such differences in behavior are pointed out as needed in the following discussions.

Because of the nature of network operations, you will use Net Lingo commands a little differently than other kinds of Lingo. Commonly, you will initiate a network operation, such as downloading a file, and then periodically query the state of that operation to check whether it is complete. When completed, you will process the data returned or the error returned. Typically, you follow this general procedure when making Net Lingo calls:

1. Begin the network operation, such as `DownLoadNetThing`.

2. Periodically call `NetDone()` in a frame loop, idle handler, or other periodic handler to determine when the operation is completed. By looping in a frame, your movie can continue with other tasks, such as animation or user interactivity, while the network operation is performed in the background.

3. After `NetDone()` returns TRUE, call `NetError()` to determine whether the operation completed successfully (returned OK) or returned an error.

4. Process the results depending on the data returned or process the error if the operation failed.

The way that you handle network operations depends on your particular application.

One possible way to set up your Director movie is to initiate the network operation in one frame, loop in a subsequent frame—periodically querying `NetDone()`—and then depending on the results of the net operation, proceed to a new frame.

For example, this handler initiates the network operation `GetNetText` from a frame script:

```
on exitFrame
global gMyID
    set gMyID = GetNetText("http://www.myserver.com/someText.txt")
end
```

To loop on a frame waiting for the network operation to complete, place this handler in a subsequent frame script:

```
on exitFrame
  global gMyID, gData
  if netDone(gMyID) then
     if NetError(gMyID) = "OK" then
        set gData = NetTextResult(gMyID)
   end if
  else
     go the frame
   end if
end
```

If `netDone` returns TRUE (that is, the operation is complete), check to make certain that no error occurred. If no error has occurred put the data that has been returned into a global variable (`gData` in this example) for further processing.

Because checking the status of a network operation requires the periodic calling of `NetDone`, this is a natural place to use Parent/Child objects, the actorList, and the `stepFrame` method. See Chapter 19, "Advanced Concepts," and Chapter 20, "Object-Oriented Programming in Director," for details on using these features of Lingo. Following is a simple plug and play script object you can use to monitor net processes. Place the following handler in a Parent script called Net Process Watcher:

```
property pURL, pID, pProcessType, pError
➥pMIME, pLastModDate,pFileName,pResultProcessor
on new me, aUrl, aMember, aProcessType,aFileName, aPostProcessor
  set pURL = aUrl
  set pMember = aMember
  set pProcessType = aProcessType
 if voidP(aFileName) then
  set pFileName = ""
  else
    set pFileName = aFileName
  end if
  if voidP(aProcessor) then
    set pResultProcessor = .EMPTY
  else
    set pResultProcessor = aPostProcessor
  end if
  set pError = ""
```

```
  set pMIME = ""
 set pLastModDate = ""
 set pID = -1
 return me
end
on StartNetProcess me
  case pProcessType of
    "GetNetText": set pID = GetNetText(pURL)
    "PreLoadNetThing":set pID =  preLoadNetThing(pURL)
    "DownLoadNetThing": set pID = DownLoadNetThing(pURL, pFileName)
  end case
  if getPos(the actorList, me) = 0 then
    add the actorList, me
  else
    netAbort()
  end if
end
on stepFrame me
if pID > -1 then
  if netDone (pID) then
    set  pError = NetError(pID)
    if  pError = "OK" then
        set pMIME = NetMIME(pID)
        set pLastModDate = NetLastModDate(pID)
      do pResultProcessor
    else
      handleNetErr me,pError
    end if
    set pID = -1
    deleteFromActorList me
  end if
end if
end
--
on handleNetErr me,pError
    alert pProcessType&&pID&&"Error returned:"&&pError
end
on deleteFromActorList me
  deleteAt (the actorlist, getPos(the actorlist, me))
end
```

To create this object in a movie or frame script use a Lingo statement such as the following:

```
gNetProcessWatcher = new(script "Net Process Watcher","http://www-
➥leland.stanford.edu/~dmiller/gmt.shtml", "GetNetText",VOID,"processGMT")
```

in which

```
script "Net Process Watcher"
```

is the name of the script object;

```
"http://www-leland.stanford.edu/~dmiller/gmt.shtml"
```

is the URL parameter to use with the specific Net Lingo command;

```
"GetNetText"
```

is the Net process to perform (either `GetNetText`, `PreLoadNetThing`, or `DownLoadNetThing`);

```
"VOID"
```

is the file name on local disk in which to save the downloaded data or file (in this case, no file name is given);

```
"processGMT"
```

is the name of a Lingo handler to process the downloaded data.

To begin a network process call the object's `StartNetProcess` handler like so:

```
StartNetProcess(gNetProcessWatcher)
```

Now your movie can play merrily along. As long as the playback head is moving and the `NetProcessWatcher` receives a `stepFrame` event, the processing of your net operation continues apace.

Initiating Asynchronous Network Operations

This section discusses the Lingo commands used to initiate an asynchronous network operation, such as downloading a file, loading another Shockwave movie, or opening a specific web page in a browser.

A new feature in Director 6 is that Net Lingo commands that initiate an asynchronous network operation return a unique network ID when the command is called as a function (that is, parameters are enclosed in parentheses), such as:

```
set myNetID = GetNetText("http://www.myserver.com/someText.txt")
```

You no longer need to call getLatestNetID() to retrieve a unique ID for a network operation. Assigning a unique ID to network operations is useful if you have more than one network operation in progress—if you are preloading an HTML file and its included graphics, for example, each of which requires a separate downloading operation. The total number of concurrent network operations possible in a Shockwave movie in a web browser is determined in the web browser preferences. It is usually set to four concurrent operations.

INSIDER TIP

Although you can have more than four concurrent network operations in a Net-aware projector, for performance reasons it generally is not a good idea.

GotToNetMovie URL

The GoToNetMovie command retrieves and plays a Shockwave movie from an HTTP server or FTP server. The currently playing movie continues to play until the new movie is completely downloaded and ready to play back.

When you use the GoToNetMovie command, be aware of the following points:

▶ The URL can specify a marker within a movie. For example:

```
set gNetID = GoToNetMovie ("http://www.myServer.com/movies/
map.dcr#intro")
```

in which intro is a marker in the movie's score.

▶ You can use relative URLs.

▶ Only one GotoNetMovie operation can be in progress at one time.

▶ When called from a Shockwave movie within a web browser, global variables persist between movies.

GoToNetPage URL browserFrameOrWindow

GoToNetPage takes an URL string as the first parameter. An optional second parameter identifies a browser frame or window within which to open the URL. For example,

```
GoToNetPage "http://www.myServer.com/myFabulousHomePage.html", "newWindow"
```

will open the specified web page in a separate window named "newWindow" if a window or frame of that name does not already exist.

In the authoring environment, GoToNetPage launches the browser identified in the Network Preferences dialog box and launches the URL. In a Net-aware projector, this command also uses the settings from the Network Preferences dialog box. In a web browser, this command uses the currently open browser.

The Lingo command GoToNetPage behaves slightly differently from other commands that initiate network operations, as follows:

▶ GoToNetPage does not return a netID.

▶ It cannot be stopped with NetAbort.

▶ When called from a Shockwave movie within a web browser, all global variables are cleared.

In Shockwave for Director 6, you can use GoToNetPage to target frames in an HTML document. One application of this would be in a two frame HTML document. One frame could contain a Shockwave navigation bar or Control Panel and the second frame could contain content accessed from the Shockwave Control Panel. Shockwave for Director Control Panels can have features such as button and rollover feedback and context-sensitive help. Figure 15.2 illustrates rich, responsive Shockwave Control Panels created using the interactivity features in Director and the frames parameter in GoToNetPage.

The Net Lingo syntax for targeting frames is as follows:

```
GoToNetPage "chapter1.html","content"
```

in which "chapter1.html" is the HTML document that will be loaded into the frame named "content". To integrate this into a navigation bar or Control Panel, place this command in the mouseUp handler of a button. For example:

```
on mouseUp
GoToNetPage "chapter1.html","content"
end
```

Figure 15.2

Shockwave control panels illustrating rollover feedback and context-sensitive help.

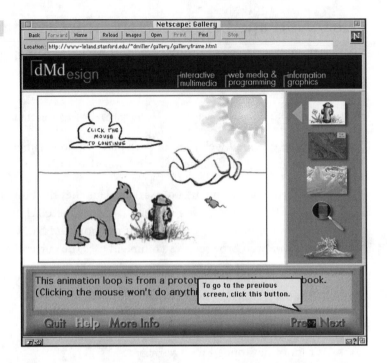

GetNetText URL

GetNetText is available in a web browser, a Net-aware projector, or in the authoring environment. It begins retrieving data from the specified URL, which can be an FTP or HTTP server. Use NetTextResult() to get at the data. For example:

```
set gNetID = GetNetText("ftp://ftp.myserver.com/someText.txt")
```

and

```
set gData = NetTextResult(gNetID)
```

PreLoadNetThing URL

PreLoadNetThing is only available in a web browser or in the authoring environment.

It takes one parameter, an URL string that can be an FTP or HTTP address, to a file on the Internet. This command attempts to download the specified file to the browser cache. Be aware that even if the download is completed successfully, you have no guarantee that the file will be present, because the browser cache can be emptied automatically by the browser at any time—for example, when the cache becomes too full—or the cache can be emptied by the user explicitly.

More details on the use of this command are covered in Chapter 14 in the section, "Using Lingo to Provide Run-Time Content Linking."

DownloadNetThing URL localFile

`DownloadNetThing` is a new command in Director 6. This command is only available in a Net-aware projector (that is, a projector that includes the Net Xtras that ship with Director 6) or in the authoring environment.

`DownloadNetThing` takes two parameters. An URL string is the first parameter. The URL can be an FTP or HTTP address to a file on the Internet. A second parameter identifies a path name and file name for the downloaded file. For example:

```
set gNetID = DownLoadNetThing( "http://www.myServer.com/someFile.gif", the
➥application path& "myDownLoadedFile.gif")
```

More details on the use of this command are covered in Chapter 14's section entitled, "Using Lingo to Provide Run-Time Content Linking."

State of Network Operations

This section discusses commands you can use to determine the state of a network   operation.

NetDone netID

`NetDone` returns TRUE if:

▶ No net operation has been started.

▶ A net operation has been started and it has either completed successfully or has returned with an error.

Typically, you call `NetDone` repeatedly after initiating a network operation such as `GetNetText`. The following handler loops in a frame waiting for the most recent net operation to complete.

```
on exitFrame
if netDone() then
```

```
   go the frame + 1
else
   go the frame
end if
end exitFrame
```

You also can pass a unique Net ID to determine whether a specific net operation is completed. For example:

```
on exit frame
global gNetID1,gNetID2
if netDone(gNetID1) then
   go the frame + 1
else
     if netDone(gNetID2) then
     go the frame + 2
   else
        go the frame
     end if
end if
end exitframe
```

NetError netID

This command returns the error for the specified net operation. If no network
ID is specified, the function returns the error from the most recent network
operation. Error codes returned for this operation were still being finalized as
of this writing. Error codes returned include the following:

- ▶ **"OK":** The operation completed successfully

- ▶ **4159:** The URL is invalid

- ▶ **4165:** The URL was not found

GetLatestNetID()

This function returns the network ID of the most recent network operation.

FrameReady frameNumber

FrameReady() returns TRUE if all media in the specified frame are present on
local disk. The following frame script, for example, loops in the current frame
until all the media for Frame 10 has been downloaded to local disk:

```
on exitFrame
 if frameReady(10) then
    nothing
 else
  go frame
 end if
end
```

MediaReady of member memberNumberorName

MediaReady returns TRUE if the specified cast member is present on the local disk. For example:

```
on exitFrame
if the mediaReady of member 10 = TRUE then
   alert " Member 10 is on disk!"
else
   go the frame
end if
end
```

on StreamStatus URL, state, bytesSoFar, bytesTotal, error

New in Director 6 is the streamStatus Lingo event handler. The streamStatus Lingo event handler enables you to keep track of a network operation while it is in progress. You can use the streamStatus report to provide a progress bar or other status display for your user during download. Continuous report of status eats up CPU cycles, so test your movie with this feature activated to see whether an unacceptable performance hit is present.

To enable streamStatus reporting in your movie, place the following line of Lingo in your on PrepareMovie handler:

```
tellStreamStatus(TRUE)
```

To report streamStatus into a field cast member named "status bar", place this handler in a movie script:

```
on streamStatus URL, state, bytesSoFar, bytesTotal, error
  set statusreport =
  ➥"File:"&&URL&&state&&bytesSoFar&&bytesTotal&&"Error:"&&error
  set the text of member "status bar" = statusreportend
```

NetAbort netID

NetAbort stops the specified network operation or the most recent operation if no network ID is specified.

Processing Results

This section discusses some of the Net Lingo commands you can use to process results of your network operations.

NetTextResult netID

NetTextResult is a command you will probably use often. NetTextResult returns the text from the last network operation or returns the text of a particular network operation if you pass in a specific network ID.

NetMIME netID

NetMIME returns the MIME type and subtype of data retrieved from the last network operation or returns the MIME type and subtype of data retrieved of a particular network operation if you pass in a specific network ID. It must be used immediately after a network operation has completed to report accurate results.

NetLastModDate netID

This command returns the file's last modified date as indicated in the HTTP header.

Querying the Network Environment

The following Lingo commands enable you to determine information about the operating environment.

netPresent()

The netPresent returns TRUE if the Network Lingo Xtras are present. It does *not* determine whether the user has as an active network connection. For example:

```
if netPresent() then
    put "got Net Xtras"
else
```

```
    put " no Net Xtras"
end if
```

browserName()

In the authoring environment and Net-aware projector, this function returns the path name of the browser specified in the Network Preferences dialog box. You can also use this function to set the path name to a browser.

For example:

```
browserName("myHardDisk:Netscape Navigator:Netscape Navigator 3.0.1")
```

sets the default browser to the Netscape Navigator that exists at that path name.

You can test to see whether browser launching is enabled by using the following:

```
if browserName(#enable) then
    put "got Browser Launching"
end if
```

You can turn on browser launching with:

```
browserName (#enable, TRUE)
```

You can turn off browser launching with:

```
browserName (#enable, FALSE)
```

ProxyServer

The following Lingo enables you to configure your Shockwave application to interact with a local proxy server:

The following Lingo sets the URL and port for an HTTP proxy server:

```
proxyServer #http, HTTPServerNameAsString, HTTPPortAsInteger
```

The following Lingo sets the URL and port for an FTP proxy server:

```
proxyServer #ftp, FTPServerNameAsString, FTPPortAsInteger
```

And this Lingo disables use of the local proxy servers:

```
proxyServer #ftp, #stop
proxyServer #http, #stop
```

You also can set these parameters in the Network Preferences dialog box discussed previously.

the runMode

the runMode property contains one of the following string values:

▶ **Author:** If the movie is running in Director

▶ **Projector:** If the movie is running as a projector

▶ **Plugin:** If the movie is running as a Shockwave plug-in or ActiveX control

You can use the runMode property to determine the environment in which your Director movie is playing and perform the appropriate actions. For example:

```
if the runMode = "Plugin" then
    do "Web_Plugin_Stuff"
else
    if the runMode = "Projector" then
        do "NetAware_Projector_Stuff"
    end if
end if
```

the version

You can also test for playback within Shockwave in a web browser by using the version property. For example:

```
if the version contains "net" then
    put "I'm in a browser"
end if
```

Preferences

Preferences are a handy way to save state or user data—such as game scores or user names—across sessions. Preference settings were originally designed for use in Shockwave movies playing in a web browser. See Chapter 14 for a detailed discussion of these commands.

In a Net-aware projector, you can also use standard FileIO commands to save and load user preferences from a write-enabled folder or directory. The command setPref does not work in a projector on a locked volume such as a

CD-ROM. These commands use the same folder as the projector to store preferences if the Net-aware projector is on a write-enabled disk.

SetPref prefFileName, prefString

When you first use the setPref command within your Shockwave movie, the file is automatically created in the local Shockwave support folder.

For example:

```
setPref gamepref.txt, score1:456
```

creates the file gamepref.txt in the Shockwave support folder of the local hard disk and appends the string "score1:456".

getPref prefFileName

This function, getPref(prefFileName), returns the content of the file named prefFileName that is present in the special Shockwave support folder. If the file does not exist, getPref returns VOID. For example:

```
set myPrefText = getPref("gamepref.txt")
```

loads the variable myPrefText with the contents of the text file "gamepref.txt" in the special Shockwave support folder.

Interface

This section looks at Lingo and HTML tags that you can use to control the web browser interface.

NetStatus()

In a web browser, you can use NetStatus() to set the text displayed in the Netscape Navigator's status bar. It doesn't work with the ActiveX control.

PALETTE Attribute of the EMBED Tag

In a web browser, you can use the PALETTE attribute of the EMBED tag to create a custom palette in your Shockwave movie and force the browser to use this palette. Set PALETTE = FOREGROUND to assert a custom Shockwave palette. A custom palette shifts all the colors in the rest of the display, which can be disorienting for some users. Also, if the user jumps to a new page, the palette may not get reset. See Chapter 15 for details on using palettes.

BGCOLOR Attribute of the EMBED Tag

In a web browser, you can use the BGCOLOR attribute of the EMBED tag to set the background color of the Macromedia wallpaper that displays while your Shockwave movie downloads and before it begins playing. For example:

```
"BGCOLOR" =#FFFFFF
```

sets the background color to white.

AUTOSTART Attribute of the EMBED Tag

Use the AUTOSTART attribute of the EMBED tag to present the movie initially in a stopped state and then use JavaScript or VBScript, as subsequently described in the "Browser Scripting" section, to start the movie, based on user input or another event. For example:

```
AUTOSTART = FALSE
```

presents the movie in an initially stopped state.

Browser Scripting and Interapplication Communication

New in Director 6 is the integration of Shockwave movies playing in web browsers with the browser's external scripting environment such as JavaScript or VBScript. This means you can use JavaScript and VBScript functions to communicate with your Shockwave movie and pass data from your movie to the scripting environment. You can also pass external parameters from an EMBED or OBJECT tag to your Shockwave movie.

External Parameters

Shockwave plug-in for Netscape Navigator supports user-defined custom attributes in the EMBED tag. Custom attributes are ways to get information from the HTML document into your Shockwave movie. Custom attributes enable you to change aspects of your Shockwave movie without recoding and recompiling a new Shockwave movie. These attributes follow the standard NAME = VALUE syntax of most HTML tag attributes. You place these custom attributes within the EMBED tag in your HTML document. These attributes and their values are accessed from within your Shockwave Director movie with the following Lingo functions:

▶ `externalParamValue(ParamNameInQuotesOrNumber)`

▶ `externalParamName(ParamNameInQuotesOrNumber)`

▶ `externalParamCount()`

The functions `externalParamValue()` and `externalParamName()` can take either an integer representing the number of an external attribute or a string in quotation marks representing the NAME in a NAME = VALUE pair.

The function `externalParamValue` returns the VALUE in the NAME = VALUE pair for the specified attribute. If you EMBED a Shockwave movie with the following HTML, for example:

```
<EMBED SRC="custattr.dcr" WIDTH=160 HEIGHT=64  myCustomAttribute=OFF>
```

the function `externalParamValue(1)` returns the string `"custattr.dcr"`. The function `externalParamValue("WIDTH")` returns the string 160.

The function `externalParamName` returns the attribute NAME for the specified attribute.

The function `externalParamCount()` takes no parameters and returns the total number of attributes. The total number of attributes includes the SRC, HEIGHT, and WIDTH attributes and any other attributes. If you EMBED a Shockwave movie with the following HTML, for example:

```
<EMBED SRC="custattr.dcr" WIDTH=160 HEIGHT=64  myCustomAttribute=OFF>
```

the function `externalParamCount()` returns the integer 4.

You cannot use custom attributes with the Shockwave ActiveX control. But you can use predefined external parameters, of which there are many, to communicate with your Shockwave movie. See the Director documentation for details.

Browser Scripting Environment

By integrating Shockwave in the browser scripting environment, you can pass data from the HTML page to your Shockwave movie and vice versa. As of this writing, browser scripting is supported only in Navigator 3 Mac68K, PPC, Windows 95/NT4, or Internet Explorer 3 on Windows 95/NT4.

You address your Shockwave movie differently in Navigator and Internet Explorer.

Enabling Browser Scripting for Netscape Navigator and Internet Explorer

1. Put the following script within the HEAD tag of your HTML document:

```
<SCRIPT Language ="JavaScript">
var gXPlatformMovieName    //global variable for movie name
var myAppName = navigator.appName
foundOffset = myAppName.indexOf("Microsoft Internet Explorer")
   if (foundOffset < 0) {
      gXPlatformMovieName  =  document.SWMovie;  //in Navigator
   } else {
      gXPlatformMovieName  = SWMovie;  //in IE
   }
//SWMovie is the NAME attribute used in the EMBED or OBJECT tag
</SCRIPT>
```

2. Include a NAME attribute in the EMBED or OBJECT tag. For example:

```
<EMBED WIDTH=160 HEIGHT=120 SRC="myMovie.dcr" NAME="SWMovie"
PLUGINSPAGE = "http://www.macromedia.com/">
```

3. Then call scripting functions from JavaScript, as follows:

```
function tellSWMovieToPlay() {
   gXPlatformMovieName.Play()
}
```

You can now use the following JavaScript and VBScript methods to communicate with your Shockwave movie:

▶ **Play():** Starts the movie playing if it is stopped.

▶ **Stop():** Stops the movie.

▶ **Rewind():** Rewinds the movie.

▶ **GetCurrentFrame():** Returns the number of the current frame.

▶ **GotoFrame(frameNum):** Tells the movie to go to the frame specified by frameNum.

▶ **GotoMovie(URL):** Tells the movie to go the specified URL, similar to a GoToNetMovie command in Lingo.

▶ **EvalScript(AString):** This JavaScript command calls an EvalScript handler in the Shockwave movie. Use this handler to run a Lingo script from JavaScript. An EvalScript Lingo handler must be present in the

Shockwave movie. `AString` can be any parameters you want to pass to the `EvalScript` Lingo handler. You can also return a result from Lingo, which will be returned to the calling JavaScript script.

▶ **AutoStart(trueOrFalse):** Sets the `AutoStart` property of the movie.

To communicate from your Shockwave movie to the browser scripting environment, you can use `EvalScript` as discussed previously or the following Lingo command:

`ExternalEvent(AString)`

In Netscape Navigator, `ExternalEvent` calls a JavaScript function named `AString`.

Internet Explorer receives `AString` as an event. You must have an event handler set up to accept the event.

Shockwave for Audio Net Lingo

Shockwave for Audio provides a rich set of Lingo commands that you can use to control and monitor playback of and determine the properties of Shockwave for Audio files. These commands include the following:

▶ `bitRate of member`	▶ `percentStreamed of member`
▶ `bitesPerSample of member`	▶ `play member`
▶ `copyrightInfo of member`	▶ `preLoadBuffer member`
▶ `currentTime`	▶ `preLoadTime member`
▶ `duration of member`	▶ `sampleRate of member`
▶ `getError`	▶ `soundChannel of member`
▶ `getErrorString`	▶ `state of member`
▶ `mostRecentCuePoint`	▶ `stop member`
▶ `numChannels of member`	▶ `streamName of member`
▶ `on cuePassed`	▶ `URL of member`
▶ `pause member`	▶ `volume of member`

In addition to the discussion in this chapter, Chapters 11 and 14 also cover a subset of these Shockwave for Audio commands in some detail.

Security Features

Any time you are downloading files and executables from unknown sources, consider the security issues. Macromedia has been careful to make Shockwave and related technologies as secure as possible, with a minimum trade-off in functionality.

Many of the features of Director are disabled in the Shockwave web browser plug-in and ActiveX control.

The following list identifies some of the Director features that are disabled in the Shockwave web browser plug-in. Check Macromedia's web site for the latest security enhancements for Shockwave.

▶ You cannot use Director's Movie in a Window feature.

▶ Many of the Lingo commands that provide access to the client hard disk, file system, or operating system have been disabled. The disabled commands include:

```
openResFile

closeResFile

open window

close window

pasteFromClipboard member x of castLib y

saveMovie

printFrom

open, openDA, closeDA

quit, restart, and shutdown

moviePath

pathName

searchCurrentFolder

searchPaths
```

▶ mci commands in Windows are disabled.

▶ FileIO, SerialIO, OrthPlay XObjects/Xtras are disabled.

▶ XObjects, XCMDs, XFCNs cannot be embedded as resources in a movie, but can be used in the Shockwave support folder.

The following Lingo commands and features have restricted usage under Shockwave. You can use these commands to access external files in the special Shockwave disk cache or support folder. See Chapter 14 for details on the Shockwave support folder.

```
openXLib

closeXLib

open castlib x
```

In addition, a Security dialog box appears at the outset of any downloading operation such as `GetNetText`, `PreLoadNetThing`, or `DownLoadNetThing`. This dialog box enables the user to deny the downloading operation.

In a Net-aware projector, many of the features disabled in the Shockwave web plug-in are enabled.

Dynamic Content and Shockwave Streaming Audio

This section takes a tutorial approach to teach you how to accomplish the following:

▶ Add streaming audio files to your Shockwave movie.

▶ Access and use custom, user-defined attributes in the EMBED tag inside your Shockwave movie. Custom, user-defined attributes enable you to get information into your Shockwave movie from the HTML document.

▶ Use these custom attributes to provide dynamic content.

The technique described here requires Netscape Navigator 2 and later or a browser that supports JavaScript version 1. The tutorial requires the Shockwave for Audio Streaming Xtra to be in the Shockwave Support folder in your Netscape plug-ins folder and in your Director 6 Xtras folder for authoring. If you performed the standard install of Shockwave, you should be all set up.

This tutorial uses the following files:

► SWA.HTM

► SWATUTOR.DIR

► CITYNITE.SWA

► MORNING.SWA

The file SWA.DIR is the final version of the Director movie used in this tutorial. The HTML document SWA.HTM uses JavaScript and custom, user-defined attributes in the EMBED tag to provide different audio content depending on the time of day that the page is visited. The custom, user-defined attribute in this case is swaURL. The value of this attribute is an URL to a valid SWA file for playback by the Shockwave movie.

For this tutorial you can create your own HTML file using the following JavaScript code or use the file SWA.HTM on the CD. Here is the JavaScript code:

```
<script language="JavaScript">
<!-- hide this script tag's contents from old browsers
var myDate = new Date();
var myHour = myDate.getHours();
if (myHour < 12){
        document.write('<EMBED SRC="swa.dcr" WIDTH=160 HEIGHT=64
          ➥swaURL="morning.swa">');
}
else {
        document.write('<EMBED SRC="swa.dcr" WIDTH=160 HEIGHT=64
          ➥swaURL="citynite.swa">');
}
<!-- done hiding from old browsers -->
</script>
```

This JavaScript runs in Netscape Navigator 2 or later, or on a browser that supports JavaScript version 1.

Chapters 11 and 14 provide details on creating and using .SWA files. If you don't want to create your own external .SWA files, two .SWA files are provided for you for the following tutorial: CITYNITE.SWA and MORNING.SWA. These files were created from sample digital audio files provided on the SoundEdit 16 CD—the files City Night Amb and Birds Desert Morning. Both files are stereo, 16-bit, 44 kHz sound files several second long. They both contain various environmental sounds. These files were converted to mono files with data rates of 8 Kbps (the lowest data rate possible) in SoundEdit 16 by using the Shockwave for Audio Export Xtra. Original file sizes were more than 7 MB and 4.9 MB. These files were converted to 41 KB and 29 KB size files, respectively, for a compression ratio of over 170 to 1.

Creating Dynamic Content, Custom Attributes, and Shockwave Streaming Audio

1. Open the Director file SWATUTOR.DIR.

2. Insert a cast member reference to an external .SWA file. Steps 3–6 detail how to do so.

3. Open the Cast window by choosing Cast under the Window menu, pressing Command+3 on a Mac, or pressing Ctrl+3 in Windows.

4. Click on an empty cast slot to select it.

5. Choose Other:SWA Streaming Xtra under the Insert menu.

6. With the cast member still selected, click in the Cast Member Name text entry box at the top of the Cast window and enter **swa**. You can use any name you want, but swa is used in this tutorial.

7. Double-click on cast member 4 in the Cast window to open the Script window. You will find an on startMovie handler in the Script window.

Figure 15.3

Startmovie handler for playing an .SWA file.

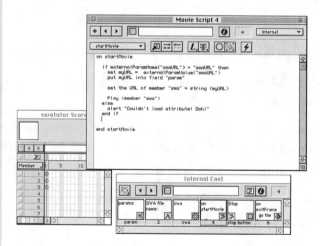

continues

Creating Dynamic Content, Custom Attributes, and Shockwave Streaming Audio continued

8. Type the following handler between the on startMovie and end startMovie lines:

```
if externalParamName("swaURL") = "swaURL" then
    set myURL = externalParamValue("swaURL")
    put myURL into field "param"
    set the URL of member "swa" = string (myURL)
    Play (member "swa")
else
    alert "Couldn't load attribute! Doh!"
end if
```

This handler is called when the movie first starts. It looks for the custom, user-defined attribute "swaURL" within the EMBED tag of the HTML document in which it is embedded as a Shockwave movie. The EMBED tag looks like this:

```
<EMBED SRC="swa.dcr" WIDTH=160 HEIGHT=64    swaURL="morning.swa">
```

You can look at the file SWA.HTM to see what the HTML looks like. Then, the handler sets the local variable "myURL" to the value of the swaURL custom attribute, which should be a valid URL to an .SWA file, in this case "morning.swa". It sets the URL of the SWA cast member reference you just created (which you named "swa") to the URL stored in the variable myURL with the following line:

```
set the URL of member "swa" = string (myURL)
```

Next, this handler starts playing the SWA sound file with the Play command.

9. Now add a button so that the user can stop playback. Steps 10–17 detail how to do so.

10. Open the Tool Palette by choosing Tool Palette under the Window menu, pressing Command+7 on a Mac, or pressing Ctrl+7 on Windows.

11. Click on the Button tool to select it.

12. Drag across the Director stage to place a button on the stage.

13. Type **Stop** inside the button.

14. Open the Cast window.

15. Select the button you just created in the cast.

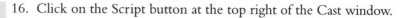

16. Click on the Script button at the top right of the Cast window.

    A Script window containing an empty mouseUp handler with a blinking insertion point should appear.

17. Type **Stop(member "swa")** between the on mouseUp and end lines.

Figure 15.4

Handler to stop playing the .SWA file.

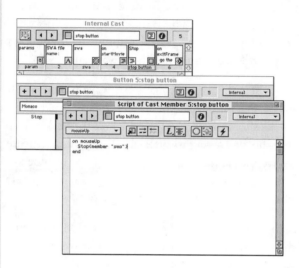

18. Now you instruct the movie to loop on frame 1. Double-click on the Script channel in frame 1.

    A Script window containing an empty exitFrame handler with a blinking insertion point should appear.

19. Type **go the frame** between the on exitFrame and end lines.

20. Choose Save As under the File menu.

21. Save the movie as SWA.DIR.

22. Choose Save As Shockwave under the File menu.

23. Name the movie **SWA.DCR**.

You can now test your movie. Make sure the files SWA.HTM and SWA.DCR are in the same directory and open the file SWA.HTM in your web browser. Or you can just drag and drop the SWA.DCR into an open Netscape Navigator window to test playback.

In Practice

This chapter has only scratched the surface of things you can do with Shockwave and Director. Consider it a place to get started using Shockwave, or, if you already use Director, to master some techniques for creating high-quality Shockwave movies. This chapter concludes the consideration of Director on the Net. Chapter 16, " Lingo: The Basics," begins the next major part of this book, a thorough look at Lingo. Keep in mind the following practical techniques when you are working with Shockwave movies:

▶ Some browsers that reach your Shockwave movie will not have the Shockwave plug-in installed. Accommodating such browsers is easy. This chapter has shown how to provide a link to the Macromedia Shockwave page; use the <META> tag to offer alternate content; create a very small Shockwave movie that can be "hidden" from browsers without the plug-in; use a JavaScript workaround; or use JavaScript to determine whether the Shockwave plug-in is present.

▶ Use both OBJECT and EMBED tags in your HTML documents to accommodate the maximum number of users and browsers.

▶ Use Net Lingo to start and manage network operations.

▶ Create dynamic documents using run-time content linking and browser scripting.

PART V

Lingo

chapter 16

Raúl Silva
Gretchen Macdowall

Lingo: The Basics

You can make useful movies in Director without typing a line of Lingo. Almost any linear movie that plays from start to finish, with occasional pauses to wait for a mouse click, can be created by using the score alone. These linear Director movies work well for such things as presentations.

Lingo enables you to break away from this sequential model. With Lingo you can make "smart" movies that take the user's input, evaluate it, and respond accordingly. This may be a task as simple as having buttons to go backward or to skip a section, or it can be as complex as creating a full-blown arcade game.

Is Lingo hard to learn? No! Although the Lingo Dictionary now contains more than 700 entries, the bulk of everyday coding centers around the 16 commands outlined in the "Essential Lingo Commands: Coding a Simple Movie" section of this chapter. Learn these terms and you're halfway there.

NOTE

The *Lingo Dictionary* is one of the reference books included with Director. It includes all the Lingo commands and functions available, as well as syntax and examples. Keep it nearby!

The biggest challenge in learning Lingo is understanding how Lingo interacts with cast members and the score, and where to place your scripts so that they behave properly.

This chapter will cover the basics of Lingo as follows:

▶ Basic components of Lingo

▶ The location of Lingo: Scripts

▶ The message hierarchy

▶ Essential Lingo commands

Key Concepts

You know by now—from creating movies exclusively with the score—that a Director movie that contains no Lingo plays from frame 1 straight through to the last frame, displaying and playing the cast members that you have placed in each frame of the score. When Lingo executes a movie, it controls playback in place of the score. A Lingo script can do the following:

▶ Jump to another part of the score or to another movie

▶ Change the cast member and other properties of any sprite channel

▶ Keep a Director movie paused by looping continuously in one frame

▶ Detect and respond to a particular user action, such as a mouse click in a certain area of the screen, or a key press

▶ Generate new score frames on the fly and fill them up with members

With the score alone you can create movies that *entertain* your audience. With Lingo you can create experiences that *include* the audience. Essential Lingo commands will be discussed soon, but to use these commands effectively you must first understand a little about the Director environment.

In an interactive Director movie, the user runs the show. You can't tell from looking at a still screen, but behind the scenes Director is constantly checking to see whether the user has moved the mouse or pressed a key. The bulk of Director programming lies in telling Director how to respond to the user, but it can also include details such as detecting when the user has done nothing for a while and programming some enticement to continue.

This section takes you on a tour of the two sides of that behind the scenes environment: yours and the user's. On your side you have commands and functions. These are the actions you can perform. Most commands and functions work on objects in the Lingo environment, such as sprites, cast members, or windows. Commands and functions make something happen that the user can see. On the user side are events and messages. Every action the user takes (or doesn't take) with the mouse or the keyboard is an event that generates a Director message.

Your job is to use commands and functions to write message handlers that tell Director how to respond to messages. This section introduces you to these and other basic components of Lingo. After reading this section you will understand Director's system for letting you know about user events, and you will know where to place your scripts to respond to those events.

Commands and Functions

Commands and functions are the building blocks of Lingo. Almost every line of code you write contains at least one command or function. *Commands* make something happen. The following lines of code all contain commands. In each line, the command is in bold. Each command line is followed by a comment line that explains what the command does.

```
sound close 1
-- stops the sound playing in sound channel 1
preLoad 12,15
-- loads any cast member in the score between frames 12 and 15 into memory
put " " into field "Question 1"
-- clears field "Question 1" by filling it with a space
```

Functions return a value that you can test, or store in a variable. Some functions require you to pass values to them when they are called.

Functions that require values are documented with parentheses after them in the *Lingo Dictionary*. The following lines of code contain functions. In each line the function is in bold, and the comment that follows each code line explains what it does.

```
if the stillDown = TRUE then go the frame
-- The stillDown function returns TRUE or FALSE
-- This line of code tests if the user is holding down the mouse and
-- continues to loop in the same frame as long as the user is holding down
-- the mouse.
--

put list( 4, 8, 12 ) into buttonSpriteList
-- The list function takes the values you pass in parentheses and returns a
-- list containing those values-- in other words the list command makes
-- a list for you.
-- This line of code makes a new list and saves it in the variable
-- buttonSpriteList for later use.
--

set nextFreeCast = findEmpty(member "ButtonZ")
-- The findEmpty function takes the cast member value you pass in
-- parentheses and returns the number of the next empty cast slot.
--
-- This line of code sets variable nextFreeCast to the number of the next
-- empty cast slot after cast "ButtonZ".
--
```

INSIDER TIP

Inserting two hyphens in front of a code line creates a comment line. Get into the habit now of documenting your Lingo as you go along. Not only does this you make it easier for another person who may have to read your code, but you help yourself as well. It's almost a given that you will have to revise your creation somewhere down the line. Months after the fact, when you're busy on new projects, you may find it hard to remember what a certain block of code in your old project is supposed to be doing. Comment everything—Director has no performance penalty for heavily commented code. Comments are stripped from the code before it loads into memory and runs.

Now it's time to fire up Director and try some Lingo commands and functions out for yourself. The first action you need to take when creating a movie in Director is to open up the Message window. Press Command+M (Ctrl+M for Windows) to open the Message window. The Message window is an indispensable tool for testing out your Lingo code. Normally, you must play the movie to see your code in action, but the Message window enables you to test out just one line of code at a time, regardless of whether the movie is running.

The Message window opens with a commented line:

```
-- Welcome to Director --
```

All of Director's responses appear in the Message window as comments, which makes system responses easy to distinguish from your input.

Position your cursor under the `-- Welcome to Director --` line and enter the following:

```
put 5 + 3
```

After you press Return, Director evaluates your code and responds as follows:

```
-- 8
```

The `put` command evaluates the Lingo expression following it and displays the result in the Message window.

Next, enter these two lines:

```
set myVariable = 4
put myVariable
```

Director responds as follows:

```
-- 4
```

The `set` command puts a value into a variable. When you use the `put` command on a variable, the Message window shows you the variable's contents.

Now try a command and a function. Enter the following line:

```
put length("habitat")
```

Director responds as follows:

```
-- 7
```

The `length` function takes a string of characters as an argument and returns the length, or number of characters, in the string. The `put` command displays the result of the `length` function.

Figure 16.1 shows what the Message window should look like after you have entered the sample commands.

Figure 16.1

The Message window after you type the sample commands.

You can use the Message window for analyzing and debugging the code in your movies, as well as testing individual lines.

Objects and Properties

Objects are the parts of the Director environment that you can control with Lingo. *Properties* are object characteristics that you can check or change. Most Lingo coding involves checking and setting the properties of objects to change the action on the stage (for example, changing the position of a sprite). Following is Lingo code that gets or sets object properties. In each line, the object name is bold and the object property is italic.

```
set the locH of sprite 1 to 101
-- Moves sprite 1 to horizontal location 101 on the stage
set the boxTypeof member "Address" to #scroll
-- Changes the text field "Address" to a scrolling field
put the filled of member "Small Box"
-- displays whether or not the shape cast "Small Box" is filled with a
pattern
```

The movie itself is an object. To change one of the movie's properties, enter the following in the Message window:

```
set the stagecolor to 255
```

When you do this, the stage turns black. `stagecolor` is one of the properties of the movie.

The built-in Director objects include sprites, cast members, and windows. In this chapter, you learn how to use Lingo to control Director's built-in objects by changing their properties. You also can create your own Lingo objects with properties that you choose.

Chapter 20, "Object-Oriented Programming in Director," covers creating and using custom Lingo objects.

Events, Messages, and Handlers

Everything in Lingo happens as the result of an event. Some events are user actions like mouseUp and keyUp. Others are generated by the system, such as timeout. Lingo recognizes the events listed in Table 16.1, among others. Note that some events can be triggered by more than one kind of action.

Table 16.1

Standard Lingo Events

Event	Happens When
mouseUp	User releases the mouse button
mouseDown	User presses the mouse button
mouseEnter	The pointer moves into a sprite
mouseLeave	The pointer moves out of a sprite
mouseWithin	The pointer is inside a sprite
cuePassed	Every time a cue point is passed by a sound, QuickTime digital video, or Xtra that supports cue points
beginSprite	The playback head reaches a sprite
endSprite	The playback head exits a sprite
prepareFrame	Before the current frame is imaged; only sprites receive this message
rightMouseUp	User releases the right mouse button (Windows) or releases the mouse button while holding the Control key (Macintosh)
rightMouseDown	User presses the right mouse button (Windows) or presses the right mouse button while holding the Control key (Macintosh)
keyUp	User releases a key
keyDown	User holds a key

continues

Table 16.1	continued

Standard Lingo Events

Event	Happens When
startMovie	User launches a Director projector
	The Lingo command `play movie` is executed and the next movie loads
	The Lingo command `go movie` is executed and the next movie loads
	The first time the Lingo command `open window` is executed for a Movie in a Window
stopMovie	User presses Command+Q or Command+. (period)
	The Lingo command `quit` is executed
	The Lingo command `play movie` is executed and the current movie is unloaded
	The Lingo command `go movie` is executed and the current movie is unloaded
activateWindow	User clicks on a Movie in a Window that doesn't currently have the focus, bringing that movie to the front
moveWindow	User drags a Movie in a Window
resizeWindow	User resizes a Movie in a Window
deactivateWindow	User clicks on a Movie in a Window that does not currently have the focus, and the current movie moves behind the movie that does have the focus
closeWindow	User clicks the close box of a Movie in a Window
	The Lingo command `close window windowName` is executed
	The Lingo command `set the visible of window windowName to FALSE` is executed
enterFrame	Playback head enters a frame in the score
exitFrame	Playback head leaves a frame in the score
idle	Director is not processing any events
timeout	The system property `timeoutLapsed` is greater than or equal to the system property `timeoutLength`

When Director senses that an event has occured, it creates an event message. Director then looks through the Lingo scripts in the movie to find the code that handles that message. A message handler is a block of code that starts with on *messageName*.

A Lingo script consists of one or more message handlers. Message handlers always start with on and end with end. They look like the following:

```
on messageName
    Lingo statement
    Lingo statement
    ...
    ...
    Lingo statement
end
```

You use the Lingo statements to tell Director what to do after it encounters a particular event message. The following are some simple examples of message handlers. The comments following each handler explain what the respective handler does:

```
on exitFrame
    go the frame
end


-- loops the playback head continuously in the same frame


on keyUp
    global score
    if the key = RETURN and field "Quiz Question 1" = "nuclear reactor" then
        set score = score + 20
        alert "That's right!"
    end if
end


-- When the user presses RETURN, Director checks the text field "Quiz
-- Question 1"
-- If the user has typed "nuclear reactor" into the text field the user's
-- score will be incremented by 20 and the system will display a dialog
-- box with the message "That's right!"
```

You can create your own events and event handlers in addition to the ones built into Director. Custom handlers fit the following basic mold:

```
on handlerName
    Lingo statement
    Lingo statement
end
```

The following code is an example of a custom handler:

```
on cleanUp
    puppetSprite 3,FALSE
    puppetSound 0
    updateStage
    sound stop 1
    set score = 0
end


-- returns a sprite to score control and turns off sound
-- in preparation to move to another part of the game
```

Unlike predefined handlers, which are called by Director in response to a detected event, custom handlers must be called explicitly in your script. To call a custom handler, you simply use its name in your code. The following code generates a `cleanUp` event that goes to the `on cleanUp` custom handler.

```
on mouseUp
    cleanUp
    go frame "Game 2"
end
```

The Location of Lingo: Scripts

You may have been wondering, having read the preceding examples, how you control when and where a message is handled. How do you specify which frame should loop or which text field should check key presses for the Enter key? The type of script you place your handlers in determines what messages it will receive. This next section describes how messages and scripts work together.

Introducing Scripts

The four different kinds of scripts in Director are sprite, cast member, frame, and movie. Sprite scripts and frame scripts are also known as behavior scripts. The kind of script in which you place the handler determines when and where it can handle a message. (There is also a fifth type of script: parent scripts. *Parent scripts* do not receive messages about user events. Parent scripts are covered in Chapter 20.

The kind of script in which you place the handler determines when and where it can handle a message.

Behavior Scripts

Behaviors are scripts associated to the Score. They enable you to easily create a sequence of actions that will be taken when certain events (both standard and custom) occur. You can attach multiple behaviors to sprites, but frames can only have one behavior. Behaviors are covered in detail in Chapter 19, "Advanced Concepts."

Sprite Scripts

A sprite script is linked to a sprite in the score. You create a sprite script by highlighting that sprite in the score, and selecting New Script from the Script pop-up menu (see fig. 16.2).

Figure 16.2

Create a sprite script by highlighting that sprite in the score and selecting New Script from the Script pop-up menu.

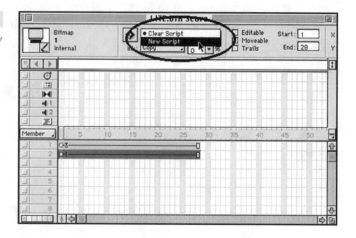

Cast Member Scripts

A cast member script is linked to the cast member. It receives a message when the user clicks or types into that cast member, provided the cel it occupies does not have a script that processes a mouseUp event. If you want a cast member to behave the same way everywhere it occurs in the score, use a cast member script. You create a cast member script by highlighting a cast member in the Cast window, clicking on the cast member properties button to bring up the Cast Member Properties window, and then clicking on the cast member's script button (see fig. 16.3).

Figure 16.3

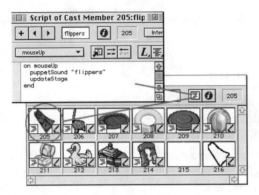

Create a cast member script by highlighting the cast member, clicking on cast member properties, and then clicking on the script icon.

Frame Scripts

Frame scripts receive messages when the playback head enters or exits the frame they are in. They also receive any mouse and key press messages not already handled by sprite or cast member scripts. The most common use of frame scripts is navigation and to keep the playback head looping over one frame or a series of frames. You create a frame script by double-clicking in that frame's Script channel (see fig. 16.4).

Figure 16.4

Create a frame script by double-clicking in the frame's Script channel.

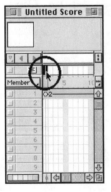

Movie Scripts

Movie scripts receive all messages that are not already handled by sprite, cast member, or frame behavior scripts. You create a movie script by clicking on the script button for an empty cast member (see fig. 16.5).

Figure 16.5

A movie script.

Figure 16.5

A movie script.

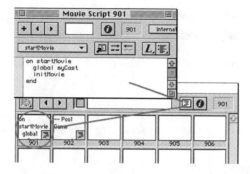

Movie scripts are a good place for default message handlers. Suppose you want the program to display an error message any time the user clicks on an area that is not hot. Normally, if you have two buttons on the stage, each with a mouseUp handler, nothing happens if the user clicks anywhere outside the two buttons. If you place a mouseUp handler in the movie script, it catches any mouseUp messages that the buttons don't handle. The mouseUp handler in the movie script could display a message that tells the user where the active areas are.

Using Scripts to Make an Interactive Movie

Now let's make a small movie that uses all four kinds of scripts. To begin, open the LITE.DIR movie from the Chapter 16 folder on the accompanying CD-ROM.

A light switch appears on stage because two cast members have already been placed in frame 1 of the score. No scripts have been placed yet (see fig. 16.6).

Figure 16.6

The movie LITE.DIR.

You want this movie to do the following:

1. When the user clicks on the switch:

   ▶ Make a click sound.

   ▶ If the switch is up, change it to the down position, and darken the stage to make it look like the lights are off.

▶ If the switch is down, change it to the up position, and lighten the stage to make it look like the lights are on.

2. When the user clicks anywhere else on stage, beep to let them know it isn't an active area.

Armed with a plan, you are ready to get started scripting the Lingo. The following tutorial takes you through scripting step by step.

Scripting a Simple Interactive Movie

The first thing you want to do is make the movie loop. If you play the movie now, it plays all the occupied frames and then stops because no more frames exist. You must keep the playback head moving if you want the movie to continue playing. Frame scripts are a good place to put the code to make the movie loop. Make sure Loop is turned off in the Control Panel or you will be tricked into thinking your movie will loop on its own. When you make a projector, it won't loop. You have to loop it yourself with Lingo.

1. Double-click in the Script channel over the last frame in LITE.DIR and type the following script:

```
on exitFrame
     go frame 1
end
```

If you play the movie again, it continues to play indefinitely because the playback head is always directed back to the first frame. (Press the Stop button on the Control Panel when you want to stop the movie.)

Now you are ready to program the interactivity for the switch. First, you want to make it animate when you click on it so that it moves up or down. You do this by switching the cast member that is in that sprite cel. When cast member 1, the ON switch, is in that sprite channel and the user clicks on it, you want to replace it with cast member 2, the OFF switch, and vice versa.

2. Open the cast script for cast member 1 by highlighting member 1 in the Cast window and clicking on the Script button. Enter the following script:

```
on mouseUp
     set the memberNum of sprite 2 to 2
     updateStage
end
```

This script changes the artwork in sprite 2 from the ON switch to the OFF switch when a user clicks on the switch in the ON position. The updateStage command redraws the stage after you change the sprite with Lingo. Whenever you change things on the stage with Lingo, you must update the stage to show your changes. updateStage is an essential Lingo command covered in more detail in the next section.

3. Rewind and run the movie again. Now when you click on the light switch, it changes it to the OFF position. But when you click on it again (while it's in the OFF position), it doesn't do anything. That's because cast member 2, the OFF switch, doesn't have a mouseUp handler—yet.

4. Open the cast script for cast member 2, and enter the following script:

```
on mouseUp
    set the memberNum of sprite 2 = to 1
    updateStage
end
```

5. Rewind and run the movie again. Now clicking on the light switch turns it ON or OFF, depending on the cast member on which you click (see fig. 16.7).

Figure 16.7

The switch in the ON and OFF positions.

The code you were asked to enter into the cast scripts:

```
set the memberNum of sprite 2 to 1
```

works just fine, but if this were a real project, using sprite and cast numbers in your scripts wouldn't be a good idea because doing so makes changing things later difficult. If you refer to sprite 2 in many different places in your scripts and then later need to move that artwork to a different channel, you have to go back through your scripts and change the sprite number everywhere it occurs.

continues

Scripting a Simple Interactive Movie   continued

In Chapter 19, the section "Defensive Programming" explains in detail how to write your scripts so that you can change and reuse them easily. For now, it is best to leave this code alone.

The next step is to make it appear as though the light is going off, which you can accomplish by changing the stage color of the stage from white to black.

6. Add the following line of code to the cast script for cast member 1, right after the set the memberNum line:

```
set the stagecolor to 255
```

This code sets the color of the stage to position 255 in the color palette, which is black. You need another line of code to set it back to white.

7. Put this line in the script for cast member 2 after the set the memberNum line:

```
set the stagecolor to 0
```

The two cast scripts for the switch casts should look like this:

```
on mouseUp
    set the memberNum of sprite 2 to 2
    set the stagecolor to 255
    updateStage
end

on mouseUp
    set the memberNum of sprite 2 to 1
    set the stagecolor to 0
    updateStage
end
```

8. Now play the movie and click on the switch. The switch moves up and down and the light goes on and off.

The only thing absent is sound. You want the sound to play as soon as the user clicks the switch, so you should include sound in a mouseDown handler. You want the sound to play when the user clicks on sprite 2, whether the cast member in that channel is the ON switch or the OFF switch. A mouseDown handler in the sprite script for sprite 2 accomplishes just that.

9. Highlight the sprite on channel 2 and select New Script from the Behavior Selector pop-up menu to open a Script window. Enter the following script:

```
on mouseDown
    puppetSound "click"
    updateStage
end
```

puppetSound puts a sound cast member under Lingo control. You must use updateStage after puppetSound to make the sound play.

10. Play the movie again. The switch now makes a clicking sound.

Finally, you want to let the users know when they are clicking on an area that is not hot. You can make a movie script by using a mouseDown message handler that catches all clicks that fall outside the switch sprite.

11. Highlight an empty cast member and choose Window, Script from the menu bar to open a new movie script. Type the following:

```
on mouseDown
    beep
end
```

The beep command plays a system beep.

12. Now play the movie. When you click on the light switch, the sprite script for channel 2 handles the mouseDown message, so that it never gets to the movie script handler. When you click outside the light switch sprite, the movie script handles the mouseDown.

The movie LITEDONE.DIR in the Chapter 16 folder on the accompanying CD contains the finished code for the preceding example.

The Message Hierarchy

As you just saw when building your movie, Director passes messages to the different kinds of scripts in a particular order. This order is called the *message hierarchy*. The general message hierarchy order is sprite, cast, frame, movie, but not all messages go to every type of script. Only movie scripts receive all messages. If you want Director to pass messages to your message handler, you must put it in the type of script that can receive that message. Table 16.2 shows the four script types and the list of messages that each receives. (To refresh your memory as to what user events trigger messages refer to Table 16.1.)

Table 16.2

The Four Script Types and the Messages They Can Receive

Script Type	Message List
Sprite	mouseEnter
	mouseLeave
	mouseWithin
	mouseUp
	mouseDown
	rightMouseUp
	rightMouseDown
	keyUp (editable-text sprite only)
	keyDown (editable-text sprite only)
	beginSprite
	endSprite
	prepareFrame
Cast	mouseEnter
	mouseLeave
	mouseWithin
	mouseUp (not to editable-text sprite)
	mouseDown
	rightMouseUp
	rightMouseDown
	keyUp (editable-text cast only)
	keyDown (editable-text cast only)
Frame	enterFrame
	exitFrame
	mouseUp
	mouseDown
	rightMouseUp
	rightMouseDown
	keyUp
	keyDown
	timeOut
Movie	enterFrame
	exitFrame

Script Type	Message List
	mouseUp
	mouseDown
	rightMouseUp
	rightMouseDown
	keyUp
	keyDown
	idle
	startMovie
	stopMovie
	activateWindow
	moveWindow
	resizeWindow
	deactivateWindow
	closeWindow
	timeOut

The Sprite Hierarchy

If a mouse event occurs and more than one sprite is under the mouse, Director sends the mouseUp or mouseDown message to all sprites under the mouse. The message is passed in order from top (120) to bottom (1) until the message reaches a sprite that has a message handler for that message. Messages pass right through sprites with no message handlers or sprites with their visible property off ("set the visible of sprite 3 to FALSE"). A script that consists only of the following is enough to intercept an event and not allow it to pass further down the hierarchy:

```
on mouseUp
end
```

Primary Event Handlers

The message hierarchy has one additional level, called the primary event handlers. Primary event handlers differ from the other event handlers (such as sprite, cast, frame, and movie handlers) in two ways:

▶ The other handlers do not receive messages unless the messages pass through all the higher layers of the hierarchy. Primary event handlers receive messages first, before any other handlers.

▶ The other handlers "eat" any messages that they receive. They do not pass messages any further through the hierarchy. Primary event handlers act on a received message and then send it further down the hierarchy.

The primary event handlers are as follows:

▶ mouseUpScript

▶ mouseDownScript

▶ keyUpScript

▶ keyDownScript

▶ timeOutScript

You can set a primary event handler from any script type by using the following syntax:

```
set the eventScript to "code line to execute"
```

Examples of an event handler follow:

```
set the timeOutScript to "go frame 10"
set the mouseUpScript to "beep"
```

The code line to execute an event handler can also be a custom handler name:

```
set the mouseUpScript to "myMouseUpHandler"
```

The primary event handler remains in effect within that movie until you set it to a new line of code or disable it using the following syntax:

```
set the eventScript to EMPTY
```

Following is an example that resets the mouseUpScript:

```
set the mouseUpScript to EMPTY
```

Use primary event handlers when you want to temporarily intercept a message. Dissolve transitions, for example, take twice as long to finish if the user clicks while they execute. To work around this problem, you could set a primary event handler to ignore mouse clicks immediately before the transition, and then turn the primary event handler off immediately after the transition. The code would look like this:

```
set the mouseUpScript to "tempLockOut"
   on tempLockOut
      dontPassEvent mouseUp --keeps primary event handler from passing the
                       --mouseUp further down the hierarchy
end
```

Without a primary event handler, you would have to add code to every sprite or cast on the stage to handle this temporary situation.

Another good use for a primary event handler is when you want to deal with an event in the same way throughout an entire movie. A movie may not have a text entry, for example, so it would not generally have handlers for keyDown, except to check whether a user had pressed Command+Q to quit. That handler would look like this:

```
on startMovie
   Set the keyDownScript to "checkQuit"
end

on checkQuit
   if the commandDown and the key = "q" then
      cleanUp
      quit
   end if
end
```

Setting the keyDownScript to checkQuit at the beginning of the movie handles keyDown events for the rest of the movie with no additional coding.

Modifying Hierarchy Behavior: pass and stopEvent

Normally, the first sprite, cast, or frame message handler to get a message "consumes" the message and it does not get passed any further down the message hierarchy. But sometimes you want more than one script to receive a message. If you put a pass command in a sprite, cast, or frame handler (movie scripts don't need pass commands because they are already at the bottom of the hierarchy), it acts on any message it receives and then passes it on to the next level of the hierarchy. In the following example, one button cast has been placed on the stage twice, creating two sprites. When clicked, each sprite plays the sound that its sprite script specifies. Then they both call on the same cast code to animate. In this example, mouseDown is the message that both levels of the hierarchy receive: The sprite level receives it as a prompt to play a sound, and then the cast level receives it as a prompt to animate.

```
-- Sprite 2
on mouseDown
    puppetSound "horn"
    updateStage
    pass
end

-- Sprite 3
on mouseDown
    puppetSound "bagpipe"
    updateStage
    pass
end

-- Cast script for both sprites
on mouseDown
    set the locH of the sprite clickOn to the locH of sprite the clickOn + 1
    set the locV of the sprite clickOn to the locV of sprite the clickOn + 1
    -- make the button move slightly
    updateStage
end

on mouseUp
    set the locH of sprite the clickOn to the locH of sprite the clickOn - 1
    set the locV of sprite the clickOn to the locV of sprite the clickOn - 1
    -- return the button to original position
    updateStage
end
```

The pass command in a sprite script cannot pass a message to sprites in other channels lower than the sprite that is clicked. The message gets passed to the next level of the hierarchy, not to the next sprite; the next level of the hierarchy would be the cast script.

Primary event handlers do the opposite of what the other handlers do. Primary event handlers act on the event and then always pass it on. Using the stopEvent command in a primary event handler keeps it from passing the event.

```
on startMovie
    set the keydownscript to "myKeyProcess"
    stopEvent
end
```

```
on myKeyProcess
   beep
   stopEvent
end
```

This example defines a primary event handler for a `keyDown` event to execute a handler called `myKeyProcess`. `myKeyProcess` first emits a system alert sound and then instructs Director not to pass the `keyDown` event. This could be used if you wanted to prevent people from editing text fields that you may want to lock on a particular situation. If `stopEvent` had not been issued and if there were any editable text fields on the stage, the computer would still beep but it would also modify the text fields. This may be what you want. You could play a typewriter sound instead of a system beep every time a user hits a key.

Bypassing the Message Hierarchy

You can bypass the hierarchy completely and send an event message directly to any script by using the following syntax:

```
messageName(script "ScriptName")
messageName(script scriptNumber)
```

An example of this follows:

```
mouseUp(script "Exit Button")
```

If `"Exit Button"` is the name of the sprite or cast script for a button on the stage, the button behaves as though the user had clicked on it even when no action occurs. This feature is convenient for making self-running tutorial demos that simulate user actions.

Deciding Where to Put Handlers

The message hierarchy sounds like a complicated system, but it actually increases your flexibility, therefore, making your job easier by increasing your flexibility. There isn't always one correct spot to place a script. You usually can accomplish the same thing in a couple different ways. The following are some guidelines that you can use until you develop your own style:

▶ Put code that moves or changes sprites in sprite scripts.

▶ If a cast member should always behave the same way throughout the whole movie no matter where it appears in the score, use a cast script instead of multiple sprite scripts.

> ▶ Use frame scripts to keep the playback head looping in an area of the score.

> ▶ Put your custom handlers in movie scripts. You can then call to them within cast or sprite scripts.

Remember, not all messages are received by all hierarchies. Table 16.3 shows the order in which each Lingo event passes through the four layers of scripts. Draw a line from the event on the left, straight through the layers on the right to see which types of scripts receive that event message, and in what order.

In this section you have learned how to use commands to change the properties of Lingo objects. You now know how to write a handler, and where to place the handler to intercept a message. With these fundamentals of Lingo under your belt, you are now ready to learn about some essential Lingo commands in more detail.

Essential Lingo Commands: Coding a Simple Movie

With the new commands in version 6, the *Lingo Dictionary* now has more than 700 entries. Fortunately, you don't have to be familiar with all of them before you can begin working. In fact, the bulk of everyday Director programming centers around fewer than 20 commands and key words. In this section you'll build a movie that uses 15 of these essential commands.

The essential Lingo commands are as follows:

▶ append   ▶ quit

▶ count   ▶ repeat while

▶ getAt   ▶ set

▶ global   ▶ the clickOn

▶ go   ▶ the cursor of sprite

▶ play   ▶ the loc of sprite

▶ point ()   ▶ updateStage

▶ puppetSound

Table 16.3

The Lingo Message Hierarchy

Event	Primary Event Handler	Sprite Script	Cast Script	Frame Script	Movie Script
enterFrame				on enterFrame	on enterFrame
exitFrame				on exitFrame	on exitFrame
mouseUp	the mouseUpScript	on mouseUp	on mouseUp	on mouseUp	on mouseUp
mouseDown	the mouseDownScript	on mouseDown	on mouseDown	on mouseDown	on mouseDown
mouseEnter		on mouseEnter	on mouseEnter		
mouseLeave		on mouseLeave	on mouseLeave		
mouseWithin		on mouseWithin	on mouseWithin		
cuePassed		on cuePassed	on cuePassed	on cuePassed	on cuePassed
beginSprite		on beginSprite			
endSprite		on endSprite			
prepareFrame		on prepareFrame			
rightMouseUp		on rightMouseUp	on rightMouseUp	on rightMouseUp	on rightMouseUp
rightMouseDown		on rightMouseDown	on rightMouseDown	on rightMouseDown	on rightMouseDown
keyUp	the keyUpScript	on keyUp	on keyUp	on keyUp	on keyUp
keyDown	the keyDownScript	on keyDown	on keyDown	on keyDown	on keyDown
idle					on idle
startMovie					on startMovie
stopMovie					on stopMovie
activateWindow					on activateWindow
moveWindow					on moveWindow
resizeWindow					on resizeWindow
deactivateWindow					on deactivateWindow
closeWindow					on closeWindow
timeOut	the timeOutScript				on timeOut
yourCustomEvent					on yourCustomEvent

The Chapter 16 folder on the accompanying CD contains two Marble movies: MARBLE.DIR and MARBLEDN.DIR. Choose one of these movies and follow along with the text to learn the primary Lingo commands. MARBLE.DIR has all the cast members in place but includes only the movie script and a frame script that keeps the playback head inside the Main Menu section. MARBLEDN.DIR contains the finished movie. You can follow along using the finished MARBLEDN.DIR, or you can start with MARBLE.DIR and construct the movie yourself as you read along.

Open the movie MARBLEDN.DIR, a tiny movie with a main menu and two sections of "lessons" about marble (see fig. 16.8).

Figure 16.8

The MARBLEDN.DIR movie's main menu.

The marble movie is not a terribly interesting multimedia experience, but it does illustrate the typical user-interface features that you will want to include in your projects. Check marks on the main menu indicate that a section has been visited. The cursor changes to a hand when a user moves it into clickable areas on-screen. Buttons provide feedback when a user clicks on them. The next section of this chapter uses code from the movie to show the most common Lingo commands in action.

The rest of this chapter teaches you the 15 common Lingo commands by implementing showing them in use, in the Marble movie. The movie will be broken up by generic tasks for easier consideration; then the common commands used to perform those tasks will be examined more closely. Keep in mind, though, that the commands are flexible and can be used in many different contexts and to solve many different programming tasks, not just the ones in our sample movie.

Realistic Buttons: Controlling Sprites

When a user clicks in an active area on-screen, something should happen—and the sooner the better. Buttons that don't respond when a user clicks on them are lifeless and confusing. The buttons in the finished Marble movie depress and make a sound when the user clicks on them.

The buttons all share one cast and one `mouseDown` script. The code is attached to the `mouseDown` rather than the `mouseUp` to give the user the most immediate feedback. The code is in the cast script rather than the sprite scripts for each button, because the button should animate the same way everywhere it appears in the score.

Open MARBLE.DIR, the unfinished version, and play it. The playback head stops on frame 2 because it contains a `go the frame` handler, but none of the buttons work yet. The following is the `mouseDown` handler for the button cast script:

```
on mouseDown
    set btn = the clickOn
    puppetSound "Mouse Down"
    set the loc of sprite btn = the loc of sprite btn - 1
    updateStage
    repeat while the stillDown
      updateStage
    end repeat
    set the loc of sprite btn = the loc of sprite btn + 1
    updateStage
    puppetSound 0
end
```

Type this handler into the cast script for the button cast (cast number 14). (Don't worry for now about understanding the fine points of how the code works; it will be explained in the subsequent syntax discussions.) Play the movie again. All the buttons now depress and make a sound when you click them. That's because they all share the same cast and cast script. The next section describes the Lingo commands used in the button cast script.

set

Syntax:

```
set variableOrProperty = value
set variableOrProperty to value
```

Example:

```
set score = 0
```

The set command names a variable or property and sets it equal to some value. If you're familiar with other computer languages, you probably already know that a *variable* is a container that enables you to save data that you want to use later. *Properties*, as mentioned earlier, are characteristics of objects in Director. Variables and properties you declare within a handler are *local*—meaning that they are discarded as soon as the handler finishes and they cannot be used by other handlers in the script unless you explicitly declare them as globals.

The first line of code for the button cast script sets the variable btn to the value of the clickOn, as follows:

```
set btn = the clickOn
```

Other lines in the handler can then use variable btn.

the clickOn

Syntax:

```
the clickOn
```

Example:

```
if the clickOn = 7 then go "Main Menu"
```

the clickOn is a Lingo function that returns the channel number of the most recently clicked on sprite channel. If the user clicks on the stage, the clickOn function returns 0. the clickOn makes it possible for the same cast script to work with multiple sprites, because it tells the cast script which sprite triggered it. The first line of code of the button cast script saves the clickOn into the btn variable. This is important because the clickOn updates with every user click—even a click that occurs during the time the handler is performing its task. If you refer to the `clickOn` directly at the beginning of a script and also further down, and the user clicks somewhere in between, the value of the `clickOn` changes. By storing the `clickOn` in variable `btn`, and referring to `btn` instead of the `clickOn` directly, you ensure that you are always working with the sprite that triggered the handler.

puppetSound

Syntax:

```
puppetSound [soundChannel,]"castName"
```

Examples:

```
puppetSound "Bird Call"
updateStage
```

```
puppetSound 1,"Bird Call"
puppetSound 2,"Dog Bark"
updateStage
```

The `puppetSound` command plays a sounds via Lingo, in a specified sound channel. The sound doesn't start to play unless you include an `updateStage` command after it or until the playback head enters the next frame. By default, `puppetSound` takes control of sound channel 1. After you play a `puppetSound`, any sound placed in the score in sound channel 1 will not play—even after the puppeted sound has finished—until you return control of the sound channel to the score with:

```
puppetSound 0
```

You can puppet up to 8 sound channels. To puppet a channel other than channel 1, include the channel number you want on your definition:

```
puppetSound 3,"chirp"
puppetSound 4,8
```

INSIDER TIP

To turn off puppeting for a channel other than channel 1, use `puppetSound channelNumber, FALSE#`. For example, if you're playing a sound in channel 3 using `puppetSound 3, "chirp"` you would stop it with `puppetSound 3, FALSE`.

The sounds you play with puppetSound must load completely into memory before they can play; therefore, puppetSound is good for button clicks and other sounds that don't take too much memory to run. The following code line plays the cast member sound "Mouse Down" in channel 1:

```
puppetSound "Mouse Down"
```

sound playFile

The sound playFile command is a better choice for large sounds. The syntax for sound playFile is as follows:

```
sound playFile soundChannel,"filename"
```

sound playFile streams the sound straight from the hard disk or CD rather than playing it from memory. You may experience a slight delay before the sound starts, especially if you play from the CD, because Director has to find the file on disc and the disc head has to move to the file before it can play.

updateStage

Syntax:

```
updateStage
```

Example:

```
set the forecolor of sprite 8 to 0
updateStage
```

Changes you make with Lingo to a sprite or to a puppeted sound channel generally do not register until you issue an updateStage command. The command name updateStage implies that only visual changes update, but updateStage actually does more than that. updateStage redraws the sprites on stage to include your Lingo changes, plays puppeted sounds, and updates digital video. If you plan to change several sprite properties at the same time over several lines of code, you can use one updateStage command after code to display all your changes at once. The following code plays the button click and moves the button at the same time when updateStage executes on the third line of code:

```
puppetSound "Mouse Down"
set the loc of sprite btn = the loc of sprite btn - 1
updateStage
```

You also could write the code as follows:

```
puppetSound "Mouse Down"
updateStage
set the loc of sprite btn = the loc of sprite btn - 1
updateStage
```

In this case, the button click would start a fraction of a second before the button moves, when the first updateStage executes.

the loc of sprite / point()

Syntax:

```
the loc of sprite whichSprite
point (horizontal, vertical)
```

Example:

```
set the loc of sprite 10 = point(100,120)
```

the loc of sprite is a sprite property that determines the location of the sprite on the stage relative to the top-left corner of the stage, which is point (0, 0). Director measures in pixels from point (0 horizontal, 0 vertical) to the sprite's registration point to determine the sprite's position. You set the registration point for a bitmap sprite in the Paint window. The registration point for shapes drawn with the tool palette, digital video, text fields, and buttons, is the top-left corner of the sprite (see fig. 16.9). the loc of sprite is stored as a special type of list called a *point*. *Lists* are Director variables that can store more than one piece of information. They are like arrays in other languages. Chapter 17, "Managing Your Data," covers lists in detail.

 NOTE

Lists are Director variables that can store more than one piece of information. They are like arrays in other languages. Chapter 17 covers lists in detail.

Figure 16.9

*The registration point
of the butterfly bitmap
is in the middle of the
image. The registration
point of the shape is the
top-left corner.*

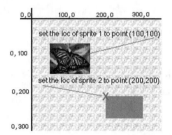

Figure 16.9

*The registration point
of the butterfly bitmap
is in the middle of the
image. The registration
point of the shape is the
top-left corner.*

In the MARBLE.DIR movie, highlight a sprite cell in the score and type the following in the Message window:

```
put the loc of sprite 5  -- the number of the sprite you have highlighted
```

Director returns the following:

```
point(100,200) -- the numbers will vary depending on where the sprite is
```

The first number, 100, is the horizontal location—the distance in pixels from the left of the stage. The second number, 200, is the vertical location—the distance in pixels from the top of the stage.

The following code line takes advantage of a nice feature of Director lists. When you use a mathematical operation on a list, it applies the operation to every item on the list.

```
set the loc of sprite btn = the loc of sprite btn - 1
```

Subtracting 1 from point (100, 100) gives you point (99, 99). The code moves the button one pixel up and to the left to make it look like the button is depressing when it is clicked.

repeat while

Syntax:

```
repeat while condition
    statement
    statement
end repeat
```

Example:

```
repeat while soundBusy(1)
   go the frame
end repeat
```

repeat while executes the statements inside the loop until the condition is no longer TRUE. A repeat loop stops the action on a stage and grabs a big share of the processor while it runs. Including an updateStage or go the frame inside a repeat loop when possible keeps other animation and QuickTime moving. Repeat loops also lock out user mouse and keyboard events. To continue accepting mouse events within a repeat loop, include a test for the mouseDown, such as the following:

```
repeat while testCondition = FALSE and not the mouseDown
```

This repeat loop continues to loop as long as the user holds down the mouse button:

```
 repeat while the stillDown
 updateStage
 end repeat
```

The button sprite the user clicked on will remain in a depressed position as long as the user holds down the mouse button.

You now have all of the buttons responding to user clicks now. In the next section you will program the buttons to take the user to other sections of the movie.

Navigation and Keeping Track of Completed Sections

The buttons click in the Main Menu section, but they don't take you anywhere. The next code you need to add should contain the commands to take you to and from different parts of the movie. This is the point where each button behaves differently; therefore, the code must go into the sprite script of each button. To attach the correct sprite behaviors to the buttons, you'll need to be able to select the sprite spans in channels 8, 9, and 10 in the Main Menu

These sprites span frames 1 and 2. They're easier to select if you change the zoom of the score to 200 percent. To do that, click on the Zoom menu on the right hand side of the channel number maker. Pull down to 200 percent. This enlarges the score. Select the sprite span in channel 8, frames 1–2. Enter the following script. Do the same for channels 9 and 10. If you don't get the whole span selected, don't worry. You'll receive an alert asking you if you want to select the whole sprite span before applying the new behavior script. Choose Select Complete sprites before attaching.

```
-- put on History button
on mouseUp
    global gVisitedHistory
    go "History"
    set gVisitedHistory = TRUE
end

-- put on Fun Facts button
on mouseUp
    global gVisitedFunFacts
    go "FunFacts"
    set gVisitedFunFacts = TRUE
end

-- put on Quit button
on mouseUp
    go "AreYouSure"
end
```

Play the movie. When you click on any button in the Main Menu section, the button now takes you to another section of the movie. But right now, you still have no way to get back to the Main Menu. Add the following handler to button sprite 14's cast script. Don't worry about what customCursorsOff does yet.

```
on mouseUp
    -- turn off custom cursors before going to a new section
    customCursorsOff
    go "MainMenu"
end
```

Play the movie again. Now, pressing the Main Menu button on the Marble History and Fun Marble Facts screens, as well as on the No button of the "Are You Sure?" screen, takes you back to the Main Menu. These buttons have no `mouseUp` sprite scripts, so they use the cast script. The buttons on the Main Menu have `mouseUp` sprite scripts that catch the `mouseUp` message before it gets to the cast script. Currently, the Yes button on the "Are You Sure?" screen also returns you to the Main Menu screen, but that's not what you want to occur. If you want to quit when the user presses the Yes button, add the following sprite script to the Yes button to override the cast script:

```
on mouseUp
    quit
end
```

go

Syntax:

```
go [to] [frame] frameNumberOrLabel
go [to] [frame] frameNumberOrLabel of movie movieName
go [to] movie movieName
```

Example:

```
go to 1
```

This example moves the playback head to frame number 1 of the current movie.

```
go to frame "first frame"
```

This example moves the playback head to the frame labeled "first frame" of the current movie.

```
go frame (the frame)
```

This example loops the playback head in the current frame. The `the frame` function returns the number of the frame the playback head is on; therefore, issuing a `go frame` command with `the frame` as its argument causes the playback head to loop on the current frame.

```
go movie "my movie"
```

This example moves the playback head to the first frame of a movie called `"my movie"`.

```
go frame "third frame" of movie "my movie"
```

This example moves the playback head to a frame labeled `"third frame"` of a movie called `"my movie"`.

The `go` command moves the playback head to the specified frame or frame label or the specified movie. If a `go movie` command is issued without specifying a frame number or label, the playback head moves to the first frame of the specified movie.

Using frame labels rather than frame numbers is a good idea because the numbers change as you insert or delete frames. By labeling frames, you save yourself the time of going back through your score and renumbering.

If any commands follow the go command in the handler, they still execute. A go command moves only the playback head—it doesn't interrupt the script in progress. In this example, you are setting a global variable to execute after the go command in the button scripts (global variables are covered in more detail later in this chapter):

```
on mouseUp
   global gVisitedFunFacts
   go "FunFacts"
   set gVisitedFunFacts = TRUE -- still executes after the "go"
end
```

play

Syntax:

```
play [frame] frameNumberOrLabel
play [frame] frameNumberOrLabel of movie movieName
play movie movieName
```

Example:

```
play movie "my movie"
```

This example moves the playback head to the movie called `"my movie"`.

```
play frame "Baseball"
```

This example moves the playback head to the frame labeled `"baseball"` of the current movie.

```
play 5
```

This example moves the playback head to frame number 5 of the current movie.

A `play` command, such as `go`, also moves the playback head to another frame or movie. The movie continues to play from that frame forward, until it hits a `play done` command. Then, if the playback head was called from a sprite script, it returns to the frame and movie where `play` was called. If `play` was called from a frame script, however, the playback head returns to the frame directly *after* the frame and movie that called it.

Unlike the `go` command, `play` suspends execution of any commands in a handler after the `play` until the playback head hits a `play done`. Only at this point do the remaining commands in the handler execute.

Altough `go` and `play` seem similar they work slightly differently. A good rule of thumb is this: If you don't intend to come back, use `go`; if you want to return, use `play`.

```
on mouseUp
    play "SingALong"
    -- Handler is suspended here while the "SingALong" section plays
    -- Playback head hits a "play done" in "SingALong"
    -- Playback head returns to the frame where this handler was called
    -- The rest of the commands now execute
    puppetSound "All done"
    updateStage
    go frame "Time For Work"
end
```

The buttons on the Main Menu of the Marble movie could have used the `play` command to take the user to the Fun Facts and History sections. The return buttons in Fun Facts and History could have had `play done` scripts. But `play done` would not have returned the playback head to the frame labeled Main Menu—it would have returned it to the frame directly after it, bypassing the first frame, which has an important setup handler located in it. Using `go` Main Menu for the return buttons ensures that the playback head always goes through Main Menu's setup handler.

Notice that each section of the movie consists of two frames: a setup frame and a looping frame. The setup frame does work that is necessary only when the playback head is entering the section. After the section has been set up, the next frame traps the playback head in a looping frame.

quit

Syntax:

```
quit
```

Example:

```
on enterFrame
  global timeAllowed
  if the timer - startTime > timeAllowed then
    cleanUp
    quit
  end it
end
```

The quit command terminates Director if you're in authoring mode, and terminates a projector at run time. The Marble movie is too small to have any cleanup work to do, but it's a good idea to call a cleanup handler before you quit. Your cleanup handler should dispose of any open Xtras or xObjects and return the user's system to the state it was in when your program started. Some externals misbehave if Director quits while they're still active, and it's only polite to leave things the way you found them on the user's system. If you have changed the user's monitor color depth for instance, you should restore it to its original settings.

Now that the buttons are all functioning, you can navigate to all sections of the movie, as well as quit. The movie is not, however, keeping track of where you go. No check marks appear, although the score does contain sprites for them (sprites 5 and 6). Where are the checkmarks? Why don't they appear on the stage?

When the movie starts, the check mark sprites are off-screen, above the menu bar at a vertical position of −500. Positioning a sprite outside the stage enables you to place it in the sprite channel without making it visible to the user. Moving a sprite on and off the stage to make the sprite visible works better than using the visible property.

This code shows the sprite for a split second before making it invisible:

```
on enterFrame
   set the visible of sprite 5 to FALSE
end
```

Add the following handler to the first frame of Main Menu:

```
on enterFrame
   displayChecks
   mainCursors
end
```

displayChecks and mainCursors are two custom handlers defined on the movie script. displayChecks checks if the user has visited a section, and if he has, it displays a check mark. mainCursors give the buttons on the Main screen a hand cursor.

Play the movie. Now the check marks show for each section that you visit.

INSIDER TIP

Version 6 gives you yet another way to hide a sprite with Lingo by setting its member number to 0. The following code makes a sprite disappear by removing the cast member from the sprite channel:

```
on enterFrame
   set the memberNum of sprite 5 to 0
   updateStage
end
```

A sprite channel with a cast member number of 0 still executes sprite scripts if the user clicks over the area where the last cast member in the channel was.

global

Syntax:

```
global variableName
```

Example:

```
global highScore
```

Declaring a variable `global` makes it available to all handlers in the movie. To use a `global` in a handler, you must declare it before you use it, as seen in the following:

```
on mouseUp
   global nextScene
   go nextScene
end
```

Refer to Chapter 17 for more information on using and declaring globals.

The globals used in MARBLEDN.DIR are first declared in the `startMovie` script:

```
on startMovie
   global gDoneFunFacts,gDoneHistory
   global gCustomCursorList,gPointerCursor
   set gDoneFunFacts = FALSE
   set gDoneHistory = FALSE
...
...
...
end
```

Globals `gDoneFunFacts` and `gDoneHistory` are flags that keep track of whether the user has visited the Fun Facts or History section. Both globals are set to FALSE at the beginning of the movie because the user hasn't gone anywhere yet.

The initial frame of the History section sets global `gDoneHistory` to TRUE:

```
on enterFrame
   global gDoneHistory
   -- mark this section as visited
   set gDoneHistory = TRUE
...
...
end
```

When the user goes back to Main Menu, the first frame of Main Menu checks looks at global `gDoneHistory`. If it returns TRUE, the History check mark is displayed by moving it from its place over the menu bar to a new position on the stage:

```
on enterFrame
   displayChecks
end
```

```
--Custom handlers in movie script

on displayChecks
    global gDoneFunFacts,gDoneHistory
    if gDoneFunFacts = TRUE then set the loc of sprite 6 = point(39,137)
    if gDoneHistory = TRUE then set the loc of sprite 5 = point(39,90)
    updateStage
end
```

Custom Cursors

The last thing you want to add to the Marble movie is custom cursors. These will alert the user when the mouse rolls over a hot spot. Add the following line to the script for frame 1:

```
-- frame 1
on enterFrame
    displayChecks
    mainCursors -- add this line
end
```

Add the following scripts to the first frame of History, Fun Facts, and Are You Sure?:

```
-- frame script 10
on enterFrame
    -- give the button a custom cursor
    histCursors
end


-- frame script 20
on enterFrame
    -- give the button a custom cursor
    funFactsCursors
end


-- frame script 28
on enterFrame
    -- give the button a custom cursor
    areYouSureCursors
end
```

Play the movie. When the cursor rolls over a button, the cursor changes to a pointing hand.

the cursor of sprite

Syntax:

```
set the cursor of sprite channelNumber to list
```

Example:

```
set the cursor of sprite 9 to [4,5]
```

The `set the cursor of sprite` command makes a custom cursor appear over a sprite on the stage. The command applies to the entire channel, not just to a sprite on one frame. If you change the cast member in the sprite channel, the custom cursor appears over the new sprite. You must keep track of custom cursors so that you can turn them off when you don't need them anymore—otherwise, you get cursors appearing in places you don't want them. You turn off a custom cursor by setting `the cursor of sprite` to `0`, like this:

```
set the cursor of sprite 10 to 0
```

When you set a custom cursor, you specify the cursor art that you want to use as a list of two cast members. The first cast member 1 is the cursor image and the second cast member 1 is the mask image. Without a mask, the cursor artwork is transparent and hard to see. The mask travels behind the cursor art, keeping the stage from showing through the cursor. The cursor cast and the mask cast must be 1-bit (black-and-white) cast members, and at least 16 pixels×16 pixels in size. Cast members 19 and 20 are the custom cursor casts in the Marble movie.

In the `startMovie` handler of the Marble movie, the custom cursor list is assigned to a global variable, as follows:

```
set gPointerCursor = [the number of member "HandCursor",the number of member
➥"HandCursorMask"]
```

You also could have coded it like the following:

```
set gPointerCursor = [19,20]
```

Using `the number of member castName` instead means that you don't have to change the code if you move those cast members to other cast member slots. Another global variable is set up in this line:

```
set gCustomCursorList = []
```

The movie is going to use gCustomCursorList to keep track of the sprite channels to which custom cursors are assigned. Each time the program goes to a new section, it uses the list to find the channels to which custom cursors are assigned and turns off the cursors before moving to a new section.

The following code on the movie script sets up the custom cursors for the Main Menu section:

```
on mainCursors
   repeat with buttonSprite = 8 to 10
     customCursorOn(buttonSprite)
   end repeat
end


-- Custom movie script
on customCursorOn whichSprite
   global gCustomCursorList,gPointerCursor
   set the cursor of sprite whichSprite to gPointerCursor
   append gCustomCursorList,whichSprite
end
```

The handler customCursorOn gives whatever sprite channel is passed to it, a custom cursor. The last line of customCursorOn adds the new sprite channel number to a list of sprite channels that have custom cursors assigned to them.

append

Syntax:

```
append list, value
```

Example:

```
append groceryList,"lima beans"
put groceryList
-- ["ham hocks","lima beans"]
```

The append command adds the item you specify to the end of a list. If the list is empty, it puts one item in the list.

The custom handler customCursorOn assigns a custom cursor to a sprite channel. It then adds that channel's number to the custom cursor list. After the custom handler mainCursors finishes, gCustomCursorList looks like this:

```
[ 8, 9, 10 ]
```

Each of the buttons that goes to a new section calls the following custom handler customCursorsOff on the movie script to turn off the current cursors. customCursorsOff uses the custom cursor list to find the sprite channels that have custom cursors:

```
on customCursorsOff
   global customCursorList
   repeat with listPosition = 1 to count(gCustomCursorList)
   set the cursor of sprite getAt(gCustomCursorList,listPosition) to 0
   end repeat
   set customCursorList = []
end
```

count

Syntax:

```
count(list)
```

Example:

```
put count(groceryList)
-- 2
```

The count command returns the number of items in a list. This code line repeats for each item on the list:

```
repeat with listPosition = 1 to count(gCustomCursorList)
```

getAt

Syntax:

```
getAt(list,position)
```

Example:

```
if getAt(groceryList,2) = "lima beans" then beep
```

The getAt command returns the value of the list item at the position specified. The first time the following line executes, listPosition is 1:

```
set the cursor of sprite getAt(gCustomCursorList,listPosition) to 0
```

If gCustomCursorList were to contain [8, 9, 10], the value at list position 1 would be 8, so the custom cursor for channel 8 would be turned off.

Adding custom cursors to the movie was the final step. If you have been building the movie MARBLE.DIR it should run as expected, if you were following along with MARBLEDN.DIR you should be able to code the MARBLE.DIR movie with Lingo. You now have the skills required for general Director programming and the foundation for learning how to construct more complex movies.

In Practice

You've covered a lot of ground in this first Lingo chapter. First you learned about the parts of the Lingo environment: objects, properties, events, messages, and messages handlers. You learned that you can use commands and functions to build message handlers that respond to user events by changing object properties. Then you were introduced to the essential Lingo commands that almost every interactive movie requires.

In the next chapter, you learn how to make more intelligent interactive movies—ones that can remember user responses to a quiz, for example, or fetch information about a certain car model from a database.

Keep in mind the following key points about Lingo:

- ▶ Remember to document your Lingo code thoroughly for efficiency in correcting and maintaining it.

- ▶ Use the Message window to test your code a line at a time, before committing it to your movie.

- ▶ Events and event handlers are at the heart of interactive movies. With Director's predefined event handlers and custom handlers, which you can write, you have almost unlimited scope to craft opportunities for users to interact with your movie and for your movie to respond.

- ▶ When deciding where to put handlers, keep in mind the message hierarchy (script, cast, frame, movie), as well as the ways to circumvent the hierarchy (primary event handlers, pass, stopEvent, and sending an event message directly to a script).

- ▶ A subset of Lingo commands is used in virtually all interactive movies; if you know and understand them, you can begin producing simple, Lingo-controlled projects.

- ▶ The updateStage command is critically important; whenever you change things on the stage with Lingo, you must update the stage for your changes to take effect.

chapter 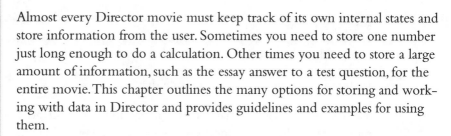 17

Rob Dillon
Gretchen Macdowall

Managing Your Data

Almost every Director movie must keep track of its own internal states and store information from the user. Sometimes you need to store one number just long enough to do a calculation. Other times you need to store a large amount of information, such as the essay answer to a test question, for the entire movie. This chapter outlines the many options for storing and working with data in Director and provides guidelines and examples for using them.

Additionally this chapter discusses methods for controlling the flow of data in a movie. This section shows you how to preload and unload cast members. Controlling how much of your movie is in memory at any time keeps your movie running smoothly and keeps its impact on system memory as low as possible.

This chapter includes information on the following topics:

▶ Types of variables

▶ Lists

▶ Multidimensional arrays

▶ Naming variables

▶ Permanent data

Types of Variables

The following two sections discuss variable types: local variables (those used only inside one handler) and global variables (which may last for the duration of the movie, or longer). A local variable has a unique identity inside just one handler. A global variable has a unique identity throughout the movie and can be referred to by any number of handlers.

Local Variables

A local variable exists only for the life of the handler that declares it. The local variable is not available outside that handler; it doesn't save its value. You declare, or create, local variables inside handlers by using the put command or the set command, as follows:

set [var] = [value]

or

put [value] into [var]

[var] is the name of the local variable that you are declaring.

[value] is what you are storing inside that variable.

You can use the same variable name in any number of scripts. The Director movie sees each of these local variables as several completely independent variables. Although the following scripts both use the local variable boundary, the two local variables are independent of each other. Setting one does not affect the other in any way.

```
on mouseUp
   set boundary = 320
   if the mouseH > boundary then
      put "You clicked in the right half of the screen."
   else
      put "You clicked in the left half of the screen."
   end if
end

on checkSprite
   set boundary = 50
   if the locH of sprite 3 >= boundary then
      puppetSprite 3,TRUE
      -- don't let sprite 3 move past a certain point on the screen
      set the locH of sprite 3 = boundary
      updateStage
   end if
end
```

One caution about creating variables: Name them sensibly. This isn't algebra or trig class. You don't have to give terse names to variables, such as x or y. You're writing this code so that you can understand it. If you name a variable something such as `startingLength`, you might not have to comment that line. You'll know right away what that variable is for when you read that line of code a week, a month, or even a year later. Also remember that you may not be the only person to ever read that code. Some clients can become seriously humor-impaired if they happen to come across a handler named `goofyClientUglyLogoRect`.

You cannot use a local variable without first setting its value. If you try to, you get a `variable used before assigned value` error.

Use local variables to hold temporary data that you do not need throughout your entire movie. The content of a local variable is purged after you exit a handler, whereas the content of a global variable is not. You save memory by using local variables wherever you can. A variable only holds one item at a time, unless it's a list. If you set a variable to an initial value and then put something else into that variable, the original value is gone.

Try this in the Message window:

```
set thisWord = locust
put thisWord
--locust
```

In the first line, you set the variable `thisWord` to the value `locust`. Then you use `put` to print out the value of the variable `thisWord` to the Message window.

```
put grasshopper into thisWord
put thisWord
--grasshopper
```

Now you put a new value into the variable. The old value, `locust`, is replaced with the new value.

Global Variables

A global variable exists in memory for the entire Director session. It can be examined or set from any handler and from any movie, including a Movie in a Window (MIAW). If you set a global variable in movie A, that global variable holds the same value in movie B. You declare a global variable as follows:

```
globalglobalVariableName
```

Example:

```
global errorCode
```

You can declare a global variable inside or outside a handler. You do not have to assign a value to a global variable before referring to it. Its initial value is <Void>.

If you declare a global variable inside a handler, any other handler that wants to get or set that global variable must also declare it. If you declare a global variable in one handler, and then try to refer to that global variable without declaring it as a global variable in a second handler, Director assumes that you are creating a local handler variable with the same name.

Here's an example to demonstrate the principle. In the following group of handlers, global variable userEntry is declared first in startMovie and then declared and used in keyDown and userCheck. The handler wontWork intends to check the length of the global variable userEntry but never declares it. In handler wontWork, userEntry actually refers to its own local variable userEntry. Because you must set local variables before they can be used, handler wontWork generates a variable undefined error.

```
on startMovie
  -- first declared here
  global userEntry
end

on keyDown
  global userEntry
  if the key = RETURN then put line 1 of field "UserName" into userEntry
end

on userCheck
 global userEntry
   if voidP(userEntry) then
     put "No name has been entered yet."
   else
     put "The current user is: " & userEntry
   end if
end
```

```
on wontWork
  set tempName = userEntry -- variable undefined error
  if length(tempName) > 25 then
    beep
    put "Your name is too long"
  end if
end
```

If you declare a global variable outside any handler at the top of a movie script, the global variable is available to any handler in that movie script. If a global variable has been declared outside a handler, handlers that use that global variable do not have to declare it. Here is how the same set of handlers would work with the global variable userEntry declared outside a handler. In the following movie script, global variable userEntry is declared on the first line, before the first handler—startMovie.

```
-- This is a movie script

global userEntry

on startMovie
  -- do some movie initialization stuff
end

on keyDown
  if the key = RETURN then put line 1 of field "UserName" into userEntry
end

on userCheck
  if voidP(userEntry) then
    put "No name has been entered yet."
  else
    put "The current user is: " & userEntry
  end if
end

on willWorkNow
  set tempName = userEntry
  if length(tempName) > 25 then
    beep
    put "Your name is too long"
  end if
end
```

Why declare global variables inside handlers? Declaring the global variables you want to use in a handler makes it clear which variables are local to the handler and which variables are global. It could help someone reading your code. On the other hand, you can use a naming convention for global variable names, such as putting a "g" in front of them, to help you distinguish them from local variables:

```
global gPlatform,gColorDepth
```

If you do so, you might also prefer to declare all your global variables in one place, such as at the top of a movie script.

Use global variables to hold data that must be available to all your movies throughout an entire Director session. You might want to store user preferences, for example, in a global variable, because you access this data at many points throughout your movies.

INSIDER TIP

Use global variables sparingly.

Consider what you need that variable for before you declare a global variable. An unnecessary global variable, once declared, takes up memory for the life of your Director session.

Name globals carefully.

You can easily get confused about the purpose for each global variable when you have a large collection of them, so be careful in naming those globals. The more globals you have to keep track of, the more likely you are to accidentally use the same global variable name more than once for entirely different purposes. This can lead to many headaches and much confusion.

Use showGlobals to help you keep track of your global variables.

Remember to use the showGlobals command in the Message window to give you a listing of the current values of the global variables. This can help to keep names and uses for these variables sorted out.

Lists

Lists are a type of variable that can hold many items at one time. You use lists to store several variables in one place. Lists work in Lingo as you would use an array in another language, and more. A list can contain any kind and combination of Lingo variable types, including strings, constants, floats, integers, symbols, and even other lists. You can use the list itself as a local, global, or property variable.

The two kinds of lists are linear lists and property lists.

A linear list looks like the following:

```
[#Introduction,#MainMenu,#Health,#FunFacts]
```

or

```
[1,3,5,6,7,9,21]
```

The four elements in the first list are all symbols. In this case, the list is being used to track the sections of a project the user has visited. After the user finishes a section, that section's name is added to the list.

INSIDER TIP

> **A Few Words About Symbols**
>
> A symbol is a special data type in Lingo. It always begins with a pound sign, #, an alphabetical character, and then any combination of alpha and numeric characters, such as #Introduction, or #Level5.
>
> Symbols take up less space in memory than strings, they can be manipulated, and they are evaluated much more quickly than strings.
>
> Symbols replace the actual string with a compact internal representation.
>
> This means that you can set up lists of symbols and manipulate them with the ease and speed of manipulating lists of numbers but keep the list contents easy to understand.
>
> The symbol can be converted to a string if necessary. Just use the `string()` function.
>
> ```
> put string(#Introduction)
> ```
>
> ```
> -- Introduction
> ```
>
> There is no function to convert a string to a symbol.

The second is a list of numbers. These could be sprite channels or members, or the scores of a test or game.

A property list looks like the following:

```
[#Introduction:66,#MainMenu:88,#Health:152,#FunFacts:84]
```

Each element of a property list consists of a property, a colon, and the property's value. The preceding list is more useful as a property list. Each element now contains the name of the section the user visited as a property, and the score the user got on the quiz at the end of that section as the property's value. The preceding list tells you, for instance, that the user visited the Introduction section and scored a 66 on the quiz at the end of the Introduction section.

You create a linear list by using the list() function or by enclosing the elements with brackets. Both of these following statements create the same linear list:

```
set myList = list(1,2,3,4)
set myList = [1,2,3,4]
```

This statement creates an empty linear list:

```
set myList = []
```

You create a property list by enclosing the property value pairs you want to include in the list with brackets:

```
set myList =["Russell":1,"Sarah":0,"Betty":1]
```

Enclose a colon with brackets to create an empty property list:

```
set myList = [:]
```

You can use any type of Lingo value for a property or a property value. All the following lines contain valid property lists:

```
[ "dog" : 1, "cat" : 2,"bird" : 99 ]
[ 1 : 98.6, 4 : 98.7, 8 : 98.4 ]
[ #pink : #warm , #blue: #cold, #amber : #warm ]
```

Table 17.1 shows an alphabetical listing of the list functions and commands. You can use this table for quick reference to how the commands operate in a linear or a property list.

findPos and findPosNear are listed as working with linear lists. This is unsupported Lingo. If the linear lists are sorted, these commands will work. If you use either of these commands, be aware that their functionality may change in later releases. These commands have worked this way since version 5.0.1.

Please open the movie LISTCOM.DIR in the Chapter 17 folder on the accompanying CD-ROM. This movie demonstrates each of these list commands. If you drag a copy into your Xtras folder for Director you can open it at any time for ready reference.

Table 17.1

List Commands

Command	Must the List Be Sorted?	What the Command Does in a Linear List	What the Command Does in a Property List
add	No	Adds a value to a linear list. If the list is sorted, the added value is placed in order; if the list isn't sorted, the value is placed last.	Returns an error alert.
addAt	No	Adds a value to a specific position in a list. If the new position is outside the range of the current list, the intermediate positions on the list are set to 0.	Returns an error alert.
addProp	No	Returns an error alert.	Adds a new property and value to a list. If the list is sorted, the property and the value are placed into the order of the list. If the list isn't sorted, the property and the value are placed at the end of the list.
append	No	Adds a value to the end of a list. Always adds to the end whether the list is sorted or not.	Returns an error alert.
count()	No	Returns the number of items in the list.	Returns the number of items in the list.
deleteAt	No	Deletes the value at the position specified. Gives an alert if the position is out of range.	Deletes the property and the value at that position in the list. Gives an alert if the position is out of range.

continues

Table 17.1   continued

List Commands

Command	Must the List Be Sorted?	What the Command Does in a Linear List	What the Command Does in a Property List
deleteOne	No	Deletes a value from the list. Gives no alert if the value is out of range.	The value is specified, the command deletes the property, and the value from the list gives no alert if the value is out of range.
deleteProp	No	If you use the position and not the value, command works like deleteOne.	Using property not in list returns nothing.
duplicate (list)	No	Duplicates the list.	Duplicates the list.
findPos	Yes	If the list is sorted, command returns the position of the value.	Returns the position of a given value in a list whether sorted or not.
findPosNear	Yes	If the list is sorted, the command returns the position closest to the given value.	Works with sorted lists; returns wrong value with unsorted list.
getAt	No	Returns the value at a given position in a list.	Returns the value of the property in the given position.
getLast	No	Returns the last value in list.	Returns the value of a the property in the last position in a property list.
getOne	No	Returns the position of the value.	Returns the property that has that value.
getPos	No	Returns the position of a given value in a list.	Returns the position of that value in the list.
getaProp	No	Works like getAt.	Returns a value for a specified property.

Command	Must the List Be Sorted?	What the Command Does in a Linear List	What the Command Does in a Property List
getProp	No	Returns error.	Returns a value for a specified property. Works exactly like getaProp except that getProp returns an error message if the specified property is not in the list.
getPropAt	No	Returns error.	Returns the property at a specified position.
listP()	No	Returns TRUE if the item specified is a list.	Returns TRUE if the item specified is a list.
max()	No	Returns the highest value in the list.	Returns the highest value in the list.
min()	No	Returns the lowest value in the list.	Returns the lowest value in the list.
setAt	No	Replaces a value at the specified position. The command pads the list with 0s to fill empty spaces.	Replaces the value of a property at the specified position in the list. If the position specified is not in the list, an alert is given.
setaProp	No	Works like setAt.	Replaces the property at the specified position in a list. If the property isn't in the list, a new property and value are added to the list.
setProp	No	Returns error.	Works like setaProp except that setProp returns an error alert if the property isn't in the list.
sort		Sorts the list in alphanumeric order.	Sorts the list by property in alphanumeric order.

Using Lists

Now it is time to look at some examples of lists at work. Lists can be used to organize data. They can be used to manage the use of data, and they can even help you to use data stored outside a list.

Open the movie MARKER.DIR in the Chapter 17 folder on the accompanying CD-ROM. Now open script member 10. The first script shows a list that organizes a series of items. Suppose that you want to let a user backtrack through the areas she has visited by pressing a Back button. You can do this easily by using a list.

Now look at the frame scripts attached to any of the frames with markers. You see that the script calls the handler shown following:

```
on recordLocation
  global locList,currentLabel
  if voidP(locList) then set locList = []
  put the frameLabel into currentLabel
  if not getOne(locList,the frameLabel) then
    append locList,the frameLabel
  end if
```

The handler recordLocation declares a global variable, locList. locList is a linear list. The third line of the handler checks to see whether the variable has anything in it. If voidP returns <void>, it creates a new empty list. The fifth line adds the name of the current frameLabel to the list. The fourth line checks to see that the frameLabel isn't already in the list.

The code will make a list that looks like the following:

```
["globe","ring","pyramid","cone"]
```

The handler in this script for your Back button takes you to the last section visited before the current section:

```
on goBack
  global locList,currentLabel
  set prevSection = getOne(locList,currentLabel) - 1
  -- the very last item is where the user is now
  if prevSection >=1 then
    go frame getAt(locList,prevSection)
  end if
```

The handler `goBack`, also in cast member 10 of the movie, uses the same global variable, `locList`. In line 3, you create a new local variable, `prevSection`. This third line sets the new variable to a value of the position of the latest frame label in the list, `locList` minus 1. The sixth line of the handler moves the playback head to the previous frame marker. It does this by getting the name of that marker from the list by using the `getAt` command. Using the preceding list, for example, `getAt(locList,prevSection)` returns `pyramid`. The current count of values in the list is 4. So `prevSection` will be 3, and `pyramid` is the third value in the list.

The marker name for the current section of the movie is kept in another global variable, `currentLabel`. This global variable is used by both the `recordLocation` and the `goBack` handlers. You have to keep track of where you are to know where `Back` refers.

Run the movie MARKER.DIR. You'll see that the Forward button steps through each of the markered sections of the movie and loops back to the start. Each time that you use the Back button you jump to the previous section of the movie. The Back button stops working when the playback head reaches the first section.

List Math

You can use the arithmetic operators on lists to perform an operation on all the items in the list. Suppose that you have a game in which you keep track of players and their points with a list called scoreList:

```
[#Mary:12,#Harry:15,#Paul:6]
```

The game has one bonus situation in which everybody gets 50 points added on to his score. You can use a repeat loop to iterate through all the items on the list and add 50 points to each one, or you can take advantage of list math and do it like this:

```
set scoreList =scoreList + 50
```

Director increments all the property values simultaneously:

```
[#Mary:62,#Harry:65,#Paul:56]
```

Copying Lists

When you put a list into a new variable, you are only setting the new variable to point to the list. You are not making a new copy of the list. After the following code executes, the variables newList and oldList both point to the same list. Try this in the Message window:

```
set oldList =["pig","dog","goat"]
set newList = oldList
```

If you make a change to newList, and then examine oldList, you notice that oldList also shows your change:

```
append newList,"canary"
put oldList

--["pig","dog","goat","canary"]
```

The duplicate command makes a new independent copy of a list. If you substitute the duplicate command and use the sameList example, you now have two independent lists:

```
set oldList =["pig","dog","goat"]
set newList = duplicate(oldList)
append newList,"canary"
put oldList
-- ["pig","dog","goat"]

put newList

--["pig","dog","goat","canary"]
```

Adding Lists to Lists

Open the movie ADDLISTS.DIR in the Chapter 17 folder on the accompanying CD-ROM. Open the movie script in cast member 10. The first three scripts in that movie script are discussed following.

If you want to add the contents of one list to another list to create a larger second list, you can do that very simply. For linear lists do this:

```
on addOneToAnother
   global listOne,listTwo
   set thisMany = count(listOne)
   repeat with n = 1 to thisMany
      set thisItem = getAt(listOne,n)
      add listTwo,thisItem
   end repeat
end
```

The two lists, listOne and listTwo, are created outside this handler. They are brought to this handler, addOneToAnother, as global variables. In this example you take each item in the list listOne and use the add command to put it into the list listTwo.

To see this handler run, start the movie ADDLISTS.DIR and click on the Set up example 1 button. You'll see the two lists displayed. Next click on the Run example 1 button. Now you see the expanded listTwo displayed in the third area.

Adding the contents of one property list to another is a similar operation. You can't get a property and its value from a list in one operation. Look at the handler that follows or in the movie script for ADDLISTS.DIR. You'll see that the value and the property are each copied to local variables. This is done in lines 5 and 6 of the handler addOnePropToAnotherProp. Then they are added to the second property list in line 7 using setaProp.

```
on addOnePropToAnotherProp
  global propListOne,propListTwo
  set thisMany = count(propListOne)
  repeat with n = 1 to thisMany
    set thisValue = getAt(propListOne,n)
    set thisProp = getPropAt(propListOne,n)
    setaProp propListTwo,thisProp,thisValue
  end repeat
end
```

You can see an example of this handler, addOnePropToAnotherProp, by clicking on the Set up example 2 button in the movie ADDLISTS.DIR. You'll see two property lists displayed. Now click on the Run example 2 button. You'll see the expanded propListTwo displayed in the third area.

If you need to create a new list that contains the values of both the old lists but still keeps the old lists intact, first create a duplicate of one of the lists. Add the contents of the other list to that duplicate.

```
on makeUniqueCombinationList
  global listOne,listTwo,newList
  set newList = duplicate(listOne)
  set thisMany = count(listTwo)
  repeat with n = 1 to thisMany
    set thisItem = getAt(listTwo,n)
    add newList,thisItem
  end repeat
end
```

The handler makeUniqueCombinationList gives you a new list, newList, that is the combination of listOne and listTwo. All three lists can now be used independently of each other.

You can see an example of the makeUniqueCombinationList handler by clicking on the Set up example 3 button in the movie ADDLISTS.DIR. Doing this shows two new linear lists. Now click on the Run example 3 button. You see a new list displayed in the third area.

Using these three handlers as examples, you should now be able to write the fourth variation: a unique property list that holds the contents of two other property lists. Your handler should look something like makeUniquePropList, which is at the bottom of the movie script window, member 10 of the movie ADDLISTS.DIR.

Specialized Lists

A few specialized lists are used in Director, including the following:

▶ rect of member

▶ rect of sprite

▶ point

Rect of Member

Rect can be used alone or with sprites or members. A *rect* and a *point* are really just specialized lists that hold more than one value in the variable. A rect holds four values and a point holds two.

The rect of a member gives a set of coordinates for a member as it resides in the cast. This is a list of the left, top, right, and bottom coordinates. It can be tested but not set in Lingo. The values for the left and the top are always 0,0. You can quickly get the dimensions for a cast member by looking at the last two values in the list. The third value is the width, and the fourth value is the height. Of course, it's far simpler to use the `width of member` or the `height of member` functions if you just need to get the width of height of a cast member.

Rect of Sprite

The *rect* of a sprite is a list of coordinates for a sprite as it resides in a window. The `rect of sprite` can be set for bitmap, shape, movie, or digital video sprites. You can use the `rect of sprite` to enlarge or reduce the size of a sprite or to change its position on the stage. It is much simpler, however, to use the `loc of sprite` to change a sprite's position on the stage.

Open the movie MOVE.DIR in the Chapter 17 folder in the accompanying CD-ROM. Open the movie script in cast member 11. You'll find the `makeItSmaller` handler at the top.

```
on makeItSmaller spriteList
  set thisMany = count(spriteList)
  repeat with n = 1 to thisMany
    set thisSprite = getAt(spriteList,n)
    put the rect of sprite thisSprite into sizer
    setAt sizer,1,(getAt(sizer,1) + 5)
    setAt sizer,2,(getAt(sizer,2) + 5)
    setAt sizer,3,(getAt(sizer,3) - 5)
    setAt sizer,4,(getAt(sizer,4) - 5)
    set the rect of sprite thisSprite = sizer
  end repeat
  updateStage
end
```

The `makeItSmaller` handler uses two lists, the first being a list of sprites. You will see that the ball and its shadow change size as you click on the smaller button on the stage. The two sprites in the list are the ball and the shadow sprites. This handler takes each of those sprites and reduces its size by changing the `rect of sprite`.

Changing a Sprite's Size by Changing the Rect of Sprite

All of this is done inside a repeat loop with one loop for each sprite in the list.

1. Set a local variable to the number of items in the list.

2. Set another local variable to the sprite that you get from the list. The first line inside the repeat loop gets a sprite from the list, `getAt(spriteList,n)`. n is a local variable that holds the value of the increment in the repeat loop. The first value is 1. This line retrieves the first value in `spriteList`, in this case 2.

3. Operate on the `rect of sprite` for that sprite. For convenience, put the values of the `rect` into a new local variable. This makes writing and reading the handler easier.

   To change the size of a sprite, change the values of the left, the top, the right, and the bottom of the sprite. You don't have to count the number of variables in this list. It is a rect—it must have four variables. If it were a point, as in the `moveItLeft` *or* `moveItRight` *handlers, it would have two variables.*

   To make a sprite smaller on the stage, you need to move its top down, its left edge to the right, its right edge to the left, and its bottom edge up. For simplicity, this example uses a change value of 5.

4. `setAt sizer,1,(getAt(sizer,1) + 5)` gets the first value in the rect and adds 5 to it.

5. `getAt(sizer,1)` gets the first value and adds 5 to it.

6. `setAt sizer,1,the new value` sets the new value back into the variable sizer. You do this one time for each variable in the rect.

   Add to the top value to move it down, add to the left value to move it right, subtract from the right value to move it left, and subtract from the bottom value to move it up.

7. Take these new values and put them back into the rect of that sprite, and then do the same thing for each subsequent sprite in the list.

8. Finally, `updateStage` and see the result of the changes.

   Start the movie and click on the smaller and the larger buttons. You'll see the ball and its shadow change size.

Point

The *loc* of a sprite (the position of a sprite's registration point on the stage) and the *clickLoc* (the position of the last mouse click) are expressed as points.

Click anywhere on the stage and then type the following in the Message window:

```
put the clickLoc
--point(25,50)
```

This point describes a position on the current window and is relative to the upper-left corner of the current active movie window. The values of points and rects are expressed in pixels, so the value is related to the resolution of the current monitor. The upper-left corner of the current window is always `point(0,0)` as far as sprites are concerned, regardless of the window's position on the monitor screen.

The two handlers, `moveItLeft` and `moveItRight`, in the movie MOVE.DIR use the loc of sprite to move a sprite on the stage.

```
put the deskTopRectList
[rect(0,0,1152,870]
```

Multidimensional Arrays

A list can contain lists, which also can contain lists, and so on. This functionality enables you to create a multidimensional array.

Open the movie LIST.DIR in the Chapter 17 folder on the accompanying CD-ROM. This movie demonstrates the basics of using lists within lists.

Suppose that you are writing a Tic-Tac-Toe game in which the user plays against the computer. You need to keep track of what each square already contains before you can calculate the next possible move. The first step is to come up with a numbering system for the squares. In this case, it is pretty easy (see fig. 17.1).

The next step is to decide on a symbol for each possible state. You could use #X, #O, and #none. The third step is to build a list in which all the initial values of the squares are set to none:

```
on buildList
  global squareList
  set squareList = []
  repeat with row = 1 to 3
    set aRow = []
    repeat with column = 1 to 3
      setAt(aRow,column,#none)
    end repeat
    setAt(squareList,row,aRow)
  end repeat
end
```

Figure 17.1

Numbering system for the positions on the game board.

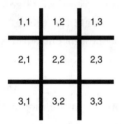

Building the Multidimensional Array for Tic-Tac-Toe

1. Declare a new global variable for the list, squareList.

2. Set that variable to a new empty list.

3. Build three new lists, one for each row of positions on the game board. This is done inside a repeat loop.

4. Start by setting a new empty list, aRow.

5. Add to that list the initial value of #none for each of the columns in that row. In the repeat loop in lines 6, 7, and 8, the symbol #none is added to the list three times.

6. The outer repeat loop then puts three copies of the list aRow into the list squareList. This is done using the setAt command on line 9.

Now you have a list called squareList, which contains three—one for each row of your Tic-Tac-Toe board. Each row sublist has three items‑‑one for each square in that row (see fig. 17.2).

Figure 17.2

The list representing the game squares at the start of the game.

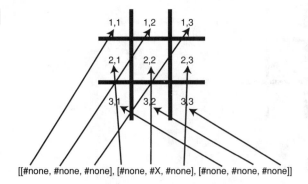

[[#none, #none, #none], [#none, #X, #none], [#none, #none, #none]]

Now you need a handler that adds new moves to the list:

```
on newMove  row,col, XorO
  global squareList
  setAt  getAt (squareList,row), col, XorO
end
```

If the first player puts an "X" in the center square, call the handler with these arguments:

```
newMove (2,2,#X)
```

No game pieces are placed to start, so the list looks like the following:

```
[[#none, #none,#none],[#none, #none, #none],[#none, #none, #none]]
```

getAt (squareList,row) refers to one of the sublists:

```
[#none, #none,#none]
```

If you substitute a sublist for the getAt statement and actual values for the argument names, the line of code in the newMove handler looks like this:

```
setAt  [#none, #none,#none] , 2 , #X
```

After newMove runs, squareList now looks like figure 17.3:

The movie TICTAC.DIR is a full Tic-Tac-Toe game that pits a human against a computer. It uses a list to keep track of where the pieces are so that it can determine the remaining legal moves. Look at the code in TICTAC.DIR for more examples of the setAt and getAt commands at work. TICTAC.DIR uses a code object to organize the game code. Chapter 20, "Object-Oriented Programming in Director," covers code objects in more detail. You may want to return to TICTAC.DIR again after reading that chapter.

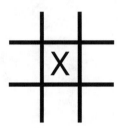

Figure 17.3

*The second sublist,
which represents row 2
of the game board,
shows an X in item 2.
The items in the second
sublist represent the
three squares in row 2.*

Naming Variables

The kindest thing you can do for anyone who might have to read your code in
the future (including yourself!) is to give significant variables meaningful
names. What does the following code do?

```
on whoKnows a,b
   global f,g
   set c = a * 12
   set d = b * 12
   set h = c - d
   if h > 0 then
      put f into field "r"
   else
      put g into field "r"
   end if
end
```

The following explains it:

```
on returnOnInvestoldMonthlyCost,newMonthlyCost
   set oldCostPerYear = oldMonthlyCost * 12
   set newCostPerYear = newMontlyCost * 12
   set savings = oldCostPerYear - newCostPerYear
   if savings > 0 then
     put "You'll save $" & savings & " with the new plan." into field"Result"
   else
     put "You won't save with the new plan." into field "Result"
   end if
end
```

No significant space or performance penalty occurs for using long variable
names. When Director compiles your Lingo, it tokenizes the variable names.
Tokenizing replaces the actual string with a compact, internal representation.

On the flip side, not every variable is significant. Scratch variables, like counters, don't need meaningful names. In fact, your code is more readable if you follow the common programming convention of using one-letter variables for these throwaways.

For example:

```
repeat with x = 1 to 100
doSomething
end repeat
```

In this example x is a scratch variable. It's completely understandable named just x.

Code that uses meaningful variable names is almost self-documenting, but you can increase the readability even further by including comments. You create a comment line by preceding it with two hyphens. The following function is easy to understand at first glance because of the comments:

```
on stripCharsinputString,charToStrip
  -- INPUT:    inputString - string to strip characters from
  --              EX: "beauty shop"
  --              charToStrip - which character to strip off
  --              EX: " "
  -- RETURNS: a string with the specified character
  --              stripped off
  ------------------------------------------------------------
  set ln = length(inputString)
  repeat with lastGoodChar = ln down to 0
    if char lastGoodChar of inputString <> charToStrip then
      exit repeat
    end if
  end repeat
  -- at the end of the repeat loop lastGoodChar will contain
  -- the number of the last character that is part of the string
  -- string
  if lastGoodChar > 0 then
    return char 1 to lastGoodChar of inputString
  else
    return ""
  end if
```

The comments at the beginning of the handler explain what it does, what arguments it expects, and what it returns. This information is extremely helpful to others who may have to work with your code. It's also helpful to you if you have to come back to this code after six months or a year. Comments are stripped out of the code when the movie is compiled, so you don't have to worry about them taking up space or affecting performance.

Permanent Data

Suppose that you are keeping track of user game scores in your application by storing them in a list. While your application is running, you can retrieve scores from the list, but as soon as your application quits, the scores are gone. If you want to save the game scores to use the next time you run the application, you need more permanent storage for the data. You can store permanent data in fields inside the Director movie or write it to separate files outside the Director movie.

Storing Data in Fields

You can save information that the user enters into fields on the stage, and you can create fields that you never place on the stage just for storing data. You use the saveMovie command to save the contents of these fields with the movie. If you don't use the saveMovie command, the fields revert to their original state when you quit the movie and any data entered during the session is lost.

You can read or write to the fields directly or use them to store lists that contain your data. If you have a very small amount of data, reading and writing directly to fields is easier. For larger amounts of data, reading the field contents into a list and using the list to access the data while the program is running is much faster. When it is time to quit the program, you can write the data back out to the field to store it.

Suppose that you have a single-user application that needs to store a small amount of information about the user's preferences. You might want to keep track of where the user was when she quit last, so you can return her to that spot as well as to her current score.

You would create a field to directly store this small amount of data. The following code writes this user data to the field "User Information":

```
on staveTheData
  global currentArea
  global score
  put currentArea into item 1 of line 1 of field "User Information"
```

```
      put score into item 2 of line 1 of field "User Information"
      saveMovie
   end
```

Call this handler from your cleanup routine that you run when the user quits. If you call this handler from a `stopMovie` handler, it runs every time you move from one movie to another.

Now imagine that you have many people using your program, and that you must store this information for every person. When the program is launched, you prompt each user to enter her name so that you can link the saved information to the correct person.

One way to do this would be to have each line of the User Information field store the information for one person. An information line would be added to the end of the field for each new person.

But how would you retrieve one user's information under this scheme? You could read through each line of the field, examining the first item of the line (the user name) until you found the right entry, but this would not be very efficient, for a couple of reasons:

▶ If you look for the name of someone who was the 200th person to sign in, you have to cycle through 199 lines in the field before you find him.

▶ Chunk commands (`item`, `char`, `word`, `line`) are slow.

A better solution is to use a property list. If you store each name as a property and use the `sort` command on the list, the user information is automatically indexed by user name. Now you can retrieve the entry you seek without cycling through all the others.

The following is a property list that contains the same information as discussed earlier. The main list is a property list of user names. The value for each name in the main list is also a property list, containing the data for one user.

```
["David": [#currentArea:"Fitness Tips",#score:40],"Marlene":  [#currentArea:
➥"Quiz", #score:80],... "Zane": [#currentArea: "Library",#score:99]]
```

You add an item to the list like this:

```
on addUser userName,area,score
   global userList
   if voidP(userList) then set userList - [:]
   set miniList = [:] -- sublist of one user's data
```

```
      setaProp miniList,#currentArea,area
      setaProp miniList,#score,score
      setaProp(userList,userName,miniList)
  end
```

You retrieve user data from the list like this:

```
on getCurrentArea userName
  global userList
  set miniList = getProp(userList,userName)
  return getProp(miniList,#currentArea)
  -- you can nest list commands. Another way to
  -- write this would be:
  -- getProp(getProp(userList,userName),#currentArea)
end
```

Lists are only temporary storage, like variables. At the end of the Director session, you must store your list data to a field and do a saveMovie to preserve it. Fortunately, you don't have to write out the list item-by-item to the field. You can put the entire list into the field at one time. Director converts the list to a string first and then puts it into the field:

```
put myList into field"Storage Field"
```

A field can hold up to 32 KB of text. A list that you store this way must be able to fit entirely into the field. Otherwise, the data at the end of the list that does not fit gets cut off.

When you restart your program, you load the data back into a list from the field with code such as this:

```
on loadList
  global myList
  put value(field "Storage Field") into myList
  sort(myList)
end
```

The value function converts the string in your storage field back into a list. Then you must sort the list to restore the internal indices that make searching fast. You lose these when you convert a sorted list to a string.

INSIDER TIP

saveMovie is a useful command but it only works in certain circumstances.

▶ You cannot use saveMovie if you're running a movie from a CD. You can't write to the CD; thus, you can't directly overwrite that movie on the CD. The full syntax for the command is saveMovie [pathName:fileName]. This means that you can save a copy of the movie with the new data onto your user's hard drive. You can even save the movie with a new name on the hard drive.

▶ If you install a projector and additional movies onto your user's hard drive, you can use saveMovie to save updates of those movies.

▶ You cannot use saveMovie from within a Windows projector. If your movie is completely contained in a projector, saveMovie won't work. If you have a projector that opens other movies, protected or not, you can use saveMovie to save an updated version of one of those movies.

If you need to use saveMovie from a Windows projector, keep the movie that you need to save as an external movie. It can be protected.

▶ You cannot use saveMovie from within a Shockwave movie. The command is disabled in Shockwave.

INSIDER TIP

save castLib can also be used to save data. save castLib also has restrictions, more severe than saveMovie.

▶ Save castLib doesn't work with internal casts. The cast must be external to the movie for the save castLib command to work.

▶ If a cast is protected before you use the save castLib command, it won't be after the cast is resaved. The icon will show an unprotected external cast. Although this is slightly more secure than saving the data to an external text file, an external cast should not be considered a safe way to hold sensitive data.

▶ To save the data changes in an internal cast, use saveMovie.

Using External Files

You can manage a small-to-moderate amount of permanent data just by using fields inside your Director movie. This is a good strategy for data that is not going to grow beyond the limits of a 32 KB text field. Although spanning data over multiple fields is possible, storing large amounts of data this way is not practical. Data internal to the movie increases the movie's file size and memory requirements. Storing data inside the movie also makes it impossible for someone else to do data entry.

External files are a better choice for storing large amounts of data because they keep your Director movie size small and reduce your memory requirements. You can retrieve data from a file one record at a time.

The movie DATABASE.DIR demonstrates data entry and retrieval for a small fixed-length record database. The text file CATFILE.TXT contains the database. The code in this movie is similar to the code that will be discussed later. This movie is in the Chapter 17 folder of the accompanying CD-ROM. Copy DATABASE.DIR and its data file CATFILE.TXT into the same folder on your hard drive before you start working with it. If you run DATABASE.DIR from the CD, it will not be able to write to the data file on the CD.

The FileIO Xtra enables you to read and write to ASCII (text) files. The FileIO Xtra should be in your Xtras folder/subdirectory. As with any Xtra, you should include a copy with your finished production. Create an Xtras folder/subdirectory and put a copy of all of the Xtras that you use into this folder/subdirectory. Put this folder/subdirectory into the same folder/directory as your projector.

You can also have Director do this for you when you create the projector. Open the Modify menu, select Movie, then select the Xtras dialog box. From this window you can select which Xtras you want to have included in the projector. If no Xtras are listed when you open this window, click on the Add button. This opens a dialog box for selecting Xtras to be added to the list.

When you create the projector you must select the Check Movies for Xtras option in the Projector Options dialog box. These two steps automatically include those listed Xtras into your projector.

The FileIO Xtra opens automatically if you do this. Please read all the FileIO documentation.

INSIDER TIP

To find out which XObjects and Xtras are loaded and available to you, type:

`showxlib`

in the Message window. XObjects and Xtras are self-documenting. To get a list of an Xtra's methods, type the following in the Message window:

`putmMessageList(xtra "fileio")`

The FileIO Xtra, as you would expect, works differently from the XObject. The XObject would only enable you to read from a file *or* write to a file. To add to a file, you used the append mode. The append mode would put the addition to the file at the end of the file that you opened. This was very handy. That has changed in the Xtra. FileIO is still modal, but the modes are slightly different. You now have a readWrite mode as well as a read and a write mode. The append mode is gone. You will use the setPosition method to write to a particular place in the file. You can use getLength to move to the end of the current file. The process is slightly different, but the result is the same.

You open a file by creating a new instance of the FileIO Xtra with the new command and assigning it to a variable. You can open multiple files. The following code opens a file that already exists and writes new data to it. Including the RETURN character at the end of a string signals the end of the record:

```
on appendMode oneRecord
    -- oneRecord is a string that looks like this:
    -- "Garden Hose,XRP2132,32.99"
    global catalogItems
    if objectP(catalogItems) then catalogItems(mDispose)
    -- if this file is already open then close it
    set catalogItems = new(xtra "fileio")
    openFile(catalogItems,"cat.txt",2)
    -- "cat.txt" would need a full file path if it was not located in
    -- the same directory as the calling movie
    -- the last parameter, 2, is a flag to tell FileIO how to open the file
    -- 0 is Read/Write, 1 is Read and 2 is Write
    setPosition(catalogItems,getLength(catalogItems))
    -- sets the write position to the end of the open file
    -- getLength will return the length of the open file in characters
    writeString(catalogItems,oneRecord & RETURN)
    -- The RETURN character separates lines in the file. The
    -- ReadLine method reads up to a RETURN character (10).
    -- If you will be using ReadLine on the file, or you need
```

```
-- to look at the data in the file with a text editor, you should
-- separate lines with the RETURN character
put integer(field "Record Count") + 1 into field "Record Count"
-- keep a count in another field of the number of records in the file
-- closeFile (catalogItems)
set catalogItems = 0
-- closes the file and deletes the instance of the xtra
end
```

WARNING

Cross-Platform Alert!

Mac text files only use the RETURN character (ASCII 13) to end lines, but PC text files use RETURN (13) and LINE FEED (10). FileIO uses the Macintosh convention to detect the end of a line on both platforms.

If you write a file using FileIO that you are only going to read through FileIO on the PC, you do not have to worry about this. If your PC users are going to use PC programs to view text files that you have created with FileIO, you should end lines with RETURN and LINE FEED.

The data file in the preceding example collects new catalog item data as it is entered, but the data won't be sorted by any data field. To retrieve a particular item's record, you must start at the beginning and read through each record until you come to the one you want. The more records you have in the file, the longer retrieving one record takes. You can speed things up considerably by maintaining an index of the file and using the setPosition method to start reading at the beginning of the record you want.

In this example, the catalog items file is built by data entry. At the same time that you add a new catalog item record to the file, you can add an index entry to a list for the record. The index entry includes only the data field you want to use to retrieve records later and the number of the record—in this case, you would use an item number. This code adds an item number to the index:

```
on newIndEntry itemNumber
  global itemNumberIndex
  if voidP(itemNumberIndex) then
    set itemNumberIndex = [:]
    set lastRecord = integer(field "Record Count")
    setaProp(itemNumberIndex,itemNumber,lastRecord + 1)
  end if
end
```

The item number index list looks like the following:

```
["ARX111":1,"BT833":8,"LR222":55, ...  "XR59393":200]
```

The index is much smaller than the data file because it contains only one data field's worth of data. You might, therefore, be able to use fields in your movie to store your index lists. Otherwise, you can write the index list out to a second file.

Having an index for a file that contains records of varying lengths solves only half the speed problem. To get to record 15, you still must use readLine to read and discard records 1–14 before you arrive at 15. You can get around this by writing fixed-length records to your file and using the setPosition method to start reading at a particular place. setPosition positions the read before the character number specified. If you know that every record contains exactly 100 characters, for example, setPosition(100) positions you before character 101, which is the beginning of record 2.

The easiest way to write a fixed-length record is to pad the end of the string with a character that does not appear in your data. Here is a record padded out to a length of 50 with the ^ character:

```
GardenHose,XRP2132,32.99^^^^^^^^^^^^^^^^^^^^^^^^^^
```

If you make certain that the character you choose for the pad character does not occur in the data itself, using the item delimiter makes it easy to strip out the padding when you read in the record:

```
set the itemdelimiter = "^"
put item 1 of recordReadIn
GardenHose,XRP2132,32.99
```

The record length you choose needs to be as large as the maximum length of all the fields. This means you limit the amount of characters the user can enter into a field at data entry. The RETURN character counts toward the length of the record. A 100-character record contains 99 characters of data and a RETURN character.

The following code uses a record number to read in a record from a file that contains fixed-length, 50-character records:

```
on getOneRecord recordNumber
  set recordLength = 50
  -- these records are padded out to character 50 with ^
```

```
      set catalogItems = new(xtra "fileio")
      openFile(catalogItems,"catfile.txt",1)
      setPosition(catalogItems,recordNumber * recordLength)
      set record = readLine(catalogItems)
      set the itemDelimiter = "^"
      set strippedRecord = item 1 of record
      return strippedRecord
   end
```

Large Databases

"What's the largest database that Director can handle?" is a question that comes up often in Director support forums. The question does not have a hard-and-fast answer because it depends on the size of one record, the projected size of the entire database, and what you want to do with the data. Because every situation is unique, the best way to test performance is to build a dummy text file similar in size and record length to your proposed database, and test access times by using FileIO. Performance is not the only factor, however. Other limitations include:

▶ The database itself can reside in a file outside Director, but the indices must fit into Director's memory. If your database is static—included on a CD with your project, for instance—growth is not a concern. If your database will expand, you run the risk of overflowing memory or field size limits.

▶ You can't delete a record from an external file by using FileIO, although you can flag records for deletion and write a maintenance program that periodically reads through the data file and writes it back out minus the deleted records.

▶ Report printing, using Director's printFrom command, requires that all the data you want to print per page fits into a field on-screen.

▶ You have to write your own utilities in Lingo to handle data entry, database queries, and report generation.

Fortunately, other options are available if your database requirements go beyond what Director can handle. As of this writing, two Director Xtras, FileFlex and V12, enable Director to create and manage an external database.

In Practice

In this chapter, you have learned many ways to store and manage information with Director. Variables, lists, and fields help you organize data during a Director session. Lists are especially versatile. They enable you to sort and index many types of data for quick retrieval.

If you want to save data between Director sessions, you have several options. You can save the data inside the Director file, write it out to a text file, or purchase a database Xtra.

The key advice to remember from this chapter includes:

► Using global variables enables you to move data values between handlers, even across different movies.

► Use symbols instead of strings for values in lists whenever possible.

► Use lists to store collections of related data.

► Use lists to cycle through items quickly.

► Use global variables sparingly. Consider the variable's purpose before you declare a global variable. An unnecessary global variable, once declared, takes up memory for the life of your Director session.

► Give significant variables meaningful names, and give Scratch variables, like counters, one-letter names.

► Variables, global or otherwise, are only temporary storage for data used in your movie. If you want to store this data permanently, you must move that data to a field or to an external file outside the movie.

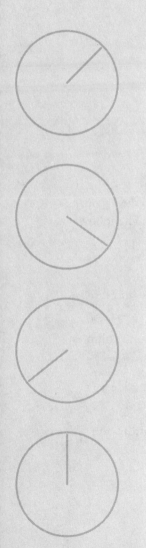

chapter 18

Raúl Silva
Gretchen Macdowall

Movie in a Window

Before Macromedia introduced the Movie in a Window feature in Director 4, Director could play only one movie at a time. The `go movie` and `play movie` commands were the only way to switch movies then, but these commands replaced one movie on the stage with another. A Movie in a Window (MIAW) is a Director movie that opens in its own window and plays simultaneously with the movie on the stage.

MIAWs are fully interactive Director movies that can execute Lingo scripts and play media independently of each other. You can open as many MIAWs as memory will enable. Playback performance depends on how many are open at a time.

Movie in a Window is a versatile Director feature available only through scripting or behaviors. The size, location, appearance, and stacking order of MIAWs are all controlled through Lingo and behaviors. You also use Lingo to pass messages back and forth between MIAWs and the stage. Director 6 ships with a few sample behaviors to work with MIAWs.

Because MIAWs are self-contained and completely independent of each other and the stage, you can use them for special functions that you don't need for the entire session. This independence makes MIAWs great for help systems and programming utilities, especially because MIAWs continue to run independently of the stage movie, even when the stage movie is being edited. Because you can create windows that the users can position wherever they want on-screen, MIAWs are also a good way to implement tool palettes and controls. Finally, MIAWs are a more flexible alternative to Director's standard "alert" box. You can simulate a dialog box with a MIAW that accepts user choice input—something Director's alert command does not do.

In addition to the MIAW tools that you can make for yourself, expect to see more commercial MIAW add-ons as well. You now can open protected MIAWs in the authoring environment; this feature enables third-party developers to write utility MIAWs, but still protect their code. The new Xtras menu will list any MIAW you place in the Xtras folder for easy access. Try placing the MEMMON.DIR movie from the accompanying CD there.

This chapter explains how to create and manage your own MIAWs, and covers the following topics:

▶ The basics

▶ Window types

▶ Panning and scaling

▶ Window messages

▶ Managing multiple windows

▶ Creating reusable MIAWs

The Basics

Take a look at the five sample MIAWs in the Chapter 18 folder on the accompanying CD-ROM to get an idea of the range of uses for MIAWs. The following list summarizes their uses:

▶ **Clock:** A moveable window that displays the time.

▶ **Memmon:** A programming utility that loads and unloads cast and shows the memory freed by each action.

▶ **MixBot:** A programming utility that records and saves the sound volumes you set for sound channels as you play your movie.

▶ **Presentation Tools:** Windows that a presenter can open alongside a main presentation and use to navigate and take notes.

▶ **Alert:** A generic dialog box that contains OK and Cancel buttons and adapts itself for Macintosh or Windows.

You can create a MIAW with one line of Lingo code, as follows:

```
open window "Movie File"
```

In one step this creates a new window, looks for the Director file Movie File in the default directory (the moviePath), assigns the Director file Movie File to that window, and opens the window. This is an easy way to open MIAWs via the Message window for quick testing, but scripts that open MIAWs are more flexible if you separate the processes of creating and opening the window.

Creating a Window

Windows and movie files are two distinct Director elements. A *window* is a porthole through which the Director movie displays. When you create a MIAW, the movie and its window default to the same size. You can, however, change the size of the window and the area the movie plays in with the rect of window and drawRect of window commands. When you make the window assigned to a movie smaller than the movie itself, the window displays only the part of the movie that fits inside the window. Position the window outside the viewable desktop area and it disappears altogether. Don't be fooled, however; the Director movie assigned to that window remains in memory and continues to play, even though you can't see it anymore.

You create a window the first time you refer to it by using the following:

```
window "windowName"
```

The string "windowName" becomes the window's name. If "windowName" is a valid path to a Director movie, the path becomes the window's name and the movie it points to is assigned to the window. Otherwise, the string just becomes the window's name and no movie is assigned to the window. Nothing will open if you use an open command on a window without a Director movie assigned to it because there is nothing yet to display.

Each of the following lines of Lingo, because it contains the phrase window "*windowName*", will create a window—if a window by that name does not already exist.

```
set helpWin = window "Macintosh HD : Project : HELP"
put window "newWindow"
set helpWin = window "helpWindow"
set the filename of window "aWindow" to "Macintosh HD: NAV"
```

Director has an internal list—called *the windowList*—to keep track of MIAWs. As soon as you create a window, even if the window has not been assigned a

Director movie yet, it appears on the windowList with the name you assigned to it. Here is what the windowList looks like after the code in the preceding example runs:

```
[ window "Macintosh HD:Project:HELP", window "newWindow", window
➡"helpWindow", window "aWindow" ]
```

As you can see, windows with short names make it easier to decipher the windowList. It is a good idea to name your windows rather than use the file path name. If you don't assign a title to a window, the window name displays by default in the title bar. You probably would not want the file path to display there.

INSIDER TIP

> If your Director movies are going to play on Windows machines as well as Macs, you should name them from the start with .DIR file extensions. The 8.3 DOS naming convention is required for playback on 16-bit Windows machines. You do not have to include file extensions when you specify a Director file name in your scripts. If you ask for movie Help, Director will first look for movie Help, and then HELP.DIR, and then HELP.DXR. If you don't include extensions in your code, you won't have to change anything later if you decide to protect the movies. Protected movies have a .DXR extension.

Making constant references in your code to window `"windowName"` is cumbersome. You can get around this by setting a variable to the phrase `window myWindowName`. If you make the window variable a global variable, you have the added convenience of making it available throughout your project.

```
global navWin
set navWin = window "Navigator"
```

You now can use the shorthand `navWin` anywhere you would have typed `window "Navigator"`. The following two statements do the same thing:

```
moveToBack window "Navigator"
moveToBack navWin
```

Opening a Window

The Director movie assigned to a MIAW does not load into memory and begin to play until you open its window. The first two lines of the following code link a Director movie to a window and assign the window to global `helpWin`. The third line then displays the window.

```
global helpWin
set helpWin = window "Hard Drive: HELP"
open helpWin
```

Why would you separate these steps? Why not just use the following:

```
open window "Hard Drive:HELP"
```

The answer is that when you open a window, if you haven't specified any window properties, the window defaults to a non-modal, moveable window with close and size boxes, and opens in the middle of the desktop. If you want to customize any of these window properties, you should create the window, modify the window properties while it is still invisible, and then open it.

NOTE

The word *modal* comes from *mode*. In the past, computers locked you into modes; you could not, for example, select a font while on the editing mode, you had to switch to the font selection mode and then back to the editing mode. When a window is modal it forces you to dismiss it before you can do anything else; for example, a Save File dialog box won't let you work on your document until it is dismissed—it locks you into its mode. A non-modal window enables you to work on your document while it's open. The Message window in Director enables you to work on any other window (including the stage) while it's open.

The following code creates a non-modal window:

```
on newStatusBox
    global diaWin, miawPath
    set diaWin = window (miawPath & "DIALOG")
    set the windowType of window 1 to 1
    open diaWin
end
```

In this example, the first line defines a custom handler called newStatusBox, which can be called from anywhere else in our code. The second line declares two global variables: diaWin and miawPath. The third line sets diaWin as the full path name for the file used by the window. miawPath is a global variable defined elsewhere that contains the directory path to the folder where movies used as MIAWs are found. The fourth line sets the windowType for the window, and finally the fifth line opens the window.

When you assign windows to files in one step and open them in another, you should find that they are easier to manage. Because assigning a Director file name to a window does not actually load the movie until you open the window, you can lump all these assignments in one place at the start of your first movie. That way they are easy to locate and easy to change, if you decide to change the names of the Director files:

```
on assignMIAW
    global miawPath
    set miawPath = "Hard Drive: MIAW:"
    global helpWin, dialogWin, paintPaletteWin
    set helpWin = window (miawPath & "TEMPH")
    set dialogWin = window (miawPath & "TEMPD")
    set paintPaletteWin = window (miawPath & "TEMPP")
end
```

All the code outside the `assignMIAW` handler can use the globals `helpWin`, `dialogWin`, and `paintPaletteWin` to refer to the MIAWs. Later in production, if the file names of the Director files linked to these windows change, it will be a simple matter to change them in one place in the `assignMIAW` handler.

Positioning a Window

The `rect of window` property specifies the window's size and its position in relation to the top-left corner of the desktop. The following code creates a window 400 pixels wide by 300 pixels tall, and positions its top-left corner 100 pixels away from the top-left corner of the desktop (see fig. 18.1).

Figure 18.1

The dialog window has a rect of (100, 100, 500, 400).

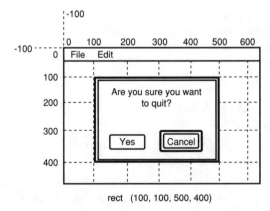

rect (100, 100, 500, 400)

```
on quitDialog
   global quitWin,MIAWpath
   set quitWin = window (MIAWpath & "QUITDIA")
   set the rect of quitWin to rect(100, 100, 500, 400)
   open quitWin
end
```

The four values in a MIAW rect and their representations are found in Table 18.1.

Table 18.1

rect(A,B,C,D)

Value	Representation
A	Pixel distance of top-left corner of MIAW from the left edge of the desktop
B	Pixel distance of top-left corner of MIAW from the top of the desktop
C	Pixel distance of bottom-right corner of MIAW from the left edge of the desktop
D	Pixel distance of bottom-right corner of MIAW from the top edge of the desktop

INSIDER TIP

You can determine the size of a MIAW from its rect values. An example of rect(A,B,C,D) follows:

Width in pixels = C–A

Height in pixels = D–B

A window with the dimensions of rect (100, 100, 500, 400) would have a width of 400 (500–100) and a height of 300 (400–100).

By specifying negative coordinates, you can position a window above and to the left of the desktop—out of sight. You can use this no-man's-land coordinate space to stash windows that you want to load, but that are not yet ready to display.

Sometimes, a noticeable delay occurs when you open a large MIAW that contains many sprites because the movie is loading from the disk or CD, and then imaging on to the desktop. You can minimize the delay by using the preLoadMovie command to preload any cast that will appear in the first frame of the MIAW, and opening the window beyond the visible desktop. This part is transparent to the user.

```
on openLargeMovie
      global bigWindow,MIAWpath
      preloadMovie MIAWpath & "BIGWIND"
      -- BIGWIND is the file name of the movie to be used as a MIAW
      set bigWindow = window (MIAWpath & "BIGWIND")
      -- the rect of bigWindow is rect(50,50,500,400)
      set the rect of bigWindow = the rect of bigWindow - 10000
      -- subtracts 1000 from each item in the rect
      -- the rect of bigWindow is now rect (-9950,-9950,-9500,-9600)
      open bigWindow
      -- window opens outside of the visible stage
end
```

INSIDER TIP

> Why a negative coordinate of 10000? Director assigns the coordinate (0, 0) to the top-left corner of the primary monitor. On the Macintosh you can have a second monitor (actually you can have as many video cards as you can squeeze in the box but it is unusual for a system to have more than two) placed to the left of the primary monitor. That second monitor will be in the negative horizontal coordinate space. Using a high number, such as –10000, reduces the chance of the MIAW you are trying to hide showing up on the second monitor on a Macintosh, because you have specified negative coordinates occupied by that monitor.

When you are ready to display the MIAW, you reset the rect of window to the correct position on the desktop. Because the movie has already loaded from disk, it displays much faster.

```
on fastDisplay
   global bigWindow
   set the rect of bigWindow to rect(50,50,500,400)
   -- preloaded window appears on the desktop
end
```

Closing a Window

The close window command makes a window invisible, but does not unload the movie linked to it from memory. The Director movie assigned to a closed window continues to play in the background. All you have done is hidden the window from view.

The forget window command removes the window and its associated Director file from memory. Use close or the visible property when you want to temporarily hide a window. This prevents a time-consuming reload of the movie from disk. Use forget when you want to clear a window from memory that you are not going to use again or when you need to free up memory.

INSIDER TIP

Setting the windowList to an empty list as follows forgets all MIAWs:

```
set the windowList = []
```

Window Types

You can customize your MIAW window frames by using the following command to set the windowType property:

```
set the windowType of window "windowName" to typeNumber
Ex: set the windowType of window "Main" to 1
```

Director's built-in window types are the standard window types available in the operating system. When you specify a particular window type, Director makes a call to the operating system to create that type of window. Window borders are useful as well as decorative, but they also tell the user how that window is going to behave. Each window type behaves the same way across all system-compliant applications, making it easy for users to get around. If you ignore interface conventions when you choose window types (for example, you create an alert box framed by a document window just to be different), you won't be doing your users any favors.

Table 18.2 lists Director's built-in window types for the Macintosh.

Table 18.2

The Standard Window Types for the Macintosh

Type	Description	Appearance
−1	Default Director window type	
0	Standard document	
1	Alert	
2	Plain	
3	Plain with shadow	
4	Document without size box	
8	Document with zoom box, with size box	
12	Document with zoom box, no size box	
16	Curved border	

Table 18.3 lists Director's built-in window types for Windows 95.

Table 18.3

The Standard Window Types for Windows 95

Type	Description	Appearance
–1	Default Director window type	
0	Standard document	
1	Alert	
2	Plain	
3	Plain	
4	Document without sizing	
8	Document with minimize and maximize	
12	Document with maximize, no minimize	
16	Document without sizing	

Panning and Scaling

The previous section described the use of the rect of window to change the position of the movie on-screen. You can also use the two rect commands, rect of window and drawRect, to create special visual effects by making the window larger or smaller than the size of the Director movie it displays.

rect of window

Setting the rect of window positions the window on-screen starting at the screen coordinate specified for the top-left corner. The rect of window command aligns the top-left corner of the Director movie with the top-left corner of the window and displays as much of the Director movie as will fit inside the rectangle it defines (see fig. 18.2). The rect of window command does not resize or reposition the Director movie within the window.

If the window rectangle is smaller than the size of the movie, part of the movie will be cut off (see fig. 18.3). You can use this feature to create a panning effect by sizing a window to show just part of the Director movie's stage, and then moving a sprite that is under the viewable area. The movie SCROLL.DIR on the accompanying CD shows a simple example of this effect.

Figure 18.2

The window at normal size (160×151), with top-left corner at (100, 100)—rect (100, 100, 260, 251).

Figure 18.3

The window rect (100, 100, 200, 200) is smaller than the movie's rect.

If the window rectangle is larger than the size of the movie's stage, the empty space below and to the right of the movie has a solid fill the color of the movie's stage color (see fig. 18.4).

Figure 18.4

The window rect (100, 100, 350, 350) is larger than the movie's rect.

drawRect of window

The `drawRect of window` positions and resizes the Director movie within the window relative to the top-left corner of the window, which is (0, 0). If you set the `drawRect` smaller than the size of the Director movie stage, the Director movie stage will shrink to fit into the space (see fig. 18.5).

Figure 18.5

The movie's rect (0, 0, 100, 100) shrinks to fit in the allotted stage space.

If you set the `drawRect` larger than the size of the Director movie, the movie expands to fill the space (see fig. 18.6).

Figure 18.6

The movie's rect (0, 0, 320, 321) stretches.

If you specify coordinates that do not start at (0, 0), the top-left corner of the movie will display that distance away from the top-left corner of the window (see fig. 18.7).

Figure 18.7

The movie's rect (75, 75, 175, 175) now begins 75 pixels away from the window's top-left corner.

The drawRect of window does not resize the window; it resizes the Director movie that displays within the window.

Resizing a Director movie with drawRect slows performance because the new size of every sprite must be recalculated with each frame. Resizing with drawRect is more effective on shape sprites than on bitmaps.

Window Messages

When a user interacts with a window by bringing it forward or moving it, for example, Director sends a window event message to the window. You can trap for these events with on eventName handlers in your MIAWs. You might have an on closeWindow event, for example, that closes all open MIAWs if the user clicks on the close box of one.

In most cases, user activity, not Lingo, generates window messages. A Lingo resize of a window, for example, does not generate a resizeWindow message. Table 18.4 lists the MIAW-generated messages.

Table 18.4

MIAW-Generated Messages

Message	User Action
activateWindow	Clicks on a window that is not the currently active window.
deactivateWindow	Clicks on an area outside an active window.
closeWindow	Clicks on a window's close box. Window types without a close box do not receive this message. The closeWindow message can also be generated by the Close window and set the visible of window commands.
moveWindow	Drags a window by the drag bar. (Windows without a drag bar do not receive this message.)
resizeWindow	Drags in the Resize box. (Only window types that enable resizing receive this message.)
zoomWindow	Clicks in the Zoom box. (Only windows with a zoom box receive this message.)

Managing Multiple Windows

After you have learned to create and control MIAWs, you will think of many ingenious uses for them and will soon wind up with several MIAWs open simultaneously. One common setup is the stage, a navigation palette, and a help window. You can ensure that all the windows work together smoothly if you know some basics about how MIAWs interact with each other and with the stage.

The Stage Runs the Show

The stage is not just another window—the stage is king. The stage establishes the palette and serves as communications central for all windows.

The `tell` command sends Lingo commands from the stage to a window or from a window to the stage. This enables you to control one window independently of another. (As the Director manual describes, you can use `tell` with other Lingo objects as well, but it is most useful for working with windows.) The syntax for using `tell` with windows is as follows:

```
tell window windowName to lingo statement
tell the stage to lingo statement
```

For example:

```
tell window "Controls" to moveToBack
```

For a multiple-line `tell`, use:

```
tell window windowName
   lingo statement
   lingo statement
end tell

tell the stage
   lingo statement
   lingo statement
end tell
```

For example:

```
tell window "Help"
   moveToFront
   puppetTransition 20,1,1
```

```
      set the locV of sprite 5 to 200
      updateStage
end tell
```

One helpful way to use a MIAW is as a navigation tool for a presentation. The MIAW displays a field with a list of all the labels in the main movie. When the presenter clicks on one of the label names, the MIAW tells the stage to go to that frame. The following code, in the sprite script for the label field in the MIAW, communicates the requested label to the stage:

```
on mouseDown
    if the mouseLine > 0 then
        set ln = the mouseLine
        put line ln of field "Presentation Screens" into newLoc
        hilite line ln of field "Presentation Screens"
        tell the stage to go newLoc
    end if
end
```

You might have a situation in which one MIAW needs to communicate with another MIAW. Although Lingo enables you to send a `tell` from one MIAW to another, it does not work very well. The best way to handle communication between MIAWs is through the stage. If MIAW1 wants MIAW2 to do something, it should wrap the message in a `tell` to the stage, as follows:

```
tell the stage
    tell MIAW2
        message for MIAW2 here
    end tell
end tell
```

Suppose that you have added a window to the presentation described previously. This moveable window contains a text field for the presenter to record audience comments. Now when you use the navigation palette, you want the stage to go to a particular frame and you want the MIAW that displays the audience notes to display any comments that were recorded for that screen. You can expand the `tell the stage` section of the preceding code sample to accomplish this:

```
on mouseDown
    if the mouseLine > 0 then
        set ln = the mouseLine
        put line ln of field "Presentation Screens" into newLoc
```

```
        hilite line ln of field "Presentation Screens"
        tell the stage
           go newLoc
        tell window "Audience Notes"
              go newLoc -- the "Audience Notes" MIAW uses the same label names
                      -- as the main movie.
              end tell
        end tell
     end if
end
```

The stage rules palette control as well as communications. Because only one palette can be active on-screen at a time, the stage "owns" the palette. When a MIAW opens—if it was created with a different palette than the stage movie's palette—its art will use the colors in the stage's palette. That means that an area of the image that uses the color in palette position 5 that was brown under the MIAW's palette, for example, could turn green if that is the color in palette position 5 in the stage's palette.

A MIAW can change the current palette, but only by telling the stage to do so:

```
tell the stage
   puppetPalette 14
   updateStage
end tell
```

Because only one palette can be active at a time, after the MIAW changes the palette, the MIAW's art will display correctly. But if the stage is visible, the stage art will look incorrect.

Another way to handle a situation in which the MIAW has a different palette than the stage is to include code in the MIAW's startMovie that remaps the MIAW's artwork to the stage's palette. Rather than just changing the colors of the artwork to whatever colors are in the same palette positions in the new palette, palette remapping tries to find colors in the new palette similar to those in the original palette. The following code, taken from a Macromedia tech note, enables palette remapping in a MIAW:

```
on startMovie
  set myName = getAt(the windowList, count(the windowList))
  -- This line puts the name of the Movie in a Window (MIAW) that
  -- was just opened into a temporary variable called myName.
```

```
    tell the stage to tell myName to set the paletteMapping to TRUE
    -- We are telling the stage to instruct the MIAW to enable its
    -- "Remap Palettes When Needed" option. For more information,
    -- see paletteMapping in the Help System.

    tell the stage to tell myName to updateStage
    -- Here we are telling the stage to instruct the MIAW to refresh
    -- its playback area.
end
```

Event Handling

User event handling usually happens independently in each MIAW. A mouseUp event, for example, is trapped by the topmost MIAW under the mouse and is not passed to any other windows.

The following sections describe a few noteworthy exceptions to this.

mouseDown

If a QuickTime movie is playing on the stage and the user holds down the mouse over a button or field in a MIAW with a mouseUp or mouseDown handler, the QuickTime on the stage stops playing until the user releases the mouse. This can be a problem if you included some kind of slider or moveable sprite on the MIAW that requires the user to hold down the mouse. You can get around this by inserting a repeat loop under the offending object in the MIAW to constantly update the stage:

```
on mouseDown
    repeat while the stillDown
        tell the stage to exitFrame( script the frameScript )
    end repeat
end
```

Key Events

If you have an editable text field on the stage and an open MIAW, the key events are always trapped by the MIAW, making it impossible to edit the field on the stage. This happens in a projector, but not in authoring. It is best to avoid this problem by designing the interface so that editable text fields always only display one movie at a time.

If you must have the MIAW open while the user edits the field on the stage, you can put a `keyDown` script in the MIAW that passes the typed key back to the stage's field, as follows:

```
on keyDown
   tell the stage
      put field "Input" & the key into field "Input"
   end tell
end
```

Rollovers

Unlike other user events, rollovers leak through MIAWs and are detected by the stage's `rollOver` handlers if the MIAW is positioned over the stage. If you are going to be using `rollOver` handlers and MIAWs, you should script the stage rollovers with this in mind.

Shared Resources and Events

Although MIAWs are generally independent of one another, they share parts of the Director environment. One movie's behavior can affect other movies, if it alters a shared resource. Following are potential problems to keep in mind:

▶ Each MIAW uses memory and processor cycles, even when it is closed or invisible. Keep this in mind when you are planning multiple window projects. The number of open windows affects animation performance.

▶ All movies running during a Director session, including MIAWs, have access to globals. Your MIAWs can use globals to pass information back and forth.

▶ If you declare an object as a global, it resides in memory for the duration of the Director session and is available to all movies. You can create a new object from a script that resides in a MIAW and "forget" the MIAW afterward. The object remains accessible even after the movie script it was created from is not.

▶ If you link MIAWs and the stage movie to the same external cast, they will share the scripts and members from that cast. Changes to the cast by one movie—such as duplicating, copying, or changing the script text of members—are immediately reflected in other movies sharing the same cast members.

▶ The timeout is reset by user events in any movie, although each MIAW can have its own `timeoutScript`. If a `timeoutScript` is in Movie A and the user clicks on Movie B, the timeout is reset.

▶ `Idle` events are sent to all resident MIAWs. MIAWs that have been closed but not "forgotten" still receive `idle` events and still execute their `idle` handlers.

▶ The windowList is a list of all resident windows. The windowList is accessible to all movies. Windows that have been closed but not "forgotten" still appear on the list.

▶ Movies do not share the actorList. (The actorList is discussed in Chapter 20, "Object-Oriented Programming in Director.") Each movie has its own actorList. MIAWs that have been closed but not "forgotten" still receive `stepFrame` events, and objects on an open MIAW's actorList still execute `stepFrame` handlers.

Creating Reusable MIAWs

Most MIAWs are small movies built for a particular kind of task. Many of these tasks, such as dialog boxes, come up again and again in projects. If you spend a little extra design time up front, you'll be able to write your MIAWs one time and then reuse them in later projects with little or no modification. Try to design your MIAWs without dependencies on any external casts and with as few dependencies as possible on global variables set outside the MIAW. Such design makes it easier to plug them in to other projects later. Table 18.5 lists all the MIAW commands and functions. You will need to know these to create reusable MIAWs.

Table 18.5

MIAW Commands and Functions

Command	Description
open window	Makes a window visible on the desktop if the window's rect coordinates are within the desktop.
close window	Makes a window invisible. The movie assigned to the window is still in memory and still processing, though not visible.

Command	Description
`forget window`	Unloads a window and the movie assigned to it from memory. The movie is no longer active.
`windowType of window`	Specifies the kind of frame and window controls (such as a zoom box) that the window should have.
`modal of window`	Specifies whether the movie should enable the user to click outside of it or beep when the user clicks outside of it.
`filename of window`	Specifies the Director movie to display inside the window. Multiple windows can have the same file name. Windows sharing the same file name display the same movie.
`name of window`	Specifies the text to use for window name. The default name of a window is the file path to the MIAW. The title bar displays the window name if you do not set the `title` property.
`title of window`	Specifies the text to use in the window's title bar.
`rect of window`	Specifies the location and size of the MIAW relative to the desktop.
`the drawRect of window`	Specifies the location and size of the Director movie relative to its window. Can be set for the stage.
`the visible of window`	Specifies whether the window can be seen. Can be set for the stage.
`moveToBack`	Moves the target window behind all other windows. Can be sent to the stage.
`moveToFront`	Moves the target window in front of all other windows. Can be sent to the stage.
`the activeWindow`	Identifies the window name linked to the movie executing the line of code containing `the activeWindow`. Similar to the way other languages use `me`. Returns (`window "windowName"`) for a MIAW. Returns `"the stage"` for the stage.
`the frontWindow`	Identifies the top window. Returns (`window "windowName"`) for a MIAW. Returns `"the stage"` for the stage.
`windowPresent ("name")`	Reports TRUE if the window exists, whether it is "closed" or "open."

In Practice

The Movie in a Window feature extends your interface options and enables you to create modular tools that you can easily share with others. As you continue to experiment with MIAWs, you will undoubtedly find many uses for them in your projects.

This chapter, combined with the information in Chapter 16, "Lingo: The Basics," and Chapter 17, "Managing Your Data," introduced you to the various parts of the Director tool set. In the next chapter, "Advanced Concepts," you learn how to apply that tool set to some of the most common development problems.

Remember the following important aspects of working with MIAWs:

▶ The process of creating a Movie in a Window requires creating a window and opening a Director movie within it.

▶ When you open a window, the movie associated with it loads and begins to play. Even if you subsequently close the window, the movie continues to play in the background, out of the user's view. The forgetWindow command deletes the MIAW from memory.

▶ If you want to temporarily hide a MIAW from a user, and make it visible again later, use the close or visible property; doing so prevents time-consuming reloads of the movie from disk. If you want to clear a MIAW from memory because you are not going to use it again, use forget.

▶ Use rect of window to position and set the dimensions of the MIAW window. You can use this feature to create a panning effect.

▶ Use drawRect of window to position and set the dimensions of the MIAW movie.

▶ The best way to handle communication between multiple MIAWs is through the stage. Although they can communicate directly, with Lingo, this does not work very well.

▶ Be aware of which events happened independently in multiple MIAWs and which resources and events are shared between them. Shared events and resources can cause one movie's behavior to affect other movies.

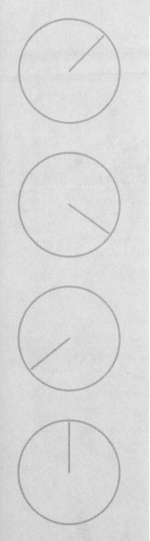

Matt Kerner
Gretchen Macdowall

chapter 19

Advanced Concepts

If you've read this far in the book, chances are that you are already familiar with what you can do with Director. This chapter covers some of the more challenging areas of developing a project in Director.

Specifically, we'll discuss the following topics:

- ▶ Score animation versus Lingo animation
- ▶ Making games
- ▶ Behaviors
- ▶ Making libraries and tools
- ▶ Performance and benchmarking
- ▶ Defensive programming
- ▶ Coming to Lingo from C

Score Animation Versus Lingo Animation

Now that you have completed some development and played with the sample movies, you can see that animation in Director can be completed in two ways. The first and easiest method of animation uses the score. This technique is illustrated in Chapter 6, "Director as an Animator." It creates movies with rather long scores and a high level of redundancy. The second animation style produces movies by using Lingo to build the score and place objects on the stage.

No one way to do animation is the best way. Both styles have their benefits. Score-based animation is relatively easy to put together in a short period of time. Lingo-based animation, on the other hand, can be extremely flexible and precise. It is best to find a happy medium between producing animation exclusively in the score or exclusively in Lingo. Components of your movie that are suited for Lingo animation are those that have a high level of user interactivity.

Think, for example, about building a training tool with several sections, each corresponding to one of four training objectives. The user can complete the objectives in any order; the only requirement is that the user must finish all four objectives before completing the training. There should be a list of the objectives and a way of indicating which ones have been completed. The list of objectives might contain these items:

▶ Product information

▶ Customer service

▶ Team structure

▶ Quality control

It is possible to design a movie that contains only limited Lingo. The score would contain all the possible sequences for completing the objectives (in this example 24 possibilities exist). After a user completes an objective and identifies the next one on which he wants to work, you would simply need to send him to the appropriate section of the score. This method of developing a project has two shortcomings. The first shortcoming is that it is extremely repetitive. Each section would have to have the training information for all the other objectives not completed because the user can complete them in any order. The second shortcoming is that it is not very flexible. Creating a movie using only score-based animation would require you to produce all 24 possible sequences.

If you instead build the training animation by using Lingo, it is possible to use a property list to check which objectives have been completed. After an objective is met, you can check off the box or dim the item. This method requires you to only build each section once as opposed to including it with the others in the package. Using Lingo also makes it easier to later add objectives for the training. Using the score, it is necessary to rebuild the entire application to add an additional objective, but with Lingo you only need to add the new section and change a bit of code.

A maze game like PacMan is another example that requires Lingo. PacMan starts out in the middle of the maze and the user can move him with the arrow keys—up, down, left, or right. Again, the minimal Lingo solution requires a separate section in the score for every possible move PacMan could make. But wait—what about the bad guys? They're moving in the maze, too. Now you need a separate score section for every move that PacMan could make and every move the bad guys could make. In this scenario the score becomes impossibly complex. Using Lingo to move objects within the maze is the only way to solve this problem.

Complex movies like the preceding examples are not always the goal, however. Presentations and support tools have only limited need for animation. Some training tools only use limited animation. For these types of movies it is best to use a combination of score and Lingo-based animation. In most cases duplicating the linear animation sequences with Lingo is not necessary. Doing so can be time-consuming and can cause problems if artwork changes, because every modification requires changing the code instead of changing a few cells in the score. The previous training tool is a good example of using the score to produce an interface and using Lingo to create changes as a user progresses. Lingo-based animation does have speed advantages; however, the speed gain may not be great enough to justify the difficulty of coding an animation.

When using Lingo to control the animation it is best to limit the action to just a few frames. Many developers find that a three frame approach works best. Use the first frame to initialize values and set up the animation. In the second frame, loop while the animation takes place, and use the third frame for clearing out the animation. If the entire movie is within the first set of animation the third frame is not necessary.

Speed Benefits

Using Lingo to perform linear animation may not give speed increases on some systems. Lingo within a repeat loop executes more quickly than score-based animation, but may not provide a beneficial increase because the speed gained may be offset by the difficulty in programming the animation. These caveats aside, let's see just how much faster than score-based animation Lingo animation can be. The following tutorial illustrates the speed differences.

Comparing Score to Lingo Animation Speed

1. Open a new movie in Director, and create a movie script that contains the following Lingo:

```
on moveRight channel
    repeat with x = 1 to 200
        set the locH of sprite channel = the locH of sprite channel + 1
        updateStage
    end repeat
end
```

2. Put the following score script into the first frame:

```
on exitFrame
    puppetSprite 3, true
end
```

3. In the second frame create a score script that calls the moveright handler:

```
on enterFrame
    moveRight 3
end
```

These three scripts set up a simple Lingo-based animation that moves the sprite in the third channel 200 pixels to the right.

4. Use the paint window to create a graphic and place it in channel 3 in both the first and second frames.

5. Now play the movie.

The object you created should have moved smoothly across the stage to the right. It's moving as fast as your computer can redraw it.

6. Using the same image, create a similar animation by using the score.

You may be surprised by the results. Be sure to set the tempo to a high setting. You can also use the SPEED.DIR movie that can be found in the Chapter 19 folder of the CD-ROM that accompanies this book to view this test (see fig. 19.1).

Figure 19.1

The SPEED.DIR movie enables you to compare animation speeds between score- and Lingo-based animation.

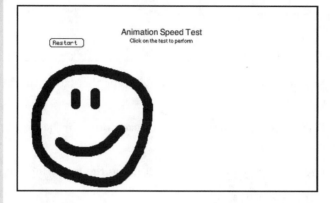

As you can see, using Lingo to perform animation can make the performance considerably faster than using the score. Repeat loop animation does have some drawbacks. While in a repeat loop Lingo takes complete control of the computer and does not enable the user to perform any actions. The repeat loop keeps the computer from noticing other activity. Background applications, the network, and user action are completely ignored while the repeat loop runs. The three major disadvantages to using repeat loop animation are the following:

▶ A repeat loop buys its speed by ignoring user events and dominating the processor.

▶ The playback head does not advance during a repeat loop, so that you must script all the activity on the stage during the repeat loop—not just the sprite you're interested in speeding up.

▶ Animation programmed within a repeat loop runs relatively faster or more slowly, depending on the speed of the machine on which it's playing. Repeat loop animation is difficult to synch to other events.

Flexibility and User Action

Using Lingo to control animation also gives a great deal of flexibility to a project. This is most evident when the user is controlling the actions. In the example of the training tool, the user's choice of individual objectives controlled the display on the screen. Another situation develops in any application that has buttons that provide visual feedback. When the user clicks on a button it should react in some way. The most common response is for the button to depress while the mouse button is pressed. If designed properly you can build a button script that creates universal actions for all buttons of a specific type. This technique is explored in a tutorial on behaviors later in the chapter. Now let's create a simple button.

Building a Simple Button Animation

1. In a new movie create a button graphic that has both an up and a down position.

2. Place these two graphics next to each other in the cast with the up button first.

3. Create a new score script that contains the following Lingo:

```
on mouseDown the rollOver
    set mouseSprite to the rollOver
    set dnbtn to the memberNum of sprite mouseSprite + 1
    puppetSprite mouseSprite, true
    set the memberNum of sprite mouseSprite to dnbtn
    updateStage
end

on mouseUp the rollOver
    set mouseSprite to the rollOver
    set upbtn to the memberNum of sprite mouseSprite - 1
    set the memberNum of sprite mouseSprite to upbtn
    updateStage
    puppetSprite mouseSprite, false
end
```

Place the up button cast member into any channel of the score, and assign the button script as a sprite script. Create a frame script that contains go to the frame on the exitframe in the first frame of the movie. When you play the movie the button should depress when you click on it and pop back up when you release the mouse button. This movie is included in the Chapter 19 folder of the accompanying CD-ROM as BUTTON.DIR. This movie can be used later in this chapter to create a behavior.

Making Games

The kinds of games people create with Director fall into two categories— slower-paced children's educational games and fast-paced action games. The graphics might differ, but when you dig through the code you'll find the same underlying techniques in each type of game. The following sections highlight the essential coding areas of each type of game, but the example movies are too involved to reconstruct in detail on the page. One heavily commented sample movie exists for each type of game on the *Inside Macromedia Director 6 with Lingo* CD-ROM.

Before we get into specifics, the following are some general game coding tips to keep in mind:

▶ Be careful with repeat loops. A repeat loop stops all other motion on-screen. Use repeat loops where smooth motion of one sprite is critical. In other circumstances, it's better to crank up the frame rate and loop over frames.

▶ Don't try to move too many large bitmaps at the same time.

▶ When you program a particular type of game for the first time, try to break the code into small modules that aren't hard coded to particular sprites or cast numbers. If the code is generic enough, you'll be able to use it again for a similar game.

▶ Director script objects are especially helpful in game programming in which you often have several game sprites that share basic behavior but with a few variations. The examples that follow do not use script objects because they would make the examples harder to understand. You could, however, incorporate the sample code from the CD examples into script objects. Script objects are covered in detail in Chapter 20.

Painting and Erasing

The trails ink property is the ticket for painting and erasing. Trails causes the sprite to make copies of itself on every frame as it moves across the screen. Increase your frame rate to make the sprite's trail as smooth as possible. Paths painted on the screen by sprites with their trails turned on are erased when other sprites move over them. The bounding box of any sprite moved over the trailed sprites erases your paintings. For the most realistic erasing, make your erasers rectangular.

The following code turns a sprite into a brush:

```
on mouseDown
  set brush = the clickOn
  puppetSprite brush,TRUE
  set the trails of sprite brush to TRUE
  set the forecolor of sprite brush to random(254)
  repeat while the stillDown
    set the locH of sprite brush to the mouseH
```

```
      set the locV of sprite brush to the mouseV
      updateStage
   end repeat
end

on mouseUp
   set brush = the clickOn
   set the trails of sprite brush to FALSE
   puppetSprite brush,FALSE
   set the forecolor of sprite brush to 255
   updateStage
end
```

The movie GENRAB.DIR in the Chapter 19 folder of the accompanying
CD-ROM is a children's painting program that uses trails ink for the paint (see
fig. 19.2).

Figure 19.2

*The movie
GENRAB.DIR
illustrates using Lingo
to make a simple paint
program.*

Matching

Matching games present a jumble of game pieces each hidden under a cover. As
the user clicks on a piece, the cover of the piece lifts off to reveal the piece
underneath. The object of the game is for the user to uncover matching pairs
until all the game pieces are matched.

This game wouldn't be much fun if the objects always appeared in the same
order on the game board. You need code to randomize the game pieces, to
keep track of which piece is in what spot, and to detect whether the user has
made a match.

The following handler takes a range of sprite channels and a range of cast members and returns a list of the sprite channels with cast members assigned in random order:

```
on scatter spriteList,castList
  set gamePieceList = [:]
  set counter = 1
  repeat while counter <= count(spriteList)
    --pick a random position in the castList
    set randomCastListPos = random(count(castList))
    --get the next channelNumber in the sprite list
    set spriteChannel = getAt(spriteList,counter)
    --get the member at the random position of the castList
    set assignedCast = getAt(castList,randomCastListPos)
    --put this sprite channel and random member on the new list
    setaProp(gamePieceList,spriteChannel,assignedCast)
    --delete the chosen member from the castList
    deleteAt(castList,randomCastListPos)
    set counter = counter + 1
  end repeat
  return gamePieceList
end
```

Next, you need code to make sure that the user can uncover only two pieces at a time. You also need code to detect a match. You should place this code in the cast script of the cast that acts as the cover.

```
on mouseUp
  global gamePieceList,turnedOverList,coverCast
  --gamePieceList: property list of sprites and the cast that will
  --               be revealed when the cover is up
  --               EX: [6:23,7:45,8:23,9:45]
  -- turnedOverList: list of pieces that have already been turned over
  --               EX: [6:23,7:45]
  -- coverCast: cast number of the cast that acts as a door, covering
  --               the member you are trying to match
  set mySprite = the clickOn
  puppetSprite mySprite,TRUE
  --coverCast is set here for clarity. It would be better to set
  --this variable once in another script rather than every time
  --a game piece is clicked
  set coverCast = the memberNum of sprite mySprite
  --reveal up transition, half-second duration, smallest chunksize,
  --changing area
```

```
    puppetTransition 15,2,1,1
    --determine which member should be revealed
    set uncovCast = getProp(gamePieceList,mySprite)
    set the memberNum of sprite mySprite = uncovCast
    updateStage
    --add this sprite to the list of turned-over sprites
    addProp(turnedOverList,mySprite,uncovCast)
    --will never have more than 2 sprites on this list
    if count(turnedOverList) = 2 then
      --if there isn't a match then turn them back over
      if getAt(turnedOverList,1) <> getAt(turnedOverList,2) then
        --let user see the 2 uncovered sprites for a sec before
        --covering them back up
        wait(60)
        --cover sprites back up
        repeat with x = 1 to 2
          puppetTransition 19,2,1,1
          set the memberNum of sprite getPropAt (turnedOverList,x) to
          ➥coverCast
          updateStage
        end repeat
      end if
      --if they match then leave them uncovered but reset the turned-over list
      --to get ready for next match
      set turnedOverList = [:]
    end if
end

on wait numTicksToWait
  set startWait = the timer
  repeat while the timer - startWait < numTicksToWait
    --keep other action going on stage during repeat
    updateStage
  end repeat
end
```

The movie BRAIGAM.DIR (see fig. 19.3) in the Chapter 19 folder on the accompanying CD-ROM is a concentration game in which the object is to match the sense organ to something in the world that it can sense. For example, a nose matches to a flower.

Figure 19.3

The movie BRAIGAM.DIR shows how Lingo can be used to build a simple matching game.

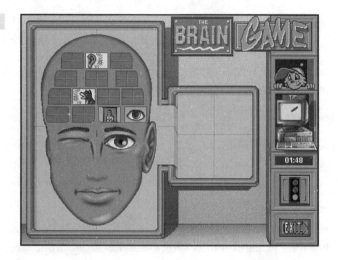

Puzzle Game

The object of a puzzle game is to drag a sprite into the correct area on the screen and drop it. You could, for instance, have the outline of a map of the US on one side of the screen and a pile of state sprites on the other. The user must drag and place the state sprites into their correct positions on the map.

The first thing you must do is arrange the puzzle piece sprites on-screen in their final positions so that you can note their correct locations. You need to compile a list containing the correct placement location for every piece to help you determine if the user has placed a piece correctly. Use the following utility handler to record the correct piece positions into a list:

```
on recordPositions startingSprite,endingSprite
  set positionList = [:]
  repeat with curSprite = startingSprite to endingSprite
    setaProp positionList,curSprite,the loc of sprite curSprite
  end repeat
  return positionList
  --looks like this--sprite number followed by correct hor and ver position
  --[3: point(78, 97), 4: point(138, 97)]
end
```

This handler is used during the development process to create a list of correct locations. Call it as follows from the Message window:

```
set correctPosList = recordPositions(5,15)
```

Make sure the movie is playing when you call the utility handler. If a movie is not playing, Lingo sometimes returns inaccurate sprite locations.

Then, arrange the pieces on-screen in their starting positions, and record those positions into another list, once again from the Message window:

```
set startingPosList = recordPositions(5,15)
```

Next, you should enable dragging of the pieces. The easiest way to accomplish this is to use the moveablesprite property. When you turn on this property for a sprite, it follows the user's mouse after the user clicks on it, for as long as the mouse button stays down.

You should also have mouseUp handlers for the pieces that check whether the user drops the piece into the correct spot. It's almost impossible to place a sprite with exact pixel accuracy, so you must have a placement tolerance—the number of pixels around the target location in which you'll accept the drop as a match.

The following startMovie code sets the moveableSprite property for the game sprites and the placement tolerance:

```
on startMovie
  global tolerance
  --if the user drops this piece within 10 pixels of the target it
  --will be considered a match
  set tolerance = 10
  --the puzzle pieces are in channels 3 through 6
  repeat with x = 3 to 6
    puppetSprite x,TRUE
    set the moveableSprite of sprite x to TRUE
    updateStage
  end repeat
end
```

The following code, when placed in the cast or sprite handlers for the pieces, checks whether the piece has been placed correctly:

```
on mouseUp
  --startingPosList: list of the unplaced piece positions
  global startingPosList
  set mySprite = the clickOn
  --check if where the user dropped the piece is correct
  if posOK(the loc of sprite mySprite) then
    puppetSound "that's right!"
```

```
  else
    --find the position to send the sprite back to and send it back
    set the loc of sprite mySprite to getProp (startingPosList,mySprite)
  end if
end
```

The function posOK, called in the preceding handler, should be placed in a movie script so that it is available to all the sprite handlers:

```
on posOK aPoint
  global tolerance,correctPosList
  set mySprite = the clickOn
  --get the exact point that is the correct position in the puzzle for
  --this sprite
  set exactPoint = getProp(correctPosList,mySprite)
  --use list math to get the range around the correct position that
  --would still be a match
  --For example point(100,100) - 20 = point(80,80)
  set lowerLimit = exactPoint - tolerance
  set upperLimit = exactPoint + tolerance
  if aPoint > lowerLimit and aPoint < upperLimit then
    return TRUE
  else
    return FALSE
  end if
end
```

The movie SKELGAM.DIR (see fig. 19.4) in the Chapter 19 folder of the accompanying CD-ROM has the user build a human skeleton by dragging bones from a pile.

Figure 19.4

The SKELGAM.DIR movie shows how sprites can be positioned precisely with Lingo after a user places it in roughly the correct position.

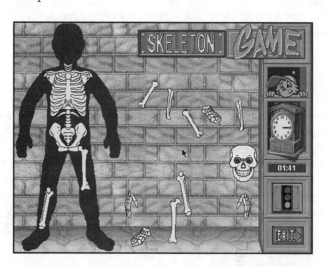

Maze Chase

In maze chase games, the user moves an animated character—by using the mouse or arrow keys—through a maze avoiding bad guys and other hazards. The biggest challenge is to keep the character moving in the direction the user specifies and inside the confines of the maze. You can define a maze in two ways.

One way to lay out the maze on the stage is by using transparent rectangle shapes. After laying out the rectangles, you must constrain the position of the sprite to stay within the shapes. The property constraint of a sprite does most of the work for you. The command for constraining a sprite follows:

```
set the constraint of sprite 5 to 7
```

Set up sprite 7 as a containing sprite for sprite 5. The regpoint of sprite 5 now always stays within the bounds of sprite 7. The constraint of the sprite property overrides any sprite location you set with Lingo.

This script sets up the constraints of your moving sprite.

```
on startMovie
    puppetSprite 2,TRUE
    set the constraint of sprite 2 to 1
    updateSTage
end
```

This script controls the motion of the sprite constrained to sprite 1.

```
on mouseDown
    set the locH of sprite 2 = the locH of sprite 2 + 4
    updateStage
end
```

The transparent rectangle method is fairly easy to set up and also easy to change. You can change the layout of the maze by rearranging the rectangle shapes. You're limited, however, to 120 channels for the maze shapes and other game sprites.

A second way to lay out the maze logically is by defining lists of points that represent the paths in the maze. With every move you can compare the sprite's position against the path lists to see whether it can continue moving in that direction. This does not limit you to 120 channels, but it's more time-consuming to code.

The core of a maze chase game is the code that moves the character sprite. Before advancing the sprite in the current direction, the code must check to see that the new position is inside the maze walls. The code also must check to see whether the sprite has hit any bad guys or other hazards. The best place for this code is in an enterFrame handler. Because the code executes with every frame, the challenge is to keep it spare so that it doesn't slow down the game.

The following code is the enterFrame handler for a simple maze that is constructed by using the first method—a maze defined with transparent rectangle sprites:

```
on enterFrame
  global characterSprite,badGuySpriteList,direction,curSegType
  --characterSprite: the dot
  --direction: current direction chosen by user(up,down,left,right)
  --badGuySpriteList: list of sprites that the dot can collide with
  --curSegType: is the current constraining rectangle horizontal or
  --vertical?
    repeat with listPos = 1 to count(badGuySpriteList)
      if sprite characterSprite intersects getAt(badGuySpriteList,listPos)
then
        --check for collision first because that resets game
        gameOver
        exit
      end if
    end repeat
  set savH = the locH of sprite characterSprite
  set savV = the locV of sprite characterSprite
  --save old positions to see if move was successful
  tryToMoveSprite(savH,savV)
  --advances sprite if it can stay within bounds of current maze segment
  --otherwise sprite does not move
  if (the locH of sprite characterSprite = savH and curSegType = "H") then
    --if the sprite didn't move check to see if it's at an intersection and
    --change current maze segment so it can continue moving
    checkCorner("Ver")
  else if (the locV of sprite characterSprite = savV and curSegType = "V")
then
    checkCorner("Hor")
  end if
```

The movie MAZE.DIR (see fig. 19.5), found on the accompanying CD-ROM in the Chapter 19 folder, is a simple movie that contains the previous code. The handlers that are not explained in that code are detailed in this movie.

The movie HEARGAM.DIR, also found on the CD-ROM in the Chapter 19 folder, is a more complex maze game. The object of the game is to guide a blood cell through the circulatory system ahead of the viruses that are chasing it.

Figure 19.5

The movie MAZE.DIR uses sprites to constrain animation to a specific area.

Adjust the score tempo to adjust speed
of dot. Close all windows before
running or the key presses won't
register. Use arrow keys to move.

Creating Behaviors

With the Behavior Inspector, Director 6 introduces the capability to reuse code blocks in the form of sprite-based behaviors. This capability serves two important purposes. First, it enables people to develop in Director without having to understand a lot of Lingo by using the libraries of behaviors that are already created. Secondly, it gives the Lingo programmer an extremely easy way to build code libraries. Building code libraries is discussed later in this chapter.

Chapter 5, "Working with Director 6: Understanding the Metaphor," covers the basics of using behaviors to add interactivity to your project. Director comes with many behaviors, and the following tutorial produces a fairly common behavior script.

The following tutorial shows how to build a simple behavior. The finished behavior creates a button behavior that swaps a graphic when clicked and highlights the button when the cursor is focused above it (see fig. 19.6). The movie used is based on the BUTTON.DIR movie used earlier in the chapter. A finished copy of the movie and behavior can be found in BEHAV.DIR in the Chapter 19 folder on the accompanying CD-ROM.

Figure 19.6

*The completed
BEHAV.DIR movie.*

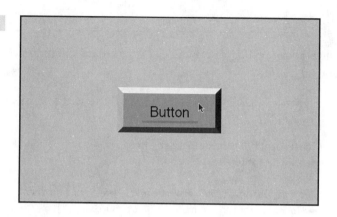

Building Behaviors

1. Open the movie BUTTON.DIR from the Chapter 19 folder of the CD-ROM and save a copy to your hard drive (this is the movie used to create a simple button script).

2. Create a new score script member in the cast and call it `btn behavior` (see fig. 19.7).

Figure 19.7

*The Behavior
Inspector window.*

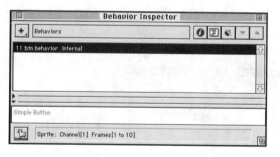

3. Enter the following code into the script:

```
property upMember, downMember, hiliteMember
```

This code sets the properties of the behavior. The three properties are as follows:

`upMember`: The cast member that contains the graphic of the normal button.

`downMember`: The cast member that contains the graphic of the depressed button.

continues

Building Behaviors continued

hiliteMember: The cast member that contains the graphic of the high-lighted button.

4. Enter the following block of code into the script. It asks for the location of the down and hilite graphics.

```
on getPropertyDescriptionList
  set description = [:]

  addprop description, #downMember, [#default:"btndn",
➡#format:#string, #comment:"Pict for Down:"]

  addprop description, #hiliteMember, [#default:"btnlite",
➡#format:#string, #comment:"Pict for Hilite:"]

  return description
end
```

The handler getPropertyDescriptionList is used to get the values for the behavior properties defined in step 3. These values can be set by double-clicking on the behavior in the Behavior Inspector dialog box (see fig. 19.8).

Figure 19.8

The Customize Behavior dialog box can be accessed through the Behavior Inspector.

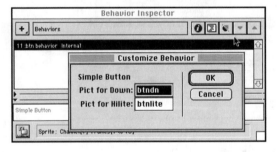

5. Set up a behavior description as follows in the behavior script:

```
on getBehaviorDescription
  return "Simple Button"
end
```

6. Enter the following script into the behavior script. This step provides the real coding of our button. These handlers provide all the information the behavior needs to make the button usable.

```
on beginSprite me
  set the upmember of me = the member of sprite (the spriteNum of me)
  puppetSprite the spriteNum of me, TRUE
end
```

```
on endSprite me
  puppetSprite the spriteNum of me, FALSE
end
```

The `beginSprite` handler is called in all behavior scripts. It is used to initialize the values of the behavior. In this example the `beginSprite` handler checks to see which channel the button selected is in, sets the `upmember` property, and puppets the channel. The `endSprite` handler is used for cleaning up any action the behavior causes. In this example, it unpuppets the appropriate sprite. The `me` property is used in most behavior scripts to act as a pointer to the behavior. Chapter 20 has a more in-depth discussion of using `me` with parent scripts.

```
on mouseDown me
  set the member of sprite (the spriteNum of me) = member the
  ➥downMember of me
end
on mouseUp me
  set the member of sprite (the spriteNum of me) = member the UpCM of
  ➥me
end
```

The `mouseDown` and `mouseUp` behavior handlers in the score script we are creating for the behavior establish the action that occurs when the mouse is clicked on the sprite.

```
on mouseLeave me
  set the member of sprite (the spriteNum of me) = member the upMember
  ➥of me
end

on mouseEnter me
  set the member of sprite (the spriteNum of me) = member the
  ➥hiliteMember of me
end
```

The `mouseLeave` and `mouseEnter` behavior handlers tell the behavior what to do when the cursor rolls over the button. In our example, it swaps the picture of the button for the button image with a red line under the word Button.

7. Recompile the script by clicking on the lightning button in the script window and then close the window.

continues

8. Open the score and remove the scripts associated with sprite 1 by selecting Script menu, Clear Scripts on the score.

9. Open the Cast window (make sure you can still see the stage), and apply the button behavior to sprite 1 by dragging the script onto the sprite.

10. Select sprite 1, and open the Behavior Inspector dialog box by selecting Window, Inspectors, Behaviors.

11. Set the properties for this instance of the behavior by double-clicking on the behavior line. Enter the names of the cast members for each property; then click OK.

   Each time you apply a behavior you can change the properties for that specific application. This button behavior, for example, may be used on any set of button graphics.

12. Run the movie and observe how the behavior works.

This is a simple example of what can be done with behaviors. You can use your creativity to make elaborate behaviors that do most anything possible within Lingo. Behaviors also provide an extremely easy base for producing reusable code libraries. The completed exercise can be viewed in the movie BEHAV.DIR found in the Chapter 19 folder on the accompanying CD-ROM.

Making Libraries and Tools

The more people developing multimedia titles, the more competitive the industry becomes. This competition drives developers to find new ways to save time in building projects. One way is to create libraries of handlers that are useful in many settings. The behaviors discussed in the preceding section lend themselves to this type of application. Director 6 ships with a library of behaviors that are already written for you to use, or you can write your own. Another way to help aid development is by producing Lingo tools that can be used in Director.

Director 5 enabled developers to use multiple cast libraries for a project. This capability continues in Director 6 and makes using code libraries extremely easy. Director 6 also adds the capability to use networked cast libraries. This feature enables multiple programmers to use one consistent library for multiple parts of a project. Linking to networked casts is discussed in detail in Part IV, "Multimedia on the Web with Director and Shockwave."

Time-Saving Library Handlers

As you develop multiple titles you most likely have found that you use the same code over and over again for certain purposes. Any time code is used in multiple projects it is beneficial to include the code in a shared library of handlers.

In almost any movie that uses Lingo-based animation, you need to puppet sprites. Traditionally, you use Director's built-in `puppetSprite` handler:

```
puppetSprite 1,TRUE
puppetSprite 2,TRUE
puppetSprite 3,TRUE
```

If you are puppeting and unpuppeting numerous sprites, a utility handler for puppeting sprites can save a lot of time. You can call the following handler with one sprite, a list of sprite channels, or the start and end points of a range of sprite channels:

```
on pup param1, param2, param3
  if paramCount() = 3 then
    --called with pup(1,5,TRUE)
    --want to puppet sprites 1 through 5
    repeat with spriteNum = param1 to param2
      puppetSprite spriteNum,param3
    end repeat
  else if listP(param1) then
    --called with pup([4,6],TRUE)
    --want to puppet sprite numbers 4 and 6
    repeat with listPos = 1 to count(param1)
      puppetSprite getAt(param1,listPos),param3
    end repeat
  else
    --called with pup(4,TRUE)
    --want to puppet just sprite 4
    puppetSprite param1,param2
  end if
end
```

You can call this handler as follows:

```
pup(2,TRUE)
pup([5,6,9],TRUE)
pup(3,10,TRUE)
```

The previous handler evaluates the number of arguments passed to it and performs the correct action by using the function `paramCount()` to determine how it should puppet the sprites. `paramCount()` returns the number of parameters that were passed to a handler.

As you build your handler library, try to create handlers that will work everywhere—not just with certain sprite or cast numbers. It's also a good idea to limit the number of parameters a handler takes and give handlers a simple name so that you can remember how to use them.

Making Tools with the Score Generation Commands

This section discusses producing tools that can greatly speed production time when dealing with casts and the score. These Lingo handlers can be used in a variety of situations.

The Lingo command `beginRecording` enables you to make changes to existing sections of the score or to populate completely empty sections with sprites.

Score generation uses `beginRecording` to automate tasks that would otherwise be very tedious to complete manually. In a large project, for instance, in which art is being continuously updated, it's possible to end up with a movie that includes one piece of art that appears in multiple cast slots. If these identical cast members are all used in different places in the score, it wastes memory and uses unnecessary space on the disk. Previously, the only way to remove these duplicate cast members from the score was to highlight every occurrence and manually switch the cells to the correct cast member by using the Edit, Exchange Cast Member menu command. You now can automate this and similar processes with score generation.

You don't need to learn many new commands to use score generation. Score generation relies on familiar commands for setting sprite properties, such as the `memberNumber of sprite` or the `forecolor of sprite`. During score generation, you advance to the frame you want to create or change, make changes to sprite properties, and issue the new Lingo command `updateFrame` to save the changes.

You issue the command `beginRecording` to start making changes to the score, and issue the command `endRecording` when you finish. The following handler uses score generation to search an existing score for a list of cast members and replace them with either one member or a corresponding list of new members. You call the handler with the following:

```
findDupes([2,5,8],[3,4,88],1,80)
```

This handler replaces cast member 2 with 3; 5 with 4; and 8 with 88 in frames 1–80.

Or you call it with the following:

```
finddupes([2,5,8],[3],1,20)
```

This example replaces cast members 2, 5, and 8 with member 3 in frames 1–20.

The following handler performs the automated cast member replacement:

```
on findDupes lookFor,replaceWith,startFrame,endFrame
  --lookFor: list of duplicate members to look for
  --replaceWith: list of members to replace dups with
  --             If this list has one item then all dups will be replaced
  --             with the same member
  --             If this list has the same number of items as the list of
  --             duplicate member it will replace each item on "lookFor"
  --             with the corresponding item on "replaceWith"
  --startFrame: frame to start looking in
  --endFrame: frame to end looking
  --
  beginRecording
    set numMembers = count(lookFor)
    set numReplacements = count(replaceWith)
    if numMembers <> numReplacements and (numReplacements > 1) then
      alert "Replacement list has to have one item or the same number of
      ➥items as the list to search for."
      exit
    end if
    repeat with frm = startFrame to endFrame
      go to frame frm
      repeat with curSprite = 1 to 48
        --cycle through every sprite channel
        repeat with listPos = 1 to numMembers
          --see if this channel contains any cast in list "lookFor"
          if the memberNum of sprite curSprite = getAt(lookFor,listPos) then
            case (numReplacements) of
              1:set the memberNum of sprite curSprite
              ➥to getAt(replaceWith,1)
              otherwise:set the memberNum of sprite curSprite to
              ➥getAt(replaceWith,listPos)
            end case
```

```
            --if there is only one replacement cast then use it, otherwise
            ➟find
            --the corresponding cast member in list "replaceWith" and use
            ➟that
          end if
        end repeat
      end repeat
      updateFrame
      --record the changes to the frame
    end repeat
  endRecording
end
```

Score generation is a powerful tool, but it is potentially lethal to your score. If you run a handler that accidentally uses score generation and you realize it immediately, you can use the menu command Edit, Undo score to undo the changes. If you don't realize your mistake immediately and make other changes afterward, the Undo command won't work.

Performance and Benchmarking

Every year the average consumer machine becomes more powerful, and with the same regularity, new technology steps in to use the extra CPU cycles. Eight-bit color is slowly giving way to 24-bit color; 16-bit stereo sound is more common now; digital video movies are larger and display at higher frame rates than they did just last year. Multimedia programming is always a balancing act. You will get the best possible performance out of Director by understanding and minimizing these three major bottlenecks:

▶ Load time

▶ Display time

▶ Processor time

Memory and Load Times

On the Macintosh, a Director projector must play within the memory partition allotted to it in the Preferred Size box of the Get Info dialog box. (Highlight a Macintosh application and choose File, Get Info from the menu bar to use the Get Info dialog box.) Director creates Standard Macintosh projectors with a Preferred Size of 4096 KB, but you can change the setting. In an ideal world, your entire movie and all its media fit into this 4096 KB partition and play directly from memory after an initial load. That's not usually the case, however. If all your cast members cannot fit into memory, then Director unloads cast members when it determines that they are no longer needed, to make room for new ones. In Windows, memory is dynamically allocated and the user doesn't worry about it as he would on the Macintosh.

Director's built-in memory management is good for score-based movies. Not only does Director anticipate in advance what cast members it needs and preloads them, but it also writes internal cast members to the Director file in the order that they appear in the score—not the order that they appear in the cast. Writing cast members to disk in score order minimizes the distance the disk head has to travel during playback to load the cast members needed in any part of the score. This is quite a performance help, especially for pieces destined for CD, because CD reads are very slow. Linked cast members do not get this performance boost, however, because they are written to disk in cast member order.

If you are using puppet commands to place cast members in sprite channels, Director does not preload those cast members because they don't appear in cells in the score. You can still take advantage of score-order optimization by reserving empty frames at the beginning of your movie and placing the cast you plan to preload and puppet in the empty frame cells in the order you are going to preload them. Your startMovie handler or the first frame of the movie can use a go to command to hop over the dummy frames to the first "real" frame where the action starts. The technique of using dummy frames to optimize loading order is affectionately known as "Schusslerization," named after creator Terry Schussler, former Director product manager.

Remember to take advantage of the Save and Compact feature at the end of the authoring cycle. All saves write the cast in score order, but a Save and Compact gets rid of the dead space taken up by cast members that were deleted or moved around in the score during the course of authoring.

Even intelligent memory management schemes do not do much to speed the load times for large cast members. The best way to optimize load time is to keep your media as small as possible. For graphics this means 8-bit (256 color) casts, and 8-bit, 22 KB sound, or the use of compression. Some developers use QuickTime to display JPEG-compressed 24-bit still images and IMA 4:1 sound compression to play 16-bit, 44 KB stereo sound.

You can further economize by looking for wasted space. If a graphic is black and white, reduce it to a color depth of 1 bit. If a button-click sound lasts only one second, try reducing it to an 11 KB sampling rate, and see if you can tell the difference. Delete any duplicate cast members. Use external AIF sounds with the sound playFile command whenever possible. The sound playFile command streams the sound from disk instead of loading it into memory. Sounds fully imported (not linked) into the cast, placed in the score, or played with puppetSound have to load into memory before they play.

If you have reasonably sized cast members (the majority under 300 KB) and your movie is score-based, you can enable Director to automatically do all the memory management for you. If you have larger cast members or your movie relies on Lingo rather than the score, you can take advantage of several Lingo features designed to make playback as seamless as possible; these features are discussed later in this chapter.

Determining the Amount of Memory You'll Need

If you have a fairly small Director movie, you might be able to preload all the cast members before you begin playing. (Choose Modify, Cast properties to set the Preload property for the cast to Before Frame One or After Frame One.) Preloading requires a longer load time to start, but it enhances playback performance because no further delays for disk access exist. Director stores cast members in a compressed form inside movie files. The movie file size in the Get Info dialog box or the Windows Explorer is not the true measure of the actual space the movie takes up in memory. After it loads and the cast members have been decompressed, the actual size of your movie is much larger.

To determine the true memory requirements of your movie, perform the following:

1. Give Director as generous a memory partition as possible (on the Macintosh, this is in the Get Info dialog box; in Windows, run Director as the only application) before launching Director and opening your movie.

2. Temporarily set the preload properties of all casts to Before Frame One.

3. Play the movie through the first frame and stop it.

4. Choose Window, Inspectors, Memory from the menu bar to open the Memory Inspector window shown in figure 19.9.

Figure 19.9

The Memory Inspector window.

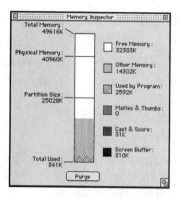

The Total Used portion on the graph is the amount of memory your movie takes up when loaded. Add another 500 KB to 1 MB to this for the projector, depending on the type of projector. The projector type is established when you specify the platform on which the movie is to be played. The total is the amount of memory your projectorized movie requires for preloading all cast members. You can add this number to the amount of memory used by the system software to determine a base memory requirement.

You can find out how much memory an individual cast member will occupy in memory by clicking on the Info button in the Cast window. This brings up the Cast Member Properties window. The member size shown is the amount of memory the cast will occupy when loaded. The Lingo property, the `size of member`, also returns this information.

The `ramNeeded` command returns the amount of memory needed to display a particular frame or range of frames. This command is useful in determining the minimum memory requirements for your movie. The minimum memory requirement is the amount of memory needed to display the frame with the largest size requirement, plus approximately 500 KB to 1 MB, depending on which projector is used.

If Director does not have enough memory to display the current frames, a variety of events could occur. The first glitch in your movie will be the dropping of digital video and sound. White boxes may also begin to appear around graphics, and some graphics could disappear altogether. The frame rate slows down as Director frantically tries to juggle the cast members needed for the current and immediately following frames.

Controlling Cast Member Loads

If you find that your movie is bogged down with too many loads in the same area or has display problems caused by low memory, several Lingo commands and features can help. The following sections describe these commands and features.

Cast Member Load Properties

You can adjust the loading properties of an entire cast and fine-tune things for individual cast members with the load settings available in the property windows for casts and cast members. The Cast Properties window (selected with Modify, Movie, Casts, Properties from the menu bar) has a preload field, which specifies a preload option that applies to the entire cast. Programmers familiar with earlier versions of Director will recognize this as the old movie preload property. The Cast Properties dialog box is shown in figure 19.10.

Figure 19.10

Use the Cast Properties dialog box to set the preload properties of a cast member.

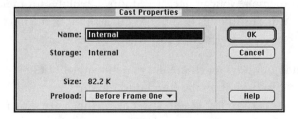

Set a general Preload preference that applies to an entire cast in the Cast Properties window. The choices for Preload are Before Frame One, After Frame One, and As Needed. Before Frame One and After Frame One are for those rare situations in which you can load the entire movie into memory. When you create a cast, the cast starts off with the default As Needed, because that is the most appropriate setting. With this setting Director preloads cast members on or before the frame in which they first appear in the score.

You adjust the unloading properties of individual cast members with the Unload field in the Bitmap Cast Member Properties window, as shown in figure 19.11.

The Unload options are Normal, Next, Last, and Never:

▶ **Normal:** Leaves the unloading of the cast completely up to Director.

▶ **Next:** Places the cast member at the top of the queue for deletion as soon as the cast member no longer appears in a frame. Choose this option for a large cast member that only appears once in the movie.

▶ **Last:** Places the cast member at the end of the queue for deletion. Director does not remove the cast member from memory unless no more members are on the queue with priorities of Normal or Next.

▶ **Never:** Retains the cast member in memory for the duration of the movie if there is enough memory to keep all the cast members with a priority of Never loaded. If you assign all cast members a priority of Never, but the movie does not have room to keep them all in memory, Director cannot keep all the cast members loaded.

Preload Commands

If you are controlling your cast members through Lingo, you have a better idea of when you will need them than Director does. In this situation, you can use Lingo `preload` and `idleLoad` commands to load the cast members that you need, and `unload` to remove the ones that you don't need from memory.

The `preload` commands enable you to specify the loading of a cast member at a particular time. The `idleLoad` commands were new in Director 5. With `idleLoad` commands you can load a large cast member or a list of cast members while the user reads something on the screen or decides what to do next. Except for the tell-tale disk activity light, idle loads are transparent to the user. If the user moves the mouse, you can abort the load and control is immediately returned to the user.

The `idleLoad` commands work during down time between frames. Each frame has a set duration dependent on the frame rate. If a frame finishes drawing and finishes executing its `enterFrame` handler before the frame duration is up, Director just waits. The idea is to use this "idle" time to load cast members when the processor is not otherwise occupied.

Table 19.1 shows the tasks that Director executes for each frame. Keep in mind that at a frame rate of 10 frames per second, all this must happen in no more than 1/10th of a second. The durations next to the events are example times. The duration of any one event will depend on the movie and the machine on which it's running.

Table 19.1

Example Durations for the Events in One Frame

Task Number	Description	Time Required (in System Clock Ticks)
1	Director draws the frame	2 ticks (including any transition)
2	enterframe handler executes (if there is one)	.5 ticks
3	Idle period—idle messages sent repeatedly until the frame duration is over; Not much happening here unless there is an idle handler or there are idleLoads to perform	3 ticks
4	exitFrame handler executes (if there is one)	.5 ticks

All this must happen in the time allotted for the frame—6 ticks in this case. If the `enterFrame`, `exitFrame`, `idle` handler, or `idleLoad` take longer than the time allotted per frame, it slows the frame rate. The processor may be idle when you start an `idle` handler or an `idleLoad`, but if the `idle` handler takes too long, it holds up the events that should happen after it.

The rest of this section lists the `preload` commands and gives a brief description of each.

▶ **preloadMember:** The `preloadMember` command loads a cast member or range of cast members into memory. The following command loads cast members 1–5:

```
preloadMember 1,5
```

▶ **preload:** `preload` loads all the cast members needed for a frame or range of frames. The following command loads all the cast members needed for frames 6–12:

```
preload 6,12
```

This command loads all the cast members needed to build the frames from the current frame through frame 21:

```
preload 21
```

▶ **freeblock:** The `freeblock` function returns the largest amount of contiguous memory available to load in a cast member. If the freeblock is smaller than the size of the cast member you are about to preload, Director is not able to preload the cast member. The following code checks to see whether enough memory is available to preload a cast member:

```
if the freeblock > the size of member 4 then preloadMember 4
```

▶ **idleLoadMode:** The `idleLoadMode` property determines whether cast members load immediately when you issue the `load` command, or wait for idle time to load. The default `idleLoadMode` is 0, meaning that idle loading is turned off. Under an `idleLoadMode` of 0 the following command immediately loads cast members 5–10:

```
preloadMember 5,10
```

If a group of cast members is large enough, playback pauses while they are loading. Instead, you may want to spread out the loading over idle periods until all the cast members are loaded. To do this, you first turn on idle loading by setting `idleLoadMode` to 1, 2, or 3. Modes 1, 2, and 3 control the degree of frequency during an idle period that Director attempts preloads.

idleLoadMode	Effect
1	Preloads during the idle period between the `enterFrame` and `exitFrame` handlers
2	Ties idle preloads to the interval that was set for other idle events with the `idleHandlerPeriod` property
3	Preloads during the idle period between enter and exit frames and again at `exitFrame`

After you have chosen the desired `idleLoadMode`, you can label the group of cast members or frames that you want to preload. Labeling groups you want to preload enables you to keep track of the progress of that group's loading. You can use any number for a label tag. The following code turns on `idleLoad` and sets it to the highest frequency. Then it creates the `idleLoadTag` 20, which applies to the cast members assigned to preload in the next line:

```
set the idleLoadMode to 3
set the idleLoadTag to 20
preLoadMember 100,102
```

▶ **idleLoadPeriod:** The `idleLoadPeriod` controls the frequency in ticks with which Director attempts an `idleLoad` between frames. The default value is 0, which attempts idle loads as frequently as possible during an idle period. If you set the `idleLoadPeriod` to 5, and you enter a frame with an idle period of 16 ticks, Director attempts three idle loads—one every five ticks until the 16 ticks are up.

Sometimes during the movie you may want to suspend idle loading temporarily—for instance, if you are about to play streaming media, such as QuickTime or sound. Temporarily setting the `idleLoadPeriod` to an interval higher than the ticks per frame effectively suspends idle loading.

▶ **idleLoadDone:** You can keep track of the loading progress of a labeled `idleLoad` group with the `idleLoadDone()` function. The following command returns TRUE if cast members 100–102 (`idleLoad` group 20) are successfully loaded:

```
put idleLoadDone(20)
```

▶ **cancelIdleLoad:** You can abort idle loading for an `idleLoad` group with the `cancelIdleLoad` command. The following line aborts idle loading for idle load group 50:

```
cancelIdleLoad(50)
```

▶ **finishIdleLoad:** The `finishIdleLoad` command loads whatever remains to be loaded from the `idleLoad` group all at once. The following line will finishes loading idle load group 50:

```
finishIdleLoad(50)
```

▶ **idleReadChunkSize:** The `idleReadChunkSize` property determines how much of a cast member Director tries to load during one idle read. The default value is 32 KB. If you find that idle loading is interfering with playback, you can decrease the `idleReadChunkSize`. This increases the number of idle loads that it takes to load a cast member, but decreases the amount of time that each load attempt takes. Macromedia does not recommend increasing the `idleReadChunkSize` beyond 32 KB because it interferes with performance.

▶ **preloadEventAbort:** When the `preloadEventAbort` is set to TRUE, user activity such as clicking the mouse or pressing a key stops a preload event. If the `preloadEventAbort` is set to FALSE, a long preload can lock out the user until the preload is finished. The `preloadEventAbort` is turned off by default.

▶ **traceLoad property:** The `traceLoad` logs information to the Message window about cast members as they are loading. The `traceLoad` is set to 0—turned off by default. Set the `traceLoad` to 1 to display cast members' numbers as they load. Set it to 2 to display more information, including the `fileSeekOffset`.

The `fileSeekOffset` number is the distance in bytes that the disk head must travel to load a cast member. The smaller the `fileSeekOffset` between cast member loads, the faster that group of cast loads. This is especially helpful in assessment of CD performance. The Schusslerization technique described earlier keeps `fileSeekOffset` low because related casts are physically near each other in the movie file.

Display Time

Display time is the second of the three major bottlenecks to Director performance. Display time is the time it takes Director to composite all the sprite layers and to draw the finished image to the screen. It can, for example, figure out which parts of a sprite with the Matte ink effect ought to enable the layers below it to show through. Five variables are at work here:

▶ **Video card speed:** Accelerated graphics cards draw the screen faster. This especially helps with 24-bit images.

▶ **Screen technology:** Notebook LCD (Liquid Crystal Display) screens display more slowly than regular desktop monitors.

▶ **Color depth:** 24-bit cast members not only take three times as much time to load, but also require the video card to move around four times as much data.

▶ **Processor speed:** Director must take into account all the sprite layers and determine which parts of overlapping sprites should be visible. A fast processor helps display speed.

▶ **Ink effects:** Some ink effects take more time than others to composite and display, especially when you use them on moving sprites. If a sprite takes more time to draw than the time allotted for the frame (four ticks per frame at 15 frames per second), the frame rate slows down to enable each frame time to draw. There is an excellent example of this on the Director 6 CD-ROM. It is in the Show Me directory and is called INKEFFECTS.DIR.

Copy, Matte, Background Transparent, and Transparent are the most commonly used inks. Of the four, Copy performs the best on moving sprites. The following chart uses Copy ink as a baseline and assigns it a value of 1. The values assigned to the other inks tell you relatively how much more time it takes to draw a sprite assigned that ink from one frame to the next. A sprite with Background Transparent ink, for example, takes 1.2 times as long to display from one frame to the next as the same sprite with Copy ink applied. The following values are examples and will vary slightly between processors and video cards.

Copy	1.0
Matte	1.5
Transparent	1.5
Background Transparent	1.1
Blend %50	4.3

Processor Time

Processor time is the third bottleneck in Director performance. *Processor time* is the amount of time the processor spends interpreting the score and executing your Lingo code. If the processor cannot finish its work for a frame in the time allotted for the frame, the frame rate slows down. Fortunately, you can do several things to optimize your Lingo code, as discussed in the following sections.

Cast Member Name Versus Number

The first time you refer to a cast member by name, as in the following:

```
set the memberNum of sprite 7 to the number of member "Turtle"
```

Director 6 creates an internal cross reference of cast member names and numbers. This can take awhile. Name references to cast members after the index exists are quite fast. If, however, any cast member changes during the Director session—the user edits a field or you edit a cast member on-the-fly with Lingo, Director stops to re-create the index.

If you find cast member name access bogging down, create a property list that links cast member names and numbers. Whenever you want to refer to a particular cast member by name, look it up in the list instead:

```
set the memberNum of sprite 3 to getProp(castList,"Turtle")
```

Repeat Loops

A repeat loop locks out the user and prevents advancement of the playback head. To enable user actions to interrupt the repeat loop, you must build in detection for mouse events:

```
repeat while [condition] and not the mouseDown
```

Don't include lines of code in a repeat loop that don't need to execute with every repeat. The following code, for example, is inefficient:

```
repeat while done = FALSE
    set counter = counter + 1
    set defaultName = "John " & "Smith"
    setAt aList,counter,defaultName
end repeat
```

The third line sets the variable *defaultName* to a value that stays the same for every repetition of the repeat loop. It should be set outside the repeat loop, like the following example, to speed progress:

```
set defaultName = "John " & "Smith"
 repeat while done = FALSE
    set counter = counter + 1
    setAt aList,counter,defaultName
 end repeat
```

Don't use an expression that must be evaluated as a counter in a repeat loop. In the following repeat loop, the number of words in field "Story" is evaluated with every repetition:

```
  repeat with x = 1 to the number of words in field "Story"
    if word x of field "Story" = "Steve" then
      set nameCount = nameCount + 1
    end if
  end repeat
```

Setting the end point of the counter beforehand eliminates this unnecessary repetitive calculation:

```
set numWords = the number of words in field "Story"
repeat with x = 1 to numWords
  if word x of field "Story" = "Steve" then
    set nameCount = nameCount + 1
  end if
end repeat
```

If/Then and Case

If you're using an if/then or case statement, place the most likely condition at the beginning. An if/then or case statement stops executing as soon as it hits a matching condition. This is especially important when the if/then or case is executed repeatedly inside a loop. The first two conditions of the following exitFrame handler are only fulfilled for brief periods of time, and not until the video has been playing for eight minutes (movieTime of 18000). Because of the way the loop is structured, it must go through both conditions to get to the one that applies to the first seven minutes of the video.

```
on exitFrame
  if the movieTime of sprite 21 > 36000 and the movieTime of sprite 21 <
  ➡36720 then
```

```
--at 10 minutes into the movie, start animating a sprite (puppeted
--elsewhere)
   set the castNum of sprite 6 to random(5)
  else if the movieTime of sprite 21 > 28800 and the movieTime of sprite 21
➥< 29000 then
    --at 8 minutes into the movie, animate another sprite
    set the castNum of sprite 4 to random(5)
  else
    --from 0 - 8 minutes, loop a background sound
    if not soundBusy(2) then
      puppetSound "intro loop"
      updateStage
    end if
  end if
end
```

It is better to place the most likely condition first so that most of the time the loop exits before the other conditions:

```
on exitFrame
  if the movieTime of sprite 21 < 28800 then
    --from 0 - 8 minutes, loop a background sound
    if not soundBusy(2) then
      puppetSound "intro loop"
      updateStage
    end if
  else if the movieTime of sprite 21 < 36000 then
    --between 8 and 10 minutes into the movie, animate another sprite
    set the castNum of sprite 4 to random(5)
  else
    --at 10 minutes into the movie, start animating a sprite (puppeted
    --elsewhere)
    set the castNum of sprite 6 to random(5)
  end if
end
```

Save Frequently Used Properties into Variables

If code refers to a property more than once, save the property into a variable. This also makes the code less verbose. In the examples that follow, the first handler is less efficient than the second. In the first handler the `forecolor of the clickOn` has to be evaluated multiple times. In the second handler, it is evaluated once and saved into a variable for quick retrieval.

```
on mouseDown
  if the forecolor of the clickOn <> 25 and the forecolor of the clickOn <>
  ➥13 then
    puppetSound "beep"
    updateStage
  end if
end

on mouseDown
  set fc = the forecolor of the clickOn
  if fc <> 25 and fc <> 13 then
    puppetSound "beep"
    updateStage
  end if
end
```

Fields

Parsing text in fields is one of the slowest operations in Director. Read a large field first into a variable before performing chunk operations on it. The following code takes the text of a field called "Story" and replaces the placeholder "insertName" with the user's name. It reads the field into the temporary variable temp first, performs the text operation on temp, then writes temp back out to the field when it's done.

```
on insertName userName
  put field "Story" into temp
  set numWords = the number of words in temp
  repeat with x = 1 to numWords
    if word x of temp = "insertName" then put userName into_word x of var
  end repeat
  put temp into field "Story"
end
```

Symbols

When possible, use symbols instead of strings in property lists. Using the getProp command is faster with items on the list that follows:

```
[#dog:1,#cat:2,#pig:3,#squirrel:4]
```

Using the getProp on the following list with strings instead of symbols slows progress:

```
["dog":1,"cat":2,"pig":3,"squirrel":4]
```

Testing the Efficiency of Your Code

Director books and discussion groups can only give you general guidelines for efficient coding. You can gauge the efficiency of various techniques by using Lingo's built-in timer to compare them. Elements of the timing system are as follows:

- ▶ **Ticks:** A running tally of the elapsed time in ticks since the Director application launched.

- ▶ **Timer:** Also a running tally of the elapsed time in ticks since the Director application launched, or the elapsed time since the last startTimer command.

- ▶ **startTimer:** Resets the built-in timer to 0, similar to clicking a stopwatch. Make sure that only one handler is using the timer at a time when you use startTimer. If you need multiple timers, save each starting time to a variable and use the ticks instead. For an example, see the following:

```
on stopWatch1On
    global watch1On
    set watch1On to the ticks
end

on stopWatch1Off
    global watch1On
    set elapsedTime = the ticks - watch1On
end
```

Testing Score-Based Techniques

You can test the effects of various score properties—such as sprite sizes, ink effects, and transitions—by placing two animation sequences in the score that are identical except for the variable you want to test. If you wanted to test and compare the animating speeds of Matte ink and Background Transparent ink, for example, place two identical animation sequences in the score. Assign one or more sprite channels Matte ink in one sequence, and assign Background Transparent ink to the same sprite channels in the other sequence. Don't include the first or last score frames in test sequences because both of these frames have extra overhead that biases the test.

To test the performance of the two sequences, first maximize the frame rate to 120, and then time each sequence by using the timer. Because few current machines are capable of playing multiple-channel animation at 120 frames per second, setting the frame rate to 120 plays the animation as fast as possible. If you set the frame rate to 120, any difference in the time it takes to play one sequence versus the other is due to the score property you are testing.

Testing Lingo Code

It's hard to time the difference between a few lines of Lingo code because running three or four lines once might not register any elapsed time—you'll get a time of 0 ticks. You can still compare the two approaches by running them for the same number of repetitions inside of a repeat loop. The following two handlers compare the relative efficiency of setting the end point of a repeat loop to a variable before the repeat loop, or reading it with every repeat:

```
on propSetInsideRepLoop timesToRepeat
  set savtime = the timer
  repeat with y = 1 to timesToRepeat
    repeat with x = 1 to the number of words in field "Story"
      --nothing
    end repeat
end repeat
  put "Prop read inside repeat loop: " & the timer - savtime
end

on propSetBeforeRepLoop timesToRepeat
  set savtime = the timer
  repeat with y = 1 to timesToRepeat
    set numWords = the number of words in field "Story"
    repeat with x = 1 to numWords
      --nothing
    end repeat
  end repeat
  put "Prop set before repeat loop: " & the timer - savtime
end
```

Called from the Message window, the handlers produce the following output:

```
propSetInsideRepLoop(100)
--"Prop read inside repeat loop: 22"
propSetBeforeRepLoop(100)
--"Prop set before repeat loop: 1"
```

Testing Tips

To ensure the closest comparisons possible, preload all the cast members your tests use. That way, the first test run doesn't reflect the added overhead of loading the cast.

Run several repetitions of a test, and average them to minimize the impact of extra overhead that may only happen the first time you run your test.

Defensive Programming

The more multimedia production you do, the more you realize that the only constant is how quickly things change. Design changes, product changes, and hardware changes all influence the development of a final product. Developing cross-platform titles brings in an entirely new dimension. For that reason it is important to test early and often as discussed in Chapter 4, "Delivering the Goods." Some techniques of defensive programming exist that make your code easier to change and your development more flexible. This section discusses some of those methods.

Don't Use Sprite or Cast Member Numbers in Your Code

Sprite numbers change whenever you have to rearrange channels to accommodate new art. Cast member numbers change when you rearrange cast in the Cast window. If you refer to specific sprite numbers or cast member numbers in several places in your code, you then have to find all those places and update the numbers. If you don't catch and change all the places, this leads to errors. It's a much better idea to create a variable name for the sprite channel or cast member, set it once to the correct number, then use the variable name in place of the number. The following code references the same sprite channel several times within just one handler:

```
on animateKey
  global locked
  if locked = TRUE then
    puppetSprite 10,TRUE
    set the memberNum of sprite 10 to 9
    if inside(the clickLoc,rect(100,100,200,200)) then
      set the loc of sprite 10 to the clickLoc
    end if
  end if
end
```

Code is easier to change if you store the sprite and cast numbers in variables that are set once in one location. Using variables in place of sprite and cast numbers also makes the code more readable.

```
on startMovie
   global keySprite,lockArea,movingKey,memberList
   set keySprite = 10
   set lockArea = rect(100,100,200,200)
   set movingKey = getProp(memberList,"MKey1")
end

on animateKey
  global locked,keySprite,lockArea, movingKey
  if locked = TRUE then
    puppetSprite keySprite,TRUE
    set the memberNum of sprite keySprite to movingKey
    if inside(the clickLoc,lockArea) then
      set the loc of sprite keySprite to the clickLoc
    end if
  end if
end
```

Use a Small Separate Movie for Each Logical Section

Small movies load faster than large ones with many cast members, even if you specify the loading for each cast as As Needed. Thumbnails and header information are still loaded for each cast member at startup, even when As Needed is on.

If no backup exists and one large movie is corrupted, you lose everything. If, however, you divide the movie into component movies, you lose only the corrupted component.

Finally, dividing a project over several small self-contained movies enables you to pass off part of the project to another person if you need help in finishing the job. Each person can work on one or two movies independently.

Leave the Higher Numbered Channels Empty

It used to be a habit to leave the last 5 or so (43–48) channels free; in Director 6 this is less of a concern (now 120 channels exist), but it should still be considered. If you fill the top channels early in development, for some reason or another, you will always need them later on. This requires shifting your current score and Lingo to work around the fact that the higher channels are already full. If possible you do not want to have to shift sprites in the score. Doing so could require major rewrites of any animation Lingo in the movie.

Coming to Lingo from C

Darien Fitzgerald programs edutainment titles in Director for publisher Virtual Entertainment of Needham, Massachusetts. Darien came to Virtual Entertainment with several years of development experience in C and C++, and he learned Director on the job. In this interview, he discusses some of the adjustments a C programmer makes when learning Director and offers some tips for getting up to speed on Lingo quickly.

What do you think you brought from your experience programming in C that helped you in Director?

The ability to organize my code and certain concepts in C, such as modularization. Also, just by having programming experience, not necessarily C, there are a lot of problems that you end up solving in Director that you would also have to solve in C. You can pretty much apply the same algorithms.

Did working with an OOP language like C++ help you to understand Director's OOP concepts and terms?

I think the semantics they use are a little bit confusing—the Parent, Child, Ancestor. They do mention in the manual that the Ancestor is sort of like a base class and the Parent would be the class that had inherited the base class. The big difference with Director is that you can actually change the base class on-the-fly. You can set the Ancestor of me to one thing and then further down the line you can set the Ancestor of me to another thing. You would never be able to do that in C. One of the problems is that you are more likely to have a situation where you would want to work in a C-like system where the base class could return a reference to the class that inherited from it.

What was difficult in the transition?

The first step was learning the relationship between all the components in Director. I think that's difficult for anyone, whether they know C or not.

If Macromedia could have described their whole environment in more technical terms, I would have had a much easier time. If you just have a little information about what's going on behind the scenes, you have a better idea of what to do when something goes wrong. Instead of just thrashing about trying to get Director to work, you can take some sort of logical action.

Initially it's hard to know what is the most advantageous structure for your code. Normally if you're a C programmer you are setting up the environment, or you're using an API, but generally the API has few restrictions about what you're actually going to do and how you're going to set up your code.

As a C programmer I had a certain programming style that I was eventually—but not immediately—able to incorporate. One of the first things you notice if you don't use objects and you're writing movie scripts—there's no scope for any of the global variables, but you really want to have scope within one script. The workaround for that is obviously to use Parent scripts.

Certain things in C are just missing [in Director]—like data structures. There are two ways to work around that. One is to birth objects and use properties. The other is to use property lists with symbols. That's relatively fast. It's a pretty verbose way of referencing though, compared to C.

Another thing that caught me is that you can't pass strings by reference in Lingo. If you pass one as an argument, you're really passing a copy. To change the string, you have to pass it back as a return value. If you're passing a string a lot, say in a repeat loop, it makes a copy every time and slows things down.

Do you have any tips for managing the transition?

Before you jump into coding, experiment with the score. My tendency was to do everything in code instead of using the score, when in fact often you can implement something much quicker just by jumping to different parts of the score. And use the object features of Lingo as a method of modularizing your code.

It's been two years since you started using Director. You've shipped two titles and you're working on a third. How are things going now?

I eventually learned how to do just about everything I need to do in Lingo. When I was first starting, I would know exactly how to do what I wanted to do in C, and there would be apparently no equivalent way to do it in Lingo. I don't seem to be running into that lately. Lingo turned out to be more powerful than I thought it was.

In Practice

All the concepts dealt with in this chapter take thinking about development to a higher level. The concerns of putting together a product in a timely fashion necessitate using consistent, reusable code fragments from a library to speed development. By following the guidelines established here and by building tools and behaviors for many purposes you can produce a library that will be useful for many future development efforts.

Chapter 20, "Object-Oriented Programming in Director," takes the idea of coding efficiency to the next level. Director script objects enable you to organize your code and to create a collection of self-standing Lingo templates that you can reuse in many projects.

Keep in mind the following advanced approaches:

▶ Aspects of your movie that lend themselves to Lingo control usually involve a high level of user interactivity, repetition, or both.

▶ Aspects of your movie that lend themselves to score-based control usually involve linear, non-interactive animation, static items, or both.

▶ Although looping with Lingo is sometimes the best solution for a particular task, keep in mind its disadvantages: In a nutshell, it takes complete control of the computer for the duration of the loop.

▶ Director can be a very powerful tool for creating games. It is possible to use Lingo to make games that paint, invent puzzles, do matching, and follow a maze path. It is also possible to make more complex games that use a lot of Lingo animation. Your imagination is the only limit.

▶ Although coding action specifically for a sprite or cast member can be beneficial, you can save a lot of time by producing a library of behaviors.

▶ Lingo can be used to produce a library of development tools as well. A collection of handlers in an external cast that can be linked to any movie is very useful.

▶ Creating development aids in Lingo is also a way of saving time. You can build handlers that perform repetitive tasks and function similar to a macro that you call from the Message window.

▶ Many factors determine the performance of a movie. Load time, display time, and processor time all have an impact. You can't do a lot about processor time, but you can optimize your movie so load time and display time have less of an impact.

▶ Programming style can have a large impact on the final product. Using the defensive programming techniques discussed can help to speed development and limit the time testing and fixing bugs takes.

▶ It is possible to move to Lingo from a higher-level programming language. There are some shifts in thinking that need to take place, but programming in any language helps you develop with Lingo.

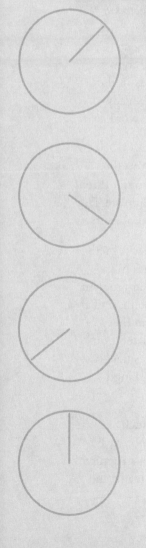

Matt Kerner
Gretchen Macdowall

chapter 20

Object-Oriented Programming in Director

If you've read any technology magazines over the past several years you have undoubtedly come across praise for object-oriented programming languages. The transition to being highly object-oriented is what gives C++ the plus–plus over traditional C. What you should know is that nothing terribly difficult exists about object-oriented programming in Director. If you've never done any object-oriented programming in the past, Director is a good place to start because you can use objects to any extent that you want. Code objects in Director (or Parent/Child scripts), for example, can be integrated easily with more traditional Lingo programming. It is possible to build projects that use nothing but objects, or to build a project that just uses an object here and there for organization.

This chapter covers many concepts related to building objects in Director. Using only the first section you should be able to build objects for the purpose of organization. Continuing further, you will be able to build a library of objects that serve many purposes. Each section of this chapter builds on the previous sections, so it is important to start from the beginning. To build the knowledge base needed to construct a variety of objects, we discuss:

- ▶ What is an object?
- ▶ Reasons to use objects
- ▶ Creating an object
- ▶ Object properties
- ▶ Using multiple objects from the same Parent script
- ▶ Ancestors

▶ The actorListactorList

▶ Escaping the score

What Is an Object?

In Chapter 16, "Lingo: The Basics," the word *object* describes something in the Director environment that you can see and control with Lingo, such as a sprite channel, a cast member, a Movie in a Window, or the stage. You control objects in the Director environment by setting their properties. Objects respond to messages with the behavior you write to them in message handlers.

This chapter introduces you to another type of object—a code object. A *code object* is a self-contained unit of code in memory that keeps track of its own internal data. Code objects share some traits with other Director objects. Code objects have internal variables called *properties*, and they too respond to messages with behavior you write for them. But unlike the other objects in the Lingo environment, you can't see code objects and they don't come ready-made. For the sake of brevity, the remainder of this chapter uses the word *object* to refer to *code objects*.

In Lingo, you define an object template by writing a Parent script. You then create an object from that Parent script by sending a new message to the Parent script. You can create as many objects as you want from the same template. The Director manuals call the objects created from a Parent object Child objects.

You get a Lingo object to respond by sending it a message. The object's methods (*method* is a fancy word for *handler*) determine to which messages it responds. An object can have a method for just about anything you can program in Lingo. Director objects also have a built-in data management system, similar to structures in more traditional programming languages. Other than the messages sent to and from an object, the objects are completely isolated from each other. The OOP word for code that manages its own data and shields its internal workings from the outside is *encapsulation*. By this standard, Lingo objects are encapsulated.

If you are coming to Lingo with experience in an OOP language such as C++, it may take you some time to get your bearings. Lingo does not have a ready-made class library, nor does it impose many rules about object structure, but it uses its own unique terminology. Table 20.1 compares OOP terms and their Lingo equivalents.

Table 20.1

Object-Oriented Programming Versus Lingo Terms

OOP Term	Lingo Equivalent
Base class	Ancestor script
Class	Parent script
Instance variable	Property variable
Class instance/object	Child object
Method/member function	Method

Reasons to Use Objects

Almost everything you can do with objects in Lingo can be done without much difficulty using Director's score-based environment. So why use objects? Objects offer advantages of efficiency, flexibility, and optimal use of processing and memory resources. Following are five reasons to use objects.

Objects Organize Your Code

Better organization is achieved with objects because the Parent contains both the code and the variables that the code relies on. If all your code and variables related to printing a report or playing digital video are in the same place, it's easier to maintain.

Objects Preserve the Global Space

Like globals, an object's property variables maintain their state over time; unlike globals, the properties are known only to the object maintaining them. This keeps the properties out of the global pool.

Suppose that you have a catalog application. In each product section—Electronics or Clothing, for example—you are keeping track of the number of products the user has bought, the number of items for which he has looked, and how long he has spent in each section. This enables you to track the user's buying preferences. All these variables must be globals (or part of a global list) to be able to maintain their contents over time. You would end up with a lot of global variables all named with some variation of a product section name and counter or timer—all available everywhere in the project. How long before you accidentally use the same global name twice for two different purposes?

Alternatively, you could make an object for each section with property variables for the number of products bought, the number of items looked at, and the time spent in that section. The Electronics object can have a `productsBought` property variable, and so can the Clothing object. Neither of these variables is part of the global pool because their scope is restricted to the object to which they belong. This way you don't have to worry about using a variable name multiple times for a different purpose; you can instead reference the properties of each object.

Objects Are Easy to Test

An object is self-contained. Because it is not dependent on any code outside of itself, an object can be tested before other parts of the project are finished. After an object is coded, you should be able to test it by sending messages to all its methods. If the methods set the correct property variables or return the correct values, you know that the object is functioning properly and can be integrated into the larger project. Easy unit testing is another benefit of encapsulation.

Objects Make Coding Easier and More Efficient

Using objects makes coding easier and more efficient through the concept of inheritance. *Inheritance* is an OOP term that refers to the capability of one script to incorporate the methods and properties of another script. Inheritance is a way of reusing existing code for similar programming problems, rather than writing code completely from scratch every time.

In Lingo, inheritance works like this: A Parent script defines the methods and properties any object created from it will have. The created object inherits the methods and properties of the Parent. Multiple objects can be created from the same Parent, and if appropriate, individualized with their own additional properties and methods.

An Ancestor script is another level of script in Lingo that utilizes the concept of inheritance. A Parent script can link to an Ancestor script. In this way, all the Ancestor script's methods and properties become part of the Parent script and are, in turn, passed on to the Child object. The Child object inherits the Ancestor's methods and properties, plus any of the Parent's methods and properties that are also needed. Ancestor scripts are discussed in more detail in a tutorial later in this chapter.

Objects Can Be Reused

If you create objects with reuse in mind, eventually you will have a library of objects that you can put together to handle much of your routine coding. Director has the capability to link a movie to more than one cast; this capability enables you to maintain a code library containing library objects that you can easily link to any movie. Almost any object you create has the potential to be reused, and if it is an external cast library, reuse is easy. If you create an object to handle grading a quiz, for example, the same object can be used in any quiz by simply changing a few of the properties.

Creating an Object in Lingo

To create an object, you must first create a Parent script. As mentioned in the previous section, a Parent script defines the methods and properties of objects created from it. The programming problem you are trying to solve determines the methods and properties that you should include in your Parent script. The basic method required by all Parent scripts is the new method.

The new method creates a new object from a Parent script. A Parent script is like a template document in a word-processing program. Just as you can create any number of identical documents from one template, you can create any number of identical objects by calling the new method of a Parent script. Each time you send a Parent script a new message it creates a new object from that Parent script.

The syntax for the new method is as follows:

```
on new me
    return me
end
```

It is important to use the word me in the line beginning with on. me holds a pointer to the location in memory of the object created from the Parent script. It is also important to include the return line inside the new method. This returns a pointer to the object. If you don't include this return you have no way of communicating with the object after you create it.

Director has a Parent script type, available through the script window, which is the proper place for creating Parent scripts. If you accidentally create an object from a movie script and send it a message, Director looks through all the movie scripts for a handler for that message. If you have a movie script handler with the same name as one of your object methods, the movie script handler gets the message instead of your object.

After you are ready to create objects from a Parent script, it's a good idea to store them in globals so that the objects are available to code anywhere in the movie where you want to use them.

Global objects, like any other globals, persist across movies. After an object is created from a Parent script, it exists independently in memory. The object no longer references the Parent script. If you go to another movie that does not contain the object's Parent script, the object still works. The object is using its own copy of the code defined in the Parent script that it has stored in memory. If you change a Parent script's code after you have created an object from it, you do not change the object already in memory. You must create a new object from the edited Parent script; if you want to update multiple objects created from the same Parent script you must create a new object to replace each of the older ones.

With these background facts in mind, we can turn to a tutorial on building an object. The object that we build contains the minimum necessary code to work. It illustrates how an object is made.

Creating a Minimal Object

1. Open the movie MINIMAL.DIR in the Chapter 20 folder on the accompanying CD. A button has already been placed on the stage for you (see fig. 20.1), and a loop in the frame script keeps the movie running when you play it. No other scripts exist yet.

Figure 20.1

The movie MINIMAL.DIR contains the basic materials to create a simple object.

2. Create a new, empty Parent script by clicking on the + button in the Script window. Click on the Info button in the Script window and use the Type pull-down menu to change the script's type property to Parent (see fig. 20.2). Enter the name minimal in the script's Name field.

Figure 20.2

Use the Type pull-down menu to create a Parent script.

3. Enter the following code into your minimalist Parent script (shown in fig. 20.2):

```
on new me
    return me
end
```

4. Create a new object by typing the following Lingo into the Message window:

```
set minimalObj = new(script "minimal")
```

The code line you entered created a new object from the minimal script and put it in the global minimalObj*. (Any variable you declare in the Message window is global.) It's a good idea to store your objects in globals so that they will be available to code anywhere in your movie where they are needed.*

5. Enter the following in the Message window and press Return or Enter to see whether or not you created an object:

```
put minimalObj
```

Director returns the contents of the object variable, which confirms that the object was successfully created:

```
-- <offspring "minimal" 2 8daa90>
```

The significance of this returned information is explained at the end of this tutorial.

minimalObj *was created successfully, but the object can't really do anything yet—it cannot receive any messages other than new, and it has no property variables to store data.*

6. Add a script to make the button the vehicle for creating a new object, so that you will not have to do so by typing commands in the Message

continues

Creating a Minimal Object continued

window every time that you play the movie. Make a `mouseUp` script that handles creating the object, as follows:

```
on mouseUp
  global minimalObj
  set minimalObj = new(script "minimal")
end
```

7. Rewind and play your movie and create a new object by clicking on the button on the stage. Check to see if the object was properly created by typing **put minimalObj** in the Message window and pressing Return or Enter.

8. Create a `hello` method for the object that makes the object beep. Edit the Parent script to contain the following code:

```
on new me
   return me
end

on hello me
   beep
end
```

9. Rewind and play your movie and create a new instance of the object by clicking on the button you created on the stage. You should now be able to type the following code into the Message window. If everything worked correctly your computer should beep.

```
hello minimalObj
```

As illustrated in step 5 of the preceding tutorial, object variables contain three pieces of information:

▶ The Parent script of which the object is an offspring (that is, from which the object was created), in this case, `minimal`.

▶ The number of references to the object. The Parent script always counts as the first, and the object created from it counts as the second. Any variable you set to the object increases the number of references to it. If, for example, you type the following code into the Message window:

```
set x = minimalObj
put minimalObj
```

The Message window returns:

```
"<offspring "minimal: 3 8daa90>"
```

▶ The object's location in memory, in this case, `8daa90`.

Creating Object Properties

So far we have created a simple object that beeps if you send it the hello message. This object isn't terribly functional, though. To add greater functionality to an object it needs more than methods. The minimal object is missing the second component of truly functional objects in Director—properties. The property variables of an object can be used to hold any type of data and are unique to each instance of the object.

You declare an object's property variables at the top of the Parent script in the same manner as you can declare globals. Properties are declared with the following syntax:

```
property varName, varName, varName …
```

The property declaration tells Director that the following variable names are properties of the objects to be created by a Parent script. It is followed by a list of variable names that are noted as `varName`. As you can see, you can define more than one variable at a time with the property command.

The syntax for referring to an object's property variable from outside the object is this:

```
the property of object
```

`property` is the name of the property variable and `object` is the name of the object possessing it.

If you finished the preceding tutorial, continue to use that movie; otherwise you can use MINIMDN.DIR, which is located in the Chapter 20 folder on the CD that accompanies this book. The next tutorial shows you how to create object properties for the minimal object.

Creating Object Properties for the Minimal Object

Figure 20.3

The minimal object script is used to teach you about properties.

1. Open the minimal object Parent script again (see fig. 20.3), and insert the following line at the top, before the new method:

```
property name
```

2. Recompile the script, rewind and play the movie, then click on the button on the stage to create a new object. Type the following in the Message window:

put the name of minimalObj

The Message window returns with the following:

```
-- <Void>
```

The property variable name has not been set by the object yet, so the Message window returns <Void>.

3. Go back to the minimal script and add the following line to the new method:

set name = "fred"

The new method of the Parent script should now look like the following:

```
on new me
    set name = "fred"
    return me
end
```

4. Recompile the script, rewind and play the movie, then create a new object with the button on the stage. Look at the name object property again by typing the following in the Message window:

```
put the name of minimalObj
```

Now the Message window returns:

```
-- "fred"
```

The object property name is now `"fred"` *because it was set in the* new *method of the object's Parent script.*

5. The object still doesn't do much that is useful. Make an addition to the `hello` method of the object to put `"Hello, my name is"` and the name of the object. The new `hello` method should look like this:

```
on hello me
    beep
    put "Hello, my name is" && name
end
```

6. Recompile the script, and create a new object by restarting the movie and clicking on the button. Type the following code into the Message window:

```
hello minimalObj
```

The message window returns:

```
-- "Hello, my name is fred"
```

As noted earlier in this chapter, you can produce multiple identical objects from the same Parent script. You can then individualize the objects by giving them different properties. In this way, you can enjoy the efficiency of not rewriting code for methods and properties that are the same from object to object. Yet, you still have the flexibility to create unique objects as your programming problem demands.

Using the minimal Parent script we created, let's make a second object.

7. In the Message window, type the following lines of code:

```
set newobject to new(script "minimal")
set the name of newobject to "sally"
```

This code produces a new object called `newobject`*. The second line of code sets the name property variable to be* `"sally"`*.*

8. Send a `hello` message to both `newobject` and `minimalObj` to see that the names of each are different.

continues

```
hello newObject
```

When you type the preceding code in the Message window, it returns:

```
-- "Hello, my name is sally"
```

The following code addresses the "old" object:

```
hello minimalObj
```

The preceding line of code returns:

```
-- "Hello, my name is fred"
```

A finished version of this movie, PROPERTY.DIR, can be found on the accompanying CD in the Chapter 20 folder.

You just created your first pair of Director objects and learned the following:

▶ An object is a self-contained unit of code and data.

▶ You define an object's characteristics by writing a Parent script. The Parent script declares the object's internal variables (properties) and contains the handlers (methods) to handle messages that are sent to the object by other scripts.

▶ You create a new object by sending a new message to a Parent script. All Parent scripts must have a new method. The Parent script's new method returns an object that you must store in a variable.

▶ Each object contains its own set of data that is unique from other objects, even if the objects are created by the same Parent script.

Using Multiple Objects from the Same Parent Script

Child objects are alike in that they all contain the same methods, but each Child object keeps track of its own property variables. If you have come to Director from a traditional OOP language, you can think of a Parent script as a class and a Child object as an instance of a class. In this section we create more multiple objects that illustrate this principle.

The movie MULTI.DIR demonstrates a situation in which creating multiple Child objects saves coding. This movie can be found in the Chapter 20 folder on the accompanying CD. It's a fictional on-screen quiz for new cashiers on product codes (see fig. 20.4). The screen contains five fields where the user must enter numeric data.

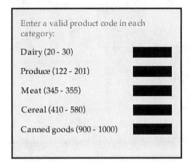

For our purposes, the correct range for each question appears on-screen beside the question for convenience. If this were a real quiz screen, it obviously would not be a good idea to show the answers on the screen. Also, the user cannot tab between questions. Adding the code to make tabbing between questions possible would make the example too complex, but any real product that includes data entry should enable the user to tab between fields. Chapter 10, "Text: The Story," explains how to handle tabbing in editable fields.

Suppose that on this screen you want to check to see if the number the user entered in each field is correct—in this case, "correct" means that the number falls within a certain numeric range. If it's wrong, you want the program to beep and erase the entry. After three wrong entries in any field, you want to prevent the user from entering any more data in that field to discourage random guessing.

Two differences between the fields are as follows: Each field has a different valid numeric range, and each field has to keep track independently of how many wrong guesses it has had. That means you can create one Parent script template to handle the code for the fields and use property variables to hold each field's valid range and wrong answers.

Open the movie MULTI.DIR. The screen shot and data entry fields are already laid out. A looping frame script keeps the movie running when you play it. The movie also already contains a Parent script in cast member 13. Now, let's take a look at the code in the Parent script to see how it works:

```
property myField,validRange,wrongAnswers,limit
```

The first line of the code, as shown in the preceding line, sets the object's properties. Two of the properties, `myField` and `validRange`, are going to be passed to the object when it is created. This enables each object to check a different field and to use a different valid range to check the field's entry. The property `wrongAnswers` is a tally of how many times the user has entered the wrong data into the field. `limit` is the number of wrong answers enabled before the user is locked out of the field.

The second section of the code is as follows:

```
on new me,passedField,passedRange
  set myField = passedField
  set validRange = passedRange
  set wrongAnswers = 0
  set limit = 3
  resetField me
  return me
end
```

The first method is the `new` method. This `new` method is waiting to receive a field number and a `validRange` list. A `new` message sent to this Parent script looks like this:

```
set fieldObject = new(script "FieldCheck",7,[50,120])
```

This code creates a new object called `FieldCheck`, with a `myField` property of 7 and a `validRange` property of [50,120].

The following shows the third section of code:

```
on checkValue me
  set aValue = integer(field myField)
  if aValue < getAt(validRange,1) or (aValue > getAt(validRange,2)) then
    set wrongAnswers = wrongAnswers + 1
    if wrongAnswers < limit then
      wrongAlert me
    else
      shutOffField me
    end if
  else
    rightAnswer me
  end if
end
```

```
on wrongAlert me
  beep
  put " " into member myField
end

on rightAnswer me
  set the backcolor of member myField to 114
end

on shutOffField me
  beep
  set the editable of member myField to FALSE
  set the backcolor of member myField to 255
end

on resetField me
  set the backcolor of member myField to 0
  set the editable of member myField to TRUE
  put " " into member myField
end
```

The checkValue method is the meat of the object that is created. The checkValue method handles the checkValue message sent from a field script. This method evaluates the data in the field and decides what action to take. If the data is wrong, the object beeps. If the user has answered the same field incorrectly too many times (more than the set property limit), the object locks the field, which prevents further data entry. If the data is correct, the object turns the field blue.

The rest of the methods are internal methods—they do not receive messages from outside of the object. Internal methods are called inside the object itself. If you have come to Director from a traditional OOP language, you can think of internal methods as private methods. But be aware that in Director, private methods do not generate errors when they are sent messages from outside the object.

The code that is located outside each object creates and sends messages to the objects. In this example the startMovie handler handles creating the objects. Five fields exist, so five objects must exist. These objects use field numbers 7–11. The startMovie handler looks like this:

```
on startMovie
  global field1Obj,field2Obj,field3Obj,field4Obj,field5Obj
  set field1Obj = new(script "FieldCheck",7,[20,30])
  set field2Obj = new(script "FieldCheck",8,[122,201])
```

```
   set field3Obj = new(script "FieldCheck",9,[345,355])
   set field4Obj = new(script "FieldCheck",10,[410,580])
   set field5Obj = new(script "FieldCheck",11,[900,1000])
end
```

If you start the movie you can see that the objects are created. Type the following in the Message window:

put the validRange of field1Obj

Director responds:

```
-- [20,30]
```

Now, try the same thing with the last object:

put the validRange of field5Obj

Director responds:

```
-- [900,1000]
```

An object has been created for each field with unique property values for the field. The only other code needed is for each field to send the checkValue message to the object responsible for the field.

The following sprite script is entered for the sprite in channel 7:

```
on keyUp
  global field1Obj
  if the key = RETURN then
    checkValue(field1Obj)
  end if
end
```

Give the next data entry field (in channel 8) the same sprite script, but change the object name to field2Obj:

```
on keyUp
  global field2Obj
  if the key = RETURN then
    checkValue(field2Obj)
  end if
end
```

INSIDER TIP

You can create this score script in the form of a behavior as is discussed in Chapter 19, "Advanced Concepts." You would then have to assign the object property with the Behavior Inspector. The script as a behavior looks like this:

```
on getPropertyDescriptionList
  set description = [:]
    addprop description, #Object, [#default:"field#obj",
    ➥#format:#string, #comment:"Object Name:"]
return description
end


on keyUp
if the key = RETURN then
    checkValue(the object of me)
  end if
end
```

Each field accepts a different range of correct answers, but behaves the same way after it detects a correct or incorrect answer.

In this section we produced a usable example of creating multiple objects from the same Parent script. You should have learned the following:

▶ You can create many Child objects from the same Parent script.

▶ Child objects operate independently and contain their own unique values for property variables.

Ancestors

So far we've seen how to create multiple objects, which possess different *properties*, from the same Parent script. Ancestor scripts provide a convenient way to create multiple objects, which possess different *methods*, from the same Parent script.

Suppose that you have finished programming your cashier quiz screen and the owner of the grocery store reviews it. "Oh dear," she says. "We forgot to tell you about the special requirements we have for the Produce and Dairy fields." She goes on to tell you that Dairy is the most-entered category of product code—all cashiers should know Dairy inside and out. If a cashier taking the quiz gets Dairy wrong even once, the owner wants an alarm to sound and the screen to lock immediately. She'll have to let that cashier go. On the other hand, Produce codes are difficult to remember. The owner wants the cashier to have no limit on the number of tries it takes to get that question correct.

Do you have to rewrite entirely new scripts to handle these exceptions? No. You can make new Parent scripts for the Dairy field and the Produce field that use the original FieldCheck script as an Ancestor. Objects created from the new Parent scripts inherit all the Ancestor script's methods. In each new script, you need to write only one new method to make the requested change.

Figure 20.5 shows a new object created from a Parent script that declares an Ancestor. The new object combines the properties and methods of the Parent and Ancestor. A method from the Parent replaces a method from the Ancestor with the same name.

Figure 20.5

An object created from a Parent script and an Ancestor script contains the methods and properties of both the Parent and the Ancestor.

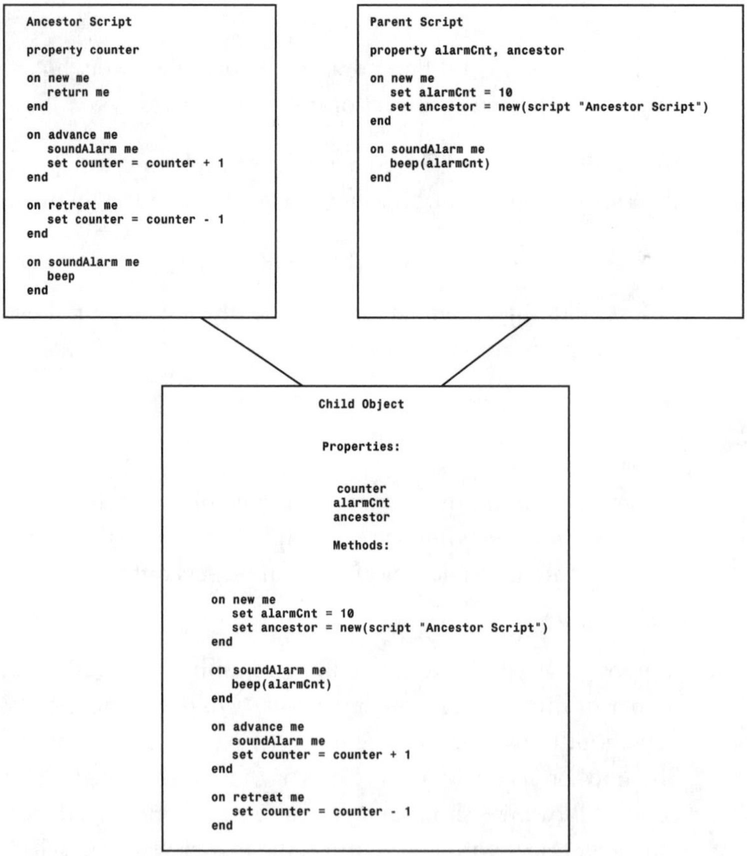

```
Ancestor Script

property counter

on new me
    return me
end

on advance me
    soundAlarm me
    set counter = counter + 1
end

on retreat me
    set counter = counter - 1
end

on soundAlarm me
    beep
end
```

```
Parent Script

property alarmCnt, ancestor

on new me
    set alarmCnt = 10
    set ancestor = new(script "Ancestor Script")
end

on soundAlarm me
    beep(alarmCnt)
end
```

```
Child Object

    Properties:

        counter
        alarmCnt
        ancestor

    Methods:


on new me
    set alarmCnt = 10
    set ancestor = new(script "Ancestor Script")
end

on soundAlarm me
    beep(alarmCnt)
end

on advance me
    soundAlarm me
    set counter = counter + 1
end

on retreat me
    set counter = counter - 1
end
```

Revising Code with Ancestor Script

Let's make the Dairy field changes first. The Dairy field must sound an alarm now and shut down all the fields the first time it receives a wrong answer.

1. Make sure the movie MULTI.DIR is still open, then review the methods in the FieldCheck script to see whether you can find the method that you would have to change for Dairy:

```
on resetField me
  set the backcolor of member myField to 0
  set the editable of member myField to TRUE
  put " " into member myField
end

on checkValue me
  set aValue = integer(field myField)
  if aValue < getAt(validRange,1) or (aValue > getAt(validRange,2))
then
    set wrongAnswers = wrongAnswers + 1
    if wrongAnswers < limit then
      wrongAlert me
    else
      shutOffField me
    end if
  else
    rightAnswer me
  end if
end

on wrongAlert me
  beep
  put " " into member myField
end

on rightAnswer me
  set the backcolor of member myField to 114
end

on shutOffField me
  set the editable of member myField to FALSE
  set the backcolor of member myField to 255
end
```

continues

Revising Code with Ancestor Script　continued

The wrongAlert method would have to change, because that is the method that handles wrong answers.

2. Create a new Parent script and name it DairyCheck. You will put the new wrongAlert method into this script, but first, you have to tell it where to get the rest of its methods. At the top of the script, declare an Ancestor property that uses your original Parent script:

```
property ancestor
```

Ancestor is a reserved word in Director. Setting the Ancestor property of one object to another object enables the first object to inherit the methods of the second.

3. Now, enter the following code for the DairyCheck's new method:

```
on new me,passedField,passedRange
  set ancestor = new(script "FieldCheck",passedField,passedRange)
  return me
end
```

4. Change the line in the startMovie handler that creates the object for field 7 to use the new DairyCheck script as a Parent:

```
set field1Obj = new(script "DairyCheck",7,[20,30])
```

The first line of the new method for DairyCheck is as follows:

```
set ancestor = new(script "FieldCheck",passedField,passedRange)
```

DairyCheck is creating a new "FieldCheck" object and storing it in its Ancestor variable.

The new DairyCheck object passes the field and range arguments on to "FieldCheck" because "FieldCheck's" new method will be looking for them.

At this point, DairyCheck has a new method and one property variable, but no other properties or methods of its own.

5. Rewind and play the movie. The Dairy field behaves exactly like the other fields. The DairyCheck object inherited all the methods from its Ancestor script.

6. Open the DairyCheck script again and add a new wrongAlert method:

```
on wrongAlert me
  global field2Obj,field3Obj,field4Obj,field5Obj
  puppetSound "alarm"
  shutOffField me
  shutOffField field2Obj
  shutOffField field3Obj
  shutOffField field4Obj
  shutOffField field5Obj
end
```

The new wrongAlert method sounds the alarm. It then sends a shutOffField message to itself and the same message to all of the other field objects, causing them to shut off too.

7. Recompile the DairyCheck script, and rewind and play the movie again. This time when you enter a wrong answer in the Dairy field, the wrongAlert method of DairyCheck receives the message and an alarm sounds.

8. Now you need to make a new Parent script for the Produce field and name it ProduceCheck. Give it the same property and new method as the DairyCheck:

```
property ancestor

on new me,passedField,passedRange
  set ancestor = new(script "FieldCheck",passedField,passedRange)
  return me
end
```

9. Change field2Obj in the startMovie handler so that it references the new script:

```
set field2Obj = new(script "ProduceCheck",8,[122,201])
```

The Produce field must not put a limit on wrong answers. In this case, ProduceCheck has to override the checkValue method. It omits the lines that keep a tally of wrongAnswers and compares the number of wrong answers to a limit.

10. Add the following method to ProduceCheck:

```
on checkValue me
  set aValue = integer(field the myField of me)
```

continues

```
      if aValue < getAt(the validRange of me,1) or (aValue > getAt(the
    ➥validRange of me,2)) then
        wrongAlert me
      else
rightAnswer me
    end if
  end
```

ProduceCheck inherits the property variables myField *and* validRange *from the Ancestor* FieldCheck *object. Notice that* ProduceCheck *has to use a different syntax to access the inherited properties. When an object refers to an inherited property, it must use the following syntax:*

```
the propertyName of me
```

11. Recompile the script, rewind, and play the movie. The Produce field accepts any number of wrong answers because the checkValue method of field2Obj is overriding its Ancestor's checkValue method.

With minimal extra coding, you have been able to make the requested changes. As you can see, tapping the capability of an object to inherit behavior from an Ancestor object can save you time.

In step 4 of the preceding tutorial, we set the object's Ancestor property in the new method, but it is possible to change an object's Ancestor property to point to a new object at any time.

When you switch an object's Ancestor from one object to another, the object immediately inherits the methods of the new Ancestor object and loses the methods of its previous Ancestor. This capability to switch an object's Ancestor on-the-fly is unique to Director. Most traditional OOP languages don't allow it.

A script declared as an Ancestor script can declare an Ancestor of its own. The number of Ancestors you can nest together is not limited. An object created from a Parent script with a chain of Ancestor scripts inherits the methods of the Parent and of all the Ancestors. If, for example, script A declares script B as an Ancestor, and script B, in turn, declares script C as an Ancestor, an object created from script A will contain methods from scripts A, B, and C.

If more than one method has the same name, the methods of the Parent script override the Ancestor methods of the same name. In the preceding example, if Parent script A had a method called display and Ancestor script B had a method called display as well, an object created from Parent script A would use Parent script A's display method.

If more than one Ancestor method with the same name exists, the methods of the Ancestor closest to the Parent script override the other Ancestors' methods. In the preceding example, if Ancestor script B and Ancestor script C both contained move methods, an object created from Parent script A would use Ancestor script B's move method.

The actorListactorList

The objects in the previous examples have all been controlled by user action. Either typing in the Message window, or clicking and typing in a field have caused all the object's methods to be called. This is not at all necessary. If you don't want the passage of messages to depend on the user, you can send a message to an object using the actorListactorList. The actorList is a reserved list that is maintained by Director. Director sends a stepFrame message to objects in the actorList at every frame, before sending an enterframe message to the frame. Any object in the actorList that contains an on stepFrame handler will receive the stepFrame message and perform the actions defined in the handler. Understanding how to use the actorList and stepFrame handlers is an important concept; it enables your objects to perform an action in a scheduled manner every time a frame is entered.

The actorList can be used for many purposes. One object that works within the actorList is a Timer object. It records a start time, amount of time you want to wait, and then keeps track of whether the time is up or not. You can use a timer for games with a time limit or for triggering events at particular intervals. Timer objects are more versatile than Director's built-in startTimer and the timeOutScript commands, which only enable you to have one timed event going at a time. Let's look at a timer script that is already built. Open the movie TIMER.DIR from the Chapter 20 folder of the accompanying CD-ROM (see fig. 20.6).

The first cast member contains the timer Parent script. Look at the first section
of code:

```
property startedAt, stopAfter

on new me
  return me
end
```

You should be familiar with the new method at this point. The timer's new
method takes no arguments, so you can create a new timer by typing the
following:

```
set stopWatch = new(script "timer")
```

The next section of code is used to initialize the timer:

```
on startTiming me,forHowLong
  set startedAt = the ticks
  set stopAfter = the ticks + forHowLong
  putMeOnactorList me
end
```

But stopWatch doesn't really start doing anything until it receives the
startTiming message. The property startedAt gets set to the ticks. The *ticks* is a
Director function that returns the number of ticks since the Director session
started. You can try it by typing the following in the Message window:

```
put the ticks
```

Director returns the number of ticks since your session started:

```
-- 90201
```

The forHowLong argument passes in the number of ticks the timer should wait
before going off.

The following code sends a `startTiming` message to `stopWatch`, telling it to go off after five seconds (5×60 ticks = 300 ticks):

```
startTiming(stopWatch,300)
```

The `stopWatch` object stores the time it started in the property variable *startedAt* and the time it should go off in the property variable *stopAfter*.

After you have captured the starting time, you need some way of continually checking to see whether the timer should go off yet. That's where the actorList comes in. After this object is on the actorList, its `stepFrame` method executes automatically at every frame. The `stopWatch` object uses its `stepFrame` method to check regularly to see when to go off.

The next section of code, the actorList, acts like a global, but doesn't have to be declared as a global or a list. It's always available.

```
on putMeOnactorList me
  takeMeOffactorList me
  append the actorList,me
end
```

You manage the actorList with regular syntax for lists. You can add an object to the actorList with `append` or `setAt`, just like you'd add an item to any other list. The first line of the preceding method takes any old timer off the actorList before adding a new timer.

INSIDER TIP

> The actorList persists across movies and between runs of the same movie just like any other global. Objects remaining in the actorList that try to operate on sprites that do not exist in the current movie can wreak havoc. It's a good idea to clear the actorList in your `startMovie` handler with the following code:
>
> ```
> set the actorList = []
> ```

The next section of code tells your timer object what it should do when it receives a `stepFrame` message:

```
on stepFrame me
  if the ticks >= stopAfter then
    timerDoneEvent me
    stopTiming me
  end if
end
```

After stopWatch is on the actorList, Director sends it a stepFrame message on every frame. (Because the stepFrame message is dependent on the frame rate, stopWatch will only be accurate within a few ticks. If, for example, the frame rate is 15 fps, stopWatch only gets a stepFrame message every 4 ticks, because there are 60 ticks in a second.)

StopWatch's stepFrame method checks to see whether it is time for the timer to go off. If it is time for the timer to go off, a timerEvent message and stopTiming message are generated.

Now we need to tell stopWatch what to do when the timer is done (this code is found within the timer's Parent script):

```
on timerDoneEvent me
  beep
end

on stopTiming me
  takeMeOffactorLis me
end
```

stopWatch beeps when the time is up. Although the line of code in the timerDoneEvent method could easily have been included in the stepFrame, having it as a separate method enables another object using this script as an Ancestor to override the timerDoneEvent with its own method.

In the stopTiming handler, stopWatch calls a handler to take it off the actorList. Following is the code for this handler:

```
on takeMeOffactorList me
  set myPos = getPos(the actorList,me)
  if myPos > 0 then
    deleteAt the actorList,myPos
  end if
end
```

After the stopWatch object has gone off, it takes itself off the actorList by finding its position on the actorList and deleting itself.

The stopWatch object is not tied to any sprites on the stage. You can try it out by playing the movie and typing the following in the Message window:

```
set stopWatch = birth(script "timer")
startTiming(stopWatch,180)
```

The timer beeps after three seconds.

You can customize the `timerDoneEvent` to stop a sound or play an animation in synch with a certain point in a musical piece. Take a look at the `frisbeeTimer`, `fishTimer`, and `stageColorTimer` scripts to see how they have used the timer script as an Ancestor, but customized the `timerDoneEvent` method. Play the movie and enter values in the fields to send each object a `startTiming` event.

INSIDER TIP

> There has been a lot of discussion among developers about the use of the actorList and some fairly serious speed concerns. Many developers have decided not to use the built-in actorList and to build their own instead. A script that can be used as a substitute for the actorList is discussed later in this chapter.

Escaping the Score

A criticism frequently leveled against Lingo is that you can never hope to do "real" object-oriented programming with it because Lingo is hopelessly tied to the score. This just isn't true. The score is a great tool for sequencing animation, but if you are more comfortable controlling everything through Lingo objects, you need put nothing more in the score than one `go the frame` script.

Two ways to fill empty sprite channels on-the-fly are as follows:

▶ You can puppet the sprite and use the `set memberNum of sprite` command to place a cast member in an empty channel. (You must set the forecolor of the sprite to 255 first for this to work.)

▶ You can use score generation to place permanent cast members in the cells. Score generation is covered in Chapter 19, "Advanced Concepts," in the section titled "Making Libraries and Tools."

Open the movie NOSCORE.DIR on the accompanying CD in the folder for Chapter 20. It contains one frame script in the score and nothing else. Play the movie (see fig. 20.7). Forty-eight interactive sprites appear on the stage and begin moving. Click on a sprite and it changes direction.

Figure 20.7

The NOSCORE movie.

Forty-eight objects created from the same Parent script control the appearance, movement, and interactivity of each sprite on the stage. Look at the part of the startMovie script that creates the objects:

```
on startMovie
   global objectList
   set objectList = []
   set the actorList = []
   repeat with x = 1 to 48
   setAt(objectList,x,new(script"genSprite",random(6),random(30)))
      appear(getAt(objectList))
      append the actorList,getAt(objectList,x)
   end repeat
```

It's difficult to come up with meaningful names for 48 objects that are all doing the same thing. And if you do come up with a naming scheme like circle1, circle2, circle3, and so on, sending a message to all the objects in sequence is still difficult. If you have a group of like objects that you will be sending messages to in sequence, it's more convenient to store them in a list than to name each one individually.

In the following line of code, the global objectList is the container list that stores each new object as it is created:

```
set objectList = []
```

In the following line of code, each position in objectList is filled with a new object created from script "genSprite":

```
setAt(objectList,x,new(script"genSprite",random(6),random(30)))
```

The following lines of code are inside a repeat loop. The repeat loop makes it easy to send the appear message to all 48 objects and append each one to the actorList:

```
appear(getAt(objectList,x))
append the actorList,getAt(objectList,x)
```

The appear method of script "genSprite" finds an empty spot in the score and fills it with a cast member:

```
on appear me
  set spriteNum = findSpace(me)
  puppetSprite spriteNum,TRUE
  set the forecolor of sprite spriteNum to 255
  set the ink of sprite spriteNum to 8 - matte
  set the loc of sprite spriteNum to point(random(the stageleft),
    ➥_random(the stagebottom))
  set the memberNum of sprite spriteNum to mymemberNum
  updateStage
end

on findSpace me
  repeat with x = 1 to 48
    if the memberNum of sprite x = 0 then
      return x
      exit repeat
    end if
  end repeat
  return 0
end
```

The following line of code calls the findSpace method and looks for an empty sprite channel to use in the score. Empty sprites have a memberNum of 0:

```
set spriteNum = findSpace(me)
```

The following line of code sets the forecolor of the sprite to black. If you place a cast member in an empty sprite channel by setting its member number, you must also set the forecolor of the sprite to 255 to make it work reliably.

```
set the forecolor of sprite spriteNum to 255
```

In the following line of code, setting the memberNumber of the sprite makes the sprite appear in the empty sprite channel.

```
set the memberNum of sprite spriteNum to mymemberNum
```

The objects in NOSCORE.DIR do not have complex behavior, but they all operate independently of each other and the score. With this knowledge who knows what imaginative and ingenious objects you can create.

Based on what we know from looking at NOSCORE.DIR, let's expand what we can do with objects. Objects can also be used to assign properties to cast members and then to place those cast members in the score.

Score Generation with OOP

1. Open a new movie and create a `startMovie` handler in a movie script that contains the following code:

```
on startMovie
    global objectList
    set objectList to []
    repeat with x = 1 to 10
        add objectList, new(script "Object Parent", x)
    end repeat
end
```

This script establishes a list, or an array, of objects that will be created by our Parent script, which is called "Object Parent." This objectList will be an easy way to reference each of the 10 objects that are created. It will also act as a substitute for the actorList if used in an enterFrame script.

2. Now we need to create our "Object Parent" script. Create a new Parent script and include the following properties:

```
property myCast, myColor, mySprite, myNumber
```

3. The next step in creating the Parent script is to provide a `new` method:

```
on new me, whichnumber
   set myNumber to whichnumber
   putInCast me
return me
end
```

The new method of this script does three things. First, it sets the myNumber property to the location of the object in the list. This can be used to reference neighboring objects. Secondly, it calls the putInCast method and the randomize method. (These methods will be defined next.) Finally, the new method returns the location of the object in memory to be pointed to by the list.

4. Create the `putInCast`, `randomize`, and `putInScore` methods:

```
on putInCast me
    set myCast to findempty(member10)
    put "Object" && myNumber into member myCast
    putInScore me
end
```

The `putInCast` *method uses the* `findempty` *handler to locate the first empty cast member after number 10. It then assigns the* `myCast` *property to this number and puts some text into the cast member.*

```
on putInScore me
    set mySprite to myNumber
    puppetsprite mySprite, true
    set the forecolor of sprite mySprite to 255
    set the membernum of sprite mySprite to myCast
    randomize me
end
```

The `putInScore` *method illustrates one of the ways you can place a cast member associated with an object in the score. In this example the cast member is a field, but it can be a bitmap also.*

```
on randomize me
    set the forecolor of field myCast to random(256)
    set the loch of sprite mySprite to random(the stageright - the
    ↪stageleft)
    set the locv of sprite mySprite to random(the stagebottom - the
    ↪stagetop)
    updatestage
end
```

The `randomize` *method positions the sprite randomly on the stage and assigns a random color to the text.*

5. Place a `go to the frame` script in the exitFrame of frame 1.

```
on exitFrame
    go to the frame
end
```

6. Play the movie. You should see 10 text fields pop onto the stage in random locations. If you restart the movie multiple times the fields should relocate and multiply.

continues

Score Generation with OOP   continued

7. The next step is to make the objects jump around. Do this by adding the following `enterFrame` handler to the score script in frame 1:

```
on enterFrame
   global objectList
   repeat with sprites in objectList
      randomize sprites
   end repeat
end
```

This script sends the randomize message to all the objects in objectList (in a similar fashion to the actorList).

8. Restart your movie and watch the text dance around the stage (see fig. 20.8).

Figure 20.8

The CSTGEN.DIR movie.

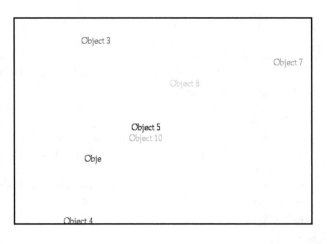

This exercise produced a movie that contains several useful code techniques. To view a finished copy of the movie you can use CSTGEN.DIR found in the Chapter 20 folder on the CD that accompanies this book. The techniques introduced in this movie are as follows:

▶ You can create cast members with a method in an object.

▶ Child objects can place themselves in the score and reposition themselves as well. Although this example is not true animation, it illustrates the potential.

Further Reading

Object-oriented programming is a popular subject for computer books these days. Visit any technical bookstore, and you will find several shelves devoted to OOP books. Unfortunately, most of them are very thick and tend to describe in great detail a particular OOP methodology or language.

Lingo Sorcery by Peter Small is an excellent book on designing object-oriented projects within Director. It deals specifically with versions through Director 5, but covers many important concepts that are still relevant with Director 6. It is full of helpful examples and is well written. Small builds a biological metaphor for programming in Director, comparing cells constructed from the same DNA in an organism to objects from the same Parent script in Lingo. Design metaphors such as this lead to innovative projects that change the way we look at multimedia.

Designing Object-Oriented Software by Rebecca Wirfs-Brock, Brian Wilkerson, and Lauren Wiener (Prentice Hall) is a good choice for introductory reading because it explains the concepts underlying object-oriented design, and then presents several project design walk-throughs. It is not language-specific, so you can apply your new tricks to Lingo right away. All this happens within a mere 233 pages of clear writing.

For more information about OOP, consider the following pages on the web:

▶ *What Is Object-Oriented Software?* By Terry Montlick. Find this at the following:

   `http://www.soft-design.com/softinfo/objects.html`

   Illustrated, humorous, and down-to-earth explanation of what OOP is and what the benefits of OOP design are.

▶ The IBM Smalltalk Tutorial: *What Is Object-Oriented Programming?* You can find this at the following:

   `http://www2.ncsu.edu/eos/info/ece480_info/project/spring96/proj63/www/`
   `tutorial/oop.html`

   Explains OOP concepts using diagrams. This web page is very approachable, and not specific to Smalltalk.

▶ The Object Orientation FAQ can be found at the following:

   `http://iamwww.unibe.ch/~scg/OOinfo/FAQ/oo-faq-toc.html#TOC`

This FAQ is an exhaustive collection of information on OOP concepts, languages, books, and other resources. It is not a good learning tool, but it is an excellent reference.

In Practice

If you feel at home using Director objects, you may want to explore object-oriented design. Object-oriented design solves programming problems by defining the problems entirely in terms of cooperating objects. The resources in the previous section are a good starting point for learning how to "think in objects." Thinking in objects gives you a new outlook on software design.

If you've exhausted your bag of programming tricks, object-oriented or otherwise—and you want to make Director do something more, consider Xtras. *Xtras* are third-party extensions to Director (and other Macromedia products) written in C or C++. Xtras are covered in the next chapter. Even if you can solve your own programming problems, it makes sense to check whether an existing Xtra provides a built-in solution.

Keep in mind the following practical guidelines with respect to object-oriented programming in Lingo.

▶ The beauty of object-oriented programming is in the way it blends the capability to duplicate code with the capability to customize code. Use Lingo's Parent/Child paradigm to avoid repetitive coding of repetitive tasks while still customizing the unique aspects of the objects.

▶ Test your objects as you complete them and before integrating them into your larger project. Send messages to each object method, and check to see that they set the correct property variables, return the correct values, or both.

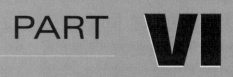

PART **VI**

Extending Director with Xtras

The Xtra Step

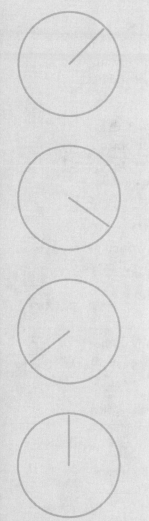

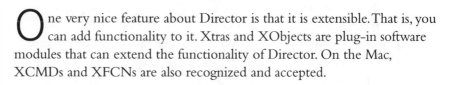

One very nice feature about Director is that it is extensible. That is, you can add functionality to it. Xtras and XObjects are plug-in software modules that can extend the functionality of Director. On the Mac, XCMDs and XFCNs are also recognized and accepted.

This chapter covers the following topics:

▶ What are Xtras and XObjects

▶ Types of Xtras

▶ Finding and obtaining Xtras

▶ Using Xtras

▶ Using XObjects

▶ Learning to make your own Xtras

From XObjects to Xtras

XObjects are the original form of the plug-in module for Director. Originally intended as a way to interface with external devices (such as a video player), XObjects are software modules written by programmers. An XObject might be available to run a videodisc player, for example, or use a modem, draw something on-screen, or save and retrieve information from files.

Although XObjects are wonderful from the point of view that they extended the functionality of Director, they have a few failings that caused Macromedia to phase them out in favor of the new and exciting Xtras. One of the difficulties associated with XObjects is that they are controlled exclusively from Lingo. If you are not willing to use Lingo, you cannot use XObjects.

XObjects also have difficulty in communicating with the Director program, finding out what Director is doing, and making things happen within Director. They are better at controlling things outside Director.

Finally, the internal structure of XObjects differs between the Mac and Windows platforms, making it difficult for programmers to provide both versions. As a result, most XObjects have been either Windows-specific or Mac-specific. Few were written for both platforms.

A couple of years ago, Macromedia, which was then starting to assemble a series of multimedia-related products, began looking at ways to integrate their products. That is, they started to make the architecture (the internal software design) similar in certain ways across all the products: standardizing, if you like, but standardizing internally.

Moving to a common architecture makes possible the creation of tools that work in multiple products. This, in fact, is the strategy: to get all Macromedia products using a common architecture so that design improvements can quickly be integrated into all products, and so that plug-in software modules can be utilized by multiple products where appropriate.

The common architecture is called *Macromedia Open Architecture* (MOA). MOA makes certain elements of Director accessible to software modules written to "fit" with MOA. These elements are more far-reaching than anything that was ever available to XObjects.

Software modules written to MOA are called *Xtras*.

What are some of the benefits of Xtras? To begin, Xtras address many of the deficiencies of XObjects. The following list identifies some of the ways in which Xtras differ from XObjects:

▶ Xtras are not restricted to Lingo. There are Xtras to make special sprites, transitions, and tools, in addition to those that add on to the Lingo language.

▶ Xtras have access to a wide range of Director functionality. This means that in addition to having full access to the "outside world," Xtras also have extensive access to the world inside Director.

- ▶ Xtras are more likely to be available in all platforms, because MOA is cross-platform "friendly."

- ▶ Xtras can be cross-product, when appropriate. It is possible for the same Transition Xtra, for example, to work in both Director and Authorware or any other product that supports transitions.

- ▶ Xtras can also be 32-bit (on the Windows side). XObjects are restricted to 16-bit only.

Types of Xtras

Let's take a look at the four different types of Xtras that Director allows.

Transition Xtras

A Transition Xtra can perform custom transitions. No longer are you restricted to the standard wipes and fades. Transition Xtras can give you many special effects when moving between screens.

One popular transition package is SharkByte's Killer Transitions, created by SharkByte Tools, Inc. and distributed by g/matter, inc. (415-243-0394). This package provides a wide variety of customizable transitions.

Sprite Xtras

A Sprite Xtra is probably the most powerful Xtra (and the most involved to write from a programmer's point of view). Whereas a regular sprite is just a bitmap or text cast member on the stage, a Sprite Xtra has whatever power was programmed into it. It may have real-time special effects (such as alpha-channel support), it may be "alive" and aware of other things on the stage, or it may not even have a visible presence at all but instead manage other sprites or elements on the stage.

INSIDER TIP

> Infrequently, the terms Asset Xtra, Media Asset Xtra, and Cast Xtra are used by programmers who develop Xtras. Should you run into one of these terms, remember that they are other terms for Sprite Xtras.

One example of a popular Sprite Xtra is AlphaMania, by Media Lab (www.medialab.com). AlphaMania enables you to import alpha-channel images (such as Photoshop images) and use them as sprites that can take advantage of the alpha-channel information at run time.

Generally speaking, no rules govern what can be programmed into a Sprite Xtra. They are limited only by the imagination of those who program them (well, imagination plus time and money).

Script Xtras

Formerly called Lingo Xtras (in Director 5), Script Xtras are accessible only through Lingo. Some extend the Lingo language by adding commands that you can use just like regular Lingo commands. Others also provide special functions but do not directly extend the language. (That is, you can use them, but you have to go through an extra hoop or two to do so.)

Script Xtras run the gamut, from adding additional printing functionality, to connecting you to the web, to doing enhanced image manipulation. One such Xtra is CastEffects from Penworks Corporation (`www.penworks.com`), which enables you—from Lingo and at run time—to break images into smaller parts and flip and rotate them. These functions can be used in everything from games to image cropping. Other Xtras enable you to interact with the operating system or play CD audio. See Appendix D, "Xtras Reference," for a complete list of scripting Xtras and the companies that provide them.

Tool Xtras

Unlike the previous three kinds of Xtras, Tool Xtras are only available in authoring mode. That is, they are not anything you use at run time in your projector; rather, they are available only while you are running Director by itself.

A Tool Xtra may provide special authoring assistance; it may apply a special effect to a cast member; it may export your movie to a particular file format.

One such Tool Xtra is Anecdote, by NEC USA, Inc. (`http://ccrl.neclab.com/Anecdote`), which is a multimedia storyboarding tool. With it, authors can create scenes, simulate the execution of the scenario, track all the media data being created, and then automatically create a Director movie, replete with any necessary Lingo.

Combination Xtras

An Xtra does not need to be just one of these types. It is quite possible that a given Xtra is two, three, or all four types in combination.

A Transition Xtra, for example, may have a Tool component by which you can pull down a menu item to open a dialog box to help you design your transition during authoring. Then, during run time it may be a regular Transition Xtra that you can insert for a custom transition. Further, it may have a Lingo component enabling you to give it Lingo commands at appropriate times.

Such an Xtra, although primarily meant to provide custom transitions, actually consists of three Xtra components: the Tool Component (to design), the Transition Component (to implement), and the Lingo Component (to control). This capability to combine components can result in powerful Xtras.

Finding and Obtaining Xtras

Before you can use an Xtra, you must have an Xtra to use. Where do you get Xtras?

Director 6 CD-ROM

A number of sources are available for obtaining Xtras. The starting point is the Xtras found on your Director 6 CD-ROM. These are the most accessible, and therefore an obvious first stop on the road to "Xtrafying" yourself. Be aware, however, that most Xtras that appear on the Director 6 CD-ROM are actually written for Director 5. That does not mean that they don't work, but rather that they may not take advantage of Director 6's new features.

The reason that the Xtras on the Director 6 CD-ROM may not be updated to Director 6 has to do with the deadlines involved in having Xtras ready for inclusion on the CD-ROM. There was not enough time between the early developer release of Director 6 and the deadline for most developers to get out updated Xtras.

Many of the Xtras on the Director 6 CD-ROM work just fine with Director 6's new features. For others, you will need to get the current version from the Xtra publisher, which may entail little more than a quick trip to the publisher's web site. Remember that the Xtras on the Director 6 CD-ROM date from the end of January, 1997; consequently, many months have elapsed to allow for improvements, updates, and new products altogether. It would be a good idea to check for a current version, regardless.

Inside Macromedia Director 6 with Lingo CD-ROM

The second place to get Xtras is on the CD that comes with the book you are holding in your hands. This is not an all-inclusive collection either, but you can find some goodies there. Dig around!

The Macromedia Web Site

The best place to look for directions to the top Xtras is at the Macromedia site. Go to `http://www.macromedia.com/software/xtras/director`. Although a delay may occur between the time an Xtra is announced and the time it appears on the Macromedia site, this is the best place to start looking around at what is out there.

You should also find some of the top developers of Xtras and make it a point to visit their sites on a regular basis. Companies such as g/matter, Penworks Corporation, Zeus Productions, Media Lab, Xaos, Component Software, and others are always releasing new Xtras that may not have made it on to the Macromedia site yet. Contact information for most of these companies can be found in Appendix D.

Paying for Xtras

Some Xtras are free, but most are not. Typically the Xtras that you find on the CDs or web sites are either demos or limited versions (either limited in functionality or limited to authoring mode only), and you get the full version only after you register the product with the company. Prices range from merely tens to hundreds of dollars, depending on the functionality you get and how greatly it can improve your life and fortunes.

Using Xtras

Assuming that you have found an Xtra you particularly like, now you need to put it to use. The first step is to follow the instructions that come with the Xtra. Those instructions should detail what you need to do.

In general though, two or three steps are involved in installing and using an Xtra, depending on its type. Keep in mind that companies do not usually advertise the Xtra type per se; that is, they don't necessarily say "Tool Xtra." But you can figure out what type of Xtra it is based on what it is supposed to do. Something you pull down from the Xtras menu and that only works in authoring mode is most likely a Tool Xtra. A new transition you can use comes from a Transition Xtra.

Installing Xtras

For an Xtra to be available in Director, it must go in the Xtras subfolder or subdirectory under wherever you installed Director. This folder was created when Director was installed and may already contain some Xtras used by Director or otherwise made available to you. (That is, they may have been pre-installed for you from the CD-ROM.)

Note that any given Xtra has at most three or possibly four variations. These correspond to the three or four platforms for which you can create projectors.

On the Windows side are 16-bit Xtras (for Windows 3.1) and 32-bit Xtras (for Windows 95/NT). 16-bit Xtras almost always have an .X16 extension and reside (for safekeeping) in the XTRAS16 subdirectory. 32-bit Xtras almost always have an .X32 extension and reside in the Xtras subdirectory mentioned previously.

Macintosh Xtras do not necessarily have extensions; consequently their names (and their type and creator) usually differentiate the various kinds. Typically, Mac Xtras are made as "Fat Binaries"—they have code for both regular 68K Macintosh computers and the newer PowerMacs.

Usually a cross-platform Xtra is distributed with 16-bit and 32-bit Windows versions, and also a Mac version. The Mac version runs on both 68K Macs and PowerMacs. These are the three primary variations.

The fourth variation arises because a Mac Xtra might be specific to a 68K machine or to a PowerMac. In that case, you may find Xtras restricted to that particular platform, but the name of the Xtra will probably be a clue, such as Super Xtra 68K or Super Xtra PPC (PPC being shorthand for PowerPC or PowerMac, and 68K being shorthand for everything that is not PPC. The name derives from the 68000-series of Motorola processors used in the non-PowerMacs).

Although all Xtras can comfortably fit in the Xtras folder, after a while it might get a bit crowded in there. Because Director looks in not only the Xtras folder but also any subfolders beneath the Xtras folder, you might prefer to collect your Xtras into groups, giving each group its own subfolder (one for Tools, one for Transitions, and so on). Figure 21.1 shows Script Xtras collected in a dedicated subfolder.

Figure 21.1

Script Xtras organized into a subfolder.

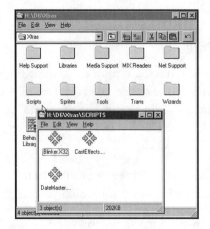

Using Tool Xtras

After installation, if your Xtra is a Tool Xtra, you can probably find a new listing for it under the Xtras menu. The Xtras menu has subcategories. This means that the new Tool Xtra may instead be listed under the name of the company that makes it.

You can also place any .DIR file you commonly use in the Xtras folder, and it too will show up on the Xtras menu. The Animation Wizard that appears on the Xtras menu, for example, is really a regular Director movie. Because it is kept in the Xtras folder, however, it appears on the Xtras menu.

To use a Tool Xtra, just select it from the Xtras menu (see fig. 21.2) and it will be invoked for you. What happens next depends on the Xtra. Some may perform a function quietly, others will bring up a dialog box with which you then do something. At any rate, you select it from the menu and the Xtra takes it from there.

Figure 21.2

Choosing a Tool Xtra from the Xtras menu.

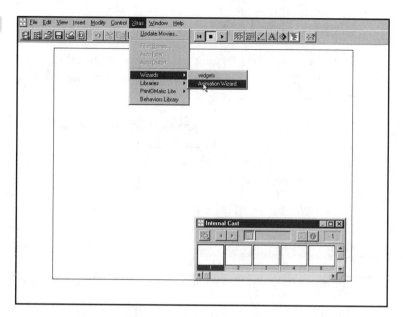

Following is a brief tutorial showing you how to use a simple Tool Xtra.

Installing and Calling a Tool Xtra

1. If you're in Director, save your work and exit.

2. Find the Xtras for the Chapter 21 tutorials.

   Mac: You will use the BeepToolFat file.

   Win: You will use the BEEPTOOL.X32 file.

3. Place the appropriate Xtra in the Xtras subfolder under Director 6.

4. Launch Director 6.

5. From the Xtras Menu, choose Tool Examples, Beep Tool.

6. Listen to the beep. You've now used a Tool Xtra!

   Note that a "real" Tool Xtra will be more functional, but the point of this tutorial was to take you through the basic mechanics of installing and calling a Tool Xtra.

Using Sprite Xtras

Sprites are made by dragging a cast member from the Cast window on to the score or on to the stage. A Sprite Xtra works the same way, but you first must make it a cast member.

To make it a cast member, open the Cast window and select an empty cast member. Then, from the Insert menu select the Sprite Xtra you want, and it will be inserted into the cast (see fig. 21.3). That cast member can now be dragged to the stage or score where it becomes your new high-tech sprite.

It's possible that upon inserting, or dragging, the inserted Sprite Xtra, you may have to customize or prepare it for use. If further such requirements or features exist, they should be listed in the instructions that come with the Xtra. Figure 21.4 shows the special features of the TARGA Xtra, which enables you to adjust its image display characteristics before placing the sprite on the stage.

The following tutorial is an example of using a Wacky Oval Sprite Xtra that you can try now.

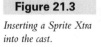

Figure 21.3

Inserting a Sprite Xtra into the cast.

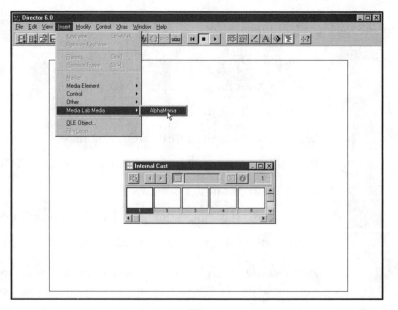

Figure 21.4

Sprite Xtras may have special features.

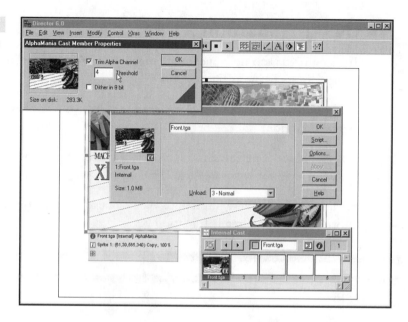

Using a Wacky Oval Sprite Xtra

1. If you're in Director, save your work and exit.

2. Find the Xtras for the Chapter 21 tutorials.

   Mac: You will use the OvalSpriteFat file.

   Win: You will use the OVAL.X32 file.

3. Place the appropriate Xtra in the Xtras subfolder under Director 6.

4. Launch Director 6.

5. Open the Cast window (Ctrl+3 in Windows, Command+3 on the Macintosh).

6. From the Insert menu choose Sprite Examples, Wacky Oval.

   The selected cast member will now contain an instance of the Xtra (displaying the four-arrow Xtra symbol in the left-corner of the cast member).

7. Drag the cast member to the stage. The sprite will appear.

8. If you want, you can now tell Director to run. The sprite will change.

9. Marvel at the amazing power of even a very simple Sprite Xtra!

Using Transition Xtras

Transition Xtras do not appear on a menu, but rather appear in the Transition listing you use to insert transitions.

Open the Transition channel in the score just like you would do to insert a regular transition.

You should see your Transition Xtra's category listed there as well. Choose the transition style you want (see fig. 21.5).

Because I'm sure you're just itching to try a custom transition, following is a tutorial on using a Stretch Transition Xtra.

Figure 21.5

Transition Xtras appear in the Transitions selection window.

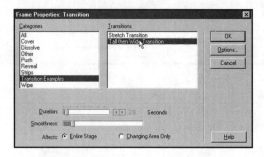

Using a Stretch Transition Xtra

To make a transition we need something to transition between. The first part of this example deals with making two cast members in adjacent frames so we'll have something to transition between.

1. If you're in Director, save your work and exit.

2. Find the Xtras for the Chapter 21 tutorials.

   Mac: You will use the StretchFat file.

   Win: You will use the STRETCH.X32 file.

3. Place the appropriate Xtra in the Xtras subfolder under Director 6.

4. Launch Director 6.

5. Open the Cast window (Ctrl+3 for Windows, Command+3 for Macintosh).

6. Open the Paint window (Ctrl+5 for Windows, Command+5 for Macintosh).

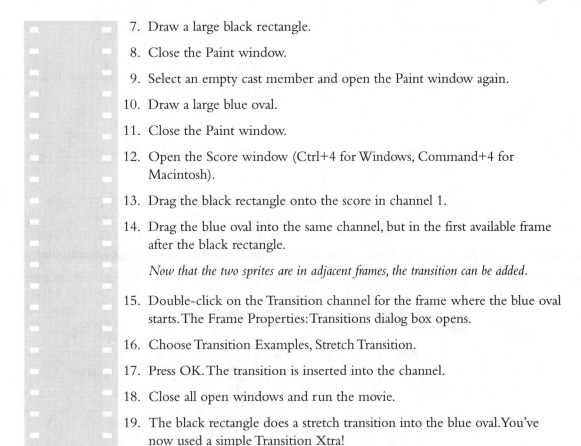

7. Draw a large black rectangle.

8. Close the Paint window.

9. Select an empty cast member and open the Paint window again.

10. Draw a large blue oval.

11. Close the Paint window.

12. Open the Score window (Ctrl+4 for Windows, Command+4 for Macintosh).

13. Drag the black rectangle onto the score in channel 1.

14. Drag the blue oval into the same channel, but in the first available frame after the black rectangle.

    Now that the two sprites are in adjacent frames, the transition can be added.

15. Double-click on the Transition channel for the frame where the blue oval starts. The Frame Properties: Transitions dialog box opens.

16. Choose Transition Examples, Stretch Transition.

17. Press OK. The transition is inserted into the channel.

18. Close all open windows and run the movie.

19. The black rectangle does a stretch transition into the blue oval. You've now used a simple Transition Xtra!

Using Lingo Xtras

Lingo Xtras, because they add power and functionality to the Lingo language, must be used from within Lingo. A Lingo Xtra can implement each of its commands in different ways. Depending on the way the commands are implemented, you will experience various levels of complexity when using the Xtra.

Simplest—Global Lingo

The most accessible way for a Lingo Xtra to implement its commands is by a Global Lingo command. It is called *Global* because with the Xtra installed, the commands are globally known; that is, you do not have to do anything special to make them available. An example of a Global Lingo implementation is the

Blinker Xtra (from Penworks Corporation, available on the accompanying CD in the Chapter 7 folder).

Blinker makes it easy to make sprites blink on the stage. You can just put the commands in your Lingo script. For example:

```
blink mySprite
```

(Blinker also requires you to issue a `blinkUpdate` command that updates the blinks for you).

Some Xtras that implement Global Lingo commands may also require you to "initialize" or prepare the Xtra. The CastEffects Xtra, for example, which enables you to flip and rotate sprites and extract sub-images on-the-fly from Lingo, requires that `castFX_Init()`, a function it provides, be called before the other functions will work. Similarly, a `shutdown` function must be called. If an Xtra requires that such functions be called, its documentation points this out.

Global Lingo Glut?

One problem with having Global Lingo commands is that more than one Xtra can implement the same command. Two separate Xtras might implement the `"Print"` command, for example.

Duplicating commands is not in anyone's best interest, but it may happen. A number of Xtras prefix their commands with a few letters to make the command distinct, which is a good start, but it is not universal. The CastEffects Xtra mentioned earlier, for example, does a combination of both. The initialization function is `castFX_Init()`, but the rotation function is simply `rotate()`, with no prefix.

The reason that `rotate()` has no prefix is because it is a pretty unique command, whereas `init()` is too generic, and too many Xtras might also want to have an `init()` function. It is better to keep `init()` distinct by prefixing it.

Another problem with global commands is that it is not obvious that these commands come from an Xtra. Does the `rotate()` command that was just mentioned come from Lingo, from an Xtra, or is it a handler in the movie? If it does come from an Xtra, which Xtra?

The *Lingo User's Journal*, a publication on Lingo programming, is trying to help resolve problems of conflicting names and names of unclear origin by creating an online *Global Lingo Dictionary* (http://www.penworks.com/LUJ/glingo). It is a registry of all submitted Global Lingo commands, organized alphabetically and by Xtra, with instructions for each command.

Director users can use the *Global Lingo Dictionary* to see where a given command came from (or what its syntax is), and Xtras developers can use it to see whether another Xtra has implemented the same command they might want to use.

Non-Global Lingo

There are non-Global commands, too. These are object-like, in that you must create, or *instantiate*, the object first, before you can use it.

As you learned in the preceding chapter, when you *instantiate* an object (create a specific instance of it), that object gets its own set of properties, while keeping the same handlers as the original object. This enables each instance of the object to have the same capabilities as its sister objects, although with its own private data and attributes.

Similarly, non-Global Lingo commands can be both copied and customized, to optimize the Director author's task. A Communications Xtra, for example, might have a separate instantiation for each communications port it controls. The FileIO Xtra (for doing file operations) has a separate instantiation for each file it is managing. Typically these instantiations are called *Child objects* because the instance is a child of the Xtra (from which the child inherited its capabilities). The original Xtra is sometimes called a *Parent*.

The extra difficulty of working with non-Global Lingo Xtras is a small price to pay for the benefits.

Directions for implementing these types of Lingo commands are usually provided with the Xtra, but it is helpful to take a quick look at how implementation works.

Speaking of which, let's quickly try an example of both a global Lingo command and a non-Global (object) Lingo command:

Examining Xtras Using a Global and Non-Global Lingo Command

1. If you're in Director, save your work and exit.

2. Find the Xtras for the Chapter 21 tutorials.

   Mac: You will use the BeepFat file.

   Win: You will use the BEEP.X32 file.

3. Place the appropriate Xtra in the Xtras subfolder under Director 6.

4. Launch Director 6.

5. Open the Message window (Ctrl+M in Windows, Command+M on the Macintosh).

6. Type **showxlib** and press Return. All the loaded Lingo Xtras will be listed. You will see Xtra: beep listed.

7. List the beep functions by typing the following: **put mMessageList(xtra "beep")**, then pressing Return.

8. Command beepTwo is marked as a global method. In the Message window type **beepTwo** and press Return. You will hear your computer beep once.

9. Now you can try calling the child object's handlers, such as beepOne. Type the following, then press Return:

   set beepObj =new(xtra "beep")

   That created a child object. Now you can call the beepOne function, which also takes a parameter of the number of beeps to generate. Try with different numbers to see what happens.

10. You can call the beepOne function like this:

    ```
    beepOne(beepObj, 30)
    ```

11. When you're finished, you need to dispose of the object you created:

    ```
    set beepObj =0
    ```

12. All done!

Implementation of Lingo commands involves the following five stages:

▶ Opening the Xtra

▶ Creating an instance of the Lingo object

▶ Using the Lingo object

▶ Destroying the Lingo object

▶ Closing the Xtra

Opening the Xtra

Opening prepares the Lingo Xtra for use by Director. If the Xtra resides in the Xtras subdirectory or is bundled with the projector, it should be opened for you automatically. Bundling is explained in the "Distributing Xtras" section later in this chapter.

If, however, the Xtra is neither bundled nor in the Xtras subdirectory, you must open it explicitly. You can do so with the `openxlib` command.

```
openxlib "filename"
```

To open `"c:\myxtra.x16"`, for example, you could use the following:

```
openxlib "c:\myxtra.x16"
```

You should be able to realize that the ability to open by name enables you to rename your Xtras to something inconspicuous, such as INFO.DAT, keep them in the same directory as the projector, and open them explicitly if you want to (and if you did not want to bundle with the projector). This is a potentially valuable capability if you have an Xtra that you want to keep hidden.

By default, the `openxlib` command assumes the file to be in the same folder as the projector, making it easy to open the file without having to deal with path names. You simply must specify the name.

```
openxlib "myxtra.x16"
```

If, however, the Xtra is somewhere else, you must provide either a full or relative path to the Xtra so that Director can find the file.

```
openxlib "c:\myxtra.x16"
```

Naturally, you must open the Xtra before using it, and you only need to open it one time. That is, you do not need to open it before every call you make to it. The on startMovie handler is a good place to open your Xtras.

Still, if you choose to bundle your Xtras or keep them in the Xtras subdirectory, you can avoid this extra work and jump to the next section, "Creation."

The Message window, as you may already know, provides an easy way to tell which Xtras are already open: the ShowXLib command. To use this command, open the Message window (Window, Message or press Ctrl+M in Windows or Command+M on the Macintosh) and type **showxlib**. Then press Return. A list of open XObjects and Xtras appears (see fig. 21.6).

Figure 21.6

Listing open Xtras from the Message window.

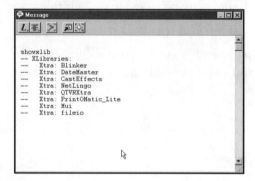

Creation

Before you can use a Lingo Child object, you must instantiate it.

To do so, use the new command.

```
set myXtraObj =new(Xtra "myXtra")
```

This command creates a version of myXtra as an object. The identification number (or, ID) for this object is saved in a variable, myXtraObj.

It is possible (likely, even) that certain information must be provided to the Xtra when you instantiate it. The Xtra documentation should specify what is needed.

If the Child object requires a file name, for example, you might have to use the following command.

```
set myXtraObj =new(Xtra "myXtra", "C:\WINDOWS\MYFILE.INI")
```

Notice that the Child object was named `myXtraObj`. You can name it whatever you want, but for generic Xtras sometimes it is easier to use the name of the Xtra with `obj` tacked on the end so that you remember it for what it is.

The Child object (in this case, `myXtraObj`) is your "key" to the instance of the Xtra. It is important that you do not lose the key. Therefore, if you are not fully creating, using, and destroying the object in the same handler, you need to make the Child object variable global so that it survives the trip across handlers. Otherwise it will appear to be undefined later, even though you may swear you had instantiated it correctly.

Finally, you should check whether creation of the Child object was successful. You can do so by testing the variable to see whether it is an object variable.

```
if not objectP(myXtraObj) then
  alert "Couldn't load myXtra!"
  exit
end if
```

Usage

Now you have an object. What you do next depends on the functions that the Xtra provides. Assume, for example, that the Xtra provides a function called `Scream` that takes a parameter that is the words to scream (the parameter is a string). You would call it like this:

```
scream(myXtraObj, "I LOVE XTRAS!!")
```

Note that the command comes first and then `object ID` is a parameter. This may seem unusual, but it is in keeping with the way that Director handles objects.

INSIDER TIP

> If Director complains that `scream` is an undefined handler, and you know it should be valid, it is quite possible that the object was not created properly (or that you did not save it in a global variable). If the object is invalid, Director complains that it cannot find the handler. For the user, this seems backward, but that is what's going on.

You can list the handlers provided by the Xtra by using the `mMessageList` function (previously `mDescribe for XObjects`). To do so, open the Xtra if it is not already loaded or open, and then from the Message window, type the following:

```
put mMessageList(xtra "myxtra")
```

substituting the name of the Xtra for "myxtra". Figure 21.7 shows a listing for a Scripting Xtra.

Unfortunately, not all descriptions can be explicit. You will invariably need to consult the documentation for the product. Some, like the example in figure 21.7, list the commands but do not make clear what the parameters are. The asterisk (*) to the left of some commands indicates that these are global commands, and the asterisk to the right, where the parameters would normally go, indicates that these commands accept a range of parameters or parameter types. Comments to the right of a few Xtras help describe the command; some Xtras, for reasons of space limitations, are forced to leave these off.

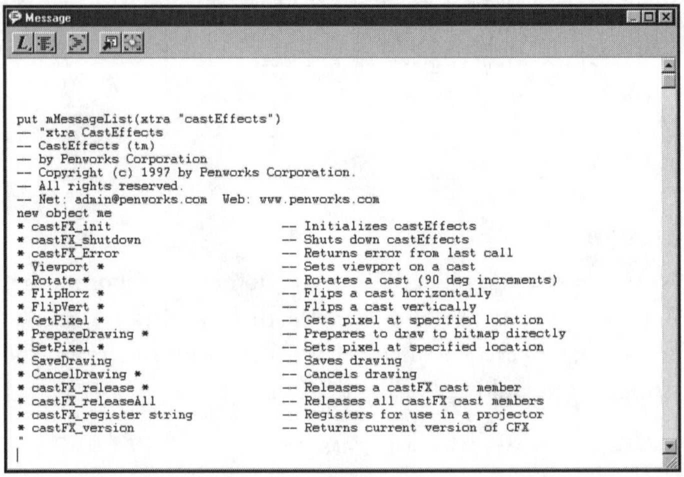

Figure 21.7

Listing Scripting Xtra functions.

```
 Message                                                      _ □ ×
 L E ≥ D
 put mMessageList(xtra "castEffects")
 -- "xtra CastEffects
 -- CastEffects (tm)
 -- by Penworks Corporation
 -- Copyright (c) 1997 by Penworks Corporation.
 -- All rights reserved.
 -- Net: admin@penworks.com  Web: www.penworks.com
 new object me
 * castFX_init                    -- Initializes castEffects
 * castFX_shutdown                -- Shuts down castEffects
 * castFX_Error                   -- Returns error from last call
 * Viewport *                     -- Sets viewport on a cast
 * Rotate *                       -- Rotates a cast (90 deg increments)
 * FlipHorz *                     -- Flips a cast horizontally
 * FlipVert *                     -- Flips a cast vertically
 * GetPixel *                     -- Gets pixel at specified location
 * PrepareDrawing *               -- Prepares to draw to bitmap directly
 * SetPixel *                     -- Sets pixel at specified location
 * SaveDrawing                    -- Saves drawing
 * CancelDrawing *                -- Cancels drawing
 * castFX_release *               -- Releases a castFX cast member
 * castFX_releaseAll              -- Releases all castFX cast members
 * castFX_register string         -- Registers for use in a projector
 * castFX_version                 -- Returns current version of CFX
 "
```

Destruction

After you finish making calls to your object, you need to release the object, enabling the Xtra to do some cleanup work; without this cleanup, certain Xtras might cause the computer to crash later. Releasing objects also frees up the memory; too many created objects that are not freed after they are created might cause your program to run out of memory and crash.

Director frees an object when no more variables reference it. If the extent of what you have done is this:

```
set myXtraObj =new(Xtra "myXtra", "C:\WINDOWS\MYFILE.INI")
scream(myXtraObj, "I LOVE XTRAS!!")
```

To release an object, set myXtraObj to any other value. This reduces what is called the *reference count* on the object. When no variables remain that refer to an object, that object is automatically released from memory. The most typical way is simply to set it to 0, as shown here:

```
set myXtraObj =0
```

INSIDER TIP

The statement made earlier, that Director frees an object "when no more variables reference it," is critical. Every time you copy a variable that references the object to another variable, you increase the number of references by one. For instance:

```
set myXtraObj =new(Xtra "myXtra")
```

```
set savedObj =myXtraObj
```

Now the object has two references. Both references would each have to be set to something different to free the object.

Closing the Xtra

If you opened the Xtra yourself (via openxlib), you need to close it. If the Xtra was bundled or in the Xtras subdirectory, it opens and closes for you automatically.

Closing the Xtra is essentially the reverse of opening it. Just use closexlib rather than openxlib. For instance:

```
closexlib "c:\myxtra.x16"
```

INSIDER TIP

Because you must provide a path name for both the openxlib and closexlib functions, it is a good idea to store the path name in a global variable (unless this is all done in the same handler) and refer to the path name instead. For example:

```
global myXtraName
```

```
set myXtraName ="c:\myxtra.x16"
```

```
openxlib myXtraName
```

```
...
```

```
closexlib myXtraName
```

Storing the path name in a global variable instead of specifying it to each of the openxlib and closexlib calls is much cleaner and keeps you from having to change references to file names in multiple places.

Using XObjects

Working with XObjects is similar to working with the non–Global Lingo Xtras. In fact, the Lingo Xtras derived from XObjects, so it is actually more true that Lingo Xtras work like XObjects.

You must explicitly open XObjects with `openxlib` and close them with `closexlib`.

To instantiate an XObject, you typically use the name of the XObject to call the `mNew` function (predecessor of `New`). After finishing, you must call `mDispose`, which is the equivalent of setting the variable to 0 with Xtras.

The `scream` example shown for the Xtras would be done like this:

```
openxlib "myxtra.dll"
set myXtraObj =myXtra(mNew, "C:\WINDOWS\MYFILE.INI")
myXtraObj(mScream, "I LOVE XOBJECTS!!"
myXtraObj(mDispose)
closexlib "myxtra.dll"
```

The following are the significant differences in calling XObjects instead of calling Child Lingo Xtra objects:

▶ Commands all start with "m" (for "method").

▶ The object comes first, and then the method (as opposed to an Xtra where the function name comes first, and then the object).

▶ You must explicitly open and close an XObject.

▶ You must call `mDispose` when you finish.

Note that Macromedia is working to phase out XObjects. In deference to the huge existing base of XObjects, Director still supports them internally, and probably will for a few more versions to come. You should, however, plan on their eventual departure.

In Windows, all XObjects are 16-bit .DLLs and, although they will run under Windows 95 projectors, they will do so only in Windows 95. They will not be available in Windows NT because of the Windows NT architecture. On the Mac, HyperText XCMDs and XFCNs can be loaded as XObjects; this provides a slightly more formidable base of available plug-ins than on Windows (where the XObjects have to be specifically written for Director).

Nonetheless, it is in your interest to use an equivalent Xtra if one is available to help guard against obsolescence. Macromedia, for example, recommends using the FileIO Xtra rather than the FileIO XObject, even though the latter is still available.

In summary, the behavior and use of XObjects is almost identical to that of a Script Xtra's child handler. As with Xtras, consult the documentation of XObjects for specifics on using them.

Distributing Xtras

The Xtras you use while authoring are kept in an Xtras subfolder under Director. If your projector makes use of Xtras, it must obtain them from somewhere. You cannot just make a projector, put it on your desktop, and expect it to find the Xtras it needs. The user probably does not have Director and its Xtra collection; therefore, the projector must carry along any Xtras it uses.

Knowing What to Distribute

As you know from the early chapters of this book, although you author in a particular version of Director (say PowerMac or Windows 95), you can create various types of projectors; you are not restricted to that in which you author.

The Windows 95 version, for example, can make a 16-bit Windows 3.1 projector that runs under Windows 3.1 (or under Windows 95 as a 16-bit program). The Mac version can make either PowerPC or 68K projectors, or a bundle of both.

This brings up a problem for projectors. Which version of your Xtra do you need to ship? If you authored in Windows 95, for example, but were making a Windows 3.1 projector, would you include, MYXTRA.X32 (which is what you use in Director), or would you include MYXTRA.X16? In this case, you would include MYXTRA.X16.

You must provide the Xtra that goes with the type of program that will be running it. The Windows 95 version of Director is a 32-bit Windows 95 program; thus, it uses (when you are authoring) the 32-bit .X32 Xtra. If you create a 16-bit Windows 3.1 program, however, you must provide the 16-bit Xtra.

If you make a 16-bit Windows 3.1 projector because it can run in either Windows 3.1 or Windows 95, you only need to include the 16-bit Xtra, because that Xtra is loaded by a 16-bit program (regardless of which operating environment is loading the 16-bit program).

On the Mac side, a "Fat binary" Xtra—which is very common—can be included with either a PowerPC projector or a 68K one, because the Fat binary Xtra includes code for both platforms. If you do not have a Fat binary Xtra (that is, if it is explicitly restricted to 68K or PPC), it can only go with the equivalent type of projector. Shipping a PPC Xtra with a 68K projector does not work.

If you ship both types of projectors (for example, both a Windows 95 and Windows 3.1 projector), both types of Xtras (.X16 and .X32) can go in the Xtras subdirectory. The projector is smart and will only load the one that matches; the same is true on the Mac side.

The Xtras Subfolder

Xtras are distributed in two primary ways. One is to place the Xtras your program uses in the Xtras subdirectory under the projector. This is the same approach as Director 5. When the projector starts up, it looks for a subfolder called Xtras. If the projector locates the subfolder, the projector loads any Xtras it finds.

You can make subfolders within the Xtras subfolder and organize your Xtras that way. This may make keeping track of an ever-expanding collection of Xtras easier, particularly when you distribute.

Bundling

The other method is to bundle the Xtras with your projector. Bundling incorporates the Xtras into the projector so that you have a self-contained projector that needs no external files.

The drawback is that bundling incorporates the Xtras into the projector, resulting in a larger projector. Further, if you get a later version of one of the Xtras, you are forced to remake your projector to incorporate the newer version of the Xtra.

You can decide whether bundling or placing Xtras in the Xtras subdirectory works best for your situation. If you have only a few small Xtras, it might be easier and cleaner to bundle them all up. If you have many Xtras, however, you might not want to burden your projector with all the extra bytes (small projectors load faster).

To bundle Xtras, you must first list them as "belonging" to the movie. You do this by adding them to the Xtras list for the movie under Modify, Movie, Xtras (see figs. 21.8 and 21.9).

Figure 21.8

Selecting the Xtras list for the movie.

Figure 21.9

Adding Xtras to be used by the movie.

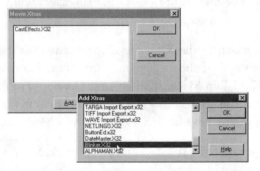

Director may add some Xtras of its own, such as sound or Internet Xtras, if you use such features. Leave these additional Xtras; they are necessary to the proper functioning of your projector.

After you have listed the Xtras to be used by the movie, choose Options when you are ready to create the projector and check the Check Movies for Xtras check box, thereby ensuring that the Xtras are bundled (see fig. 21.10).

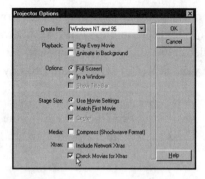

Figure 21.10

Bundling Xtras with your movie when creating the projector.

When you create your projector, the Xtras are now included with the projector; conceivably, you don't have to have separate files.

An added benefit of bundling is that the users get the Xtra you ship to them—it is not likely that they can accidentally delete a support file or replace it with another. A drawback is that if you want to update a bundled Xtra, you must ship an entire replacement product.

Rolling Your Own

It is possible to write your own Xtras, but it is not a task for the squeamish. To begin, you need to be proficient in C. Other languages will work, but they are more involved to implement.

To start, visit the Macromedia Xtras Developer Center for the current XDK (Xtras Developer's Kit) of choice. Second, print the documentation (print double-sided). Third, join Macromedia's Xtras Developer's Program. As this book goes to press, the cost is $249 and it is well worth it. (You are going to want it!) You get online help (in listserv form) from Macromedia Engineers.

Finally, set aside several calendar days and go to work. Macromedia has made things much easier—with better examples—than "in the old days." Still, however, a lot of work is involved, particularly if you are going cross-platform. It is rewarding, but a learning curve is involved.

In Practice

Although the folks at Macromedia are smart, they are not in a position to imagine and create everything you might want. That is why Xtras are so great—if someone needs particular functionality or knows of a special effect that would be terrific to have, he can make an Xtra available for it. Companies coming out with new equipment or technologies (such as QuickTime VR) can provide Xtras that can make the power of that new technology available to Macromedia Director users. Xtras really open up a new world.

Appendix D contains a list of Xtras organized by category and a list of companies developing Xtras. Of course, this is not a comprehensive list—if you need something, ask around. Check the sources mentioned in the section entitled, "Finding Xtras," earlier in this chapter.

Keep in mind the following issues with Xtras:

- ▶ To find Xtras, check the Director 6 CD-ROM, the accompanying CD, Macromedia's web site, and Appendix D of this book, for starters.

- ▶ Xtras always go in the Xtras subfolder under Director.

- ▶ Your two choices for distributing Xtras with a projector are to include them in the Xtras subfolder under the projector, or to bundle them with the projector. Bundling has the benefit of not adding external files to your projector, but the drawback of making the projector larger and potentially slower to load.

- ▶ When distributing projectors with Xtras, include the version of the Xtra that matches the platform on which the projector will be running.

- ▶ Consider organizing your Xtras in groups and giving each group its own subfolder for easier management and location.

- ▶ Remember the different types of Xtras: Scripting (Lingo) Xtras, Sprite Xtras, Tool Xtras, and Transition Xtras.

- ▶ Commands from Lingo Xtras may be automatically defined, or they may need to be instantiated (depending on the Xtra).

- ▶ To check which handlers are available for a Lingo Xtra, use the `mMessageList` function in the Message window.

- ▶ To release a Lingo Xtra object, set every variable that references the object to some other value.

- ▶ Sprite Xtras are placed in the cast from the Insert menu.

- ▶ Tool Xtras are invoked from the Xtras menu.

- ▶ Transition Xtras will appear in the Transitions dialog box.

▶ Read the documentation that accompanies each Xtra. The Xtras are all very different.

▶ Always check with the publisher of the Xtra for the most current version.

PART VII

Appendices

Lingo Library

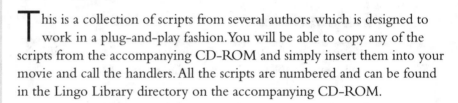

This is a collection of scripts from several authors which is designed to work in a plug-and-play fashion. You will be able to copy any of the scripts from the accompanying CD-ROM and simply insert them into your movie and call the handlers. All the scripts are numbered and can be found in the Lingo Library directory on the accompanying CD-ROM.

Scripts for the Lingo Library were created and contributed by the expert Lingo programmers Rob Dillon, Al Hospers, Tab Julius, Glenn Picher, and Kathy Kozel.

Rob Dillon founded the Digital Design Group in 1993 to produce CD-based and web-based digital media for business. He began using Director in 1984 when it was called VideoWorks. Rob is also a contributing author to this book and can be reached via e-mail at rob@ddg-designs.com.

Glenn Picher, principal of Dirgo Multimedia, is a freelance multimedia consultant specializing in Macromedia Director, Lingo, Xtras, and XObjects. He has developed a number of shareware and freeware Director plug-ins and multimedia authoring utilities in response to some of the most commonly expressed needs of the community of Director developers. You can reach Glenn at gpicher@maine.com.

Tab Julius is President/CEO of Penworks Corporation, a leading developer of software written with, and Xtras written for, Macromedia Director. He is also publisher of the *Lingo User's Journal*, author of *Lingo! An Advanced Guide* (New Riders, 1996), and a contributing author to this book. He can be reached at tab@penworks.com.

Al Hospers' software design and development consulting company, A.L. Hospers & Associates, has a client list that includes Papyrus Design Group, Kinderactive, *The Princeton Review*, and Harmonix Music Systems. Al programmed the latest version of "Inside the SAT '97," the CODIE award-winning SAT preparation title, and is currently the Executive Producer for Harmonix Music Systems, Inc., an interactive music software game developer. You can write Al at `Al_Hospers@msn.com`.

radioGroup   01
Rob Dillon

Purpose

This script handles the visual representation of a set of radio buttons in which one is always ON and the rest of the group is OFF.

Syntax

`highlight whichSprite`

▶ `whichSprite`: The spritenum of the sprite that serves as a marker

Usage

Place `highlight` into a mouse event script.

`highlight 5`

▶ `5`: The `spriteNum` of the checkmark that notes a selection

filmLoopCheat   02
Rob Dillon

Purpose

This script is used to cycle through a series of cast members for an animation. It is used in place of a film loop.

Syntax

```
filmLoopCheat whichSprite, memberList
```

- ▶ whichsprite: The sprite to be animated
- ▶ memberList: The list of sprites to be cycled through for the animation

```
wait howlong
```

- ▶ howlong: The value for 1/60th of a second to delay

Usage

Place filmLoopCheat into a mouse event script.

Place wait into any handler that you need to delay before continuing an action.

```
filmLoopCheat 2, [27,28,29,30]
```

- ▶ 2: The sprite to be animated
- ▶ [27,28,29,30]: The list of cast members used in the animation

---

filmLoopEnd   03
Rob Dillon

Purpose

This script detects the end of a film loop and resets a sprite to another member when the loop is complete.

Syntax

```
filmLoopEnd loopSprite,switchMember,loopList
```

- ▶ loopSprite: The sprite where the film loop is running
- ▶ switchMember: The new member to be substituted at the end of the loop's running
- ▶ loopList: The members in the film loop that is running

Usage

Call `filmLoopEnd` from another handler that controls a film loop animation.

```
filmLoopEnd 2,31,[13,14,15]
```

- ▶ 2: The number of the sprite to be acted on
- ▶ 31: The number of the cast member that will be put into sprite 2 at the end of the animation
- ▶ [13,14,15]: The list of members in the animation that is running

---

moveTo   04
Rob Dillon

Purpose

This script moves a sprite from point A to point B in increments using Lingo.

Syntax

```
moveTo startList, steps, endList, whichSprite
```

- ▶ startList: The location point for the start of the move
- ▶ steps: The number of steps this move takes
- ▶ endList: The location point for the end of the move
- ▶ whichSprite: The sprite to be moved

Usage

Call this handler from a mouse event or from inside another handler in response to something.

```
moveTo [22,100],5,[192,48],1
```

The first argument, [22,100], is the starting location of the sprite to be moved. 5 indicates the steps in the animation, which places the sprite at [192,48]. The final argument, 1, is the sprite to be animated.

scrollPict

Rob Dillon

05

Purpose

This script scrolls a bitmap in multiple directions.

Syntax

```
scrollPictLR whichSprite,whichMember,where
```

- ▶ whichSprite: The sprite to be scrolled across the stage
- ▶ whichMember: The member to be used in the scroll
- ▶ where: The starting horizontal or vertical point

scrollPict has four variations: left to right (LR), right to left (RL), top to bottom (TB), and bottom to top (BT). Each operates the same way, but moves the sprite in a different direction.

Usage

Call scrollPict from a mouse event or from another handler in response to some other event.

```
scrollPictLR 1,26,60
```

- ▶ scrollPictLR: The left to right variant
- ▶ 1: The sprite to be used
- ▶ 26: The number of the member to be used in sprite 1
- ▶ 60: The locV for the scroll to use

popUpHelp

Rob Dillon

06

Purpose

This script makes fields pop up with text at the mouse location.

Syntax

```
popUpHelp rollList, showList
```

- ▶ `rollList`: A list of sprites that activates this handler
- ▶ `showList`: The list of field sprites that move to the mouse location

Usage

Put `popUpHelp` in a frame script and call it like this:

```
popUpHelp [1,2,3],[6,7,8]
```

The first list items are the actual sprites to be tested for `rollOver`. The second list items are the sprites that will be made visible. If `rollOver(1)` is TRUE, for example, sprite 6 is visible.

cursorMan   07
Rob Dillon

Purpose

This script keeps track of custom sprite cursors to get rid of them later.

Syntax

```
cursorMan
```

Usage

Put `cursorMan` in a `mouse` event handler like this:

```
cursorMan
```

popUpList   08
Kathy Kozel

Purpose

This script displays a non-scrolling field (like a `popUpList`) when the user clicks a button; enables the user to select from the list. Also highlights the user selection based on author `textStyle` preference.

Syntax

`popListWasClicked whichField, actionCode, unlitStyle, litStyle`

- ▶ `whichField`: The cast name or number of the popUp field.

- ▶ `actionCode`: Lingo to be executed when the popUp is clicked.

- ▶ `unlitStyle`: The default text style of the popUp field, formatted as a string; for example, `plain`, `bold`, `italic`. If not specified, the default is `plain`.

- ▶ `litStyle`: The text style of the line while it is being highlighted by the user (`mouseDown` over the line). If not specified, `bold` is used.

`PopButtonClicked popSprite, popField, listOfStringsOrField, unlitStyle`

- ▶ `popSprite`: The spriteNum of the button.

- ▶ `popField`: The castName or number of the text field that is being used as the popUp. Note: Must be a field, not rich text.

- ▶ `listOfStringsOrField`: This tells the code where and how to get the text that fills the popUp field. If you are passing in the strings yourself, they must come in formatted in a list: `[item 1, item 2, line 3]`. If the code does not find a list, it assumes that you've passed the cast name or number of a field where the text can be found, and it places the entire field into the popUp field. You can specify the same field as the popUp field.

There is no protection from making a list so large that it will move off the top of the screen.

▶ unlitStyle: The default text style for the popUp field, because it always comes up with nothing highlighted. Must be sent as a string (plain, italic) and should obviously match the unlit style specified in the popListWasClicked handler. If not supplied, the default is plain.

Usage

Put the complete set of handlers in a movie script, to make available through-out the movie. The two main handlers are called from a sprite or cast script—one for the button, one for the popUp field. Requires a text field sprite to be placed off-screen—for example, –500,–500—which will display the lines of text (passed as a list of strings or retrieved from a text field). Note: This field sprite should not be set to invisible; the script does not check for visibility. It assumes the sprite is merely outside the stage rectangle. User selection is processed based on which LINE was selected (an integer).

```
PopButtonClicked "myPopField", ["mary", "fred", "sue"], "plain"
```

myPopField is the name of a field to act as the popUp. mary, fred, and sue are the individual items in the popUp. The text of the popUp should be formatted as plain.

```
PopButtonClicked 22, "TextStorageField"
```

The button is sprite 22 and the text for the popUp is in the field "TextStorageField".

popUpScrollList   09
Kathy Kozel

Purpose

Displays a scrolling field (like a popUpList) when user clicks a button; enables the user to scroll and select from the list. Also highlights the user selection based on author textStyle preference.

Syntax

```
popScrollListWasClicked whichField, actionCode, unlitStyle, litStyle
```

```
PopButtonClicked popSprite, popField, listOfStringsOrField, unlitStyle
```

The syntax for the arguments for these handlers is identical to the arguments for `popUpList`.

Usage

Put the complete set of handlers in a movie script, to make available throughout the movie. The two main handlers are called from a sprite or cast script—one for the button, one for the popUp field. Requires a text field sprite to be placed off-screen—for example, –500,–500—which will display the lines of text (passed as a list of strings or retrieved from a text field). Note: This field sprite should not be set to invisible; the script does not check for visibility. It assumes that the sprite is merely outside the stage rectangle. User selection is processed based on which LINE was selected (an integer). The `popButtonClicked` handler is identical to the `popButtonClicked` from the `popUpList` movie, but the handler for selecting from the popUp is different. For an example of the usage, see `popUpList`.

keyMove   10
Rob Dillon

Purpose

This handler enables a user to use arrow keys to move a sprite, cross-platform.

Syntax

```
keyMove thisSprite
```

▶ `thisSprite`: The sprite that moves in response to arrow keys

Usage

Call `keyMove` from a frame handler, from inside another handler, or from the `startMovie` handler.

Call keyMove from a frame handler like this:

```
set the keyUpScript = "keyMove 3"
```

This handler as written requires the sprite to be puppeted outside the handler. It is better to puppet the sprite in a frame before the handler. In this example the sprite is puppeted in the `exitFrame` handler.

trapQuit   11
Rob Dillon

Purpose

This script traps the Escape key or command "q" or command "." cleanup and quit.

Syntax

```
trapQuit
```

Usage

Call `trapQuit` from the `startMovie` handler like this:

```
set the exitLock = true
```

```
set the keyDownScript = "trapQuit"
```

This handler does not work properly in authoring mode, with the exception of the Escape key. You must create a projector to see it in actual use.

stillThere?   12
Rob Dillon

Purpose

This script detects user inactivity with `timeOutLength`, lapsed.

Syntax

`stillThere waitHowLong, whatToDo`

▶ `waitHowLong`: A value in seconds for the length of time to wait

▶ `whatToDo`: The handler to be run when a `timeOut` occurs

Usage

Call `stillThere` from inside the `startMovie` handler like this:

`stillThere 10,"wakeEmUp"`

`10` is the number of seconds that the projector will wait with no user input. It is then put into the `timeOutLength`. `"wakeEmUp"` is the handler that is called in response to no user input. It is the `timeOutScript`.

mouseMoved   13
Rob Dillon

Purpose

See if the mouse has moved with Lingo.

Syntax

`mouseMoved`

Usage

Call this handler from a frame script like this:

```
go to the frame

mouseMoved
```

playQTSection   14
Rob Dillon

Purpose

This script sets up to play a section of a QuickTime movie.

Syntax

```
playQTSection whichQTSprite
```

> ▶ whichQTSprite: The sprite that will be played

```
stopQTSection whichQTSprite
```

> ▶ whichQTSprite: The sprite that will be played

```
playQTSection2 whichQTSprite, startNum, stopNum
```

> ▶ whichQTSprite: The sprite that will be played

> ▶ startNum: The number, in ticks, where the QT sprite will begin to play

> ▶ stopNum: The number, in ticks, where the QT sprite stops playing

Usage

Call `playQTSection` from inside another handler like this:

```
playQTSection 5
```

5 is the digital video sprite number.

The handler `stopQTSection` works in the same manner.

Call `playQTSection2` from a frame handler like this:

```
playQTSection2 5,120,380
```

`5` is the sprite number for the QT sprite to be played. `120` is the number of ticks into the movie that the movie will begin to play. `380` is the number of ticks into the movie where it will stop playing.

playQTWait   15
Rob Dillon

Purpose

This script causes a movie to wait until a QuickTime movie has finished playing and then proceeds. It works as an alternative to the Tempo settings and enables continued user interaction.

Syntax

```
placeQTSprite whichQTSprite,where
```

- ▶ `whichQTSprite`: The sprite number to be puppeted and moved

- ▶ `where`: The locV, or locH, to position the sprite to

```
playQTWait whichSprite
```

- ▶ `whichSprite`: The sprite number that will be tested to see if it's playing

```
cleanUpQT whichSprite,destination,transList
```

- ▶ `whichSprite`: The QT sprite that was playing

- ▶ `destination`: The new frame number to send the playback head to

- ▶ `transList`: A list containing arguments for a puppetTransition

Usage

Call `playQTWait` from a frame handler like this:

```
playQTWait 3
```

3 is the sprite number for the QT member.

This handler requires a `setup` handler.

Call `placeQTSprite` in a frame handler before the frame that holds `playQTWait` like this:

```
placeQTSprite 3
```

3 is the sprite number for the QT member.

`cleanUpQT` is called from inside another handler like this:

```
on playSomeQT theQTSprite

  -- do some stuff

  if the movieRate of sprite theQTSprite = 0 then

    cleantUpQT theQTSprite,goWhere,transitionList

  end if

end
```

`theQTSprite` is, of course, the same sprite used in the calling handler. `goWhere` is the marker or frame to move the playback head to when the QT movie is finished playing. The `transitionList` argument is a list of arguments for a `puppetTransition` command. The `puppetTransition` is to ensure that the QT sprite is wiped from the stage.

puppetSoundWait   16
Rob Dillon

Purpose

Play a `puppetSound` and then wait for it to be done.

Syntax

```
playSound thisChannel,thisSound
```

▶ `thisChannel:` The sound channel in which the sound will play

▶ `thisSound:` The name of the sound file to be puppeted

```
puppetSoundWait thisChannel,thisSprite,thisMember
```

▶ `thisChannel:` The sound channel to be watched by `soundBusy()`; the same channel as was used in `playSound`

▶ `thisSprite:` A sprite that will be puppeted for a visual cue

▶ `thisMember:` A cast member number that will be used in a cast swap

Usage

Call `playSound` from a mouse event handler like this:

```
playSound 2,"someSound.aif"
```

2 is the channel number for the sound to play in. `"someSound.aif"` is the name of the sound cast member to be played.

Call `puppetSoundWait` from a frame handler like this:

```
puppetSoundWait 2,3,39
```

2 is the sound channel that will be watched by `soundBusy()`. It must be the same channel as was used in `playSound`. 3 is a sprite that's puppeted to provide a visual cue. This is incidental. 39 is a cast member number to be used in the incidental visual cue.

SoundWait   17
Rob Dillon

Purpose

This handler performs a sound playFile and then waits for the sound to be finished.

Syntax

```
playTheSound whichSprite,whichChannel,whichSound
```

▶ whichSprite: A sprite number to be changed

▶ whichChannel: The channel number that the sound file will use

▶ whichSound: The .AIF or .WAV sound file to be played

```
SoundWait whichChannel,whichSprite,whichMember
```

▶ whichChannel: The channel number that the sound file will use

▶ whichSprite: A sprite number to be changed

▶ whichMember: The member to be used by the changing sprite

Usage

Call playTheSound from a mouse event handler like this:

```
playTheSound 3,1,"someSound.aif"
```

3 is the sprite number to be puppeted. This is incidental. 1 is the channel number that the sound will use. "someSound.aif" is the actual sound file to be played.

Call soundWait from a frame handler like this:

```
soundWait 1,3,75
```

1 is the sound channel number that the sound is using. soundBusy() will use this argument. 3 is the sprite number for the visual cue sprite. 75 is the cast member number for the member used by the puppeted sprite.

SoundLoop   18
Rob Dillon

Purpose

This script loops a sound played with sound playFile.

Syntax

playTheSound whichSprite,whichChannel,whichSound

- ▶ whichSprite: A sprite number to be changed

- ▶ whichChannel: The channel number that the sound file will use

- ▶ whichSound: The .AIF or .WAV sound file to be played

SoundWait whichChannel,whichSprite,whichMember,whichSound

- ▶ whichChannel: The channel number that the sound file will use

- ▶ whichSprite: A sprite number to be changed

- ▶ whichMember: The member to be used by the changing sprite

- ▶ whichSound: The .AIF or .WAV sound file to be played

stopSound whichChannel,whichSprite

- ▶ whichChannel: The channel number that the sound file will use

- ▶ whichSprite: A sprite number to be changed

Usage

Call playTheSound from a mouse event handler like this:

playTheSound 3,1,"someSound.aif"

3 is the sprite number to be puppeted. This is incidental. 1 is the channel number that the sound will use. "someSound.aif" is the actual sound file to be played.

Call soundWait from a frame handler like this:

soundWait 1,3,75,"someSound.aif"

1 is the sound channel number that the sound is using. soundBusy() will use this argument. 3 is the sprite number for the visual cue sprite. 75 is the cast member number for the member used by the puppeted sprite. "someSound.aif" is the actual sound file that is running.

Call `stopSound` from a mouse event handler like this:

```
stopSound 1,3
```

1 is the sound channel to be checked. 3 is the sprite that will be unpuppeted.

QTSoundSynch 19
Rob Dillon

Purpose

This script uses list of movieTimes and handlers to synch screen action or sounds.

Syntax

```
QTSoundSync whichSprite
```

▶ `whichSprite`: The QuickTime sprite to be used

```
setThisText "whichField"
```

▶ `"whichField"`: The field that holds the text to be used in the property list

```
showNum thisWord,thisField
```

▶ `thisWord`: Text to be used by the handler

▶ `thisField`: A field cast member's name to be used by the handler

Usage

Call `QTSoundSynch` from a frame handler like this:

```
QTSoundSynch 3
```

3 is the digital video sprite number.

Call `setThisText` from a frame handler like this:

```
setThisText "textFile"
```

`"textFile"` is the name of the field member to be used.

Call showNum from the QTSoundSynch handler as a do function like this:

```
on QTSoundSynch 3

    -- lots of things happening

    -- an if condition then

    do anotherVariable

    -- some other things

end
```

The handler showNum gets called through a variable that's referenced from the property list, not by its actual name.

Each action is controlled by a unique handler. These handlers are called by a procedure that looks up a value in a property list. The property list is created from a field.

Enter the information into the field in this order:

1. The movieTime of sprite that you want to use

2. A colon

3. The handler to be executed at that movieTime

4. Any arguments for that handler

Enter everything as it would normally be used. Don't add spaces where they don't need to be.

addComma   20
Kathy Kozel

Purpose

This handler inserts commas into a numeric field.

Syntax

```
addCommas theString
```

▶ theString: This is a numeric string

Usage

Put this handler in a movie script to make it available everywhere in your movie.

```
addCommas "123456789"
```

addCommas will return "123,456,789"

---

password   21
Kathy Kozel

Purpose

Enables you to capture keyboard input and display a disguise character (for example, an asterisk) for each key typed.

Syntax

```
disguisePassword nameOfStorageField, nameOfDisplayField, keyToShow
```

▶ nameOfStorageField: The cast name (or memberNum) of the text field that holds the actual user entry (the real password).

▶ nameOfDisplayField: The cast name (or memberNum) of the editable text field into which the user types, but which displays the disguise key. (Note: This will also be the sprite in which you will place the sprite script to call the disguisePassword handler).

▶ keyToShow: The character you want to display as the disguise key. (This is an optional parameter; if you don't supply it an asterisk is used.)

Usage

Requires two field cast members: one editable text member on the stage to which the user types, and another field to store the user's actual typed entry for later checking or display. Place the `disguisePassword` handler in a movie script to make it available anywhere. Call this handler from the SPRITE script of the editable text cast member.

```
disguisePassword "PasswordStore", "PasswordEntry",  "#"
```

needPassword   22
Kathy Kozel

Purpose

Accepts a user name and password and compares it to an internal list.

Syntax

```
CheckThePassword userName, passString, passwordList
```

- ▶ userName: A string, typically from an entry field where the user has typed, but could also come from a pop-up list. Must be only one word (for example, `Fred`, `John_Smith`).

- ▶ passString: A string, almost certainly from an entry field where the user has typed. Can be multiple words.

- ▶ passwordList: A property list, formatted with the property key as a symbol and the value as text. Example: [#Fred: "pancake", #Mary: "whatever"]. The symbol formatting is to prevent problems with case-sensitivity. The list can be a global variable, can be passed in as code, or can come from a text field. If it comes from a text field, it must be converted from string to value. Example: If the text field contains [#bill:"gumbo", #ted:"theToad"] (the text field must include the brackets), use `set passwordList = value(the text of field "storedList")`.

Usage

Requires a password list to be passed in; it could be a global or just built locally within the script that calls the handler. The list must be formatted as follows:

[#username: "password", #anothername": "password2"]. The username must be one word only, must begin with a letter character, and must be formatted as a symbol rather than string (to prevent case-sensitivity).

```
CheckThePassword(the text of field "nameinput", the text of field
"passinput", [#zeus:"theMoose", #joe:"wildman"])
```

cutPaste   23
Glenn Picher

Purpose

The cutPaste handler gives Director's editable text fields all the standard system keyboard shortcut behaviors for cutting, copying, selecting, and pasting text. Supporting handlers used by cutPaste can also perform cut, copy, and paste operations in response to other user interface events, such as mouse clicks on button bar icons.

Syntax

cutPaste theField

▶ theField: Integer of the memberNum (or string of the name) of an editable text field

performPaste theField

▶ theField: Integer of the memberNum (or string of the name) of an editable text field

performCut theField

▶ theField: Integer of the memberNum (or string of the name) of an editable text field

```
performCopy theField
```

▶ `theField`: Integer of the `memberNum` (or string of the name) of an editable text field

```
performSelectAll theField
```

▶ `theField`: Integer of the `memberNum` (or string of the name) of an editable text field

Usage

These handlers should be copied to a movie script in your own Director movie and called in the following manner.

The `cutPaste` handler dispatches control to other supporting handlers to perform cut, copy, paste, and select-all operations when the proper key combinations are pressed. The handler assumes that the insertion point or selection is currently located within field `theField`. This will always be true if `cutPaste` is called from a `keyDown` handler in the editable text sprite's sprite script or in its cast script. Normally the `cutPaste` call will be followed by the use of Lingo's `"pass"` function to deliver regular keystrokes to the text fields in which they belong. When a special keystroke is detected, `cutPaste` will never return execution to the `keyDown` script because it uses the Lingo `"abort"` keyword.

Because Director's own menus intercept standard cut, copy, paste, and select-all keystrokes while authoring, you must use other keystrokes to test these functions within the Director authoring environment.

Mac authoring keystrokes:

Cut:	Shift+Command+x
Copy:	Shift+Command+o
Paste:	Shift+Command+v
Select all:	Shift+Command+e

Windows authoring keystrokes:

Cut:	Shift+Ctrl+x
Copy:	Shift+Ctrl+o
Paste:	Shift+Ctrl+v
Select all:	Shift+Ctrl+e

From a projector, all the authoring keystrokes will still work, but the system standard keystrokes will work as expected:

Mac standard keystrokes:

Cut:	Command+x
Copy:	Command+c
Paste:	Command+v
Select all:	Command+a

Windows standard keystrokes:

Cut:	Ctrl+x
Copy:	Ctrl+c
Paste:	Ctrl+v
Select all:	Ctrl+a

A global string variable `PNP057_pasteBuffer`, private to Director or the projector, is used to store the text to copy or paste. This buffer is not made available for copying and pasting between other applications. If you must provide that capability, you can modify the `perform` handlers to use Lingo's `copyToClipboard/pasteClipboardInto` keywords on field members instead of using a global string variable. Unfortunately, it's impossible to know from Lingo what is currently in the paste buffer—possibly a bitmap instead of text, for instance. A large bitmap on the system-wide clipboard, pasted with `"pasteClipboardInto"`, could use much or all of Director's available memory, and a large chunk of text on the system-wide clipboard could overrun Lingo's 32K limit on field contents. For these reasons, these handlers are provided using a string variable buffer instead of `copyToClipboard/pasteClipboardInto`.

hypertext 24
Kathy Kozel

Purpose

Supports hypertext by highlighting "hot" words when the cursor is over them, and by going to a specific frame when a hot word is clicked.

Syntax

`CheckForHyperText listOfWords, fieldCastName, hiliteStyle, unlitStyle`

- ▶ `listOfWords`: Can be either a global or passed in at the time of the call. It can be either linear or property, but if it is a property list, the actual hot words must be in the value position—the right side of the colon (see examples that follow). Note: List text is case-sensitive! You must supply the hot words in all lowercase, regardless of how they appear in the hypertext. They will be converted as they are checked.

- ▶ `fieldCastName`: This is the name (or memberNum) of the text field that displays your hypertext to the user. It's the text the user moves the cursor over to highlight and clicks on to actually make the link.

- ▶ `hiliteStyle`: This is the style the hot word will change to when the user rolls the cursor over it. Text styles are formatted as strings: `"plain"`, `"underline"`, `"bold"`, `"italic"`.

- ▶ `unlitStyle`: This is the default, normal style of the text when it is unlit.

`CheckForLink listOfWords, unlitStyle`

- ▶ `listOfWords`: Can be either a global or passed in at the time of the call. It can be either linear or property. If a linear list, the destination frame must be named the same as the hot word. If it is a property list, you can use the "key" (the left side of the colon) to indicate the destination frame for the corresponding hot word. If it is a property list, the actual hot words must be in the value position—the right side of the colon (see examples that follow). Note: List text is case-sensitive. You must supply the hot words in all lowercase, regardless of how they appear in the actual hypertext. As the user rolls over or clicks on a word, the word will be put through an upper-to lowercase converter automatically.

▶ `unlitStyle:` This is the text style for the field words when not highlighted. They are formatted as strings: `"plain"`, `"bold"`, `"underline"`, or `"italic"`.

Usage

Both handlers can be placed in a movie script. This requires a text field that contains the text with hot words, to be placed on the screen. The `CheckForHyperText` handler can be called from a frame script to manage highlighting the words. The actual linking handler `checkForLink` is called from the text field sprite script (on `mouseDown`).

```
CheckForHyperText ["some", "word"], "hyperField", "underline", "plain"
```

or

```
CheckForHyperText ["myFrame":"some", "destination":"word"], 26, "bold",
➥"italic"
```

```
CheckForLink ["some", "word"], "plain"
```

or

```
CheckForLink ["myFrame":"some", "thisFrame":"word"], "plain"
```

Gravity   25
Kathy Kozel

Purpose

Moves an object (created from a parent script) under the influence of "fake" gravity, with the option of an elastic bounce.

Syntax

```
MoveYourselfWithGravity me
```

> ▶ me: The object. If you have more than one object, you may be calling a list of objects, updating each one in turn.

Optional object creation script:

```
new me, whichChan, hVel, vVel, startingV, startingH, elastic,
groundZero, gravity
```

> ▶ me: The object (required).

> ▶ whichChan: The sprite channel of this particular object.

> ▶ hVel: The horizontal velocity (in pixels) of the object. This refers to the number of pixels the object will move—horizontally—with each update. Positive numbers will move from left to right, negative numbers from right to left.

> ▶ vVel: This is the object's starting vertical velocity. If you are dropping the object from a standstill, this value should be 0.

> ▶ startingV: The vertical starting location of the object.

> ▶ startingH: The horizontal starting location of the object.

> ▶ elastic: The "bounceability" of the object. A value of 0 means no bounce at all. Numbers must be negative, and must be less than 1. −0.9 is a big bounce, −0.2 is a much lower bounce (less elasticity). A value of 1 bounces the object higher than it started!

> ▶ groundZero: The vertical location of the ground or object to be bounced from.

> ▶ gravity: This is the "fake" gravity acceleration factor whose range begins at 0.1 (very slow—lots of air resistance). A number such as 30 causes it to drop like a big stone—very, very fast. Experiment.

Usage

Place the MoveYourselfWithGravity in a parent script for the objects that will be moved with gravity. Use the optional new script in the Parent script, or make your own. *All* objects must have the following object properties: velocityH, velocityV, myElastic, myGravity, spriteChan, and groundZero.

```
MoveYourselfWithGravity getat(myObjectList, 1)

new(script "GravityObjectParent", the clickon,3, 0, the locv of sprite
➡the clickon, the loc of sprite the clickon, -0.4, the locv of sprite
➡3, .8))
```

bounce   26
Kathy Kozel

Purpose

Detects a collision between an object and a wall, or any two objects, and then adjusts the horizontal and vertical velocity of the objects to make the bounce.

Syntax

```
checkforAWall me, aBoundaryRectangle
```

▶ me: The object being tested.

▶ aBoundaryRectangle: This is the rectangle representing the walls. If you want to use the full stage, you must create an adjusted stage rectangle; the rect of stage function gives you the stage relative to the user's full screen, when it really needs to use the same coordinate system as the sprites (0,0, right, bottom).

```
CheckForSpriteObjects me, listOfBounceObjects
```

▶ me: The object being tested.

▶ listOfBouncingObjects: A list of actual objects (created from a Parent script) to be checked for collision with the current (me) object. If an intersection is detected (sprites should be set to matte ink), the hVelocity and vVelocity of both the current object (me) and the object being tested (an object x in the listOfBouncingObjects) are modified to reflect their new angles and momentums.

Optional:

```
MoveAndBounceYourself me
```

▶ me: The object being tested.

Usage

These are method handlers to be used within a parent script for bounceable objects. The bouncing things must be actual sprites, and they must be objects (created from a Parent script). The objects that are bounceable must be in a list passed to the CheckForSpriteObjects handler. Each bounceable object must have three properties: hVelocity, vVelocity, and spriteChan. The velocity properties (measured in pixels) will be adjusted by the two bounce handlers. These handlers do not actually make the sprite move. You must still update the locv and loch, referring to the new velocity properties. Bouncing objects that are not rectangular should be set to matte ink—otherwise, the collision will occur on the sprite bounding rectangle rather than the sprite shape.

```
checkforAWall(me, rect(0,0,336,240))

--if this is within a parent script

--if checkforAWall(me, myBoundaryRect) then

set the loch of sprite mySprite = the loch of sprite
➥mySprite = HVelocity

set the locv of sprite mySprite = the locv of sprite
➥mySprite + vVelocity

updatestage

end if

checkForSpriteObjects me, bounceObjectList
```

barGraph   27
Kathy Kozel

Purpose

Takes a rect, a top and bottom number, values, and a starting sprite channel and builds a bar graph.

Syntax

```
makeBarGraph theRect, BottomNum, TopNum, valList, firstSpriteChan,
➡boxSpriteChan
```

- ▶ theRect: This defines the boundary of the entire bar graph and placement on the screen. The format must be as a rect, or a list in rect order (left, top, right, bottom). Note: If the rect is not large enough to support drawing all the bars, they simply won't show up at all. You won't get fewer bars—you'll get no bars if the individual bars are calculated to be less than two pixels.

- ▶ BottomNum: The lowest number on the scale.

- ▶ TopNum: The highest number on the scale.

Note: The topNum must *always* be greater than the bottomNum. If not, the code will assume that they are reversed, and it will automatically reverse them. All graphs go from lowest to highest numbers vertically.

- ▶ valList: This is the list of one or more values, one per bar. If only one value exists, it must still come in as a list, for example, [23]. Note: Bars whose value exceeds the top of the scale will simply go to the top and stop (effectively "cropped" at the top). Bars whose value is below the bottomNum (the beginning of the scale) will not be drawn at all.

- ▶ firstSpriteChan: The sprite channel of the first bar sprite.

- ▶ boxSpriteChan: Optional. The sprite channel of the draw shape or bitmap that will be used as a border or background to the graph. If it is a nonfilled outline draw shape, it will be a border. A filled shape must be placed in the lowest (deepest) sprite channel so that bars will be drawn over the top of it.

Usage

Place the `makeBarGraph` handler in the movie script. Requires one sprite channel per bar; these sprites must contain a bitmap or draw shape and be in consecutive sprite channels (they can be placed off-stage).

```
makeGraph [40,40,200,200], 0,1000,[300,500,800],2,1
```

---

drawLine   28
Kathy Kozel

Purpose

Takes two points and draws a shape line.

Syntax

```
drawLine aSprite, startPoint, endPoint, leaningRightCast,
leaningLeftCast
```

▶ `aSprite`: The sprite channel for the line.

▶ `startPoint`: One of the two points. This must be formatted as a point: point(1,2).

▶ `endPoint`: The other point.

▶ `leaningRightCast`: The member name or `memberNum` for a line shape cast member that is diagonally leaning to the left.

▶ `leaningLeftCast`: The member name or `memberNum` for a line shape cast member that is diagonally leaning to the right.

Usage

Requires two shape (line) cast members: one leaning to the left, and one leaning to the right. The names or numbers of these cast members will be passed in.

```
drawLine 7, point(10,10), point(30,30), "leaningLeft", "leaningRight"
```

drawBox   29
Kathy Kozel

Purpose

Takes a rect (four coordinates) and draws a shape or bitmap box on the screen.

Syntax

```
drawBox aRect
```

▶ aRect: Coordinates of the corners of the box

Usage

The rectangle parameter must be formatted as a rect: rect(1,2,3,4) or a linear list: [1,2,3,4]

```
drawBox rect(10,20,30,40)
```

userCircle   30
Glenn Picher

Purpose

The userCircle handler enables the user to draw a circle by dragging the mouse, either by selecting corners or by selecting a center and a radius.

Syntax

```
userCircle howToDraw, drawChannel
```

▶ howToDraw: A symbol representing a method with which to draw the circle; #fromCenter specifies that the center of the circle is chosen by the mouseDown and that the radius is selected by dragging the mouse, and

#byCorners specifies that the mouseDown chooses an anchor point for the circle, and the diameter and location relative to the anchor are chosen by dragging the mouse.

▶ drawChannel: An integer representing a sprite channel from 1–120 in which userCircle will position a supplied circular shape sprite to match the user's choice. This parameter is optional.

Usage

In addition to the userCircle handler script text, you should also copy to your own movie the range of cursor bitmaps and shape member in cast member slots 23 through 35 inclusive. The handler uses those bitmaps and the shape member to provide feedback to users as they draw the circle. This handler can be called from any mouse event script.

```
global PNP069_nextSprite

userCircle(#fromCenter, PNP069_nextSprite)

--Set up for next circle to be drawn

set PNP069_nextSprite = PNP069_nextSprite + 1

--Reuse the first sprite if we just used the the last

if PNP069_nextSprite > 34 then set PNP069_nextSprite to 15
```

shuffleList   31
Kathy Kozel

Purpose

Accepts a linear or property list and returns a randomly shuffled copy of the list.

Syntax

```
shuffleList aList
```

▶ aList: A linear or property list.

Usage

The value passed in must be an actual list. The handler exits if it does not receive a linear or property list. The handler creates a working copy of the list so that the original remains untouched.

```
shuffleList [1,2,3,4,5]
```

---

scatterSprite   32
Kathy Kozel

Purpose

Randomly scatter sprites on the screen or within any rectangle. Ensures the sprites are fully contained and visible.

Syntax

```
scatterSprite firstChan, lastChan, aRect
```

▶ firstChan: The first channel holding a sprite to be scattered.

▶ lastChan: The last channel holding a sprite to be scattered.

▶ aRect: This is an optional parameter. If passed, it must be formatted as a rect. If this parameter is not passed, the default boundary for constraining the sprites will be the stage.

Usage

ScatterSprite assumes that sprites are placed in consecutive channels in the score. If not, the handler will have to be called more than once.

```
ScatterSprite 1,5

--will scatter sprites in channels 1 through 5 randomly on the stage

or

ScatterSprite 1, 5, the rect of sprite 4

--will scatter sprites in channels 1 through 5 randomly, constrained to
--the boundary of the sprite in channel 4
```

hang   33
Kathy Kozel

Purpose

This handler causes a movie to do nothing for a period of time. Enables you to insert a "pause" within a script.

Syntax

hang howLong

> ▶ howLong: This is a number variable for the duration of the pause in ticks.

Usage

Hang can be called from any script that needs a pause inserted in the following manner:

hang 120: Hangs for 120 ticks or 2 seconds

countDown   34
Kathy Kozel

Purpose

Creates and displays a stopwatch-like timer that can count.

Syntax

```
startCountDown startNum, endNum, incrementSize,timerRez, displayField
```

- ▶ `startNum`: The starting number for the counter; for example, 0 or 1.

- ▶ `endNum`: The number the counter will stop on or before. Note: The counter will never exceed this end number, so depending on your increment size, the counter may not actually reach the end number. It always stops at the last number it can without going over the `endNum`.

- ▶ `incrementSize`: the counter will increment or decrement by this number. (It will increment if the `endNum` is greater than the `startNum`; otherwise it will decrement, or subtract, this amount.)

- ▶ `timerRez`: In ticks, the time between updates of the counters. A `timerRez` of 60 will update once per second (assuming it gets called frequently enough). A `timerRez` of 1 will go as fast as it possibly can.

- ▶ `displayField`: The text field name or number where the counter will be displayed.

```
CountDown displayField
```

- ▶ `displayField`: The text field name or number where the counter will be displayed.

Usage

Put both handlers in a movie script. The `startCountDown` can be called from anywhere; the `CountDown` handler should be in a looping frame script or an idle handler. The script creates one global list variable and requires a text field to display the counter.

```
startCountDown 1, 10, 1, 60, "counterDisplay"

CountDown "counterDisplay"
```

startCheck   35
Rob Dillon

Purpose

This script checks numerous settings when the movie starts. It checks colorDepth, platform, whether the CD is in the drive, whether QuickTime is installed, and whether the projector is running from the hard drive or from the CD.

Syntax

```
startCheck

macSetUp colorNum

isItInMac fileName

winSetUp colorNum,QTversion

isItInWin subDirName,fileName
```

Usage

startCheck is called from the startMovie handler of your projector like this:

```
startCheck
```

getCD   36
Rob Dillon

Purpose

On a PC this script checks for the CD and then returns the drive letter of the CD.

Syntax

```
getCD thisSubDir, thisFile
```

- ▶ thisSubDir: The name of a subdirectory on the CD
- ▶ thisFile: The name of a file on the CD

Usage

Call this handler from the startMovie handler like this:

```
getCD thisSubDir,thisFile
```

---

stopCheck   37
Rob Dillon

Purpose

This script will restore the color depth (Mac only) and sound volume and save data.

Syntax

```
stopCheck thisCast
```

- ▶ thisCast: The name of a cast library to be saved

Usage

stopCheck is called from the stopMovie handler of your projector like this:

```
stopCheck "storage"
```

---

startedFromCD   38
Rob Dillon

Purpose

This handler returns TRUE if the projector was started from the CD.

Syntax

```
startedFromCD thisSubDir,thisFile
```

> ▶ `thisSubDir:`The name of a subdirectory on the CD

> ▶ `thisFile:`The name of a file on the CD

Usage

Call this handler from the `startMovie` handler like this:

```
startedFromCD thisSubDir,thisFile
```

---

encrypt   39
Kathy Kozel

Purpose

These handlers take a string and return either an encrypted string or a decrypted string.

Syntax

```
encryptText aString
```

> ▶ `aString:`A string to be encrypted

```
decryptText aString
```

> ▶ `aString:` A string to be decrypted

Usage

No special usage or cast members, but new encryption sequences can be added to the handler set. The encrypted or decrypted string is returned in the result. An encrypted string will include a one character "key" and will therefore be one character longer than the original string.

```
encryptText "hello world"
```

```
decryptText "nfakjkukqj'"
```

aListCheat   40
Kathy Kozel

Purpose

Enables you to call your own procedures on idle, by sequencing through a list.

Syntax

```
aListCheat theDoList
```

▶ theDoList: A linear list of strings, which are handler names (or scripts)

Usage

Place the handler in a movie script to make it available anywhere. The scripts in the do list must also be in a movie script. You can then call aListCheat in an on Idle handler either in a frame or in the movie script. Requires one global variable that tracks which procedure in the list was last called.

```
aListCheat ["handler1", "handler2", "beep 3"]
```

Constrain   41
Kathy Kozel

Purpose

This handler returns a number that is either an input number or the constraint boundary it is closest to (if the input number falls outside the boundary).

Syntax

```
Constrain aNumber, min, max
```

▶ aNumber: Number to be tested

▶ min: Minimum constraint value

▶ max: Maximum constraint value

Usage

Place constrain in a movie handler.

Constrain 10,20,30: Will return 20

Constrain 20,10,30: Will return 20

Constrain 30,10,25: Will return 25

MinMax   42
Kathy Kozel

Purpose

minMax returns the larger or lesser of any two numbers.

Syntax

minMax firstNum, secondNum, minORmax

- ▶ firstNum: This is the first number to be tested
- ▶ secondNum: This is the second number to be tested
- ▶ minORmax: This is the test criteria

Usage

This handler can be called for any suitable purpose from any script.

minMax 10,20, "min": Returns 10

Navigator   43
Kathy Kozel

Purpose

These handlers manage a browser-style "Back" button so that the user can retrace his steps through a navigational path.

Syntax

```
Navigator navList
```

- ▶ navList: A global variable holding the list of navigational points. These can be marker names, frame numbers, list keys, and so on.

```
AddToNavList navList, markerOrKeyName
```

- ▶ navList: The global navigational list. If the global is not a list, the script will not execute, so you must be sure to have previously declared the global *and* initialized it as a list (that is, `global gNavList, set gNavList = [ ]`)

- ▶ markerOrKeyName: Whatever you are using for navigation. In a score-based program, where destinations are separately labeled frames, you will probably be using marker names. For a single-frame movie, you may be recording background screens or a key into a navigational database property list.

Usage

Both handlers must be used together; place them in a movie script to make them available anywhere. The Navigator handler should be called when the user clicks on the Back button. The `AddToNavList` should be called from anywhere the user makes a navigational choice. Requires one global variable to be previously declared as a list, which is passed to both handlers (that is, `set gNavigationList = [ ]`).

```
go to frame Navigator gNavList
```

```
addToNavList gNavigationList, MarkerNameTheUserJustChose
```

---

plainDialog   44
Glenn Picher

Purpose

The `plainDialog` handler is a flexible replacement for the Lingo `"alert"` command. It fixes several problems with the Lingo `"alert"` command, such as improper string handling, improper screen redraws, and palette errors.

Syntax

`plainDialog messageString, adjustToFit, positionRect`

▶ `messageString`: The string to be displayed by the dialog box

▶ `adjustToFit`: A boolean that determines if the dialog box will be enlarged to show `messageString` (optional, default = TRUE)

▶ `positionRect`: The dialog box is displayed at the position and size dictated by this rect

`plainDialogAnswer`

`plainDialogAbort`

Usage

`plainDialog` requires that the dialog MIAW, PNP02402.DIR, be in the same folder as the movie that calls `plainDialog` (or in a folder listed in the Lingo property the `searchPath`, which is a list of full pathName strings). `plainDialogAnswer` and `plainDialogAbort` are called when a user clicks on the OK and Cancel buttons respectively.

yesNoDialog   45

Glenn Picher

Purpose

The `yesNoDialog` handler displays a text message in a Movie in a Window and enables the user to make a yes or no choice with button presses.

Syntax

`yesNoDialog messageString, adjustToFit, positionRect`

▶ `messageString`: The string to be displayed by the dialog box

▶ `adjustToFit`: A boolean that determines whether the dialog box will be enlarged to show `messageString` (optional, default = TRUE)

▶ `positionRect`: The dialog box is displayed at the position and size dictated by this rect

`yesNoDialogAnswer`

`yesNoDialogAbort`

Usage

`yesNoDialog` requires that the dialog MIAW, PNP02502.DIR, be in the same folder as the movie that calls `yesNoDialog` (or in a folder listed in the Lingo property `the searchPath`, which is a list of full pathName strings).

The MIAW can be customized with particular artwork or colors using the stage's current palette. You can specify the location of the dialog box on the screen (or allow the handler to set a default location and size and enlarge the dialog box if necessary until all the text message fits on the screen without being chopped off). Finally, you can continue doing work in the movie that requests the `yesNoDialog`, checking periodically to see whether the user has answered the dialog box, or you can dismiss the dialog box after a certain time has elapsed without requiring the user to answer.

Use `yesNoDialogAnswer` to check whether the user has made a Yes or No button click yet. If the dialog box is still displayed, this handler will return the symbol `#notYet`. If the dialog box has been answered, the handler will return the symbol `#yes` or the symbol `#no`.

Use `yesNoDialogAbort` to automatically dismiss the dialog box without requiring the user to answer. This can be useful in a kiosk environment where you want to ask a yes or no question but you want to move on to another part of your project if no user is present at the kiosk. Returns TRUE if the dialog box was dismissed as a result of `yesNoDialogAbort`, or FALSE if the dialog had already been answered by the user. Ensure that `yesNoDialogAnswer` is not used after you use `yesNoDialogAbort`.

listDialog   46
Glenn Picher

Purpose

The listDialog handler displays an instruction message and multiple lines of
text in a Movie in a Window and enables the user to select one item (or
optionally, more than one item) from a scrolling list box. This could be useful,
for instance, in a project in which you want the user to make a choice of one
or more topics to visit.

Syntax

```
listDialog message, items, selections, mustSelect, allowMultiple
```

▶ message: A string with instructions to the user about the choice he is
making.

▶ items: A string with all the items from which the user can select. Different items are separated by Return characters.

▶ selections: A linear list of integers indicating which items, if any, should
be initially displayed as selected. Each integer in the list corresponds to
the line number supplied in items. Use an empty list [] if nothing should
be selected initially. Supply no larger than a one-item list if allowMultiple
is FALSE.

▶ mustSelect: TRUE if the user must make at least one selection before the
dialog can be dismissed with the OK button; FALSE if OK can always
end the dialog box.

▶ allowMultiple: TRUE if the user can select more than one item from the
list, FALSE if only one item can be selected.

▶ where: A rect specifying exactly where the dialog box should be displayed.
Optional.

```
listDialogAnswer
```

```
listDialogAbort
```

Usage

Puts the handlers into a movie script to make them available anywhere in your movie. Also requires that the dialog MIAW, PNP02602.DIR, be in the same folder as the movie that calls `listDialog` (or in a folder listed in the Lingo property `the searchPath`, which is a list of full pathName strings).

Use `listDialogAnswer` to check whether the user has answered the dialog box yet. If the dialog box is still displayed, this handler will return the symbol `#notYet`. If the dialog box has been answered, the handler will return the symbol `#cancel` if the Cancel button has been pressed, or a linear list of integers (possibly an empty list) with the numbers of all items that the user had selected when pressing the OK button.

Use `listDialogAbort` to automatically dismiss the dialog box without requiring the user to answer. This can be useful in a kiosk environment in which you want to the user to select from a list, but you want to move on to another part of your project if no user is present at the kiosk. Returns TRUE if the dialog box was dismissed as a result of `listDialogAbort`, or FALSE if the dialog box had already been answered by the user. Ensure that `listDialogAnswer` is not used after you use `listDialogAbort`.

radioDialog   47
Glenn Picher

Purpose

The `radioDialog` handler displays an instruction message and two or more radio-style buttons with text in a Movie in a Window, and enables the user to select one setting. This is useful, for instance, in a project in which you want the user to make a selection among mutually exclusive choices, such as age or income brackets.

Standard OK and Cancel buttons are provided. You can specify the initial radio button choice. You can specify the location of the dialog box on the screen (or allow the handler to set a default location and size, and enlarge the dialog box if necessary). Finally, you can continue doing work in the movie that requests the `radioDialog`, checking periodically to see whether the user has answered the dialog box, or you can dismiss the dialog box after a certain time has elapsed without requiring the user to answer.

Syntax

`radioDialog message, items, selection, where`

- ▶ `message`: A string with instructions to the user about the choice he is making.

- ▶ `items`: A string with all the radio button items from which the user can select. Items are separated by Return characters. There must be at least 2–25 radio buttons (due to limited sprite channels in the dialog MIAW).

- ▶ `selections`: An integer indicating which radio button should be initially selected. The number provided corresponds to the line number supplied in items.

- ▶ `where`: A rect specifying exactly where the dialog box should be displayed. Optional.

`radioDialogAnswer`

`radioDialogAbort`

Usage

Puts the handlers into a movie script to make them available anywhere in your movie. Also requires that the dialog MIAW, PNP02702.DIR, be in the same folder as the movie that calls `radioDialog` (or in a folder listed in the Lingo property the `searchPath`, which is a list of full pathName strings).

Use `radioDialogAnswer` to check whether the user has answered the radio dialog box yet. If the dialog box is still displayed, this handler will return the symbol `#notYet`. If the dialog box has been answered, the handler will return the symbol `#cancel` if the Cancel button has been pressed, or an integer indicating the number of the radio button that the user had selected when pressing the OK button.

Use `radioDialogAbort` to automatically dismiss the dialog box without requiring the user to answer. This can be useful in a kiosk environment in which you want the user to select a button, but you want to move on to another part of your project if no user is present at the kiosk. Returns TRUE if the dialog box was dismissed as a result of `radioDialogAbort`, or FALSE if the dialog box had already been answered by the user. Ensure that `radioDialogAnswer` is not used after you use `radioDialogAbort`.

`radioDialog message, items, selection, where`

showTrans   48
Glenn Picher

Purpose

The `showTrans` handler is an authoring-time utility to print information about Director's built-in transitions in the Message window. You can get information for a specific transition name or number, or you can get information about all transitions listed alphabetically, numerically, or by transition group.

The `showTrans` demo movie PNP10901.DIR contains an interactive transition browser that builds on the `showTrans` handler to sample and experiment with settings for all of Director's built-in transitions.

Syntax

`showTrans nameOrNumber`

 ▶ `nameOrNumber`: Optional argument; an integer representing a transition number, a string of a specific transition name, a string of a transition group, or a symbol describing a sort order for printing a list of all transitions.

`insureTransitionList`

`transitionDetails theNumber`

 ▶ `theNumber`: Integer of a built-in transition number (1-52 inclusive)

```
padRight theString, padTotal
```

> ▶ theString: A string of information to return with a uniform width

> ▶ padTotal: An integer describing the number of characters that should be returned

Usage

Although it is doubtful that you would need to incorporate the showTrans handler in your final Director presentation, all the scripts you need to use showTrans in the Message window are contained in the PNP10901_CODE member of the demo movie PNP10901.DIR. The demo movie is by far the easiest place to experiment with transitions because of its interactive browser.

drawCircle   49
Glenn Picher

Purpose

This script draws a circle using a centerpoint and radius you specify. Also moves a sprite along a circular path. Use this handler when the dimensions of the circle you want to place on the stage will vary at run time.

You can create interesting animation effects by turning trails on for a bitmap sprite and calling the handler repeatedly with different parameters.

Syntax

```
drawCircle centerPoint, radius, spriteChannel
```

> ▶ centerPoint: A Lingo point, such as point(24,75) or the loc of sprite 23. This syntax is useful when a circle should be drawn at another sprite's location, or at a particular distance from a location using list arithmetic, such as (the loc of sprite 1) + [5,13].

> ▶ radius: Floating point or integer value. Floating point values will be rounded to integer values before drawing. A 0 radius will draw nothing. Negative radii are permitted.

> ▶ spriteChannel: Integer value from 1–120 inclusive.

Usage

This handler uses a one-pixel draw sprite or a bitmap sprite on the stage to draw the circle. Place this handler in a movie script. Call it from any script.

easyPlayMIDI   50
Al Hospers

Purpose

easyPlayMidi will play MIDI on either a Mac or PC. The handlers control a MIDI file through MCI on the PC and a sound-only QuickTime MIDI file on the Mac. You supply the file path of the MIDI file or QuickTime member in a setup handler.

You can play sound-only MIDI QuickTime files on either platform. Doing so enables you to use the same code for both platforms, but requires that you install QuickTime on the PC. Use this code if you want to avoid installing QuickTime on the PC to play MIDI files.

Syntax

OpenMidi (midiFileName, midiFilePath, QTsprite)

▶ midiFileName: The name of the MIDI file on the PC or the name of the QuickTime cast member on the Mac.

▶ midiFilePath: Path to the MIDI file on the PC (long file names in paths are not supported by MCI). On the Mac set this to "" because it's not necessary.

▶ QTsprite: Set this to "" on the PC because it's not necessary. On the Mac this is the sprite number of the MIDI QuickTime movie.

CloseMIDI

PlayMIDI

RewindMIDI

StopMIDI

Usage

These handlers require an external MIDI file on the PC or a MIDI QuickTime cast member on the stage on the Mac.

Place all the handlers in a movie script. Call openMidi from your startMovie handler to set up MIDI for the rest of the handlers, like this:

```
on startMovie

  if the machinetype = 256 then

    set QTsprite = ""

    -- this could be any path to where the MIDI file is

    set midiFilePath = the moviePath

    set midiFileName = "pnp04402.mid"

    -- open the MIDI file with the appropriate parameters

    OpenMidi midiFileName, midiFilePath, QTsprite

  else

    -- the sprite number of the QuickTime MIDI file placed
    -- in the score

    set QTsprite = 7

    -- the path to where the MIDI file is

    set midiFilePath = the moviePath

    -- the name of the QuickTime member

    set midiFileName = "pnp04401.mov"

    OpenMidi midiFileName, midiFilePath, QTsprite

  end if

end
```

The other handlers (`CloseMIDI`, `PlayMIDI`, `RewindMIDI`, `StopMIDI`) perform the playing, rewinding, and stopping of the MIDI file. `CloseMIDI` closes the MCI drivers on the PC and is unnecessary on the Mac.

EasyPlayWAV (PC-only MCI)   51

Tab Julius

Purpose

Play and control external .WAV files using MCI (Windows platform only).

Syntax

```
wavePlay whichFile, doWait, from, to
```

▶ `whichFile`: The file name of the Wave file to be played

▶ `doWait`: TRUE/FALSE causes the function to wait until the sound is finished playing (Optional; default = False)

▶ `from`: Time to start playing in seconds (Optional)

▶ `to`: Time to stop playing in seconds (Optional)

```
wavePause
```

```
waveResume
```

```
waveStop
```

```
waveCleanup
```

Usage

Place this code in a movie script. No initialization calls are needed, but you should probably call `waveCleanup` before exiting to free up the sound card.

EasyPlayAVI (PC-only AVI) 52

Tab Julius

Purpose

Play and control external .AVI files (Windows platform only).

Syntax

```
AVIPlay whichFile, doWait, from, to
```

▶ whichFile: The file name of the .AVI to be played

▶ doWait: TRUE/FALSE causes the function to wait until the video is finished playing (Optional; default = False)

▶ from: Time to start playing in seconds (Optional)

▶ to: Time to stop playing in seconds (Optional)

```
AVIPause
```

```
AVIResume
```

```
AVIStop
```

```
AVICleanup
```

Usage

Place this code in a movie script. No initialization calls are needed, but you should probably call AVICleanup before exiting to free up the sound card.

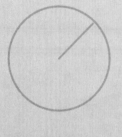

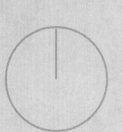

appendix B

New Lingo Terms in Director 6

New Terms

Following is an alphabetical list of all of the new Lingo terms in Director 6. You'll notice that event handlers have been categorized alphabetically and not under the letter "O" for "on."

A

activeCastLib

on alertHook

applicationPath

B

on beginSprite

behavesLikeToggle (member)

behavesLikeToggle (sprite)

bitRate of member

browserName

C

cacheDocVerify

cacheSize

call

callAncestor

castLibNum of member

clearCache

cpuHogTicks

on cuePassed

cuePointNames

cuePointTimescurrentSpriteNum

currentTime

D

duration of member

E

on endSprite

on EvalScript

externalEvent

S

scriptList of sprite

searchPaths

sendAllSprites

sendSprite

setPref

SPACE

spriteNum

state of member

stopEvent

stop member

on streamStatus

symbol

T

tellstreamStatus

tracking

tweened of sprite

U

URL of member

V–Z

VOID

Lingo That Has Changed

Following is a short list of the Lingo that has changed between Director 5 and Director 6.

Lingo Element Changes in Director 6

Director 5 Term	Director 6 Term
dontPassEvent	stopEvent
scriptNum of sprite	scriptList of sprite

The Director 5 terms listed in the table are supported in Director 6, but will become obsolete in future versions of Director. Use the Director 6 terms instead.

Lingo That Is Outdated

The following Lingo property is outdated and unsupported in Director 6.

castNum of sprite

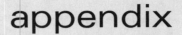appendix

Lee Allis

Contacting Macromedia

Following is contact information for Macromedia.

Office Locations

Macromedia has offices in the U.S., Europe, Japan, Asia Pacific, and Latin America.

Macromedia U.S.
600 Townsend, Suite 310W
San Francisco, CA 94103
Web: http://www.macromedia.com
Phone: 415-252-2000
Fax: 415-626-0554

Macromedia Europe (including Europe, the Middle East, and Africa)
Pyramid House
Easthampstead Road
Bracknell
Berkshire RG12 1NS
United Kingdom
Phone: 44-1-344-458600
Fax: 44-1-344-458666

Macromedia Japan
2F Deer Plaza Akasaka
4-3-28 Akasaka
Minato-ku, Tokyo
Japan 107
Phone: 81-3-5563-1980
Fax: 81-3-5563-1990

Macromedia Asia Pacific
East Kew, Victoria
Australia 3102
Phone: 61-3-9859-8325
Fax: 61-3-9859-4162

Macromedia Latin America
600 Townsend Street
San Francisco, CA 94103
U.S.A.
Phone: 415-252-2000
Fax: 415-626-0554

Sales

Domestic Sales: 800-288-4797
Product Upgrades: 800-457-1774
International Sales: Contact your local distributor

Customer Service

Phone: 800-470-7211

Product Information

Phone: 800-326-2128

Source & Center

Phone: 800-396-0129 or 415-252-7999

Contact Source & Center for training, consulting services, purchasing of Priority Access technical support, referrals for multimedia development, referrals to user groups, and authorization programs for trainers, developers, and service bureaus.

Macromedia International User Conference

Phone: 415-252-7999

For information on this year's Macromedia International User Conference, take a look at http://www.macromedia.com.

Success Stories

Have a success story to pass along to Macromedia? Contact them and let them know!

Web: pr@macromedia.com
Fax: 415-626-1502

Product Suggestions and Feedback

Web: wish-director@macromedia.com
Fax: 415-626-0554

Contact the Director Product Team with product suggestions and feedback about Director.

Made with Macromedia Program

Made with Macromedia FAQ voice mail:
Phone: 415-252-2171
Web: http://www.macromedia.com/

Macromedia offers Director 6 developers the ability to distribute applications created in Director without paying royalties. The Macromedia licensing policy enables you to distribute your Director projects royalty-free, provided that you include the Made with Macromedia logo as described in the guidelines.

Technical Support and Resources

Macromedia offers online, fax-on-demand, and telephone technical support for Director.

Online Services

Information about Director is available on Macromedia's web site, the forums on CompuServe, America Online, and also at various sites on the Internet. For an up-to-date list of all of the resources available online, call MacroFacts, Macromedia's 24-hour fax information line, and request document 3503.
In the United States and Canada, call 800-449-3329. From elsewhere, call 415-863-4409.

Web Site

For the latest technical tips, frequently asked questions, and techNotes on Macromedia Director, Macromedia's other products, and multimedia in general, check out the support section of `http://www.macromedia.com`.

CompuServe

To reach the Macromedia forum on CompuServe, use the command: `Go Macromedia`.

On CompuServe, Macromedia provides message areas for discussion of multimedia development and support of all of their products, as well as libraries that contain useful utilities and examples—including drivers, models, DLLs, XObjects, and Xtras.

America Online

In the United States, to reach the Macromedia forum on America Online, use the keyword: `Macromedia`.

On America Online, Macromedia provides message areas for discussion of multimedia development and support of all their products, as well as libraries that contain useful utilities and examples—including drivers, models, DLLs, XObjects, and Xtras.

Resources in Faxable Formats

MacroFacts Automated Fax-on-Demand System
Phone: 800-449-3329 (United States and Canada)
Phone: 415-863-4409 (Elsewhere)

Macromedia's 24-hour fax information line provides instant access to techNotes on all of Macromedia's products and services. Currently, almost 100 Director and multimedia techNotes are available.

Macromedia Direct

In the U.S, contact Macromedia technical support directly with questions or problems at the following:

Phone: 415-252-9080
Fax: 415-703-0924

For assistance by fax or phone internationally, contact the vendor or the distributor from which you acquired Director.

appendix D

Xtras Reference

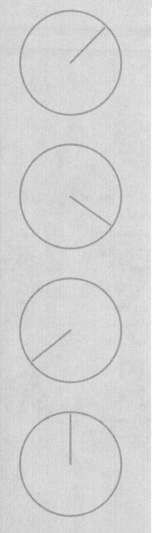

AlphaMania

Developer's Name: Thomas Summerall

Contact Information: summeral@november.diac.com

Description: AlphaMania is a sprite Xtra supporting dynamic alpha-channel compositing of graphics.

Status (shipping or beta): Shipping

Available on IDL6 CD: Yes

DirectControl

Developer's Name: Hed Arzi Multimedia

Contact Information: 3a
Yoni Netanyahu St. Or Yehuda
60376, ISRAEL
972-3-6342374
Tomer.B@ildc.co.il

Description: DirectControl is a Lingo Xtra that provides fast and consistent access to analog and digital joysticks.

It also applies to other ancillary input devices—such as a touch screen, digitizing tablet, and light pen—that track positions within an absolute coordinate system.

Each device can use up to six axes of movement, a point-of-view hat, and 32 buttons. You can use the DirectControl Xtra to determine the capabilities of the joysticks and joystick drivers. Also, you can process a joystick's position and button information by querying the joystick.

Status (shipping or beta):   Shipping (Windows 95)

Available on IDL6 CD: Yes

Price and Restrictions: $99

DirectSound

Developer's Name: Hed Arzi Multimedia

Contact Information: 3a
Yoni Netanyahu St. Or Yehuda
60376, ISRAEL
972-3-6342374
`Tomer.B@ildc.co.il`

Description: DirectSound is a Lingo Xtra that enables the use of Microsoft's DirectSound 3 API in Director applications. The DirectSound 3 API provides low-latency mixing, hardware acceleration, and direct access to sound devices. The Xtra takes advantage of Microsoft's revolutionary DirectSound APIs and enables you to mix as many sounds as you want; locate and change the sound's position, volume, panning, and frequency; control 3D sounds; and retrieve the hardware capabilities.

Status (shipping or beta):   Shipping (Windows 95 platform)

Available on IDL6 CD: Yes

f3Export

Developer's Name:	Focus3
Contact Information:	PO Box 13868
	Berkeley, CA 94712–4868
	http://www.umminger.com/focus3
Description:	f3Export enables the exportation of cast members in PICT and JPEG formats.
Status (shipping or beta):	Beta (Macintosh PowerPC)
Available on IDL6 CD:	No
Price and Restrictions:	$75

f3SoundFX

Developer's Name:	Focus3
Contact Information:	PO Box 13868
	Berkeley, CA 94712–4868
	http://www.umminger.com/focus3
Description:	The f3SoundFX Xtra provides simple Lingo functions to asynchronously record sound from an audio input device. In addition, it provides a complete set of standard audio effects that can be applied to any sound stored in AIFF file format.
Status (shipping or beta):	Shipping (Macintosh PowerPC)
Available on IDL6 CD:	No
Price and Restrictions:	$150

f3VideoCapture

Developer's Name:	Focus3
Contact Information:	PO Box 13868
	Berkeley, CA 94712–4868
	http://www.umminger.com/focus3

Description:	The f3VideoCapture Xtra enables you to simultaneously display multiple windows of live video from multiple QuickTime-compatible video input devices, capture still images into the cast, and record QuickTime movies through Lingo commands.
Status (shipping or beta):	Shipping (Macintosh PowerPC and 68K)
Available on IDL6 CD:	No
Price and Restrictions	$150

FileFlex

Developer's Name:	Component Software Corporation
Contact Information:	PO Box 201 Rocky Hill, NJ 08553 609–497–4501 http://www.component-net.com
Description:	FileFlex is the cross-platform, relational database engine for multimedia. It was designed for creating CD-ROMs, kiosks, and interactive multimedia projects. FileFlex is fully xBASE/dBASE compatible. FileFlex does not require special drivers and requires only 100K of RAM.
Status (shipping or beta):	Shipping FileFlex 2.03
Available on IDL6 CD:	No
Price and Restrictions:	$119 for each Software Developer's Kit; $100 for FileFlex runtime/License. Products distributed using FileFlex require a signed license agreement in addition to the $100 runtime fee. A separate license is required for each platform or title.

Focus3D

Developer's Name:	Focus3
Contact Information:	PO Box 13868
	Berkeley, CA 94712-4868
	http://www.umminger.com/focus3
Description:	The Focus3D Xtra enables you to display multiple 3D views containing multiple models. You can hide or show models and views; change the positions of models, lights, and the camera; and change colors and textures using Lingo. In addition, you are notified when a user clicks on a model.
Status (shipping or beta):	Shipping (Macintosh PowerPC)
Available on IDL6 CD:	No
Price and Restrictions:	$250

Inspect Xtra™

Developer's Name:	codeHorse
Contact Information:	47 Merriam Avenue
	Bronxville, NY 10708
	914-961-5636
	800-934-5636
	http://www.codeHorse.com
	sales@codeHorse.com
	support@codeHorse.com
Description:	The Inspect Xtra from codeHorse gives you a powerful inspector window that complements the message window and the debugger in the Director authoring environment. Use it to display and change everything from lists and objects to protected movies and castLibs.
Status (shipping or beta):	Shipping (Macintosh, Windows versions 3.1, 95, NT)

Available on IDL6 CD: Yes

Price and Restrictions: $99 for a cross-platform license for use on one computer of each platform.

MXCalculator

Developer's Name: Maxwell Technologies

Contact Information: 8888 Balboa Avenue
San Diego, CA 92123
`http://www.maxwell.com`

MathXtras: `http://www.maxwell.com/MathXtras`

Educational Software Group: `http://www.maxwell.com/edsoft`

Technical Contact: `mandell@maxwell.com`

Marketing and Sales: `marion@maxwell.com`
619-756-7839

Description: The MXCalculator Xtra enables the designer to present his end user with a small, attractive hand calculator. The controlling program is capable of reading the calculated result. Developers can import their custom art into MXCalculator.

Status (shipping or beta):   Shipping (Win32, Win16, PPC Mac, 68K Mac)

Available on IDL6 CD: Yes

Price and Restrictions: MathXtras Full Package: $199

MXCounter

Developer's Name: Maxwell Technologies

Contact Information: 8888 Balboa Avenue
San Diego, CA 92123
`http://www.maxwell.com`

MathXtras:	`http://www.maxwell.com/MathXtras`
Educational Software Group:	`http://www.maxwell.com/edsoft`
Technical Contact:	`mandell@maxwell.com`
Marketing and Sales:	`marion@maxwell.com` 619-756-7839
Description:	The MXCounter Xtra is used to display the value of an individual parameter, such as time or distance. It models the odometer of an automobile as a set of rolling digit wheels. All colors and the number of digits on either side of the decimal point are controlled with Lingo.
Status (shipping or beta):	Shipping (Win32, Win16, PPC Mac, 68K Mac)
Available on IDL6 CD:	Yes
Price and Restrictions:	MathXtras Full Package: $199

MXEquation

Developer's Name:	Maxwell Technologies
Contact Information:	8888 Balboa Avenue San Diego, CA 92123 `http://www.maxwell.com`
MathXtras:	`http://www.maxwell.com/MathXtras`
Educational Software Group:	`http://www.maxwell.com/edsoft`
Technical Contact:	`mandell@maxwell.com`
Marketing and Sales:	`marion@maxwell.com` 619-756-7839

Description: The MXEquation Xtra displays, modifies, and evaluates algebraic equations. Standard algebraic notation is used. Typically, an equation is initialized by the author and modified by the end user. MXEquation can be used as a calculator or as a function generator for the MXGraph Xtra or other applications.

Status (shipping or beta): Shipping (Win32, Win16, PPC Mac, 68K Mac)

Available on IDL6 CD: Yes

Price and Restrictions: MathXtras Full Package: $199

MXGraph

Developer's Name: Maxwell Technologies

Contact Information: 8888 Balboa Avenue
San Diego, CA 92123
http://www.maxwell.comMathXtras

MathXtras: http://www.maxwell.com/MathXtras

Educational Software Group: http://www.maxwell.com/edsoft

Technical Contact: mandell@maxwell.com

Marketing and Sales: marion@maxwell.com
619-756-7839

Description: The MXGraph Xtra displays points, lines, and curves on a familiar quadrille motif. End users can click to plot points, select and trace curves or lines, and manipulate lines. Scaling, zoom, pan, and curve-fit capabilities are included.

Status (shipping or beta): Shipping (Win32, Win16, PPC Mac, 68K Mac)

Available on IDL6 CD: Yes

Price and Restrictions: MathXtras Full Package: $199

MXSlider

Developer's Name:	Maxwell Technologies
Contact Information:	8888 Balboa Avenue San Diego, CA 92123 `http://www.maxwell.com`
MathXtras:	`http://www.maxwell.com/MathXtras`
Educational Software Group:	`http://www.maxwell.com/edsoft`
Technical Contact:	`mandell@maxwell.com`
Marketing and Sales:	`marion@maxwell.com` 619-756-7839
Description:	The MXSlider Xtra enables the end user to control the value of a single parameter by moving the Slider's Thumb or pressing its end arrows or cross-bar. Range and sensitivity are controlled through Lingo control, and the controlling program can get or set the slider's value. Developers can import their custom art into MXSlider.
Status (shipping or beta):	Shipping (Win32, Win16, PPC Mac, 68K Mac)
Available on IDL6 CD:	Yes
Price and Restrictions:	MathXtras Full Package: $199

MXSpeedometer

Developer's Name:	Maxwell Technologies
Contact Information:	8888 Balboa Avenue San Diego, CA 92123 `http://www.maxwell.com`
MathXtras:	`http://www.maxwell.com/MathXtras`
Educational Software Group:	`http://www.maxwell.com/edsoft`

Technical Contact: mandell@maxwell.com

Marketing and Sales: marion@maxwell.com
                            619-756-7839

Description: The MXSpeedometer Xtra displays the value of an
                            individual parameter. It is modeled after the speed-
                            ometer of an automobile. MXSpeedometer presents
                            a semi-transparent bar sliding across a horizontal
                            scale. All colors are contolled through Lingo.

Status (shipping or beta): Shipping (Win32, Win16, PPC Mac, 68K Mac)

Available on IDL6 CD: Yes

Price and Restrictions: MathXtras Full Package: $199

MXTable

Developer's Name: Maxwell Technologies

Contact Information: 8888 Balboa Avenue
                            San Diego, CA 92123
                            http://www.maxwell.com

MathXtras: http://www.maxwell.com/MathXtras

Educational Software   http://www.maxwell.com/edsoft
Group:

Technical Contact: mandell@maxwell.com

Marketing and Sales: marion@maxwell.com
                            619-756-7839

Description: The MXTable Xtra provides a simple means of
                            displaying tabular (spreadsheet-like) information.
                            Each cell may display either text or a castmember
                            bitmap. The font, alignment, backcolor, and
                            forecolor of each table cell are individually con-
                            trolled. The controlling program may get or set the
                            contents of each cell. Interaction of the end user
                            with the table is controlled with Lingo.

Status (shipping or beta):	Shipping (Win32, Win16, PPC Mac, 68K Mac)
Available on IDL6 CD:	Yes
Price and Restrictions:	MathXtras Full Package: $199

PhotoCaster

Developer's Name:	Thomas Summerall
Contact Information:	summeral@november.diac.com
Description:	The PhotoCaster Xtra is a tool that imports Photoshop files into casts. It also splits out layers, indexes, pre-positions regpoints, and so on.
Status (shipping or beta)	Shipping
Available on IDL6 CD:	Yes

Smacker

Developer's Name:	RAD Game Tools, Inc.
Contact Information:	850 South Main Street Salt Lake City, UT 84101 801-322-4300 http://www.radgametools.com
Description:	The Smacker Xtra gives Lingo programmers complete playback control of Smacker animation files. Smacker is a video, animation, and sound compressor that can compress most files from 4:1 to as much as 12:1. The Smacker Xtra does transparent playback, full-screen playback, and can even extract individual frames into bitmap cast members.
Status (shipping or beta)	Shipping (Windows versions 3.x, 95, NT)
Available on IDL6 CD:	Yes
Price and Restrictions:	$995

Speech Lingo Xtra™

Developer's Name:	Digital Dreams Talk Media
Contact Information:	4308 Harbord Drive Oakland, CA 94618 http//www.dreams@surftalk.com Tel: 510-547-6929 Fax: 510-547-6799
Description:	The Speech Lingo Xtra enables Director developers to create multimedia products and Shockwave web sites that incorporate spoken user interactions as well as spoken commands and controls. For example, "What is the capital of Kansas?" Answer, "Topeka." It requires Apple's PlainTalk Speech Recognition and Speech Synthesis.
Status (shipping or beta):	Shipping v1.3.1 (Macintosh AV, Power Macintosh)
Available on IDL6 CD:	No
Price and Restrictions:	Single-User License: $49 Commerical License: $449

The following Xtras were developed by g/matter, inc.:

Install

PickFolder

StageHandT Buttons

Director Xtras provided by g/matter, inc. Unregistered Xtras can be purchased by contacting g/matter, inc.

Contact Information:	g/matter, inc. Tel: 415-243-0394 Fax: 415-243-0396 sales@gmatter.com http://www.gmatter.com

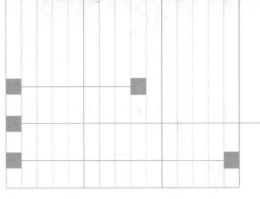

index

A

a.l. hospers & associates

Rock-solid development, analysis, and design.

a.l. hospers & associates has over 13 years experience in creating software of all types. We have developed products for a wide variety of clients ranging from game companies to children's educational software creators. As an independent software production and development group we often find solutions to problems that are not apparent to less experienced organizations. We offer an economy of scale that is extremely flexible, and which can be adjusted to fit projects of almost any size.

As management consultants we specialize in helping small and large companies evaluate their software development structure and process. We will work with you to help design a coordinated development strategy, that will allow your organization to make the maximum use of your assets.

Feel free to contact us for quotes on your next software development project, or for help in refining your software design and development process.

Recent clients list:
- The Princeton Review
- KinderActive
- Dr.T's Music Software
- Harmonix Music Systems
- Papyrus Design Group

Contact:
a.l. hospers & associates
122 West Central
Natick, MA 01760
e mail - al_hospers@msn.com

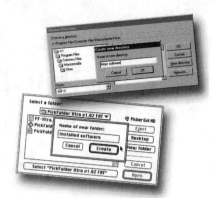

*progress*copy

Copies files with optional progress bar, cancel button, and message.

*pick*folder

Enbles users to choose a destination folder (including a New button).

authoring *utilities*

*drop*start

Set a document or application to start automatically. A Macintosh drag-and-drop application to make using QuickTime's AutoStart feature a no-brainer. Create CDs that automatically install or run when they're inserted!

*auto*run • *auto*start

Automatically install and run your presentations. Windows and Mac applications to either run your installer or run an already-installed copy of your software from the hard drive. No-brainer for your end users. Lower your tech support expenses!

*re*launch

Launch applications and return to Director. Mac and Windows applications to launch another program from Director and eventually return. Useful on low-memory machines, when you want to run a number of projectors, or when you need to install QuickTime.

Glenn M. *Picher*

50 Market Street, Suite 1A, Room 338

South Portland, ME 04106

Phone: (207) 767-8015 E-mail: gpicher@maine.com

http://www.maine.com/shops/gpicher

published by

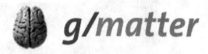

300 Brannan Street, Suite 210

San Francisco, CA 94107

Phone: (415) 243-0394 E-mail: sales@gmatter.com

http://www.gmatter.com

Glenn M. *Picher*

Freelance multimedia consulting, specializing in Macromedia® Director® Interactive design,

Lingo™ programming and Xtra™ / XObject™ plug-in C programming for Mac and Windows.

Shareware & freeware Xtras & XObjects for Director, and other multimedia authoring utilities.

dir · i · go \ 'dir-ə-go \ *v*

[Latin *dirigere*] 1: I Direct!

2: Maine's state motto

Director *plug-ins*

Xtras and XObjects for Mac and Windows

*progress*copy

ProgressCopy copies files at speeds roughly equal to the Mac Finder or Windows Explorer. You can also display a progress bar, three lines of configurable text, and a cancel button.

*pick*folder

PickFolder enables your users to choose a folder, typically useful as part of an installer or when custom information needs to be saved from a Director presentation. The New Folder button enables your users to organize their hard disks as desired.

*master*app

MasterApp launches and controls external applications— locating executables; opening and printing documents; launching apps and keeping track of their windows; simulating menu and dialog box mouse and keyboard input; rearranging window size, position, and front-to-back draw order; and quitting.

install

Install can do all the useful tasks a Director-authored Windows installer would need. It can access .INI files and program groups and icons; switch Director back to the front; detect CD-ROM drive letters, the DOS environment, command line arguments, and more.

versions

Versions detects QuickTime, DOS, Windows and file version numbers (both 16- and 32-bit); tells you if you're running under Windows 3.1, 95, or NT; and translates between long and short file names. The QuickTime methods are free to use and distribute.

free *plug-ins!*

*prefs*folder

Get the full path to the Mac Preferences folder.

*win*dirs

Get the full path to the Windows and System directories.

Get in the Pipe-Line of Director.

Lingo User's ◆◆
j o u r n a l

The Lingo User's Journal is the top publication for Lingo programmers. With current and in-depth articles for beginners, intermediates, and advanced developers, the Journal is published to over 50 countries monthly. Join us and see why!

SPECIAL! Pre-pay with your order and get 14 issues for the price of 12 (for new subscribers only).
Rates: $42/yr to US/Canada/Mexico, $64 to all other countries. Visa, MasterCard, American Express accepted. Checks and money orders only if in US funds and drawn on a US bank (your bank can help you with this. If unable to draw on a US bank, include additional US $25 to cover international banking fees). Sorry, no purchase orders accepted.

Please PRINT Clearly   **Subscription Form**   Lingo User's ◆◆
                                                    j o u r n a l

Name: _____
Company: _____
Address: _____
_____
_____
_____

email: _____
Telephone: _____

Card#: _____
Expires: _____

Signature: _____

Mail to:
Lingo User's Journal
Penworks Publishing
PO Box 531
Holderness, NH 03245-0531
USA

www.penworks.com
US/Canada Tel: 1-800-PENWORX
Int: +1 603-968-3341
Facsimile: Int: +1 603-968-3361
Fax: 1-800-PW-FAX-NUM
sales@penworks.com

◆◆ **PENWORKS**
Multimedia for the World

Light.

Director delivers the illusion of motion...it doesn't work without light. Illuminate with Penworks Xtras.

CastEffects
Subimage extractions, flips and rotates on-the-fly from Lingo!

Blinker
Create great Blinking effects for your sprites

DateMaster
Complete date functions, internationally safe, valid back to 1 A.D.!

We'll have more available by the time your read this, including the CD Toolkit Pro - the only CD Xtra for Enhanced CD's, plus others! Check out our web site to see, or join our mail-list!

www.penworks.com
Tel: 1-800-PENWORX
Int: +1 603-968-3341
sales@penworks.com

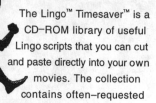

Fresh Every Morning

That's right, we grow our digital media right on our own farms. Lots of producers get their media from other growers. They buy batches of this and bunches of that. These other producers truck these ingredients in and mix them all up into what they call "multimedia."

At Digital Design we prefer to grow our own media. This way we can be sure it's grown just right. Custom made you might say. As you can see from this photo of one of our button farms, we take care to be sure that you get the freshest ingredients.

Getting Started with the CD-ROM

This page provides instructions for installing software from the CD-ROM.

Windows 95/NT 4 Installation

Insert the disc into your CD-ROM drive. If autoplay is enabled on your machine, the CD-ROM setup program starts automatically the first time you insert the disc.

If setup does not run automatically, perform these steps:

1. From the Start menu, choose Programs, Windows Explorer.

2. Select your CD-ROM drive under My Computer.

3. Double-click SETUP.EXE in the Contents list.

4. Follow the on-screen instructions that appear.

5. Setup adds an icon named CD-ROM Contents to a program group for this book. To explore the CD-ROM, double-click on the CD-ROM Contents icon.

Macintosh Installation

1. Insert the disc into your CD-ROM drive.

2. Open the CD-ROM volume by double-clicking its icon in the Mac desktop.

3. Double-click the icon named CD-ROM Contents.

How to Contact New Riders Publishing

If you have a question or comment about this product, there are several ways to contact New Riders Publishing. For the quickest response, please send e-mail to support@mcp.com.

If you prefer, you can fax New Riders at 1-317-817-7448.

New Riders' mailing address is as follows:

New Riders Publishing
Attn: Publishing Manager
201 W. 103rd Street
Indianapolis, IN 46290

You can also contact us through the Macmillan Computer Publishing CompuServe forum at GO NEWRIDERS. Our World Wide Web address is http://www.mcp.com/newriders.